HEIDEGGER IN FRANCE

HEIDEGGER IN FRANCE

DOMINIQUE JANICAUD

TRANSLATED BY FRANÇOIS RAFFOUL AND DAVID PETTIGREW

INDIANA UNIVERSITY PRESS   Bloomington & Indianapolis

This book is a publication of

Indiana University Press
Office of Scholarly Publishing
Herman B Wells Library 350
1320 East 10th Street
Bloomington, Indiana 47405 USA

iupress.indiana.edu

First published in French as *Heidegger en France*
© Éditions Albin Michel S.A., 2001
English translation © 2015 by Indiana University Press

Manufactured in the United States of America

Library of Congress Cataloging-in-Publication Data

Janicaud, Dominique, 1937–2002
    [Heidegger en France. English]
    Heidegger in France / Dominique Janicaud ; translated
by François Raffoul and David Pettigrew.
    pages cm. — (Studies in Continental thought)
    Includes bibliographical references and index.
    ISBN 978-0-253-01773-4 (cloth : alk. paper) — ISBN 978-0-253-
01977-6 (ebook) 1. Heidegger, Martin, 1889–1976. 2. Philosophy,
French—20th century. 3. Philosophers—France—Interviews. I. Title.
    B3279.H49J2713 2015
    193—dc23

                                                    2015015901

1 2 3 4 5   20 19 18 17 16 15

Contents

Acknowledgments

The translators would like to thank first and foremost John Sallis and Dee Mortensen for their support of this project from its earliest stages. Initial planning began for the project in discussions with Professor Sallis and with Dee Mortensen, senior sponsoring editor at Indiana University Press. We are grateful that Professor Janicaud endorsed our plan to undertake the translation from the outset, and for the encouragement that he addressed to us in his paper "Toward the End of the 'French Exception'?" delivered at the meeting of the Heidegger Conference in New Haven, in May 2002; it was subsequently published in *French Interpretations of Heidegger: An Exceptional Reception.*[1] Dominique was to die tragically later that summer in Nice. Subsequently, we attended a *Colloque* in Dominique's memory in Nice in 2003, and met with his family at that time. We are grateful that we received their blessings to go forward with the translation. We would like to thank especially Françoise Dastur, who organized the *Colloque* in Nice and facilitated our discussions with Dominique's family.

Based on these early discussions, we were committed to keeping our promise to Dominique to complete the translation of his book, and our commitment to that promise sustained our efforts over the years. This was indeed a massive undertaking, given the size of the two volumes to be translated. The final manuscript numbered nearly 1,000 pages with 1,500 footnotes. We are therefore deeply grateful to a number of colleagues and friends who contributed to the early stages of the work by helping with the production of first drafts of some of the chapters and interviews. We thank John Castore, Cathy LeBlanc, Gregory Recco, Hakhamanesh Zangeneh, and Susanne Schilz, in this respect. Cathy LeBlanc, in particular, helped further with an early review of a substantial part of the manuscript and some of the interviews, and for this we are grateful. Additional essential editorial assistance was received from a number of graduate students and scholars at Louisiana State University (LSU) and elsewhere, including Michael MacLaggan, Nadia Miskowiec, and Jim Ryan. We would also like to express our appreciation to Heidegger scholars in France who were consulted on various translation questions, including Jean Greisch, Pierre Jacerme, and Joseph O'Leary, all of whom actually appear in Dominique's book as part of the history of the reception of Heidegger in France.

David Pettigrew would like to thank Southern Connecticut State University for the support he received over the course of the translation, including from the Philosophy Department, the School of Arts and Sciences, and the Office of the Provost. Such support included a sabbatical, research-reassigned time, and research grants. In addition, David would like to thank Cathy LeBlanc and her family for their hospitality in Aniche, France, as well as his friends at Hotel de Senlis in Paris, and at Hotel Saraj in Sarajevo, all places where much of the work of translation and revisions was undertaken over the years.

For the support he received at Louisiana State University, François Raffoul is grateful to the College of Humanities and Social Sciences at LSU for granting him a Manship Summer Research Fellowship in 2012 to work on the translation, as well as Delbert Burkett, department chairperson, and Gregory Schufreider, from the Department of Philosophy and Religious Studies. He is thankful to Luis Daniel Venegas for his hospitality and Charlie Johnson for his friendship. Last but not least, he is deeply grateful to Melida Badilla for her unconditional support.

Finally, we have been grateful for the support and patience of Indiana University Press, and for the profoundly important contributions of many colleagues and friends. It has been an honor to have had the opportunity to bring Dominique Janicaud's extraordinary book, *Heidegger en France,* to an English-language readership. We would like to think that we have kept our promise to our friend and colleague, Professor Dominique Janicaud, and in this way, that we have honored his memory.

Translators' Introduction

Dᴏᴍɪɴɪǫᴜᴇ Jᴀɴɪᴄᴀᴜᴅ's *Hᴇɪᴅᴇɢɢᴇʀ in France* is a major work of breathtaking historical scope, a unique intellectual undertaking reconstituting in two volumes the history of the French reception of Heidegger, from its earliest stages in the late 1920s until 2000.[1] One "certainty" guided Dominique Janicaud in this enterprise, that of "the omnipresence in France of the influence, direct or indirect, of Heidegger's thought and work. Apart from the mathematical sciences and life and earth sciences, there is hardly one sector of knowledge or intellectual activity that has not been positively or negatively affected by that thought" (*HF,* 301). Volume 1 is a narrative on Heidegger's influence on twentieth-century philosophy in France; volume 2 is composed of interviews of leading philosophers and Heidegger scholars working in France, including Françoise Dastur, Jacques Derrida, Éliane Escoubas, Jean Greisch, Philippe Lacoue-Labarthe, Jean-Luc Marion, and Jean-Luc Nancy, each offering an account of their own relation to Heidegger. These interviews provide a unique perspective on the impact that Heidegger's thought has had on contemporary French thought, shedding light on their intellectual itinerary. This English edition includes the entirety of volume 1 and seven of the interviews from volume 2, which have been selected by the translators. This intellectual history of the French reception of Heidegger's work also amounts to a history of twentieth-century French philosophy itself, since, as Janicaud shows throughout, contemporary French philosophy has to a large extent constituted itself on the basis of a dialogue with Heidegger's thought, whether embracing it, rejecting it, or misunderstanding it! Jacques Derrida, for instance, explains in his interview with Janicaud that Heidegger is a kind of *contremaître* for him (literally, a *counter-master,* but the French term has the colloquial sense of a work supervisor, or overseer, someone in a position of authority who watches over someone else, often disapprovingly[2]). Derrida plays here as well on the sense of being against, as in "going against" the master: "When I say: '*counter to* Heidegger's order' (*Counterpath,* 56), it is because he haunts me, in *Counterpath* as in *The Post Card,* he is always there, watching me and reproaching me for something" (*HF,* 355). This description of Derrida's relation to Heidegger might serve as an accurate illustration of Heidegger's place in French philosophy: a master with whom and against whom one thinks.

Janicaud writes that at first he "had not envisioned a second part completely devoted to interviews with the personalities, translators, and/or interpreters who have been significant actors or witnesses in the reception of Heideggerian thought in France" (*HF,* 12). However, he then adds that the development of the work itself "obliged us to call on these witnesses" (ibid.). The interviews, in turn, further enriched Janicaud's project as they provide a source of unique personal reflections on the reception of Heidegger in France. Françoise Dastur, for example, recalls in her interview her early studies on Heidegger in 1962. She remembers encountering Heidegger's work during her second year at the Sorbonne, in courses with Ricoeur and Derrida. Ricoeur advised her to work on *Unterwegs zur Sprache,* and to study Heidegger. Dastur subsequently traveled in 1963 to Freiburg, where her "genuine" introduction to Heidegger took place. Then, in the early 1970s, Dastur participated in seminars with Fédier and Beaufret. Having become fluent in German, Dastur "rarely used French translations," and read Pöggeler, Biemel, and von Herrmann. In time, her own works, such as *Heidegger and the Question of Time,*[3] would emerge as a major resource in the French reception of Heidegger. Jean Greisch, in his interview, recalls that his first encounter with Heidegger's questioning "was connected to my studies in fundamental theology in 1965–1966 in Innsbruck, in the shadow of Karl Rahner" (*HF,* 371). When he arrived in Paris to pursue his philosophical studies, Greisch was also influenced by Paul Ricoeur. He attended his lectures at the C.N.R.S., beginning in 1972. Greisch recalls that he was "fascinated by Jean Beaufret, whom I met in the context of the discussions at Saint-Jacques du Haut-Pas, which were moderated by Odette Laffoucrière" (*HF,* 372). Due to the fact that he was from Luxembourg and taught at a Catholic institution in Paris ("which, because of a strange state restriction, is not allowed to call itself a 'university'"), Greisch remarks on his "feeling of being a rare bird," who could therefore "feel free to think whatever he wants, without any obligation to the academic authorities" (*HF,* 375). Greisch's inventive approach led him to pioneer studies related to Heidegger's *Beiträge, Besinnung,* and *Geschichte des Seins,* particularly in an essay with the "deliberately provocative title of 'The Poverty of the Last God.'"[4] In addition, Greisch translated volume 60 of the *Gesamtausgabe: The Phenomenology of Religious Life.* Additional interviews with Jacques Derrida, Éliane Escoubas, Philippe Lacoue-Labarthe, Jean-Luc Marion, and Jean-Luc Nancy reveal similar accounts of first encounters with Heidegger's work, subsequent inspirations, and deep engagements, as well as lasting contributions to the living reception of Heidegger's thought in France. For his part, Philippe Lacoue-Labarthe, in his interview, reflects on his earliest readings of Heidegger. He was captivated from the outset by Heidegger's references to Hölderlin. He states, "Soon I became a Heideggerian." In fact, he adds, "Soon Heidegger became the only philosopher that I understood" (*HF,* 384). Lacoue-Labarthe says that after the publication of Heidegger's *Nietzsche* in 1961, "I never stopped reading Heidegger, whatever the rest of my reading in the tradition of German idealism happened to be, or when I read Benjamin or Lukacs, etc. In any case, I continued to be attached to something fundamental in Heidegger's thought" (*HF,* 385). Lacoue-Labarthe concludes his interview with a poignant note about collecting Heidegger's books after his death, books that were to be donated to the library at the Strasbourg Philosophy Institute. On the night table, among the books that had been set aside, "there were books by Hölderlin, Goethe, and the Suhrkamp collection of Celan's poems." Another book on the night table included a dedication from Jacques Lacan (*HF*, 392).

Dominique Janicaud's *Heidegger in France* reconstitutes, both through synthetic analyses and in minute details, the way in which Heidegger has had a major influence—in a striking and unique way—on twentieth-century French philosophy, and in particular on such thinkers as Sartre, Merleau-Ponty, Levinas, Derrida, Lacan, Foucault, and Althusser, as well as Blanchot and Ricoeur, among others. Such an enterprise is an invaluable contribution to the discussions and debates regarding Heidegger's place in contemporary philosophy. In fact, as Janicaud notes in the opening pages of the volume: "Despite the abundance of translations, interpretations, and polemical interventions, no one has ever attempted to write in French the complete history of the singularly turbulent and unexpectedly fruitful reception of what is quite possibly the most original thought of the twentieth century" (*HF*, 13). The tone of this narration, consistently balanced and measured, combined with impeccable scholarship and documentation, is also very refreshing. Polemical works have their place and necessity, but they must yield to the serious work of the intellectual historian, a role that Janicaud deliberately assumes in this *opus magnum*. The result is a welcome departure from the intellectual terrorism that has so often affected research, a brilliant synthesis of seventy years of French philosophy that is written in a lucid and jargon-free prose.

The principal qualities of this work are first and foremost its fairness, its constant attempt at being equitable, and its effort to achieve some level of objectivity, as much as this is possible:[5] Janicaud never tries to "settle accounts"; his reading is instead one of a "generous" or "benevolent" neutrality. It also comes as close as possible to an exhaustive account, combining an intimate knowledge of the history (as attested by the more personal, autobiographical "epilogues" inserted between the main chapters) with a keen understanding of the various philosophical positions and interpretations, as well as the subtext of the history of the conflicts and interactions between the protagonists. As Janicaud explains in his introduction, it is a matter of restituting the threads of both the grand and "anecdotal" history, knitting together, as it were, *Geschichte* and *Historie* (cf. *HF*, 13). In its attention to detail, its investigative flavor, and inquisitiveness, the book reads at times like a veritable spy novel. Janicaud displays an impressive mastery of the material in question, including facts, texts, and commentaries, as well as of the underlying philosophical assumptions. The major stages of that history are revisited, from Levinas's first commentaries on Heidegger's early works (Levinas was the one who first introduced Heidegger in France); to Sartre's magisterial (mis)appropriation of the key moments and vocabulary of *Being and Time* in *Being and Nothingness;* to the explosion of existentialism after the war and the famed "Letter on Humanism" addressed to Jean Beaufret, a key figure in the French reception of Heidegger; to Heidegger's visit in France in the mid-fifties at the Cerisy meeting and his encounter with Lacan, as well as his lecture at Aix-en-Provence in 1958; to the sixties and the seminars held in France, in Provence at the Thor, near the house of René Char; to the debates in the eighties regarding the translation of *Being and Time,* which took sixty years to be completed after many vicissitudes; and, last but not least, to the cyclical reappearance on the French intellectual scene, from the thirties (but especially since 1947 through articles in *Les Temps Modernes)* to Victor Farias's infamous 1987 book, of heated debates regarding Heidegger's relation to National Socialism. Janicaud has already written an important book on Heidegger and politics,[6] and he revisits the issue in this book through an informed discussion of each and every one of its known aspects. Throughout these episodes, Janicaud discusses at length another integral and crucial part of the reception of Heidegger in France, namely, the question of the French *translation* of Heidegger's language and vocabulary, which also had (and still has) its own complicated history. In all of these cases, Janicaud provides the most informed and complete account to date, one that is destined to set a new standard and become a reference for future discussions.

Janicaud observes that the French "reception" of Heidegger has been everything but passive; in fact, it has given rise to all kinds of interpretations, appropriations, or misappropriations, not to mention misunderstandings, even if these were brilliant and inventive, as in the case of Sartre. Janicaud recounts that Heidegger, hearing of this polymorphous transformation or re-creation of his thought, exclaimed: "My God, I did not want this!" (*HF,* 427n5).[7] Much of Janicaud's book is a reconstruction of the successive stages of the reception of Heidegger's work, following a chronological order that began in the late twenties and early thirties. *Heidegger in France* comprises an introduction, twelve chapters, and a conclusion. The chapters unfold the story of Heidegger's reception in France in easily digestible parts. The transition through the years is accessible for the reader because it is organized in terms of the key figures (e.g., Levinas, Sartre, Beaufret, and Derrida) who dominated each phase—phases spanning one or more decades and in some cases overlapping. Each of these figures, in turn, passed the role of interlocutor and interpreter on to the next person in the next phase. There are seven inserted "Epilogues," or more personal accounts, which were added by Janicaud to the general narrative. These epilogues recount, in a more subjective tone, Janicaud's personal involvement in that history, and they shed an interesting light on the preceding chapters, providing a welcomed and necessary pause in a long text. One can nevertheless distinguish the following main stages in that narrative, beginning with the first introduction of Heidegger in France by Emmanuel Levinas.

Indeed, it was none other than Levinas who introduced Heidegger to France, and who played since the early thirties "an important role in the diffusion and explanation of Heidegger's thought" (*HF*, 19). Levinas held Heidegger in the highest esteem, ranking him among the great philosophers of the tradition: "I knew right away that this was one of the greatest philosophers in history. Like Plato, like Kant, like Hegel, like Bergson" (*HF*, 19). Levinas, moreover, shared his enthusiasm with Blanchot, and Blanchot credited Levinas for helping him understand Heidegger. In these early years, it is interesting to note that Heidegger was read not as an existential atheist, but rather as a deeply spiritual thinker. Indeed, Heidegger's first French translator, Henri Corbin, pursued research in Persian spirituality.

Levinas—although certainly other figures of note read Heidegger in the '30s, including Gurvitch, Koyré, Wahl, Corbin, and Aron (*HF*, 31)—was followed, in the next phase, by Sartre. Sartre, in the '40s, championed Heidegger and appropriated his thought in a highly "inventive," although ultimately misguided, way. Janicaud points out how extensively Sartre's *Being and Nothingness* drew from *Being and Time,* and notes, "A systematic index would reveal that Heidegger is omnipresent in *Being and Nothingness*" (*HF*, 37). Ultimately, Sartre's existentialism, conceived of as an essentially anthropological humanism and activism, was to be refuted by Heidegger in what Janicaud describes as the next phase of Heidegger's reception in France. Yet, Janicaud concedes that the "Sartre effect," or the "Sartre bomb," was so powerful, in and of itself, that *Being and Nothingness* was a book "which became fetishized by existentialists" (*HF*, 48).

Jean-Paul Sartre was followed by Jean Beaufret, who was to be Heidegger's host in France, as it were, as well as his main interlocutor for the next thirty years. Given Beaufret's crucial and extended position in the reception of Heidegger in France, it is all the more striking that Beaufret continues to be virtually unknown in the United States. Yet Beaufret was the recipient of the seminal "Letter on Humanism," in which Heidegger implied that he had been misread by Sartre. Beaufret came to Heidegger's attention when Frédéric de Towarnicki gave Heidegger some of Beaufret's articles (*HF*, 51). Heidegger was favorably disposed to the essay. Beaufret paid his first visit to Heidegger's hut in September 1946, and so began their thirty years of philosophical friendship. The "Beaufret phase" included the Colloque at Cerisy in 1955 (Heidegger's first visit to France), as well as the Thor Seminars in Provence in 1966, 1968, and 1969.

This thirty-year phase in which Beaufret played such a central role overlapped with Derrida's reception and dissemination of Heidegger in the 1960s. As Derrida has acknowledged himself, Heidegger has been a central presence in his work, a kind of overseer, who "haunts" him, someone who, as Derrida says, "is always there, watching me and reproaching me for something" (*HF,* 355). Moreover, Derrida and his students Jean-Luc Nancy and Philippe Lacoue-Labarthe continued to explore in various ways and expand upon Heidegger's thought until the end of the century. Many of Jean-Luc Nancy's books and articles in the last twenty years on community draw explicitly from Heidegger's analyses of being-with in *Being and Time.*

Janicaud's book is particularly noteworthy for its comprehensive and balanced treatment of the debate in France that swirled around Heidegger's affiliation with National Socialism and his rectorship at the University of Freiburg in 1933. Janicaud addresses several strands in this debate in a precise and measured way, including the work of Jean-Pierre Faye and Victor Farias, although the latter's book from 1987 is judged harshly. Most importantly, however, the reader is free to pore over the copious details of these debates, which in and of themselves constitute a significant part of Heidegger's reception.

Janicaud shows that in the '90s, "Heidegger studies" in France revolved around the question of his "turn," often referred to in terms of Heidegger I vs. Heidegger II, following William Richardson's paradigm in his celebrated 1962 study, *Heidegger: Through Phenomenology to Thought.*[8] This phase could be characterized as a time when, beyond the debate of the '80s surrounding Farias's book, Heidegger's thought was considered as a whole and the work rather than the man became the topic of study.

In a veritable *tour de force, Heidegger en France* extensively and exhaustively treats, then, in a constantly engaging style, nearly everything that has been written and said about Heidegger in France in the past seven decades. In any given instance, we receive information that provides a richly varied and layered context for the historical event or moment. In the case of Heidegger's visit to France in 1955, we learn of its organization, the dialogues that took place, the meetings and interactions with historical figures (Lacan, Braque, and Char), as well as of Heidegger's itinerary in Paris. It is fascinating, for example, to read of and imagine Heidegger's visit to the Louvre, Versailles, and to Café de Flore, that *haut-lieu* of French existentialism.

The reason for Heidegger's visit to France at that time, organized by Jean Beaufret, was the Colloque at Cerisy. Heidegger presented a paper on August 28, 1955, entitled "What Is Philosophy?," and again we are drawn in by the narrative of the context. We learn of the style and the atmosphere of the seminar, his "exchange" with Paul Ricoeur, and we read of the key philosophical points under discussion. We learn, for example, of Heidegger's announcement, at the seminar, to the surprise of those in attendance, that there was "no Heideggerian philosophy." He characterized his thought, rather, as being engaged in a "dialogue with the tradition."

As regards Heidegger's visits to Provence in 1966, '68, and '69, we learn about the circumstances of his invitation (attributed to René Char), the person who proposed and organized the seminar (Jean Beaufret), and even the person who did the driving (François Fédier). True to his statement at Cerisy, Heidegger engaged in Le Thor in a dialogue with the Greeks (in particular Heraclitus and Parmenides), as well as with Kant, Hegel, and Husserl.[9]

This work will become the standard reference for the understanding of Heidegger's reception in France, and will shed a unique light on contemporary French philosophy itself. In a glowing review of *Heidegger en France* for the January 2002 issue of the *Times Literary Supplement* (*TLS*), Georges Steiner wrote that Janicaud's book is an "intellectual history of the first rank." The aim of objectivity that guides this work is remarkable, and Janicaud's appeal to fairness and impartiality is also important in the face of so many agenda-driven works: he thus explains that "duty demands that we do all we can to avoid making this work narrow and partisan" (*HF*, 12). Objectivity may not be the ultimate horizon for matters of thought, yet it becomes indispensable in order to engage the work of interpretation of a thought that is always struggling with its *Sache*. It is that struggle which is really at stake in all the discussions on Heidegger, and ultimately it is that essential *polemos* that allows one to understand the accidental and conflictual history of the French reception of Heidegger in the last seventy years. In the end, this brilliant history will open onto the work of thinking, and it is Dominique Janicaud's extraordinary merit and impressive achievement to have first presented that history, and opened it for further thinking.

David Pettigrew and François Raffoul

HEIDEGGER IN FRANCE

PART I

Introduction

First Discoveries

Once upon a time, a poor Swabian child was born in a little village east of the Black Forest. By the sheer force of his intellect and the tenacity of his own efforts, he became world-famous and conquered the intelligentsia of the "hereditary enemy," France. How was Heidegger able to occupy, for more than half a century, the privileged position of being a fashionable philosopher, a *maître à penser* in the intellectual and cultural capital of Paris? Some Americans have posed the question more bluntly: how could minds as acute and intelligent as those of the great French intellectuals, from Sartre to Lacan, have become ensnared in the jargonistic traps of a Swabian peasant, who might have been clever, but who was ultimately a Nazi? They even made him into a *French philosopher,* by claiming that he was for fifty years the *maître à penser* of all of French philosophy (which, incidentally, would have been completely mistaken).[1]

This French "Heideggerianism" has been puzzling for some time in America, but especially in Germany. As early as 1946, Karl Löwith had this to say on the subject: "The fact that Heidegger found during the last war a wide audience among French intellectuals, in contrast to the situation in Germany at that time, is a symptom that merits renewed attention."[2] Is it yet again another almost incomprehensible coquetry on the part of those French? An indulgence? A fancy? An aberration? After all, the German expression, *Wie Gott im Frankreich,* designates a happiness overflowing with abundance, life in a land of plenty, with all of its supposed and desired delights and follies.[3] Not only do the French have the best wines and the finest cheeses, but they also decided that they can understand German philosophers—Nietzsche and Heidegger in particular—better than the Germans themselves. And they produced an unexpected and quite sophisticated French Nietzsche and Gallic Heidegger, who in many respects were more appealing and piquant than the originals. A major newspaper in Germany devoted an entire—and quite sarcastic—page to the "German philosopher's new adventures in France."[4] Those French!

Heidegger himself did not miss the opportunity to exploit his *French connection* in the last part of his life. Finding that he was no longer a prophet in his own country after the war, he received something like a consolation prize with the French. But what a prize! It was in no way restricted to a handful of the faithful around Jean Beaufret. In this affair, an even more surprising fact was that Heidegger's "influence" in France over the course of more than half a century constituted a multi-faceted intellectual adventure that was far from being a passive reception. It was rather a continual creation, a veritable dazzling display whose sparks extended well beyond the sphere of strictly academic philosophy. There really seems to have been a "French Heidegger."[5] What a contrast with Heidegger's reception in his own country! Whether hostile or favorable, that reception remained mostly confined to academic commentary, even in the cases of Jürgen Habermas and Karl Löwith, with the notable exception of Adorno, whose polemical text, *The Jargon of Authenticity*,[6] did not hold the public's attention for long. Gadamer was a sort of privileged witness and almost an arbiter of these German debates, without anyone ever knowing which side he favored.[7] Whereas in France Heidegger was the object of considerable intellectual debate, certainly with some misfiring or some duds, while serving as a catalyst for linguistic and conceptual inventions and opening new domains of research, by contrast, in Germany, the "Heidegger effect" fell flat, or nearly so: the Heidegger case was only the occasion, a particularly troublesome one, for an examination of the "German guilt." This settling of accounts was too serious and too personal to be conducive to creative thinking (not to mention the sort of intellectual playfulness found in Lacan, which was unthinkable in Germany).

Heidegger in France: would that be the best as well as the worst? Perhaps, but it would be perilous to speak as a judge here, when the first and foremost concern is to write a history of the French reception of Heidegger's thought—a project whose value nobody denies.[8] But on what conditions? First, of course, on the condition of avoiding any nationalistic pride, or its opposite: a systematically bad conscience. That should be especially easy since the word "France" designates not only a geographical entity or a national community, but also and more importantly a cultural and spiritual home expanded to include French-speaking philosophers (as well as foreign interpretations whose translations would come to enrich the debate within France). Above all, the historian must first narrate and analyze: analyze in order to narrate advisedly, narrate in order to analyze impartially, support one's analyses through the narrative—and inversely. While remaining a philosopher (as one must in order to be able to confront the difficulties of the project, both terminological and conceptual), I shall undertake first to be a historian, true to the Greek sense of *historia:* an inquiry that enables one to understand events. The effort at impartiality, however, will not rule out criticism. The reader would be rightfully disappointed if I limited myself to reviewing the various stages of an exceptional "reception," merely recording its various elements (to the extent that it would even be possible to limit oneself to such an impartial account): should one not set aside what is judged unimportant and at least lay the ground for a philosophical assessment of what is essential?

From the outset, Heidegger's name had hardly crossed the Rhine when translations and interpretations were already being put forward. It was indispensable for this study, after having introduced and presented them, to assess their philosophical scope and limits. The author, therefore, will assume the inevitable (and salutary) risks that such an undertaking entails.

From Fad to Method

Is our task, then, to give a mere digest of the history of a fad? This is a question that is partially justified, but only partially. It is clear that Heidegger's thinking came into the intellectual foreground in France at different times and that the inventiveness of that reception would not have been as intense (and perhaps would not even have existed) without the interest of a vast audience. How could the most difficult and austere philosophy have received such an exceptionally favorable reception? Even if one takes into account the temporary eclipses or the virulent reactions that attempted to get in its way, this fascination with Heidegger does not fail to surprise or trouble the vast majority of interpreters and historians of ideas. More generally: how could it be, is it even acceptable, that matters as serious as philosophical reflection and the most intimate movement of thoughts (which are going to orient action, ethics, politics, and so forth) are subject to external, sudden and superficial influences, or to circumstantial positions imitations? In philosophy, as elsewhere, "fame is in the end only the sum total of all misunderstandings gathered around a new name." In spite of himself, Heidegger assumed Rilke's disillusioned assessment for himself.[9]

The historian that I intend to remain will not censor these misunderstandings, but rather put them in context so that they may be better understood. The moralist is free to take offense, to condemn or condone. The fact is that the history of ideas is just as impure as history *tout court*: on the one hand, it is a matter of a purely intellectual analysis; on the other hand, it includes all-too-human passions, the most contradictory and violent "mass movement." Intellectual or philosophical history is no less subject to contingencies, arbitrariness, and absurdity than political or diplomatic history. Certainly, the work of the historian consists in bringing interpretive structures to light in the confused mass of traces and documents. But let the historian beware of trying to impose too much order based upon one's preferences or political or ideological orientation!

These preliminary reflections on the real difficulties of the undertaking might be discouraging. It is certain that when faced with the complexity of the "Heidegger effect" in France, considering him or herself incompetent to capture the most speculative subtleties, the historian will pass the ball to the philosopher, who will no doubt be tempted in turn to avoid overly scrutinizing such a welter, which will judged to be unrefined, journalistic, or anecdotal. Without claiming to find a definitive or indisputable balance in an inquiry that demands varied, contrasted, and even opposed perspectives, I have decided to itemize all these difficulties in order to arrive at a method *sui generis,* by weaving together—thanks to the thread of the *narration* that constitutes this first part—a text fitted to the specificities, singularities, and even the aberrations of the strange story of the eventful reception of an exceptionally difficult thought.

It is true that Heidegger was at the center of French intellectual life, but not continuously and not in the same way over the course of seventy years: before the war, after Liberation, up to "the Farias affair," and beyond. There was not a continuous expansion of his influence; rather, there were ruptures, upheavals, reversals, and strange delays, too: for example, it took nearly sixty years for two complete translations of *Being and Time* to finally appear in French!

"What is surprising in the reception of Heidegger in France is its slowness as much as its constancy and intensity," noted the greatly missed Jean-Michel Palmier.[10] Here, I will tell the tale of this unusual history—cryptic (like a mystery novel), at times dramatic (like a love story or a soap opera)—and I will tell it in its highs and lows, at its inspired peaks as well as its polemical episodes or extra-philosophical agendas. I will also endeavor to punctuate the narration with critical analyses. My aim is not only to raise the level of the debate or to restore it to its proper level, which would already be justified since the body of thought in question is so complex and demanding. Not to pursue the investigation all the way to the foundations and choices of that thought would be to condemn oneself to merely following or recording superficial effects. Is it impossible to trace these back to their presuppositions? One must at least try to address all issues throughout the many philosophical and ideological conflicts that I will analyze, in their clashes and in their truces.

* * *

This will be an interpretive text, then: no more, no less; and, in order to give it substance, to render it as interesting and as exhaustive as possible, instructive, and (why not?) useful, it is plainly necessary to be respectful of facts, dates, texts—and to meet the demands proper to the genre, by inscribing oneself within the lineage of the "histories of reception." On this path, with regard to Heidegger, this work will be pioneering, at least in the French-speaking world (whereas, with regard to Nietzsche, for example, the reception of his ideas and texts has already been the subject of significant work).[11]

These two giants, Nietzsche and Heidegger, however different they may be in other respects, share a common trait: they both were the subject of receptions in France so exceptional that they became, in a sense, "French philosophers." This recognition is more surprising in the case of Heidegger than Nietzsche: Nietzsche did not hesitate to rail against Prussian heaviness or German bad taste by contrasting them with the wit and style of the French. Heidegger, in contrast—and he has been rather harshly criticized for this—based his meditative power on the German-ness of his language, which he privileged along with Greek; he associated the tasks of essential thought with an approach that rejected universalism. Whereas Nietzsche, inspired by our French moralists and novelists, courted the support of the most distinguished French minds (to receive a letter from Taine filled him with an immense joy), Heidegger at first did little, in the early part of his career, to cultivate such connections. On the contrary, his indisputably nationalistic engagement in 1933, his attacks on Cartesianism, and the relative dearth of significant references to the great French authors (aside from the most classical, Descartes and Pascal, in *Being and Time*) did not seem destined to strike a chord in France. One should also point out that the French enthusiasm for Heidegger ran counter more than once to the prevailing cultural and political climate: before the war, when anti-German feelings were prevalent (even among intellectuals), one would think that Heidegger would have found his first admirers among those on the extreme right who had been seduced by Italian fascism, and then by Hitler. This was not at all the case, as his first admirers were on the contrary the great liberal intellectuals, who were mostly Jewish. After the war, the collapse of Nazism ought to logically have alienated the French intelligentsia from German thought in general and from Heidegger in particular. Again, this was not at all what happened; one had to wait for the publication of Farias' book in 1987 for a realignment to occur, one that nonetheless did not associate "Heideggerianism" with the extreme right.[12] The French reception of Heidegger was thus not exempt from peculiarities (which some might denounce as a kind of intellectual masochism) and it indisputably appears more disconcerting than that of Nietzsche. This paradoxical aspect, which I am not the first to note,[13] should not be minimized: instead, our task shall be to contextualize and analyze it.

Heidegger himself was surprised by this reception, but was able to turn it to his advantage, to the point of exploiting this fame among his compatriots to some extent, and appealing in a rather heavy-handed way to the fact that a few French thinkers "rallied" to his conception of the speculative privilege of the German language.[14] Thanks to the warm welcome that he gave his numerous French visitors, particularly thanks to his friendship with Jean Beaufret and then with René Char, and thanks to his sojourns in France (undertaken with great pleasure[15]), it was in the end a "new Heidegger" who came to us and whose good-natured persona prevailed until it clashed in our imaginary with the dark brown shadows evoked by Farias' book.[16] After all, he did not have to respond to Jean Beaufret with a letter as consequential as the "Letter on Humanism." Already, before the war, unable (or unwilling) to accompany the German delegation to the 1937 *Congrès Descartes* in Paris, he composed a text in which, as we shall see, he laid the groundwork—in consistently appropriate and not "imperialistic" terms—for a real dialogue between German thought and French thought. These are signs that Heidegger himself—despite his political error and his strongly held "Germanism"—did not in any way isolate himself, like a hermit lost in his meditations, but was able to be extremely attentive to his reception in France. Certainly, if his own willingness to dialogue does not explain everything, it does allow one to better understand how the paradoxical or "unexpected" character of this reception was compensated by "transmissions" and initiatives that pertain as much to "anecdotal history" as to the domain of pure thought.

In fact, the phrase "Heidegger in France" is also to be taken literally, since the Master made several visits to France, including Paris, Cerisy, Aix-en-Provence, and Le Thor—visits all the more remarkable as they were made by the most sedentary philosopher since Kant: Heidegger never left Europe and was not at all inclined to leave Germany or even his Swabian homeland. In contrast with Nietzsche's visits to Nice, Italy, or Sils-Maria, Heidegger's visits were hardly the partially touristic, partially health related escapades of a solitary person, but rather trips that were carefully planned and executed as though for a head of state.

I will not overestimate this first dimension, which, while clearly anecdotal, is nonetheless meaningful (to an extent that will have to be specified further). I will not underestimate it either. The history we are following here also plays itself out on more complex levels. Among these, we shall have to constantly address the problems of translation: indeed, "Heidegger in France" also and perhaps above all denotes an impressive collection of texts that at first glance seem nearly unintelligible, with scraps of meaning appearing gradually, which then offer more or less decipherable reference points and suggestions, and finally constitute semantic constellations that become full-fledged philosophical stakes, often reduced to their ideological currency.

The way in which Heidegger has been translated (well or poorly) has never been immaterial. Felicitous, awkward, or even catastrophic, translations always betray something of the choices, intentions, and ulterior motives of their authors. Translators are comparable to those ambassadors of yesteryears who had the power, depending on their skill or lack thereof, to bring about war or peace. They had the privilege of *being the author* by proxy, and, in this capacity, they channeled, capitalized on, and sometimes usurped something of the author's spiritual powers (attractive or repulsive, almost taboo), especially when the author found his or her prestige reinforced by his or her mystery. The translator need only say one word, hazard one expression, and immediately minds are ignited, a polemic begins to rage, the Left Bank trembles. This very French hypersensitivity to the nuances of language is probably subsiding or even disappearing because of the media. For centuries, it served as a blockade against strange or foreign [*étranges ou étrangers*] malapropisms, since French clarity and distinction had become proverbial. Did this blockade give way over the past fifty years under the pressure of the "Heidegger effect"? So it would seem, since the Germanization of French thought has wreaked havoc by rendering a language that had been previously known for its elegance (although other factors also played a role in causing this refinement to disappear . . .) heavy and "technical." One can easily imagine Fontenelle dying even younger of apoplexy while reading Sartre, or the uproarious laughter of Molière poring over the anagrams and apothegms of Diafoirus Lacan. But there is no need to go so far back, in a kind of surrealist time-travel. Only eleven years separate *The Two Sources of Morality and Religion* from *Being and Nothingness:* what happened between 1932 and 1943 such that Bergson's lucid reserve gave way to Sartre's dark and implacable rhetoric? War and the reading of Heidegger . . .

The defenders of our beautiful language should not, however, press their *lamento* too far. I will take a more serene look, although still as critical as possible, at these linguistic disruptions (which, incidentally, are not entirely new[17]); philosophy was not the only scene of these seismic events, far from it (the Anglo-Saxon invasion rushes through with other, even more powerful, channels); furthermore, a patient and precise observation enables one to realize that things are sorting themselves out gradually: many monstrosities do not survive; they are promptly cast aside into the museum of horrors or curiosities; just as Attila retreated as quickly as he had arrived, certain translators met swift defeat. I will attempt here to give an account of this sensitive question of the translations of Heidegger, a very touchy and even painful issue, without claiming to render a definitive verdict. Translating Heidegger into French was and remains a very ambiguous experience where the French language sacrifices a part of its beauty to what it believes to be profundity, but where inversely it grants the legitimacy drawn from its age-old stature and dignity to audacities that it takes to be typically Germanic. There was between the Master and Jean Beaufret, so concerned with the beauty of language, an acute awareness of these translation questions.

At a more humble but also more objective level, I shall endeavor to do the reader the service of trying to clarify debates that are often forbiddingly technical. Without claiming to resolve all the difficulties, the present work strives to be both pertinent and useful, to be cognizant of the obvious pitfalls, to respect the work done by several waves of translator-interpreters, while formulating its own propositions.

I have thus begun to take into account the abundant difficulties that stem from the richness of a reception fertile with interesting episodes, reversals, misrepresentations, and displacements. Were they a series of misunderstandings? This cannot be ruled out: but it is far too simplistic to settle the issue by claiming that the whole of the French reception was mistaken.[18] Even if this were the case, should the historian of ideas really behave like a tutor correcting arithmetic homework? The most interesting part of this history would then be missed and one would forget that philosophical hermeneutics is at least equal to literature when it comes to dramatic developments! Nor should one overlook the positive aspects of the reception of that thought, in particular the renewal of the history of philosophy, an in-depth work taking place apart from passing trends. Furthermore, it is most likely in this domain that Heidegger's influence will prove most durable and most beneficial. The "final assessment" will come in its due time.

A further difficulty—which, from another perspective, could be considered an advantage—comes from the fact that the author himself was a witness or actor, albeit modestly, in this history. The risk of being both judge and judged in the trial should not be underestimated. Paradoxically, it is this almost insurmountable *aporia* that provided the opportunity for the clearest choice concerning the method: the decision to separate the main text from the quite personal "epilogues," relating what the author experienced, thought, believed, or heard, in the first person, and reporting on encounters and exchanges with Heidegger himself, and, of course, with Jean Beaufret and other French philosophers over the course of many years. Are these the occasion for a confession? At the very least it is a testimony, perhaps a *catharsis,* in any case a clarification that allows one to put one's cards on the table and to let personal engagements and philosophical stakes illuminate each other. The development of ideas cannot be completely distinguished from human, all-too-human encounters; we shall have more than one opportunity to confirm this.

This personal involvement in the matter obliges us to raise, with complete frankness and transparency, the question of the author's impartiality, not only with regard to debates in which he was involved, but also because the issues in question remain very much alive, and often controversial. No more than in any macro-historical inquiry can absolute objectivity be achieved here. Is impartiality even possible? On the basis of his own research on texts, documents, and testimonials, the author had to recognize a fact that was not entirely unexpected: any attempt at neutrality in the reading and interpretation of this mass of information would have deprived the enterprise of its edge and almost any relevance it might have had. Respect for the facts and commitment to integrity are not to be confused with the impossible quest for a cosmic or divine vantage point from which to judge matters here below. The author must accept his limits and especially his responsibilities. Any work of reading implies a selection and choices, which are always open to criticism. Let it be perfectly clear that the philosophical history presented here is both a document and a testimonial. As serious as it may be in its intentions and in its execution (this is what I wanted and hoped for), it certainly could not avoid some deficiencies or flaws; above all, it wants to be and knows itself to be exposed to discussion as well as to new critical reconsiderations. This contribution does not intend to conclude debates that have been raging for nearly half a century, but to carry them farther, pass them on, and even renew them.

The chief obstacle remains: how could we combine narrative and analysis to account for this enormous mass of facts, events, and thoughts, in order to untangle the most essential knots, to mark the necessary divisions? A completely synchronic composition, working on the level of general themes, would drain all the life and even interest from this sequence of discoveries and episodes, which constitute a veritable intrigue, that is often fascinating and almost always unpredictable. Conversely, a purely chronological overview would miss the coherence or incoherence of the positions that are under discussion. We have therefore chosen to respect the diachronic order, punctuating it with divisions that will in each case have to be justified. Each main chapter corresponds in principle to a decade; but we have not applied this rule mechanically, which would have led to absurdities.

To begin from the beginning, let us take the exemplary cases that first come to mind: it is entirely natural and necessary to refer to the first French translations of Heidegger and to the pioneers who mentioned his name or offered introductions to his thought; but how does one discriminate? It is generally agreed that the most historically decisive moment was Corbin's 1938 translation of "What Is Metaphysics?" It seems reasonable to end the chapter devoted to the first receptions of Heidegger's work with Corbin, for the war and Sartre's publication of *Being and Nothingness* in 1943 would begin a new phase: Heidegger would be recognized as the greatest contemporary German philosopher and his main philosophical theses would help crystallize a new philosophical movement, namely, existentialism.

Even though the division of later phases will prove more delicate, I will follow the same principle: to adhere to the course of events pertaining to the reception of our author and unfold its most incontestable philosophical articulations.

What Horizon of Possibilities?

Yet this is not the most decisive element in the play of "reception." Even the word itself can be heard in French both in the abstract sense of a connection between a transmitter and a receiver and in the infinitely richer and more complex sense of receiving a guest into one's home. The case of Heidegger magnifies this complexity, since, received in France not only as an author through his texts but also in person, he provoked not only various forms of fascination and rejection, but also unforeseeably creative developments. This explains why, in its various mutations, "Heidegger in France" could have taken on specific forms in which the "original" can barely be recognized: it became, in short, a kind of mutant or even a Genetically Modified Organism![19]

Whatever the necessity of taking all the aspects of this strange "presence" into account, the main focus of the work will clearly be the texts. As for the critical assessments that will have to be made of the various stages of translations and interpretations, we should not overlook the "horizon of possibilities" out of which these emerged. The works of Gadamer and Jauss[20] taught us both to avoid separating a work from the context of its emergence and to reinscribe the readings that appropriate this work back into the living tradition that continues to enrich itself through this appropriation.

Our progression will be linear only in the sense that it will follow the chronological "framework" of events, from the 1930s to the year 2000[21]; it will nonetheless involve some interruptions and retrospective moments; its rhythm will be uneven, depending on the intensity of publications and discussions.

At first, I had not envisioned a second part completely devoted to interviews with the personalities, translators and/or interpreters who have been significant actors or witnesses in the reception of Heideggerian thought in France. It was the development of the work itself that obliged us to call on these witnesses. A living history is a history that continues to unfold. Such is the case of a "reception" that is continually being revived, revealing in the recesses of its own memory facts, aspects and ideas that until then had remained either unapparent or neglected. The aftershocks provoked by the interviews have stimulated the author's research and critical reflection. It would have been a shame not to share this with the reader. I would like to express my gratitude to the interviewees, who substantially helped enrich the initial project.

With respect to the narrative itself, the balance was intentionally broken in Chapter 12, because it became apparent that the linear progress had to give the last word to a philosophical meditation, even if any "final assessment" proves elusive in the complex field of the reception of a great thought.

One more word on the problem of impartiality. Though it is plainly necessary to distinguish it from an impossible notion of objectivity in the domain in which we are engaged (the understanding of intellectual and cultural events that are infinitely more complex than the most complex quantum events!), duty demands that we do all we can to avoid making this work narrow and partisan. This, moreover, would provide very little interest. Nonetheless, one must acknowledge that the task is not an easy one: in addition to the brilliant intellectual performances and the various achievements in writing and thought, the history we have to write has also involved some personal rivalries and polemics that were often cruel and no doubt petty. When a light skiff sets out on such tumultuous waters, can it avoid capsizing? Good intentions are never enough. Even if the author were to profess his good faith and desire for impartiality a thousand times, he could not satisfy everyone on every point. Readers will judge for themselves. Let us therefore make a pact: do not put the effort of your humble servant to maintain critical distance into doubt, but do not grant him either any particular indulgence owing to the difficulty of the undertaking. I know that the impartiality I seek is difficult to maintain, despite all the precautions that have been taken to be respectful to persons when there have been clear theoretical disagreements.

If I only manage to shed a little more light on this history, then this work will not have been a complete failure! Whatever judgment the reader finally renders on this narrative about these seventy years of intellectual and philosophical life, let him or her not forget—under the tumult of fashionable trends and cliques— the zeal and courage of those young minds who admired Heidegger's thought, the philosophical talent and selflessness of the main protagonists and of the Master himself. Let him or her find in the following pages the account of an epic, which, while concerning the "history of ideas," nonetheless touches upon the passion for truth of flesh-and-blood human beings, with all its collection of illusions and weaknesses—indissociably intertwined—brought about by a perhaps super-human mirage and its incontestably all-too-human reactions. Let him or her also recognize, then, that whatever the imperfections of the present work, it has the merit of being new, at least in its scope. Despite the abundance of translations, interpretations, and polemical interventions, no one has ever attempted to write in French the complete history of the singularly turbulent and unexpectedly fruitful reception of what is quite possibly the most original thought of the twentieth century. Thanks are due to Richard Figuier who helped launch me on this intellectual and philosophical adventure, which I surely would have not have ventured on my own. My sincere thanks also go to Hélène Monsacré, who helped at a difficult moment and very effectively supported my efforts. Incidentally, never did I see (or foresee) myself in the role of a historian, when I had the privilege of briefly meeting Heidegger in person and of being Jean Beaufret's student, disciple, and close friend. Rightly or wrongly, the author-to-be did not walk around with a notebook in hand, and he never hid a tape-recorder under his coat. He always thought that one had to respect the wonderful evanescence of exceptional moments and let memories sort themselves out. Furthermore, there is no lack of documents and texts, and, in order to enrich this book, we have solicited testimonials from the main translators and interpreters. The inevitably historiographic dimension provided here has been undertaken from the outset with an awareness of the humility and limits of this sort of work. I did not intend to bury what is essential under anecdotes or gossip, but, on the contrary, to reconstitute its native soil. This is a considered—and, let us hope, philosophical—choice: there is not, on the one hand, trivial history, and on the other, grand history. Heidegger himself may have put too much distance between the latter, *Geschichte,* and the former, *Historie.* The threads of any history are tangled and the role of the contingency of encounters is no less significant in the case of intellectual history than history itself. Ideas also have their Cleopatra's nose. Nonetheless, I have always tried to preserve the openness of the philosophical horizon. The reader will assess how well I have managed to respond to challenges that were as formidable as they were difficult to reconcile.

Finally, the author may confess that sketching this tableau has been a fascinating task, even if, on leaving the workshop, he is aware that this varied fresco might need yet a retouching or completion. At the very least, it was worthwhile to conduct this experiment on a terrain less visible, *prima facie,* than those of economics or diplomacy, but in the long run perhaps more decisive for the fate of our civilization, if it is true that in the end thoughts are what guide the world.

* * *

Let me thank here all those who, directly or indirectly, lent me their assistance: Kostas Axelos, Guy Basset, Walter Biemel, Jean Bourgault, Alain Boutot, Lucien Braun, Michel Contat, Jean-François Courtine, Marc Crépon, Françoise Dastur, Michel Deguy, Jacques Derrida, Éliane Escoubas, Jean-Pierre Faye, Didier Franck, Maurice de Gandillac, Claude Geffré, Gérard Granel, Jean Greisch, Michel Haar, Pierre Klossowski, Philippe Lacoue-Labarthe, Marc de Launay, Jean-Pierre Lefebvre, Paule Llorens, Jean-Luc Marion, Henri Mongis, Edgar Morin, Roger Munier, Jean-Luc Nancy, Jacques Orsoni, Nicole Parfait, Alain Pernet, Frédéric Postel, Élisabeth Rigal, Tom Rockmore, Claude Roëls, Michel Rybalka, Jacques Taminiaux, Claude Troisfontaines, Éric Vigne, and François Warin.

1 First Crossings of the Rhine

Heidegger's sudden celebrity following the publication of *Sein und Zeit* in 1927 did not go completely unnoticed in Paris, which was at the time, even more than today, the intellectual capital of Europe, and probably of the world. But to know a name is one thing; to enter into a thinker's thought is another. While Heidegger's masterpiece had to wait nearly sixty years before being translated in its entirety into French, reports and publications establish that distinguished university professors like Léon Brunschvicg and Xavier Léon quickly recognized, in this case, that a philosophical event had taken place in Germany.

An even more surprising fact is that in the years immediately following the publication of *Sein und Zeit,* a course was offered at the Sorbonne on contemporary German philosophy, published as *Les Tendances actuelles de la philosophie allemande.*[1] We do not have evidence that the last part, devoted to Heidegger, was delivered in 1928. In his foreword, the author, Georges Gurvitch, only mentions that the book he published in 1930 assembled four studies summarizing three courses that were delivered at the Sorbonne between 1928 and 1930. Clearly, since the two sections on Husserl, Lask, and Hartmann had already been published in journals, the chapter on Heidegger was the most recent.

Whatever the case may be, this confirms that Heidegger's name was uttered at the Sorbonne before 1930 and that a first survey of his thought was presented. In retrospect, it is rather striking that this pioneering work was done by Georges Gurvitch, who was known later by generations of students only as a sociologist immersed in his own system, and who became quite distant from Heidegger's thought. At the end of the 1920s, Gurvitch was not yet a full professor: he was only a lecturer and still affiliated with the Russian university of Prague.

The terms used to present Heidegger's work were far from neutral. Léon Brunschvicg spoke of a "profound resonance,"[2] and Georges Gurvitch presented the young German master as "the most popular philosopher in Germany today."[3] All this confirms that the impact of *Sein und Zeit* made Heidegger's name known in Paris and elevated him to prominence, though he had barely reached the age of forty.

An Existential Idealism

The thirty or so pages that Gurvitch devoted to Heidegger's "descriptive analysis of existence" presented a surprising contrast between a conscientious and relatively faithful summary of Heidegger's positions and some critical judgments that today appear peremptory, but whose coherence is worth reconstructing in light of the intellectual situation of the time.

First, the exposition adequately presented the originality of the new phenomenology, a phenomenology concerned with raising the question of being on the basis of existence alone. This questioning was not to be confused with an anthropology and was neither an idealism nor a realism.[4] The being of the human being is care (*Sorge*), and it is through anxiety in the face of its own thrownness (*Geworfenheit*) that existence "finds itself again."[5] However, one must first understand how the existent is delivered over to everydayness in the reign of the "everyman" [*monsieur tout le monde*]: this is how Gurvitch translated *das Man,* in a quaint manner, but which at least avoided the jargon of the "They." He showed clearly that humans' existence in the world is involved—prior to the knowledge of the presence of things—in a relationship that he left untranslated [the *Zuhandenes*], and he recognized that the Heideggerian existent is in no way isolated in solipsism, but open to *Fürsorge* understood as "intentional sympathy" in Scheler's sense. If an existence that is lost in the world is *fallen* [*Verfallen*], it is nonetheless an "indispensable mode" of human existence.[6] However, "Anxiety . . . frees humans and returns them to themselves";[7] next, the theme of being-toward-death was invoked; anxiety is freedom for death: this existential interpretation leads the human being to *Entschlossenheit,* translated by the expression *résolution résignée* [resigned resoluteness], which is clearly inadequate, for the theme of moral resignation is absent from Heidegger's text. This summary ended with several pages devoted to the theory of temporality and historicality: he showed convincingly that existence is concretized temporally and especially out of the future, and that the modes of temporalization determine the modes of existence, as well as the separation between the banal and the "genuine." This finite temporality, reinterpreted especially on the basis of a parallel with Bergson's theory of duration, is realized in historicality and is to be understood in terms of a truth that is prior to judgment and that is *disclosed* [*Entdecktsein*].[8]

Gurvitch did not conceal the schematic nature of his exposition, while emphasizing that *Sein und Zeit* was an unfinished work.[9] Once again, one may be surprised by this last claim, but wrongly in this case, for Heidegger had indeed announced a second part that he never published.

The importance of this first account cannot be denied. But even as we acknowledge Gurvitch's serious effort at understanding and his intellectual honesty and rigor (he also consulted *Kant und das Problem der Metaphysik,* which had just appeared in 1929), the limits of his work are all too apparent. First, with respect to the translations, which were pedagogically inclined and devoid of jargon: some are acceptable (*délaissement* for *Geworfenheit, malaise* for *Unheimlichkeit, dégradation* for *Verfallen*); others are frankly insufficient: *état émotif* for *Befindlichkeit*, a notion that, just like that of *Stimmung*, was vaguely referred to "a rather emotive state of human 'synaesthesia'"[10]; finally, it is clear that difficulties are merely circumvented, and not resolved: the problem of the translation of *Dasein* was not even raised; the *Dasein des Menschen* is simply "human existence";[11] we saw that the *Zuhandenes* was not even translated and that "resignation" was added to *Entschlossenheit*. In like manner, finite existence was presented as "humiliated,"[12] without any textual reference that justifies this interpretation.

Beyond these problems of translation, all the more understandable given that the author was the first to really face them, what matters is to evaluate Gurvitch's critical remarks on a philosophy he interpreted as an "existential idealism." How is this expression to be understood? Certainly not in the Marxist sense, which is the first to come to mind. It is in the course of Gurvitch's explication of section 43 of *Sein und Zeit* on the reality of being-in-the-world that the discussion of idealism and realism comes to the fore. But precisely, as Gurvitch himself seemed to recognize, Heidegger does not separate the world from human existence any more than he does human existence from the world: and he rejects the poorly formulated problematic concerning the reality of the external world. In this way, he rejects idealism and realism equally. If he seems at one point to favor idealism, it is inasmuch as idealism understands that being constitutes a "transcendental" for all beings, but he rejects the reduction of being to a pure "I" or subject.[13] That is quite a tenuous basis from which to claim that Heidegger's position is an "idealism"! Gurvitch nonetheless asserted just this, on the basis of the primacy of understanding [*Verstehen*], and by arguing from the fact that "all 'understanding' has pronounced idealist traits."[14] Nevertheless, this reintroduction of an "existential idealism" occurred at the price of a misunderstanding of the page of *Sein und Zeit* that was cited:[15] Heidegger does not admit in any way that he is an idealist in this passage, because he denies that the a priori character of the Existent stems from any sort of consciousness in general; always placing "ideality" in quotation marks, he underlies that, just like the affirmation of "eternal truths," such ideality, when applied to an absolute subject, belongs "to the remnants of Christian theology within the philosophical problematic that have not yet been radically eliminated."[16]

One better understands Gurvitch's aim, without for that matter being able to agree with it, when one realizes that he claimed to see a sort of Platonic dialectic in Heidegger (a reading that is all the more untenable since he attempted to justify it on the basis of Heidegger's theory of truth: in fact, truth as "disclosure" arises prior to the idea or the ideal). This erroneous reading can be clarified in light of Gurvitch's hermeneutic horizon, one that he himself elaborated in some "critical observations" that are not unimportant: the relation—which Heidegger did not thoroughly adopt—between phenomenal consciousness and the absolute in Fichte's later philosophy. Situating Heidegger in this lineage (idealist but anti-Hegelian, constructivist but irrationalist), Gurvitch denounced phenomenology's inability to ground its value judgments; the opposition between everyday existence and an existence that finds itself again seemed to him to be conditioned by a moralism that is unable to justify itself. An abyss separates the relative from the absolute.

However relevant these criticisms may be, they came too soon, so to speak, since they were addressed to an audience that was as yet innocent of any fascination with Heidegger. Paradoxically, they allow one to recognize in Heidegger—in a form still too indeterminate—a kind of ethical concern (and even a moralism) that will be later largely denied him. But there is a premonition in Gurvitch's final judgment, when he identified "the dangers that seem to threaten Heidegger's philosophy."[17]

In the end, this very first reception reveals both an effort to read and a misunderstanding that was probably unavoidable. Despite an effort to recognize his originality, Heidegger was received as a prodigal son of German idealism who turned against Hegel but lacked the stature of a Fichte.

How does one let go of oneself so as to discover the other? The recognition of a great and difficult author is a long-term project that will require many more efforts and engender further misunderstandings.

Encounters, Studies, and Pioneering Translations

Maurice de Gandillac, then twenty-five years old, had the privilege of participating, along with Léon Brunschvicg, Jean Cavaillès, and Emmanuel Levinas, in the famous philosophical gatherings in Davos, Switzerland, held during Easter in 1929. In his memoirs,[18] he recounted with an admirable intensity the famous discussion between Ernst Cassirer and Martin Heidegger on Kant. He did not leave this *grosse Disputation* with a sense of uneasiness as a result of Heidegger's allegedly arrogant (and somewhat anti-Semitic) attitude; he disagreed on this point with Mrs. Toni Cassirer, who seemed to him, in her own memoirs, to have retrospectively projected the image of a Heidegger compromised by his political activity of 1933. It is worth citing also Cavaillès's enthusiastic reaction to this exceptional philosophical confrontation: "It was with a true intellectual joy that the listeners were able to hear Heidegger—whose enthusiasm was only strengthened by the questions and criticisms—define the meaning of *Dasein* in his philosophy in impressive formulations, situate the place and function of truth in metaphysical reality, and finally bring to light the role of anxiety as revelatory of human finitude and the presence of nothingness."[19]

The French reader is fortunate to have been able to consult (although only in a library, since any reprinting of this "pirate" publication was unfortunately forbidden) a translation of this discussion, as well as related documents,[20] which provide an idea of the intellectual grandeur and philosophical stakes of these exchanges. Heidegger defended his interpretation on the basis of the role of the schematism and transcendental imagination, and Cassirer criticized it on the basis of a conception of Kant's architectonic that was at once more classical and more systematic, and that also emphasized practical reason (which Heidegger reduced, perhaps excessively, to the finitude of the Existent).

In the margins of this "summit," as one might imagine, several other discussions took place in which Heidegger was also the star. Here is an anecdote that testifies to this: the young Levinas sat on a pile of snow and read some passages from *Sein und Zeit* out loud; it was a beautiful day, the sun was shining and melted the snow; it turned out that Levinas had been sitting on a pile of manure.

Despite his youth, Levinas would also play an important role in the diffusion and explanation of Heidegger's thought. It was in Strasbourg that he discovered *Sein und Zeit,* thanks to the pastor Jean Hering, a former student of Husserl.[21] He became a student of Husserl[22] and Heidegger[23] at Freiburg in 1928–29. It was above all Heidegger who would soon fascinate him, as he went on to explain: "The great thing I found was the way in which Husserl's path had been extended and transformed by Heidegger. To speak in the language of a tourist, I had the impression that I went to see Husserl and found Heidegger. . . . I knew right away that this was one of the greatest philosophers in history. Like Plato, like Kant, like Hegel, like Bergson."[24] The same enthusiasm was in evidence in an article published in 1931 in the journal *Revue d'Allemagne.*[25] Beginning with an idyllic evocation of Freiburg, "the capital of phenomenology," the text pays homage to Husserl, but celebrates Heidegger in incomparably more flattering terms: his name "is now the glory of Germany." Levinas adds: "Endowed with an exceptional intellectual power, his teaching and his works offer the best proof of the fecundity of the phenomenological method. But already a considerable success manifests his extraordinary prestige." The conclusion takes the praise to the extreme: "While contemplating this august gathering, I came to understand the German student I had met on the Berlin–Basel express train on my way to Freiburg. When I asked him his destination, he responded without blinking: "I am going to see the greatest philosopher in the world."[26] The course given by "the greatest philosopher in the world" that Levinas attended in the winter semester of 1928 was modestly named "Introduction to Philosophy," but it was such a sensation that one had to arrive several hours in advance to find a seat![27] It was then that Levinas recommended that Blanchot read Heidegger. Blanchot confirmed this in the following way: "Thanks to Emmanuel Levinas—without whom, in 1927 or 1928, I would not have been able to begin to understand *Sein und Zeit*—reading this book really moved me intellectually. An extraordinary event just occurred: it is impossible to diminish its effect, even today, even in my memory."[28]

In the conclusion of his 1930 thesis on Husserl,[29] Levinas revealed the Heideggerian character of his interpretation of the "constitutional problems as ontological problems," and he presented Heidegger's philosophy as the bold interpretation of the *"meaning of the very existence of being"* as suggested by Husserlian phenomenology[30]: Heidegger raised the question of the ontological meaning of objectivity that Husserl had addressed without resolving it; the Husserlian overcoming of objectivism and naturalism tends in this direction, but "only Heidegger dares to face this problem deliberately."[31]

In 1932, Levinas published an article, this time on the ontology of *Sein und Zeit,* with an absolutely laudatory preamble.[32] In this article, Levinas no longer simply whets the appetites of his readers. He provided a substantial and conscientious introduction to existential ontology, and in a much different spirit than Gurvitch: the task was not first to combine some critical remarks with a schematic presentation of Heidegger's theses, but to set aside any other point of view, so as to lay bare a radically new kind of thinking. Without mentioning Gurvitch by name, Levinas refuted him, maintaining that with respect to Heidegger's ontology, "His undertaking is thus diametrically opposed to that of dialectical philosophy."[33] What followed were some very clear and pedagogical pages—devoid of any jargon or heavy-handedness (a fault that marred the translation of a certain Bessey, published in the same year[34])—in which Levinas explained in succession: the difference between being and beings, the meaning of pre-ontological understanding, and the fact that the human's mode of being is conceived of as *Dasein* in a radically finite way. Continuing with the relation to space and the world, Levinas accurately discerned Heidegger's break with the Cartesian tradition: space is to be thought on the basis of the world, itself reconceived as an "environing" world, and any theoretical perspective on the world is drawn from a more original relation, handiness [*maniabilité*], or "readiness-to-hand" [*Zuhandenheit*]. Emphasizing the positive sense of the possible in Heidegger, Levinas next explained the role of affective disposition [*Befindlichkeit*] in its relation to facticity, and in particular in the exemplary case of the existential understanding opened up by anxiety, in contrast to everyday existence. He also noted that falling [*Verfallen*] must be interpreted in a radically nontheological sense. On all these points, Levinas's article, without claiming to be exhaustive, exhibited a deep familiarity with Heidegger's text and an unfailing competence, in particular with respect to the specificity of the phenomenological method (as a *via negationis* relative to everyday existence) and concerning intentionality comprehended within immanence (a point that was not lost on Sartre). We have already noted the absence of jargon from these translations; we may add that there are even some inventive renderings (for example, *parlerie* [idle talk] for *Gerede*).

The hermeneutic horizon here, in contrast to Gurvitch, involved the reception of a new thought. Levinas recognized the extent to which phenomenology—in Heidegger even more than in Husserl—broke with German idealism. Concerning the dynamic unity of care, he concluded: "This is indeed an excellent example of the Heideggerian mode of thinking. It is not a question of reuniting concepts by a 'conceptual synthesis' [*synthèse pensée*]. Modes of existence such as these are only accessible to effective existence itself. To think their unity is to realize it in existing."[35]

Despite his perspicacity, Levinas remained nonetheless relatively conventional in comparison with the enthusiasm of Rachel Bespaloff. Unknown today, she was a friend in the 1930s of several leading intellectual luminaries, including Daniel Halévy, to whom she sent an inspired letter in the autumn of 1932. This letter, which was republished,[36] first appeared at the end of 1933, thanks to Daniel Halévy himself, with the following circumspect note (suggesting that Rachel Bespaloff's enthusiasm had surely been tempered by Heidegger's political activity): "I believe I ought to make clear that this letter was written in September 1932."[37]

The letter in question is imbued with an extraordinary spirit and intelligence: "The poignant grandeur of this philosopher is that, with an unparalleled audacity, he immediately places himself in the inextricable; he does not feign to cut the knot of Existence, but reveals its complexity to us. His conception of the world reveals this inextricable entanglement."[38] Confronting the untranslatable character of key terms in *Being and Time,* Rachel Bespaloff singled out *Erschlossenheit* ("unconcealment"? "revelation"? Perhaps rather, a "prior disclosure") as the book's central theme, in the sense of "a sort of immense *Kunst der Fuge.*" Indeed, it is in music that this ontological structure seemed to show itself most clearly to her, by unifying the two modes of disclosure (understanding and affectivity). That is why rapture [*ravissement*] seemed to her as important as anxiety in the revelation of ontological sensibility, the crux of which is being-toward-death. One must discern therein an opening onto "the imminent . . . possibility of existence."[39] In this way, the "voice of conscience" makes itself heard. The choice of authenticity is to be understood as the opening of the "visibility of being."[40] However, the state of total destitution to which Heidegger is led "does not go without provoking some resistance."[41] Must one accept that freedom refers only to itself? Rachel Bespaloff believed that what is lacking is a sense of a creative *Fiat:* "The freedom with clipped wings that unfurls its leaden flight beneath the vast and somber sky of Heidegger's philosophy, as you know, is Necessity."[42] She concluded her letter with a magnificent allusion to the end of the second *Faust:* that which resonates in Heidegger with respect to Faust is the meaning of a finite temporality in which, as in music, "all that has been still resonates, in which all that shall be can already be heard."[43] A great poetic spirit permeates Heidegger's world, a world that Rachel Bespaloff admired so profoundly, though without giving herself over to it entirely. Our description provides only an incomplete account of one of the most beautiful texts ever inspired by Heidegger, a text that testifies to the quality of this first reception, one that deserved to be retrieved from oblivion.

This enthusiasm raised expectations, only to be disappointed in the case of Benjamin Fondane: he had placed Heidegger among the "trail blazers of free thought" and discovered that the philosopher "only concerned himself with anxiety in order to describe it."[44] In sum, since Heidegger is "alas, neither a poet nor a madman,"[45] it is better to turn away from existence with the courageous rationalism of Husserl. Not expressing himself as a professional philosopher, but with a freedom of tone that is still surprising, Fondane turned away from the laicized and academic version that Heidegger seemed to give to the existential anxiety of a Kierkegaard or a Dostoyevsky: "Tragedy—even that of the gods—is neither grand nor beautiful; human 'finitude,' its 'abandoned and humiliated' character, even in the mouth of a Heidegger, has a base and guttural accent that turns one's stomach."[46]

Toward the Concrete?

In 1932, Jean Wahl published some studies on contemporary thought, gathered under the title *Vers le concret* [Toward the concrete].[47] This book had a certain impact, and particularly on Sartre.[48] Although none of the essays in the book bear on Heidegger, he is cited approvingly and substantively several times. The figure of Heidegger is certainly present in the background of explicit discussions of James, Whitehead, and Marcel; what is important now is to verify in what terms and according to what perspectives it intervenes.

Jean Wahl's approach was more cursory and allusive than systematic; his conceptualization was not always terribly precise, and the vagueness that affected his terminology conveyed the fortuitous character of a constant improvisation. The orientation of his book is nonetheless plainly perceptible in the preface. Against Hegel and the idealist critique of the sensible, it was necessary to return to the richness of immediacy and to the conditions of its emergence, which were not to be conceived in an "atomistic"[49] way. There is an empiricism that is not naïve and that recovers, indirectly, "the feeling for the given."[50] In various though convergent forms, James's pragmatism, Whitehead's philosophy of the organism, and Marcel's ontological disquiet were all searching for a concreteness that occurs prior to intellectuality and which is already, at a more existential level, the discovery of the thickness of the world. It is easy to understand how much this anti-idealist and anti-intellectual inspiration was capable of seducing a whole generation surrounding Sartre.

What function do the references to Heidegger play in this reorientation of contemporary philosophy? Wahl clarified it in a somewhat curious way in the first of the notes devoted to *Sein und Zeit,* which is worth citing, for the German philosopher is praised less for his basic originality than for his representative role: "Heidegger became acutely aware of several aspirations of contemporary philosophy, and the clear consciousness of this obscure background, combined with his remarkable ability to translate his own observations or those of his predecessors—whether Kierkegaard, pragmatism, Dilthey or Spengler—into abstract terms, and combined as well with his grand mastery of the philosophical language he created for himself, established his work as an invaluable reference point."[51] Heidegger is commended as a great "translator," the spokesperson of his time: while very favorable, this judgment misses the mark due to its oddly academic character, which was completely alien to the terms and themes that are most characteristic of *Sein und Zeit.* Readers of Gurvitch and Levinas had learned much more about Heidegger's major work.

What most of all should be retained from Wahl's attitude: his carelessness or his empathy toward Heidegger?

The carelessness can be easily explained by circumstances: in a preface to a work devoted to James, Whitehead, and Marcel, Wahl could not emphasize Heidegger's originality without putting himself in some difficulty (if Heidegger is such an important philosopher, should not an independent work be devoted to him?).

The empathy is nonetheless clear, and what really matters is that by arousing the curiosity of readers, it would start them on paths of research that would sooner or later be followed, including the factical character of the a priori, the opening onto the phenomenon as it shows itself, the nonrepresentational spatiality of *Dasein,* the sense of immanence in the world, and the pragmatic rootedness of a profoundly temporal existence.[52]

Although scattered, these allusions and references are not entirely inaccurate: the pages cited concerning "existential spatiality" are more convincing than those concerning immanence (since the page referenced by Wahl concerns *Befindlichkeit,* which he neither cites nor explains). Heidegger's "pragmatism" was mentioned too quickly without genuine attention given to equipmentality. Heidegger's interpretation of time was not really considered.

On the whole, Wahl reaps more than he sows; one has the impression that he only skimmed *Sein und Zeit.* Yet, his book helped draw attention to Heidegger, in a sense that was quite different from the "idealism" emphasized by Gurvitch; rather from the perspective of new studies centered on the immanence of being-in-the-world and on the affective and pre-predicative conditions of existence. An allusive inspiration often offers more than an exhaustive exposition: Wahl pointed out a direction that younger talents (among whom we must not forget Merleau-Ponty) found alluring.

Yet, as if he recognized that he had not yet quite done justice to Heidegger's originality, Wahl published—not long after *Vers le concret*—a very dense and important article[53] that did not escape Sartre's attention.[54] Wahl correctly noticed that, however justified they may be, the connections with Kierkegaard (his critique of diversion, existential singularization through anxiety and care, a keen sense of a thrown and even guilty finitude, and an openness to an authentic temporality reconceived in the *Augenblick*) must be completed and counterbalanced by the role assigned to being-in-the-world and equipmentality. Nonetheless, as he did previously, he made a hasty connection with Whitehead and, moreover, his terminology (subjectivism and objectivism) was completely inappropriate. Did he nonetheless achieve his goal: to identify the "original elements" in Heidegger's philosophy? Only partly, in the sense that he saw that existentiality and facticity are combined in a temporality that is at once "thrown" and anticipatory. In addition, he saw that Heidegger's critique of the *cogito* allowed for a reappropriation of the *Sum*. Finally, he perceived that the sense of the world and of "environmentality" provides the possibility of overcoming both idealism and realism (an idea that we would find again in Sartre), an "existential light" dissolving pseudo-problems.[55] The more interesting aspect of this article is probably not to be found in the positive effort it undertakes and leaves unfinished; it consists rather in the presentation of critical questions and remarks,[56] questions that are in a sense premature (since they are addressed to a public that is incapable of fully appreciating them), but that reveal—at least some of them (in particular, concerning the reduction of spatiality to temporality, a point on which Heidegger will later rethink)—an undeniable perspicacity.

This strange hodgepodge of insight and rash judgment is suggestive: the final, but certainly debatable, presentation of the situating of Heideggerian ontological consciousness in the environing world ("familiarity, trust, communion of being with what surrounds it"[57]) would not fail to provoke, as a reaction, Sartre's critique of "being-with." Finally, the ultimate rapprochement with Jaspers (on the unity of subjectivism and objectivism) is the very kind of approximation Heidegger himself would decry as "*the* misunderstanding *par excellence.*"[58]

A Groundbreaking Translation

Nineteen thirty-seven and 1938 are important years in the history of the reception of Heidegger's thought in France; 1937 could have taken on an even greater symbolic importance had Heidegger been able to realize his goal of presiding over the German delegation to the Descartes Congress. His absence did not diminish the influence of his philosophy in any way. What really mattered was Henry Corbin's 1938 publication of the first volume of Heidegger's writings in French, *Qu'est-ce que la métaphysique?*[59]

Before analyzing the composition of this volume, its choices of translation and the reasons for its success, it is useful to look back at the translator's career. Corbin read Heidegger as early as 1930:[60] "This was when Jean Baruzi planned to invite Heidegger to lecture at the '*Union intellectuelle.*'" This information, which

Corbin provided much later,[61] allows us to determine that at that time Heidegger was perceived not as an atheist existentialist (as would later be the case as a result of Sartre's influence after Liberation), but rather as a thinker fulfilling a profound spiritual expectation: Baruzi was known for his work on mystics (Saint John of the Cross, in particular) and Corbin himself would not come to see any separation between his interest in Heidegger and his studies on Iranian spirituality and its "*hiérohistoire*."[62] In fact, a first translation of the lecture "What Is Metaphysics?" [*Qu'est-ce que la métaphysique?*[63]], first rejected by the *Nouvelle Revue Française*,[64] was published in 1931 in the journal *Bifur* (where Paul Nizan was an editor[65]); yet, although the translation was enthusiastically supported by Koyré, Corbin was unhappy with it and expressly requested that "this first attempt at translation . . . not appear in his bibliography."[66]

It is worthwhile to dwell on this first attempt at translation, and first of all, on Alexandre Koyré's introduction: "In Germany's philosophical firmament, Martin Heidegger's star shines with a brilliance of the highest order. Some would say it is not even a star: it is a new sun that rises."[67] Koyré next insisted on the originality of Heidegger's philosophy, opposing (without naming him) Gurvitch, who had spoken of a weak "synthesis between irrationalism and dialectic."[68] Finally, Koyré was not afraid to praise Heidegger, in a nonconformist way (in keeping with the style of the journal), in the following terms: "For Martin Heidegger's undertaking—and there lie its value and importance—is a formidable exercise in demolition. The analyses of *Being and Time* are a kind of liberating and destructive catharsis."[69]

This provocative tone can be better understood by reading this journal more thoroughly, in order to realize that its orientation was anti-colonialist and avant-garde. A journal of high quality, though of an unfortunately short lifespan, *Bifur* included some quite beautiful photographs and some prestigious collaborations (James Joyce, Gottfried Benn, and William Carlos Williams numbered among its "foreign consultants"). An even more significant fact for us is that in the same issue as the translation of Heidegger the young Sartre published a piece called "Légende de la vérité," an ironic allegory about rational and democratic progress that leads to colonial domination. This is not yet the great Sartre: the style remains rather academic, even if in the end an almost subversive thinking can be discerned. Why should this piece by Sartre, which in itself was so minor, attract our attention? Simply because it proves that by being published in the same issue of *Bifur*, Sartre could not in 1931 have been unaware (he was only twenty-six) either of the existence of Heidegger, or of the high opinion Koyré had of him, or of the emergence of the theme of the metaphysical discovery of nothingness through anxiety. This name and these themes came to stimulate his thinking long before he himself or his interpreters have tended to admit. An amusing aside: the list of contributors provided in the issue has a certain piquancy, whether deliberate or not: "Martin Heidegger. One of Germany's greatest philosophers. Established the philosophy of nothingness. It is said that he had the idea while skiing. . . . Jean-Paul Sartre. A young philosopher. Completing a work of destructive philosophy."

Returning to more serious matters, let us quickly examine the reasons that drove Corbin to disavow his first translation of the lecture "What Is Metaphysics?" The first version does not give the impression of carelessness when one limits oneself to the lecture's "literary" passages, but the technical lexicon of Heideggerian ontology has clearly not been mastered: *Dasein* is translated as *"existence"* without any further clarification; the term *l'existant* [the existent] is also used to translate *Seiende;* more problematically, this same word is also translated as *l'Être* [being], which is definitely an error.[70]

A serious reworking of his translation and several meetings with the Master in Freiburg in 1934 and 1936 ultimately enabled Corbin to produce this "historic" work, whose virtues, limits, and considerable influence we shall now consider.

The first quality that stands out is that Corbin provides, in a single work of reasonable size, selections that were in a sense authorized by Heidegger, since he wrote a prologue for the translation that indicates he approved and sponsored it. Since the work in question is difficult, endowed with the prestige of originality and preceded by authorized complimentary assessments, one can imagine how timely this volume was: it became the only textual access to the Heideggerian mysteries. Above all, it is clear that the choice of texts received the author's approval. Corbin explains these choices in his foreword, accompanied by warnings inspired or dictated by Heidegger himself, as though the texts presented were vulnerable from the outset to major misreadings or misunderstandings.

Concerning the 1929 lecture, two misreadings are to be avoided: it is neither a "philosophy of anxiety" nor a nihilistic work. Of course, these warnings, far from preventing such misreadings, would only provoke them, not to mention that the capitalization of the word "Nothingness" made its constant evocation fascinating. Corbin claims that the second piece in the collection, *On the Essence of Ground* [*Vom Wesen des Grundes*],[71] which has today been unfortunately forgotten to some extent, enables one to better understand the "structure of transcendence." In fact, it is a text that opens every foundation onto its groundless origin, with freedom being understood as *Dasein*'s instituting of its possibilities. Some passages from *Being and Time* follow, thirteen out of eighty-three sections: on this point, as well, Corbin highlights the author's agreement as regards the difficult selection of the sections: sections 46 through 53 on "being-toward-death" and sections 72 through 76 on temporality and historicity. What is explicitly invoked here is the accessibility of these passages: and if, on the one hand, one can indeed understand why section 77 was left out (since Dilthey's and Yorck's correspondence is, as it were, overly specialized), on the other hand, nothing is said to justify the omission of the introduction and the first part of the work, which would have been very useful for understanding Heidegger's new method and its connection with phenomenology. In his clarification, Heidegger insists on the fact that the truth of being is not an anthropological question and—even more decisively—emphasizes its rootedness, since the dawning of Greek philosophy, in the horizon of time, namely, "the experience of the *present* and of pure permanence."[72] It is unlikely that many readers realized that a whole reinterpretation of the history of metaphysics was engaged. The existential character of the sections included was more important than overly elliptical cautionary notes.

In the last four paragraphs of *Kant and the Problem of Metaphysics*, Heidegger highlighted the reasons for his "repetition" of Kant's questions in terms of a fundamental ontology. The translator sought to clear Heidegger of "any charge of anthropologism or anthropocentrism." This is a new warning clearly suggested by the author himself, who would be so intent ten years later to distinguish himself from the tradition of humanism. But the irony of the situation is that by translating *Dasein* as "*réalité-humaine*" or "human-reality," Corbin does not make the readers' task any easier. A second ambiguity is added to the first, concerning metaphysics: in what sense is Heidegger still a metaphysician? With regard to these two crucial points, one must admit that the ambiguities outweigh the certainties, especially upon reading a phrase like this one: "The necessary question for a laying of the ground for metaphysics, namely, that of what man is, is taken over by the metaphysics of Dasein."[73]

As for the lecture on Hölderlin that concludes the volume, Corbin emphasizes its character as an "existential analysis" and denies that it is only an excursus. Even here, his denial, hidden behind by a convenient phrase, highlights rather than conceals a significant difficulty. However cognizant we may be today of Hölderlin's importance for Heidegger's thought, in 1938 this reference could only have confused readers. It was not known that Heidegger had taught whole courses on Hölderlin[74]—a "revolutionary" innovation from a professor of philosophy, and successor to Husserl—during the winter semester of 1934–35, that is, within a very particular political context.[75]

If these few points facilitate our appreciation of the relevance and care that attended these "selected writings," we can also begin to see the obverse of these qualities and circumstances: cuts, certain omissions, and most importantly, one particularly inopportune translation choice (which we will presently specify), all warped the understanding of texts that were already dense and difficult in their original language.

We should nonetheless take note of Corbin's reservations, which he stated thus: "In the perilous passage from one language to another, the translator must efface himself and have only one concern: to be a thought's faithful servant."[76] The intention is laudable, and one could not rightly claim that Corbin, with all the virtues of the pioneer, was completely unworthy of the initial project—quite the contrary. Yet, how does he justify his most debatable choice: "human reality" [*réalité-humaine*] for *Dasein*? He sought to avoid "unusual or irritating neologisms" as though he had a premonition of the whole future of excesses in this regard.[77] This is a precaution that is in principle respectable and that he even reinforces by the use of a hyphen, arguing that Heidegger himself makes use of it systematically. Further, he explains that "human reality" in the quite specific sense of existentiality is precisely not one reality among others, first "posited" and then qualified with the predicate "human." Despite these explanations, which invite the reader to understand the expression as an integral whole, Corbin paradoxically requires the reader to keep in mind—beyond this "human reality"—a transcendence that is precisely not an anthropological reality! His predicament is obvious, and he finds himself obligated to invoke the "intention" included in the expression as an apology of sorts. If only Corbin could have known that the ingenious compromise he believed he had found would be precisely the expression Sartre would use in a humanistic sense, he would probably have sought another solution or avoided translating *Dasein*.

It is a fact that the fate of certain translations, whether "good" or "bad," escapes their authors. The translation of *Dasein* as "human reality," one must admit, is atrocious. By contrast, Corbin ingeniously unearthed the Old French adjective *historial*,[78] which, in addition to echoing *existential* (the ontological version of the *existentiell*), allows one to differentiate between what belongs to the study of history [*historisch*] and what is intimately linked to historicality properly speaking. This discovery was salutary and would not be contested until later. Other cases raise fewer problems, though without being completely satisfactory: for instance, Corbin does recognize that *la réalité-révélée* [revealed reality] for *Erschlossenheit* impacts *la decision-résolue* [resolute decision] for *Entschlossenheit*, but his reference to "reality" seems almost obsessional, for one encounters it again in his translations of *Vorhandenheit* as *réalité-des-choses-subsistantes* [reality-of-subsisting-things] and of *Zuhandenheit* as *realité-ustensile* [instrumental-reality].

The Corbin translation was groundbreaking in several ways: its chronological priority is not the most decisive factor; we saw how the author's patronage, the translator's scrupulousness, and the range of the texts he chose gave the event a kind of exceptional, almost solemn, character, which was further strengthened by the circumstances. With the war years, Liberation, and the task of reconstruction, new translations of Heidegger were neither encouraged nor solicited. The very success of Corbin's book,[79] while reinforcing further the *aura* surrounding Heidegger, helped produce the illusion that it could serve as a sufficient basis; an illusion whose provisional character would persist for a long time . . . In addition, Sartre's rise to prominence would contribute further to this "unfortunate effect," which was neither anticipated nor wanted.

With respect to the impact of this translation and its considerable influence upon generations of students, evidence abounds: Jean-Pierre Faye and Edgar Morin said they discovered Heidegger thanks to this volume, which Jean Beaufret referred to often without contempt,[80] since it was for him, too, a first step in an initiation with Heidegger's thought that he undertook in Lyon during the Occupation, with the help of Joseph Rovan.[81] Sartre, for his part, wrote in February 1940: "Granted, *if* Corbin hadn't published his translation of *Was ist Metaphysik?*, I shouldn't have read it. And if I hadn't read it, I shouldn't have spent last Easter trying to read *Sein und Zeit*."[82] We will return later to the context and meaning of this "admission," which confirms, at the very least, the role played by Corbin's work, which was clearly more influential than Alphonse de Waelhens's book, which should also be mentioned,[83] since it served for a long time as the only access to Heidegger for non-Germanists who were cruelly deprived of a translation of *Sein und Zeit*—a situation that would persist for a long time. A straightforward summary, which was uninspired but conscientious, de Waelhens's work was originally a dissertation defended at Louvain in 1938. It had success (it was even cited by Sartre[84]) and went through several printings, for the very simple reason already mentioned: by force of necessity, the "de Waelhens" became a kind of gift of Providence in the 1950s for professors and others.

In his foreword, de Waelhens is unfairly and peremptorily harsh with respect to the first French reception of Heidegger, and particularly critical of Corbin, whom he criticized for his hermeticism and for the exclusively existential orientation of the texts that had been selected[85] (as if he foresaw the existentialist fad): this was a first muted polemic, more convincing because of its good intentions than because of de Waelhens's own performance. Let us concede, however, that Waelhens did not resort to jargon and was right to leave *Dasein* untranslated rather than give in to the temptation of "human-reality."

A Missed Opportunity, Promises of Glory

Our epilogue will first take us back to the year 1937, although Heidegger is involved here only because of a missed opportunity that takes on symbolic value retrospectively as a result of the text he wrote for the occasion. The opportunity missed was a trip to Paris for the Descartes Congress, a trip that had to be canceled. The text, *Wege zur Aussprache*, was published in an obscure, locally produced volume[86] that was unknown to the French public until relatively recently.

With respect to the Descartes Congress, what is certain is that Heidegger was officially invited and that he could not or would not accept the invitation. His version was that he was removed from the delegation by the German authorities: "This seemed so strange in Paris that the leadership of the congress there—Professor Bréhier at the Sorbonne—inquired on his own why I did not belong to the German delegation. I responded that the leaders of the congress should direct this inquiry to the Reich's Ministry of Education. After some time, a request came from Berlin that I belatedly join the delegation. I refused to do so."[87] Victor Farias challenged this account on the basis of a letter of July 14, 1937, to Professor

Metz, then rector of the University of Freiburg, in which Heidegger lays out his idea for German participation in the Congress: to respond to the French "liberal-democratic concept of science."[88] Did Heidegger himself make a discreet trip to Paris in 1935 in order to prepare for this conference to which he attached so much importance? Farias claims he did;[89] but we have found no convincing evidence of this:[90] Heidegger always claimed to have been to Paris for the first time in 1955, on Jean Beaufret's invitation, as a stopover on his way to Cerisy.

What seems to have been decisive in his restated 1937 refusal to join the German delegation is the fact that the leadership of this delegation had been granted to Hans Heyse, and not to him; but it is not impossible that he realized that the "non-Aryan" professors were excluded, in particular Husserl; and that the "military" character of the said delegation threatened to put him in an awkward position with respect to his French colleagues and the international public. In this particular case, whatever the motives for his abstaining, it was prudent, and "he was saved some embarrassment."[91]

For its part, the text develops the theme of the *entente* between France and Germany, based on the mutual recognition of their common heritage and their particular virtues. It is indeed a dignified work, but its style is edifying and somewhat solemn. Its content cannot be understood without reference to the Descartes Congress. Even the translation of the title was a problem: as always, Heidegger did not choose his words by chance. *Ausprache* can of course mean explanation, discussion, reciprocity, but we must also hear in it the emphasis of language, or one's way of expressing oneself.[92] The opening to the alterity of the Other on the basis of a mutual self-affirmation prefigures, to some extent, the orientation of the later "Dialogue on Language: Between a Japanese and an Inquirer." Descartes and Leibniz were chosen as emblematic figures of philosophical modernity, but without any aggressive, "nationalistic" overtones. Today, in light of the courses on Nietzsche, how can we avoid reading, between the lines, what is suggested by the connection between the Cartesian conception of nature and the essence of technology? This suggestive thought reached well beyond the political circumstances of 1937. In any case, the call to meditate together on the legacy of Greece is made in terms that in no way correspond to the official exaltation of the unique German *Lebensraum*. Let the text speak for itself: "If we reflect upon the possible greatness and standards of western 'culture,' then we immediately recall the historical world of the early Greeks. And just as easily do we then forget that it was not by means of an encapsulation in their own 'space' that the Greeks became what they were. It was only due to the sharpest, though creative, confrontation with what was a most foreign and difficult world for them—the Asiatic world—that this people was able to become great in the brief course of its historical singularity and greatness."[93]

It is an irony of history, in this case both mischievous and favorable, that this dignified (and quite discreet) message occurred in the context of Heidegger's "absence" from the German delegation to Paris, in the very same year when the preparation of the volume that would assure his postwar glory in France was being completed. The philosopher's absence, far from hurting him, produced some results for which the author had sagely prepared the ground. Until now, this fact has gone largely unnoticed. Of course, it is unfortunate—and this misfortune came with a heavy price, even too heavy—that Heidegger had not practiced this virtue of abstention a few years earlier. At the very least, he was beginning to learn the lessons from bitter experience and was indirectly compensated, over many years, by many expressions of friendship and support in France, while awaiting the belated return of the repressed.

But this return was also made possible by the limited knowledge in the first debates—which were already lively and thorough—about Heidegger's political activity of 1933, which took place after Liberation. Furthermore, this return should not eclipse the philosophical issues or cause us to forget the richness of the first reception of Heidegger in France, a reception that is today largely unknown. As early as 1932, René Char had heard of Heidegger from Tristan Tzara's wife;[94] in 1936, Heidegger's name even began to seep into Le Senne's classroom in Paris.[95]

If curiosity and enthusiasm prevailed, some resistance was also beginning to take shape. Hence, in the 1930s, some Marxist intellectuals such as Georges Politzer,[96] Paul Nizan, and Henri Lefebvre were rejecting Heidegger's philosophical positions.[97] At first attracted by these positions, Bataille later distanced himself from them and even became disgusted by them.[98] Another axis of resistance, this one Catholic, was developing much more discreetly not far from our borders.[99]

Long before Jean Beaufret, and even before Sartre, brilliant minds and precursors whose perspicacity deserves to be commended produced pioneering works and interpretive advances that were for the most part remarkable. In different ways, Gurvitch, Koyré, Levinas, Wahl, Corbin, and even Aron[100] laid the foundations for an understanding of this thought and lit the first fires of a paradoxical glory that Sartre, long after his time in Berlin,[101] would brilliantly establish.

2   The Sartre Bomb

IF SARTRE DESERVES his own chapter, it is not only because of the explosive eruption of his celebrity after Liberation, but also and above all because of the decisive and very personal way in which he approached Heidegger's thought—both criticizing it and integrating it into his own philosophical project. This approach transformed the conditions of the first reception of Heidegger. We have already noted the import of this first reception. Without denying his debt to this first reception, Sartre nonetheless eclipsed it through the sheer force of his style and problematic. However, the counterpart of this effect—which Sartre neither controlled nor perhaps even wanted—was the incontestable recognition of the Master of Freiburg, who was seen as an equal to Hegel and Husserl. As Heidegger is discussed and analyzed, his philosophical stature is definitively established. We shall determine how and at what cost this grand operation was carried out.

Confessions from the "Phoney War"

In February 1940, in personal notebooks we have had access to only since 1983 (three years after his death), Sartre was already producing a first account of the influence Heidegger had on him.[1] An invaluable testimony due to its candor and lucidity, this posthumous publication not only sheds useful light on the genesis of *Being and Nothingness*,[2] it also enables one to reconstruct Sartre's recognition of Heidegger from within by highlighting both the strength of its logic and also some of its weaknesses. The following dense pages from Notebook XI deserve a close reading and a thorough analysis.[3]

From the outset, Sartre announced the theme that would guide his reflection: "to understand how much there is of freedom and how much of fate in what's termed 'being influenced,'"[4] with respect to the peculiar case of his own relation to Heidegger. This, of course, meant admitting this influence, and not denying its importance. It is much more than that: it is a free appropriation of such "influence," the history of an *encounter*, the conditions of which Sartre himself analyzed and reconstructed from both sides, that of fate and that of his own perspective as a free Sand engaged person.

Sartre acknowledged that he himself had at times considered this encounter "providential,"[5] a word that ought to shock us, since one does not often find it in the writings of this unwavering atheist, for whom the human condition is absurd and contingent. Plainly, the word is not to be taken literally, but it expresses the force and the quality of Sartre's encounter with Heidegger's thought. "How much time I gained!"[6] This sincere admission is later confirmed with respect to the grand themes of Heidegger's "*pathos*": "it arrived at just the *right moment*."[7]

Of course, such philosophical encounters have taken place for centuries, but here we must recognize that a third protagonist was present in the background, namely history, which was absent when Malebranche, for example, was enthusiastically reading Descartes. When Sartre discovered Heidegger, it was not just one individual being inspired by and finding himself reflected in the writings of another: there were also fate and war, which established a new perspective and cast a new light on events and on humanity. Now, precisely, Sartre wrote that Heidegger's influence "supervened to teach me authenticity and historicity just at the very moment when war was about to make these ideas indispensable to me."[8] That is what seemed "providential" to Sartre—perhaps in the Stoic sense, to which he alluded later—namely, that circumstances offered the opportunity to better face destiny, to take it on so as to affirm freedom rather than stifle it. Heidegger became the symbolic "spokesperson" for the time.[9]

Nonetheless, Sartre quickly considered two objections that must temper any initial enthusiasm and avoid any simplification in the quest for the proper relation between fate and freedom: he was immensely aided by the publication of Corbin's book; he experienced some difficulties and even some serious reservations in the course of his reading of Heidegger.

This admission is important with respect to Corbin's translation, which, by a kind of salutary reverse effect, almost required Sartre to read *Sein und Zeit*, although only in the spring of 1939. He had bought the book in 1934 in Berlin, but had done no more than skim through it, and finally gave up on anything more than brief attempts at reading it. An avowed and intense Husserlian, he had (quite logically) promised himself to study Husserl's disciple Heidegger, but was put off by the difficulty of the vocabulary.

With respect to these difficulties, Sartre once again did not mince words: "The essential thing was certainly the revulsion I felt against assimilating that barbarous and so unscientific philosophy after Husserl's brilliant, *scholarly* synthesis."[10] Barbaric philosophy in what sense? One might be tempted to answer: by virtue of its difficult vocabulary. Sartre would not disagree, but he added that this radical break with classical vocabulary left him with the impression that, with Heidegger, "philosophy had returned to its infancy." But, in what sense? By virtue of the break with traditional problems (that is, in French philosophy between the two wars), such as realism, idealism, truth and error, and so on. While today we are more aware of the problems of method and the renewals that enabled Heidegger to revive the reading of metaphysics, Sartre emphasized the shock that was first produced by the existential interpretations of anxiety, authenticity, and choice. His confessed "aversion" primarily concerned Heidegger's terminology. However, without saying it explicitly, Sartre suggested that he would appropriate some of this terminology for himself. In any case, his unflattering judgments of Heidegger's language in no way prevented him from assimilating Heidegger's philosophy. The difficulties seem, if anything, to have stimulated him.

Having been a Husserlian for several years, Sartre stated that he found himself at an impasse (especially with respect to the question of intersubjectivity, since Husserl's treatment of it seemed problematic to him), and that it was Heidegger who reconnected him with the theme of historicity, providing him with the tools for understanding it.

That is not all. Sartre pushed the analysis farther, now reversing the providentialist perspective that he himself had established. He intended to show that he was not simply the pawn of fate or the beneficiary of an unbelievable stroke of luck: he himself (along with his friends and intellectual contemporaries) sparked the interest that allowed for the tremendous success of Corbin's book as well as the impassioned reception reserved for such existential philosophy.

It must be admitted that, on this point, his reasoning might resemble a kind of historical sleight-of-hand: since he himself acknowledged his debt to Corbin's work, he sought to show (or to convince himself) that he, Sartre, had substantially contributed to making this work possible by means of the "*élan* of curiosity" in which he actively participated: "Thus if Corbin translated 'What Is Metaphysics?' it was because I (among others) freely constituted myself as an *audience* awaiting that translation—and, in this, I was assuming my situation, my generation, and my epoch."[11]

Sartre's wish to resolve the tension (which he himself set up) between fate and freedom can easily be understood, and one can only admire the skill with which he made the case for his inventiveness in this situation: it is he who established the "horizon of possibilities" for Heidegger's thought! One must of course concede that the reception of a difficult body of thought demands not only time, but also sustained and constantly renewed attention, which could not be undertaken by passive subjects receiving a flood of ideas all at once (the way an average television viewer today is bombarded by violent images). What Sartre says of his situation (the war) is entirely true, and he is also right to note that Heidegger himself had "responded" to Germany's distress during the period between the wars. From the first war to the second, from one distress to another, between the young Sartre and his German elder, a kind of strange exchange transcending both individuals took place in which they shared the same kind of fate and the same quest for authenticity. (Sartre said nothing, however, about Heidegger's political activity, of which he could not have been unaware in 1940.[12])

Nonetheless, Sartre sensed that he was in danger of going too far by giving himself a role more important than it actually was: "I just want to show how I inserted myself as an *active* and *responsible* member into a community of interested people and scholars which designated itself spontaneously as an audience. It was *for us* that Corbin made his translation."[13]

This invaluable and assuredly sincere testimony cannot receive, however, the unconditional approval of the historian of ideas. Sartre can defend his freedom all he wants: on that level, one can only admire his intelligent rewriting of history. However, this interpretive move took place *after the fact* and rested on the considerable labors of others, especially Corbin, but also on the pioneers whom we examined earlier and whom Sartre admitted having read.[14] The entirety of the first reception of Heidegger took place without Sartre, even if he was present at the fringes and constituted (with others) an attentive and receptive audience. We have seen that in 1931 he even published a few pages on "Légende de la vérité," which followed the first translation of Heidegger's lecture "What Is Metaphysics?" in the same issue of the journal *Bifur.* Could this coincidence have completely escaped him?[15]

The truth is even more complicated than Sartre imagined. By intervening explicitly and powerfully in the debate, he would attempt (with great success) to appropriate its terms and stakes for himself, but he would also contribute to the confusion concerning the basic issues. Our only goal here is to reveal the intense complexity of a "reception" that was in no way passive, and that we will investigate in Sartre's major work.

Published in 1943, *Being and Nothingness* became—after Liberation—the most successful work of philosophy in France in the twentieth century, taking its place between *Creative Evolution* and *The Order of Things.* What was striking at the time was the forthright vigor and radical novelty of Sartre's themes and style: freedom, bad faith, the absurdity of the human condition, atheism, the look of the other, the sketch of an existential psychoanalysis, engagement. The existentialist fad that took hold immediately after the war overshadowed the questions of influence or reception of Heidegger even as it reinforced his impact. The "Sartre effect" was powerful in its own right: bolstered by literary and theatrical successes, it was also achieved by undeniable pedagogical value and some brilliant pages that compensated for many overly technical passages. In one stroke, this philosopher, the virtuoso of phenomenologico-ontological obscurity, set a scene or story with great clarity, as in these lines: "It is certain that the café by itself with its patrons, its tables, its booths, its mirrors, its light, its smoky atmosphere, and the sounds of voices, rattling saucers, and footsteps which fill it—the café is a fullness of being."[16] And, *voila!* The ontological status of the in-itself is made accessible to anyone and everyone!

It is plain that no one, or almost no one, read this hefty tome from cover to cover: *Being and Nothingness* is a book that is at once unreadable and, at the same time, all too readable. People went directly to the most accessible and most sensational passages. This helped keep the question of Sartre's debt to Heidegger in the background. There seemed to be even less reason to make this a priority since Sartre in no way denied his debt and seemed to clarify matters himself (in particular, with respect to the status of the *cogito* and the relation to others). As years passed and fascination with the work declined, a rumor initiated by the Heideggerians began to circulate: Sartre was said to have built his own philosophy by pillaging the carcass of a misunderstood Heidegger, like an overly literary elephant in a Saxon (or rather Swabian) china shop. Therefore, one should not take Sartre too seriously on "technical" matters, and for this reason, what he wrote on or about Heidegger in *Being and Nothingness* could not even be considered as an interpretation.

A serious reexamination of this question is unavoidable. In the first place, we must not forget that the book was published in occupied Paris, which means that the German censors allowed it to appear. In this situation, one was engaged in a battle of wits, and who won? Sartre could not have been unaware of the existence of this censorship—run by Gerhard Heller, a clever man closely associated with the Parisian intelligentsia—nor of the acquiescence of the great publishing houses, Gallimard in particular, to German demands.[17] We must further recognize that Sartre's main references in modern and contemporary philosophy were German (Hegel, Husserl, and Heidegger). Surely, to place Husserl in a honorable position and to cite Spinoza and Kafka was commendable, but it came at the price of some silences and omissions:[18] Marx was left out, and there were practically no Anglo-Saxon authors; nothing—not even an allusion—concerning Heidegger's political engagement in 1933 and his resignation from the rectorship in 1934. These were diplomatic silences. . . . Must we see these as complicities that sacrificed the spirit of resistance to the requirements of a literary career? The question is all the more justified since it was not the result of a retrospective illusion, for it was raised at the time, rather violently, in the form of communist tracts accusing Sartre of "being a disciple of the Nazi philosopher Martin Heidegger."[19] Furthermore, although no one is forced to write a book, as Bergson said, publishing one without delay (and under the humiliating authority of the occupiers) could have been said to be dishonorable.[20] Let us limit ourselves to noting this.

What is most crucial here, from a philosophical perspective, is whether Sartre's reading of Heidegger can be reduced to a series of misinterpretations or whether it deserves to be considered in its own interpretive coherence. We will maintain the latter position.

Heidegger Omnipresent

A systematic index would reveal that Heidegger is omnipresent in *Being and Nothingness*.[21] Yet that is not what is most decisive: this philosophical presence is overwhelming, beginning with the very title and subtitle, the introduction, and the position of the problem of the origin of nothingness.

The very title itself is modeled after *Being and Time*. We can understand why nothingness replaces time by referring to the heart of the first part of the book, on "The Phenomenological Conception of Nothingness":[22] it is human freedom that introduces nothingness into the plenitude of being. The explicit reference to the lecture "What Is Metaphysics?" rests upon the central role played by the nihilation of nothingness itself: "It is toward this new conception that Heidegger is oriented."[23] Sartre thus proceeded as though the 1929 lecture marked a change from the major work of 1927. This is quite a claim, which was not entirely innocent: it allowed him to justify the anthropologization of Heidegger's position.

The subtitle, to which one does not always pay enough attention, is no less significant: "An Essay in Phenomenological Ontology." Reference to Husserl alone would not allow one to understand the meaning of this expression. Who undertook to "ontologize" phenomenology if not Heidegger in the first pages of *Being and Time,* and especially in section 7? The same must be said about the introduction—"The Pursuit of Being"—which placed Sartre literally on the same path as Heidegger, since he was in search of that "surpassing towards the ontological, of which Heidegger speaks" and since he stipulates that "the phenomenon of being requires the transphenomenality of Being."[24]

Yet, as early as the introduction, and through a plethora of explicit references, borrowings, and allusions, Sartre appropriated this ontological quest to his own purposes. This appropriation would lead to a series of misunderstandings if it presented itself as a faithful interpretation, but such is not at all the case. While for Heidegger being [*l'être*] is always different from beings [*l'étant*], Sartre avoided that latter notion and as a result concerned himself much less with the ontico-ontological difference (of which, however, he appeared not to have been unaware) than with the much more directly comprehensible difference between being (in-itself) and nihilation (of the for-itself). Within the schema he established (without alerting the reader that he was breaking with Heidegger on this point), Sartre risked a great deal, since his "being" [*être*] is precisely what Heidegger meant by "beings" [*l'étant*]!

From this point on, the pursuit of being in Sartre took on an ironic, absurd, or desperate sense, which is not the case at all for Heidegger, despite the theme of anxiety. It became clear rather quickly that nothing is to be expected from the in-itself, for its fullness appears only on the basis of the nihilation of which the human being is the bearer. A "being of distances," as Heidegger put it,[25] for Sartre the human being is even more radically an exile who posits being only to find him or herself excluded from it. This is what the analyses of the notion of nihilation made all the more plain: the human being is both the locus and the agent of this nihilation. That being which Heidegger called *Dasein* is now taken as "for-itself," that is to say as autonomous in a face-to-face relation with the in-itself, a problematic absent from *Being and Time*.

Sartre's reading is curious: on the one hand, it is saturated with Heideggerian themes (transcendence, being-in-the-world, the difference between authenticity and inauthenticity); yet one notes, on the other hand, a firm and early stipulation that favors a dualism between the in-itself and the for-itself (a dualism Sartre will attempt to exorcize); as a result, it is a philosophy of consciousness (the philosophy of the "I think") that reappears and reasserts itself. On this point, Sartre laid his cards on the table: "Any study of human reality must begin with the *cogito*."[26] Throughout the whole of Sartre's project, reflexivity comes to the fore, on the basis of a break with Heidegger that is as avowed as it is radical.

The omnipresence of Heideggerian themes was thus paired with a constant and regulated displacement, which can be traced through the rest of the work. One notes, on the one hand, the consideration of facticity (which directly transposes Heidegger's *Faktizität*), and on the other, the transformation of the "they" into "bad faith."

Now that the omnipresence of Heidegger's thought has been demonstrated, it is important to analyze more precisely the "differences" that Sartre purposely introduced, beginning with central notions like the consciousness of freedom in the face of facticity, the role of the "I think," the understanding of others, and his positions on ethical engagement.

The Keystone: The Consciousness of Freedom

For Sartre, the center of everything is the human being; for Heidegger, it is being. This is how one might articulate a disagreement that Heidegger himself would later recognize in his "Letter on Humanism" and that is essential to grasp in its genesis. Sartre's recapitulation of Heidegger's analyses of nothingness and nihilation seemed at first to follow directly in the footsteps of the author of "What Is Metaphysics?" with the difference that the former sees the human being as the author of nihilation (he or she "makes nothingness emerge in the world"), while the latter places the Existent (*Dasein*) before a nothingness that imposes itself on him and over which it has no power.

In this connection, what is decisive is not the translation: while it is true that Sartre often reproduced the often contested translation of *Dasein* as "human reality" [*réalité humaine*], he occasionally left the word in German or simply wrote "man" [*l'homme*]. These variations did not affect his fundamentally humanistic position. Did he then misinterpret the meaning of Heidegger's *Dasein*? There can be no doubt about it, since he ignored the radicality of the singular difference by which *Dasein* is not even identified as human. Yet this misunderstanding still reveals a decisive feature: transcendence with respect to any in-itself, a transcendence that Sartre vigorously emphasized. The keystone of the Sartrean edifice is to conceive of this transcendence as conscious freedom, a human privilege. Not that Sartre failed to recognize that there is such a thing as a pre-ontological understanding, as Heidegger saw. But, for Sartre, humans' presence to themselves resides in their nihilating consciousness; Sartre will understand this as a pre-reflective *cogito*,[27] which effectively amounts to turning on Heidegger the very weapon that was stolen from him (but is this not fair game between philosophers?). The disagreement with Heidegger indeed revolves around the role of the *cogito*, a divergence that is decisive for everything else. The fact that this *cogito* is not a substantial plenitude supported by a divine veracity changes nothing. Sartre was neither willing nor able to accept that *Dasein* is transcendence by virtue of its projection alone; he would not accept an "ekstasis" without consciousness. This also means that freedom has an altogether different content in each case: for Heidegger it is an openness to the disclosure of being while for Sartre it is the determination made by a consciousness that chooses (itself) and takes on a situation. Sartre clearly emphasizes this disagreement: "Heidegger endows human reality with a self-understanding which he defines as an 'ekstatic pro-ject' of its own possibilities. It is certainly not my intention to deny the existence of this project. But how could there be an understanding which would not in itself be the consciousness (of) being understanding?"[28]

On the one hand, by claiming that this project can be reduced to a "thinglike . . . in-itself,"[29] Sartre exhibited a total misunderstanding of Heidegger's project; on the other hand, he was perfectly consistent, especially from the point of view of a practical engagement that must, in his eyes, be conscious and come to terms with itself as such. In other words, Sartre's misunderstanding nonetheless does not diminish the difficulty of Heidegger's attempt to free himself from the constraints of the sort of deliberative choice confronted by the agency of a responsible and lucid consciousness (since the difficulties in articulating ethical concern are patent in Heidegger).[30]

In a translation-betrayal of Heideggerian freedom and transcendence, Sartre's existentialism performed a brilliant transposition of these themes into the French and Cartesian horizon of thought. By reevaluating the role of the *cogito* and founding it on a vigorous, but very personal, reinterpretation of Cartesian freedom,[31] he thus offered conceptual tools that were immediately intelligible to a broad readership and, further, much more immediately useful in the practical sphere than Heidegger's unusual suggestions (which were nonetheless constantly employed). In this way, the conclusion of the article "La liberté cartésienne" situated Descartes and Heidegger along the same axis of "democratic" autonomy, which exposes both thinkers to misunderstandings.[32]

However, if Sartre had limited himself to introducing these bold moves into the sphere of classical philosophy, he would have found himself exposed to a danger to which he was extremely sensitive and which he wanted to avoid at all costs: idealism. If the consciousness of my own thought gives me from the outset a transparent certainty with respect to the world and others, then I have direct access to the truth of the essences that constitute reality. The brute weight of facticity and the irreducible struggle of consciousnesses are miraculously eliminated. Faced with two evils, Sartre must choose the lesser one: he still prefers Heidegger's ambiguities to a pure and simple return to reflexive idealism. Consequently, he must clarify the role of consciousness in the presence to self of human transcendence. When he claimed that "the sole point of departure is the interiority of the *cogito*,"[33] he was careful to specify that this reflective anchoring takes place in a situation, and cannot or should not be posited as an ontological sovereignty that obliterates the multiplicity of other consciousnesses; his philosophical adversary here is Hegel and his absolute idealism. As a starting-point, the *cogito* reveals nihilation at work in an interiority whose finite and situated character must endlessly be reiterated: neither divine veracity nor absolute knowledge can provide a basis from which this cogito could also constitute an end-point. It is in these references to the order of finitude that the "translations-betrayals" of Heidegger would prove to be invaluable to Sartre, regarding facticity, relations with others, and the moral project.

Facticity and Bad Faith

Among the themes and terms that Sartre borrowed from Heidegger, facticity is distinctive in its "advantageous" ability to directly translate the German *Faktizität*. From a philosophical point of view, it designates above all the actual anchoring point of existential thought, which no longer speculates about pure essences, but is committed to articulating our being-in-the-world as it is given in a situation as thrown. To be precise, Sartre showed, after and with Heidegger, that humans do not choose the being they are, that they are not the ground of their being, and thus that they must apprehend themselves in their radical finitude. But the word "facticity" conceals a trap; it may lead us to believe, at least at first, that our existence is reducible to the set of facts through which it apprehends itself: physical characteristics, age, nationality, social situation, and so on. In fact, it is quite the opposite.

Heidegger writes that "Dasein exists factically":[34] as Sartre understood, this means that *Dasein* is essentially transcendence, a project, or care. Facticity and transcendence cannot be separated from each other any more than the situation and the freedom that emerges from it and gives it meaning. Yet, to purely and simply equate facticity with transcendence would be to neglect the fact that transcendence is precisely not an absolute surpassing toward oneself, a pure self-identity, but an always broken and nihilated self-presence. Nothingness itself is not pure, for it is the nihilation of an in-itself. The self-presence of the for-itself is indeed conscious presence, assuming within this consciousness the ineradicable wound of contingency, that is, facticity: "This perpetually evanescent contingency of the in-itself which, without ever allowing itself to be apprehended, haunts the for-itself and reattaches it to being-in-itself—this contingency is what we shall call the *facticity* of the for-itself."[35]

Without this ambiguous and metastatic state, we would be left with a sterile dualism between the in-itself and the for-itself. Similarly, was there not already in Heidegger a risk that the ontico-ontological difference would be reduced to a rigid opposition between being and beings? The danger, which was avoided by means of an emphasis on *Dasein*'s peculiar privilege—both an entity and a questioning of its being—runs the risk of shifting toward an overly schematic opposition between the "they" and the authentic Self. Sartre saw that the "they" is also a mode of being of *Dasein* as responsible for its own being; he drew out the consequences of this in his phenomenological description of bad faith as role-playing.

On this point, for once, he may even have surpassed his master. Indeed, though Heidegger recognized the ambiguity[36] of inauthentic conduct, he described it in negative terms and with a certain heavy-handedness. Sartre, by contrast, excels at making us party to the equivocations of a hesitant woman being seduced,[37] to the dance of the waiter who plays at being a waiter,[38] and to the bad faith of the homosexual who refuses to admit his identity to himself, even as he plays the role.[39]

By renouncing the impersonal character of the Heideggerian "they" and by describing inauthenticity as a range of conducts by which human beings turn negation against themselves, Sartre relocated it in consciousness, thus giving it the phenomenality of a lie. It may lack the translucence of a lie, but it shares its outward aspects: it is a lie with respect to oneself.[40] As a result, bad faith can be analyzed in both intellectual and existential terms, depending on its constant displacements and its ever-renewed ruses within "the unity of a *single* consciousness."[41] As flight (in the face of anxiety and responsibility), it is also conscious of what it hides from itself. Thus the woman who goes to her first rendezvous knows that she is beginning to compromise herself; she nonetheless only pretends to recognize as respectful the advances of the man who tries to seduce her: the provisional solution that she adopts is to yield her hand while feigning not to notice it. In this way, she succeeds in experiencing her first physical emotion, even as she maintains distance, both here and elsewhere: "a certain art of forming contradictory concepts,"[42] Sartre noted, even as he showed correlatively that this dismantling of a contradiction would be incomprehensible without reference to the existential oscillation between facticity and transcendence: "One must affirm facticity as *being* transcendence and transcendence as *being* facticity."[43] Analogously, the exchange of looks makes possible a conduct of evasion between being-mine and being-for-others. On these various levels of bad faith, which Sartre staged as the playwright he in fact was, it is human freedom that is acted out, with all its resources and subtleties. It is therefore not a question of criticizing these attitudes, which would allow one to believe that the phenomenologist should play the moralist by showing how to rectify these various positions through which freedom abuses its powers. Although this problem should be raised again in terms of the choice of a morality (otherwise, why speak of "bad" faith?), let us first acknowledge the author's delight in his subject and the intellectual pleasure he affords us. Sartre knew perfectly well that all these ambiguities make up the stuff of existence and its richness; for what would freedom be, if it allowed no play or deception?

By comparison, the Heideggerian "they" conforms to simple structures, which are described externally: idle talk, curiosity, ambiguity.[44] Heidegger may well claim not to give everyday discourse a negative connotation or to criticize it from a moral point of view, but his description of speech reduced to an "average" or "uprooted" communication that loses itself in the public sphere without leading to any authentic decision leaves him little opportunity to refine his analyses or linger over these phenomena so as to locate them historically or socially, or distinguish them psychologically. Similarly, his evocation of curiosity, from Augustine's text on the concupiscence of the eyes, barely allows him to identify three constitutive characteristics of this phenomenon: restlessness, distraction, and homelessness; all these general and negative features, described all too quickly, are understood as fallen forms of authentic care and life. In the end, the equivocation gathers these negative features together in an ambiguous instability, incapable of an authentic understanding, without providing any certainty: "Everything looks as if it were genuinely understood, grasped, and spoken where basically it is not; or it does not look that way, yet basically is."[45]

These pages, which are not the best in *Being and Time,* lack vitality and complexity; nonetheless, they were a catalyst for Sartre's inspiration, by suggesting to him a kind of hermeneutic framework, and by implicitly presenting him with a sort of challenge: if there is ambiguity with respect to the inauthentic, must one not learn to exploit its ruses and detours? Sartre did, in fact, draw from the Heideggerian idea of a pre-ontological understanding, transforming it into a pre-reflective understanding: namely, bad faith. The inauthenticity that troubled Heidegger fascinated Sartre: since it is a phenomenon of consciousness (albeit in a pre-reflexive form), there is rich material for further intellectual analysis. Here the Parisian virtuoso turns the somewhat dull scales of the Master of Freiburg into a *tour de force* performance! This transformation occurs also in the case of the problem of the other.

What Other?

It was with respect to the problem of the other that Sartre distinguished himself most decisively from Heidegger. In the important third part devoted to the "for-the-other," what stands out is chapter 3, which is significantly titled, "Husserl, Hegel, Heidegger," and in which Heidegger, while severely criticized, was nonetheless elevated to the empyrean of great classical philosophers.

What is the disagreement about? Is it profound or superficial? A hasty reader might only note the formal rejection of equating the "for-itself" with Heidegger's "being-with" [*Mitsein*]. But why deny that the human being is a "being-with"? What is at stake in this refusal?

Having adopted an attitude of reflexive description and beginning from negative behavior and from the *cogito*, Sartre knew full well that his ontology was threatened from within by this "obstacle," namely, solitude, which he referred to as solipsism. Why does this hypothesis, even as it is rejected as perfectly unjustifiable and gratuitous, prove so dangerous?[46] Because the access to the being of the "for-itself" was immediately secured, at least at first, by the nihilation of the in-itself. Since he insisted on following the classical path of self-positing through thought, it is not surprising that Sartre repeated the logical and systematic consequence that so horrified him: idealism. Will the "for-itself" remain a pure self-relation to the end? And is its reflexive freedom not inalienable?

Sartre's solution consisted in refusing both realism and idealism (others are not those I transcend absolutely, and they do transcend me completely), so as to discover being-for-the-other as the simultaneity of nihilation and contingency. I am a transcendence-transcended; being-for-the-other and being-for-oneself are not dissociable. In this regard, there is no ontological structure of coexistence: it is in radical contingency and conflict that this nihilating opening of the for-the-other is played out.

It is on this last point that Sartre asserted his opposition to Heidegger. The latter was criticized for having erased the multiplicity of consciousnesses, and the element of radical struggle that it entails, in the name of an ontological structure (described as "being-in" [*In-sein*]) that is given the same status as being-in-the-world. "In his abrupt, rather barbaric manner of cutting Gordian knots rather than trying to untie them, he [Heidegger] gives in answer to the question posited a pure and simple *definition*."[47] Let us be clear: the definition of *Dasein* as originarily coexistent and interconnected (following an ontological structure) erases or overly obscures the problem itself: the emergence of the other as other than me, a for-itself as well, or rather: as primordial as myself. A feature of Hegel's phenomenology, the struggle for recognition, is here introduced against Heidegger, though without its totalizing and reconciliatory culmination.

Nonetheless, Sartre must concede that Heidegger's "being-with" provided him, in a way, with what he was looking for: "a being which in its own being implies the Other's being."[48] Nonetheless, he confessed that he was unsatisfied with the fact that the "with" is, as it were, given in advance. Proceeding pedagogically, he used the image of a crew in order to explain what he found lacking in Heidegger: "the mute existence in common of one member of the crew with his fellows," a common basis on which the "common solitude" of being-toward-death is founded.[49]

Sartre pressed his criticism of Heidegger further yet, accusing him of idealism, and going so far as to claim that "Heidegger's *transcendence* is a concept of bad faith."[50] Is this going too far? One suspects that he was chagrined, inasmuch as he ultimately had to admit that Heidegger—because of the sense of existence as "outside itself"—succeeded in partially overcoming this despised idealism. Above all, was it not Heidegger's many suggestions that led Sartre down the path of a sober ontology? Certainly it never occurred to him to deny the extent of his debt: however, since he did not wish to make a final accounting of it (which ought to be our task, though it may not be possible), he demonstrated a free and even carefree attitude that continues to surprise us. Sartre's situation remains unique, even to this day; no French philosopher has ever had a relationship to Heidegger that was at once so intimate and so free.

Sartre only partially justified his charge that Heidegger's concept of transcendence was in "bad faith": he would have had to show that the concept of "resoluteness" (and of a historical choice associated with a "generation") was itself in bad faith (let us defer this investigation for the moment and return to it later from a moral perspective). By contrast, the critique of the "bastard form of idealism"[51] that is discernible in Heidegger is somewhat more explicit: the fact of having understood "being-with" as a structure that is constitutive of existence constitutes, according to Sartre, a flight from the self, isolating the philosopher from the actual struggle of consciousnesses, as was already the case in Kantian transcendentalism. What is clear is that Sartre objected to the "we" as a constitutive figure of existence. Although he recognized in passing the relevance of this type of collaboration in the context of equipmentality, he was not very interested in it; for him, it was only a secondary and tenuous acquisition: "One *encounters* the other, one does not constitute him."[52]

One question we might raise is whether Sartre weighed his criticisms of Heidegger carefully. Another is whether the conceptions he proposed were coherent and original. One may deny the first while affirming the second. As has already been said, and as one might guess, this is in fact our position.

The fact that Sartre did not develop his criticisms of Heidegger with great care is not surprising. Without accusing him of attempting to conceal the extent of his debt to Heidegger's work, by means of a few strong criticisms, it must be stressed that Heidegger never deduced the existence of others from any sort of necessary structure; he in no way denied that actual encounters are contingent; rather, since *Dasein*'s self is neither substantial nor reflexive, it can never be insular, and consequently will not have to operate in terms of the tension between consciousnesses and intersubjectivity. Sartre unquestionably failed to recognize the richness of Heidegger's analyses of equipmentality, which in no way can be reduced to the use of this or that tool, but designates an ekstatic apprenticeship in an environment (*Umwelt*) that is always already shared. He also failed to recognize that understanding or *Verstehen* (which he improperly reduced to *Verstand*) and discourse or *Rede,* are primordial "*existentialia.*" Finally, one might object to Sartre that he relied on Heidegger in two respects: first, on the level of empirical description, when he must return to the "we" and make the following stipulation in response to the objection that he returned to Heidegger: "We shall only remark here that we had no intention of casting doubt on the *experience* of the 'we.' We limited ourselves to showing that this experience could not be the foundation of our consciousness of the Other."[53] Second, and more importantly, on a level that he himself calls metaphysical, during a one-page digression on the existence of others[54] and in a nearly Fichtean manner (but with a terminology that is still Heideggerian), Sartre presents a theory of the three ekstases of the for-itself, which ends up reintroducing a sort of ontological structure (in a way that is not clearly explicated): the first ekstasis is the nihilation of the for-itself with respect to the in-itself; the second is the reflexive transcending [*arrachement*] with respect to this first occurrence; the third (which particularly interests us here) is being-for-others in its conflictual dimension or its play of transcended-transcendence. In what sense can one distinguish the three ekstatic moments? What is their status? Sartre does not pause to clarify what might nonetheless have enabled him to make his relation to Heidegger explicit.

That being said, we should recognize—as we have begun to do—that Sartre's position has its own coherence, a coherence that mainly stems from its open and fully acknowledged reintroduction of the *cogito* into the central position from which Heidegger had dislodged it. Since others share my privilege of being a for-itself, one must draw all the existential and intellectual consequences from this. Sartre made the field of the struggle of consciousnesses, effectively left fallow by Heidegger, abundantly fruitful with his brilliant descriptions and analyses of the look, of the body-for-others, of love, masochism, desire, hatred, and sadism. There is no point in dwelling on these specific passages from Sartre's work, which are, moreover, intimately connected with the themes of his plays and novels. Through them, Sartre asserted his incontestable originality, which is quite distinct from Heidegger. Can one even conceive of Heidegger as a playwright or novelist? And most of all, could the profound themes of *Being and Time* easily be depicted?

Whatever the answer, we must draw two conclusions from all the above: the question of the other is the decisive ground on which a *differend*—that stems as much from differences in style and temperament as from profound disagreements—is played out. If this question is not purely theoretical, it must inevitably extend itself into the domain of morality, where nothing guarantees that its resolution (in either Heidegger or Sartre) will be satisfying.

A Deferred Morality

Was Sartre in good faith when he accused Heidegger's concept of transcendence of "bad faith"? We have begun to have doubts about this, without yet achieving any certainty on such a delicate question. Furthermore, is this concept of transcendence distinct from that of authenticity, which Sartre's morality is far from effectively rejecting? Certainly not. These perplexities, which implicitly follow from our previous discussions, invite us to complete, in moral terms, our analysis of the complex and inextricable relation of Sartre's originality with the considerable debt he had to Heidegger.

If one but refers to the table of contents of *Being and Nothingness,* one notes that only the two and a half pages at the end of the work are explicitly devoted to "ethical implications." This brief section begins by affirming that "ontology itself cannot formulate ethical precepts"[55] and ends with the pronouncement, which has become famous and, as it were, emblematic: "We shall devote to them a future work."[56] Consciously or unconsciously, Sartre pushed his imitation of Heidegger to the limit, since he managed to turn a very dense work of 722 tightly packed pages into something like the prelude to a moral treatise (that never saw the light of day), leaving the reader in suspense, just as Heidegger had announced a second part of *Sein und Zeit* that was never published. In fact, one cannot take Sartre's declarations at face value: moral considerations are explicit in the fourth part of *Being and Nothingness* ("Having, Doing, and Being"), and they are in no way absent prior to that. It could not be otherwise, insofar as this is a philosophy of existence that is oriented toward the concrete, and above all since its overarching concept is freedom, radically reconceived. Insofar as any theological or ontological order has been rejected, the for-itself is the only origin of values; every traditional form of morality has been invalidated; freedom must assume itself as such, in its situation, and so its responsibility will be absolute: "I carry the weight of the world by myself alone."[57] One cannot appeal to a *"spirit of seriousness,"* which for Sartre is a bad-faith compromise between transcendent values and everyday circumstances.[58]

It is interesting to note that the criticism leveled against Heidegger with respect to morality can be addressed to Sartre as well. Indeed, he is not wrong—concerning the call of conscience (*Ruf des Gewissens*)[59] in the context of "fallenness" and the guilt [*culpabilité*] from which it emerges—to formulate the following criticism: "In truth, Heidegger's descriptions show all too clearly his concern with establishing an ontological foundation for an Ethics with which he claims not to be concerned."[60] Was Sartre himself not in a similar situation, claiming that an ontology should not offer any moral prescriptions, but not denying himself recourse to notions as moral as those of bad faith, authenticity, and responsibility? Could this attitude be criticized as bad faith? It might be, except that Sartre fully assumed the moral project, which was not exactly the case in

Heidegger. And this is probably why Sartre, for the remainder of his life, could not complete or publish the projected volume: his ethics was already more than initiated in *Being and Nothingness.*

Now, since we have access today to the *Notebooks for an Ethics,* written in 1947–48,[61] can we discern in them a relation to Heidegger as intimate and intense as found in *Being and Nothingness*? Certainly not: not only because the direct allusions to Heidegger are few in number,[62] but also and especially because the problematic treated in this work is markedly different from the themes we have just studied. Furthermore, it would be inappropriate to claim to have found a unified problematic from these fragmentary pages. There can be little doubt that they pertain to the treatise of morality Sartre wanted to write, but the fact is that he did not complete it; one can apply to these texts what Sartre himself wrote in *Situations X* regarding his unpublished material: "They will represent what I wanted to do at a certain point and what I decided not to finish, and in that respect they will be definitive."[63]

In reading these fragments, what is in fact striking is that Sartre was already, in many ways, addressing the questions that would constitute the texture of the *Critique of Dialectical Reason.* There are many pages that concern the problem of history, the impossibility of drawing a unified meaning or definitive objectivity from it, the role of violence, and the emergence of the concrete universal. This means not that the questions of morality and psychology are missing, but that Sartre addressed them as a militant rather than as a phenomenologist: "Ethics *today* must be revolutionary, socialist ethics."[64] With this as a beginning, how could Heidegger remain useful? Sartre was not unsympathetic to the early criticisms of Heidegger by Levinas, who traced the notion of equipmentality back to the concrete, material, and sustaining conditions that precede it.[65] In a moment of Hegelian enthusiasm (which would not be repeated, at least to this extent), he went so far as to demean all that followed, including Marx, adding: "Heidegger and Husserl small-time philosophers. French philosophy zero" (*Notebook for an Ethics,* 61).

Nonetheless, Heidegger is not completely forgotten and certainly not despised, even from the perspective of the establishment of a morality, as the following surprising passage attests: "*Tough* thinkers (Heidegger) and *tender* thinkers (Jaspers). Don't wait for an ethics filled with hope. Man are ignoble. We have to love them for what they might be, not for what they are. Sketch out a *tough* ethics."[66] If it is clear that Sartre cannot stand Jaspers, whom he criticized for his "sleight of hand" in favor of Transcendence,[67] it is significant that we find him still fascinated by the very toughness of Heideggerian thought, and in particular in the moral domain where the Master of Freiburg had seemed to him to have gone astray[68] (and all this without the slightest allusion to Heidegger's activity in 1933, which revealed Sartre's almost complete lack of interest in the question).

One cannot dismiss a deep fascination so easily; but it is clear that Liberation brought about a radical shift in Sartre's attitude toward Heidegger: he would never again read him as closely. And it must be added that—beyond his increasing political engagement with the communists and the radical left—Sartre would reassert his characteristic irony or suspension of the spirit of seriousness, which strongly distinguished him from Heidegger: "If you seek authenticity for authenticity's sake, you are no longer authentic."[69] Here, it is indeed a matter of a morality in suspense, not only because it did not find its definitive expression, but because the project excluded both any objective order of values and any theory of salvation.

An Impossible Assessment

One can easily assess the damage caused by a bombardment; but in the present case, while suggested by the circumstances of the war, the metaphor should not be taken literally, for the effects of *Being and Nothingness* were deferred.

The very fact of acknowledging the great difficulty of assessing Sartre's debt to Heidegger is by itself instructive: this debt is incalculable, and Sartre knew this well from the start, when he sensed the "providential" character of *Being and Time*. But to the very same extent, we must also notice how strongly Sartre resisted being completely bewitched by Heidegger, as well as how obstinately he blazed his own thematic and stylistic trails. For him, Heidegger remained an idealist, who was crypto-religious, and deeply bound to a community to which he belonged; his ethics was not clearly delineated, because it was not founded on a reflective analysis. All these criticisms did not form a systematic whole and did not get in the way of a genuine admiration or of the quasi-mimetic adaptations we have indicated.

* * *

Sartre's early fame in 1943 and 1944 was essentially due to his first novels (*Nausea, The Wall*) and his plays (*The Flies* and *No Exit*), and certainly not due to *Being and Nothingness,* which was barely noticed.[70] From the point of view of the reception of Heidegger, the "Sartre bomb" was more like a time bomb. It was only after Liberation and in the following years that it would permanently transform the philosophical landscape. *Being and Nothingness,* a book that became fetishized by existentialists, would carry with it, in the wake of its caravan of curiosities of the moment, a Heidegger who was as prestigious as he was mysterious, already enshrouded in the myth of the founding father, solitary among the vanquished, a misunderstood genius, and a forerunner yet to be rediscovered.

3 Postwar Fascinations

It is not surprising that Liberation was not solely political, but cultural as well, and that the Sartre bomb was not the only one to explode at the time of an intense intellectual turmoil, amidst a joyous confusion. Sartre himself noted and deplored that existentialism, transformed into a fashion, became a word that "has been so stretched and has taken on so broad a meaning, that it no longer means anything at all."[1] Existentialism had almost become a slogan, whose meaning was no longer clear. "At St. Germain des Prés, the language of that time was taking shape and so was its jargon. The critics were confusing everything: Jaspers' philosophy with that of Gabriel Marcel, Trotsky with Malraux, Nietzsche with André Breton, and Kierkegaard with Heidegger."[2] Thus, there was nothing unusual in the fact that Heidegger was one of the involuntary members in this motley crew.

What is more surprising is the way in which Heidegger—his prestige suddenly at its zenith—was put on a pedestal by the snobbish Parisian intelligentsia, even though he had not done anything—at least in the beginning—to encourage such a level of curiosity and sympathy. Further, he was not being blamed for having been in the camp of the vanquished or for having compromised himself politically. Not only had the French presented themselves as victors just a few years after the worst routing in their history, but now they afforded themselves the opportunity to court and celebrate an obscure and difficult philosopher, while pretending, in a condescending way, to be unaware of his political error.

The indications of this paradoxical glory were numerous. One of the first was that as early as 1945, the French intellectuals began their visits to the Master.

Visiting the Great Philosopher

One would be hard pressed to say that people had beaten a path to Heidegger's door. The conditions of access and transportation in the occupied zone were quite difficult and controlled by the military. Given these serious obstacles, it is significant that Frédéric de Towarnicki was not the only one to use his French army uniform to go meet the Master on several occasions. He was followed by other officers, including Edgar Morin and Maurice de Gandillac, themselves forecasting the legions of French visitors from whom Heidegger would benefit later in more favorable circumstances.

It seems that Towarnicki was indeed the first to have dared to brave the many obstacles in order to venture to 47 Rötebuckweg, in Zähringen at the edge of Freiburg.[3] In the course of a first unsuccessful visit (which took place around the end of the summer of 1945), he encountered only Heidegger's wife. He returned during the fall with Alain Resnais and this time actually met with Heidegger. His very lively account of this meeting is worth reading;[4] it is incontestably in good faith, and seems as faithful as possible; but one cannot find any philosophical revelation, nor any truly precise information about Heidegger's past. This account offers the sketch of what was to become the typical scenario of the visits of the French to Freiburg—the visitors, who were visibly intimidated, would do their best to introduce themselves, inquire about the thinking of the Master and the state of his work, or even dare a few bolder questions regarding politics, while their host showed great courtesy mixed with an amused (or perhaps bemused) curiosity concerning his Parisian celebrity,[5] and asked questions about the better known philosophers (he questioned Towarnicki about Sartre and Beaufret, but also about Sorbonne professors such as Le Senne or Bréhier—to whom he had written without having received any response). While Edgar Morin had not kept any accurate records of the content of his own conversations,[6] he did recall that Heidegger was at first "extremely wary," then cordial. Maurice de Gandillac, both in his article in *Les Temps Modernes* and in his autobiography, showed himself to be less sympathetic toward Heidegger than Frédéric de Towarnicki (even though there were no noticeably different elements in their accounts) in spite of his efforts to draw out the illustrious interlocutor: "Short, stocky (the Chaplinesque mustache evoked certain comical aspects of the Führer), Heidegger seemed overwhelmed by the event. . . . Heidegger returned deliberately to the banality of everyday life. . . . Whatever his genius, how could one not take into account the contrast between the very demands of his philosophy and the vaguely evasive attitude of this 'man in situation'?"[7]

Whether the atmosphere of these various discussions was cheerful or tense, Heidegger rarely opened up, and remained reticent. It is now known that he had some episodes of depression up to 1947. Is that so surprising? His country was defeated, devastated, and dishonored by the first revelations of the horrors of the extermination camps. Heidegger was subjected to strong psychological pressures and to seizures of his personal property. Even worse: his teaching privileges were suspended and he was the object of a denazification investigation; additionally, his two sons were in a prison camp in Russia and he received no word of any kind about their fate.

The asymmetry between the visitors and Heidegger was dramatic and, truth be told, quite incredible: on the one hand, one arrived—with either a real or feigned respect—to see what the great philosopher of the day, who was already legendary, looked like. On the other hand, one could sense Heidegger's mixed feelings of sadness, of fear, and of relief as a philosopher haunted by his past, surrounded by hostility, nonetheless discovering admirers, and perhaps even unexpected friends, among the representatives of the occupying power. Did any of his neighbors believe that they were coming to arrest him?[8] It was in fact the contrary that took place: these were acts of recognition and homage, which were the precursory signs for Heidegger of the enduring support that he would find in France.

Heidegger himself was so favorably impressed by these visits[9] that he wrote to Jean Beaufret on November 23, 1945" "I sense, as far as I have been able to grasp in just a few weeks, an extraordinary *élan* which shows that a revolution is forming in this domain."[10]

At a properly philosophical level, what was actually the case? Apart from the rumors of the existentialist fad, and except for Sartre, could one detect a sophisticated philosophical receptivity in France at that time? Even if there were no doubt that the answer is yes, we would still need to clarify the basis for such an appraisal.

Communications from a Certain Mr. Beaufret

During his very first visit to Heidegger's residence, Frédéric de Towarnicki gave Mrs. Heidegger two issues of the journal *Confluences* with a series of recent articles by Jean Beaufret, "*À propos de l'existentialisme.*" A minor occurrence with great effects: this minor event occasioned one of the most profound and well-known philosophical friendships in history!

At the time, Towarnicki himself did not realize the consequences of this gesture. But he appreciated the quality of Beaufret's work and hoped that Heidegger would recognize the effort being made to grapple with his thought in its specificity without reducing it to the Sartrean horizon.

This showed great instinct, considering that there was only one text involved. It must be emphasized that personal relations between Heidegger and Beaufret came after the philosophical readings and not the reverse. It has been suggested (and without doubt believed in good faith) that Heidegger wrote his famous "Letter on Humanism," addressed to Jean Beaufret, in an attempt to establish support in France, throwing it out like a rescue buoy, when he was so terribly isolated in Germany. This last point is perhaps not completely erroneous, but prior to this, Heidegger's attention had been awakened by the reading of Beaufret's text—this act of recognition from such an exceptional reader as Heidegger had a unique value that transcended psychological or anecdotal considerations. Given the enthusiasm of some French intellectuals who had come to Freiburg, Heidegger was not lacking external "support" (was not Sartre potentially the most impressive among them?).[11] What was lacking, much more radically in 1945, was an authentic philosophical account of the path of his thinking following the publication of *Being and Time,* which was already fifteen years old. Knowing now the ever so decisive volumes of the *Gesamtausgabe,* which punctuated his itinerary from 1936—in particular, the Nietzsche lectures and the *Beiträge*—one can better measure his extraordinary intellectual isolation, which was further reinforced by circumstances. Having published practically nothing for fifteen years, although intensely pursuing his "turn" all the while, he had no real interlocutors. Perhaps only a few former students or colleagues, such as Walter Biemel and Eugen Fink, were able to sense the depth of this profound intellectual solitude. Alphonse de Waelhens referred to this solitude in 1942 in these rather unusual terms: "It is not certain—according to Eugen Fink who could be, if he wanted, the most penetrating interpreter of his thought—that the philosopher of *Sein und Zeit* could one day overcome the crisis of discouragement and weariness that he has known for several years."[12] What hidden insight had Heidegger discerned, in the fall of 1945, in these pages from Jean Beaufret?[13]

It is difficult, though not impossible, to adopt Heidegger's point of view by assuming, for a moment, his expectations and curiosity. With his keen intelligence, Heidegger had immediately grasped the obvious qualities of the text: clarity, absence of jargon and chatter, and a knack for bringing out the essential. One also notes, due to its mention in his first missive to Jean Beaufret,[14] that he had particularly appreciated (which was not surprising) the sentence, "if German has its resources, French has its limits."[15]

As for the question "What is existentialism?" Beaufret had an immediate response: "First and foremost, it is a certain way of philosophizing." But there are two breeds of philosophers, those who return to the question of the human being only at the end of a systematic enterprise and those who, on the other hand, "address the human being directly."[16] Aristotle is the champion of the first, Pascal the hero of the second. Of the latter group, Beaufret writes, in his illuminating prose, "It is by aiming at the very heart of one's 'existing' that they attempted to wrest a truth from the obscurity of one's condition, which would be from the outset attuned to our fundamental nostalgia." Each word carries weight, especially when Beaufret emphasizes the ambiguity of the word "presence" in Heidegger.[17] It is, alas, impossible here to follow the text line by line in order to reproduce all of its richness. It suffices to characterize the role of Heidegger in this first article (which in theory concerned mainly Kierkegaard) and in the second article, which was explicitly devoted to the Master of Freiburg.

Heidegger is present in the text on Kierkegaard, despite a general orientation bearing Sartre's imprint. He remained present throughout the four articles in emphatically laudatory terms. For example, we read, "Jaspers absolutely did not have the caliber, the power, or the originality of Heidegger";[18] and, "With Heidegger, indeed, everything is consistent."[19] (He goes so far as to compare the rigor of Heidegger's text to a "sequence of equations.")[20]

But these praises were neither formal nor removed: they relied on an already very astute reading of *Being and Time*—that he, Beaufret, had begun reading in German as early as 1942,[21] even translating some fragments with his friend Joseph Rovan[22]—and on a careful consideration of the specific difficulties that Beaufret was trying to resolve by himself, without any help. Sensing that Heidegger abhorred "cheap sentimentality,"[23] Beaufret showed that Heidegger rediscovered the "highest moment of openness [*Offenheit*] of philosophical thought."[24] As in this last case, Beaufret's translations were not commonplace: for example, Beaufret translated *das Seinsverständnis* as "*intelligence de l'être*" and the word *Dasein* as "the bursting of an act of presence: Here I am."[25] We note as well that he confronted the difficulties of the text when he analyzed consciousness as *Erschlossenheit* ("the disclosure" of being in the world), when he evoked the facticity and fallenness (*Verfallen*) of the existential project; but above all, in the way he made authentic temporality explicit by presenting it in a remarkably synthetic manner and without jargon: "Being-ahead-of-oneself-already-thrown-into-the-world."[26]

Finally, the significance he recognized in Heidegger's work was such that it led Beaufret to authorize himself to correct Sartre's flippant "carelessness": it is not sufficient to say that "existence precedes essence," and for existence to somehow vaguely mean "effective presence in the world." Indeed, "the presence of man in the *Da* of *Dasein* has nothing to do with the presence of a thing"[27] (we have already seen the need to be attentive to the ambiguity of presence). Further, with respect to Heidegger's involvement in National Socialism in 1933, about which he cared very little before being subjected to the psychological pressures of Liberation and denazification, Sartre had written: "Heidegger has no character, that's the simple truth."[28] Beaufret responded that Heidegger thought he had discovered an "authentic philosophy of resoluteness in the face of death." Was it simply a matter of naïveté? Beaufret's explication, opposed to Sartre's interpretation, was somewhat Marxist: Heidegger's political error could be explained by "an unreflective petit-bourgeois moment," with the Freiburg philosopher forgetting to be "attentive to infrastructures."[29]

One can guess that neither this explanation nor that of Sartre was to Heidegger's liking. But he had to make the best of the situation. Even if Beaufret was superficial or somewhat hasty on certain points,[30] his brilliant intuitions and desire to do justice to Heidegger's originality caused the Master to take careful note of his work. One must begin there to understand the thirty-year philosophical friendship between Martin Heidegger and Jean Beaufret. Their first meeting took place in September of 1946 at the Todtnauberg hut,[31] which Beaufret approached with supplies and baskets given to him by Heidegger's daughter-in-law in Freiburg. The expedition, which was captured in a picturesque account,[32] was carried out to this point in a military vehicle thanks to Joseph Katz, who at the time had the rank of commander. Katz continued on to Salzburg; Beaufret settled at the inn at Todtnauberg, where he spent two days. "It was over the course of these two days that I asked Heidegger to explain to me who he was." We do not know the answer to the first question posed: "Who is Husserl for you?" Heidegger did, however, dictate a response to the second question, "And you, who are you?" In a few pages,[33] Heidegger announced both the "Letter on Humanism" and the elucidation of the "truth of being": an explanation of his thought that he would continue to provide to Jean Beaufret, who would be his friend from then on. Beaufret later confided to François Fédier that he had immediately recognized Heidegger's greatness:[34] it was an extraordinary moment of recognition.

Parisian Minds

The proliferation of articles, lectures, and diverse discussions testified to Heidegger's fame in Paris immediately after the war: we will initially address two interviews with Jean Beaufret that appeared in *Le Monde;* we will then return to the case of Alexandre Kojève; and finally, we will analyze at length, as warranted, the more detailed philosophical testimonies of Alexandre Koyré, Jean Wahl, Emmanuel Lévinas, and Maurice Merleau-Ponty.

While Kojève could have passed for a Heideggerian reader of Hegel, it seems that his texts suggest just the opposite.[35] Raymond Queneau's 1947 publication of the *Introduction to the Reading of Hegel* in no way contributed to stimulating interest in Heidegger himself, as it was *The Phenomenology of Spirit* that remained the constant reference for any anthropology. One footnote, however, quite illuminating in this respect, is worth citing: "In our times, Heidegger is the first to undertake a complete atheistic philosophy. But he does not seem to have pushed it beyond the phenomenological anthropology developed in the first volume of *Sein und Zeit* (the only volume that has appeared). This anthropology (which is without a doubt remarkable and authentically philosophical) adds, fundamentally, nothing new to the anthropology of the *Phenomenology* (which, by the way, would probably never have been understood if Heidegger had not published his book); but atheism or ontological finitism are implicitly asserted in his book in a perfectly consequent fashion."[36] This is certainly a homage to Heidegger (whose "inspirational" role was recognized), who Kojève nonetheless resituated (with the sharp clarity that belonged only to him) as an heir to Hegel. Whatever Heidegger's place (but also Marx's place) in the incomplete yet brilliant interpretation that Kojève gave of the Hegelian dialectic, there is no longer any doubt about the decisive role that his courses played from 1933 to 1939 in the emergence of French existentialism.

"What is existentialism?" This was exactly the expected question that Beaufret, who had just become known for his articles in the Lyon journal *Confluences,* was asked to answer in two interviews with the journalist Henry Magnan in December of 1945.[37] Always the teacher, Beaufret answered in the retrospective manner of which he was fond, by resituating existentialism in the Pascalian tradition of questioning the human condition: "Being-in-the-world has the brutality of a fact without rhyme or reason."[38] The first interview almost paid more attention to Kierkegaard and Jaspers than to Heidegger. The second interview was much more interesting for us, because it concerned the "value system" of existentialism, and it required Beaufret to explain his ideas on the relationship between existentialism and fascism. Can existentialism be reduced to being the "hieroglyph of a fascism that does not admit to what it is?"[39] The answer was more brilliant than precise: Heidegger, like Rilke, Kleist, or Novalis, was the object of a "sort of appropriation by the Nazis." The journalist pressed further (it had been said that Heidegger was "the official philosopher of the Nazi party"). Jean Beaufret dismissed this objection all too easily since it was clearly constructed in inadequate terms. Recalling that he believed Heidegger was the "most important philosopher of the contemporary world," he emphasized that the Master agreed to become a member of the Nazi party only after having been elected to the position of rector "with the insistence of his predecessor who had been threatened," that he resigned a few months later so as to "not comply with Rosenberg's orders," and that finally he was critical in his courses of biologism and his publications were censored by the regime. This line of defense was—almost in the same terms— the one that Heidegger himself had suggested to Towarnicki, who was moreover cited by Jean Beaufret.[40] At that time (December 1945), Beaufret had not yet met Heidegger; he had just received his first letter from him, dated November 23, 1945, which was a response to his first friendly missive that he sent at the suggestion of Frédéric de Towarnicki, and which had been delivered by an intermediary, a friend named Palmer.[41] The personal relationship was only just beginning, but one could see that Beaufret was already a fervent defender of Heidegger. This contrasted with the more tempered, though generally favorable, attitudes of his friends and colleagues—Jean Wahl and Merleau-Ponty, in particular—who were also interested in existentialism and phenomenology.

At this point we need to address the case of Koyré. Among those who read Heidegger closely, he was certainly the most reserved. This reserve contrasted with his early enthusiasm. The crisis of 1933 and the Holocaust contributed to his change in attitude. But a long article published in two parts in the first issues of the journal *Critique* allowed Koyré to develop a careful and detailed argumentation to explain his disappointment and to conclude with respect to "Martin Heidegger's failure."[42]

This article is a very detailed report on the essay on truth (*Vom Wesen der Wahrheit*), a book published by Heidegger in 1943, which, of course, had still not been translated in 1946.[43] The fact that an important scholar as distinguished as Koyré took on the task of writing such an in-depth study, the length of which exceeded that of the original work it was addressing, could only be seen as an homage to Heidegger's philosophical importance. Nonetheless, one cannot overlook the other side of this high praise: a negative judgment on the contents of the work. The impossibility of publishing the announced part two of *Sein und Zeit* was not the result of a contingent failure: the essay on the essence of truth revealed that access to ontological authenticity was illusory and that Heidegger was constrained to abandon his existential anthropology[44] while enclosing himself in an esotericism of so-called concealment (*das Verbergen*). Without speaking of a "turn," Koyré noted rightly the profound transformation in Heideggerian terminology after *Being and Time,* and he identified in this respect a "completely anti-existentialist" orientation.[45] Human subjectivity no longer played any role in the face of the concealment and the errancy of being. "The *Irre* (darkness, errancy, confusion, alienation) is irreducible. *Dasein* is a mystery."[46] The Heideggerian rejection of the traditional concept of truth and of the Platonic understanding of dialogue only resulted in a fascination with silence, a misunderstanding of history, and a regression toward the "concealment of concealment."[47] One should not have searched for the essence of truth (and its conditions of possibility) except in truth itself. Koyré's text is an important step, and while it merited serious thought, it might be assumed that its rigor and technical difficulty must unfortunately have limited the number of its readers.

For his part, in an entirely different manner, Jean Wahl actively pursued his role as a pioneer. One finds a very interesting example of this in the journal directed by Wahl, *Deucalion:* the first issue contained a balanced treatment of "Heidegger and Sartre" by Alphonse de Waelhens, as well as an article by Wahl himself on the problem of nothingness in Sartre's work. But above all, it contained a text by Levinas on the theme of the *Il y a* [the "there is"], in which one could detect (albeit in a subtle way) a challenge to Heideggerian existentialism as trapped in an ontology of finitude and thus incapable of opening itself to the hypostasis presupposed by nothingness: "the appearance of a noun, of a name, or a particular within the anonymous and universal rustling of the *il y a*."[48] Publishing in 1947 several phenomenological studies (on fatigue, on the now, on exoticism, and on insomnia, and so on) begun before the war, Levinas stated more clearly that his research "is governed by a profound need to leave the climate" of Heideggerian philosophy, without at the same time regressing to a "pre-Heideggerian"[49] philosophy.

Wahl was something of a pioneer. This can be seen in a lecture he gave in 1946 at "Club Maintenant."[50] The lecture was interesting in and of itself, but also because of the rich discussion that followed. The lecture was very clear and didactic: it claimed to be impartial and only hinted at the political question by emphasizing that in Heidegger's work, "resolute decision" remained formal, and did not correspond to any ethics properly speaking.[51] This amounted to both lamenting a serious shortcoming and exonerating Heideggerian philosophy at its very core from any substantial association with Nazism. Wahl could not help but express his concerns, namely that Heidegger was not really able to ground an ontology on the basis of existence; furthermore, that in his later writings, Heidegger "has attempted, in certain tracts, to erect a kind of philosophy more myth-like than mystic, in which he enjoined us to a communion with the earth and the world, invoking to this end the thought of Hölderlin and Rilke."[52] In the discussion that followed, it was paradoxically the first person to have introduced Heidegger in France, Georges Gurvitch, who showed extreme hostility.[53] Moreover, he was the only one to have been critical, since Berdiaeff, Koyré, Gandillac, Marcel, and even Levinas developed clarifications of Heidegger's work rather than criticisms.[54]

Wahl's role as a pioneer was revealed in a more surprising manner (we will see why) in the course he gave on Heidegger at the Sorbonne from January to June 1946. Published in 1998 by Jean Montenot,[55] this course was unusual, first, because it was not in the strict sense a course *on* Heidegger but a commentary on a course *given by* Heidegger—obviously unpublished at the time (though it has since been published):[56] a rather unusual and somewhat odd process (especially if one notes that the author of the course had apparently not been consulted). Secondly, Jean Wahl initiated a style of commentary that he would pursue (particularly in the course entitled *Vers la fin de l'ontologie*) and that consisted in introducing—due to his multiple references to different texts of Heidegger, most notably *Being and Time*—the academic audience to some original texts that were not accessible to most people. His was a commentary on unknown texts, like a medieval preacher who could choose to cite and comment on biblical verses unavailable to the common churchgoer! After Liberation and through the 1950s, a small circle of initiates was formed, those who obviously knew German, or allegedly so, and those who had read *Sein und Zeit*, or at least claimed to refer directly to it, and who benefited from a privilege not available to the general public, due to the absence of a translation. One could wonder, moreover, if this privilege did not in fact diminish, among the initiates (Wahl, Hyppolite, Beaufret, Merleau-Ponty, Birault, among others), any genuine interest in having the texts translated.[57]

Wahl, in any case, did not justify his choice; he directly followed the very terms and progression of Heidegger's course. As Jean Montenot stated, Wahl's "goal was probably less to offer a course on Heidegger's thought than to follow step by step, sometimes critically, Heidegger's reflection as it unfolded."[58] In fact, Jean Wahl was fortunate that Alexandre Koyré apparently supplied him with a copy of the lecture course in France as early as 1929.[59]

Whatever reservations one might have with respect to the method that was used, this course was nonetheless quite interesting. The very fact that it could have taken place at the Sorbonne without incident clearly confirms the exceptional stature that Heidegger's thought enjoyed among Parisian intellectuals in 1946.

If it is certainly not a question here of examining in detail this course, which was itself already quite intricate in nature, by conducting a comparison with the Heideggerian "model," it is however quite appropriate and necessary to reveal its intention in broad strokes. One must confess a major disappointment with Wahl's text, especially since he had "just come back from visiting Heidegger."[60] What a contrast! In principle, the contents were the same, since Wahl followed the typed copy of the course. In fact, Wahl followed both parts of the course ("Philosophy and science" and "Philosophy and worldview"), and he closely followed Heidegger's analyses (concerning the specificity of philosophy; its relation to the sciences; the meaning of worldview, truth, and the modes of being; Heidegger's theses on truth, the concept of world and the Kantian interpretation; the world as a "play of life"; and finally philosophy as fundamental stance and shelter), even though he condensed the forty-six paragraphs of the course into twenty lectures.[61]

If the contrast is striking, although not flattering for Wahl, this is not only because a commentary is necessarily secondary in relation to the original that it addresses (Wahl could not have been unaware that he risked being overshadowed by a Heideggerian text); this is because, instead of effacing himself before the text to make its force and its extraordinary pedagogical virtues apparent (this is one of the best of Heidegger's lecture courses), Wahl dithered without any method, with no guiding questions, multiplying the defects of an anarchic gloss. And while he was a Germanist and a decent translator in other respects, he kept the horrid translation of *Dasein* as "human reality." Above all, he claimed mistakenly that Heidegger was criticizing the preeminence of the problem of being[62] (he wrongly assumed that Heidegger "subordinated the problem of being to the problem of the world"[63]), and he did not at all clarify his own position, while asserting that he had detected "extreme idealist elements and also extreme realist elements"[64] in Heidegger's work. This projection of a traditional terminology onto the Heideggerian horizon (when Heidegger's entire efforts had been to free himself from such a terminology) only added to the confusion without giving Heidegger his due—however debatable it might be. That being said, it must be admitted that Wahl followed Sartre, who had already resorted to the same kind of dualist reduction; furthermore, it would be out of place or unjust not to concede that he was able to identify decisive thresholds in the text (thus the passage from worldview as sheltering—*Bergung*—to worldview as stance—*Haltung*—was treated correctly in lessons 17 and 19).[65] He also appropriately noticed that the Heideggerian notion of the divine was neither pantheistic, nor theistic, nor atheistic.[66] Simply, his listeners would have needed exceptional skill in order to extract the most pertinent critical remarks from an occasionally brilliant, but most often improvised and quite disorganized, presentation. With some distance and thanks to the publication of this lecture course, we can however appraise both the strengths and the weaknesses of Jean Wahl's reading. After having been a pioneer in Heideggerian matters, he continued—in his own way and in a critical mode—to publicize this thought, by stimulating the interest of the public in Heidegger's thought.

Emmanuel Levinas, also a pioneer, and incidentally a friend of Wahl's, gave four lectures in 1946 and 1947 under Wahl's supervision at the Collège Philosophique on "Time and the Other," in which Heidegger was often cited. In his preface to these texts,[67] Levinas clarified that one must read these lectures "in the spirit of those years of openness," when "new philosophical possibilities" seemed to be promised by Husserl, Sartre, Merleau-Ponty, and "even the first statements of Heidegger's fundamental ontology."[68] This formulation from 1979 revealed some reservation that might lead one to believe that Heidegger was not as present as the other phenomenological authors. In fact, a reading of these lectures shows that Heidegger remained present throughout. He is the most cited author, whether it was on the subject of being, anxiety, equipmentality, or being-toward-death. However, it is quite interesting to note the reservations (also formulated in the introduction to the 1949 volume *En découvrant l'existence avec Husserl et Heidegger*[69]) that constitute important developments with respect to the early texts from before the war. With moderation, without direct allusion to the political question or to the Holocaust, without even really developing his new thematics of the alterity of the Other and of the "face to face," Levinas clearly emphasized that he henceforth rejected the Heideggerian conception of "being-with" as well as a solitude reduced to "the privileged experience of being-toward-death."[70] Opposing both Marxism and existentialism, Levinas outlined a phenomenology of suffering, of modesty, and of the caress, which was no longer Heideggerian. Indeed, the privilege he granted to the "future" still seemed capable of being understood in terms of *Sein und Zeit*, but this "future" was no longer essentially that of *Dasein:* it was, rather, the radicality of the Other, as such, that Levinas introduced. In relation to his teacher, Levinas thus began a change of course in which the stakes were not yet explicit. Undoubtedly, there were only a few who noticed the intensity of the tension this created. Was it even possible to detect to what extent this change of course would be radicalized?

Merleau-Ponty's approach in the *Phenomenology of Perception* was altogether different. Heidegger was integrated in a deliberate and methodical way in a long-term personal research project. As in the case of Sartre's *Being and Nothingness,* but more subtly, Merleau-Ponty took his place next to Husserl as an important figure within phenomenology. From the first pages of his preface, Merleau-Ponty constantly mentioned the names of Husserl and Heidegger, the latter having completed and corrected the phenomenological project of the former by resituating "essences back into existence."[71] Could this quite conciliatory perspective benefit either? It is difficult to determine since the two projects were so intertwined. Anticipating objections, Merleau-Ponty clarified from the outset that "one may try to do away with these contradictions by making a distinction between Husserl's and Heidegger's phenomenologies; yet the whole of *Sein und Zeit* springs from an indication given by Husserl and amounts to no more than an explicit account of the '*natürlicher Weltbegriff*' or the '*Lebenswelt*' which Husserl, toward the end of his life, identified as the central theme of phenomenology, with the result that the contradiction reappears in Husserl's own philosophy."[72] This overly subtle elliptical remark is extremely cryptic and raises more difficulties than it solves: by attempting to reduce Heidegger to an interpretation of the late Husserl, it in fact reinscribed Husserl in a Heideggerian landscape, albeit in terms that themselves were prompted by a Merleau-Pontian problematic of the pre-reflexive primacy of perception. A lot said in the space of a few lines! Mischievously, Merleau-Ponty suggested that this would discourage a "careless reader." Is this the situation in which we find ourselves? If we follow our line of inquiry patiently—that is, the reception of Heidegger's thought—what should we conclude? By indissociably mixing the names and projects of Husserl and Heidegger, Merleau-Ponty succeeded both in including himself in what he called the phenomenological "fad" and "movement" and in asserting a style that was quite different from Sartre's, namely, less aggressively "existentialist," but just as committed to retaining the lessons of *Sein und Zeit*.

How did this project actually unfold in the text of the *Phenomenology of Perception*? Heidegger, in fact, was much less present in it than Husserl, Sartre, or even a forgotten philosopher from Lyon, a certain Lachièze-Rey (at least if one is guided by the actual occurrences in the text). Apart from the foreword, this project was essentially presented in the last part, the most philosophical one ("Being-for-itself and Being-in-the-World"), on the subject of the *cogito* and temporality. It is not surprising that Heidegger is absent from all the technical discussions on the psycho-physiological roots of perception, the body, sexuality, and space—areas of study neglected or given little consideration in *Sein und Zeit*. One expected Heidegger to be more present in the chapter on "Other People and the Human World." Clearly, while acknowledging his closeness to Sartre, Merleau-Ponty was reluctant to follow in the footsteps of his comrade and to embrace all of his polemics. Thus, with respect to Heidegger, he did not adopt any of Sartre's criticisms, preferring to retain only those thoughts or themes that inspired him. In this light, the discussion of the *cogito* became very complicated; would he, like Sartre, affirm the imprescriptible rights of the Cartesian principle, or follow Heidegger on the less-traveled path of a nonreflexive openness of *Dasein* to its own transcendence? At first glance, one might think that the first was the case, since one rediscovered "an element of final truth in the Cartesian return of things or ideas to the self."[73] Very early on, however, Merleau-Ponty rejected an atemporal or purely reflexive conception of the *cogito*. The "I think" is indistinguishable from the world, and one must restore all of its linguistic and temporal depth as a "fundamental mode of the event and *Geschichte*"[74] (one senses that Heidegger's work is in the background, though it is never cited).

Without letting himself be caught up in an overly formal or dogmatic position, Merleau-Ponty thus treated the question of the *cogito* in a way that appeared compatible with the Sartrean position, although in fact it was quite similar to Heidegger's notion of being-in-the-world. Two explicit references to *Sein und Zeit* testify to this, but in an unexpected way. Evoking "one single 'living cohesion'"[75] in a thought that regains its movement [*son bougé*] in time and in the world, Merleau-Ponty incorrectly cited the expression to which he was referring: in Heidegger's text one finds the "connectedness of *Dasein*!"[76] The beginning of paragraph 75 was an appropriate reference,[77] because its theme is the historicity of *Dasein,* recognizable in its familiar world and institutions. It is strange, however, that Merleau-Ponty proceeds with a casualness that is repeated with the other reference on pages 124–125 of *Sein und Zeit* concerning the expression "Je suis à moi *en étant au monde*" [I belong to myself *while being in the world*]. This expression is not literally found in the aforesaid pages, which do not bear precisely on the relation between the self and the world, but concern, rather, being-with as constitutive of being-in-the-world. These are strange "citations," which reveal more of an appreciation than a meticulous and deep reading.

In a comparable, though much more precise, manner, Merleau-Ponty proposed with respect to temporality what was the equivalent of a "rectification" of the idealist position[78]—though this time it was Husserlian—thanks to the reference to Heidegger. All of a sudden, Heidegger is much more present (and already in the epigraph of the chapter[79]), as if Merleau-Ponty had concentrated his reading of *Sein und Zeit* on the final pages concerning, properly speaking, temporality. From the outset, what Merleau-Ponty borrowed from Heidegger is the idea that time is not a "succession of instances of now."[80] Would he, however, follow Heidegger in his radical destabilization of the "vulgar" conception of time and in his "ek-static" reinterpretation based on the priority of the future? Merleau-Ponty certainly accepted the Heideggerian reformulation,[81] although he reinscribed it within the intentional network of retentions and protentions, following the Husserlian scheme. One can discern a certain difficulty in his text,[82] when he borrowed Husserl's diagram for the sole reason that it allowed him to isolate a moment in the totality of motion, whose dynamic it was necessary to grasp.[83] Merleau-Ponty was trying to consider at the same time the continuity of time and the discordance in its three dimensions. What is not at all Heideggerian, despite an obvious desire at reconciliation,[84] is the apprehension of the essence of time as subjectivity. "We *must understand time* as the *subject* and the *subject as time*."[85]

In this chapter, which is both very rich and highly ambiguous, Merleau-Ponty seemed aware that he should continue his critical dialogue with Heidegger, a dialogue that was barely outlined by this very clever elliptical remark: "Heidegger's historical time, which flows from the future and which, thanks to its resolute decision, *has* its future in advance and rescues itself once and for all from disintegration, is impossible within the context of Heidegger's thought itself: for, if time is an *ek-stase,* if present and past are two results of this *ek-stase,* how could we ever cease to see time from the point of view of the present, and how could we finally escape from the inauthentic?"[86] At times too subtle, but always suggestive, Merleau-Ponty's intelligence was always at its peak in his engagement with Heidegger, which would never cease to deepen until his sadly premature death.

Heidegger and Politics: The Question Is Posed

At the end of the course mentioned above, Jean Wahl made only one, very discreet, critical reference to the political error of 1933: "One is compelled to say that Heidegger as a man was inferior to Heidegger as a philosopher, at least at a certain time."[87] It is even surprising, considering the "honor" he paid Heidegger by devoting an entire course to him, that Wahl never counterbalanced that homage with a more vigorous stand on such a sensitive question, given the atmosphere of Liberation. Most importantly, Wahl did not even formulate the political question in its most decisive respect. He claimed that if Heidegger the man was inferior to Heidegger the philosopher, his error can be reduced to a psychological weakness: he lacked character. One finds this "explanation" offered by Sartre in the newspaper *Action* on December 29, 1944, which clearly consisted in placing Heidegger's philosophy above reproach and not even suspecting the man of a genuine allegiance to Nazi ideology. To understand this account, one must recall the virulence of the communist attacks against Sartrean existentialism in which his subjective idealism and his Heideggerian leanings were treated as Nazi-like. "Immediately after the dissipation of the euphoria of Liberation, which had brought together Sartre and the communists, they began to attack existentialism harshly by accusing it of being a philosophy of diversion in the class struggle. The communist weekly *Action,* in its cultural section directed by Francis Ponge, served as the main instrument of these accusations, although it invited Sartre to respond."[88] What should we glean from Sartre's explanation concerning Heidegger? Sartre replied in the following way to the criticism that he relied on this "German and Nazi philosopher": "Heidegger was a philosopher well before he was a Nazi. His adherence to Hitlerism is to be explained by fear, perhaps ambition, and certainly conformism. Not pretty to look at, I agree; but enough to invalidate your neat reasoning: 'Heidegger, you say, is a member of the National Socialist Party; thus his philosophy must be Nazi.' That's not it: Heidegger has no character; there's the truth of the matter. Are you going to have the nerve to conclude from this that his philosophy is an apology for cowardice?"[89] To consider the case of Rousseau: the man who wrote *The Social Contract* also abandoned his children. One should not condemn the work on account of the weaknesses of the man. "Why then does Heidegger matter?" concluded Sartre, since one only asked of him "techniques and methods" without there ever having been a question of allegiance.

Although this position was significant to the extent that it corresponded to the prevailing sentiment of the time, it was still not unanimously shared. The communists persisted in speaking of the "Nazi Heidegger,"[90] and Camus followed suit, although without hostility.[91] Furthermore, very little was known about Heidegger's political engagement: he had joined the National Socialist party in 1933,[92] and then he resigned as rector the following year. This was almost everything that seemed to have been established at the time, although the communist Henri Mougin tried to sharpen his attacks and began publishing excerpts from the "Rectoral Address."[93] But this is not what mattered: his philosophy was the issue. Although he was a communist at the time, Edgar Morin confirms today that the mood of young people who were interested in philosophy was hardly "punitive" with respect to Heidegger.[94] It is true that there were more important matters to attend to and that the immediate political struggles, the internal purge, and postwar reconstruction were much more urgent than the reconstruction of the details of the political engagements of a great philosopher, among other intellectuals in Germany in 1933.

However, as we have seen, the question had indeed been posed. Silent during the Occupation, Sartre had to take a stand, however briefly, on this question, and then organized a debate in the pages of *Les Temps modernes*. It is worth referencing the debate and reconstituting its essential moments, because the discussion, taken as a whole, was of high quality and quite eventful, which attests that it was responding, as one could imagine, to a genuine concern and expectation.

The first installment concerning Heidegger appeared in January 1946. It contained a brief editorial note bearing Sartre's signature, and began in the following way: "The French press spoke of Heidegger as a Nazi; it is a fact that he was a member of the Nazi party. If one had to judge a philosophy by the courage or political lucidity of the philosopher, Hegel would not stand up to the scrutiny. It can happen that a philosopher be unfaithful to his best thoughts when he arrives at political decisions."[95]

The allusion to the "French press" (attacks were coming from the communists, but also from Christian democrats of the *Mouvement républicain populaire*) established that Sartre saw himself forced to take on a subject he would rather have avoided. There is no dispute with respect to the factual concession regarding Heidegger's party membership in 1933. But the sentence that came immediately after considerably mitigated the significance of his party membership: the comparison with Hegel, eminently debatable in itself, from the outset put Heidegger on a pedestal by dissociating the value of a philosophy from the actions of the philosopher. And the short following sentence strongly suggested that Heidegger's "best thinking" was diametrically opposed to Nazism. Already, on the basis of this short paragraph, which was quite skillful and worthy of a great lawyer, the reader understood that Heidegger must have lacked "courage" or "political lucidity," but that his philosophy was not challenged as such.

In the ensuing debate, a new concession was made, which was once again skillfully cloaked in the parallel to Hegel, "It is possible, it will be necessary to look into *what* in Heidegger's existentialism would motivate the acceptance of Nazism, as one could look into what, in Hegelianism, made Hegel's support of the Prussian monarchy as well as the reactionary Hegel of the last period, possible." On this point, Sartre was going farther than he had ever gone before. In admitting that he could see a link between Heidegger's philosophy and his political engagements, he invalidated his own psychological explanation. But he made this concession thanks to the parallel with Hegel, "Tailored for Hegel, this analysis exonerates most of Hegelian philosophy, that is, of dialectical thought. When that concession is made for Heidegger, it will disculpate most of his philosophy, that is, existential thought (which is not unrelated to dialectical thought). Moreover, it showed perhaps that an 'existential' politics is diametrically opposed to Nazism."

One would be justified in finding the allegation regarding Hegel debatable: not that Hegel must be "suspected" straightaway, but because Sartre hastily made two huge assumptions: the Marxist treatment of the "dialectic core" would save most of Hegelian thought by characterizing the speculative dimension as unimportant (and dangerous); dialectical thought would be politically acceptable. When one considers everything the expression "meaning of history" has justified, this last claim seems monstrous. But Sartre did not mind: he addressed a public that he knew supported "dialectical thought" and that, in the context of Liberation, had no doubt about the triumph of just causes.

The strangeness of the Sartrean intervention did not, however, stop there. By opening an inquiry, one already announces its result! Why would one undertake this inquiry under these conditions? The answer is already obvious: in order to comply with an external pressure, which was essentially communist. Furthermore, by not distinguishing Heidegger's case from his own, and by affirming the proximity between dialectical thought and existentialism ("antipodal to Nazism"), Sartre created an effective illusion. His debate with the communists would largely eclipse the more precise questions concerning Heidegger. Sartre's attitude can also be analyzed as defensive. It was because Sartre had to justify his own work that he was so peremptory. His conclusion confirmed his explanation of the mistake of 1933 in terms of Heidegger's weakness. "The reader will thus find in these texts the occasion to observe in Germany and in the work of a famous philosopher the ambiguities we have known in so many mediocre people."

It is equally significant that the two texts thus presented limited themselves to being anecdotal accounts of visits to the Master of Freiburg. Certainly, the first one, by Maurice de Gandillac,[96] revealed a strongly unfavorable and critical tone. The second visit, by Frédéric de Towarnicki,[97] proved favorable and even warm. But this opposition only gives the appearance of an actual debate. No precise fact was examined, and no clear argument was genuinely discussed. The two texts, as interesting as they were, remained personal testimonies that were rather anecdotal, and devoid of genuine conclusions (and did not bear exclusively on the political question).

I've already alluded to Towarnicki's account. We must now address, in his account, the properly political elements, and first and foremost the atmosphere that reigned at the time. "Concerning Heidegger's political past, there was little mention. Neither Sartre, nor Raymond Aron, nor Henry Corbin, his translator, dwelled on his stand in favor of National-Socialism in 1933. One might just as well say: I knew nothing." Towarnicki added, however, that "serious rumors were circulating about the philosopher."[98]

The paradox is that, because of these uncertainties, Towarnicki clearly questioned the Master concerning his relations with National Socialism and gave Heidegger the opportunity to justify himself vigorously with his wife's support. "In no way troubled, Heidegger replied that in 1933 he had welcomed a national reawakening by virtue of which he had hoped that the people of Germany would be freed from misery and chaos."[99] The rest of Heidegger's *pro domo* defense consisted of emphasizing his efforts at reforming the university and his resignation from the rectorate in February 1934 (he was silent on his public stand in favor of Hitler). Heidegger then rejected with indignation the "rumors" concerning his anti-Semitism or the actions that humiliated Husserl.[100] On this point, he was more precise and more convincing. "He had criticized in his courses—notably the ones on Nietzsche from 1936—the racial biologism of Rosenberg, as well as the pseudo-scientific mumbo-jumbo of pseudo-philosophers of the regime who had used Nietzsche (as well as Hölderlin) to feed the official doctrine and compensate for its vacuity."[101]

Without our knowing whether he literally quoted the Master, Towarnicki claimed that Heidegger pronounced the equivalent of a moral condemnation of the regime, which was so definitive that it left no room for additional commentary. "How could one not experience shame when thinking about what happened in Germany? Even if Germany had been victorious, it could not have survived such crimes. Heidegger stood up . . ."[102]

One might have expected that Maurice de Gandillac, clearly not well disposed to the Master, had put Heidegger in a difficult position by asking him more difficult questions. This was not the case. "We broached the political issue. He readily admitted that the process of changing the mind-set would be long and difficult, that Hitlerism, in a sense, was but the historical explosion of a structural illness of humanity as a whole. But he refused to incriminate specifically the 'German' man, or to confess to a sort of collective *Verfallen* of the German community. The only hope of the philosopher was to awaken in his disciples, gradually, the true meaning of their freedom. . . . He changed the topic. . . . Heidegger quite deliberately returned to trivial conversation matters. We will know nothing of his fundamental choices and of his true projects."[103]

It is interesting to analyze the quite limited subjective basis on which the difference between the two reports rests. While Towarnicki gave Heidegger the opportunity to offer a strong defense, highlighting his sincerity, de Gandillac limited himself to a more cautious position that, in the end, was similar to Sartre's psychological interpretation: "Whatever his genius, how could one not take into account the contrast between the very demands of his philosophy and the vaguely evasive attitude of this 'man in situation?'"[104]

However vague with respect to the facts themselves and their philosophical stakes, these two reports would have the positive effect of provoking other contributions. The debate would take on another dimension with the contributions of Karl Löwith, Éric Weil, and Alphonse de Waelhens. This would be one of the signs of a progressive change in the intellectual climate during the period just following the war. The euphoria and slogans, and the lack of rigor during the time of Liberation, gave way to a more critical era.

* * *

From 1946 to 1947, there would be greater scrutiny, concerning not only the question of his political engagement, but also the singularity of Heidegger's thought. Jean Beaufret's role was taking shape. Recognized as the privileged interlocutor, gradually he became a sort of personal representative of the Master in France. As such, he was Heidegger's first line of defense, especially in the leftist circles (and took this role into the columns in the *Revue socialiste*).[105]

Sartre's well-known 1946 lecture *L'Existentialisme est un humanisme*[106] marked the end of the immediate postwar era. In presenting the existential thesis in a simplified form for the public at large, Sartre occupied, more than ever, the center stage. But with respect to the content, he moved away from the high-level philosophical reflection that had allowed him to enter into dialogue with Heidegger. Sartre is cited henceforth only as the representative of "atheistic existentialism,"[107] a circumstantial expression that is based on no textual reference but that nonetheless would be repeated for years, a veritable platitude in presentations on existentialism.[108] Paradoxically, even with this intellectual distinction, which was barely perceived at the time, Sartre presented existentialism (in a critical confrontation with Marxism and Christian spiritualism)[109] as an ideological camp to which Heidegger's thought belonged. One does not find a word of reservation or criticism toward Heidegger in *L'Existentialisme est un humanisme*. However, the concerns with political and moral engagement got the upper hand from then on in Sartre's work over "phenomenological ontology," and Heidegger's very name would barely appear in his later writings.[110] The unintended consequence of this artificial ideological alignment was that it gave Heidegger the opportunity to distance himself from Sartre entirely and once and for all. By grasping the olive branch offered by a young unknown philosopher (Jean Beaufret) whom he had noticed, and by writing a reply to Sartre's lecture, he achieved a masterly coup that consisted of reclaiming the initiative on the philosophical scene by reasserting his originality. Was then the question of humanism only a pretext?

4 Humanism in Turmoil

The Letter to Jean Beaufret and the Debate on Humanism

It is unusual for an author to influence his or her own reception abroad. This is, however, what happened with Heidegger's long response to Jean Beaufret, a response that became famous under the title of *La lettre sur l'humanisme*.[1]

One is indebted to Jean Beaufret for having provided details on the circumstances at the origin of this text. It was November 1946. Jean Beaufret spontaneously drafted questions to the attention of the master, on the table of a café, intending to entrust a friend heading to Freiburg with them. He had already exchanged a letter once with Heidegger, which gave him hope for a reply, but he was still far from expecting him to take the trouble to reflect upon his questions thoroughly and to compose a powerful and well-wrought text that was destined to become famous. His wish was above all to give the dialogue he was weaving with the Master a philosophical content.

In his first question, Beaufret quoted a sentence by Paul Valéry about the "proponents of action," clearly with Sartre's theory of engagement in mind. This enables us to understand why the "Letter on Humanism" begins so abruptly: "We are still far from pondering the essence of action decisively enough."[2] The second question, which would give this text its title, appeared very early in the "Letter on Humanism": "How can we restore meaning to the word 'humanism'?"[3] While categorically objecting to the project denoted by this question (since it employs a word ending in *-ism*, a source of contention and of what he dramatically called a "misfortune"[4]), it is to this question that Heidegger responded at length, but not without resituating it in terms of his own perspective, that is, his understanding of the forgetting of being. It is only in the last few pages of his long response that Heidegger addressed the third, and quite benign, question: "How can we preserve the element of adventure that all research contains without simply turning philosophy into an adventuress?"[5]

Two clear facts (which Beaufret admitted quite freely in later conversations) emerge with respect to these questions: first, they were not carefully elaborated, as they were only meant to start the dialogue; second—and this is even more remarkable—these questions did not reveal any particular expertise in Heidegger's work. To this extent, they were less developed than the articles in *Confluences*.

What was Beaufret's thinking at that time? The fact that Heidegger began to be his main focus (as the Plato of our time) and that he criticized Sartre's "carelessness" or superficiality should not lead us to believe that Beaufret was already deeply Heideggerian at that time. As suggested by his questions, Sartrean existentialism was still for him the main reference, to the very extent that it directed philosophy toward the concrete by beginning from the facticity of situational freedom and by rethinking Husserl's intentionality in terms of openness onto things. This reconsideration of Sartre's project was nonetheless accompanied by an attempt to accommodate Marxism, a very significant approach in the intellectual and political atmosphere following Liberation. "Marxist clarifications"[6] do not have to be opposed to existentialism, but can participate in the same emancipatory project, as a philosophy of freedom returning human beings back to the truth and dignity of their condition. Ultimately, Beaufret's position proved "irenic," that is to say, entirely (and undoubtedly excessively) conciliatory between four doctrines: phenomenology, existentialism, and Marxism, but also Platonism (dear to the philosophy teacher)! This desire for conciliation was so strong that—during a lecture on "Marxism and Existentialism" given on April 8, 1946[7]—Jean Wahl confessed he was shocked, and was so bold as to reproach Beaufret for having given an academic synthesis worthy of Victor Cousin, and lectured him in this way: "The Cartesian *cogito* on which Beaufret insists has no place in Heidegger's philosophy."[8] This critical remark made by Wahl isn't unjustified; however, within a few years, as soon as Jean Beaufret seriously applied himself to Heidegger's philosophy, the situation would be reversed: it was Beaufret himself who would lecture Wahl on Heideggerian matters. This reversal of roles makes Wahl's account of May 1946 all the more interesting. Certainly, Beaufret did choose sides, but he was looking for an overly delicate balance—impossible to maintain for long—not only between existentialism and Marxism but also between phenomenology and Platonism.[9]

Heidegger's answer disrupted this very personal, Parisian, circumstantial, and dated circle of four, although crafted by a talented and overly "conciliatory" professor. Seen from Freiburg, these nuances seemed irrelevant. What mattered for Heidegger was the opportunity (which he seized in a remarkable manner) to reply to Sartre and to differentiate himself from him. More than Jean Beaufret's questions, it was the text itself (*L'Existentialisme est un humanisme*) that was at issue.

The differences with Sartre's position were clearly delineated. In this respect, one cannot ascribe to Heidegger any opportunism (as for the content). His only concession (an important one, since it will remain an exception) was to enter into an explicit and public philosophical dialogue with a contemporary philosopher.

What were those main differences? Let us briefly mention them in order to gain some perspective, and mostly to appraise the stakes of the debate on humanism, in terms of the conditions of the time.

The first difference concerns the priority of the human being and humanism, replaced by the listening to the truth of being. The second one undermines activism and the concern for a thematic ethics: Heidegger insisted on the fruitfulness of a meditative thought without which there can be no "dwelling." Finally, with respect to the status of Platonism and the question of metaphysics, Heidegger broke with what he believed constitutes the illusions of "eternal philosophy," stating instead that one has to understand philosophy on the basis of metaphysics as a destinal "sending," while preserving the possibility for a more original and authentic thought.

These themes, which have become familiar to us (even if they have not always been understood), seemed quite strange at the time. First and foremost, we have to take into account the fact that this response had been known, in France, only through a progressive wave of translations, in 1947, 1953, and 1956. If Heidegger was able to seize an opportunity, the effects of it appeared only later. Moreover, whereas Sartre addressed a wide audience and did not hesitate to proceed schematically, Heidegger, on the contrary, adopted the slow and meditative if not esoteric way of the untimely thinker (but in a style that is completely different from Nietzsche's: less exuberant, less daring, as well as more heavy and more patient at the same time).

Clearly, if Heidegger succeeded to some extent in his goal to reply to Sartre, it was by speculating on the long term and by calling for a listening entirely different from the Sartrean notion of engagement. The response is profound (if we take his reinterpretation of the history of philosophy seriously) and extremely skillful (since as it deemphasized direct action, it tended to make people forget that, not long before, Heidegger himself did not embody the detached character of a "shepherd of being").

This long reply to Jean Beaufret still needed to be understood. The addressee immediately set himself to this task, showing the way to all those who—along with great professors who had already become readers of Heidegger: Jean Wahl, Maurice Merleau-Ponty, Jean Hyppolite, and soon Henri Birault—understood the unique and difficult task demanded of them by Heidegger's thought.

With respect to the very question of humanism, there was truly an abyss, which was difficult to measure in the years 1946–47 and following, between Sartre's position—shared by many at that time, including Merleau-Ponty—and Heidegger's unusual way of questioning. Were they even speaking about the same "thing"? After the war and the Nazi horrors, under the sustained pressure of Stalinism and of the tension between the USSR and the free world, the debate on humanism reactivated the Kantian question of the priority of human dignity over any instrumentalization, but the existentialists agreed with the Marxists in their refusal of any formalism and in the recognition of power relations.

In this brutal debate, the very debate of *Dirty Hands*, the troublemaker Heidegger would introduce a prior question—that of metaphysics—and a suspicion: "You humanists, you have understood nothing of the true secret history! You blindly repeat the fundamental mistakes that have led the Western World to nihilism. Instead of being naïve humanists, we should eradicate metaphysical anthropocentrism."

At that time, and until the 1950s and even 1960s, neither Sartre nor his peers seriously paid attention to this response, which, incidentally, did not appear in the concise pedagogical form we just gave it and whose public effects were not only postponed but also to a large extent displaced (insofar as anti-humanism was transposed to a more or less epistemological status). What preoccupied them were infinitely more direct and stirring ethical and political questions: Did you accept the Nazi monstrosities without saying a word? What about the practical means sometimes used by the Resistance and the allies to fight them? Do you prefer to remain a beautiful soul? Do you agree with the Soviet regime or do you stand by the so-called capitalist reactionary camp?

To have an idea of the immense distance that still separated the Parisian intelligentsia from the genuinely Heideggerian themes, one only needs to refer to the book Merleau-Ponty published in 1947, titled *Humanism and Terror*.[10]

How is the "communism problem" presented? In terms of a very acute tension, if not contradiction, between the violence done by the state or the party on behalf of the dictatorship of the proletariat and the proclaimed goal: the restoration of man's essence and dignity: "But for man, the root is man himself," said Marx.[11] By borrowing this account of humanism for his own use, Merleau-Ponty was then—without realizing it—very far from Heidegger. He referred to him only once, and in a way that makes one shiver today: with practically nothing in common with the content of Heidegger's thought, this allusion imprudently refers to Moscow's Trials: "One is not an 'existentialist' for no reason at all, and there is as much 'existentialism'—in the sense of paradox, division, anxiety, and decision—in the *Report of the Court Proceedings* at Moscow as in the work of Heidegger."[12]

This is not Merleau-Ponty at his best; but however severely one might judge such an excerpt, one has to recognize that it reveals the attitude of a great number of European intellectuals of that time. Those "fellow travelers" of the Communist Party preferred criticizing the vices and abuses of "abstract democracy" rather than condemning too harshly the terror and repression practiced by the USSR and its allies. They (including Merleau-Ponty) were obsessed by the fear of going over to the "reactionary camp" of anticommunism. This was a very delicate balance to achieve, since their aim was to maintain a critical distance from the communists while keeping their long-term humanist goals and being aware of the unquestionable cynicism of their methods.[13]

The contrast between Merleau-Ponty's refined analysis and the violence he had to face is poignant. Is it the same situation with Heidegger's "Letter"? The following lines reveal a tenuous "bridge" between both thoughts at a determined historical moment. Merleau-Ponty writes, "This sort of conclusion is upsetting. To speak of humanism without being on the side of 'humanist socialism' in the Anglo-American way, to 'understand' the Communists without being a Communist, is to set oneself very high—in any case, way above the crowd. Actually it represents nothing more than a refusal to commit oneself to confusion removed from truth. Is it our fault that Western humanism is warped because it is also a war machine?"[14] Was this a confession or a premonition? Merleau-Ponty obviously came closest to Heidegger's mode of questioning in the last sentence, without being aware of it. He also wanted at the same time to occupy a "higher" ground than he ultimately managed, remaining too close to political events. Heidegger himself indirectly echoed these events when, for the first time in his work, he contemplated the possibility of "a productive dialogue with Marxism."[15] Though quite fragile, this possible connection between the two thinkers can be discerned except for the fact that Heidegger (whence the peculiar interest of his new attempt) broadened the horizon to include the entirety of Western history: "Homelessness is coming to be the destiny of the world."[16] One does not encounter such a thought in France at that time, neither any question on the meaning of technology (nor the stress put on the importance of language as a "house of being").

The debate between the Sartreans and Heidegger about humanism did not occur. Literally, and even essentially, the positions were diametrically opposed. On the one hand, Sartre and his followers were for humanism and engagement, while on the other hand, Heidegger stood against any engaged humanism. However, Heidegger wanted to preserve the specificity and dignity of the Existent beyond humanism and the metaphysics that constituted it. Was his critique of Western humanism not more pronounced than Merleau-Ponty's transformation of it into a "war machine"?

This question was not timely after Liberation (no more than a thinking of the sacred that would not simply be "atheistic"). The debate on humanism then gave way to immense misunderstandings, principally in politics. It is thus to this terrain that one must return if we are not to miss the actual course of the history of ideas.

The Political Debate Resurges

The discussion concerning Heidegger's political engagement, launched by Sartre under the pressure of the communist attacks, did not end with the publication, in January 1946, of the two accounts of his visits to the Master, which, as we have seen—despite their intrinsic interest—were exceedingly subjective, anecdotal, and overly partial or imprecise concerning the facts as well as the meaning to be given to them. With the publication in *Les Temps modernes,* in November of the same year, of a rich text by Karl Löwith,[17] the scope of the debate widened and its philosophical level improved. This was the case for two reasons: Löwith, who was a powerful personality, was a close friend of Heidegger's,[18] and his testimony was firsthand; moreover, he set forth a thesis that was meant to reach the core of the question while confronting the Sartrean interpretation: there is indeed a real and even profound connection between Heidegger's thought and his political failure.

This connection is striking, according to Löwith, when one compares the end of *Being and Time* (in particular section 74 on "The basic constitution of historicality") and the political discourses of 1933: there is a consonance between them that is due to the fact that the former presents a "theory of historical existence" and of "resolute decision" in the face of "current events" while the latter accomplishes the application of this philosophy according to the historicist perspective of existentialism. According to Löwith, against academic and cultural intellectualism, Heidegger developed the pathos of a heroic radicalism that had religious connotations (partly inspired by Pascal and Dostoyevsky), but that opened onto a real nihilism: "The inner nihilism, the 'national-socialism,' of this pure Resolve in the face of nothingness, remained at first hidden beneath certain traits that suggested a religious devotion."[19] The point was absolutely not to claim that the end of *Being and Time* was automatically leading to Nazism; Löwith remarked, in fact, that "Heidegger's disciples were surprised by his decision," for "he had almost never expressed his opinion about political matters."[20] For Löwith, the correspondence between Heidegger's philosophy and the national-socialist political adventure is at once deeper and more concealed: on the one hand, it is the significant (and possibly, alas, inspired) symptom of an evil that eats away at the German spirit, reflecting the crisis of that time (the *"disastrous intellectual mind-set"*);[21] on the other hand, the fact that Heidegger's involvement is not a common one and, in this sense, is more radical than any "ordinary Nazism." Löwith praised, incidentally, the philosophical quality of the "Rectoral Address," while noting its extreme ambiguity.[22] One of Heidegger's students had put this ambiguity in a nutshell, saying: "I am resolved, only toward what I don't know" (people were in doubt as to whether one should start reading the pre-Socratics or enlist in the SA![23]).

Hence this severe statement, which represents the core of the interpretation: "Given the significant attachment of the philosopher to the climate and intellectual habitus of National Socialism, it would be inappropriate to criticize or exonerate his political decision in isolation from the *very principles* of Heidegger's philosophy itself."[24] Yet, where one could expect the verdict to be a complete condemnation and the rejection without appeal of this work, Löwith's position, while implying a vivid critique of the historicism and nihilism imputed to Heidegger, was in the end more complex: Heidegger enjoyed a considerable and important reputation; his talent and the intensity of his inspiration nevertheless obviously produced a certain fascination. This oscillation between condemnation and admiration was in fact openly confessed by the author at the beginning of his study: "The reader of the essay at hand will find, at his own choosing, a significant defense of Heidegger's philosophy or a condemnation of his political attitudes."[25]

"M. Löwith is somewhat in the same situation as Balaam, a Moabite prophet . . . gone to curse Israël but whose lips only uttered blessings." Éric Weil's sarcastic judgment captures perfectly the impression of perplexity one feels when reading Karl Löwith's fascinating yet equivocal testimony. For its part, Éric Weil's brilliant formulation gives a foretaste of the style—remarkably intense and sharp—of the article that appeared in July 1947 in *Les Temps modernes*,[26] along with a polemical response by Alphonse de Waelhens to Löwith's text.

Let us note in passing the clearly stated intention of the editorial board of the journal to have a balanced debate and not to take sides at the outset. Granting Heidegger the benefit of the doubt, Sartre and his team remained faithful to their preliminary position. In the meantime, the careful reader will have learned much.

We will focus more here on Éric Weil's contribution than on Alphonse de Waelhens's interventions. Not that these were unimportant. We will cover their gist. But although Weil was more coherent and original, this does not mean that his position was unassailable.

Weil did not dwell on facts for very long; he assumed they were known. One cannot fault him entirely, although one does not read this statement without smiling, in a sense still valid fifty years later: "Heidegger's file keeps growing even though it seems the essential pieces are missing."[27] Of course many things have been discovered since, but what is essential remains in the two facts on which Weil insisted: the allegiance to the Nazi party, and a low-profile defense.

One gathers that Weil judged Heidegger's engagement of 1933 harshly, but he emphasized, with Löwith, the fact that it was made even worse by his public declarations (the call to faithfulness to the Führer, the homage to Schlageter, the approval of the break with the League of Nations) that were condemned in the following terms: "This is Nazi language, Nazi ethics, Nazi's thought (*sit venia verbo*), Nazi feeling. This is not Nazi philosophy and that is why M. Heidegger believed his arguments would prevail."[28]

It is necessary, then, to introduce distinctions according to which Heidegger's "defense" (as summarized by Towarnicki) implies necessarily a philosophical reflection on the connection between existentialist thought and political commitment. Recognizing that Heidegger was not an "orthodox Nazi," since he rejected biological materialism, Weil still did not consider that this should lead one to minimize the philosopher's responsibility, especially since Heidegger tried to benefit from this by attempting to merge his personal case with the ranks of the German people. For Weil, this trivialization is unacceptable because by becoming "representative . . . of a large part of the German people," Heidegger avoided his own responsibility, which is that of the philosopher as such: "What is unsettling in this story is not so much what M. Heidegger did first and did not do afterwards, but his very defense."[29]

This defense would be much better, and even "excellent," if Heidegger, "the philosopher of decision," assumed this decision "with full liability" and explained why he has since "understood" the immensity of his error.[30] But what Weil found intolerable is what we just called the "low-profile" defense that asks for forgetfulness, avoiding the very philosophical task that consists in posing clearly the problem of responsibility in regard to action.

Going to the core of the philosophical problem, Weil considered that Heideggerian existentialism was not capable of giving a political response. This is a most serious charge but with the unexpected implication that this philosophy can be distinguished from Nazism. Existentialism, by itself, has nothing to do with Nazism. It can lead to engagements of a completely different nature, and even politically opposite. In his positions in 1933, Heidegger "falsified" his philosophy; "he twisted it in order to extract a political response that it could not possibly give."[31]

For Weil, existentialist philosophy is a transcendental philosophy, which, in Hegelian terms, remains at the level of reflection. It cannot be articulated with a satisfactory conception of concrete totality. In proposing this explanation, Weil succeeded in exonerating existentialism as such, while noting however its weakness, and making Heidegger personally responsible for the distortion and denial of his properly philosophical role. "These considerations are not made to support Heidegger's defense; they exonerate Heideggerian existentialism. Perhaps his philosophy is insufficient but it should not be taken to be false simply because Heidegger was a member of the Nazi party."[32]

One understands how Sartre could have agreed to publish this strong article without completely abandoning his own convictions. It is also possible that he might have found grounds therein for his reflections on engagement and its application to an actual historical context. Nevertheless, Weil's article represented an important step in the critical reflection on "Heidegger's case." Though he excessively reduced the philosophy of *Sein und Zeit* to existentialism in general (a concession to the mood of the time), he was quite aware in his approach of the complexity of the connection between Heidegger's doctrine and the error of 1933: the philosopher did not feel constrained by his error, and further, the way he defended himself, far from diminishing his personal responsibility, only increased it.

This article received no response. Was it refutable? Certainly not, but it undertook an impressive effort of clarification, which was not really the virtue of

Löwith's account. If Alphonse de Waelhens directed his counterattacks exclusively against the latter, it was first for a factual reason: his text[33] appeared in the same issue as Weil's and as a response to Löwith's essay that had been published eight months earlier. De Waelhens may not have heard about Weil's article when he was writing his own text. Furthermore, it is clear that Löwith exposed himself more easily to criticism and, correlatively, facilitated a certain defense of Heidegger's position, at least from an exclusively philosophical perspective.

In fact, de Waelhens was careful not use Towarnicki's somewhat hagiographic tone. First, he differentiated between the genuinely philosophical question and the personal aspects of the Heidegger case. He did not want to advocate for the man, and he seemed to rightly reproach Löwith for citing overly subjective testimonies and even excerpts from private correspondence. Even at the theoretical level, he did not want to shield Heidegger's thought from criticism but wanted to address the only issue that mattered to him: was there a substantial link between Heidegger's thinking and Nazism? The answer was clearly negative, although it was not reached without difficulties. On the basis of the perhaps overly general premise that one cannot expect a political thought to be derived "exclusively" from a "metaphysical" work,[34] de Waelhens admitted that "the existential analytic, in its essential parts, is conceived in a purely static manner and [that] one doesn't find any effort there to describe the dialectical future of authentic or everyday existence."[35]

The acknowledgement of the relatively undetermined nature of the existential analytic seemed to be shared by de Waelhens, Löwith, and even Weil. The question is how de Waelhens managed to "make his case." He did so precisely by relying on the indetermination that has just been granted: it enabled neither the demonstration of the absence of any intrinsic link between existentialism and Nazism nor the opposite demonstration by Löwith. There is consequently a clear and even considerable distance between Heidegger's philosophy and Nazi politics. Heideggerian historicity is oriented toward the liberation of freedom of the other, whereas fascism undertakes a conditioning of masses (condemned by Heidegger through his phenomenological critique of the "They"). Furthermore, for de Waelhens the cynical pessimism of the Nazis had nothing in common with the radically ontological anxiety of existential thought. Thus, by deciding not to support Heidegger the man, and addressing only the distinction between existential philosophy and Nazi politics, de Waelhens adopted a fall-back position that clearly appealed to the editorial staff of *Les Temps modernes,* with whom he declared himself in agreement:[36] existential philosophy was thus exonerated.

Despite its relative moderation, this clarification provoked a strong response from Karl Löwith,[37] which one can easily understand since he found himself in the position of having to justify himself. His response was useful, to the extent that it enabled him to clarify his point of view, which had been ambiguous: he had not claimed that there was a *necessary* connection between existential philosophy and Nazism; he only postulated that the *possibility* of this essential connection came from its "*intrinsic* deficiency"; he perceived a homology between the key concepts of *Sein und Zeit* (*Dasein,* "existence," "historicity," etc.) and the political discourses given by Heidegger in 1933; these discourses represented one possible "practical application" of Heidegger's philosophy, but not the only one. To conclude, Heidegger, just as Ernst Jünger, was not an ordinary Nazi. His philosophical stature cannot be denied. It is out of the question to reduce it to racist biologism (with which he never sympathized). Yet, his undeniable association to National Socialism is to be understood in relation to the dynamics of this movement: "The so-called Nazism was a revolutionary movement, exceeding the cultural and racial politics of the party."[38]

I will only mention from memory the brief "Response to this response." De Waelhens maintained his position: ignoring Heidegger's personality, he focused his attention on maintaining the gap between his philosophy and fascism: "Löwith does not take into account the definition of Fascism"; he is wrong to associate it with "the actions of the former rector."[39]

What should one retain from this heated exchange? The problem for us is less to take a position on that conflict than to resituate it in its proper context and to evaluate its importance. One should note that de Waelhens had the last word, without Sartre or his editorial staff drawing any conclusion or trying to settle the matter. From the beginning to the end of that debate, a perspective was chosen and maintained: a distinction was made between existential philosophy and Nazism. While insisting on Heidegger's personal responsibilities, Weil did not really oppose this distinction: existentialism, although inadequate, was not directly suspect. Löwith alone, particularly in his response to de Waelhens, threatened this schema, for he attained a more sophisticated level of reflection concerning the connection between Heidegger's thought and a certain National Socialism: at that level, it was not the "definition" of Nazism that mattered (as de Waelhens claimed), but a certain dynamic that momentarily caused Heidegger's thought to merge with the political ideal he had constructed. However, in the face of this complexity (and in particular, the ambivalence of the "Rectoral Address"), Löwith acknowledged the correctness of Weil's objection and accepted responsibility for the ambiguity of his own position: "I in fact hold Heidegger to be the 'good' (if not the best) philosopher of a bad historical 'moment.'"[40]

This attitude was too subtle to attract the attention of a still poorly informed intellectual audience, which was in any case more interested in more definite positions. In fact, although the debate on Heidegger's political involvement would greatly intensify in the years to come, it is not certain that it got any farther than Weil, de Waelhens, and Löwith already did in 1946–48. It would have been better to resume the discussion where they had left off rather than thinking that the discovery of isolated facts would be sufficient to really improve the philosophical understanding of the Heideggerian imbroglio. But the history of philosophical thoughts, as is the case for events, is enveloped in oblivion. Our anamnesis dares to struggle against the powerful and tumultuous current of the river *Lethe* . . .

Jean Beaufret Comes to the Fore

One too often forgets that Jean Beaufret would not have achieved his fame if he had only been the passive recipient of the "Letter on Humanism." On the one hand—as we saw—he received the letter because Heidegger had already read and appreciated the quality of two of his articles. On the other hand, since Liberation he had occupied a distinctive role on the Parisian scene, which was certainly quite different and infinitely more discreet than that of Sartre, but nonetheless strategic in intellectual life, including his presence at the École Normale Supérieure of rue d'Ulm (where he taught from 1946 to 1962), his *khâgne* class at Lycée Henry IV, Condorcet, and the friendship or companionship of influential intellectuals such as Jacques Lacan, Maurice Merleau-Ponty, Jean Hyppolite, Maurice de Gandillac, Ferdinand Alquié, Louis Althusser, Roger Stéphane, Jean-Paul Aron, Gilles Deleuze, Roger Kempf, Michel Foucault—among others.[41] Haunting these places or institutions, associating with these characters: this would not have been enough by itself to ensure such a prominence unless he also had some talent. This is too often forgotten; it was as if he had been nothing else but Heidegger's assistant. Far from it! Charming and witty in conversation, unpredictable and fascinating in his teaching, informed and scholarly, quick-witted and original in his articles and public interventions, Beaufret was not just anyone. Quite simply, he was someone. You would not forget him if you met him, even if only once. Not that he imposed himself forcefully, like a lawyer or a politician: he had a gentle and sweet style, relying on patient influence. Fundamentally *kind,* he enjoyed lingering with his interlocutor or his listener, no doubt to charm them, but above all to establish a special relationship with them as one does in a village or in a family (this only made the falling-outs with certain people more painful). Of course, for bourgeois convention, he was an "eccentric." He could not have cared less about these kinds of judgments, as he chose to ignore convention. This carefree attitude explained both his friendship with Heidegger, which transcended the age difference and the academic status (for thirty years, he regularly went to Freiburg for short stays, two or three times a year) and his influence on the Parisian intellectual world, an influence that was disproportionate to his relatively modest status as *professeur de khâgne.*

Thus Heidegger did not have an ordinary "ambassador" in Paris. However, it is precisely because he did not have the solemn title or rank of an "official" representative that he was able to play a more discreet, more unusual, and probably more efficient role, at least at the beginning.

Let us return to the chronology. From 1946 (the beginning of their personal relationship[42]) to 1976 (Heidegger's death), the Master and Jean Beaufret enjoyed a philosophical friendship without interruptions or difficulties; yet the effects of Beaufret's "discipleship" were not always as continuous or as efficient as in the beginning.

Let us remain, for the moment, at the end of the forties. Beaufret was not yet "the best interpreter of Heidegger's thought."[43] He patiently placed himself under Heidegger's "schooling" as he would enjoy saying later. He felt he had to learn everything again: "It was a completely new language for me."[44] Yet, he asserted himself, as early as 1947, thanks to the publication of a brilliant text (published in the journal *Fontaine* at the same time as an excerpt from the "Letter on Humanism"[45]): "Martin Heidegger et le problème de la vérité,"[46] a title that echoed the text "On the Essence of Truth," which Heidegger gave Beaufret as a present some time earlier.[47]

This text deserves a close analysis of its main features. The polemical tone strikes one already in the first lines: Heidegger was misunderstood, as Kant was in his time; such is the fate of any great philosophy. This theme was repeated several times, as if one had to fight on all fronts at the same time: "To classify a philosopher who was constantly and genuinely concerned with the problem of truth as an apostle of the pathetic, a proponent of nihilism, or as an opponent to logic and science, is one of the strangest travesties for which the superficiality of the time was to blame."[48]

This lecture given to his contemporaries would be repeated in the future, but it was new for Beaufret in 1947. Two years earlier, Heidegger was praised, *primus inter pares;* henceforth, he was alone, unique and misunderstood. The "Letter on Humanism" produced a dazzling impression. Heidegger distinguished himself from Sartre and existentialism, from Marxism, from Jaspers, and so on. Beaufret's harsh tone can certainly be justified by a change in the climate, indicated by the political polemics. The personal attacks, which were the price of fame, did not come only from the Marxists. We are soon going to see convergent signs of it.

Far from being an academic text on the problem of truth, it was rather a quite peremptory first presentation—to an audience that was probably quite perplexed—of the singular greatness of Heidegger's thought, characterized as a thought that was in direct dialogue with the great tradition (Plato, Aristotle, Descartes) and that posed, on a completely novel basis, the question of being. Being is no longer conceived of as a Supreme Being or God, but as "nothing that is" [*rien d'étant*],[49] a first inapparent disclosure that any adequation presupposes: "Thus unconcealment means being revealing itself in its original dignity as the Un-concealed."[50] It is this alliance between being and meaning that Heideggerian ontology reinterprets on the basis of the understanding of *Dasein*. There is nothing subjective in the lightning event, here and now, of "the miracle of being,"[51] and neither is there anything idealistic or realistic. Neither Sartre nor Merleau-Ponty situated themselves at the prior level discovered by Heidegger, that of the truth of being. Beneath the *cogito,* one must rediscover the richness of the "there is." Heidegger did not ignore the *cogito,* as Sartre claimed, but rediscovered its condition. Similarly, the primacy of "ek-sistence" cannot be reduced to a sort of creative dynamism, but signifies that being never ceases to come to the encounter of human beings.[52] And it is by experiencing and assuming a resolute anxiety—not pathological but with a Mallarmean intensity—that human beings can assume their freedom and most profound destiny, especially if they know how to listen to "Hölderlin's prayer."[53]

To summarize those pages is a real challenge, due to the early appearance of Beaufret's dense and inimitable style, which would be fully evident ten years later in *Le poème de Parménide.*[54] It was an incredible blend of lyricism and brilliant references to the history of philosophy, a sort of prolonged juxtaposition of polemics and doctoral lessons, between an almost religious enthusiasm and the cold shower of a warning: "You have not understood anything. Get to work!" One can imagine the impression such a text made on the *khâgne* students and on some intellectuals dazzled by the style and the Greek, Germanic, and poetic references. It also constituted Jean Beaufret's unique position, as one who was henceforth authorized to decipher Heidegger's enigmas[55] and definitively breaking not only with Sartre and with Marxism, but above all with their political and contemporary social themes. Breaking as well with the majority of the audience that rushed barely a year earlier to his lecture on "Marxisme et existentialisme," Beaufret even chose (even if the results of this choice were not immediately felt) to concentrate on his teaching and on the circle of his acquaintances, disciples, and friends.

*   *   *

What was the status of humanism in this context? It is remarkably absent from this text. One may object that this is the theme that Heidegger addressed from beginning to end in his "Letter," which was published simultaneously in issue 63 of the journal *Fontaine.* It is nonetheless obvious that the question was asked in terms that were decidedly irrelevant to current events. From the perspective of a meditation on the fate of the Western world, Heidegger's text was infinitely richer than the great majority of partisan positions of the time. We also have to recognize that the Master of Freiburg needed a certain boldness (or recklessness?) to shift the terms of the debate to a purely ontological—and thus dehumanized—ground, only two years after the discovery of the Nazi crimes and the other horrors of the Second World War. One easily conceives that he may have wanted to remain above the political or national divisions, and for good reason! However, now that fifty years have elapsed, should we not recognize the troubling nature of his obstinate refusal to utter even one word, or acknowledge the suffering and distress of human beings, whoever they were?

The debate, obviously, was only suspended for a time. It will come back later, with the return of the political polemics. As for the structuralist displacement of the Heideggerian antihumanism, it was still completely unforeseen in the years following Liberation and even at the beginning of the next decade. Althusser admitted having read the "Letter on Humanism" only quite late, and he clarified that it "influenced" his thesis concerning the "*theoretical* antihumanism in Marx."[56] This clarification is not surprising, but is refreshingly frank. The "Letter" is indeed the text by Heidegger that had the greatest influence in France, above all in the 1960s.[57]

We saw how Heidegger radically differentiated himself from Sartre. Logically, Sartre should also have differentiated himself from Heidegger. We now have the proof that Sartre read *On the Essence of Truth* a few months after the publication of its translation in 1948: he made numerous allusions to it in the fragments assembled and published after his death, in a volume entitled *Truth and Existence*.[58] What he drew from Heidegger's text is the idea that "the ground of Truth is freedom." He immediately added: "Thus man can choose non-truth."[59] This interprets the relation between truth and nontruth—which Heidegger had situated within being itself—in a radically humanistic sense. Similarly, Sartre appreciated that this Heideggerian being historicizes itself, but not that it should do so by virtue of a "letting-be," delivering the human to pure passivity. His most radical opposition bore on the "mystical position" that he attributed to Heidegger: he refused "to define man by mystery."[60] Even if this word badly translates the Heideggerian *Geheimnis* and reduces it excessively to the Christian tradition, there is no doubt that the incompatibility of Sartre's conception of the human being with Heidegger's will only become more radical. Sartre refused to conceive of being except as an *in-itself* against which (and not from which) the *for-itself* (the human being) must assume its absurd condition. The debate on humanism cannot be separated from that which concerns ontology. Examining the Heideggerian approach to the truth of being, Sartre found nothing of interest: "Being is a congealed hyperabundance that does not fill up."[61]

A few years later, in December 1952,[62] Sartre visited Heidegger[63] for a lecture at which he was "coolly received by the students." He only remained with the Master for a short while and confided his disappointment to Simone de Beauvoir: "He was dabbling in mysticism, Sartre told me."[64] This is of course a rather superficial way of measuring a gap that would only widen between the two philosophers and that remains incontestable. They did not relate well during their meeting: Sartre found that his interlocutor had "the air of a retired colonel."[65] Henceforth, each would follow his own way, ignoring the other; and Sartre had no interest in being present at Cerisy when Heidegger came to France for the first time in the mid-50s, when the fate of his French reception seemed uncertain.

5   The Bright Spell of the '50s

IN WHAT SENSE did the 1950s reveal a generally favorable, although unavoidably ambiguous, reception of Heidegger's thought in France? Although one will discover it gradually in this chapter, one already detects that the principal criterion of this ambiguity could not reside exclusively in the division between the partisans and the opponents of that thought: that would be to confuse the scope of a philosophy with the kind of influence associated with an ideology or a political party. Of course, I will have to make room for the reservations or attacks. But one has to take other disagreements into account, and know also that one needs to differentiate between the orientations that motivated the different positions and the ambiguities they may have harbored. The existential theme would be accompanied or supplanted by other perspectives: the approach to the Sacred, the interpretation of metaphysics, and even (to a lesser extent) the question of planetary technology. This was a complex reception for a rich thought: increasingly, Heidegger's thought invited numerous approaches. As one moved further away from Liberation and the existentialist fad, the question of the uniqueness of that thought appeared more clearly, which was a favorable factor for Jean Beaufret's work. It is in this sense that one can speak of a certain "bright spell" (especially since the 1950s, which were devoted to economic reconstruction and the constitution of a new Europe resisting the Soviet threat, turned its back on the old demons of fascism and freed itself from the obsession with political purges). Undoubtedly the French university was still largely opposed to the dissemination of Heidegger's thought, but new translations gradually revealed a "Heidegger II," even though the masterpiece of 1927 was not yet translated. This was quite a paradoxical situation! A gap appeared between the interpreters who remained concerned with *Being and Time*[1] and a new generation mainly interested in the critique of the metaphysical tradition. Jean Beaufret refused to take sides: he placed his influence in Paris at the service of Heidegger's name and work, whose prestige grew (in a nonlinear expansion, provoking different kinds of resistance) before new divisions appeared in 1961–62. In the same way, indeed, as one could accept that the nineteenth century only ended in 1914, I will here argue—on a clearly more modest chronological scale—that the death of Merleau-Ponty, Jean-Pierre Faye's revival of the political polemics, and the publication of *Totality and Infinity* made 1961 a caesura that concluded the period that we are now going to examine.

We may not have given enough attention, however, to the rejections or hostile reactions that accompanied the first waves of Heidegger's reception in France. The reason is simple: even if pioneers like Georges Gurvitch or Rachel Bespaloff expressed reservations, curiosity or admiration was nonetheless predominant, which was also the case for the educated public. Only among the Marxists did one find an open hostility, and even then only after the USSR entered the war. In fact, it was at the time of Liberation that the fad of existentialism, almost automatically—through its very intensity—provoked reactions and rejections. Their immediate or raucous expressions in the press were not necessarily the most interesting or meaningful for the future.

It would be false to give the impression that these reservations or oppositions came only from the extreme left (even if it did maintain a "hard line" toward Heidegger).[2] Thus, for example, Éric Weil, author as we recall of a remarkable article in *Les Temps Modernes* on "Le cas Heidegger," published his thesis in 1951, called "Logique de la philosophie,"[3] the style and contents of which made no concession to existentialism, in general, or to Heidegger in particular. He recognized the importance and "complexity" of Heidegger's philosophy in passing,[4] but only to situate them within the limits of the category of the finite and more precisely of a philosophy of transcendental reflection on the "conditions of possibility of existence."[5] Weil referred to Heidegger's analyses of temporality, but not without emphasizing their "disputable" nature,[6] due to the fact that their horizon was limited to individual consciousness. It would be difficult to find a stronger resistance, which is expressed so clearly and firmly, in the space of a few lines, to Heideggerian themes and to their dissemination into France.

But the hostility toward Heidegger's thought has worn many different masks, including that of satire.

A Polemical Interlude

At the beginning of the fifties, Sartre paid attention only to his debate with the communists. Heidegger, on the contrary, knew enough not to expect anything from them. This is why, it seems, he was shaken by an unexpected attack (perhaps by its form more than by its content), from none other than Gabriel Marcel. During Sartre's short visit, Heidegger would speak of nothing else than Marcel's play.[7] Indeed, it was in a play, *La Dimension Florestan,* that the Master found himself ridiculed, in a very unusual attack for a German academic who was not used to seeing his own character portrayed on stage!

In fact, it is quite unlikely that Heidegger could have heard the French radio program and have been acquainted with the play whose text was published only five years later. It is more likely that he was alerted by Jean Beaufret and all the more shocked since—unable to identify the words of the polemics—he was suffering an "assault" that was as strange as unexpected. The incident, which was quickly forgotten, seems really unimportant today. It is, however, interesting to refer to the text of *La Dimension Florestan* to reveal the "grievances" that fueled Gabriel Marcel's caustic irony.

This comedy in three acts is located in a little town in South Germany, and the hero is Professor Hans Walter Dolch, "the most notable champion of contemporary atheism,"[8] who is protected by a vigilant housekeeper, Fräulein Schmuck and surrounded by a little court: a countess, a certain Frau Melitta, and a priest, Father Plantille. This is how the latter defines the main work of the Master: "The profound work titled *Die Wacht am Sein* is only a set of precautions meant to protect the integrity of being from those who, in one way or another, infringe upon its sacred essence."[9] The purpose of the—more or less successful—*lazzi* of the play was thus first and foremost the sacralization of a de-theologized being by a Master who complacently maintained an esoteric "guard" [*Wacht*], around both being and his own person. The satire was reinforced by a more direct attack against the Heideggerian abuse of tautology. Let us examine this exchange:

> THE COUNTESS: you said, the pear *pears,* and you added, with an even more imperious authority, that the apple *apples.*
>
> FRAU MELITTA (SARDONICALLY): Somebody might be tempted to ask whether the peach is the act of peaching.[10]

What stinging sarcasm! Was this some kind of joke or some clever story? If it was a joke, it was too intellectual; in the other case, it was hardly funny; it just brought a smile to a small circle of friends in the know (the satire is a victim of the esotericism it denounces). One easily guesses why the play was never performed: there would have been no audience. It is highly unlikely that the listeners of the national channel would have been able to identify the subtle allusions to texts that were not yet translated. Presumably they were able to at least appreciate the facile anti-German nuances. Who at that time could understand the satire of Heidegger's use of tautology? The allusion to the text called "The Thing," which would be transparent today, would only have been missed by almost everyone: not yet translated, the lecture "Das Ding" appeared in Germany only in 1954.[11] It was based on a lecture, first held in Bremen, then in Bühlerhöhe, and then again on June 6, 1950, at the Bavarian Academy of Fine Arts. Gabriel Marcel, whose German was excellent, was able to read it in the yearbook of that academy.[12]

The underlying philosophical stakes obviously escaped the readers. Nonetheless, this matter shed light on a strong Catholic opposition to atheist existentialism, as well as on reservations (undoubtedly more common) toward Heidegger's hermeticism.[13] Marcel also unwittingly revealed, through his violent reaction, a personal aversion (should we go as far as to say jealousy?) to both the style and the problematic of the later Heidegger. However, he insisted on qualifying his opposition.[14] Similarly, the attitude of most of the Christian intellectuals had nothing in common with the monolithic approach of the communists. Heidegger found both support and opposition among the Christian intellectuals.

The Christian Intellectuals: Between Reservation and Attraction

Christian intellectuals had no reason, in theory, to welcome a thought that was most often presented as an atheistic existentialism, destroying the metaphysical tradition and offering only resolute decision to assume finite freedom as a remedy to anxiety. Consequently, it is not surprising that a massive line of resistance would have formed on the basis of neo-Thomism. The very title of Étienne Gilson's work *L'être et l'essence,* published in 1948, is significant. We can see it as an indirect, but quite firm, critique of *Being and Nothingness.* The main theme of the book is indeed the demonstration of the noxious character of the modern dissociation of essence and existence: the reaction against absolute idealism produced existentialism, and the intellectualistic excess provoked, almost mechanically, a backlash.[15] It was necessary to go back to the Supreme Existence that gives sense to the essential determinations of life: "Existence is not the disease of essence; on the contrary it is its very life."[16] However, this refutation was directed mostly at existentialism and not at Heidegger in particular: he is barely named in the first edition of *L'être et l'essence.*[17] Gilson would clarify later: "In fact, Martin Heidegger's philosophy did not play any role in this story and I have only included it arbitrarily to respond to contemporary interests."[18]

It is indeed, in a second appendix, published in 1962 but certainly conceived earlier,[19] that Gilson felt it was necessary to answer "a few questions" concerning existentialism. He made an important terminological concession in this response. If he could rewrite the book, the author would translate *ens* by "étant." This did not change anything essential, but it revealed the entry into the French philosophical vocabulary, in the 1950s, of a word whose introduction was clearly attributable to Heidegger's translators and principally to Jean Beaufret (who identified this terminological development from 1946 on).[20]

Gilson confessed that he was unfamiliar with Heidegger's thought, and his 1962 clarifications only confirmed this admission. Even if he confessed his hesitations and proceeded with "extreme caution,"[21] Gilson distanced himself from a thought that puzzled him while he recognized its qualities and dignity. Although he continued to speak of existentialism with respect to Heidegger, without quite freeing himself from the "misunderstandings of that time,"[22] he managed to dissociate Heidegger's case from Sartre's. Whereas he was quite severe when judging Sartre's inconsistencies and "subjectivism," he was much more circumspect with respect to Heidegger. Furthermore, his references proved that he had carefully read "What Is Metaphysics?" but also the postscript whose translation appeared in 1959 in the *Revue des sciences philosophiques et théologiques* (published by the Dominicans of the Saulchoir),[23] as well as the seminar on "The Onto-Theological Constitution of Metaphysics."[24]

Gilson clearly discerned several features that distinguish Heidegger's thought: the rootedness of his thought in the German language,[25] the openness and motility of his questioning (it "may not have reached its limits"),[26] the new and disconcerting (for a classical mind) problematic of the overcoming of metaphysics.[27] Far from engaging in polemics, Gilson limited himself to preparing the ground and marking these distinctions with an unquestionable intellectual honesty. While accepting the definition of metaphysics as onto-theology,[28] he acknowledged not understanding the goal of overcoming it, since he conceived of it only as unsurpassable. There was a radical disagreement (or misunderstanding) on the notion of "overcoming." Gilson did not seem to discern the most singular specificity of the Heideggerian undertaking, for he reduced the historicity of metaphysics to a "given empirical fact."[29] However, what he did perceive remarkably was a twofold incompatibility between Thomism and Heidegger: on the one hand, in the former, there is no equivalent to an analytic of *Dasein*,[30] and on the other hand, the latter thinks the ontological difference through a radical distancing from all beings, whereas Saint Thomas returned to the pure act of being starting from beings in order to ground them.[31]

Consequently, Gilson recognized Heidegger as a "genuine philosopher"[32] (this is not insignificant coming from someone who had such high expectations); however, at the same time he did not agree with the German Master's critique of metaphysics as overly dependent on representation. Heidegger should nonetheless know that he has "unknown friends"[33] on the path of a negative ontology!

This mixture of enthusiasm and hesitation was already shared by the anonymous author of the presentation of the postscript to "What Is Metaphysics?" in 1959, in a journal edited by the Saulchoir Dominicans. The publication of this text, presented as a document, certainly qualified as a "milestone in the history of the growing influence of Heidegger's work in France within the neo-Thomist circles."[34] This hesitation was due to being cautious: "In our presentation of this document, it is out of the question to take sides for or against Heidegger's thought."[35] This caution excluded the all too quick parallels with Christian thought, whether Thomist or Pascalian;[36] yet, it became interesting to the extent that the suspicions of atheism or nihilism had to be set aside. Avoiding the "hasty baptisms,"[37] the author of the presentation noted both that the ontological difference had been accounted for—according to Thomist doctrine—in the analogy of being and that despite this important divergence, the thinking of being could never leave a Thomist indifferent. The reason for this was mentioned discreetly: redoubtable common enemies—rationalism, positivism, analytic philosophy—surrounded the horizon.[38]

Other signs testified to an attentive listening to Heideggerian themes in Christian circles. In March 1955, *Recherches et débats,* the journal of the Centre catholique des intellectuels Français (Catholic Center of French Intellectuals), welcomed Henri Birault, who gave a substantial, detailed, and documented presentation on "La foi et la pensée d'après Heidegger"[39] (Faith and thought in Heidegger's work): this impartial account, which was very attentive to all the published texts and even to the lecture "Theologie und Philosophie," which was unpublished at the time,[40] focused on showing that far from any militant atheism, Heidegger clearly delineated the respective domains of philosophy, guardian of the question of being, and of theology, science of the revealed Word.[41] Birault went further (and one then could realize how much he was attuned to the thought he was presenting): it became increasingly clear that Heidegger endeavored to overcome, along with metaphysics, the theology that it produced (a theology that should be distinguished from the strictly Christian theology involving interpretation of the Word). Heidegger came to unmask metaphysical theology (or the theologizing metaphysics) as a "phenomenon of profanation."[42] There is a resource available to the believer, although the thinking of being does not pass judgment on the question of God. Though Birault remained cautious, his presentation was as favorable as possible to Heidegger and bound to encourage the Christian intellectuals to read him: "This thought leads us to the vivid sources of being and the Sacred: they express the original deity which, at a certain level, cannot be shared by the philosopher's God and the Christian God."[43] Birault thus confirmed, though more discreetly, the both pedagogical and mediating breakthrough he had achieved as early as 1951 in a brilliant essay in which he presented Heidegger's thought as a preparation for a "possible return of God" and concluded as follows: "It is a private matter for each person to determine whether this Return is still possible and whether this Protection appears sufficient."[44]

Anecdotally, let us mention Jean Guitton, who visited Heidegger in October 1956 for a lecture in Freiburg on "Pascal and Leibniz." His narrative, which was lively and picturesque, faithfully reporting the now consecrated ritual of the visit to the Master, revealed a respectful regard toward a meditative philosopher, who was attached to the poetical experience of thought, sensitive to the quality of light, the gravity of words, the message of the country path. There are no criticisms inspired by Catholicism. On the contrary, Heidegger's return to the pre-Socratics along with his sense of the Sacred are perceived in their religious dimension (confirmed by the recourse to the mystics and mostly to Eckhart).[45]

In 1957, Roger Munier, who himself belonged to the Society of Jesus, thanked the Reverend Fathers Fessard and Jeannière[46] for their assistance with the translation of the "Letter on Humanism." During the winter of 1955–56, Paul Ricoeur gave a lecture at the Centre catholique des intellectuels français, on rue Madame. His lecture was devoted to Heidegger's text, Nietzsche's Word: "God is Dead": he gave a conscientious but pedestrian reading of *Holzwege,* a text which had not yet been translated, leading to a confrontation between Jean Wahl and Jean Beaufret during the discussion.[47] Some time before, in September 1955, Ricoeur agreed to participate in the Cerisy conference, at which Heidegger was the star and where several clergymen also attended: the Abbots Morel and Pépin, Fathers Fessard, Kleiber, and Léger,[48] not to mention the canon priest and psychoanalyst Vergotte[49]. Gabriel Marcel was also present and was to play the role of Heidegger's main interlocutor.

In this respect, an unexpected confirmation can be added to the story. Publishing *La Dimension Florestan,* in 1958, Marcel insisted on making a clarification in order to reduce the polemical character of his play. He first noted quite strangely that during his first meeting with Heidegger in Freiburg, he did not have the "slightest impression of being in the presence of a ridiculous character."[50] Then, referring to Cerisy: "I was impressed, as well as everyone there, by a certain simplicity or even modesty, almost a naivety that made a great impression upon us all. The grotesque character of *La dimension Florestan* does not look at all like the perfectly authentic thinker whose language has nevertheless given me the occasion of writing a comedy."[51] Is this a retraction? On the personal level, certainly; yet, Marcel remained critical, by focusing his attacks on the dangers of esotericism.[52] This was a compromise position that allowed him to avoid a deeper debate (in particular, on the expected question of the approach to the Sacred). And he shot Parthe's arrow by making an allusion, in a bittersweet way, to "a thought intoxicated with itself and victories all too often illusory."[53]

Between Gilson and Marcel, and between Guitton, Ricoeur, and the Dominicans of the Saulchoir, the differences of form, style, and temperament were patent. However, with respect to the content, these Christian intellectuals shared the same reservations, mixed with interest or even fascination, toward a Heidegger who was then completely dissociated from Sartre and from existentialism. Perplexity won out over hostility; and when the latter simmered, it proceeded cautiously, for there is no worse ridicule in Paris, even in the religious circles,[54] than to appear unable to understand a philosophy that is championed by many intellectuals, and that benefited in 1955 from a kind of discreet and unexpected consecration, thanks to the conference at Cerisy, which was the culmination of the Master's surprise visit to France.

Heidegger in France!

"One thing that struck Heidegger in Paris in 1955 was to have actually been there. Before he went through the gate of the *gare de l'Est,* he paused for a moment and said, pensively: *Ich bin doch in Paris.* Mrs. Heidegger asked him: And so, what's your impression? He responded: *Ich bin erstaunt—über mich!*"[55] It was with these words that Jean Beaufret began his recollection of Heidegger's first stay in Paris. The significant events of such visit included encounters with René Char, Georges Braque, Jacques Lacan, then the conference at Cerisy.

The trip was carefully planned by Jean Beaufret with the collaboration of Kostas Axelos.[56] To have Heidegger stay in Paris incognito, where everything is very public, was quite an undertaking; but the capital was deserted in August: the scheduling itself guaranteed the success of this operation. It was indeed an undeniable success since the Master was able to visit the Louvre and the château de Versailles in exceptional conditions, even having a drink on the sidewalk of the Café de Flore.[57] In addition to sightseeing, Heidegger wanted to meet with Char and Braque,[58] meetings that Jean Beaufret devoted himself to organizing. Kostas Axelos always served as the interpreter. Jean Beaufret had generously loaned his flat on *passage Stendhal,* in Ménilmontant, to the Heidegger couple. This is where the legendary dinner took place: "*sous le marronnier*" [under the chestnut tree], with René Char (and in the company of Axelos and Munier).

Most readers will be appropriately surprised that a chestnut tree could grow in the middle of a Parisian flat, which would be hardly more surrealistic than the presence of Heidegger in Paris. Let us clarify that at the time when this dinner took place, there were still some areas of greenery in Paris: the *passage Stendhal* (in fact a cul-de-sac) was one of them. Still spared by the property developers, those vultures of modernity, and mostly visited by sparrows and *khâgne* students, the place was quite calm due to its remoteness from all the busy centers of the capital. The modest apartment, wallpapered with books, located on the second floor of a building, included the use of a terrace that would have had no charm, even in summer, without the protection of the impressive foliage of a chestnut tree, which became famous thanks to a text written by Jean Beaufret, and published eight years later as a tribute to René Char.

Despite its title ("L'entretien sous le marronnier" [dialogue under the chestnut tree]), this text was not a narrative of that famous dinner. It took it as a pretext for a pleasant though quite solemn stylization of the meeting between the Poet and the Thinker. Some remarks, however,[59] in addition to another short account by Beaufret,[60] enable us to get a sense of a supper that could have been a fiasco: there was the language barrier (Char did not speak German and Heidegger refused to utter even one word in French), but there was above all the danger inherent in any "summit meeting" between great men who have to get to know each other (a formal atmosphere or shyness, and the fact that they had little in common). However, the heat in August, the simple charm of the place, and above all the kindness of Jean Beaufret and of his friends made the task easy: "We joyfully ate in the summer night, thoroughly enjoying Mrs. Heidegger's cooking. Melville and Billy Budd happened to come up during the conversation and both discovered a common admiration. Char, who was so prompt to withdraw when faced with a disagreement, felt at ease and spoke while Heidegger listened. I can still hear him saying: "The poem has no memory. What I am being asked is to go forward."[61] For once, this was a fruitful exchange: the poet spoke boldly, the thinker listened; the casting of the roles suited the foreign guest, who was in fact quite shy and who had no desire to play the role of the great professor in such circumstances; moreover, his appreciation of a reciprocal listening and of the exceptional relationship—at once frank and fraternal—between the poet and thinker, was confirmed. The latter becomes the silent guardian of memory, "even if poetry remains a resource for the thinker."[62] Char was obviously flattered to have been invited and recognized, and appreciated not having to be lectured: "This is really the first time, he said referring to Heidegger, that a man of this stature has not attempted to explain to me what I am or what I do."[63]

There is less to tell about his visit to Braque in his house in Varengeville, on a hill that dominates the sea, near Dieppe: the two great men hardly exchanged any words: "*Take a stroll and look at everything.* Braque's frail condition confined him to an armchair. It is only when we left that he stood up to accompany his visitor as far as the middle of the green in front of the workshop."[64]

Perhaps I should yield the floor to a poet who did not attend the meeting:

Braque
What was he thinking about
What was he dreaming of
in front of the sea, this nude model?[65]

Full Days in a Castle

The first castle Heidegger occupied for five or six days with Jean Beaufret and Kostas Axelos was Jacques Lacan's manor house in Guitrancourt. It was a "very pleasant stay."[66] However, we wonder if meaningful discussions really took place between the psychoanalyst and the thinker. Axelos's response was negative: they remained at the level of friendly small talk[67] and pleasant walks (in particular, a picturesque visit to Chartres cathedral).[68]

Finally, the actual purpose of the Master's visit to France was the meeting that took place from August 27 to September 4, 1955, in the castle of Cerisy, in Normandy. The program of those famed ten days was described only in vague terms, without giving the names of the directors or the participants. The theme was "What is philosophy?,"[69] which was a skillful way to announce an event without revealing the well-kept secret: Heidegger's participation.

Was it a stroke of luck for Jean Beaufret, who had proposed the idea of a meeting in France?[70] Or was it a "master stroke" for Madame Heurgon, the owner, who sensed the "propitious moment"?[71] The fact remains that this meeting took place and was a success, according to most of the participants,[72] who numbered about fifty.[73] Two incidents occurred, however: the complaint of Vladimir Jankélévitch, who would never set foot in Cerisy again;[74] and the cautious, if not hostile, attitude of Lucien Goldmann, who would nevertheless attend all the sessions.

To fully appreciate the importance and the real influence of this exceptional symposium, one has to differentiate between the anecdotal and what is important. For Jean Beaufret, who was very sensitive to encounters and friendships, it was a consecration; he thought what mattered had been attained: Heidegger was recognized and accepted by the cream of the French intelligentsia, along with a text that quickly became a classic: the lecture "What Is Philosophy?"[75] In fact, this meeting, mostly unknown to the public and quickly forgotten, probably had much less influence than Beaufret had hoped: with the passage of time, *verba volant scripta manent.* Translations or essays, favorable or unfavorable, would certainly succeed in impressing the philosophical memory more deeply. But the visit to Cerisy has taken on an almost sentimental, symbolic value. For Heidegger himself, who less than ten years earlier had been subjected to a process of "denazification" and deprived of his chair, this was quite a relief!

Anecdotally, can we mention that they went to Bayeux Cathedral to find a lectern for the Master? Or that the Heidegger couple was given the most beautiful room of the castle?[76] Or that Gabriel Marcel was forced to work hard on the classical texts included in the program by Heidegger?[77] Or that Alexis Philonenko was designated to operate the tape recorder? Or that Deleuze granted that he had spent "lovely days" at the meeting?[78] Or that Lucien Goldmann found himself on the floor at Heidegger's feet because of his refusal to get up from the bench with the other guests for the entry of the Master and his spouse?[79]

Obviously more significant was the content of the program proposed by the two organizers (Axelos and Beaufret), which provoked as early as August 27th a brief discussion during which Gabriel Marcel and Lucien Goldmann questioned the inclusion of commentaries on Kant's and Hegel's texts into the schedule (to follow the inaugural lecture by Heidegger, "What Is Philosophy?"). Both hoped that people would not feel restrained from asking questions on Heidegger's work and the "entirety of his thought." Jean Beaufret calmed things down, suggesting that the program was simply a guide that did not need to be followed to the letter: "What is important is that we manage to start."[80]

On Sunday August 28th, Heidegger delivered the lecture: "*Was ist das, die Philosophie?*,"[81] a very sophisticated text in which he remained silent concerning his own thought and confined himself resolutely to a meditation on the Greek origin of philosophy, whose point of departure was formulated in the following way: "The Greek word *philosophia* indicates the direction."[82] The following days alternated between discussions and close readings of the text. On August 29th, an intense debate between Marcel and Heidegger on the criteria of translation and interpretation took place: the former, while saluting the depth of Heidegger's suggestions, questioned their "critical basis": can there be incontestable criteria? Though Marcel and Heidegger first agreed to respond negatively, the latter emphasized the basic presupposition of his readings: to enter into dialogue with a discourse delivered by the tradition and precisely with its "unsaid" (he gave the example of the new perspectives he opened on the schematism and the "amphiboly" of the concepts of reflection in his *Kantbuch*). Marcel objected that this involved a certain kind of excessive and finally dangerous "generosity" toward the author. Heidegger replied with the example of the thought of place in Greek thought and its Galilean transformation into a conception of space: it is the play of presupposition that one should reveal in the interpretative dialogue. "Are we going to ask Braque what his criteria are?" Beaufret interjected, finally reminding everyone of the necessity to go back to specific texts. On August 30, the official program began with the explication of the beginning of Kant's essay on *The One Possible Basis for a Demonstration of the Existence of God: "Vom Dasein überhaupt"* ("Existence in General").[83] Heidegger led this seminar according to the very authoritarian method his former students (such as Biemel, himself present at Cerisy) knew well.[84] The professor requested that the participants answer a series of apparently simple and academic questions: What's the title? In what sense is the word *Dasein* used here? What about the word *Gegenstand*? The word *objectum*? And *realitas formalis*? The point was to understand why existence is not a predicate: but what is a predicate? Kant writes: "The concept of position or positing is totally simple and on the whole identical with the concept of being in general."[85] Paradoxically, the positive relation is to be understood from the relative position: what is posited is represented.

After this particularly austere session, Heidegger began August 31st with a clarification: he wanted to consider "a few difficulties" that had arisen; this was a euphemism to refer to the objections and resistances formulated in the very first session and then reinforced by his method, which was similar to that of an "elementary school teacher." As a response to those who wished to study the theses of Heideggerian philosophy, he stated (a statement thereafter often quoted by Jean Beaufret): "There is no Heideggerian philosophy; and even if it existed, I would not be interested in that philosophy." To the implicit criticisms he perceived, he replied that his method was not dictatorial, but represented an effort to answer the "dictate of being." He then returned to Kant's text and reasserted his interpretation: Kant conceived of existence as absolute position on the basis of the relative position consisting in the exercise of judgment. The following discussions remained quite "technical" and were not conducive to harmonizing the points of view: if he conceded to Jeanne Hersch that the pre-critical Kant of the 1763 essay had not yet made his "thesis about being"[86] explicit, Heidegger resisted Ricoeur (who insisted that the thing in itself escapes the sphere of representation). As an object in general = x, it is not perceptible by the senses. What matters is to understand that, for Kant, the position of existence can be conceived only on the basis of the proposition formulated by judgment.

Gabriel Marcel opened the session of September 1st with a long presentation. He first expressed his surprise at having heard from Heidegger himself that there was no Heideggerian philosophy. While admitting and even approving of the absence of a system, he nonetheless maintained that Heidegger's thought is a philosophy, if only for the fact that it is immediately recognizable and that it possesses that "unique quality" that allows it to be identified, just as one distinguishes Brahms's style from Debussy's. The question of the translation of the key words of Heidegger's vocabulary was then posed. Thus *zum-Tode-sein* ("being-toward-death") is *stumm* ("mute") for a French ear; in French, *être* can be plural (one can speak of "*un être*," or "*des êtres*"), which makes the difference between *être* and *étant* (being and beings) difficult to grasp. While admitting his agreement with the Heideggerian understanding of truth as unveiling and clearing (*Lichtung*), Marcel asked whether Heidegger could defend his absence of reference to any philosophy of values and his silence on the great Catholic tradition from Saint Augustine to Pascal. For him, as an ultimate recourse, the last word belongs "not to the wise, but to the saint." As if echoing this intervention, Ricoeur insisted on this point, but more precisely asked whether it was possible to exclude the Hebraic tradition from philosophy. Of course, one should not have the prophets philosophize as was attempted during the nineteenth century; but the translation of the Hebrew Bible into Greek was an event that had a deep significance and that one should reflect on. How can Heidegger help us in thinking these "two greatnesses" of *Denken* and prophecy, in order to rethink the difference between the philosophical path and that of divine calling?

To Gabriel Marcel, Heidegger responded that the assertion that there is no Heideggerian philosophy is rather a sign of humility [*Demut*] before the very question of philosophy as metaphysics. It would have been better to ask: "How can you characterize philosophy as metaphysics if your own thought is an overcoming of metaphysics?" Strictly speaking, it was from the perspective of a meditation on the temporal character of the being of beings that the overcoming of metaphysics was attempted, at least as a gesture, as early as *Sein und Zeit*. With respect to the question of universality, Heidegger limited himself to a purely historical clarification (the Greeks did not have the universal conception that classical philosophy attributed to them) that was immediately contested by Marcel (beyond the flat universalism of the Enlightenment, one has to be open to a genuine universality, as offered by great art). Heidegger replied that an authentic universality is never guaranteed in advance: to understand requires the productive translation of what is to be thought. To Paul Ricoeur,[87] Heidegger responded briefly and cautiously that he could not follow him in a direct confrontation between Hebrew and Greek (having forgotten the little Hebrew he had learned during his studies in theology), but above all that it was necessary to consider the twofold character, both ontological and theological, of Aristotle's metaphysics, without assuming that a word for word confrontation with the theology of the prophets would be possible.[88]

On September 2nd, after another very technical clarification concerning Kant (to reassert that the thing in itself, even if not scientifically knowable, is an object of representation), Heidegger approached Hegel through some apparently elementary observations: *Wissenschaft* (science) is synonymous with philosophy or metaphysics. And what does *Begriff* mean? Not a representation in the Kantian sense, but the free development of the absolute idea, that is to say, of being. What about God himself? His coming into being is not to be understood as if he went from nonexistence to existence, but as the auto-revelation of what was concealed in him. Why all those clarifications? To introduce the explanation of the "speculative proposition" in Hegel and more particularly in the preface of the *Phenomenology of Spirit*. Was it with the intention of "restoring calm"?[89] Heidegger proceeded in this way mostly to keep on course and to highlight his method in reading fundamental philosophical texts. The method would surprise specialists, for when Heidegger asserted that "the speculative proposition is itself being," he seemed (or wanted to seem) to ignore that for Hegel being is "in fact nothing,"[90] the most abstract and vacuous notion. However, Heidegger insisted on remaining literally faithful to Hegel's thought by contrasting term for term— and in a very academic manner—the usual form of judgment and the speculative form. He recalled that in the ordinary predicative proposition (for example, "this tree is green"), the predicate qualifies the subject, without having any substantial meaning. Reconsidering on the contrary the very example Hegel gave of a speculative proposition, "God is being," Heidegger underlined that "being" cannot be reduced to a simple predicate, but becomes in turn, subject. Hence a "counter-thrust" [*Gegenstoss*] undergone by thought, as Hegel indicated in a key sentence cited by Heidegger: "Formally, what has been said can be expressed thus: the general nature of the judgment or proposition, which involves the distinction of subject and predicate, is destroyed by the speculative proposition, and the proposition of identity which the former becomes contains the counter-thrust against that subject-predicate relationship."[91] Thus, as Heidegger explained, "God abides in the essence of being, and being is not a predicate of God." Only two brief exchanges with Jeanne Hersch and Father Fessard departed from the doctoral style of the session on Hegel's "correct doctrine" in speculative matters.

The session of Saturday, September 3rd, departed from this austere style. Those ten days concluded on a high note with the reading and commentary by Beda Allemann of Hölderlin's hymn "Celebration of Peace" (*Friedensfeier*), which was discovered in its entirety in London in 1954. Composed after the treaty of Lunéville in February 1801, the poem enthusiastically celebrated the Prince of the Celebration (Bonaparte), but far from any prosaic banality—with a delicate emotion and an ineffable sense of the Divine. To present the poem, Allemann, who was a philologist and historian of German literature, proceeded methodically, carefully explaining the composition of the work: for example, the twelve stanzas of the hymn are divided into four triads of three stanzas. The first triad is devoted to Bonaparte, the second to Christ. To understand this opposition, one must understand that Jesus is, for Hölderlin, a demi-god who leaves this earth. The aim of his return—which animates the third triad—is to bring reconciliation. The fourth triad finally resituates this reconciliation with the Divine in the midst of the sojourn of the mortals. The theme of reconciliation [*Versöhnung*]—as well as that of the historic and almost sacred role of the hero—is of course common to both Hölderlin and Hegel, but the difference between poetry and philosophy appears in the transition between the third and the fourth triads. The very rhythm expresses the essence of the poem in its gathering of the Divine. Rhythm, the importance of which Hegel did not fail to recognize,[92] is poetically enacted and yet in an undeniable proximity to idealistic metaphysics. Heidegger agreed with Beda Allemann. Gabriel Marcel and Jeanne Hersch were satisfied to ask for some clarifications. Only Ricoeur did not seem to agree, declaring himself disappointed that Hölderlin could have had such an excessive admiration for Bonaparte.

The last session of the conference took place Sunday, September 4th, and enabled Heidegger to make some final clarifications. Returning to the first inaugural lecture and to the question of the "philo-sophical" correspondence with *sophia,* he emphasized that Hegel's wish to renounce the love of *sophia* in order to incorporate it into the form of the System could in no way be understood as a return to the pre-Socratics. What Hegel aimed at was instead the idealistic accomplishment of philosophy. Heidegger confessed that the published work by Walter Schulz[93] convinced him that the accomplishment of idealism genuinely took place in Schelling's late philosophy. The guiding question of philosophy bears on the being of beings. In contrast, the basic question that Heidegger posed concerns being itself, that is to say, the difference between being and beings. But this difference should not be assimilated to a relation. How is it possible to avoid that reduction? The difficulty lies in language. Heidegger reviewed matters the audience seemed to be familiar with, but in his own style, insisting upon them patiently. It is to be noted, however, that by so doing he responded to the original request: that the meeting should also concern his own thought. The justification of the detour through the study of the major texts was the following: for Heidegger, it was above all, here as elsewhere, a matter of maintaining "a constant dialogue with the tradition." He then explained that the forgetting of the difference is not to be understood as a forgetting in the ordinary (negative) sense, but as the sheltering

[*Verbergung*] of that which is not yet manifest. Anxious to clarify again what he meant by epoch or by destinal sending [*Geschick*], Heidegger then characterized the *Grundstimmung* of his own thought by the two following words: *Offenheit* ("openness") and *Gelassenheit* ("releasement"). The first is openness to the dialogue with history, in the sense that was clarified earlier; the second seems to be its direct complement: thinking the "mutation of the forgetting of difference."

Formulating his thanks to the hostess, Madame Heurgon, to Kostas Axelos for his translations, and to Gabriel Marcel for leading the debates [*Gesprächführer*], Heidegger asked the audience to excuse him for having possibly "shocked" them when he recalled his peasant origins. One final gesture is worth noting; beyond the participants, it was addressed to the French language; Heidegger dwelled on two French words that seemed to him laden with meaning: the verb *penser* (where one should hear *peser* [to weigh]) as well), and the substantive *regard* (which refers not only to vision but also to *zurückbewahren*, the guarding that preserves and restores). About this word, Heidegger even said that it is "marvelous" and does not exist in German. He was so often reproached for exclusively privileging the German language that this exceptional homage to the French language is worth mentioning. Finally, it was a quotation from Braque with which the Master concluded the conference: "Penser et raisonner font deux" [To think and to reason are two different things].[94]

Even if it is difficult and risky to try to make a definitive statement about those days, one has to recognize that the occasion was exceptional and that Heidegger's "performance" was not insignificant: he came down from his pedestal, or from his hut, to dialogue in a very civil manner with some of his most distinguished French peers (this was a renewed recognition for Heidegger, the importance of which escaped no one in the European philosophical world) and, in this unexpected undertaking and with the efficient help of Axelos and Beaufret, he succeeded in imposing his method of reading and working. This achievement (due in large part to the devotion and skill of Jean Beaufret) was all the more remarkable since it occurred only ten years after the defeat of Germany, the destitution of Heidegger and the "denazification" process to which he was subjected. However, as we saw, there were also quite a few objections. They mainly concerned the particularities of Heidegger's language, the difficulty of translating it and making it understood in French, its inability to be universalized, his silence with respect to biblical sources and even with respect to his political involvement of 1933.[95] Jean Beaufret evoked these debates a few years later: a polemical text, admittedly, but so striking that I cannot resist the temptation to quote it: "Are you not in philosophy, Gabriel Marcel asked, a sworn enemy of universality? Don't you skip over Jaweh? Ricœur said. And Lucien Goldmann, more unexpectedly: what happened in 1930, which you would like the naïve to believe was principally the date of the first divulgation of your question concerning the essence of truth? Heidegger answered in his own way with a counter-question. To Gabriel Marcel: Universality, how do you understand it, except in the sense of what Rivarol held to be the universality of the French language? To Ricœur: is the Bible really an epoch in the history of philosophy? To Goldmann: what are you insinuating? Following this, at the request of the majority, the debate returned to Kant and Hegel."[96]

To a great extent, Heidegger managed to concentrate most of the effort of those present on the great texts of the philosophical tradition, making the debate less passionate and less personal. Was it solely a diversion to avoid embarrassing questions? One should not forget that this return to the basic texts had been at the heart of his method since his teachings in Marburg. Furthermore, the very choice of the title "What Is Philosophy?" implied a refusal to devote the seminar to the most innovative and personal developments of a thought that was perhaps considered (even in the eyes of its author) as overly secret and difficult. But one should be able to discern in this attitude a thesis that cannot in any way be reduced to a false modesty: the most urgent task that thought should impose on itself is to assume and meditate on the meaning of the metaphysical tradition. And this is why—as we saw—Heidegger was able to defend at Cerisy a surprising theme to which Jean Beaufret would thereafter continuously return: there is no Heideggerian philosophy.

This refrain could only have been irritating, for—reduced to a formula—it seemed excessively paradoxical. If one accepts the distinction between metaphysics (identified with philosophy) and thought (which thinks the "un-thought" of metaphysics and discloses new possibilities), one understands Heidegger's position, which has an undeniable coherence. But should one accept it? Should one, in particular, validate his interpretation, at once unified and representative, historical and destinal, of metaphysics? The hermeneutic choice imposed in Cerisy was perfectly consistent. It corresponded, quite obviously, to the presupposition exposed in the "The Way Back into the Ground of Metaphysics":[97] it is by returning from metaphysics back to its essence and by meditating on the scope of that essence that one begins to free oneself from the forgetfulness of the truth of being. However, to present this choice as obvious and Heidegger as the only thinker of the century, to dismiss any other attempt as an obsolete agitation, could only upset (rightly or wrongly) a large part of the philosophical community. It was thus the secondary effect—the doctrinal repetition by Jean Beaufret—that may have compromised, paradoxically and in the long run, the reception of a beautiful lecture that was translated with great care (in which, one should note, Heidegger only presented his own attempt as one possible path).[98] In fact, and in spite of the denial from the translators,[99] this lecture was a compendium of themes fundamental to the later Heidegger: philosophy is Greek "in its nature";[100] it is the source of the domination of sciences, established in the "atomic age";[101] the history of philosophy unfolds not according to a necessary dialectical process, but as a "free consequence";[102] only a meditation on language allows thought to be understood, in its proximity to and its distance from poetry.[103]

In spite of the advanced level and "consensual" character of the inaugural lecture, despite the psychological and "social" success of the meeting, Cerisy did not lead to the overwhelming support of the Heideggerian position. After all, how could it be the case? Of course, this event represented a symbolic milestone that was very significant in the diffusion of Heideggerian thought into France.[104] The bright spell would continue for a few years with a series of new translations, most of them more intelligible, while others were disconcerting, along with interpretative advances breaking with the philosophical order of the past.

A Wave of Translations

In the decade with which we are concerned, a French translation of Heidegger appeared almost every year, either as a book or in a journal.[105] This profusion was doubly paradoxical, since *Sein und Zeit* was still not translated (except for the few paragraphs included in Corbin's volume); in addition, a result of this feverish activity was that it was the later Heidegger who became the best known.[106] As regards the difficulty that appeared early on—how was it possible to render such a singular philosophical language readable and intelligible?—each translator answered as he or she could, but two antithetical tendencies clearly emerged, and the opposition would only get worse and degenerate later into an open conflict: should the priority be given to readability (by making use of transpositions, periphrases) or, on the contrary, should it be given to a "faithfulness" that would lead to esotericism (due to the creation of neologisms)? Although he seemed to offer quite a legible text (compared to the "excesses" that have taken place since then), Corbin had already been accused of the latter tendency.

The conflict did not begin straightaway: for lack of sufficient linguistic skills or style, the Louvain school took a conservative path. Thus Alphonse de Waelhens and Walter Biemel, authors of the two translations that I have to first account for, proceeded cautiously, choosing—in fact—readability. They faced a particular difficulty in the case of the redoubtably complex and bold "On the Essence of Truth."[107]

Accompanied by an introduction that was longer than the text itself and that was more of a paraphrase[108] than a genuine explanation, this translation was not aimed at a general audience and would even confuse many specialists in philosophy. One should recall that Heidegger undertook, in this work discreetly published in 1943 (but reworked from a first version dating from 1930), a completely original overcoming of the traditional concept of truth as adequation. Not contenting himself with understanding truth as freedom and freedom as unconcealment [*Entbergung*],[109] he boldly undertook an absolutely unprecedented movement of thought: to begin again from nontruth as concealment [*Verbergung*].[110] One can thus read, among other things, a cryptic little sentence like this one: "concealment [*obnubilation*] deprives *aletheia* of disclosure."[111] Without claiming to elucidate all the riddles hidden here, I will wonder whether the word *obnubilation* renders in any way the *Verborgenheit* it is supposed to translate. *Obnubiler* means, literally, to cover with clouds, to envelop in darkness, and by extension, to hypnotize.[112] Here the reader was given two false leads: *Verborgenheit* would come to obscure nontruth and would have a vertiginous or obsessional psychological nature. However, the *Verborgenheit* in question is not secondary: it refers to the most originary feature of *Dasein*'s ec-static freedom; it has nothing to do with a psychological state: to begin to understand it, one should refer to *aletheia* itself as unconcealment or uncovering, that is to say, understood in relation to its etymology, rethought by Heidegger on the basis of his return to a Heraclitean, pre-Socratic sense of withdrawal [*retrait*]. If we think of the withdrawal of *phusis* that, in Heraclitus, loves to hide,[113] we are undoubtedly in a better position to engage the meaning of the passage. Consequently, it becomes obvious that *Verbergung* should not be assimilated to any "dissimulation" that would come from human beings.[114] Instead, it belongs to a withdrawal that is here thought of as more originary than any fragment of truth that one could extract from it.

May the reader forgive me for having dragged him or her so abruptly into the center of an excessively disconcerting maelstrom! It was necessary to confront the difficulty that some courageous translators were willing to face. Their efforts had mixed success, as other examples could show.[115] What is today even clearer, from the perspective of the reception of the translation in question, is that it surprised an audience, even among specialists, which was absolutely unprepared for these kind of difficulties, despite the review published in 1946 in *Critique* by Koyré and the article by Jean Beaufret in 1947 on the same issue.[116] However, de Waelhens and Biemel were didactic enough to at least explain that a "significant evolution"[117] had taken place in Heidegger's thought; without already speaking of a "turn," they showed how the emphasis was no longer placed on the existential understanding of *Dasein* itself, but on the ontological preconditions of its attunement to truth.

Retrospectively, the most surprising lacuna in this otherwise quite valuable work was the absence of any thematic justification of the translation choices, despite the prolixity of the commentaries on the text and the fact that the translators were aware of the dangers of misunderstanding that the reader would face due to the completely new vocabulary.[118] There was a time when the translation choices of the Heideggerian texts were neither the object of a passionate debate nor sufficiently explicit: a kind of "underdevelopment" in the matter . . .

I will mention only in passing, however important it was, the translation that the same translators published in 1953 with Gallimard. *Kant et le problème de la métaphysique* [*Kant and the Problem of Metaphysics*] did not, indeed, present a level of difficulty comparable to the essay on the essence of truth. Even if the Heideggerian interpretation shook the conventional vision of Kant as a theoretician of knowledge, even if his reading of the first Critique on the basis of the role of the transcendental imagination and the schematism revealed an undeniable hermeneutic "violence" (explicitly assumed),[119] the careful work on the texts remained within the terminological horizon of Kant's critical philosophy. De Waelhens and Biemel prefaced their translation with a long introduction of fifty pages that presented the Heideggerian interpretation as an "authentic repetition"[120] of the Kantian problematic. One finds no critical or polemical element in this serious commentary that aimed at—and would succeed in—including the work into the closed circle of recognized university bibliographic references.

In contrast, the important translations that appeared in rapid succession, in 1957 and 1958, attested more vigorously to the singularity of Heidegger's thought by re-posing the question of its readability in French. Roger Munier[121] and André Préau[122] chose fluidity, indeed, elegance; Gilbert Kahn[123] did not refrain from using neologisms and proposed a translation that was noted for its "strangeness." Who was right? We should not ask the question in those terms, and Heidegger himself never weighed in. What is undeniable is that the "Letter on Humanism" would not have had the impact that it did if it had been only a collection of strange jargon. Without being Heidegger's most obscure text, the "Letter on Humanism" offered real difficulties for the translator: however, the solutions adopted facilitated the reading more than they discouraged it.[124] Roger Munier confided in me that François Fédier had reproached him for choosing intelligibility, a choice illustrated as well, and with undeniable success, by André Préau in his translation of *Vorträge und Aufsätze,* "so sober and so thoughtful."[125]

Containing crucial contributions, though very different from one another, this volume (which offered a sort of a compendium of the later Heidegger's thought, addressing contemporary technology as well as the pre-Socratics) was translated with utmost care by a scholar in German studies who included useful notes throughout the text, scrupulously limiting himself to explaining the translations and quoting the German text at each notable difficulty. From the outset, there is a surprising discovery: the use of *Arraisonnement* for *Gestell,* the essence of technology; this evocative word, borrowed from maritime vocabulary, immediately presented the advantage of suggesting the violence exercised by the scientific-technological destiny on nature and humanity itself, but the inconvenience of implicitly attributing this violence to reason, losing in the process both the gathering sense of the prefix *Ge* and any relation to the connotations of the verb *Stellen* ("to set up," "to dispose"). It was almost more of a transposition than a translation, but its success assured it an apparently definitive status as the standard translation. Some other ingenious translations deserve our attention:

the *Quadriparti* for *das Geviert,* the *Quadrature* for *die Vierung,* the *Pose recueil-lante* for *die Lesende Lege.*[126] Of course, each of these options would deserve to be discussed in detail. What should be noticed here is the pedagogical effort of Préau and his concern not to "add on" to the word games that are sometimes vertiginous in Heidegger, especially in the lecture "The Thing" [*La chose*]: thus, *le rassemblement propre à la chose* (literally: the gathering proper to the thing) does not frighten the reader, as would the literal translation of *das Dingen des Dinges:* the *"choser" de la chose* (the thinging of the thing);[127] similarly, the tautological expression *Die Welt weltet,* literally "the world worlds," appeared in Préau's translation as *le monde . . . joue-le-jeu-du-monde* (literally: the world . . . plays-the-game-of-the-world).[128] It is obvious that if all of Heidegger's translators had adopted the same policy, with comparable care and talent, the image of the Master would have been different: without being as "diaphanous" as the text on the back cover of *Essais et Conférences* wished and claimed,[129] it would have nonetheless provoked less reticence and fewer accusations of jargon; it would undoubtedly have received a better welcome and would have been better understood in its genuine intentions. One could always object that a faithful translation does not necessarily have to be low key and that Préau's Heidegger was almost too *soft* [TN: In English in the original]. He translated *ereignet sich* by *se produit* (to happen), which loses the decisive relation to *Ereignis,* translated (but partially betrayed) as *Avènement* (Advent). No translation is perfect, especially when the author has placed the bar so high: it is legitimate and necessary that the confrontation with the text should be pursued; whatever the degree of felicity of those choices, Préau never avoided it. What renders his work so praiseworthy is both its readability and the fact that the access to the original text was never occluded (the notes and the parenthetical comments keep referring to it).

For his part, Gilbert Kahn—whether or not he was being provocative—gave the impression of having pushed the opposite choice too far in the *Introduction to Metaphysics,* even though this was only a written course (Heidegger's lectures were always more accessible). The presence at the end of the volume of a double glossary did not attenuate the shock caused by the neologisms, most of which were disconcerting. The list of bizarre translation choices never ceases to amaze. Let us consider, in alphabetical order, without any intention of being exhaustive, the following neologisms: *l'adestance* [*Anwesenheit;* presence], *l'anté-spection* [*Vorblick;* preview], *la dé-latence* [*Ent-borgenheit;* unconcealment], *la discession* [*Auseinandertreten;* setting apart from one another], *l'estance* [*Wesend;* essencing], *la méversité* [*Verkehrtheit;* positive pervertedness], *la patéfaction* [*Eröffnung;* manifestation], *la per-spection* [*Durchblick,* glance], *la prépotence* [*Übergewalt,* excessive violence], *le pro-de-stin* [*Geschick,* destiny], *le pro-sister* [*entstehen,* coming into being], *le proventuel* [*Geschichtlich,* fateful]. We need to understand how Gilbert Kahn, a confirmed German scholar and well-informed philosopher, came to this, after a long work conducted in large part with a team in Freiburg, among whom were disciples of Heidegger. In his introductory foreword, he maintained that he preferred a "certain linguistic brutality" (euphemistically speaking) to capture a "change in perspective"[130] and that, in order to respect the author's perspective and his proper movement of thought, he coined new words from Latin roots. He thus attempted to undertake a real work of transposition. The result, for those who made the effort to follow him, was a complete change of scenery. This shows that, although the value of this undertaking must be recognized (for some "transpositions" are justifiable or suggestive),[131] this translation remains, on the whole, very strange, and perhaps contributed to marginalizing once more a great author whom others—at the same time—labored to render accessible.[132]

Incidentally, this seminar on the *Introduction to Metaphysics* had been analyzed in a very pedagogical manner, a few years earlier at the Sorbonne, by Jean Wahl, who re-edited—in this case from an already published text[133]—a sort of a pedestrian commentary that he had already undertaken in 1946 from the transcript of another seminar he had devoted to Heidegger.[134] This commentary, with the ambitious title of *Vers la fin de l'ontologie* [Toward the end of ontology],[135] deserves to be reconsidered, for at least two reasons. On the one hand, it has been noted[136] that Jean Wahl deserved credit for not hiding his discomfort with Heidegger's reprint of a sentence from 1935 on the "inner truth and greatness" of the national socialist movement and for not allowing this question to interfere with the properly philosophical commentary. He drew attention to that point in his introduction and did not return to it except for a brief final allusion on how "deeply distasteful"[137] this sentence was. One could not blame him; yet, what is strange, and reveals once more Wahl's amateurish approach, is his inaccurate quotation and translation of the infamous short sentence (*mit der inneren Wahrheit und Grösse dieser Bewegung*)[138] with *la grandeur ou la hauteur de ce mouvement* [the greatness or the loftiness of this movement].[139] Let us grant that the difference is small; but does such a delicate question not demand the utmost rigor? Wahl did note that the comment concerning "planetary technology"[140] (which we now know did not appear in the course of 1935) is in parentheses. However, he did not include this parenthesis where it should be in the text; further, he translated *Begegnung* inaccurately by "union." In sum, while this revision suffers from its oral, improvised, and unedited nature, the content also seems somewhat rushed. Wahl suggested that this parenthesis "perhaps diminishes the noxiousness and the unpleasant nature of the sentence," due to the fact that "Heidegger does not like technology." This is cheap psychology that overlooks an important difficulty: why open such a deep wound to immediately cover it with a bandage? The objection addressed to Wahl's gloss does not absolve Heidegger. Let us admit, additionally, that Wahl's commentary does not merely reveal a somewhat anarchic style; it also presents a subtle grasp of the four distinctions of being (in relation to seeming, becoming, thinking, and the Ought). Above all, it reveals an awareness that was uncommon at that time (revealed by the title that anticipates "the end of ontology"): far from limiting himself to introducing metaphysics, Heidegger undertook the "task"[141] of questioning being as constant presence and thus prepared, as early as 1935, the turn toward another thinking.

From a completely different source, somewhat later, in 1959, the very readable translation of a course given only seven years earlier, titled *What Is Called Thinking?*,[142] appeared. The brilliant and enthusiastic introduction by Gérard Granel, speckled with Greek and German, relying on the fact that a large part of that course was a translation of the first eight words of fragment VI of Parmenides, saluted Heidegger as the great *tra-ducteur* (trans-lator) of the metaphysical Tradition and brilliantly justified the upheaval of the linguistic scene and customs: "It is obvious that something *changes* in the Heideggerian language. Consequently, the entire Metaphysics of the Tradition, for the first time since Nietzsche and Kant, is put in perspective, including Kant and Nietzsche."[143] That same year, and in the same collection directed by Jean Hyppolite, the outstanding essay by the literary critic Beda Allemann appeared:[144] establishing precise and sober correspondences between Hölderlin's poetry and Heidegger's thought, the "return to the origin" of the first and the "turn" of the second, he avoided the traps of systematic comparison and succeeded in approaching the intimacy of the dialogue that the thinker sustained more and more intensely with the poet. Well documented, deep and measured, this book offers an irreplaceable key for the understanding of the later Heidegger.[145]

Yes, something also changed in the French philosophical field: at the end of the decade, Heidegger's influence grew considerably and in many respects. Jean Beaufret had already established himself, but the image of the Master of Freiburg had changed, as it continued to impose itself. Almost forgotten, the image of Heidegger as the father of existentialism was replaced by a new image: that of a major interpreter of the metaphysical tradition. Devil of the avant-garde not long before, angel of the bizarre at times, Heidegger became the keeper of Philosophy's temple. Was that too much?

* * *

In the end, although impressive, the result of this decade was also very ambiguous. Heidegger's magisterial image imposed itself, but was also blurred in the process. The disagreements in the methods of translation were only one of the axes of this ambiguity (this was discernable in Beaufret himself, as he wavered between an effort of pedagogical clarity and a certain esoteric research).[146] The status of ontology, the interpretation of the history of philosophy, and in particular of pre-Socratic thought, the meaning and nonmeaning of a technology thereafter conceived of as planetary, represented the new stakes of the discussion. We saw it in Cerisy. These new developments were quite varied, but no major reading emerged that engaged the depth of the Heideggerian project. In addition to *Le Poème de Parménide*,[147] a very personal essay, where Jean Beaufret applied his talent to the service of the Heideggerian theses in their entirety (the reinterpretation of Kant's transcendental schematism was even retrospectively made to clarify the scope of the Parmenidean *doxa*), let us note the unexpected comparison established by Mikel Dufrenne between "primitive mentality and Heidegger"[148] and the perplexity of Alphonse de Waelhens, who raised many questions at the end of a quite awkward presentation of the *Holzwege*.[149] For his part, Kostas Axelos introduced the group of the journal *Arguments* to a progressive reception of Heidegger's meditation on the essence of technology, by articulating a dialogue with Marxian themes:[150] on four occasions, the journal published texts by Heidegger.[151] Axelos initiated a debate in 1959 with Jean Beaufret, François Châtelet, and Henri Lefebvre on the theme of "Karl Marx and Heidegger":[152] a surprising consensus emerged to emphasize the convergences between the two most radical thinkers of modernity; Henri Lefebvre went so far as to claim that "Heidegger is indeed a materialist,"[153] and Jean Beaufret, for his part, emphasized that Heidegger encouraged a debate *with* Marxism rather than *against* it.[154] Finally, the *Revue internationale de philosophie* devoted a special issue to Heidegger,[155] in which a beautiful text by Birault on *Heidegger et la pensée de la finitude* [Heidegger and the thinking of finitude] stood out.[156] In this case, the relation to the Christian message was no longer at the center of the discussion. Beginning instead from a quotation by Kojève, who recognized Heidegger as "the first to undertake a complete atheistic philosophy,"[157] Birault distinguished Christian finitude from Judaic finiteness [*finité*] or Hellenic completion [*finition*]: he sought to explain why "the notion of *Endlichkeit* or finitude was abandoned by Heidegger and what was the ultimate signification of this abandonment."[158] Insisting on the "step back" [*Schritt zurück*] of the thought of being with respect to metaphysics, it marked the disorientating originality of an approach that understood the nothing as the veil of being, and nontruth as an essential element for truth. This thought of being had "no worse enemy" than onto-theology.[159]

In 1960–61, Heidegger was thus omnipresent on the French philosophical scene and his stature more recognized than ever. In this respect, Jean Beaufret could not be more satisfied:[160] He even managed to facilitate Heidegger's visits to France after Cerisy with lectures at the Faculté des lettres of Aix-en-Provence,[161] in 1956 and 1957, and above all in 1958, where the lecture "Hegel and the Greeks" was successfully given on March 20, "in front of a thousand captivated people."[162] Pierre Aubenque, who was then teaching in that university, reflected on the exceptional atmosphere of the lecture in these terms: "Heidegger's entry was almost unnoticed because of his diminutive stature. At that moment, the Greek scholar Louis Moulinier, who was in charge of welcoming the lecturer on behalf of the dean, who was 'unable to be present' that day, found just the right words. He told the story that one day, in a gathering, somebody suddenly noticed the presence of J.-S. Bach, told his neighbor and then three words were whispered a hundred times, spreading through the crowd: *Bach ist da.*" Aubenque added that the connection with the famous cantor was not unjustified.[163]

The text of that lecture, "Hegel and the Greeks,"[164] was so austere and formal that it demanded intense concentration from the audience: Hegel's judgment on Greek philosophy—reconsidered on the basis of the four fundamental sayings (of Parmenides, Heraclitus, Plato, and Aristotle)—was finally redirected by Heidegger toward the "truth" (*aletheia*) that remains to be thought within the destiny of Western thought. Heidegger disappeared, as it were, within Hegelian thought only to "subvert" it at the last moment. This was a subtle operation, but one that could only be lost on the majority of those in attendance. No doubt foreseeing this difficulty, Heidegger attempted to be especially "charming" in the foreword in which he declared his love for Provence and his admiration for Cézanne.

> *Why do I speak here in Aix en Provence?*
> *I love the sweetness of its regions and its villages*
> *I love the rugged terrain of its mountains*
> *I love the harmony of both*
> *I love Aix, Bibemus, the montagne Sainte-Victoire*

And he concluded:

> *I love all that because I firmly believe that there is no essential spiritual work unless it is rooted in an original soil on which one must stand.*[165]

It seems, indeed, according to all accounts, that he "won over" a patient audience, which then listened carefully to the German text, translated paragraph by paragraph by Pierre-Paul Sagave[166] and Jean Beaufret.

Such breakthroughs and successes did not overcome the deep resistances that would soon be expressed in a quite virulent manner. As if he could anticipate it, Jean Beaufret accentuated the polemical nature of his interventions: he prefaced his beautiful translation of "Georg Trakl" with a warning in which he foresaw an "unavoidable misunderstanding," and he resolutely separated Heidegger from "literary criticism, aesthetic delectation," as well as "metaphysical reflection."[167] All the same, instead of presenting the content of the texts of the volume in detail—although so rich—he gave in his preface to the *Essais et Conférences* (*Vorträge und Aufsätze*), and not without panache, the resolute tone of a defense of the Master, apart from philosophy and from intellectuality, completely removed from cultural agitation: "This strange carnival, as Valéry would say, where theological virtuosity and humanistic passion, verbiage of values and scientific claims, dialectical conceit and phenomenological improvisation unfolded, in the wake of the death of God, such a rich collection of prestigious alibis: how could a peasant from Messkirch possibly feel at ease there?"[168] This exaltation of the great thinker, alone against all, would irritate more than one reader and produce the opposite of the desired effect. Was this a backlash from Cerisy? Jean Wahl, who, as we saw, made an important contribution by making Heidegger's thought known, seemed to harden his position and became quite critical: "There is a good deal of mythology in all this Heideggerian thinking";[169] while defending himself against the charge of "jealousy" or "negativity," he launched a sharp attack about the political question: "It is only an appearance that Heidegger separated himself from Nazism after the first anti-semitic demonstrations."[170] Wahl did not conceal the fact that he thus aimed to respond to Kostas Axelos, who had claimed that Heidegger was the only genuine interlocutor of Marx and derided the hostile conspiracy of conservative institutions.[171]

The polemics would be revived in an unexpected and much more violent way, not by Axelos but by René Char. In *Autres pages de journal,* Wahl attacked two contemporary poets who appeared to him as unworthy of Claudel's stature: "We ended up with Char and Ponge . . . I do not understand Char."[172] Heidegger seemed to have been forgotten. But he appeared again in the thundering reply that Char addressed to Wahl, reviving the surrealist tradition of insult for "a good cause"—a postcard that "well-intentioned" people published quickly in *La Nouvelle Revue française* entitled "Polemics and Violence": "With you Sir, the shit no longer climbs up on the horse, as Kierkegaard enjoyed saying, it falls down to the pot." Char also reproached Wahl for both his misunderstanding of Ponge and his "recent ugly comments against Heidegger."[173] In contrast, he wrote in his most inspired style a few lines of homage to Heidegger for the volume that appeared in Germany on the occasion of his seventieth birthday.[174] The only other French figures present in the volume were Beaufret, Blanchot, and Braque.

Whether admiring or polemical, did these blows announce the brutal end of the bright spell of the fifties? The interview published in May 1959 in *France-Observateur* suggests a more nuanced interpretation: Jean Beaufret and Kostas Axelos engaged in an amicable discussion with François Châtelet and Henri Lefebvre on "Karl Marx and Heidegger."[175] Each side made an obvious effort at a rapprochement: Lefebvre said he had been "delighted and taken by a vision"[176] during the reading of the *Holzwege* and asserted that "following Engels' famous definition, Heidegger is indeed a materialist";[177] Axelos and Beaufret delineated the strict limits of the involvement of 1933 and insisted on the fact that Heidegger's thought, thereafter turned toward the future, absolutely excluded any activism of that kind; Châtelet, the most hesitant, nonetheless conceded that Heidegger helped him in his reading of Marx;[178] Beaufret went so far as to assert that "Heidegger essentially intends to help us understand Marx."[179] One can see that Heidegger remained *persona grata* within the intellectual left. However, it was with the university that relations were strained: Jean Wahl, one of its most influential representatives, had been the director of Beaufret's thesis (never completed); he had then become his ideological adversary. The misunderstanding between them would only continue to grow.

The counterpart of the bright spell would soon itself be revealed: the unconditional defense of the Master's theses, the very success of their diffusion (soon sustained by an exclusive contract with Gallimard) paradoxically made his thought—which had gained an almost classical stature—lose a part of the mysterious and prestigious aura it enjoyed and also contributed to violent reactions. Overall, the climate would change radically with respect to Heidegger in particular, but also more generally; new stars would twinkle in the intellectual firmament. The exposure of those contradictions obliged people to seriously consider questions that the closing decade had not managed to answer clearly: What was Heidegger's true face? How could one deepen the understanding of his thought, and maintain a critical distance so as to avoid polemical rejections and hasty schematizations?

Epilogue I

The first reception of a great thought is always uncanny in its singularity. First there is a name, a shell empty of intuitions that one supposes to be profound and original. This is how the three syllables of that heavily Germanic name struck my ears during the summer of 1954 (I was sixteen), as I leafed through textbooks and books to begin my education in philosophy. Unlike what would have been expected, retrospectively, it was not love at first sight. On the contrary, I did not succumb to its charms, any more during that summer than during my first year of Philosophy. I was taken with Bergson and I became Bergsonian, combining momentarily my Catholicism with a philosophy of vital dynamism. However, André Jacob, my professor at the lycée Lakanal, made me enthusiastic about Heidegger. I remember, not without emotion, the wonder I immediately felt before that young professor who was doing us the honor of thinking before us! For the first time, knowledge was not imposed on us: we were thinking for ourselves! André Jacob's first words are almost literally engraved in my memory: "One traditionally defines philosophy as the love of wisdom. Heidegger proposed the opposite definition: the wisdom of love." This initial reversal was not pursued: a paradox thrown to young minds, overly eager to go farther, it did not lead to any "Heideggerian" development. Jacob considered himself mostly as a follower of Piaget and he was quite eclectic. Thus, this allusion to Heidegger long remained a riddle (that even Jean Beaufret, when questioned later on that matter, could not decipher) until the publication of a course given by Jean Wahl in 1946 allowed me to find the origin of this allusion.

It was above all as a precursor of Sartre that Heidegger was presented, though still mysteriously. To this "atheistic existentialism," I preferred Kierkegaard, even

Jaspers or Simone Weil. A deep believer, I wrote a mystical interpretation of what I knew of Heidegger: I interpreted the opening to being as akin to Simone Weil's concept of "décréation." For a short while during the summer of 1956, I contemplated writing a "mystère" à la Péguy with, as an epigram, this thought of Heidegger's: "The darkening of the world never reaches the clearing of being." I debated the theses of Being and Nothingness *with my friend Jean-Philippe Guinle point by point. The difference between being and beings and the radical encounter with nothingness are the themes I started to discover the following year, in* hypokhâgne,[180] *studying Corbin's book and consulting the volume from 1942 in which de Waelhens summarized* Being and Time. *My professor of philosophy in* hypokhâgne *and in* khâgne, *Jean Brun, who was an eloquent, efficient, and undeclared Protestant, could only have encouraged my attraction for Kierkegaard and Bergson: he had little taste for Heidegger, but did not suppress him or his work. After an oral presentation on "boredom and angst" in which, for the first time, I devoted myself to the reading of "What Is Metaphysics?," he warned me: "Citing Heidegger from the outset and continuously as you have done could get you into trouble!" This was my first exposure to the disturbing nature of the "Heidegger case"!*

I was no less astonished when I attended, dumbfounded, and unaware of all the stakes, a brief confrontation between Jean Beaufret and Jean Wahl at the end of a lecture by Paul Ricoeur on Heidegger and the death of God. This scene took place at the Centre catholique des intellectuels français located on rue Madame, most probably in February or March of 1956. Beaufret, whom I could only see from behind, was in the first row on the left; Wahl was seated in a symmetrical position on the right. The discussion did not bear on the lecture itself. It was a serious summary of the famous Holzwege *text, which had not been translated yet. At the podium, Ricoeur seemed uncomfortable and out of his depth on the occasion of this strange confrontation between Beaufret and Wahl. Insisting on what Heidegger said in Cerisy (and repeatedly pronouncing this name that meant nothing to me at the time), Beaufret would say: "Philosophy is not out of date, it is dead"; Wahl responded: "Unfortunately." Beaufret, in his soft and singular voice, replied: "Fortunately." The misunderstanding was total and heads turned back and forth. I cannot remember how the moderator (Étienne Borne, I think) put an end to that bizarre duel.*

I did not dare approach Beaufret that night. His personality intrigued me all the more as he was a mythical figure in my family: they told me about "cousin Beaufret" without my being able to know exactly what they meant, or how or why my parents had lost contact with him for such a long time. I was told he was a "maverick" who never responded to letters. This left me unsatisfied and curious to know more. The opportunity to satisfy this curiosity came, in the spring 1956, with the publication of one of his books, Le Poème de Parménide. *One could hardly imagine the incredible impression that this little book made on me, among others, for there were many* khâgne *students, at that time, to devour it, dazzled perhaps more by the brilliant and enthusiastic insolence of a new tone than by the content itself, many elements of which remained out of reach (Parmenides's Greek, the problem of the unity of the Poem, the interferences with the reinterpretations of modern philosophy and of Kant in particular). However, what stood out was the idea that Heidegger revolutionized thought through an unprecedented understanding of being itself (distinct from the being of metaphysics, the being of beings, which I discussed as the "God of philosophers"), thanks to the rediscovery of the pre-Socratics. What thus announced itself was a totally renewed interpretation of the history of philosophy. Impossible to classify, Heidegger seemed infinitely more profound to me than Hegel or Schelling.*

This was Jean Beaufret's perspective when I finally met him. Having waited for three months to answer a letter of admiration that I had sent him after much hesitation, he came to the house for lunch with his elderly parents in April 1957 (it was then because of philosophy that my family reconnected with him). On that day and during the meetings that followed (first in a class on Bergson at the École Normale, where Jean Beaufret brought me along with my friend, Jean-Philippe Guinle), we spoke little of Being and Time, *but almost exclusively of the classical authors and the light Heidegger shed on them. Thus Heraclitus was reduced to a universal movement, and thoughtlessly opposed to Parmenides's permanence, when his fragments shimmered with an incredible richness in which the first experience of being as "One-Whole" can be read, prefiguring metaphysics but without its onto-theological structure. Similarly, Aristotle was completely unknown to French idealism: this required a return to the texts, to learn to listen to the Greek with a Greek ear and to decipher the "multiple significations" of being. One had to free oneself from the conventional interpretations of metaphysics and even of their foundations: already the principle of identity was a "leap into being"; Cartesian objectivity was made possible by the cogitative reflection and not the contrary.*

Heidegger appeared, in the course of long conversations with Jean Beaufret, as the only thinker of the twentieth century who was able to appreciate the "monumental continuity" of metaphysics from its Greek origins, and who, beyond conventional academic oppositions such as that between idealism and realism, made the texts as well as the tension they harbor with their "unsaid" speak again. Paradoxically, this patient teaching (which was also constantly polemical toward the standard university interpretations) led one to delve less into Heidegger, at least exclusively, than to reread the great texts of the tradition with new eyes (including Spinoza, on whom Heidegger himself was almost completely silent).

All those dialogues, which were conducted amicably, either at Sceaux or at passage Stendhal, *advanced my knowledge of those authors significantly, encouraged me to study Greek and German, and made me progressively abandon my "early" Bergsonian and Kierkegaardian philosophy. It was through Jean Beaufret that I heard for the first time the name of Althusser, who also seemed to me an un-*

approachable and already mythical character (although he was not yet famous). I could not dare to imagine that I might be a Normalien[181] *and that Althusser would be my "caïman";[182] yet, this is what would come to be after the entrance exam of 1958: during the fall, Beaufret became one of my professors at the École Normale Supérieure (rue d'Ulm). It was thus my destiny to have met him. However, as far as the content was concerned, his "official" teaching did not change my philosophical orientation in any way: I pursued the same interest until I left the École in 1962. I often learned more in "freewheeling" conversations with Jean than through his classes, which were devoted to themes essentially dependent on the program of Agrégation (successively, if my memory does not betray me: Aristotle's metaphysics, Descartes and Leibniz, Kant and his third Critique, Plato's great dialogues), although his style was so unique (a binary rhythm: at times the dictation of a very carefully composed text, at times slow, brilliant, and casual improvisations— "divagations . . . in the Mallarmean sense," Hyppolite would say).*

As far as Heidegger himself was concerned, I read everything that appeared in French (including, as early as 1954, the first translations of the "Chemin de campagne" (Feldweg) and "Sur l'expérience de la pensée" (Die Erfahrung des Denkens) in the NRF edition); I was very impressed by the "Letter on Humanism" and I started to work through a few original texts. I engaged in passionate discussions with Michel Haar, who, in 1960 (I think), suddenly "converted" to become a Heideggerian after having heard a presentation on the Introduction to Metaphysics *(organized, incidentally, by Jean Hyppolite, who in his classes almost spoke more often about Heidegger than Beaufret—though obviously in a more critical way). Should one interpret metaphysics as a forgetfulness of being? How is the Heideggerian reinterpretation of the essence of truth to be understood? Or his "overcoming" of metaphysics? How should one understand the essence of technology? All these questions preoccupied us and would become the themes of discussions that Michel Haar organized with Hubert Dreyfus and even Henri Birault, who was kind enough to join us.*

A great event: during the winter of 1960–61, Sartre gave a private lecture to the philosophers-normaliens. Hyppolite, Merleau-Ponty, and Canguilhem were seated in the first row; I think Jean Beaufret also attended. Althusser was in a corner on the right in the salle des Actes, *surrounded by his friends. After having read one of his unpublished manuscripts on* The Critique of Dialectical Reason *for more than two hours, Sartre took questions. Althusser asked the most difficult questions. At the last moment, as the exchange of questions and answers was about to conclude, I gathered all my courage and dared to ask Sartre more or less the following: "You never responded to Heidegger's critiques in his famous 'Letter on Humanism.' What is your current position toward those critiques?" I expected to be rebuffed in a few words, but to my great surprise, Sartre gave a benevolent and lengthy answer, conceding that he had really not followed the recent evolution of Heidegger toward a philosophy of thinking and poetical language, but that he maintained a great debt to Heidegger, that he still granted him a decisive importance and did not intend to take his objections lightly. He returned to the points of disagreement, but ended by almost apologizing for not having read Heidegger's latest works as of yet. Later, I was told of this piece of Sartre's conversation with Hyppolite and Merleau-Ponty in a café: "Perhaps I should read Heidegger?" Sartre had asked. Hyppolite answered: "But no, you are a genius: you should give priority to the pursuit of your own work."*

From these heights, I had to return to the duties of student life. The inexorable pressure of a foreseeable "fate" (the approach of the Agrégation examination) dampened my passion for reading Heidegger; it was, however, to resurge during my "supplementary year" at the École, in 1961–62: the time in my life when I probably worked most under the inspiration of Jean Beaufret, when I applied myself seriously to learning German and when I was led—almost in spite of myself—to finally meet Heidegger. This was an unquestionable caesura.

6   Renewed Polemics, New Shifts

When it comes to the climate, whether in meteorology or in philosophy, changes can be sudden. At the beginning of the 1960s, the bright spell Heidegger had enjoyed did not of course come to an end in one day. Heidegger's influence continued to inspire original research.[1] The work of translation—distinguished, in particular, by the publication of *Chemins qui ne mènent nulle part*,[2] an important volume published only five years earlier in Germany—continued,[3] but a few signs announced the end of the most favorable years. Furthermore, a page was also being turned in another domain. In politics, the Fifth Republic was being installed, and the Algerian war ended. With respect to the economy, a consumer society was taking shape, growth accelerated, and France was becoming industrialized and "adapted to its time." Similarly, the intellectual and cultural climate changed quite quickly: the *nouvelle vague* in cinema and the *nouveau roman* in literature disrupted the unity of the narrative. Lévi-Strauss, who had already published two major works,[4] was elected in 1959 at the Collège de France, where he delivered the inaugural lecture on January 5, 1960: structuralism made its entry on the intellectual scene. The following year witnessed the sudden death—on May 3rd—of Maurice Merleau-Ponty, whose last works revealed a sustained interest in Heidegger[5] (and who was working on having the Collège de France officially invite Heidegger).[6] That same year, May 1961, Michel Foucault published his thesis, *Madness and Civilization: A History of Insanity in the Age of Reason*, which caused a sensation. There is no reference to Heidegger in this structural study,[7] which situated itself mainly under the patronage of two masters of the theory of myths and of the history of scientific concepts, who were unknown to the German thinker: Georges Dumézil and Georges Canguilhem.[8]

Jean Beaufret gradually realized that he was no longer at the center of the Parisian debates. One unpleasant sign, among others, was Althusser's nonrenewal of his teaching appointment at the École Normale of the rue d'Ulm at the start of the new academic year of 1962.[9] With respect to Heidegger, a certain indifference, which was at first insidious, difficult to identify, and often tainted with hostility,[10] was spreading. More precisely, in 1961, the political polemics returned, unexpectedly, regarding a problem of translation that at first seemed minor.

Inconvenient Documents: The Return of Politics

"Should we translate *Volkswagen* by *voiture de la race* ["race car"]?" Aimé Patri[11] asked, responding to the translation proposed in volume 3 of the journal *Médiations* by Jean-Pierre Faye. This strange question, asked in jest, challenged Faye's translation of the adjective *völkisch* by *raciste*. The stakes were obvious: was Heidegger guilty of racism because he unfortunately yielded to the dominant terminology of 1933? Apart from this problem of translation, it was the question of Heidegger's "Nazism" that was posed once again.

Engaged in a long-term study on the genesis of "ideological speech" in the extreme right wing German discourse,[12] Faye discovered previously unknown texts in Freiburg in 1958–60: statements in support of Hitler, signed by Heidegger while he was rector. On the basis of conversations with young faculty [*Dozenten*], of a citation found in the student newspaper, as well as of a brochure published by Guido Schneeberger,[13] he decided that these forgotten pages were significant and deserved to be brought to the attention of the French public. This occasion was given to him, when he returned to Paris, by Jean-Louis Ferrier, director of the review *Médiations*, who was looking for original texts.[14]

Faye's commentary[15] follows six texts that he translated himself, all dating from 1933, except a "Call to the Labor Service" of January 23, 1934.[16] Formulating first the question that everyone would ask: "How were these statements possible?" Faye immediately focused on a reflection on the linguistic affinities between Heidegger's language and "an all too recognizable ideological language":[17] namely the *völkisch* ideology of the "national-conservatives" and the Nazis. And these affinities fed his perplexity: how is it that the ontological decisionism and the "revolutionary" pathos suddenly tended to coincide? This convergence cannot be explained without reference to the political and social climate in which Heidegger lived in the 1920s: "It was as a contemporary of the revolution of the spartacists and the social democrats . . . that the Heidegger of 1920 engaged himself on the path of a 'phenomenological destruction.'"[18] Relying on the critical reflections formulated after Liberation by Éric Weil and Karl Löwith in *Les Temps Modernes*, Faye supplemented and nuanced them by pointing out that "from *Vom Wesen der Wahrheit* . . . the decisionist pathos . . . is in the process of *returning* toward a renewed language of 'essence.'"[19] The unusual ambivalence of the Heideggerian discourses of 1933–34 was reflected in the expression *völkisch*, which, "more vague, less literally biological than the word 'racist,' bridges the gap between the 'national' and the 'racist' properly speaking."[20]

In the end, Faye's judgment appears to us today to be relatively measured (and certainly much more so than Farias's condemnation): while judging "unbearable" the impression that comes from these calls and speaking of Heidegger's "misfortune,"[21] he in no way reduced his thought to an ordinary Nazism; he clearly emphasized that Heidegger "strongly condemns" biologism, and he even possibly goes too far when asserting that Heidegger's faithfulness to Husserl proves the absence of any anti-Semitism.[22] And he concluded, not without relevance, with a moving allusion to the paradox of Heidegger's "engagement" with Trakl's poetical vision: although his desire (already with this poet and with Hölderlin) was to break with the modern decline, he was forced to participate in "the great weakening of a people."[23]

At the time, Jean-Pierre Faye did not intend, by translating these historically incontestable documents, and by accompanying them with a commentary more or less respectful of the tragic dignity of an authentic thinker,[24] to stir up a controversy. But the fact is that he had just challenged the image, until now relatively spared—at least in France—of a giant of contemporary thought, who had succeeded, for more or less a decade, to reduce, even in his own country, the circle of hostility or suspicion that formed against him after the war.[25]

In private, Jean Beaufret reacted strongly, but—entertaining good relations with Faye until then—he allowed his colleague Patri to voice publicly the Heideggerian response, but not without telling him what was important to say. In a very blunt tone, Aimé Patri first sarcastically mocked Jean-Pierre Faye for "being too late, and for revealing what was already well-known,"[26] then he insisted on the serious error in interpretation that resulted from the translation of *völkisch* by *raciste,* and in the process criticized Jean-François Lyotard for also being guilty of a malevolent inexactitude toward Heidegger.[27] That being said, he had to recognize that Faye's position was not so reductive as to transform Heidegger into an unconditional disciple of Hitlerian anti-Semitism,[28] and he did not refuse to take both the arguments of the defense and those of the prosecution into account. But this concession was immediately withdrawn, because of Faye's "confusion."[29] In the end, he was reproached for using Heidegger's silence since 1934 (on the political question) as a way to fuel hostility against him: had he come out in favor of Stalin—even once—he would have been forgiven for many things![30]

One can hardly understand the virulence of these polemics if one does not place it in the political context of the time: the journal *Le Contrat Social* (in which former communists such as Boris Souvarine and Kostas Papaioannou participated) was virulently anti-Stalinist; the other journal, *Médiations,* directed by Lucien Goldmann, remained Marxist. Heidegger became, at least in part, a "lure" in the settling of accounts in which his thought itself became almost secondary. And yet, the original intention of Faye, who had been a sincere admirer of Heidegger at the outset, was above all to bring new elements of critical reflection to a case that was triggered at the time of Liberation. Aimé Patri, who was himself mistaken when he reduced Heidegger's rectorate to three months,[31] considered himself above the need to inform people about the rector of the University of Freiburg's declaration of allegiance to the Führer. The question of the translation of the word *völkisch* then risks being the tree that conceals the forest. Even if Faye can be criticized on this very point, he was able to show that the adjective *völkisch* has a history and a connotation (different from the substantive *Volk*) that were so influenced by the extreme right wing that its usage was banned after the war and had to be abandoned (which was not the case with the word *Volk*).[32]

The Debate Worsens

The most important episode, however, was yet to come. In addition to the immediate polemical effects, the debate concerning Heidegger's political involvement resurged dramatically, from elements that were not entirely new (because Löwith and Weil had alluded to them and even had quoted a few excerpts), but whose publication was impressive as a whole as well as because of its vehement tone. After reading these texts, one is no longer able to maintain that Heidegger's affiliation with the party had been merely tentative; one is even obliged to recognize that, as Löwith noted, some keywords of these political statements betray, to a certain extent, a troubling terminological analogy with the ontological vocabulary of *Sein und Zeit*.

These hostilities were only the prelude to a more massive attack, coming from Switzerland, and to the polemics that followed and intensified. Given the success of his little book in 1960, Guido Schneeberger published in 1962, at his own expense and in house, a beautiful red hardcover volume containing 217 documents referring to Heidegger's political involvement in 1933–34.[33] This book, which has never been completely translated into French (in the meantime some of the more important documents have been translated), nevertheless abundantly fueled the French debates in the 1960s. Jean Beaufret often referred to it at that time, in his numerous conversations on the subject, to claim that nothing damaging to Heidegger could be found there. François Fédier responded to it a few years later in *Critique*,[34] as well as to two other German publications (the most notable of which was Adorno's *The Jargon of Authenticity*).[35]

Fédier's article aimed to brush aside all the attacks against Heidegger in one fell swoop. This goal was all the more ambitious since this counterattack claimed to be above the fray by revealing the presuppositions of the hostile arguments against Heidegger. To elevate the level of the discourse was, in principle, laudable; to act as if it were not in the context of a polemics seems, however, less tenable. Fédier found himself in a delicate position: although he wanted to appear impartial, he could neither deny the authenticity of the documents produced by Schneeberger nor genuinely set aside the hostility of his adversaries. However, it was understandable to express one's opposition on a more philosophical ground rather than in the context of base polemics. As for Schneeberger, Fédier objected that out of the 217 documents that the book contained, 100 of them (almost half) had no direct relation to Heidegger (newspaper articles, proclamations from students and even from Rudolf Hess) and that 38 others related only indirectly to the philosopher; finally, even among the "direct" documents, only 18 were by Heidegger himself and 17 dated from May 1933 to March 1934. Moreover, from the very beginning of the text, in the second document, the volume contained an excerpt of Madame Toni Cassirer's autobiography, written well after the events and stating that Heidegger had a certain "inclination to anti-Semitism." Fédier emphasized that having placed this very subjective testimony in the book (and the only one referring to the philosopher's anti-Semitism) revealed its biased nature, which did not deserve to be considered objective since it included only hostile testimonies and documents against Heidegger (excluding the fact that he had resigned from his functions as a rector). Its design sought "to present a defamatory image of Heidegger."[36] Schneeberger's book was also silent concerning the attacks on Heidegger as early as 1934–35 from different Nazi groups. Analyzing the presuppositions of the book, Fédier denounced "a socio-political treatment," along with a psychological caricature, with no consideration for Heidegger's evolution (nor for the properly philosophical dimension of his thought). These psycho-sociological presuppositions are confirmed by a moral presupposition that considers the engagement of 1933 as an "absolute" without recognizing that it lasted only ten months and that it had been "strictly conditional."[37]

One sees that Fédier's method is exactly that of an attorney who focuses more on discrediting his opponent than on really addressing the contents of the case. To have succeeded in showing that Schneeberger's book was neither complete nor impartial was for the most part emphasizing the obvious: nobody expected such a book to be published without any ulterior motives. There is still the matter of the texts signed "Heidegger" where he claimed an unconditional allegiance to Hitler: having circumscribed the flaws of Schneeberger's book, Fédier managed to avoid comment with respect to the content of the most embarrassing texts. The same was at stake in his discussion—albeit less detailed—of Adorno's book entitled *The Jargon of Authenticity.* He did not take the opponent's thesis seriously by renewing the debate over Heidegger's *Eigentlichkeit.* Adorno's thesis was reduced to a reflection theory; the jargon was so generally imputed to philosophy that Heidegger himself became one symptom among others of numerous stand-ins for Nazism. Adorno's book, considered as a product of the Marxist reduction of language to an expression of socioeconomical infrastructures, does not seem to present any interest in and of itself. Since Adorno did not make an effort to understand Heidegger,[38] why should he receive any greater consideration?

We will not dwell on the third part of Fédier's article that attacks a clearly mediocre text by Paul Hühnerfeld.[39] However, the last pages are more interesting. Preceding a testimony showing that in his courses from 1935 to 1944, Heidegger had the courage to note how he differed from the regime, Fédier presented, as a return to "reality," a summary of Heidegger's defense, always as an advocate: he did, however, recognize "Heidegger's most serious political failing."[40] But in the same way that the adversaries were reproached for not being sufficiently philosophical, the links between Heidegger's thought and his involvement were not examined.

Fédier's vehement article was nonetheless precise and elegant; it remained a minutely detailed defense of Heidegger the man, and remained silent on the most embarrassing texts. He did not discuss, as he initially claimed he would, the "presuppositions" and the crux of the problem of Heidegger's engagement. If his goal was to control the discourse with a kind of "barrage" responding to the anti-Heideggerian attacks, it was a success. On the contrary, if the aim was to silence Heidegger's opponents through incontestable argumentation, it was a complete failure: he only managed to relaunch a polemic that was smoldering like an unextinguished fire.

In fact, three months later, the same journal published a new issue, "À propos de Heidegger."[41] In a few scathing pages, Robert Minder, an eminent Germanist and a professor at the Collège de France, put his finger on an essential and sensitive point that was ignored by Fédier: the close connections between the language of Heidegger's statements in 1933 and Nazi terminology: "Heidegger literally wallowed in that jargon, just as the cohort of the *Blut- und Bodendichter* themselves wallowed in it, prostrated before Hitler."[42] Minder also recalled that the elegies Heidegger devoted to his fellow citizens of the town of Messkirch, Conradin Kreutzer and above all J.-P. Hebel, put excessive emphasis on the "virtues of the Earth and the dead."[43] Considering Heidegger as a representative of the "malaise of contemporary Germany," Minder imputed a twofold responsibility to the philosopher: his silence after the war only worsened his error of 1933. However, Minder weakened the scope of his intervention by completely neglecting to examine the philosophical dimension of the work that he intended to condemn and that he reduced to the expression of a rustic, reactionary, Swabian Catholicism.[44] Heidegger's style was summarized as a set of puns or verbal tics; above all, Minder did not seem to be able to finally repress his anger, which compromised the scientific nature of his contribution as a linguist: was it necessary to characterize some of the last communications of the elder Heidegger as "ludicrous" or as "ridiculous"? Even if he was not completely wrong to deplore the fact that Heidegger was "sacralized" in France, Minder gave the obvious impression that instead of the balanced and thorough analysis of a work that he himself recognized "will have marked its time,"[45] he succumbed to a kind of allergic reaction.

In the same issue of *Critique,* Jean-Pierre Faye, for his part, responded directly to Fédier.[46] After having referred sarcastically to the "Paris Heideggerians" who protect their Master in the same way that the SPA (Society for the Protection of Animals) protect a special pet, Faye returned in the first part of his response to the problem of the translation of that "very singular word," *völkisch:* the history of the uses of that word, from Fichte to Hitler, including "social Darwinism" and the "German National" party of Ludendorff in the 1920s, carried a heavy connotation that Heidegger could not be unaware of: "Could we possibly imagine Sartre, for example, being unaware of the meaning of the word 'ultra,' after one year of the Algerian war?"[47] The "apologists" portrayed Heidegger either as naive or as ignorant, thus erasing the tragic dimension of a "thinking that was both blind and insightful,"[48] and which allowed its language to be contaminated by the gravest peril.

The second part of the response, less directly polemical, intended to reflect on the complexity of a hermeneutical situation characterized as follows: "Heidegger the ontologist was influenced by semantic usage, forcefully operative at that time, against the obvious and hidden backdrop of a certain economic process."[49] Certainly, after he resigned from the rectorate in February 1934, Heidegger freed himself from direct complicity, but—weakened by the attacks of a certain Krieck, who was rector of Heidelberg—he tried to answer the charges by rejecting the accusation of nihilism and by ascribing it to the errancy of Western metaphysics. Faye went as far as to assert: "What has most fascinated the Parisian left in the work of the late Heidegger, i.e., the fall of Western metaphysics as logos and concept, comes directly from the Rector Krieck." This reductive suggestion was, however, compensated by a conclusion on the complexity of the "transformational levels"[50] of the Heideggerian texts: avoiding both censure and blind defense, one must take Heidegger at his word, and respond to the duty to explicate matters, in the light of a rigorous reading, "under the most dangerous light of day."[51]

These hostilities ended with a new intervention by François Fédier in July 1967.[52] Returning to the translation of the word *völkisch*, a decidedly ultra-sensitive word, he argued that Faye implicitly recognized a general, and not racist, connotation of the term: if the word involves the struggle between two senses, one has to examine Heidegger's use of it "with greater appreciation of its *nuances*."[53] Consequently, in the "German Students" of November 3, 1933, did Heidegger actually intend to speak of the "racist (*völkischer*) vocation of the state"? But the substantive Faye translates by "vocation" is a masculine plural dative (*in den Berufen*). Arguing that in this context it could not mean "vocation," Fédier noted that Faye had to slightly modify the German text to adapt it to his translation (by transposing the masculine plural into a feminine singular). While admitting that Heidegger spoke over the course of ten months using some "contaminated" words, he argued that it was preferable—in the interest of interpretation—not to adopt an external point of view, but to be able to question these texts by constantly relating them to the work of the philosopher.[54]

After having made that point, although on the basis of a position that was less ambitious than it had been previously (since it conceded Heidegger's "philosophical failing" more explicitly),[55] Fédier proceeded in a much less convincing way by challenging Faye on issues of translation:[56] Fédier's purpose was to cleanse Heidegger's language of any contamination by Nazi ideology. It was quite a task to claim that Heidegger was not Hitlerian when he wrote: "The Führer alone is the present and future German reality and its law." For Fédier, Heidegger limited himself in 1933 to believing that Hitler was an authentic leader and his mistake was precisely not to have seen, from that moment on, the real Hitler. That being said, Heidegger's oath of allegiance in 1933 shows that he had been—however briefly—Hitlerian, even if one agrees that this does not imply an adherence to the Nazi *ideology* in its entirety (and, in particular, to the doctrinal racism—a point on which Faye agreed). Reproaching Faye for always choosing the *lectio pessima*, Fédier always chose the *lectio optima*. The fact that it should be necessary to "interpret" the unconditional allegiance to the Führer on the basis of Heidegger's other texts and in the light of his thought does not mean that we should minimize, as much as Fédier did, the extreme and unconditional character of this allegiance. The texts themselves provide extremely embarrassing testimony to this allegiance.

It is time to draw some conclusions about the argument,[57] certain nuances of which may have seemed Byzantine. The discussion seems endless and vain when it loses sight of something essential that Éric Weil had discerned in a magisterial way, in a few pages, as early as 1947. Since the facts were established, the texts known and indisputable, what was the point of the disagreement? With respect to the preferred interpretative method: the apologist favored an internal critique, and the accuser an "inter-semantic" approach. Are the two methods incompatible? One must understand what Heidegger felt he had to accept based on the presuppositions of his thinking (which does not diminish his responsibility) and resituate his personal comments in their historical, semantic, ideological, and even psychological context (although some "allegiances" or "contaminations" appeared then, they seemed less ideological than psychological). The difficulty of finding a balanced view in such a delicate task explains that the debate was destined to return and to intensify.[58]

"And Now, We Will Have to Take Levinas into Account"[59]

Nineteen sixty-one was a decidedly eventful year for Heideggerian matters. Emmanuel Levinas came on the scene with two texts of uneven importance that appeared almost simultaneously: an article about "Heidegger, Gagarin and Us" and his thesis, which would become famous: *Totality and Infinity.*

The article could obviously not be placed at the same level as Levinas's *magnum opus.* Aimed at a readership consisting of nonphilosophers, that of *Information juive*,[60] it was nonetheless very significant. On the occasion of the first successful space flight by Yuri Gagarin on board the vessel *Vostok I,* on April 12, 1961, Levinas proposed a few reflections on technology. They are very polemical and essentially directed against Heidegger, whose critique of contemporary technology was briefly presented as a "declamation"[61] containing, nonetheless, some truths: technology threatens human identity and even the survival of our planet. Was it really necessary to oppose it in order to seek the secret beauty of the world? In this approach (that he presented in a schematic form, while recognizing paradoxically that it was "subtle and new"), Levinas unmasked "the eternal seductiveness of paganism," by clarifying that "Judaism is perhaps no more than but the negation of all that."[62] Consequently, Gagarin's exploit was praised as admirable, for he opened new possibilities for a humanity henceforth capable of liberating itself from belonging to a Place. In diametrical opposition to Heideggerian rootedness (already figured in various forms, before the letter, by Catholicism), Judaism demands the destruction of idols and the demystification of place. In the same way as technology. Hence, Levinas aligned himself with both.

What should we think of this short article? It is absolutely not what one would expect from Levinas. Overly schematizing Heidegger's thinking with respect to technology, Levinas embraced an unconditional "technicism," without recognizing (at least at the end of the text where the initial concessions seemed forgotten) that technology could, in turn, produce idolatry, and moreover without even considering that the concern for the secret of the world does not necessarily entail a contradiction with the respect for the human being in "the nakedness of its face." But this polemical episode should not cause us to forget the main work: *Totality and Infinity*.[63] To believe, however, that this work had a major impact at the time would be a serious mistake. Published by Nijhoff in the Netherlands (thus at a relatively high price, with negligible distribution in France), plagued by quite a large number of typographical mistakes in its first edition, the book was read at first only in limited circles.

However, the henceforth uncompromising opposition to Heideggerian ontology did not escape the specialists, who were all the more aware of this reversal since Levinas had been one of the most enthusiastic early readers of Heidegger's thought in France. Furthermore, if anyone approached *Totality and Infinity* without knowing a thing about Heidegger, many allusions would be lost on him or her. One could even wonder if the main thrust of the text would not be missed in these conditions. Indeed, it is from the outset, in the preface, that Heidegger is targeted: "We do not need obscure fragments of Heraclitus to prove that being reveals itself as war."[64] Ontology is conceived of as the primordial grasp of totality, the affirmation of mastery of beings, the abstract expression of violence and valorization of war. Being itself neutralizes any relation to the Other through an impersonal knowing. By affirming the priority of being over beings, Heideggerian ontology subordinates "the relation with *someone*" to the relation with impersonal being, allowing the domination of beings: it "subordinates justice to freedom."[65] Certainly, Heideggerian ontology is granted a certain "primacy,"[66] a certain radicality as first philosophy, but by that very fact it is rejected, because it reduces the Other to the Same: "Ontology as first philosophy is a philosophy of power."[67] On the contrary, it is metaphysical transcendence, subjectivity, and ethics that are not only revalued, but absolutely affirmed in a radical exteriority prior to any recuperation of identity. Levinas goes beyond any "clearings," any disclosure in the Heideggerian mode[68] in favor of events or "conjunctures" that are indescribable and even go beyond the face.

I will not insist here on the fundamental themes of a philosophy that has become well-known, since we should not let go of the guiding thread of an extremely conflictual relationship with Heidegger. Even limiting ourselves to the analysis of the Heideggerian corpus, which is always present as a foil, it would be possible to identify the details of a rewriting of the existential themes of *Being and Time* in a strictly opposite or in a radically different sense; joy and love of life replace anguish and being-toward-death, sensitivity, enjoyment, and the face-to-face rupture the affective neutrality of beings: "It is interesting to observe that Heidegger does not take the relation of enjoyment into consideration. The implement has entirely masked the usage and the coming to term of satisfaction. *Dasein* in Heidegger is never hungry. Food can be interpreted as an implement only in a world of exploitation."[69] And at the end of the book, it is the infinite nature of fecundity that overflows the possible, and it is the positivity and the novelty of the temporal beginnings that are contrasted with the radical finitude of time and mortality: "It is not the finitude of being that constitutes the essence of time, as Heidegger thought but its infinity."[70]

One has to recognize that Levinas has taken (no doubt half-heartedly at first) a completely radical turn with all of its consequences: Heidegger, whom he had so admired, became the emblematic thinker of totality, as well as of war and violence, in an intolerable complicity with Nazism. A careful study by a historian of contemporary philosophy should be able to show whether this turn led Levinas to exaggerate matters, sometimes by doing violence to the texts, in particular concerning the use of the concepts of "totality" and "violence," which cannot be imposed on the analytic of *Dasein* without betraying it—especially since Levinas failed to address the theme of the call of conscience [*Gewissen*] and solicitude (*Fürsorge*).

But my perspective is not that of a historian of philosophy. It is neither that of a judge deciding whether Levinas—in spite of his concern for justice—has ultimately been unfair to Heidegger. In fact, he never ceased oscillating until the end of his life between nuanced homage and devastating critique. There are two inescapable facts. On the one hand, Levinas himself accepted the consequences of an "anti-Heideggerian" (hence, excessively reactive) reading of *Totality and Infinity*. On the other hand, he had certainly "found his voice" and the relative reserve, which was still apparent in his writings just after Liberation, had disappeared. One saw evidence of ethical concern, of the welcome of the stranger, of the widow, and of the orphan, but without the radical incompatibility with the Heideggerian ontology being emphasized. In this clarification, the decisive turn against Heidegger played an absolutely pivotal role. There is no possible doubt about that, even if the text of *Totality and Infinity* offers other perspectives, and, in particular biblical eschatology, as well as the metaphysical and ethical rereading of Plato or Descartes.

Why has such an important, personal, authentic book taken so much time to become known? No doubt its uncompromising style, its publication in The Hague, and its relatively "confidential" mode of distribution were all factors. But the cryptic nature of the conflictual relation with Heidegger must have also played a role. The resistance from the "Heideggerian circles" was insufficient to discourage the average reader. In fact, it was necessary to have been very well versed in the debate on the "end of ontology" to grasp the profound stakes of the book. And it required the exceptional lucidity of some particularly attentive minds such as Wahl, Ricoeur, Blanchot, or Derrida[71] to recognize that these stakes—apart from any narrowly partisan position—were on par with the most far-reaching intuitions of the Master of Freiburg.

It was precisely this particularly delicate work that Jacques Derrida undertook in 1964 in one of his major texts, "Violence and Metaphysics." It would be a complete mistake to present this essay as a Heideggerian refutation of Levinas. On the contrary, Derrida went to great lengths to take the specifically Levinasian questions into account: the objection to the "violence of light" that phenomenology still relied on following the Western tradition, the opening to the radical difference of the Other conjuring the logic of the Same, the quest for the radical exteriority of transcendence, even beyond the face itself. Nevertheless, Derrida contrasted the revival of metaphysical and ethical transcendence with the essence of metaphysics and Western Logos. He undertook this patient operation by following Levinas's itinerary: "The respectful, moderate reproach directed against Husserl in a Heideggerian style will soon become the main charge of an indictment this time directed against Heidegger, and made with a violence that will not cease to grow."[72] Resituating Levinas's choices in the "powerful architecture" of *Totality and Infinity,* Derrida exposed them to their linguistic and ontological presuppositions: those of a nonviolence that has to assert itself in the very words of an economy that it sought to exceed: the "non-Greek" must speak Greek: "In addition, metaphysics, unable to escape its ancestry in light, always supposes a phenomenology in its very critique of phenomenology, and especially if, like Levinas's metaphysics, it seeks to be discourse and instruction."[73] The metaphysical revival of ethics was less disputed than related to its transcendental preconditions: Derrida undertook a return to the destinal character of the Heideggerian listening to Western metaphysics. "Levinas' metaphysics in a sense presupposes—at least we have attempted to show this—the transcendental phenomenology that it seeks to put into question."[74] The result is that the debate with Heidegger should not be reduced to a frontal contradiction but would require a much deeper dialogue. To have this dialogue, one should first not try to schematize Heidegger's thought under the influence of polemics: to reduce being to a neutral principle, separated from beings, is to misunderstand the ontological difference; to reduce the question of being to an ontology, or to a "philosophy of power," when Heidegger meant to begin again from the very possibility of naming, amounts to being closed to the question of being: "It is thus paradoxical to see the Heideggerian city governed by a neutral power, by an anonymous discourse, that is, by the 'one' (man) whose inauthenticity Heidegger was the first to describe."[75] The "letting-be" in the sense Heidegger understood it does not mean that beings should first be reduced to objects of understanding in order to then speak to the interlocutor: it immediately refers to the possibility of the approach of the other. Further, Levinas, who had been able to recognize the nontheoretical nature of the Heideggerian understanding of being, thereafter identified it as a conceptual knowledge, just as he (wrongly) identified the Same in Heidegger as a generic unity. In fact, through all these polemical operations, Levinas presupposed the very concept of being that he meant to overcome: by so doing, "Levinas confirms Heidegger in his discourse,"[76] that is to say, by virtue of the fact that the very gesture of metaphysics is the forgetting of the ontological difference (metaphysics refuses to pose the question: "What Is Metaphysics?"). From the Heideggerian point of view, it was Levinas who regressed toward a humanism *and* a metaphysics. The question of being, returning to the ground of the great metaphysical distinctions, "is simply forever out of reach"[77] for the operation of the reversal (of ontology) proposed by Levinas. But in the end, if there is a certain legitimacy in Levinas's approach, it is that he returned to the priority of beings within the natural attitude, while imprisoning himself in the contradiction of the affirmation of a pure nonviolence, through which he revealed, by relying on a trans-historicity, his theological intention.[78]

At the end of this extremely dense and subtle confrontation, Derrida identified a relative complicity between Levinas's metaphysics and a certain empiricism, but not without recognizing the dignity of the play between philosophy and nonphilosophy, between the Greek Logos and its other (that never ceases reappearing within the same), and between the Greek and the Jew. He concluded, by quoting the end of Joyce's *Ulysses,* that the extremes (the Jew and the Greek) meet in an undecidability that requires that the indissociable marks of the two heritages be recognized simultaneously in our Western world.

One would also be tempted to characterize Blanchot's writing in terms of undecidability, in its complex relation to Heidegger's influence, an influence that was increasingly questioned due to Levinas. Long before his reflections on the Neutral and quite early on (before 1930), at Strasbourg, Blanchot had been exposed to phenomenological, and then more specifically Heideggerian, themes.[79] These themes can be perceived in *Thomas the Obscure*, although never in the form of a thematic review or of explicit references: "Each time, Thomas was thrust back into the depths of his being by the very words which had haunted him and which he was pursuing as his nightmare and the explanation of his nightmare."[80] If there is, then, an undecidability, it is that of the relation of language to truth and to death. Consciousness is certainly no longer a sovereign self-presence. One can perceive the mute proximity of the existential anguish of the early Heidegger; however, nothing allows us to impute Blanchot's continuous development of a work on the secret and "central point" of literature, namely, the "concentration of ambiguity" and paradoxical opening of *désœuvrement*[81] in Mallarmé, Rilke, Kafka, Hölderlin, and Char, to Heidegger's influence alone. Though these last two names evoke a different Heideggerian "legacy," Blanchot's interest in them developed in an autonomous way, and to such an extent that, as early as 1956, Levinas was able to discern in art, such as Blanchot conceived of it, a very penetrating questioning of Heidegger: "Does Blanchot not attribute to art the function of uprooting the Heideggerian universe?"[82] Blanchot's "turn" away from a thought that undeniably was relevant to his aesthetics[83] thus seemed clearly anterior to *Totality and Infinity*;[84] it would become even more pronounced thereafter. The attention to the most refined nuances of Heideggerian translations[85] did not prevent Blanchot from distancing himself from, among other things, the political involvement of the philosopher (and above all, in this respect, from the very complicities of the philosophical language):[86] anonymous, without reason, without face, without definitive value, the Neutral escapes any grounding, any reappropriation, even that of an originary event. Is the part of night and silence that Blanchot shelters from any ontology, from any "clearing" of being, not evocative of "language in archipelago," which, in Char himself, remains apart from the Heideggerian approach?[87] Even in 1959, Blanchot paid tribute to Heidegger in a few pages for the philosopher's seventieth birthday. This text, entitled "L'attente" (Awaiting),[88] could seem Heideggerian to an overly hasty reader who would only retain, from the title, the connection to the patient endurance of the preparation for *Ereignis*. In fact, this tribute was anything but a show of support. The awaiting according to Blanchot is an impossible, paradoxical waiting, without content, mysterious and ineffable, "without anything being hidden."[89] The question raised by the awaiting even escapes meditative questioning: "It was neither a question that he could find and make his, nor a proper manner of questioning."[90] This is a disconcerting expropriation of the words that were most dear to the thinker, and on his own ground . . .

The debate having been opened by Levinas, and carried on by Blanchot and Derrida, plowed a new furrow into the reading of a work about which it was no longer a question of introducing or even interpreting, but rather of rethinking at its true height, and in its deepest stakes (essentially, the status of metaphysics, the uncovering of its un-thought, the resources of language and writing, and, the possibility of an ethics). These works—closely followed by young students who, like Jean-Luc Nancy and François Warin, did not hesitate to translate Heidegger's difficult pages[91]—sowed new interrogations.

The Text Makes the "Différance"

Were the first writings of Jacques Derrida Heideggerian? That question exceeds the scope of the present work. It has to be formulated in more strictly limited terms: although it is true that the young Derrida, who began his philosophical career with a work on Husserl[92] and who was neither a translator of Heidegger nor a member of Beaufret's circle of close friends, was interested in the Master of Freiburg, can it be said that this interest really marked a stage in the reception of Heideggerian thought in France? An entire part of this interest was expressed in Derrida's teaching at the Sorbonne, where, as an assistant from 1960 to 1964, he gave "entire courses" on Heidegger.[93] Can the signs of this interest be considered as interpretations or as already original reconsiderations? We will address two texts in which the reference to Heidegger is the most explicit: "Ousia and Grammē," in homage to Jean Beaufret, which I will treat of after the lecture "Différance," given January 27, 1968 before the Société française de philosophie.

This lecture was disconcerting for more than one reason. I will not undertake an inventory of the discordances that were deliberately and strategically introduced in the usual philosophical discourse. We have a sufficient number of systems of classifications concerning the connections and caesurae with respect to Heideggerian thought. The title, before one notices its strange orthographic feature, is consonant with the theme of the "ontological difference." The author's skill (should we add his boldness or mischievousness?) is precisely not to have written a lecture *on* this basic question, but to literally have reinscribed it into a text where this question is newly rearticulated against the Heideggerian alliance of the word and of speech. This perspective, which ultimately focused on the Heideggerian Proper (in order to contradict it) confirms, if it was necessary, that it was above all Heidegger with whom Derrida was debating (although Freud and Nietzsche figure importantly as well in this questioning of difference). However, one should obviously add that this lecture cannot be included in the economy of a classically academic "reception." It is unlikely that the great majority of the listeners, or readers, were really able to follow Derrida in this excessively subtle operation of a deconstructive reappropriation of Heideggerian thought, which was focused on one of his most difficult texts, "Anaximander's Saying."

How does the substitution (apparently a misspelling) of a single letter in a single term—even if it is an important word—constitute an event of thought? Could we not see, then, the particularly bizarre Heideggerian use of etymologies and translations taken up again in ways that were as ingenious as baroque by an (almost) too clever doctor? In order to understand this gesture without condemning it too quickly, one should be willing to listen to and to read the "accused."

Although inaudible, *différance* can be marked and remarked upon only through reading: such is the first stratagem, playing on a difference between meaning and trace, between logos and its written form. Let us call this first difference grammatological, insofar as it allusively points, in an orthographic *hapax,* to the critique of logocentrism already undertaken by the young Derrida. With this first difference at the level of the signifier, there is also a second difference that plays within the signified: between *différance* as temporization and *différance* as spacing.

Derrida admits straightaway that this set of distinctions is both "strategic and adventurous."[94] The strategic aim is the introduction of an operation exceeding any ontological and/or theological reappropriation. The adventurous part comes from the absence of any "finality" in this operation (a boldness that will return at the end of the text, with Nietzsche, "in a certain laughter and a certain step of the dance").[95]

How is Heidegger then put into question? He is put into question in two respects, through a gesture that is accomplished with him and that turns against him. With him: to think what differs from any being (even in the form of the being of beings) is to radically criticize the presence of the present and to deconstruct onto-theology (which is constituted as an economy and hierarchy of presence). Against him: the project consists in reinscribing in the play of an endless text the aim of a linguistic reappropriation of a single word (being or *Ereignis*) such that *différance* would no longer appear as an ultimate word, and on the contrary, appearing as a "metaphysical name,"[96] all the while subverting, however, that same metaphysics (of language, within language, and through language).

Such an intense discussion with Heidegger had to be undertaken, according to the very logic of a textual deconstruction, including finding the trace (*Spur*) of the forgetting of being in the 1946 text, "Anaximander's Saying."[97] Without being able to address this reading in detail here, I will note that Derrida's originality does not limit itself to repeating that the forgetting of being reveals itself in its very essence, but rather finds in the Heideggerian deciphering of one of the most enigmatic documents concerning the Greek "origin" of philosophy the play of a trace that is both early and already (barely) erased, a trace of the difference between the present and the withdrawal of its presence. Avoiding "criticizing" Heidegger, but seeking to imbue his text with its "power to provoke,"[98] Derrida went as far as possible in the decryption of the play of a difference, and questioned whether it pertains to being. And this is why he concluded the essay with a radical and elliptical interrogation of one of Heidegger's key sentences: "Being speaks always and everywhere throughout language." Does being speak? For Derrida, it traces itself, writes itself, and disseminates itself. But should one still refer to it as to a subject? The very unity of being is undermined and under erasure. The "Heideggerian hope" (of a proper, unique word) is put into question. By so doing, Derrida uses and turns the play of the crossing out of being [*la rature de l'être*][99] against the master, but he does so on the basis of an *affirmation* (suspending questioning) that we have just seen introduced elliptically with Nietzsche in laughter and dance, without further explanation. Nietzsche against Heidegger, but which Nietzsche? This relation to Heidegger is certainly not easy to "narrate," since it is such a close reading of the Master's text. It does not so much undertake to enrich its "margins" as to displace its literality.

Do we find the same situation in "Ousia and Grammē"? This "note on a note from *Being and Time*" presents itself overtly as a commentary in a classical sense. Before addressing it, it is necessary to recognize how it was included in a book that was a homage to Jean Beaufret. A casual reader could think it is a pure and simple act of allegiance to the inner circle of the French Heideggerian school. This is not at all the case, for the publication of *L'Endurance de la pensée*[100] was not an easy matter. It is necessary to briefly recount its entangled circumstances.

It seemed that it was François Fédier who initiated the project of a volume in homage to Jean Beaufret and was indeed the editor of the project. It is not impossible that the idea was suggested by Heidegger himself, who was fond of the academic practice of the *Festschrift,* which was bestowed on him on his sixtieth birthday. Might not the master have wanted to honor his disciple and friend in this way, even though he never really understood the idiosyncratic, uniquely French, and apparently modest status of a "*khâgne* professor"? Whatever the case may have been, beyond the quite laudable intention to "please" the person concerned and to render him a fitting tribute, this strange initiative (normally appropriate to the retirement of a "distinguished university professor," it did not correspond, in this case, to the retirement of Jean Beaufret, which would take place five years later) seemed to involve the will to express, in relation to Heidegger himself, an exceptional recognition of the intellectual pedagogical and philosophical stature of an authentic master (and in this way to "put to shame" the French academics for not granting him the first rank that he deserved). Well intentioned in principle, this project, controlled by François Fédier, who himself had strangely hidden his role as the "editor" of the volume,[101] would encounter unforeseen obstacles that were quite unpleasant for the "recipient" of an undertaking that had, however, been (almost too) carefully prepared. The project was perhaps too ambitious, and its (relative) failure needs to be carefully considered, even if (and precisely because) a bitter irony emerged. Of course, the volume seems successful if one approaches it without knowing anything about the context. Opening with a page by René Char, who saluted Beaufret as "philosopher of origins" with "eminent presence," it then included Heidegger's important lecture "On Time and Being," followed by a very respectable collection of contributions bringing together authors of diverse renown from France and Germany.[102] But besides the fact that no prominent figures of the French university (or of the German university)[103] of that time were present, one detail should not escape the attention of the careful reader. Maurice Blanchot's text is dedicated to Emmanuel Levinas with this mention, both explicit and disturbing: "For Emmanuel Levinas, with whom, for forty years, I have been linked by a friendship that is closer to me than I am to myself: in a relation of invisibility with Judaism." Thus is not the "gift" singularly "poisoned"? Is that the fate of any *gift*? Or does this gift, in particular, not indicate, in spite of itself, its "lacks" or un-said, if only through the typographical error that had surreptitiously slid into Parmenides's epigraph?[104] How could good intentions have resulted in this strange situation that could only engender malaise or, at least, confusion? What one absolutely wanted to avoid took place, as the return of the repressed (Heidegger's "Nazism" in the form of an anti-Semitism that he would have "bequeathed"—or passed on—to his disciple and friend). I will not arbitrate what had become the first *affaire Beaufret*[105] and the fall of the noble quest for truth in a succession of accusations and of exonerations where *L'Endurance de la pensée* seemed to be symbolically put through the mill. Briefly put: Roger Laporte, thinking he heard Jean Beaufret making an anti-Semitic remark, reported it to Jacques Derrida, who became upset and wrote to Fédier. The latter protested and asserted Beaufret's innocence. Maurice Blanchot, also informed, considered pulling his text from the collection. Beaufret, accusing Laporte of slander, justified himself to Derrida and Deguy. Blanchot's and Derrida's texts barely made it into the collection, but Blanchot added the dedication to Levinas along with a justification.[106]

Much ado about (almost) nothing? It is impossible not to mention this succession of incidents that one should neither exaggerate nor underplay. Even if public rumor did not benefit from adjudication of this "matter," the textual trace deliberately left by Blanchot would deserve some clarification. And this information is necessary to understand how and why Jacques Derrida kept his text in the volume, thus recognizing (in spite of everything) his debt toward his former professor at the École Normale Supérieure. To overemphasize the incident would be, additionally, to erase this recognition of debt, and to risk, as well, causing Derrida's very important text to be forgotten, despite its ironically modest subtitle.

This "Note on a Note from *Being and Time*"[107] is in fact far from unimportant. We can give only an incomplete account of it here. What is striking at the outset is the accuracy of Derrida's "insight," which located a crucial passage from paragraph 82 of Heidegger's master work.[108] Although it appears to be concerned only with Hegel's debt toward Aristotle in the determination of the now, of the limit, of the point, and of the "this," this note raises anew the meaning of being as presence of the present throughout the history of metaphysics. On the basis of a very careful commentary on its literality, on its references and allusions, Derrida succeeded in widening the horizon to the very limits of the enclosure that metaphysics circumscribed by privileging the now, as a result both of the "self-evident" character of the ordinary concept of time and of the "exorbitant privilege"[109] afforded to the "now" by Western thought, from Parmenides and Aristotle to Hegel and Bergson. Could this privilege of the present be "destroyed"? Although it seems obvious and steadfast, nevertheless, this privilege can be deconstructed, insofar as, by thinking what could not have been thought, one will produce "a certain difference, a certain trembling, a certain decentering that is not the position of an other center."[110] Applying a meticulous double reading that was not immediately apparent, Derrida first proposed a new "paraphrase" of Heidegger's text and of its harmonics, showing the extent to which the analyses in Book IV of Aristotle's *Physics* are determinative for the establishment of the traditional concept of time as "number of movement" (and in this way Derrida followed in Heidegger's footsteps), but he also initiated in these very analyses the discernment of premises of an "instability" that the author of *Being and Time* would have controlled.[111] Thus, he gradually inserted into the scrupulous commentary on the Heideggerian note a text that overflows or exceeds it, a text that, while claiming to work within the Heideggerian question, displaced it. It is indeed the theme of the oblivion of being that was being transposed into the theme of (the trace) of the erasure of the trace in the metaphysical text, so that the elliptic conclusion points at a difference that is even more unthought than the difference between being and beings: the unsettling *différance* that would be "the first or the last trace."[112]

This is an important text, but a very strange homage to Jean Beaufret! We first encountered it in its context; we can understand it better now on the basis of a reading that reveals the extent to which Derrida undertook a work of critique from within, with virtuosity, a work that until then had not been accomplished by the French Heideggerians. Further, a note denounced both "the camp of Heideggerian devotion and the camp of anti-Heideggerianism," allied "in the same refusal to read."[113] We will have to return to it to clarify how Derrida inscribed, more and more vigorously, the singularity of his themes in an intellectual concert that often became cacophonous.

Between Things and Words: From Foucault to Lacan

Among all the contributions that added, in the most intense moments of the sixties, to the complexity of the debates owing to an intellectual inventiveness that was labeled "structuralist" too hastily, one led Michel Foucault to present a brilliantly erudite history of the life sciences, of political economy, and of language as a genealogy of the "death of man." It is essentially in the tradition of Nietzsche that the author of the successful although austere book called *Les Mots et les Choses* situated himself when he reflected on the "uprooting of Anthropology"[114] to which contemporary thought seemed (to him) to be devoted. As was the case in the thesis on madness, Heidegger is never cited. Should we, nonetheless, suspect his hidden presence in the critical distance from humanism, but above all in the genealogical undertaking that redefines the caesura of modern rationality? Emphasized and systematized, this hypothesis becomes an interpretative frame that is no doubt too ambitious, recomposing Foucault's itinerary and even indicating a somewhat Heideggerian "turn."[115] The risk is then to transform a useful reference into a *cliché*. Foucault himself confessed, a short time before he died: "My whole philosophical development was determined by my reading of Heidegger"; he nevertheless added the following, which considerably attenuates the scope of these words: "I nevertheless recognize that Nietzsche outweighed him. I do not know Heidegger well enough: I hardly know *Being and Time* nor what has been published recently."[116] This ambivalent confession does not permit one to distinguish between those who want to "Heideggerianize" Foucault and those who refuse to do so. As he asserted in the interview we just cited, there is no question that Foucault read Heidegger as early as 1951 or 1952. That Nietzsche "prevailed" is an obvious fact confirmed constantly by the reading of the work in its totality. There remains, as far as the relation to Heidegger's thought is concerned, an immense margin of uncertainty that it is important to be able to recognize rather than question. In this respect, Hubert Dreyfus seemed to have gone too far in the connection he established between Heideggerian being and Foucaldian power. To read Heideggerian ontology as "the unthought of Foucault's *œuvre*" requires hermeneutical and scrupulously critical deciphering work.[117] A "happy positivist," who occasionally cited René Char (which was not that frequent in the neopositivist circles), Foucault was too intelligent and too lucid to have "censured" Heidegger's name and direct references to his themes, without consideration or cause. The work, such as it is, is silent on this point, although its constant concern to draw the limits of rationality and to establish its genealogy could be interpreted as the most subtle of "positive" translations of an essentially Heideggerian questioning.

Things are different with Lacan. In spite of his taste for the secret, or even for mystification, he offered, in the matter, some traces and testimonies that can be identified more easily despite their constantly cryptic opacity. First of all, commentators have not been inattentive to the facts and events attesting to Lacan's interest in Heidegger's work beyond the first "existentialist" approaches. Did the fact that he became Jean Beaufret's psychoanalyst in April 1951[118] provide an initial access to a formidably hieroglyphic thought? Yet, the "cure," soon interrupted, gave way to a very Parisian friendship rather than to a genuine philosophical exchange, despite some efforts.[119] Did a visit to Freiburg in 1955, as well as the hospitality offered that same year to the authoritative Master, on the occasion of the famous conference of Cerisy (which Lacan did not attend), indicate more than a fascination toward an oracle from which one grasps fragments? It is necessary, no doubt, to return to the texts, which, as it turns out, provide less information than one would have hoped.

In the intellectual fireworks of the sixties in Paris, the highpoint was probably the publication of Jacques Lacan's *Écrits*. Produced thanks to the efforts of François Wahl and Jacques-Alain Miller, this huge book contained a collection of articles and interventions of the mysterious doctor whose seminar had been attracting intellectuals in Paris for years already. It contained thirty-four titles, with some unpublished texts.[120] If we keep to the letter of the text, the relation to Heidegger's thought comes up only incidentally. However, Lacan is not someone who would allow just anything to appear in his texts, so that the least allusion requires a decoding, which, in turn, indicates a path of research that until now had not been considered.[121]

In "The Seminar on 'the *Purloined Letter*,'" we read: "Thus, when we are open to hearing the way which Martin Heidegger uncovers for us in the word *aletheia* the play of truth, we narrowly rediscover a secret to which truth has always initiated her lovers, and through which they have learned that it is in hiding that she offers herself to them *most truly*."[122]

This valuable (since it is rare) allusion to Heidegger deserves to be savored as such and demands to be examined according to its scholarly intentions. One should note that, far from clarifying the paradox of the "Purloined Letter" (invisible because it is so obvious) on the basis of the Heideggerian understanding of *aletheia*, it submits the discovery of the word "truth" to the always valid logical paradox of a hide-and-seek game in which what seems to be "the most true" is known only to its "lovers." Nothing was more foreign to Heidegger than such eroticized mind games in social circles that would be more germane to the eighteenth century than to any so-called original Greek thought.

Thus, more than the parsimony of allusions, it is the very nature of this wink that should caution us from "acceding" to the Heideggerian hermeneutic field. It is extremely difficult (and it would most probably be in vain) to want to decide whether this allusion is a kind of *coquetterie* (precisely since this kind of step is never so simple), or if it is not rather, in the guise of a tribute, the mischievous reduction of the Heideggerian discovery of a key word to a kind of eternal truth for a few privileged minds, or if—third possibility—it manifests a profound fascination masked by the veil of ellipsis, for fear of misunderstanding.

Nothing would be more superficial and vain than to begin a quest for traces of Heideggerianism in Lacan. This is, incidentally, what a knowledgeable interpreter, Gérard Granel, avoided. While devoting a text to "Lacan and Heidegger,"[123] he avoided any comparisons[124] and on the contrary emphasized the distance [*Entfernung*] between both thinkers. He showed that it is the same refusal to treat humans as objects that is at stake in both cases, an extreme attention paid to the "gestures of language in language."[125] And the unexpected "fraternity" that Granel discerned between Lacan and Heidegger, despite everything, concerned the very idea of science with regard to its "subject" as well as its "model": "The subject of science is the narcissistic constitution of the Western World."[126] To exorcize this historical fixation in a new way, Granel proposed and outlined a new epistemo-logical task beyond the currently authorized disciplines.

In any case, Lacan himself, as if he were extraordinarily sensitive to the precious singularity of the Heideggerian thought, showed a discretion and a prudence that was unusual for him.[127] His only audacity—which was quite significant—was to publish a very personal translation of the essay "Logos." In May 1957, at the end of "The Agency of the Letter in the Unconscious," discerning in Freud the "symptom of and prelude to a reexamination of man's situation in the midst of beings [*dans l'étant*]," he forestalled, with a conspicuous verve,[128] any "neo-Heideggerian" labeling of the perspective thus advanced, concluding nonetheless this clarification with a strong tribute: "When I speak of Heidegger, or rather when I translate him, I strive to preserve the sovereign signifyingness of the speech he proffers."[129]

A master of sovereign utterance allows us to appreciate that more sovereign still is the word whose oracle is in Freiburg. This also clarifies that the effort of translation is to be taken seriously as well as taken as a homage that is superior to any ordinary reference or allegiance. The translation of "Logos" was thus not unimportant, although the Heideggerians made no comment on it.[130] Strange and very "Lacanian" through its apparently unusual choices and further encryption of the original text, this attempt could only have discouraged the reader further, given that Heidegger's text was not an easy one to begin with. More poetical than pedagogical, but especially thoughtful, this translation merits our full attention.

Without attempting to "summarize" Heidegger's words in this text, let us indicate the main orientation: what is at stake is to rethink the very meaning of logos from what is probably Heraclitus's most celebrated fragment.[131] To recognize the ordinary and prevailing sense of the verb *legein* (to speak, to say, to tell) does not prevent one from mentioning a sense that is at least as archaic (and understood as more originary by Heidegger): to gather (in the sense of the Latin *legere:* "to lay in order to gather"). Two German verbs are then used to restore the rich semantic range of *legein: lesen* (to gather, to read) and *legen* (to lay, to lay out), which, it is noted, is homonymic with the Greek word. How is it possible to conceive of the unity of this meaning? Does the saying allow itself to be thought as the Laying that gathers [*La Pose recueillante*]?[132] If this was the original meaning, how did it come to signify speech? Returning to Heraclitus's sentence, Heidegger suggested that the listening to the One-All to which we are invited is that of the truth of being, which was unthought by the Greeks and even by Heraclitus: the Laying that gathers of logos is the sheltering of *aletheia*. As in a lightning bolt, one thus catches a glimpse of "the storm of being"; our task is now to think what first imposed itself as destiny.

Aware of the risks and after having warned the reader,[133] Lacan undertook a bold initial move: translating the German verb *legen* by *legs* [legacy]. This was apparently an arbitrary suggestion, though ingenious, for in the French, it is a play on the homonymy (or homophony) evoked by Heidegger with respect the Greek *legein* and the German *legen*. Lacan defended himself by translating *legen* more adequately by "putting to rest" and emphasizing that "he uses a spontaneous equivocation of our language" (between legacy [*legs*], lay [*lais*], letting [*laisser*]).[134]

Obviously, Lacan enjoyed taking Heidegger at his word and adding to his disconcerting language games, causing them to proliferate in French, almost *ad infinitum*, without one being able to know exactly when the quest for the originary stops and when the puns begin. One should be able to follow, in all of its details, this high-stakes game in which Jean Bollack discerned a salutary and liberating subversion of the Heideggerian account of the Greek origin that privileged the authenticity of the German language: "Lacan's translating method is very free and high-handed. He wrenches the text in the direction of science, art, and language and accords more importance to hearing than to speech. He adds a touch of Mallarmé."[135]

Indeed, when Lacan retranslated the Heideggerian translation of the Heraclitean logos [*die lesende Lege*] by the "lay in which what is being elected becomes legible" [*le lais où se lit ce qui s'élit*],[136] he almost succeeded in using the French language in a completely unexpected, albeit baroque way, and at the cost of a radical departure from the ontological gathering of the "Laying that gathers," as André Préau would translate it more literally. The stakes, as Bollack pointed out, was the interpretation of Heraclitus and—on that basis—the philosophical decision to be taken: was it necessary to follow Heidegger in his ontological conception of language?[137] One would look in vain for an explicit response from Lacan, who took great care to respect Heidegger from a distance and to maintain toward him the dignity of a power addressing another power.

The fact is that until now there have been very few readers, even among the most experienced philosophers and psychoanalysts, of this outstanding translation by Lacan. One can regret this while appreciating that such a cultivated singularity could discourage readers. From a more general perspective, one should certainly be able to recognize the unexpected complicity between Lacan and Heidegger with respect to the originary ground of a revelatory truth that, far from being reduced to enunciation, conceals as much as it shows, such that the theory of repression as the truth of desire becomes intelligible in terms of the Heideggerian *aletheia*. In this sense, some have gone as far as to assert that "Heidegger dominates Lacan's entire strategy."[138] However, as one has judiciously noted elsewhere, "Lacan's truth, no matter how unfathomable and repressed, remains none the less the truth of a desire—that is, of a *subject*."[139] Between this theory of the speaking subject (an auto-enunciation that has to elucidate its desire) and Heidegger's nonsubjective approach to language, there is a greater distance between them, finally, than the signs of proximity and compatibility have indicated.

Such is the esoteric other side of a reception that has been, on the contrary, often trivialized. Throughout this chapter we have established its anguished character[140] (which we would still need to analyze further), which is strangely punctuated by discreet inflexions,[141] unexpected[142] latencies and caesurae, which will undergo new developments after 1968.

* * *

Epilogue II

I have said that my first encounter with Heidegger, in early June 1962, was almost imposed on me. I would never have dared to disturb the great thinker unless exceptional circumstances had constrained me to do so. The sudden death of my father had put an end to my language instruction near Lake Constance. Sensing my disarray, Jean Beaufret strongly advised me to go back to Germany by way of Freiburg. A letter was to precede my arrival and prepare the way for my meeting with the Master.

With respect to this meeting, which was approached apprehensively by a shy young man, I will only focus on what pertains to the relation of the Master to French thought. Not daring to ask fundamental questions, and assuming that Heidegger did not intend to hold a work session with me, I answered his amiable questions about Jean Beaufret, my life as a Parisian student, and the philosophical situation in France. What were Wahl, Hyppolite, and the Parisian professors doing? He most appreciated my report on Sartre since it was of greatest interest to him, namely the lecture Sartre had given the previous year at the École Normale mentioned in Epilogue I.

The Master was very glad to hear this story. He asked about the news from Paris as would the people of the countryside who enjoy a calm and regular life, far from the capital of which they had formed a mythic idea. Anxious to ensure that his Nietzsche volumes were well translated, he asked me about Pierre Klossowski, the translator who had been proposed by Gallimard, and seemed very interested to learn that he was a maverick, well-read, and an author of somewhat mystical and inventive libertine stories. Evoking Kostas Axelos's name warmly, he seemed amused by a sentence of his about "the erotic life of Heraclitus." More seriously, the conversation also included Kant and interpretations that I was able to recall: he seemed surprised by Jules Vuillemin's reduction of the Kantbuch *to an exclusive treatment of the transcendental Aesthetics: "No, really?" he asked with an air of incredulity. He showed me the books he loved (Kommerell, Jünger, Stifter). He opened his copy of Ernst Jünger's* Der Arbeiter, *to which he had devoted a seminar: the important passages were underlined in red, blue, and yellow, as if the text had been submitted to a thorough X-ray revealing its various layers of meaning!*

Seeing me out after more than an hour of conversation, Heidegger found Jean Beaufret's letter that was supposed to announce and introduce me in the mail box. Jean was indeed always late! This contretemps *made the Master smile one last time and filled me retrospectively with confusion: I had dared to knock at his door and to disturb him without having been announced! I only had one wish: to continue my trip and to discover a stream or a swimming pool, to swim in fresh water to gather my spirits . . .*

When I saw Heidegger again, almost one month later in his hometown of Messkirch, I had gained some confidence and I was able to ask questions about Hölderlin, Nietzsche, Plato, and Kant. The conversation was less concerned with France and the French philosophers. But I remember that Heidegger seemed surprised to learn that Jean Guitton had wanted to join the Académie française (clearly, this institution did not mean anything to him); more significantly, he asked me questions about structuralism: he wanted to know exactly what that label meant. I did my best, although not being knowledgeable enough to satisfy him completely!

What lessons shall we draw from these encounters for our inquiry? I have never overestimated their philosophical importance, neither at that time, nor since. They did not change my admiration, nor my subsequent concerns about the thinker. They simply—and this is not trivial—played an important role in modifying the image I had of the man as a great German authoritarian and magisterial professor. The man I encountered was not at all like that (I am not the only one to have noted it). He was short, active, mischievous, with an unforgettably penetrating gaze, very attentive to his interlocutor, giving the impression of being friendly, and able to be humble enough to learn from another person, the very opposite of a pontificating Master. Undoubtedly, he could play several characters; but I felt a fragility, even a shyness, a reserve, which was quite surprising when one thinks of the demonized image his opponents have spread.

His interest in what was taking place in France appeared to be genuine. Having become well-known early on in our country, having made friends there (not only with Jean Beaufret and his close associates), he showed a real admiration toward the French intelligentsia that was tempered by a critical distance. We have seen how, after the war, he found a kind of antidote in and consolation from his exchanges with "die Franzosen." Of course, the cynics would say it was in his own interest; and it is probable that he hardly read French works (and nor even his

German contemporaries . . .). But sometimes heart and reason are in unison. Heidegger would not have known such a sustained and multifaceted glory in France if his interlocutors, on this side of the Rhine, had felt only reserve and hostility from him. Those who exploited his praise of the German language to suggest that he despised all kinds of non-Germanic thought were mistaken. And first, the thinker who was so attached to great texts could not ignore the heritage of Descartes and Pascal (cited in French in Sein und Zeit); the admirer of Nietzsche could not completely ignore or disapprove of the tributes that the author of Zarathustra addressed to the moralists of the Enlightenment: to Bayle, to Fontenelle, to Voltaire, and to Stendhal. If there was a German philosopher permeated by historicity, it was Heidegger; that is why the dialogue he had with French thought was essential for him, for it was the very opening of the space of listening in which the fate of modernity unfolded between rationality (in which France excelled, at least in principle . . .) and the Germanic concern for the fundamental and the originary. But this "polarity" is recalled only for the sake of context. Why, in this matter, should we yield to clichés that bar access to the most essential thoughts? Heidegger also read the French poets, including, among others, Baudelaire, Rimbaud, Mallarmé, Valéry, and René Char, who was to become his friend.

As for me, more modestly, my encounters with the Master could only have been an incentive to improve my German so as not to be dependent on translations. I then immersed myself in the Nietzsche volumes (whose translation appeared only in 1971), especially the second volume, more decisively turned toward the future (the determination of nihilism and the question of the overcoming of metaphysics). My readings of Heidegger—in particular, Unterwegs zur Sprache, Der Satz vom Grund*—constantly accompanied the more "academic" work that I undertook for my thesis on "Hegel and the Destiny of Greece." I have never worked more closely with Jean Beaufret than at the end of my time at rue d'Ulm, in 1961–62, during the extra year Althusser granted me after my* agrégation*: I began making constant connections between the great texts (first those of Aristotle) and Heidegger. Noticing, however, for the first time, a reserve or hostility among some of the students and* normaliens *toward Beaufret, I wrote in my notebook: "If a Frenchman had spoken in an intelligent manner and faithfully of Hegel in Paris in 1820, would he have received any better welcome?" Returning to this today, my judgment would be more nuanced: the hesitancies of most of the* normaliens *did not only concern Heidegger, but also Beaufret's style, which was considered to be inappropriate for* agrégation*. Half the time he improvised. Too many of his allusions escaped most people: he was a fireworks display with rockets bursting out in Greek, German, and everything was being done to discourage the uninitiated. Sensitive to this brio, always happy to catch an essential thought in the making, I was not shocked by his casual approach; on the contrary, it seemed to me to be one of the qualities of somebody I deeply admired and who was, incidentally (in his unconventional manner), an admirable* *pedagogue. Moreover, I did not perceive any hostility coming from Althusser, but rather a distant sympathy: very kindly, he had established a convivial atmosphere that pleasantly surprised me: "We are in the same situation: Marx and Heidegger are both excluded from the University," he confided to me.*

Althusser was certainly not motivated by a personal hostility when, at the new term of 1962, he did not renew the classes Beaufret had been teaching for more than fifteen years: coinciding with my departure from the École, the disaffection of the normaliens *was obvious: most philosophers were turning toward Althusser himself, Canguilhem, or even Lacan, and the* Cahiers pour l'Analyse *was founded, articulating a Marxist reading of epistemology through a structural interpretation of Marxism. Twenty-three years of age at the time and thinking mostly of the future, I did not feel that I belonged to any "Heideggerian old guard," an expression I find, in retrospect, quite funny, if it is true that this "old guard," in the eyes of our slightly younger colleagues, was essentially composed of Michel Haar and of myself!*

Peace was declared in Algeria: I had worked with the socialist left (a breakaway group from the SFIO party, the French Section of International Workers) in order to achieve this goal; but—an irony of history—it was obtained thanks to de Gaulle; a page was turned; other tasks, new curiosities, emerged.

I was not overly concerned by this transition; I had prepared myself for it in two ways: with Heidegger's thought itself and with Jean Beaufret's "ultra-minority" mentality. Was the age of Technology not the reign of nihilism? It was to be expected that authentic thought would remain unknown. As for the French university, it remained stuck in its habitual patterns: a self-satisfaction and a rhetoric that a nonconformist professor of khâgne *used to laugh at. He was brilliant, almost famous because of his exceptional friendship with the greatest philosopher of the century, and—furthermore—he was surrounded by disciples (which was generally not the case with respect to the professors at the Sorbonne). Consequently, I was in no way put off or shocked by Jean Beaufret's quasi-marginal situation: the joy of listening to him, the force of his knowledge and of his kindness, the youth that surrounded him: was that not equal to all the Sorbonnes of the world?*

How did this situation evolve between 1962 and 1968? Without returning to the changes in the Parisian intellectual climate, what was the situation in the more restricted circle that I am considering here? Nothing was too overwhelming or shocking. With respect to Beaufret, the retreat to the khâgne *at Condorcet and to the circle of the faithful was perhaps conducive to a routine, interrupted by two or three trips to Freiburg each year; the wings of glory and carefree readings were reined in, to do research and gain some "distance." However, on April 21, 1964, in the large hall of the UNESCO headquarters, which was completely packed, Jean Beaufret took his place at the head table next to Jean-Paul Sartre and Gabriel Marcel. The occasion was a tribute to Kierkegaard. It was almost like a dress rehearsal of some of the events of May '68: the crowd of students, who had been excluded from the room reserved for the invited guests, violently clamored at the doors and succeeded in forcing their way in; they settled on the steps and overflowed throughout the room. What accounted for this almost insurrectional insistence? Was it to listen to Sartre, who delivered a remarkable text—"Questions of Method"—in a dry and monotone voice that was too difficult for an otherwise quiet and respectful audience? What about Beaufret? He spoke "on behalf of" Heidegger who had asked him to translate a lecture that had nothing to do with Kierkegaard: "The End of Philosophy and the Task of Thinking" (subsequently published, along with Sartre's text, in* Kierkegaard vivant *by Gallimard). Beaufret read this very "Heideggerian" text slowly, and as it were with devotion. The master made no accommodation to any audience. Heidegger undertook, however, a very interesting self-critique of his interpretation of truth in Parmenides, referring to the* Lichtung *(the "clearing of unconcealment"). But as for the audience, Beaufret might as well have been from another planet. I was quite aware of it at the moment and was sincerely distressed, noticing the incredible gap between the importance of this text and the catastrophic impression that it made on the audience. A short while after, in October of the same year, 1964, in Royaumont, during a Hegelian symposium, I had the unpleasant occasion to hear Hyppolite tell Gadamer about this session: "It was a caricature of the caricature" (to be clear: a caricature by Beaufret's translation of Heidegger's caricature of himself). I completely disagreed with this judgment, whose sincerity or motives I did not question (for if the translation in question, made in collaboration with François Fédier, was accurate, it had no pedagogical virtue; as for the text, it was not adapted to the circumstance at all, and Heidegger had made no effort in that regard). Thus the gap became abysmally more obvious, and although it had nothing to do with the political question, that question would only widen it further. At the same time, it seemed that everything was conspiring to increasingly isolate Jean Beaufret as well as the people close to him: it was an irresistible phenomenon of fragmentation, where fate and the quasi-mechanical effects of a psychosocial logic of "isolation" reinforced each other. The word "sect" had always been used with malevolence by adversaries. There had never been, on Jean Beaufret's part, the least authoritarian or sacral affectation of a guru, or attitude of "devotion" from the faithful of the "inner circle," properly speaking. Everything was philosophical, free, and disinterested, in the erudite or critical discussion and the Socratic exchanges punctuated by anecdotes: this was what I always experienced. Why, then, these misunderstandings, these accusations that would only worsen until the intolerable and pathetic* affaire Beaufret *that began in 1967–68, according to Christophe Bident in his book on Blanchot? Having followed the genesis of the* Festschrift *to Jean Beaufret from a distance, entitled* L'endurance de la pensée *[The endurance of thought] (not having been associated in any way with this project), I can provide only a limited testimony. No longer living in Paris, I heard only Jean Beaufret's version, in which he depicted himself as a victim of slander and persecu-*

tion. What is certain is that, far from trying to escape his psychological isolation, he was doing everything (without being aware of it?) to sink into it even more.

While respecting his courageous support of Heidegger and his work, I understood less and less its unconditional nature, and—already for several years- I tried unsuccessfully to introduce more flexibility and a critical distance in our conversations (they became more and more sporadic because of my military service, my stay at the Fondation Thiers, but mostly due to my academic appointment in Nice dating from the fall of 1966). Simple common sense, sustained by a sound and critical philosophical tradition, seemed to recommend a disjunction (which was accepted and even thematized by Heidegger himself) between life and work: a great thinker could have personal weaknesses (Jean admitted this only in relation to the several months of the political error in relation to the rectorate). However, the recognition of the "historical" importance of his thought did not imply an allegiance to all of his theses: even the thinker Heidegger remained fallible! Of course, Beaufret did not deny this in principle, and he never went so far as to grant the Master of Freiburg "pontifical infallibility" in any sense. Further, in daily practice and in the very exercise of argumentation, it was always the defense that prevailed over criticism (which at times allowed for minor concessions). Consequently, one was getting tired of exercising a censorship that would unavoidably encounter a series of obstacles (for one had to follow the extremely slow and convoluted rhythm of the conversation). One should not overlook all the knowledge, the intelligence, the presence of mind and the humor that Jean placed at the service of this good cause (which he instead presented as the correction of misunderstandings, of the malevolencies, and of the "rubbish" repeated about Heidegger). Nonetheless, his extreme concern for details, his deep and sincere friendship for Heidegger the man, his approach to personal relations such as one would find in a local village (he was from the department of the Creuse), sometimes made him go astray, a nearby tree occluding the forest. And the result was, over the course of the years, an increasingly inextricable blending of the personal and the philosophical, the anecdotal and the essential.

I felt it was an opportune time to take some distance. But that was not really a "solution." It was a stopgap measure.

At the same time, if my work at the Fondation Thiers on an almost unknown philosopher, Ravaisson, seemed to distance me from Heidegger, I was very aware of the metaphysical character of this thought and I started to discreetly sow, in a part of the history of philosophy (that had not been explored until then), seeds from a Germanic ground.

It was also necessary to pursue other ways to access or critique Heidegger's thought: in 1965, informal discussions took place at the Fondation Thiers with Jacques Derrida, Hubert Dreyfus, and Michel Haar. However, we hardly addressed the reinterpretations of the metaphysical tradition (which were Jean Beaufret's main concern, since he was reluctant to take Heidegger's more personal questions seriously: even in his reading of Sein und Zeit, *the pages on conscience, being-guilty, and* Fürsorge *did not seem to retain his attention for long). Other questions interested us more: Did* Sein und Zeit *succeed in overcoming the anthropological point of view? Is "authenticity" possible, and how? As appropriation? Under what conditions? How should one conceive of the famous "turn," its connection with the political mistake, the essence of technology? Could one overcome nihilism? I list these questions in no particular order, not to give an exhaustive or faithful list of them, but to show the directions our friendly discussions took, discussions that were not arguments, but rather provocations, stimulations, and common research projects: moments of philosophical joy that one could only hope to recreate again at another time, in another place!*

7 Dissemination or Reconstruction?

THE YEARS THAT led from the events of 1968 to the death of the Master in 1976 cannot be characterized in one way. On the contrary, the French reception of Heidegger split up into different, if not contradictory, camps. The appropriation of his thinking became dogmatic in each camp, each closing in upon itself; marginalizations, and indeed, excommunications, proliferated. In acknowledging this dissemination, we are not forgetting what this allusion to the title of Jacques Derrida's book (which appeared in 1972) connotes:[1] threads become woven with more specialized research and with Heidegger's most difficult, ambitious, and inapparent themes; one should neither sever them nor forget them. But did this "dissemination" foreshadow a reconstruction of the philosophical landscape?

Mysterious Barricades

If we borrow this expression from François Couperin, it is because he liked to give his compositions for harpsichord poetic and fantastic titles, whose secrets we still do not know how to decipher. It is also because, all things being equal, the events of May '68 in France remain enigmatic (why this unpredictable, sudden, and intense explosion?). Allow me to make a discreet admission of my own perplexity, especially with respect to the years immediately following 1968, faced with a shifting and highly volatile intellectual situation, where certain cases proved to be extremely complicated. This is a troublesome knot for our inquiry, reminding us that the history of thoughts, like history as such, does not follow an unambiguous, calm, and transparent course.

A preliminary question has to be examined: did the year 1968 constitute a break in the reception of Heidegger in France, which was comparable to the break that took place in the political world? Although the series of causes and events were quite different from each other, and although the analogy has to be handled with caution, it remains that the shock of the "events" was such that, in the university as well as in intellectual circles, one must at least raise the question of the pertinence of the relationship—positive or negative—between the rebellious spirit of May and Heideggerian thought. In fact, is there such a thing as a

"French Philosophy of the '60s"?[2] And if so, was Heidegger one of its instigators or one of its foils? From one myth to the other, finding one's bearings is not so easy here.

First myth: May '68. Taking the time to demystify the myth is not our intention. However, this implies that we ask whether Heidegger's thinking intervened in any significant sense in the references and the themes of the workers' and student movements. The answer is obviously negative; but it was only indirectly, due to the sudden onset of the climate of "protest" and of the more or less overt intellectual terrorism, that Heidegger was rejected as a "bourgeois" philosopher, without the question of his "Nazism" intervening in any explicit or specific manner.

Even in this tumultuous climate, Heidegger was not always subjected to accusations or rejections. At the time when a translation of Pöggeler's important work was published[3] and the series of volumes of *Questions*[4] began to appear with Gallimard, a book by a young assistant professor at the University of Nanterre, Jean-Michel Palmier,[5] presented a heroic and combative image of Heidegger that was thoroughly Marcusian.[6] Without ignoring the gravity of the error of 1933, without attempting to excuse him, without even denying that the language of *Sein und Zeit* can be discerned in the political proclamations of 1933–34[7], Palmier intended to resituate these facts and these writings within the properly philosophical horizon of the accomplishment of metaphysics in technology. The question: "was Heidegger a Nazi?" made "no sense" to him.[8] Instead, he maintained that Heidegger's position remained incomprehensible if one did not consider it in the context of Ernst Jünger's book *Der Arbeiter* (The Worker), published in 1932, to which Heidegger accorded a great importance, and more generally, in the context of the accomplishment of nihilism proclaimed by Nietzsche. For Palmier, the short sentence from 1953 concerning "the inner truth and greatness of this movement" makes no sense outside of this interpretative horizon. Further, Palmier diligently reconstructed the attacks directed against Heidegger from as early as 1934 by certain Nazi authorities and in particular by Rector Krieck. At the end of the volume, Palmier included the "Rectoral Address" and a few articles. Overall, this book, laudable for its careful documentation and philosophical quality, was generally well received,[9] although no one assumed that it had settled the case (which, incidentally, it did not claim to do). François Chatelet praised it as "a courageous enterprise," while continuing to question the "ideological situation" that allowed such a remarkable German intellectual to be led astray.[10]

For his part, like almost everyone else, Jean Beaufret found himself out of step with the events. In the midst of May '68 and apart from the turmoil of the Faculté des Lettres—in a room reserved at the last minute—Beaufret decided to give a talk in Aix-en-Provence on "Heidegger and the Thinking of Decline,"[11] far from the preoccupations of the time and leaving his listeners stupefied (as in Nice where the talk was repeated, without disruption, in university facilities). Highly stylized, a partial defense (Heidegger is presented as the sole thinker of our Western destiny), and somewhat polemical (against the "academic establishment"), this text engaged the "entire scope" of metaphysics from the early dawn of Parmenides and Heraclitus to the modern "downfall" in the scientific and technical domination of nature, in order to express in one word—decline—a situation designated by Heidegger first as *Verfallen*[12] and then as *Abfall.*[13] The inauthenticity first attributed to our everyday existence ("distracted" from its more originary condition) was historicized, which is to say placed back into the perspective of its Greek origins: the thinking of being as such. Philosophy pronounced both the opening to the being of beings as well as the withdrawal of the enigma of being. "If metaphysics, then, is declining in its history—let us say, rather, *in decline*—then we are dealing here with a wonder at which we will first learn to marvel in order to then be able to meditate upon it."[14] Refusing to understand the decline of the West in a purely superficial Spenglerian sense (this refusal also applied to the interpretation of *Verfallen* as a secularization of the Christian doctrine of original sin), Jean Beaufret (this was his Aubussonian side[15]!) wove a rich tapestry whose philosophical threads and Heideggerian knots were so dense, so consecrated by the beauty of the writing, that one would almost have to untie every single knot in order to explicate, discuss, and meditate upon it. What a challenge to give such a talk at such a moment! It was the sign of a break. This time, no quarter was given! The man who had devoted twenty years of his talents to the exclusive service of the singular genius of Heidegger no longer made any concessions to current trends. It was as if, having noted that the vast majority of the philosophical public no longer followed him, he told himself: "They no longer want to be either converted or convinced. Let us confuse them!" The discomfort of certain conventional rationalists and Bachelardian colleagues was visible by the end of the lecture. To them, this stylistic exercise seemed mercurial or insane, even though it was so carefully written, so intelligently informed by the loftiest thoughts. One felt that they would have preferred a frankly reactionary presentation in order to have been able to reject it out of hand. Instead they found themselves, like most of the students, utterly flabbergasted. It could not have gone otherwise, since the art of being "untimely" was Beaufret's style—and not without panache.

As for the *Zeitgeist,* it was far from clear or unified. An ideological camp cannot be formed in a few days or weeks. Further, although a few leaders or groups shouted Maoist, Trotskyite, or liberal slogans, the immediate benefit of May '68 was "freedom of speech" in the halls of the Sorbonne, in city squares and many other public places: the buzzing of questions, the ebb and flow of opinions of all types, and indeed, an enjoyable but pointless "anarchy." "May '68" was, at first, reduced to a syncretistic mix where militant reactualization of Marx combined with basic demands, anarchist slogans, and the creativity of "imagination in power." It was only after the party, in the postcoital sadness, that Marcuse was said to have been its leader.

A second "mythologizing" operation can be seen in the severe diagnosis offered by Ferry and Renaut, who—many years later[16]—produced questionable amalgams of quite different thinkers. For some of them, their relation to May '68 was negligible or even nonexistent (Derrida's case is the most obvious one: his complex and patient work of deconstruction started much earlier, was carried on much later, and had, strictly speaking, nothing to do with May '68. And what can be said of Lacan in this respect?) Nonetheless, it is necessary to examine how the challenge to Heidegger, rightly or wrongly, intervened on this occasion or under this pretext. It was the question of antihumanism (already emphasized by Dufrenne[17] in '68) that provided the polemical guiding thread of Ferry and Renaut's polemical text, even though it was tied up with many other themes: the end of philosophy, the paradigm of genealogy, the dissolution of the idea of truth, and the historicization of categories.[18] We shall return to these different points at the right moment in order to measure "Heidegger's influence"—which, in our opinion, the text in question largely overestimates.[19] Let us for the moment mention the fact that this work dedicated only a single chapter to "French Heideggerianism"[20] and was concerned only with Derrida: a double reduction, from the said "Heideggerianism" to the work of Derrida, and from the latter to May '68. In fact, this late reconstruction of the intellectual landscape of the end of the sixties risked misunderstanding a much more decisive trait of the ideological realities of those years: the diminishing influence of Heidegger in favor of structuralism, of linguistics, and of a renewed Marxism. At the same time, other philosophers displayed their originality and their work: thus Gabriel Marcel reiterated his critiques of Heidegger in 1968, but also his points of agreement in his *Entretiens* with Paul Ricoeur,[21] who would publish the following year, in spite of his own troubles at the university, a first collection of "hermeneutical essays," one of which stood out as a dense and solidly constructed text on "Heidegger and the Question of the Subject."[22]

In this text, Paul Ricoeur advanced and connected two theses: the Heideggerian critique of the cogito does not eliminate all subjectivity; it is "the reverse side of a hermeneutics of the 'I am.'" This hermeneutic persists throughout his work: the later Heidegger remained faithful, like the early Heidegger, "to the same pattern of a 'backward relatedness' from being to man."[23] This hermeneutic unification of Heidegger's path is highly clarifying, but also has a limitation. It is based on a precise and pertinent analysis of the relationship between *Dasein* and being in *Being and Time:* the "destruction" of the *cogito,* far from implying the renunciation to all self-relation, makes possible the de-substantification of the self and its authentic unfolding.[24] Its limitation is perhaps to be found in its very formal skillfulness: by maintaining that "one and the same formulation" organizes the entire Heideggerian path, and by reducing the thought of the later Heidegger to a "philosophy of language" that only displaces the terms of a hermeneutics of the *I am,* in place from the very beginning, Paul Ricoeur risked being schematic. For if it is true that Heidegger maintained a hermeneutical circularity, it is not enough to say that poetic authenticity now occupies the space previously reserved for freedom-toward-death. The entire questioning of the essence of metaphysics (and the metaphysical status of subjectivity) is thus ignored. Formalizing an analysis that had a certain initial pertinence, Ricoeur reconstituted the unity of the Heideggerian path abstractly, causing it to lose the fragility of its course. The "hermeneutical" operation provided an understanding of Heidegger in terms of a philosophy of reflection. Did this not miss the most critical aspects? One may wonder whether, due to his unwillingness to confront a thinking that he so strongly disliked, Ricoeur did not prefer to recuperate the offending "object" by sterilizing it. This is a question that will have to be posed in the light of other texts, in which, thanks to hermeneutics, the project of restoring metaphysics and morality is explicitly avowed.

More generally, what is in any case incontestable is that the style of the 1960s—in literary as well as in philosophical matters—(in the case of Barthes, for example, but also Lévi-Strauss, Dumézil, and Foucault) is absolutely not Heideggerian. As far as the "content" was concerned, to the extent that it could be separated from the style, the issue would have to be discussed on a case by case basis. We have begun, and will continue, this examination. In fact, if Heidegger's thought is reintroduced into the ideological horizon of the time, it is rather through Marcusian protest—also relayed by Kostas Axelos—against the one-dimensionality of technology and the increasing tyranny of a society of production and consumption on the road to globalization, suffocating the message of thinkers and word of the poets.

A clear sign of Heidegger's withdrawal—willing or forced—was the extremely discreet and private character of the seminars that Heidegger gave in Provence starting in 1966. One must understand the logic of dissociation (and of a correlative "sectarian" fragmentation) to which these events corresponded. To propose only one reading of them would be reductive.

The Thor Seminars

Why hold seminars in Le Thor, in Provence, during the month of September, on three occasions (1966, 1968, 1969), and under such private conditions? The simplest question to answer is the choice of place, which was closely tied to the occasion: René Char invited Heidegger for a visit and lodged him in Le Thor, at the Hotel du Chasselas, a few kilometers from Char's small property, Les Busclats, situated in L'Isle-sur-la-Sorgue. The poet and the thinker would meet in the afternoon for conversation and for walks. René Char never involved himself in philosophy;[25] he remained an outsider to the seminars (even though the discussion of September 9, 1966, took place in his house, at Les Busclats[26]).

Before addressing the seminars, we must pause to emphasize the extent to which Heidegger's repeated visits to the "precious soil of Provence" took on a meaning laden with affective attachments: Char's friendship, the appreciation of Cézanne, and the admiration for the landscape that was evocative of Greece blended together in the same crucible and formed a precious and rare alloy. Jean Beaufret, who did so much to ensure that there would be an invaluable collegial climate of collaboration and complicity, spoke of the sojourn as follows: "He loved above all the site of the Rebanqué, where a Delphic cliff towered over an olive grove." He recalled an unforgettable evening at the Grand Camphoux: "Christian and Yvonne Zervos came to join us, led by René Char, while Madame Mathieu, discreetly attentive, reigned over a domain where the gods of Greece were present, as in Heraclitus' saying."[27]

Who had the idea of holding a seminar during Heidegger's stay? Not René Char, it would seem, but Jean Beaufret. Beaufret obtained Heidegger's agreement since he himself "managed," together with the two François (Fédier and Vezin[28]), "the details," including the transportation (Fédier had a car and was the Master's chauffeur, thus sparing him any inconvenience, if not fatigue[29]).

Heidegger never conceived of a seminar except as organized formally around a theme: there was no question of "having a discussion" around a vague or general theme; rather, the goal was to gather in a most rigorous and academic fashion around the professor to study a text prepared in advance; for each session, a student had the task of writing a "protocol," which was then reviewed at the beginning of the following session. The professor constantly held the initiative. What distinguished the seminar from a classical lecture is that the Master often paused in order to question his interlocutors, whom he considered not as "partners" but as students whom he even bullied on occasion! This very Germanic method—to which Heidegger added his personal touch—could have become more flexible; after the last war and especially since the end of the 1960s, this was the case in Germany in different ways, but not for Heidegger, who held on to this classical model, which was for him the only serious one. One might have thought a "private" seminar would be an occasion for more equal exchanges and that it would take place in a more "informal" atmosphere, especially in the case where the participants would not all be young students. Kostas Axelos reported[30] that he suggested this to the Master, but to no avail. At the beginning of the 1960s, the editorial committee of the journal *Arguments* would have gladly organized a discreet and friendly round table around Heidegger; the text of the encounter would then have been published in the journal. But the Master did not even take such an exchange into consideration—he would consider only the formal lecture format, which obviously was of no interest to Axelos and his friends.

At Le Thor, the 1966 sessions were not as "structured" as those of 1968 and 1969.[31] The German edition indicates that the seminar of 1966 had not been planned as such,[32] but was decided upon following conversations that took place during joint excursions. This also explains why Heraclitus would be at the center of these discussions: at the time, Heidegger was preparing the Heraclitus seminar that he would give together with Fink during the winter of 1966–67.[33] The "protocol" (which had been composed only after the fact and by only one person, namely Jean Beaufret) was presented as incomplete (having been written on the basis of the participants' notes) and reported on only three "conversations" bearing primarily on Heraclitus, out of the seven that actually took place. Furthermore, there was no particular text that formed the basis of the study; the first two conversations were said to have dealt with Parmenides and the following five with Heraclitus. Beaufret himself furnished these details at the beginning of his protocol, published ten years later in *Questions IV*.[34]

"Upon its poetic cliffs, Le Thor rose up. Mont Ventoux, the mirror of the eagles, towered into view" (*FS*, 1). This is how Jean Beaufret "set the scene" for the session that took place September 5, 1966, using a citation from René Char, as he would for the other two sessions. It was at once an elegant and clever way to pay homage to Char, who was the "welcoming power," and to insist on the "proximity" between the poet and the thinker, while easing the strangeness—and unprecedented nature—of this distance. René Char succeeded in maintaining this sovereign autonomy, in perfect accord on this point with Heidegger, who applied the verse from Hölderlin's *Patmos* to the relationship between poets and thinkers: "close on mountains most distant." In fact, the way Heidegger approached Heraclitus was so precise and "technical" that it did not lend itself easily to dialogue with a "non-philosopher," as intelligent and inspired as Char might have been. In the first session, a commentary on the beginning of fragment I in the Diels-Kranz edition proposed a more "paratactical than syntactical reading."[35] Singling out the genitive *eontos*, Heidegger saw therein the being of beings, thus bringing Heraclitus into maximal proximity with Parmenides instead of focusing on the singular specificity of his logos or of seeing in it the prefiguration of a quasi-sophistical linguistic game.

The session in Rebanqué, on September 8, 1966, revealed once again the proximity between Parmenides and Heraclitus, but this time on the basis of a reading of fragment II, where the *xunon* must not be understood as general or generic but rather as a co-belonging, like that of day and night. In contrast to the everyday view (as in Hesiod), which sees nothing but the succession of light and darkness, Heraclitus's thinking is that of an "unfolding of contraries and grounded in the inapparent character [*Unscheinbaren*] of *logos*."[36] This welcoming logos announces, but does not yet engage directly, the dialectical method; nor does it transform being into an object, but attunes thought to it.[37]

The conversation of September 9, 1966, at Les Busclats, Char's house "at the edge of lavender fields,"[38] almost exclusively concerned the Heraclitean *kosmos*, with Heidegger attempting to stress its polysemy (at once an ordering, a shining and an ornamentation).[39] This protocol was the most elegant, which was characteristic of Jean Beaufret's style. It was also the most surprising since "the poet" (Char) appeared on the scene to note that "Heraclitus stands among the poets"— a remark that was not of a transcendent originality but that allowed Heidegger to oppose the modern will to domination to the richness of the Greek language in its opening to nature, an openness that is today preserved by poetry. Philosophical thought, for its part, was left to assume the heavy fate of a world that has lost "the site."[40]

Were we to venture a critical appraisal of these conversations from 1966, as they were recorded in the French edition,[41] two points would have to be established. With respect to Heidegger's interpretation of Heraclitus, the "seminar" teaches the contemporary reader nothing more, indeed even less, than the one held a bit later with Fink, and which was subsequently published. Thus the "scholarly" interest of this seminar is quite limited. The second point is more significant: it concerns the tone and style that reveal the original style of Jean Beaufret, not just in the staging (or the decor) that we have already alluded to ("at the edge of the olive trees" at Rebanqué, "at the edge of the lavender fields" at Les Busclats), but more decisively in the superimpositions (between Heraclitus and Char—or Heidegger himself,[42] between Provence and Delphos) that tend to endow, in an almost religious way, the Heraclitean logos with a real presence: "Behind us rests a Delphic mountain range. This is the landscape of Rebanqué. Whoever finds the way there is a guest of the gods. . . . Heraclitus remains near to us."[43]

Did the seminar of 1968 have the same characteristics? Held from August 30 to September 8, 1968, this time only in Le Thor,[44] it was prepared more carefully, and Heidegger insisted that it had to be a "model seminar."[45] The participants, noticeably more numerous than in 1966,[46] did not number more than fifteen: they were selected on the basis of "non-academic"[47] criteria (actually, according to the personal preferences of Beaufret and his two "co-organizers"). The text that served as the basis for the work was *The Difference between Fichte's and Schelling's System of Philosophy,* a work dating from the end of Hegel's youth (1801), an important but austere and difficult text for a nonspecialist. Heidegger knew, of course, that Beaufret and his friends were not well-versed in German idealism and would not have been able to read the text with ease—it is after all not one of Hegel's most famous works, not even in Germany. Furthermore, and above all, this choice was unexpected because the Master, who did not search for his most intimate inspirations in Hegelian sources, even thought of himself as Hegel's "adversary" (*Gegner*): in the texts dedicated to Hegel, there was always a radical distancing that prevailed in the end, specifically concerning the idealist accomplishment of metaphysics. The last Thor seminar concluded by asserting "the most pointed contradiction to Hegel."[48] How can such a decision be explained? Aiming at a "model seminar," Heidegger himself evoked his teaching at Marburg, which "aroused criticism"[49] because of its slow and deliberate quality, but above all because of its method of reading—which was extraordinarily careful and detailed about a few passages of a major text. It can hardly be doubted that he was somewhat nostalgic for those Marburg years and had sincerely wanted to have his young French friends benefit from this exceptionally authoritative approach (which he himself compared to a "kindergarten"[50]). All things considered, there was a "doctrinal" reason also at play: Heidegger conceived of the "overcoming" of metaphysics only as the result of an entry into its essential domain: the appropriation of the very heart of metaphysics must uncover the possibility of "another thinking." Nonetheless, a less apparent motif can be added to these two reasons: the choice of such a difficult and poorly known text—especially when one considers the language barrier—was a sure means of maintaining absolute control of the seminar and of avoiding any "slippages," in the sense either of digressions or of troubling questions (too contemporary, too politicized).

The philosophical substance of the commentary on the Hegelian text was not negligible, although it was not one of Heidegger's most unforgettable achievements. A phrase of Hegel's was at the center of the commentary: "When the power of conjoining vanished from the life of man, and the oppositions lose their living connections and reciprocity and gain independence, the need of philosophy arises."[51] This sentence accounts for the "need of philosophy" that arises from the division [*Entzweiung*] that causes the loss of the primary and living unity: this *Vereinigung* cannot be thought as a progressive "unification," but as the originary unity that is already "an indication of the Absolute."[52] In the following sessions, Heidegger explored in a patient and precise fashion this "need of philosophy" (which must be read as both a subjective and an objective genitive), in order to emphasize what separates the absolute position of self-consciousness (in the sense of Hegelian or Fichtean idealism) from the Greek experience of the One-All. However, starting with the session of September 4th, and especially that of September 5th, the accomplishment of metaphysics (or its "acceptance") was interpreted from the ontological difference, itself reinterpreted "as difference":[53] Hegel's text passed into the background and was replaced by a formal lecture, in which the Heideggerian reading of the history of metaphysics was unfolded; Hegel's text returned to the center stage on September 6 with the remarkable explication of the fundamental statement in which Hegel characterized his dialectical method as "infinite world-intuition" (*unendliche Weltanschauung*).[54] The seminar ended on September 8 in a more heterogeneous fashion, always in a tension between the projects of explicating Hegel's thought (namely: what is a "speculative proposition"?) and of practicing phenomenology in a radical sense (namely: what does it mean to posit?), and not without a note of dissatisfaction expressed by the Master: "Heidegger makes the observation that the seminar did not go as far as he had wished to take it. This, however, is neither a regret nor a reproach to anyone."[55]

In sum, it cannot be denied that Heidegger made a considerable effort (especially considering his age) in these eight sessions, in which he had wanted to apply his method of reading and interpretation in the most rigorous manner and without any concession to fashionable trends (let us emphasize that we were in 1968!) or to any group.[56] In this respect, a piece of his advice is worth being mentioned: "What remains essential is to continue along the same path without concern for any of the publicness around us."[57]

Did the six sessions in 1969 follow the same model? Yes, as far as the discreet nature of the gathering and the limited number of participants were concerned.[58] No, with respect to the methodology: although a classical text was again chosen, it was never discussed! At issue was a precritical text of Kant's, from 1763, *The Sole Possible Basis for a Proof of the Existence of God,* and more specifically the first chapter: "Of existence in general." Heidegger's choice[59] of a text in which the status of *Dasein* was addressed is perfectly understandable (even if he did not necessarily want to uncover the sense he had given this term in *Being and Time,* he tried to show the status of existence within classical philosophy, and then in critical philosophy). The reasons for abandoning the method of literal explication that he had vigorously defended the previous year is less obvious. The text of the protocol of September 2, 1969, did specify that "This seminar aims to elucidate Kant's text *indirectly*";[60] however, the text was so indirectly clarified that it was completely forgotten! A plausible explanation for this state of affairs was the recognition that leading a "model seminar" in the Marburg method would be difficult with French participants, regardless of their good will. In fact, even when previous questions by Roger Munier concerning the essence of modern technology were inserted, there was still no other theme treated than Heidegger's own thinking with respect to the destiny of metaphysics since the Greeks. This made things no less interesting. The style became somewhat improvisational, essentially connected to key words from the tradition: *hypokeimenon* (traditionally translated by "subject"), *eidos* ("idea"), form, beings, and phenomenon. This terminological summary did nonetheless follow a guiding thread: the Greek meaning of appearance was objectified by modern subjectivity, making possible the reduction of the world to a manipulable and technicized ensemble. Thus, Kant was relevant in the sense that he contributed, starting with his text of 1763, to an understanding of being that determines modern science and its technological unfolding: being as "position"[61] (with the added provision that the *Critique of Pure Reason* subjected this position to the capacities and limits of our understanding). The world would be reduced to what it became for Wittgenstein: "that which falls under a determination, lets itself be established, the determinable" (*was der Fall ist*),[62] "actually an eerie statement,"[63] added Heidegger, who thus prepared the group for a meditation on technology understood as *Gestell,* which, for its part, prefigured the appropriation of *Ereignis*. Refusing to present the planetary domination of technology as a "negative occurrence," Heidegger nevertheless concluded with a one-sided account based solely on the fact that "the human is challenged forth to comport himself in correspondence with exploitation and consumption." This seminar was the only text to present the possible passage to *Ereignis* as direct and almost mechanical: "The photographical negative of *Ereignis* is *Gestell.*" One can wonder whether this metaphorical formulation was genuinely Heideggerian or whether it had not been accepted, after the fact, by an elderly man who lacked the time and the energy to weigh every formulation with the same care as he had earlier. Neither the German nor the French edition mentioned the name of the person responsible for each protocol in 1969. However, the private version of the seminar of 1968 did mention the names of the responsible parties[64]—useful information that was eliminated in the final edition. Another unusual aspect of these seminars is that they constituted the only texts by Heidegger (at least among those published under his name) that had first been written in French and then translated into German.[65] I am not suggesting that their "authenticity" should be questioned. But when it pertains to philosophical thought, and at this level, the slightest nuance matters: it is legitimate to raise the same kinds of questions about pages that do not stem from Heidegger's own hand—taking appropriate differences into account—about Hegel's courses and their additions, which were not texts written by the Master himself.

If we take an even more critical perspective with respect to the seminars of Le Thor as a whole, two remarks can be made: one concerns the timeliness, the other the spiritual impact of the seminars. Their confidential, almost clandestine, character cannot be solely explained by the Master's preferences (he had not always refused to appear before a large public). There were mitigating circumstances behind this "low profile": we have seen that the climate of the 1960s was no longer as favorable to Heidegger's thought as it had been; not to mention the years 1968–69, when the very style of a "formal lecture" was called into question. Furthermore, Jean Beaufret's successful "coups" (Cerisy in 1955, and Aix-en-Provence in 1958) inspired countercoups as well as direct or indirect reactions. Heidegger himself, having weathered many unpleasant episodes, had to have realized that the conditions had changed, that the prior visits to France could not be repeated in the same form. However, to settle for these explanations would be shortsighted: at his age, and given his international reputation, nothing obliged the Master to accept the work and make the effort. He could have easily used the private nature of Char's invitation to limit himself to walks and conversations or simply to *taking it easy.* One might consider the Thor seminars repetitive, insufficiently open to real discussion of Heidegger's presuppositions, and one could certainly find other failings. Can one deny, however, their rigor, their erudite quality, impartiality, and absence of narcissistic complacency (for Heidegger never spoke of himself)? It was clear that he intended this work to be a testament for posterity: he worked less for the participants and less for the short term than for the image of the work of thought he wanted to communicate (he was undoubtedly happy as well to show his compatriots that he was amicably received on the other side of the Rhine). This is also what explains why he allowed his name to be used on texts that he did not himself write.[66]

Toward a Recomposition?

It was no small paradox that the Thor seminars—in any case, those of 1968 and 1969—were exclusively dedicated to meditations on the thinking of the Master, at the time when the critique of traditional hierarchies was unleashed in the universities and in the intellectual world. It was no small feat for an older Heidegger to have been able to discreetly "stay the course" and to have done so in France. One had wanted to avoid embarrassing questions and to achieve absolute discretion: the instructions were respected: no "leaks" and no incidents disrupted the sessions. Yet, while these sessions were quietly taking place (as intended and as it should have been), intellectuals were mostly occupied with the many and various repercussions of the events of '68. Most surprising, however, was the belated appearance, with Deleuze and Guattari[67] and with Lyotard,[68] of a liberating and "libidinal" philosophy that continued the defiant ardor of the mad days gone by, aiming to give them a theoretical coherence: now that was the "*pensée '68!*" Heidegger was absent from the discourse, for the question posed was that not of being, but rather of power—and in terms of desire, affects, or intensities. It was a creative reading of the Nietzschean "Will to Power" that came to fuse the apparatus of displacement of the Marxist and Freudian texts, all the while contesting, in passing, the conception of desire and repression professed by another Master (Heidegger's "friend"), Jacques Lacan.[69]

It would be too facile, however, to focus only on those who made the most noise in order to gather a crowd, whatever their talents. I recalled only this in order to underline the great diversity and even the dissemination that characterized the philosophical landscape of these years,[70] as soon as one takes the trouble to broaden the horizon, within which the "Heideggerians" remain present although not in dominant way (this is the case, as well, of Michel Serres, an independent spirit, who always remained unaffected by Heidegger's thought). Another pioneer, Jacques Derrida, whose work developed at the beginning of the 1970s, deserves a more refined consideration than the "all or nothing" practiced by many. A representative of "French Heideggerianism" (according to the authors of *La pensée 68,* but also to many Americans), he was completely exiled to the wilderness by the "orthodox" Heideggerians (there would never even have been a question, it appears, of inviting him to the Thor seminars).[71]

I have already indicated that I would not be satisfied with the simple question: was Derrida Heideggerian? Let us recall that he denounced the "complicity" that united the anti-Heideggerians and the repetitive rephrasing of the Heideggerians in the same "refusal to read."[72] He thus seemed to situate himself above the fray, while in fact he was at the center of the liveliest philosophical research, when he published successively three volumes: *Dissemination, Margins of Philosophy,* and *Positions.*[73]

Although the title of this chapter alludes to it, *Dissemination* is, of these three works, the one that deserves the least attention here. The complex topic of that work is to relate the question of "paleonymy" to that of polysemy, to allow the old names to circulate[74]—including that of the book—in order to displace them toward an "outside-the-book" and an "outside-the-text," beyond explicit meaning, toward the randomness of numbered information, toward the blank and the outside of the canonic Western text that was woven from Plato to Hegel and that Mallarmé disrupted. Not only is it the case that none of the three texts gathered there[75] refers to Heidegger, but the question of the text replaces the question of being, and a writing of dispersion and of the trace disjoins the gathering meditation of Language. The deconstructive work seemed to particularly upset, among other Heideggerian presuppositions, the reappropriation of the truth of being. And yet, various allusions or references to the closure of metaphysics,[76] the contestation of truth as presence,[77] the discernable fold between adequation and disclosure,[78] and the crossing of being,[79] all signaled discreetly the grafting of Heideggerian themes. In order to go further and determine more clearly the stakes of the "double game" that Derrida thus put into operation with respect to Heidegger, one should turn above all to *Positions,* where he accepted the ambiguity of his reading of Heidegger, a reading whose finesse I have already analyzed with respect to the two principal texts collected in *Margins.*[80]

The clarifications one finds in *Positions* do not add anything new, strictly speaking, in comparison to the two concluding pages, of an almost solemn tone, of the famous lecture "Différance": a recognition of an absolutely essential debt with respect to Heidegger ("What I have attempted to do would not have been possible without the opening of Heidegger's questions"[81]), as well as a critical reversal and "demarcation" from this decisive advance (a demarcation that concerns the concepts of origin, of fall, but above all of the proper, properness and appropriation[82]). The terrain of this twofold reading was strategically extended to all textuality but was delimited with and against Heidegger in relation to a "metaphysics" whose "closure" was affirmed while being thought as incessantly mobile and displaceable. With and against Heidegger: Derrida was thus on the razor's edge; he knew that the equilibrium between the "for and against" was infinitely difficult to maintain, and he understood better than anyone else that the only way to resolve this aporetic situation was to advance, that is to say, to balance the "for and against," not under the pressure of circumstances, but rather through the patient deconstruction of the key concepts of metaphysics, and of the Heideggerian text. No serious philosopher can doubt that the word "deconstruction" is undisputedly Heideggerian, since it translates the *Abbau* of metaphysics, even if the stakes of this translation are still debated and remain debatable. As we have just seen, in pursuing the project of deconstruction, Derrida remained to a large extent bound up in the network of Heideggerian presuppositions, and he admitted this himself.[83] What is less clear, however, is the extent to which he distanced himself from the letter of the Heideggerian texts. Although this uncertainty is not surprising (since, as we have seen, the nature of the criticism is modified by the questioning), it is increased by Derrida's style, which is not content to oppose "thesis to thesis," but prefers to put deconstructive practice into play through a writing that multiplies "audacities" and modes of intervention (one sees in particular this textual proliferation at work in the opening text of *Margins,* "Tympan"). Far from attempting to stabilize these shifting frontiers, Derrida already gives the impression of doing his utmost to blur the fragile boundaries even further. Not placing any principled limit on a general interrogation (which is as wide-ranging in its references as in its modes of inscription), his enterprise, on the one hand, can appear more Heideggerian than Heidegger's own work (since the issue is one of contesting, even more radically, the economy and hierarchy of onto-theology), and on the other hand, can seem a radical challenge, whose laughter and dance recall Zarathustra, in order to derail any path to the Proper.[84] The very formulation of this reversal against Heidegger is not conclusive: "I sometimes have the feeling that the Heideggerian problematic is the most 'profound' and 'powerful' defense of what I attempt to put into question under the rubric of the *thought of presence.*"[85]

A feeling can change; it can be reversed. In any case, deconstruction is an infinite task, increasingly exposed to the undecidable. With respect to the magisterial element in Heidegger's discourse, we thus witness displacements that are tantamount, of their own admission, to borrowings, deviations, or appropriations, thus contesting any doctrinal understanding of Heidegger in terms of "revelation." It was thus also the Lacanian reading that finds itself challenged: Derrida *literally* purloined the "purloined letter."[86]

Mines had thus been laid throughout the terrain of deconstruction. Some would not detonate until much later. For the moment, in the middle of the 1970s, the confrontations concerning Heidegger would be more clear-cut. With the sufficient hindsight that we have today, the examination of the chronology leaves no room for doubt: the publication in 1973–74 of Jean Beaufret's three volumes of his *Dialogue avec Heidegger* was followed in 1975 by an aggressive anti-Heideggerian offensive by Pierre Bourdieu, which seemed to be a strategic reply to Beaufret's advocacy. Of course, Bourdieu's enterprise did not present itself as such: it would be, let us be plain, difficult to "refute" Beaufret on his terrain (the history of philosophy). In ideological matters, as elsewhere, modern warfare demands mobility.

How did Jean Beaufret, who never ceased his patient work despite the difficulties,[87] regain the initiative?[88] His friend Kostas Axelos had pressured him for a long time to publish a collection of texts in Axelos's series *Arguments* at Éditions de Minuit, supplemented perhaps by new material. This detail about the publisher is not without import: the publisher in question was also Bourdieu's publisher. With a "leftist" reputation, this publisher offered Beaufret an almost ideal support to "clear" Heidegger of all remaining suspicion. However, this was obviously not the main purpose of *Dialogue avec Heidegger,* and it would be regrettable if one reduced the purpose of this work to these circumstantial facts. Let us say that without being hasty (for that would be out of character for him), Beaufret managed to seize this opportunity so as to bear witness to the philosophical work accomplished over almost thirty years with Heidegger and his school.

This accomplishment turned out to be a considerable one. The three volumes[89] cover all of philosophy: the first, dedicated to Greek thought, contains two previously unpublished texts, a "Note on Plato and Aristotle" and a detailed analysis of the Latin translation of the key Aristotelian word *energeia;* the second covers the path from Christian philosophy (principally medieval) to Nietzsche, with patient and knowledgeable sections on Descartes, Pascal, Leibniz, Kant, and Hegel. It was only in the third volume that Beaufret addressed Heidegger himself, insisting on the fact that his thought is not a new "thesis" about being, but an unprecedented and irreplaceable listening to the unsaid of the entire Western metaphysical tradition: the question of being in its forgotten truth.

His former students and auditors found in these volumes—alas, without the gentle and slow rhythm of his voice—the inimitable conjunction of two great pedagogical qualities: a reliable and precise knowledge of the fundamental texts, and a disconcerting talent for distinguishing and confronting the texts casually and at times carelessly (though always with a very firm command of the French language). One will not be surprised to find out that the weft of this meticulous weave was the Heideggerian reading of metaphysics (which was above all legible in the interpretations of Descartes and of Nietzsche). But what is most surprising for the unprepared reader is that the most specifically Heideggerian themes were not obvious until the third volume, and even then only by way of a rereading of the monumental history of philosophy. This was not an accident. Beaufret's motivation was not merely a defense and illustration of Heidegger's oeuvre; this first task was inseparable according to Beaufret from the reappropriation of the philosophical tradition. Beaufret, the philosophy teacher, rediscovered the essence of philosophy thanks to the ideal professor: Heidegger. This is why he minimized or even objected to the theme of an "overcoming of metaphysics,"[90] in favor of the inverse: the wonder before the presence and the exaltation of a thinking resituated in its abode, thanks to the openness to the secret of being and the listening to the legacy of the tradition.[91]

Nothing in this paragon of philosophical sobriety and didactic care would seem to incite fierce and hostile reactions. Alain Renaut, still a Heideggerian at the time, noted both his admiration and his reservations, particularly concerning Beaufret's "pessimist lyricism" and his way of settling "certain accounts."[92] Indeed, as always with Beaufret, the seriousness of "the thing itself" is not without irony. The best example thereof is the conclusion of his preface: his letter to Heidegger, which takes up the theme of the thoughtful dialogue between Germany and France since Leibniz, and ends on La Fontaine's little known fable, *The Serpent and the File*. The last verses were directed at the superficial minds who dared criticize Heidegger too quickly:

> *Your teeth will leave their marks*
> *Upon the deathless works you criticise?*
> *Fie! fie! fie! men!*
> *To you they're brass—they're steel—they're diamond!*

The ending is admirable. But one can guess that it was not to everybody's taste among intellectuals in Paris and within the university. What must have been irritating was precisely that this manner of lecturing, always at the highest level, with great flair and without jargon, expressed open contempt toward anything ideological or coming from the university, and with no consideration whatsoever for the champions of the "social sciences." In a certain sense, Beaufret reached his goal effectively: stinging his adversaries, with a very Nietzschean bite. But was it necessary to put Heidegger so high on a pedestal? A more measured defense would certainly have been better received. But those who knew Beaufret well could not doubt his sincerity for an instant: it was at once his strength and his Achilles' heel. He never sacrificed this sincerity for the sake of efficacy. Furthermore, he would have been hard pressed to introduce criticisms against Heidegger that he did not agree with merely in order to "provide a balanced view." One can apply Heidegger's "confession" to Beaufret: "When you are able to see my limits, you will have understood me. I cannot see them."[93]

These were the limits that Gérard Granel sketched out, for his part, with his singular writing talent.[94] Going back to the heart of *Sein und Zeit*, he emphasized the difficulties with great finesse, but did not offer the reader simple and straight "access": the absolute singularity of Heidegger's thought is its "unapparent" relation to metaphysics (freed from it and entirely turned toward it[95]); his rediscovery of the world is a (non-)description that forms a circle with the description of *Dasein*. One must enter into the withdrawal of this radical transcendence while grasping its differentiated unity, which constitutes the fecundity of finitude.[96] Neither empirical, nor psychological, nor transcendental, this Heideggerian phenomenology is ontological in a completely new sense, which is no longer metaphysical, and which constitutes—in its "earth shaking quality"[97] and its untimeliness—a "scandal for our time."[98]

Is this "introduction" to Heidegger in the form of a learned manifesto really to be taken as pedagogical in nature? One can have one's doubts, since it did not hesitate to play on and exacerbate the semantical and methodological aporias of the Master. While in no way imitating Beaufret, Granel shared with him an immense admiration for Heidegger and the taste for challenging, under his banner, the vain group of pedantic academics. Is it then surprising that the academics censured, in turn, a singularity that had wanted to be so provocative?

Bourdieu's Attack and Discord

Heidegger's destiny was to provoke hostility as well as adulation. Things could have certainly been different if he had not made the "great blunder" of 1933. However, even his political involvement, its assumptions and implications, were subjected to successive waves of critiques, which were only repeated in part, and in fact reinforced each other.[99] Even before Bourdieu's scathing critique, Jean-Pierre Cotten published a short book in 1974, called *Heidegger,* in the excellent series *Écrivains de toujours.*[100] Well-written and beautifully illustrated, this book attempted to do justice to the internal coherence of the work and to subject it to a vigilant critique. This critique was guided by a Freudian and above all a Marxist perspective. The issue was to show that Heidegger, without being a Nazi or even "a reactionary," shielded himself from the sociohistorical reality by way of denial: "Heidegger is sequestered in a certain library."[101] This was an eminently peremptory expression that illustrated the ambiguity of this little book: not clearly distinguishing introduction from critique, it carried out—under the appearance of an introduction to an oeuvre—a veritable project of demolition! Reducing the existential analytic in *Sein und Zeit* to a preanalytical anthropology,[102] he acknowledged that Heidegger, "in his own way," conceived of the development of power-knowledge in terms of technicism and positivism, but without extricating himself from the "final phase of imperialism" and from "its denial."[103] This essay, which certainly meant to avoid being reductive in a mechanistic sense, left one perplexed.[104] Although the author's attempt at a critical explication is undeniable, his readings of Heidegger turned out to be superficial, and his own assumptions were not made explicit. In such a limited space, he proposed to do either too much or too little.

Levinas pursued his questioning of Heidegger's thinking from what was obviously a completely different perspective when he published *Otherwise Than Being or Beyond Essence* the same year.[105] This book was neither explicitly nor principally devoted to the Master of Freiburg, who is hardly ever mentioned[106] (he was certainly less in question in this text than in *Totality and Infinity*). Nonetheless, an informed reader would not have missed the extent to which a quite personal and intense debate with Heidegger's thinking was being pursued. The very title indicates that thought, which is responsible in the face of the infinity of the other, goes beyond ontology and even beyond the ontological difference. To the latter, Levinas opposed the more originary alterity of infinite subjectivity. This "exception" disrupts all ontological conjunction,[107] transgresses the obsession of the anonymous *il y a* [there is] (a Heideggerian theme)[108] so as to rediscover the sense of justice and the absolute transcendence of God as "not contaminated"[109] by being. Levinas turned Heidegger's weapons against himself, even more radically than in *Totality and Infinity*: the search for an origin inscribed at the heart of existence, the non-ontical character of transcendence, the concern for Difference assumed in the verbality of the "saying" at the limits of the unsayable.

The attack launched by Pierre Bourdieu in 1975, entitled "Heidegger: un professeur ordinaire" [Heidegger: an ordinary professor],[110] entailed a new and interesting dimension. It did not concentrate on the facts that testified to Heidegger's political involvement with the Nazis, but introduced the interpretative perspective on the inscription of his professorial discourse in the sociopolitical conditions of his milieu, of his country, and of his epoch. The irony of reducing the great Master to an "ordinary professor" played on the German term *Ordinarius*, a term generally reserved—contrary to what one might expect—not for teachers of a modest rank, but on the contrary for university professors occupying a chair. Bourdieu's essay presented its goal at the outset: to reveal—beneath the mask of a great philosopher, by way of a critical analysis of his "professorial" discourse—a skillful operator, representing a certain class and dated interests. This "act" of social research was also a militant text: after being ground in the mill of its pitiless denunciation, not much remained of the "greatness" or even of the originality of Heidegger's thinking. One might use the explicitly polemical and even reductive character of this essay as an excuse to ignore it. This would be to misunderstand the work that it represents, and the skillful passion that it involves (an involuntary homage to his ideological adversary?), not to mention the influence that it would exercise on the subsequent reception of Heidegger's work in France.

We have noted the minute and detailed quality of this long essay, which attempted to combine, as one might expect, an "external" and overtly reductionist reading (sociohistorical as well as ideological) with an "internal" reading that claimed to be familiar with the latest refinements of the "self-interpretation" of the Master (in particular, the distinction between "Heidegger I" and "Heidegger II," which became canonical after Richardson's book[111]) as well as with the most subtle virtuosities of the clarifications and puns of the thinker. The issue was one of demystifying, by way of "effects" and of "discursive strategies" (terms dear to Bourdieu) the *distinguished* status granted to Heidegger for many decades[112] in the French ideological field, and of unmasking in the work itself "the corrections, rectifications, clarifications, and refutations through which the author defends his public image against criticism—in particular politically based criticism—or, worse, against all forms of reduction to a common identity."[113]

The goal of this corrosive text was twofold: to give an exemplary illustration of the critique of literary work, broadly conceived (as developed in that issue of the *Actes de la recherche en sciences sociales*) and to liquidate the "Heidegger myth" in the French philosophico-ideological field (in this respect, the irony was scathing and willingly feigned familiarity to attack the Heideggerian hagiography and even—in less acceptable fashion—attack the friendship between Beaufret and Heidegger).[114]

To what extent did Bourdieu achieve, exceed, or miss his goal of attempting to unmask the Heideggerian "double-game" between ontology and politics, the occultation of the latter to the benefit of the former (always wrapped up in a "linguistic alchemy")? We will refrain, here as elsewhere, from attempting to offer a sort of Last Judgment on the issue. We shall simply limit ourselves to giving the reader a few elements of a critical appreciation of the debate that ensued.

In relation to a brutal "sociologism," and even a first-rate Marxist reading, this essay was interesting in that it combined the contributions of Freudianism (censorship, denial, sublimation) with a linguistic analysis of the "euphemistic" and "formal" style of professorial discourse. It extended and broadened Löwith's criticisms and Faye's research beyond the relatively limited question of Heidegger's political involvement in 1933–34. One can ask, however, if it really went farther than the aforementioned authors in the denunciation of the ambiguities of Heidegger's language and of its contaminations by (or with) the "conservative-revolutionary" discourse. In fact, Bourdieu's essay was more heterogeneous and itself more ambiguous than it may appear at first glance: heterogeneous (between an appropriation of the sociolinguistic critique of the *völkisch* ideology of the 1930s[115] and a theoretical inquiry—peremptory if not pretentious—concerning the symbolic strategies of literary work, related to the social conditions of its production[116]); and ambiguous, for it masked—to a large extent but not entirely—its ambivalence between a critical discourse of pure scientific research (praising, with some affectation, scientific reason,[117] and claiming to be in possession of the sociological "truth" of the processes that it analyzed[118]—a truth that can be found only in "the academic fraction of that class"[119]) and the militant passion that led to Jdanovian denunciations, and almost to insults, aimed at the all-too famous "professor ordinarius."[120]

Hence, if it is undeniable that Bourdieu's work calls for a reflection on Heidegger's language and on its relation to the historico-social conditions of its production, it also sheds some light, despite itself, on Bourdieu himself, on his militancy, his style of "righting wrongs," and his resolutely reductionist approach. To what understanding of Heideggerian philosophy does Bourdieu's critique of the critique of reductionism lead? It leads to a degree zero that is in fact assumed as such. I can easily concede that the "haughty philosophical tone" invites questioning and critique, especially in the context of the sociohistorical conditions of Hitlerian and post-Hitlerian Germany. But Bourdieu goes much farther and even too far when—transforming his critical analysis into an inquisition, and bordering on intellectual terrorism (every "distinction" becoming suspect, even Rilke is not spared[121])—he disputes the autonomy and pertinence of the questions that Heidegger poses concerning the forgetting of being, the essence of truth, temporality, and so on. What remains of this thought? "Verbal incantations!"[122] Is Heidegger really a guru calling his disciples to repeat his formulations without understanding them? He instead asks his disciples to put his formulations into question and to think them through. These invitations are merely rhetoric for Bourdieu, a smokescreen that served to maintain a dominant academic, and even sacred, position. Finally, for Bourdieu Heidegger was just a *sordid* trickster. One almost expects the revelation of a connection to some sort of mafia. In belittling his ideological adversary to this extent, does not the attacker belittle himself? At the risk of reintroducing a "distinction" that would incur Bourdieu's ire: should we not here distinguish the point of view of the servant from that of his master?

Just a few months after this virulent attack, discord would be prevalent in a Heidegger "camp" that was already quite divided. In fact, a personal break had already taken place earlier, between Roger Munier and Jean Beaufret, albeit discreetly. After the last "private" seminar held in early September 1973 at Freiburg,[123] Munier addressed a letter to the Master drawing his attention "to the fact that the closed circle where Beaufret and his friends had enclosed him risked depriving him of contact with other French *Heideggerians* who resented this monopoly, notably Birault."[124] Beaufret, who was informed of this by Heidegger himself, did not forgive Munier, who would take the initiative again in 1976.

The publication of *Questions IV*[125] instigated a heated polemic, of a somewhat private nature, in any case not carried out in public. Taking the unprecedented form of a letter addressed to Heidegger himself in March 1976 (two months before his death) from "numerous French readers and translators,"[126] the polemic concerned a certain number of key translations of essays, lectures, and speeches gathered in this volume—decisive texts of the later Heidegger.[127] "Surprised and indignant," the signatories to the letter claimed a "mass of mistakes and sloppiness," and then concentrated their critiques on "key terms."

Given the technical nature of the debate, we shall limit ourselves here to three significant expressions, *Die Unverborgenheit, Zur Sache des Denkens,* and the *Schritt zurück,* translated respectively as *l'Ouvert sans retrait* [The Open without withdrawal],[128] *Droit à la question* [Straight to the question],[129] and *le pas qui rétrocède* [The step back].[130] All these translations resulted from Beaufret's "inventions," and one must admit that they worked better orally than in writing. In the first case, the literal translation would be *décèlement* [unconcealment] or *désabritement* [uncoveredness]; for the second, *contribution à l'affaire de la pensée* [contribution to the task of thinking]; for the third, *le pas de recul* [the step back]. The uninformed would be completely fooled.

In fact, what accounted for the strong reaction of the signatories was less the intention (nonetheless proclaimed and indeed legitimate in principle) to correct errors or mistakes than a complete rejection of the "spirit" of the translations in question: a somewhat baroque quality and a certain linguistic license (thus *la traque* [the hunt] for *Nachstellen,* and *saisonnement du temps* [seasons of time] for *Die Zeitigung der Zeit*). At the same time, the end of the letter formulated an opposition, now personal, against those "who are currently in charge of the complete translation of *Sein und Zeit* and the first volume of the *Gesamtausgabe.*" One could not have more clearly accused Jean Beaufret, François Fédier, and François Vezin of taking the heritage hostage, by referring to the essential stakes of the protest: the translation—still unfinished—of the *magnum opus* of 1927 and, in the long term, of the announced *Collected Works.*

Did the signatories really expect the Master to give a formal response? Even if his impending death could not have been anticipated, the fact of his age and of his close relationship with Beaufret made such a response highly improbable.[131] However, this letter took on the meaning of a declaration of war against the enemy "camp" and wanted to make a point to the supreme authority, Heidegger himself (but also, and above all, to his French publisher Gallimard, to whom the letter had also been sent).

It is not hard to imagine to what extent the "accused" could have been outraged. At the time, there was no direct response,[132] and even less when the Master's sudden death came, the 26th of May 1976. A schism was thus consummated between the "faithful" around Beaufret and the "critical Heideggerians."[133] But the truce brought about by the period of mourning suspended the polemic, which would only return and turn bitter in the course of the following years.

Epilogue III

The attentive reader will have no doubt noticed that my name is mentioned among the participants present "for a day or two" at the second seminar of Le Thor, in 1968. In fact, things happened as follows: I found out about this seminar only at the last minute, two or three days beforehand, at a time when I had expected to be leaving for Corsica with friends. I confess not having appreciated this late notice, given that the text chosen was none other than Hegel's Differenzschrift. *Hegel was the author I was working on in my main thesis. Since I was the sole "Hegelian" in Beaufret's circle of friends and students, should I not have been notified early enough to be able to study the text carefully? Did the quality of the seminar not demand such preparation from the participants? Had they neglected to inform me or had they deliberately delayed notifying me? I never found out. In any case, I must admit that I was unhappy, and I almost stayed away from the seminar. But they had after all notified me, and I knew that this was a "privilege." I had already missed the 1966 seminar, but that was not my doing: if I remember correctly, I had found out about the seminar only after the fact by way of a postcard, incidentally a very kind one, signed by Jean Beaufret, Heidegger, and the two François.*

Returning to the end of August 1968 and to my dilemma: "Should I go or should I not go?" As a good Norman (at least half-Norman, and this fact is the perfect Norman logic), I chose the conciliatory solution; I would spend a few days in Corsica as planned, but would return sooner than planned by plane, to participate on the last day of Heidegger's seminar. This delay allowed me to read the text thoroughly—a precaution that turned out to be unnecessary (as one will see).

The morning of September 8, 1968, I attended the last seminar session. Under the shadow of a tall tree, around a long rectangular table, a dozen participants were seated and were taking notes. Heidegger sat at the end of the table at my left; he seemed tired and had a blanket on his knees. His interlocutors were Beaufret, Fédier, and Granel (who recorded the protocol). The other participants were silent and seemed intimidated. The Master seemed dissatisfied by the pace and the quality of the exchanges. Nothing of what I heard was extraordinary: every experienced reader of Hegel knows that it is not sufficient to reflect on the Absolute for it is the latter that reflects itself in us. But how? Not in an enclosure, but according to the modern sense of representation. What does it mean to represent? I think: the Louvre is in Paris. For us, at this moment, this is a "representation." Where is it? . . . Granel's protocol did not conceal that the Master was irritated by how we were floundering: "Everyone was surprised to be so lost in the discussion. It was a long and beneficial wandering." I thought to myself that it had been unnecessary to read the Differenzschrift *so thoroughly, for the Master stated: "the phenomenological exercise is more important than the reading of Hegel." As far as* Aufhebung *was concerned, we dwelled on its negative sense, which is not surprising. The seminar ended with the explication of the speculative proposition: "God is being itself," where the predicate can also become subject, but not according to a merely mechanical reversal. There were many clarifications, certainly pertinent, but which would only disappoint someone seeking "discoveries." Granel nonetheless concluded his protocol with panache: "The session ended on the silence created by the winds of speculation, with each person content and exhausted." I remember above all the silence—and the feeling of Heidegger's unhappiness (or fatigue). But perhaps I was mistaken.*

In the afternoon we were allowed to rejoin the group at Char's house, where we were quite welcome. Heidegger did not say very much. Char, on the other hand, proclaimed in his strong voice: "Poetry is without walls." There was a general accord. The surrounding youth took notes or maintained an admiring silence. Shortly after, Heidegger left, driven away faithfully as ever by François Fédier.

Had I made the right decision to attend? Should I have taken part in the whole seminar? It is not clear. Having always thought that the anecdotal should be sub-

*ordinated to what is essential in matters of thought (a Heideggerian position, inci-
dentally), I did not dwell on this perplexity.*

*Let us go back a few months earlier, to the famously merry month of May 1968.
I alluded to the audience's lack of understanding on the occasion of Beaufret's lecture on "Heidegger and the Thinking of Decline." These memories must be analyzed
further: the public can be excused; they could not understand because they were
not expected to understand! When I reread this lecture, it became clear to me that
Beaufret did everything he could to encrypt his theme; the brilliant style of presentation was not able to mask an esoteric bent, punctuated as it was with polemical
allusions. This style was not new, but it was more accentuated. Why? At the time, I
did not know the whole story: I knew almost nothing of the "Beaufret affair"; I only
heard from afar of the discussions (often turning bitter) that Jean deemed necessary in order to defend Heidegger. A little later, two years away from retirement,
he applied to the University of Aix for a position as* chargé d'enseignement: *he was
entitled to do so, having been on the list of those who were qualified, which was then
called the* liste large. *Professor Granger resolutely and successfully opposed his can-
didacy (which was supported, on the other hand, by Gérard Lebrun), not because
of personal hostility but due to philosophical and ideological reasons (he did not
realize that it would have been better to be open-minded, and to have offered Jean
Beaufret a dignified and entirely reasonable, time-limited, end to his career). Beaufret did not take this failure well (even though it was highly predictable): he had the
impression (evidently mistaken) that there was universal malice toward Heidegger
and him. He developed what one would have to call a sort of persecution complex
that would only intensify in the last years of his life.*

*Of course, I—1,000 kilometers away—did what I could to combat this isola-
tion: in 1972–73, if I remember correctly, I managed to have Beaufret invited to my
university to give a few classes on Merleau-Ponty (the* Phenomenology of Perception *was on the reading list for the Agrégation). But I could not do more than this,
for my new and highly eminent colleague Éric Weil, with whom I had good relations despite our philosophical differences, could not keep himself from making a
horrible grimace upon hearing the name Heidegger. In any case, for Beaufret, the
merciless age limit for retirement would soon fall like an axe.*

*In 1974–75, my distance from this situation was only greater since I spent an
academic year in the United States, in Pennsylvania. This helped put things in context: I realized that the French polemics must be put into perspective, since serious
and friendly students, at a university where the philosophy department was largely
"continental" and phenomenological in orientation, were requesting a methodical study of Heidegger's texts (an author who was considered a classic on par with
Husserl or Hegel).*

*On my return, after a summer of "reacclimating," I eagerly awaited the pub-
lication of* Questions IV *announced by Jean Beaufret, but—alas!—once again the
all-too-French polemic continued, first with the publication of Bourdieu's essay in*

the fall, and second, with the unrest surrounding Questions IV *barely two months later.*

Reading Bourdieu obviously had an effect on me, but I cannot say that I was profoundly impressed: surprised by the effort at documentation and almost taken by a certain insolent tone, I found this essay nonetheless a terribly reductive sociological approach that barely concealed its hostility toward everything that questioned its neo-Marxist and positivist assumptions. Despite the alacrity of style, the goal was to flatten and ideologically "liquidate" Heideggerian discourse. At the time, it did not escape my attention that this operation could succeed and that it could even ravage the young left-wing intellectuals (the terrain that Axelos and Palmier had covered). But—out of laziness or indifference to these power issues?—I did not feel like responding (this was undoubtedly a mistake).

As far as Questions IV *were concerned, I was completely perplexed and in a quandary. On the one hand, with Michel Haar, I found that more prudent and more literal translations would have better rendered Heidegger's thought—certainly better than a mannered style whose strengths and weaknesses had the disadvantage of erecting a barrier to the German instead of facilitating access. On the other hand, I still respected and admired Beaufret's offhand approach, which could be questioned but which was never mediocre. Further, I found that my personal relation with Jean prevented me from joining the detractors, whose tone, on closer examination, was extremely severe. Was I wrong? Would it not have been preferable—in a complicated field where divisions into "camps" and where personal animosity risked compromising all understanding, all collaboration—to undertake a patient dialogue concerning true difficulties of translation? I thought then and I still think now that jargon could be avoided, as shown by André Préau's success (which was commended by Heidegger himself in my presence). I myself participated in a patient and faithful collaborative translation with Beaufret, on a brief text,* Hegel and the Greeks, *published in* Questions II, *in 1968.*

Going back to the affair of Questions IV, *I must alas acknowledge my helplessness. I could not prevent a schism that took on an almost fatal character. No longer living in Paris, I could no longer participate in the debate with the accusers. In any case, they were so "vehement" that it would have been very difficult to convince them to be more moderate in their approach. But I knew from experience how outraged Jean would be at this method (the appeal to the Master was the most severe blow that one could have delivered) and how his position would harden. Most certainly, "the business of thinking" was not and is still not free of passion!*

8 Death and Transfiguration?

Heidegger's Death and Its Repercussions in France

Heidegger passed away in his sleep, the morning of May 26, 1976. He was buried in his birthplace, Messkirch, in a special ceremony that he had carefully organized with his friend Bernhard Welte, the Catholic priest who delivered the homily in the cemetery's chapel. Before the open grave, Hermann Heidegger read the prayer, Our Father, followed by excerpts from Hölderlin's poetry.[1] The tombstone is adorned with a small star, however, and not a cross.

Without making any reference to these ritual nuances, Beaufret, who was present at the ceremony with Fédier and Vezin, would remember Heidegger in the following terms, in the sober obituary notice published in *La Quinzaine littéraire:* "Such was, apart from all honors, the private ceremony, which gathered around him those who accompanied him that spring to his last abode where he rests in his country close to his kin."[2]

The event did not make it into the newspaper headlines nor the television news, but was nonetheless the subject of an important dispatch from the Agence France-Presse,[3] which was released in the media and received a "headline" on the front page of *Le Monde* on May 28, 1976.[4] It thus did not go unnoticed, in contrast to the silence that had surrounded Husserl's death forty years earlier. In the meantime, the cultural and social status of philosophy had changed: the public had heard of existentialism, most of all because of the political debates that it had incited. Of course Heidegger's name was constantly implicated in these debates, as well as in their existential and political stakes.

Yet, at the end of the spring of 1976, the climate was less volatile.[5] There was an attempt to take a step back and to pay homage to the thinker ("the greatest philosopher of our times," according to Jean Lacroix),[6] although it was more difficult to do justice to the man whose complex personality was still a mystery. The allusion to the involvement of 1933 in *Le Monde* was discreet and measured.[7] Clearly, it was a reflective moment, and this was no doubt the reason why *Le Monde* published an article by the Catholic philosopher Jean Guitton, entitled "A Peace

That Emanates from a Long Rest of Being," in which he used his picturesque[8] memories of his visit to Freiburg to salute Heidegger as a spiritual master. In the same issue of *Le Monde,* the longest article was by Jean-Michel Palmier,[9] which was an undeniable effort to do justice to the thinker, and to the richness of his oeuvre, without becoming a mere defense. Certainly at the time it was unimaginable that the political polemic would return with the same intensity, as there had already been so many developments. It was thought that everything about the involvement of 1933–34, its effects and implications, had been well-known. There was greater interest in the news of the monumental *Gesamtausgabe,* prepared by the Master during the last years of his life. This interest accentuated the profound significance of the passing of a philosophical giant. It was also in these terms that he was saluted in *Les Nouvelles littéraires* in a dossier entitled "The Loneliness of the Long Distance Thinker," in which the moving testimony of the young philosopher Henri Mongis[10] stood out. There was also a vibrant tribute on France-Culture radio.[11]

One must nonetheless nuance this quasi-universal expression of appreciation. On the one hand, an event willed by Heidegger himself followed his death, namely, the publication, on May 31, 1976, in the weekly *Der Spiegel,* of a conversation held ten years earlier between the philosopher and the magazine's director. Although the highly awaited clarification of his political involvement was not immediately translated into French, it was said to be ambiguous. Produced fairly rapidly, the French translation appeared in March 1977.[12] It was received with interest but without much excitement: a general relief was felt as Heidegger finally emerged from his silence—albeit postmortem—and refuted some accusations,[13] but also there was also a disappointment as his personal self-justification seemed to blind him to the intrinsic perversity of the National Socialist movement (the specificity of which he continued to dilute in the global movement of planetary technological nihilism).

However, while the disappearance of a great figure deserves respect and circumspection as well as an analysis of an entire oeuvre, it would be naïve to think that Heidegger would experience a transfiguration—all things being equal—comparable to the apotheoses of Roman emperors! One must know how to differentiate silence and reticence.

Thus, if one takes the trouble to compare the way in which the main French philosophical journals reported Heidegger's death, one notices a surprising contrast between restraint or discretion on the part of some (the majority)[14] and cautious homage on the part of others.[15] Among the latter, only one text stands out, the truly affectionate "In Memoriam," in which Pierre Aubenque skillfully wove personal memories and substantive appreciation. Confessing his "painful and deep conviction that one of History's few great thinkers in history had passed,"[16] Aubenque recalled Hannah Arendt's observation: the initial shock of Heidegger's teaching was due to an unprecedented combination of a return to the "things themselves" with a renewed attention to the fundamental texts of the metaphysical tradition. Emphasizing the extraordinary exegetical contribution made by Heidegger's interpretations, Aubenque criticized the caricatures often given of the Master: "The grotesque image of a pompous and presumptuous thinker—a sublimated hypostasis of an oppressive society—is the view of Heidegger promulgated by the Frankfurt school."[17] Nonetheless, he also distanced himself from the French Heideggerians, from a few translators[18] as well as from—without naming him—Jean Beaufret (concerning the connection between Heidegger and neo-Platonism[19]). Sensitive to the complexity of the famous "turn," which seemed to produce a shift from fundamental ontology to the "overcoming" of metaphysics (he saw it more as a slight shift than as a complete reversal), Aubenque concluded this careful and measured essay in an unexpected fashion, that is to say, in an apologetic mode concerning the political question. Vigorously opposing Bourdieu,[20] he defended Heidegger by recalling the circumstances and reasons for his acceptance of the rectorship, namely, his assumption of the responsibility for a university aware of its mission: "He wanted to reaffirm its necessary autonomy by opening it onto the outside world. Who, today, would reproach him for this?"[21] Falsely naïve, this question stands out at the conclusion of this talented and captivating essay by the great Aristotle scholar, and it was thus important to note its significance.

A few months after his death, the *Magazine littéraire* published a special issue dedicated to the philosopher. The editors' desire for balance was obvious. In the introductory note, one reads the following question: "Was Heidegger's philosophy intrinsically a Nazi philosophy?," but this was immediately counterbalanced by the recognition of his "incomparable language" and by the fact that he opened new perspectives for "thinking outside the domain of economic production."[22]

Whereas Jean-Paul Dollé hailed Heidegger as a "messenger" [*passeur*] who came to poetry through metaphysics, Jean-Marie Benoist was more critical. Recalling the more compromising declarations of 1933, he drew a comparison to the bloodstains on Lady Macbeth's hands, probably unaware of the extent to which this assertion would be proven right: "Periodically, the French intelligentsia was occupied with washing Heidegger's brown shirt."[23] He wanted to give this polemical statement a philosophical scope: referring to the critical works by Faye, Bourdieu, Bollack, and Derrida, he gave the last word to the latter in order to challenge the return in Heidegger's work of "the great shadow of Unity and of a totalizing and totalitarian discourse."[24] In a less obvious way, he praised Beaufret sarcastically: "Heidegger's ontology carries out definitively—Beaufret was not mistaken in this—a triumph of Parmenidean ontology over the decorative ruins of a Platonism that had been shaken in order to be better invested with being."[25] Opening genuinely new pathways: Heidegger thus failed in this difficult task, which he barely glimpsed, a task that must now be undertaken by interweaving texts and discourses, apart from any tyranny of unity.

Whereas other articles gave a precise account of the relations between Heidegger and the philosophies of Nietzsche, Marx, and Sartre,[26] the most notable contribution was a brief conversation with the expert of German literature Robert Minder.[27] While confirming his earlier severe criticisms (above all concerning the "interpretation" of Johann Peter Hebel), he situated Heidegger politically in the wake of the nationalist conservative agrarian Friedrich Naumann, and linguistically (due to the "taste for assonance") in the heritage of Wagner. In sum, he did not deny Heidegger's originality, but deemed it to be less significant than what was thought in France. Particularly, he found Heidegger's approach to the poets rather limited (yet he did not consider the reinterpretation of Rilke).

Manifesting their concern for relevance, the editors followed these highly critical considerations with an excerpt from a televised interview from 1969, followed by notes illustrated with photographs taken by Frédéric de Towarnicki. A brief comment concerning Heidegger's *Spiegel* interview (published posthumously) noted correctly that Heidegger attempted to justify himself while skillfully evading the most embarrassing questions, and that the interview failed to add anything new.[28]

However, what are all these comments, pertinent and interesting as they might be, compared to the few lines written by the poet and friend René Char, the very day of Heidegger's death?

> *Martin Heidegger died this morning. The sun has laid him to rest along with the tools. Only the work remains. This threshold is constant. The night opens itself with love.*[29]

Two days later, Char wrote a letter to two young friends from which the following lines deserve to be recalled:

> *We will go to Rebanqué with Heidegger's friends from Provence this afternoon. There, at least, our sadness, perhaps, shall be attenuated when we draw water from the deep well into which Heidegger gazed and meditated on the spark twinkling between darkness and day, making them communicate.*[30]

It was thus up to the last moment and even beyond it that the poet and the thinker pursued their friendly dialogue. A few months after Heidegger's death, the translation of one of the most important of his later works appeared, *On the Way to Language.*[31] The French translation[32] carried a particularly warm dedication to René Char.[33] Heidegger himself chose three of Char's sayings, which "attest to the proximity of poetry and thought," while adding: "Is dear Provence the secret invisible arch that connects the inceptual thought of Parmenides to the poem of Hölderlin?" This attention given to the "nearness" of the poetic word corresponds intimately to the spirit of this volume in which a study on Trakl was juxtaposed with meditations on poems by Stefan George, Gottfried Benn, and once again Trakl, not to mention the "conversation with a Japanese." This latter text would quickly become emblematic of the Heideggerian encounter with Eastern thought and of his respect for the singularity of linguistic alterity.

As an unexpected epilogue, let us note the posthumous homage, quite indirect, which was paid to Heidegger a year after his death. In 1977, André Glucksmann published *The Master Thinkers.*[34] This book attracted a good deal of attention and inserted itself into the offensive of the *"nouveaux philosophes"* against totalitarianism, Stalinism, and the ideologies of state power. Four criminals of thought were thoroughly dismantled, thinkers of the State and of the Will to Power: Fichte, Hegel, Marx, and Nietzsche. Not only did Heidegger escape the pillory, but his thinking was clearly used to give thought to this power and to the "will of the will"[35] that subtended the catastrophes of the twentieth century. Glucksmann saluted Heidegger as the "greatest of contemporary German thinkers"[36] in the chapter "Why We Are So Metaphysical" (a telling title) and even absolved him of any Nazi tendencies, since the Master confirmed after 1940 that the French were "not sufficiently 'up to the level'" of the demands of modern technology.[37] No doubt, Glucksmann did not engage in "Heideggerian jargon" in a manner that was overly ostentatious, but it is clear that he sought recourse to a true thinker who had the "honesty" to publish his thoughts on Nietzsche and not remain "settled" there.[38]

Reasons for a Quarrel

In the course of 1978, a number of texts, which were very different in both spirit and form, would be published. At the outset, one must pay particular attention to a polemical response that Jean Beaufret addressed to the detractors of the translation of *Questions IV,*[39] and specifically to Alain Renaut,[40] who had become the spokesperson of these critiques. Without alluding to the letter addressed to Heidegger a year earlier, without mentioning the details of its argumentation (which he only summarized by insisting on two points: we do not know who really authored the texts of the seminar protocols; the general allure of the translations revealed "a preference for a style that was quite affected," "a deliberate search for the unusual and the archaic"[41]), Renaut went further: he made the debate public and did so in severe terms, for he openly suspected that the translators of *Questions IV* wanted to "render the text *unreadable* and thus beyond critique." Renaut thus unmasked their "insidious hagiography."[42]

One thus understands that Beaufret himself felt obligated to exercise his right to respond in the same journal. The response obviously had no bearing on Renaut's philosophical choices ("to read Hegel in order to finally work at the heart of that which is"[43]), but it does have a bearing on the justification of the incriminated translations and, more generally, on the type of work he carried out with his students and disciples in relation to reading, understanding, and translating Heidegger. Much more than a simple "response," this was an important and significant text of self-justification. Beaufret, once again, revealed his talent as a polemicist in an embarrassing and paradoxical situation, since in this case he condescended to quarrel in public with a young man who had until only recently been his disciple.

Denouncing from the outset "the atmosphere of suspicion" that Renaut set out to create around *Questions IV,* Beaufret recalled that the seminar "protocols" had indeed been verified, reread, and authorized by Heidegger; he admitted, at most, a "lack of coordination, since each person had worked on his own."[44] This concession was all the more noteworthy since it was the only one made in the text: it amounted to admitting that someone should have been designated as "responsible for the editing." Further, the most rigid position was taken with respect to the translations that were called into question, especially with respect to "the Open without withdrawal" ["*l'Ouvert sans retrait*"] as a rendering of *Unverborgenheit.* In a Parmenidean context, the essence of truth is not thought in its most intimate essence, but rather as "clearing of presence."[45] In his counterattack, Beaufret himself alluded to the famous "protest letter" to express his indignation with respect to Renaut's tactics and pointed out that Renaut proceeded by hiding his sources. The other signatories were not named, but ridiculed as "clandestine letter-writers" or as the "collective."[46]

Yet this was not the most interesting element of this text. Having been personally attacked, Jean Beaufret intended to address the accusation of hagiography. It was thus the very spirit of his lifelong work, in Heidegger's footsteps, that he intended to defend and to illustrate. This was the heart of the debate: was there a guardian angel protecting Heidegger from all criticism and choosing intentionally abstruse or affected translations in order to rebuff the critics? Beaufret was not content with denying it, preferring, as was his habit, to recount (rather than to demonstrate) how his patient pedagogical and hermeneutical labors had gained him the loyalty of excellent students (certain of whom, including Renaut, were beginning to make a name for themselves). He accused his former disciple, who had become his adversary, of being involved in a "partial recuperation" of Heidegger, based on a distinction between an "acceptable" and an "unacceptable" Heidegger.[47] This precisely consisted in implicitly recognizing that the reception of Heidegger was no longer carried out in terms of an "all or nothing," but also explicitly in refusing to enter into a heated philosophical discussion with Renaut,[48] who found himself rejected as one of those who understood nothing, such as . . . Gabriel Marcel![49] In his inimitable style—more an amusing conversation than a philosophical discussion—Beaufret clearly managed to win over the audience. Was this, however, not accomplished at the price of a few distortions?

More precisely, was it true that the "official university curriculum" categorically refused to address Heidegger? And was it true that Beaufret had encountered a "climate of prohibition or intimidation, albeit muffled?"[50] Did these allegations stem from what could be called a persecution complex? The question must be posed with frankness and clarity. If one were to respond honestly, one would have to take into account the evolution of the question itself over the course of the French reception of Heidegger's thought. To take sides in this emotional quarrel would be tantamount to dismissing, all too quickly, the entire achievement of the present study. Let us go back to the facts. It is clear that Jean Beaufret was never prevented from teaching either in *khâgne* or at the École Normale Supérieure, nor was he subjected to any pressure; on the contrary, it is difficult to imagine a greater pedagogical freedom than the one from which he benefited. One can also present Birault's case as another counterexample: he followed a classical university career, concluding at the Sorbonne, even though he wrote a dissertation on Heidegger, without either abandoning his admiration or joining the accusers. There never was any implacable ban at the pedagogical level; however, it is true that Beaufret's university career had been blocked, once by Jean Wahl (in 1953 or 1954) and a committee (having determined that he had not made sufficient progress on his dissertation); then, much later, in 1969–70, when his application was turned down at Aix-en-Provence. Even taking these facts into account, the expression "implacable ban" seems exaggerated. On the other hand, was Beaufret right to speak of a "muffled" climate of intimidation? By definition, such an atmosphere is infinitely less clear than an explicit ban. What is true, we have observed, is that this climate (at once intellectual, academic, and cultural) evolved considerably between Liberation and 1978. This change was not an unambiguous one (in the sense of being favorable or unfavorable to Heidegger): the reception became more complex, the critiques (external and internal) became more sophisticated, and the popularity of other philosophies (structuralism, Wittgenstein—to mention just two) competed with the exceptionally favorable reaction Heidegger initially received. That Beaufret did not take well to these evolutions and reversals and remained proud of the work accomplished, sheltered from publicity, is undeniable. But it is equally clear that certain misunderstandings that separated him from Renaut (whose good faith cannot be put into question) were due to his approach to personal relationships, where arguments were often less important than allegiances. The all-too-easy accusation of sectarianism was not Renaut's fabrication; it had been formulated for some time from many sides, since Beaufret's attitude had very quickly become one of an unconditional and polemical defense of Heidegger, the man and his oeuvre. Renaut perhaps went too far when he spoke of "hagiography"; it is nonetheless obvious that for his part Beaufret—as respectable as his true motives might have been—refused to take seriously criticisms of a thinking whose resources he had wanted to illustrate in purely philosophical terms and had thus always treated as conducive to reflection and meditation. Thus put in perspective, the quarrel with Renaut can be situated in a series of different disputes that had crystallized around Heidegger's name since Liberation and that Beaufret had wanted to handle personally. As the years passed, the dossier thickened for the person who had made himself the defender of the Master, who had become his friend (choices became a destiny, although not an inevitable fate: Merleau-Ponty's case shows clearly that a very different attitude, which was open and nonconflictual, was also possible—certainly easier for a chair at the College de France . . .). Let us recall that Renaut belonged to a completely different generation (forty years younger than Beaufret!): for him, Heidegger was a classic whom he at first idealized and then almost "abhorred": personal allegiance to a classic was not possible!

Between Critique and Hermeneutics

What kind of critique is desirable? Is the distinction between an "external" and "internal" critique pertinent? This problem of a hermeneutic-critical deepening of Heideggerian thought arose again in 1978, although in a less contentious manner and in radically different texts, which were barely comparable. On the one hand, there was a severe article by two young, still unknown, writers who proposed an "internal critique" of Heidegger,[51] and on the other hand, there was a long-awaited, voluminous book by a distinguished Heideggerian that offered, in elegant language, an equally "internal" commentary that was hardly critical of Heidegger.[52] This disparity went unnoticed at the time. It was instructive nonetheless, both as regards the interpretative sophistication that was carried out in the 1970s and in relation to the widening gap that would increasingly separate the adversaries of the Master from his staunch supporters.

While it would be inappropriate to establish a parallel between (or even equate) Ferry-Renaut's article and Birault's volume, their contemporaneous appearance nonetheless deserves some attention. Let us note—without making any judgment as to their respective value—the symbolic opposition that separates them, despite their simultaneity.

Indifferent to current affairs, Birault finally gathered together the fruit of many years of work; his brilliant commentary came at the end of the first wave of Heidegger's reception—the one that welcomed a great thinker with admiration and paid attention to a philosopher taken to be one of the greatest. Ferry and Renaut, on the contrary, presented a new style, which was rather irreverent toward the Master, closely tied to ideological and political contexts, and aiming to put into practice a project of "internal critique" (they would not be the only ones to make this claim).

Each attempt must be given its due, but Ferry and Renaut's "attempt at an internal critique" cannot occupy us for too long (it is after all just an article; furthermore, and more importantly, more elaborate forms of that same approach in the later works of the same authors will be subsequently considered). This article—where Renaut's complete turnaround with respect to Heidegger[53] became visible for the first time—revealed a strange disparity between its stated goal (to replace the "external" critiques of Ladmiral, Cotten, and Bourdieu[54] with a truly "internal" critique) and its actual outcome: a virulent denunciation of an "impasse," even of a "deception," indeed of a "failure" bordering on mystification (one gets the impression that in fact a new form of "external" criticism prevailed). What happened between these two extremes—against the "external" critiques and against Heidegger himself? There was the identification of a "remainder" that would have been missed by the "external" critiques and that, once identified, would be subjected to critique, a critique so acute it would silence Heidegger's thought. The transition from the "external" to the "internal" was conceived not as a hermeneutical deepening but rather as a radicalization that turned into a rationalist and critical position. Although they showed clearly that the challenge from "external" readings to the autonomy of Heidegger's work folded these readings back onto the sociological or ideological "interests" that they claimed to represent (while failing to address the core of Heidegger's thought), Ferry and Renaut's reading itself sought to be efficacious.[55] However, the aim of the reflection (which was opposed to the Heideggerian "dignity" of said thought) was never made explicit. Although they claimed to follow the Hegelian model of internal refutation, the method used was less a dialectical and comprehensive overcoming than an ostracizing, which, in the end, was as polemical as the "external" critiques. The accusation of "deception"[56] also carried a moralizing connotation that was in no way justified by the authors themselves. Their final judgment, however, attempted to balance the failure imputed to Heidegger with the acknowledgment of two essential achievements of his thinking: the grasp of the onto-theological structure of metaphysics, and the identification of an irreducible (ontological) difference.[57] This was a somewhat peremptory conclusion to ingenious analyses of the relation between being and language, which—while succeeding in unmasking the Heideggerian "double game" between the mirage of a new instauration and the conservation of the status quo—remained completely foreign to the question of the meaning of history under the effects of a henceforth planetary technology.

What a contrast with Henri Birault's work, where one has the impression of being on a completely different planet! It is not just that the latter limited himself to thinking *with* Heidegger without attempting to criticize him, but that he took care to carry this out with style, in a personal manner, and with a probing method. In this case we are dealing with an attempt similar to that of Jean Beaufret: a similar studious admiration for an oeuvre, which is taken to be profoundly innovative and already a classic, a similar recounting of a pedagogical experience, and a similar interest in style (in both cases sustained by the art of rapproche-ments and the talent for introducing new perspectives).[58] This connection must of course be nuanced: Birault's style is more eloquent, and also more academic; his tone is also less insolent or polemical; he does not offer Beaufret's inimitable mix of depth and anecdote.

Indeed, Birault's intention was to rise above the fray. He achieved this by conducting his dialogues only with the greatest figures associated with Heidegger: Kant, Hegel, and Nietzsche. His strategy of in-depth readings (following the great themes: knowing, desiring, willing, questioning truth, being, and time) was complemented by the constant play of a "double reading": Heidegger on the basis of Kant, and then the reverse; similarly for Heidegger's other great "partners." This confrontation was not limited to a repetition of the teachings of the Master of Freiburg, but enriched them by multiplying the angles of attack—a method that nonetheless was faithful to the fundamental project of unearthing the "unthought" of the great metaphysical worldviews: "In its very path, Heideggerian thought is inseparable from a renewed reading of the entire metaphysical tradition."[59] The accuracy of this remark is especially attested in his work in the field of modern philosophy. Although Hegel is not neglected (he appears in the chapter "The Adventures of the Concept"[60]), we should note that this rereading is principally inscribed within the Kant-Nietzsche-Heidegger "triangle." This triad is thought to circumscribe our modernity: Kant as the critical refoundation of a "metaphysics of metaphysics" on the basis of transcendental subjectivity; Nietzsche as the destabilization of such subjectivity in terms of a will whose nihilism becomes apparent; Heidegger as the questioning of all the assumptions of this tradition and as the preparation of a completely different thought.

A significant hesitation, however, appeared in this scholarly interpretative ballet, and one should not think that it was settled once and for all in Heidegger's favor. It was Nietzsche who introduced and imposed this hesitation, to the extent that the chaotic character of his thought resists Heidegger's reading, as penetrating as it might have been. Thus, one must resist "subscribing too quickly to the Heideggerian interpretation according to which Nietzsche's philosophy is purely and simply a metaphysics of the will to power."[61] Not rejecting, for all that, Heidegger's interpretation (and above all not its genealogical character, following the guiding thread of the accomplishment of metaphysics), Birault did not intend to reduce this tension the way that one solves a problem: he preferred to open the horizon to a "double reading" of Nietzsche (either chaotic or "despotic").

However clever (albeit sincere) such a model might have been, it becomes clear—above all at the end of the book—that Birault remained split between Nietzsche and Heidegger. It is not just the interpretation of the former by the latter that gave rise to his perplexity: the stakes of thinking lay in that interpretation, as thinking was determined by Nietzsche's quest for the "eternal now" and

Heidegger's disposition for "another beginning." Birault did not really decide: he left two irons in the fire for the future.[62]

A Resurgence of the Heideggerian Left?

The hostility or admiration toward Heidegger was not always directly linked to clearly defined political orientations. The two cases just mentioned are good examples of this—especially that of Henri Birault, who was quite unlikely to take a political position. Another memorable example of a study of Heidegger that is difficult to classify politically is George Steiner's book, which appeared in a French translation in 1981[63] and was hardly noticed at first. It was an introduction to Heidegger intended for an English-speaking audience, and its more original aspects were largely ignored (an acute sensitivity to Heidegger's language and a passionate effort at making a distinction between the greatness of his thinking and the intolerable character of his silence about the Holocaust).[64]

Furthermore, the very idea of a "Heideggerian left" could be disputed since there had never been—to my knowledge—an explicit claim to such a title, by either a single person or a group. Would it thus not be odd to be satisfied with such a label to describe Jacques Derrida? In 1980 he published a large work of more than 500 hundred pages entitled *The Post Card,* which was difficult to categorize according to conventional genres and whose "subject" was in no way Heidegger.[65] In fact, was there even a subject in this text (or collection of texts)? Starting with a "sendings" of a correspondence, (with) a postcard that strangely depicts Plato standing behind his teacher, and reversing their roles by having Plato seem to dictate something to Socrates, who functions as a scribe, Derrida inserted many allusions to Heidegger into a lover's correspondence, caught up in the pleasure of his own text. Under what pretext did this take place? Under a critical reflection on destinal "sending" in Heidegger, a *Geschick* more proper and more decisive than being itself. When Derrida opposed Heidegger with "the Postal Principle as differantial relay,"[66] the unprepared reader risked getting lost and giving up. Nonetheless, one must understand—as strange as this may appear—that Derrida is much more serious here than he lets on. What he is putting into question is the Heideggerian return to an original gathering or gift. If nothing is destined at the heart of being itself, there is, in some sense, no privileged sender: there are only networks, intermediaries, multiple sendings; there would be only "the postal" without destination, neither originary nor final.[67] Hence the erasure or disintegration of the notion of a destiny of being and even of the idea of a unity of metaphysics[68] in favor of an ever-reiterated, albeit elusive, *différance* through the textuality of the proposed fragments. This ironic and coded critique of the Master's assumptions seemed clearly unacceptable or unnecessarily insolent to "strictly obedient" Heideggerians; it was, however, accompanied by a gesture of homage ("we will not get around Freiburg"[69]) and other signs, where a decisive debt to Heidegger is unquestionably confirmed. This is particularly the case with a questioning of Lacan's logocentrism and the meditative retrieval of the question of truth within and without the psychoanalytic field.[70]

Regardless of the limits or the relative legitimacy of the label "Heideggerian left" (which was obviously insufficiently clarifying in the case of Derrida), it is undeniable that it at least allows a provisional orientation within a complex intellectual and ideological landscape. It is in this respect that one can consider Kostas Axelos as the most noteworthy representative of an early "Heideggerian left," which was certainly small in number and more of a minority among Heideggerians than the left Gaullists were in the large family of the supporters of the General! To seek a convergence between the goals of emancipation in Marx and the preparation of "another thinking" in Heidegger is certainly neither a reactionary nor a conservative approach. It is also a more radical project than an enlightened liberalism or a socio-democratic progressivism, not to mention its clear rejection of an allegiance to the Stalinist or even "revisionist" systems. As contextualized as every political "classification" must be, it does not seem unjustified to consider two publications from 1982 as belonging to the left, if not the extreme left: first, a remarkable accomplishment by Gérard Granel, and second, an unexpected theoretical advance by Reiner Schürmann.

The accomplishment consisted in the publication of a bilingual edition of the famous "Rectoral Address"[71] and of an explanatory text: "Why have we published this?"[72] Oft cited and added to the accusatory dossier against Heidegger, this address had, until then, hardly been read closely in France. Publishing it while proclaiming its value as a great text was perceived as a provocation, especially since it was accompanied by virulent contestations of the "capitalist-fascist" order instituted by developed capitalism in Europe. Far from limiting himself to a defense of Heidegger the man, and by wisely inscribing his contribution within the limits of the ongoing debate around Heidegger's political error, Granel shook up the landscape of this controversy by almost turning the "Rectoral Address" into a contemporary text. Thus, managing to catch Heidegger's enemies off balance, he attempted more audaciously (but also more decisively) to explain the urgency of a meditation on the joint effects of technicized science and of neo-capitalism.

We cannot dwell on the French context—largely forgotten today—surrounding this operation: the student demonstrations and the protests surrounding the "Higher Education Laws" imposed by Madame Saunié-Séïté, then state secretary of higher education. This context, although significant, was the technocratic conception of the university that was rejected by a large number of students and faculty. This allows us to understand the surprising comparison of the French situation of 1976–77 with the German one from 1933. Granel turned the "Rectoral Address" into a crucial reference, in the sense that Heidegger proclaimed therein "the self-affirmation of the German university" in order to thwart the politicization of the university disciplines that was advocated by the Nazis. He also attempted to initiate a more radical questioning concerning the essence of science. Of course, Granel had to concede the legitimacy of the question: "How could Heidegger have made such a mistake?" He responded that it was a question of "false expectations".[73] Heidegger had thought (clearly in error) that he could make a compromise with a movement whose positive possibilities he had overestimated. This was an enormous mistake, but one that was shared at the time by the German bourgeoisie and by many others as well—including in France.[74] This "logic of compromise" (found, *mutatis mutandis,* among the "comrades," as Granel cruelly recalled) does not negate the call of the address to rethink the "existential" founding of the sciences, to free them from their functionalist closure, and to tirelessly question their meaning.[75] Read in this light, the "Rectoral Address" was, according to Granel, a text of great importance whose lesson must be heard. Considering the "constitutive ambiguity"[76] of this text (which was rooted in its historical inscription and in the fragility of a personal choice), we must relate its finding to those of Marx in order to interpret technocratic modernity (in its neo-liberalism as well as in its fascist dementia) as "the total mobilization of the individual in service of infinite production."[77] Despite the homage paid to Jean Beaufret,[78] this latter point clearly differentiates them.

At the same time, this gap also explains how Granel, in his very excess, and even if he did not convince everyone, managed to influence the "vanguard." Instead of limiting himself to defending Heidegger the man, a task where many failed, he set forth a skillful assessment and attempted to open up a philosophical discussion. The assessment concerned the importance of the "Rectoral Address" that was to be read as the great text that it was (which did not mean that one had to accept all its assertions[79]); to reduce the address to its Nazi elements was to misunderstand what was crucial to it. However, the open perspective toward philosophical discussion concerned the convergence of irrationality (indeed of dementia) and efficiency in the contemporary forms of domination at the heart of which science and technology play a decisive role. Granel discerned that as early as 1933, Heidegger paved the way for giving thought to the "monstrous nature" of modern technology: did Heidegger not have a premonition of the incommensurable complicity that would unite—in hitherto unknown forms—technological neutralization and mass extermination when he denounced hyper-specialization and called for questioning? However, what was lacking in this unfinished text[80] was a more precise determination of Heidegger's "error" and of the specificity of political tasks, to the extent that these provide scant resources for exorcising the excess produced by the convergence between the capitalization of the means of production and the technicization of scientific knowledge.

The intentionally provocative character of Granel's contribution, his audacity and his panache (within the limits we just mentioned) gained him, if not respect, then at least its equivalent in our intellectual jousts: no one challenged him directly. Just as unexpected, but in a completely different style and on a completely different register, was the publication, in 1982, of an original work by a German philosopher teaching in the United States: Reiner Schürmann.[81]

In an impeccable French and with abiding elegance, Schürmann turned away from any sort of historiographical or biographical consideration in order to envisage the legacy of Heideggerian thought on its own terms. His question was precisely that of *archē,* the grounding principle understood as the economy of presence. Schürmann begins at Heidegger's ending point: the presumption of an end or a closure of metaphysics. The task of thinking should be one not of repeating or saving that which is inscribed in this closure of the figure of presence, but rather of completing the decay of the epochal principles, a decay that, by disrupting the dyad of theory and praxis, impels thinking beyond their difference. "Action itself, and not only its theory, loses its foundation or *archē.*"[82] Such a conception of the deconstruction of metaphysics seems to lead to a paradox, indeed to a contradiction: how can there be a principle of that which withdraws from any principle?[83] Schürmann acknowledges this possible misunderstanding, the reality of this paradox or even contradiction, from the outset: he turns it into the "dazzling"[84] theme of his reflection. "Anarchy," in the sense in which he meant it, in following Heidegger (a name that points to a "discursive regularity"[85]), designates an enterprise that is conscious of its own impossibility: the search for the Principle is dislocated. Deconstruction is not a purely theoretical gesture; it is on the contrary the expression of a dispossession of all principled mastery of action. It opens the "releasement" (*Gelassenheit*) and the explosion of a pluralization of action, announced in poetical mode by Char:

> *That part never fixed, asleep in us, from which will spring TOMORROW THE MANIFOLD.*[86]

To remain at this preliminary level might give the impression that Schürmann's work advances provocative propositions without argumentation. As a matter of fact, nourished as it was by meticulous Heideggerian interpretations of the history of metaphysics, the book is solidly constructed around a core that undertakes a historic deduction of the categories of presence by distinguishing three decisive moments: the "prospective" categories of the pre-Socratic beginning,[87] the "retrospective" categories (essentially Nietzschean) of the technological accomplishment of metaphysics,[88] and finally the transitional categories resulting from Heidegger's own "turn."[89] Schürmann is most original when he shows precisely how Heidegger reworks his own conceptuality (that initially corresponded to his fundamental ontology) in order to be able to indicate, or at least begin to indicate, what is left in reserve beyond the closure of metaphysics and the economy of presence. It is also this elaboration of the transitional categories that lends support to the paradoxical principle of anarchy itself: the mutation that announces a completely different thought is first translated into the language that it destabilizes. The closure of metaphysics is not to be confused with the end of history: it creates rather a tension internal to our actions, and the conditions of a transition whose stakes we are only beginning to glimpse.

Although we cannot here enter into more "technical" considerations, we can nonetheless mention the attention Schürmann paid to the objections made against him.[90] He reconstitutes them systematically and responds to them in detail at the end of his book. Indeed, he establishes his position without hesitation by almost teaching a lesson to his elders: against Derrida he shows that the Heideggerian concept of "presence" utterly destroys the "complete possession of self by self,"[91] and in sharp opposition to Birault, he maintains that the latter ignored the "hypothesis of closure" and that he does not understand that with the lecture "On Time and Being" a new turn sets in, allowing us to think that epochality itself is overcome.[92]

Such a masterful book, having marked a turning point in the Heideggerian literature, could not provoke, as one might have guessed, immediate reactions. Nonetheless, not only did it not go by unnoticed,[93] but it contributed to a resurgence of interest[94] in Heidegger, which was seen at the beginning of the eighties, from an innovative and progressive perspective.

The most notable text in this respect is nonetheless difficult to characterize in these terms. In a long reflection, the principal concern of which is the "Rectoral Address," Philippe Lacoue-Labarthe posed anew the question concerning Heidegger's political involvements by trying to maintain two positions at the same time: refusing any complacency toward the "unforgivable" while still recognizing the "greatness" of the thinker in question.[95] The issue then was to avoid slipping back into the rut of the polemics around Heidegger's personal guilt, in order to identify that which in this thinking "made possible—or more exactly, did not forbid—the political engagement of 1933."[96] The axis followed was the one that led to a gesture of foundation (or refoundation) of Germany's spiritual mission: this gesture was both philosophical (hence radically metaphysical) and political (in an equally fundamental sense).[97] This "overvaluing" of the philosophical and this overestimating of the political intersected in the exaltation of the Nietzschean model and crystallized in a twofold way: in the interpretation of events based on the will to power and the ideal of refoundation in terms of Spirit (Derrida, a few years later, would return to this crucial point). What did the failure of this attempt lead to? It led undoubtedly to "the pure and simple *collapse* of fundamental ontology."[98] But this negative result (whose counterpart would be the famous "turn") could not cover up a "formidable assumption" or, if one prefers, a Heideggerian unthought: "Heidegger's constant refusal, as it seems to me, to take seriously the concept of *mimesis*."[99]

Lacoue-Labarthe thus gave the impression (for those looking for a conclusion that could easily be exploited in a politico-ideological sense) of finding a way out that may seem too academic or subtle: Heidegger's political error would be due to the mimetical mythification (investing history) of the German possibilities seen in relation to the Greek model (inimitable). The impossible "repetition" of this model would find its confirmation in the failure of the political involvement, but would nonetheless not be radically placed into question by Heidegger. "It seems to me more and more difficult not to see a fundamental mimetology at work in Heidegger's thought."[100] What was thus proposed was less a definitive response than a working hypothesis, a path for further research that Lacoue-Labarthe intended to explore and deepen.

A Cascade of Tributes

A delayed effect of the Master's death? The discovery of new aspects of a thinking approaching monumental status thanks to the gradual publication of the *Gesamtausgabe*? These explanations are not mutually exclusive when it comes to explaining the flourishing of studies[101] and tributes (the most interesting of which—especially, *Heidegger et la question de Dieu*[102]—were not exempt from critiques or questions). These years were also marked by the passing of Jean Beaufret,[103] who, until his last days, never ceased working along "Heidegger's path."[104] Beaufret's final texts, collected in the fourth volume of *Dialogue avec Heidegger*, testify to his careful work, which was always attentive to the quality of the writing, and aimed to show that "with Heidegger, everything is reversed."[105] He was no longer interested in "converting" anyone to this thinking (if he had ever tried). From then on, with no more illusions about support or success, he concentrated on coming to terms with what he liked to call Heidegger's "enormity," and on formulating scrupulous clarifications on the oblivion of being, Aristotle's metaphysics, his interpretation of tragedy, the question of "Christian philosophy," and that of the "humanities." If one of the texts in this collection was openly polemical (the reply to Renaut, "A propos de *Questions IV* de Heidegger"), the book is permeated from one end to the other by a scathing irony that in no way impeded highly scholarly explanations, whether on "the enigma of Z3" (a subtle questioning of the formulations of the multiple senses of being in Aristotle) or—in following a digression on technology—on the discussion of "Marx's exact point of confusion." Marx posited a priority of the practical over the theoretical even though the two always correspond to each other: "To juggle, in regards to modern technology, the twin concepts of theory and *praxis*, amounts quite simply to repeatedly raising the insoluble question of the chicken and the egg—which comes first?"[106]

Even though the order would have to be reversed from a strictly pedagogical point of view, a reading of these studies should be completed by reading the interviews[107] Beaufret gave in his last years. In those interviews, once again, his inimitable style of joining what was important with the anecdotal by explaining them together shone forth. Beaufret managed once more to amaze, not only by his pedagogical talent in the domain of the history of philosophy, but also by his ability to make the past palpable: for example, in his *Entretiens avec Frédéric de Towarnicki,* by discussing the specifically Greek wonder before what is, but also, more subtly, in discussing the Hellenistic sense of oblivion, that "great withdrawal from everything" that, according to Thucydides, had beset the Athenians on the occasion of the famous plague.[108] Suddenly, with the passage of time, one understands why the Cartesian search for certainty could have only given rise to sarcasm on the part of Pythagoras[109] and in which sense the Greeks "had no concept of consciousness."[110] One then understands Archimedes's protest against the Roman soldier about to kill him: "Do not disturb my circles!"[111] And then, there is this privilege afforded to Beaufret, rare enough among philosophers: a pure and sober language that is no less for having been spoken, like a table set impeccably (and yet spontaneously), clear and ironic, like Valery, but suddenly delicate and poetical like Nerval. Thus, a childhood memory arises and carries us to this "almost sacred" moment when, at twilight, the ceremony of the lighting of gas lamps took place.[112] Thanks to these traits of originality, the faithfulness to Heidegger's inspiration takes on its own unforgettable life in the French language.

Jean Beaufret's death in August 1982, six years after the death of the Master, justly conveyed the impression that an era was drawing to an end. The hero and his principal confidant had withdrawn from the scene of history. Hence, one turned to an immense field for research, for decades to come: the German publication of the *Gesamtausgabe* and its French translations.[113] Would there be anything more than interpreters, commentaries, or obtuse adversaries from that point on?

The most notable tribute, in *Cahier de l'Herne,* which appeared in the fall of 1983 (preceded, incidentally, by an equally remarkable edition of *Exercices de la patience*[114]), seemed to exclude such a pessimistic reading of the evolution of Heidegger's French reception. The challenge was successfully met: the horizon was opened up to as many as possible, to persons and orientations, breaking with all strict "orthodoxy." The inclusion of voices from other countries was also notable: German and American contributors were almost as numerous as the French. The purely "French" divisions were skillfully displaced or effaced. An undeniable care for quality presided over the endeavor. Even the photograph adorning the cover attempted to break with the academic or imperious images of the Master: there he was, pictured intimately, at work, lost in thought, on the verge of writing, perhaps signing his name.

Michel Haar's preface had the virtue of explaining the spirit and the goals of the project with great clarity. As a recognition of an "immense debt" that nonetheless avoided uncritical allegiance, the endeavor aimed to distinguish itself from any school: "We are students of Heidegger, but there is no Heideggerian school." This statement seemed somewhat defensive: on the matter of the difficulty and the "hermeticism" of Heidegger ("obscurity is the index of the *finitude* of presence"), and on the debatable or unfortunate nature of certain translations ("some have circulated a heavy and precious jargon for the initiates"). A "freer and more lucid" reading—which, however, must always be accompanied by a "critical view"[115]—would have to hasten the overcoming of "the old dilemmas wherein we tread," authorizing what Derrida had called "Heideggerian hope." This preface was accompanied by a liminal text, "The banished biography,"[116] in which Michel Haar emphasized that Heidegger always discouraged biographical questions: if it is true that deep reserve in this matter is compensated by a careful "self-interpretation" of the path of thinking, can nothing more than the "natal" be retained as an autobiographical element? This summary was skillful for it avoided allusion to the political involvement of 1933. Further, the latter is present in the chronology that opens the volume. It is admitted that a series of calls and discourses from 1933 revealed "the allegiance to certain Nazi ideological themes,"[117] but it is also noted that the "Rectoral Address" defended a conception of the independence of the university "which in no way corresponds to the views of the party." Above all, it was clarified that after stepping down from the rectorate in 1934, Heidegger "was completely skeptical with respect to Nazism."[118] These details barely maintain a fragile equilibrium between a few cruel truths and their comprehensive reevaluation—Jean-Michel Palmier's text "Heidegger and National-Socialism"[119] developed this line of thought.

Palmier's text aimed to assess, as impartially as possible, a "dossier" that at that point was already quite large.[120] It was as if he was having premonitions of an unavoidable rebound; he resigned himself to affirming that texts dedicated to Heidegger's political involvement were without any doubt more numerous than those dedicated to his ontology. In attempting to avoid the excesses of an accusation as well as those of an unconditional defense, he recalled first of all—as an illustration of the former—a certain number of inexactitudes bordering on calumny and then examined more sophisticated critical analyses (particularly those from Lukacs, Adorno, and Steiner). Along the way, he tipped his hat, so to speak, to Jean-Pierre Faye's *Langages totalitaires*, which he called "a special contribution to the sociology of language," without necessarily finding the parallel between Heidegger's metaphysics and the Rector Krieck's discourses convincing.[121] In denouncing the retrospective illusions and the absence of questions concerning what Heidegger during that period "understood precisely by National-Socialism,"[122] he attempted to reconstitute the facts. His presentation of the involvement from 1933 (which could not be exactly the same today) carried two sections: one relatively favorable to Heidegger, the other hostile. His acceptance of the rectorate at the insistence of the dismissed Social-Democrat Rector Möllendorf was described as an attempt to defend the university from the threat of a brutal "reorganization": the "Rectoral Address" was a truly philosophical text that was distinguished from Nazi ideology in many essential respects (the autonomy of the university, the conception of science, and the absence of anti-Semitic biologism). Yet, the text and the proclamations from 1933 (support for Hitler, tribute to Schlageter, and support for the withdrawal from the League of Nations) were "absolutely indefensible" and testified to Heidegger's political blindness.[123] Balancing this criticism, Palmier credited Heidegger with a certain courage for carrying out of his functions as rector (his refusal to allow anti-Semitic posters and his refusal to allow the burning of "banned books" in the university), as well during the period after his resignation when he was attacked and isolated by the regime. Moving on to the political implications of Heidegger's ontology, Palmier was in no way dismissive of Bourdieu's critical analyses, recognizing what was pertinent and even notable in his approach to the complexity of Heidegger's discourse read in the highly variegated context of the German intellectual life of the period. But he could approve of neither the unproven accusation of anti-Semitism nor the arbitrariness of the examples, nor the ambiguity of the irony regarding the rural tastes of the "professor." Recalling the apolitical nature of the German university and the prevailing disdain for politics at the time, Palmier maintained that one could not understand Heidegger's case outside of its context, but that the sociological explanations in and of themselves could not account for the complexity of the situation in which the strictly philosophical stakes were so high. It was toward these philosophical stakes that it was necessary to turn, in order to understand how Heidegger could have paid tribute to the "inner greatness" of the National Socialist movement in 1935. Was this a naiveté? Perhaps not only, for it was a grave error to have projected a spiritual possibility upon reality. Finally, the most "embarrassing" question was that of the silence after the war. Perhaps due to the thinker's pride, this "ambiguous silence" loomed large, but should not become the object of a trial.[124]

In the conditions of the moment, and whatever the unavoidable corrections might be made in the event of a reprinting, Palmier's text seems to have represented a worthy effort at a sincere assessment, which was intellectually honest in a domain that was particularly sensitive and delicate. This is also what Roger-Pol Droit acknowledged in a review[125] where he praised the qualities and the importance of the *Cahier de l'Herne* as a whole.[126]

We cannot examine the other essays in the *Cahier* in detail, among which the text by a young Jean-Louis Chrétien[127] stands out due to its distinctive quality of writing. It is useful nonetheless to characterize more precisely the principal orientation of the volume in order to complete our remarks concerning the spirit of the endeavor. If we put aside the personal testimonies and the documentary elements, what were the major themes that were explored? The main chapter headings[128] were predictable. Yet, a critical distance allows us to discern that the guiding thread was the completion of metaphysics in the age of technology—a central question that was not the only question subtending the section entitled "The Age of Technology." If it had been published two decades earlier, this *Cahier* would have given more importance to the question of existence and to the early Heidegger. Assembled more recently, it would have no doubt given more space to Heideggerian interpretations of the entirety of the history of philosophy and to the numerous volumes of the collected works that remain untranslated. It is not surprising that the balance (due also in great part to the fact—well understood and exploited by Michel Haar—that Heidegger's death required that one be imaginative in order to ensure that the awaited tribute would not be conventional) was marked by the historical moment when the critique of the society of production and consumption was no longer carried out in the overly passionate terms of 1968, but benefited rather from reflexive and critical distance, specifically due to a more developed meditation on Nietzsche. Of course, many of the questions posed in the *Cahier* transcended the circumstances, particularly the perplexities concerning the question of God, concentrated in this remark by Jean Greisch: "Everything takes place as if the sacred as divine milieu absorbed the figure of God."[129] Heidegger's tomb carried no cross but rather a small, eight-pointed star. The "god to come" is not identified.[130] Always enigmatic, the thinker preferred instead a more sober and more exacting legacy: awaiting.

We spoke earlier of transfiguration. At a more modest level than that of glory, of immortality, or waiting for God, we must consider the enigma that figuration posed to thought, and to the *polylogue* that Derrida organized around the Heideggerian interpretation of Van Gogh's famous painting of the worn-out shoes.[131] This was a seemingly marginal and yet decisive debate (for it thematized the status of truth in Heidegger's discussion of painting—the credibility of the latter having been put into question by Meyer Schapiro, the renowned art historian). It was under the ironic title "Restitutions of the Truth in Pointing [*pointure*]"[132] that Derrida led a complex discussion, whose starting point was the opposition of the two "truths" concerning the famous painting: were the shoes those of a peasant (as Heidegger suggested) or those of a city-dweller, the artist himself (Schapiro's thesis)? At first, Derrida had no difficulty in showing the narrowness of the dilemma, as it was brought about by the very specificity of Schapiro's "expertise": the issue can only be, instead of the shoes painted by Van Gogh, the canvas referenced as "*de la Faille n.225.*"[133] Heidegger acknowledged having seen the painting to which he was referring in an exhibition in Amsterdam in March 1930. This "admission" caused him to fall into a trap. But where was the trap? Should the restitution of the "truth" of/in the painting be limited to this narrow dispute—city mouse against country mouse? Schapiro never considered that what was at stake in Heidegger's text went well beyond the question of whether or not the shoes belong to a peasant woman (with restitution to their "owner"). For the issue was much more fundamentally the critique of metaphysical truth and, with it, of the notion of the subject—truth and the subject as well as the truth of the subject, both confronted by the question of the work of art, and with the origin of the work itself, thrusting into a world. Henceforth, "is it a matter of rendering justice to Heidegger, of restituting what is his due, his truth, the possibility of his own gait and progress?"[134] No doubt: the explication of the text is scrupulous, even meticulous, showing the subtle progression that allowed the thinker to choose the example of Van Gogh's painting in order to allow the work—which cannot be reduced either to the insignificance of a thing nor to the elaboration of a finished product—to appear as the opening of an entire world. The truth that was thus evoked no longer had anything to do with a mere attribution. The Van Gogh painting was chosen by Heidegger as "an intuitive accessory"[135] in a process of evocation (which was in no way dependent on the "peasant" character of the shoes) that unfolded beyond any narrow relations of correspondence between reality and representation. "Let us not forget that *The Origin* deals with the essence of truth, the truth of essence and the abyss (*Abgrund*) which plays itself out there like the 'veiled' destiny (*fatum*) which transfixes being."[136]

If Heidegger was incessantly defended, other voices from the polylogue can be heard in order to cast doubt on him for a certain "monoreferential naïveté."[137] Indeed, he could not have overlooked the fact that Van Gogh had often painted such shoes; above all, with the attribution of the shoes to a peasant woman, "Heidegger falls short of his discourse on the truth in painting."[138] Irony wielded as a weapon also made use of sexual and psychoanalytical connotations that were completely absent from Heidegger's text ("sex of reattachment,"[139] the form of the shoes, the role of the laces, etc.). Moreover, despite the credit given to Heidegger for having overcome the conception of a shoe-wearing subject outside of the painting, it was necessary to go so far as to identify an ultimate limit of the horizon of his thought: "in the belonging (corresponding) to the silent discourse of the earth."[140] And, in fact, is it possible to approach Van Gogh's work in terms of a pre-originary ultimate reconciliation (an alliance or a gift) worn secretly by the Mother-Earth? Finally, the last word—if there is one—belonged not to Heidegger but to a poet paying tribute to the "occult strangeness" in Vincent, his fellow artist in despair. Listening to Artaud in order to learn to look at Van Gogh? This unwritten moral message of *The Truth in Painting* is a declaration of the failure of all restitution: "but never to be possessed."[141]

Was Heidegger more disfigured than transfigured? Jacques Derrida's surprising polylogue left the question open. Along the way, a voice registered the following furtive tribute: "It was indeed Heidegger's text that opened this debate."[142]

Epilogue IV

We noted the stark contrast that characterized 1976: it was the year of the Master's death, and his disciples were divided regarding the translations of his texts. Obviously this was about the sharing of his legacy. Every empire meets such a destiny upon the death of the founding sovereign. But one might have thought that in intellectual and above all philosophical matters, the stakes would not involve ownership or even an editorial authority. Did the "critical Heideggerians" have the right to complain of being excluded in this respect? Would they not have preferred, after all, to privilege philosophical freedom over unconditional allegiance, since a recognition of a philosophical approach cannot be reduced to fealty or to a personal fidelity? For my part, even if I complained of certain of its effects, I was not scandalized that the publisher Gallimard followed the Heidegger family's instructions to the letter: Jean Beaufret, and then Fédier, would have the last word concerning the choice of translators of the collected works. The problem should instead have been reversed: it is normally the case that the responsibility for choosing translators would be confided to those who had Heidegger's or his family's confidence; it was less justifiable that the choices seemed determined more by a degree of faithfulness to "orthodoxy" (or to the inner circle of the faithful) than by competence. Among the "excluded," only one would experience a dramatic outcome. The reason for this is clear. Emmanuel Martineau was precisely not to be counted among "critical Heideggerians"; his disillusionment (and his "revenge") would be in proportion to his absolute admiration for Heidegger. We shall return to this.

Disconcerted by the growing divisiveness, at a time when the passing of the great thinker should have imposed a thoughtful critical distance, I attempted to clarify my own contribution to this task. Sketched out in "L'apprentissage de la contiguïté" (an article that appeared in June–July 1976 in the journal Critique*), this work was completed by combining three dialogues ("De la domination," "Heidegger à New York," "La rationalité comme partage"), which I intended to publish under the title "L'Expérience dite" (the first article is to this day unpublished; the two others would be reedited and published later, one in* Heidegger from Metaphysics to Thought, *the other in* Rationalities, Historicities*). During the years immediately following Heidegger's death, I became very aware that the period of "admiration" (with the pioneers Beaufret and Birault) had run its course and that a new critical effort would be absolutely necessary. Not that the value of this first reception would be annulled; on the contrary, it was precisely its assimilation that made new advances possible and necessary. I will not dwell here on the lack of preparation of the philosophical public for the nuances of such an internal critique. During a lecture given in December 1976 at the* Collège de philosophie, *I noted the change in Alain Renaut and the even more radical neo-Kantianism of Luc Ferry. Our friendly yet vigorous debate revealed our disagreement: they did not join me in pursuing a linguistic dimension preserving the gains of Heideggerian hermeneutics in relation to the "dominant language" of metaphysics (my interlocutors rejected the Heideggerian contribution out of hand). At a time when I thought of myself as more and more critical (or "diacritical"), engaged in a difficult dialogue with Heidegger's thought, I was surprised at being perceived as still (too) Heideggerian.*

This misunderstanding would only grow. I have had to admit that the reception of Heidegger did not escape a highly classical "rule": the reversals from for to against, exercising an irresistible power of fascination, captured the imagination and held the public's attention, and even the attention of the supposedly more informed interpreters, who were repelled by the critical interpretative refinements or were insensitive to its nuances. I had to slowly accept this situation, whether I liked it or not.

In 1977, on the 22nd of May, Jean Beaufret celebrated his seventieth birthday. His close friends organized a celebration dinner at the Bofinger brasserie, near la Bastille. The invitation card bore the following quote from Simone Weil: "A man who has something new to say can only be heard at first by those who like him." In fact, snubbed by the "powers of the establishment," Beaufret was always surrounded by friends and young auditors—a privilege that many professors holding prestigious chairs at the Sorbonne or elsewhere did not enjoy.

Yet, it was in that same year 1977 that the feud between Renaut and his former teacher was consummated and made public, through an article by the former and a reply by the latter, the following year. Was it really necessary for Beaufret himself to reply and to turn this response into a matter of self-justification? He could have simply endorsed a summary prepared by the "accused," the translators of Questions IV. *It would even have been possible for him to hide behind a supreme contempt and to allow them to reply without him. For some time, and increasingly in his last years, Beaufret never hesitated to engage in polemics that turned sour. In fact, he did everything in order to involve himself in polemics. Without saying he was entirely wrong, I must admit having perceived a certain uneasiness that I had trouble understanding at the time, but that had less to with the issues than with the modalities and circumstances. Did a respected master have to accept a sort of public duel with one of his close disciples? His* pro domo *defense put him on the defensive. Whatever the quality of the text, whatever the validity of the arguments and the liveliness of the formulations, there was something inappropriate or unbalanced, as when a family quarrel—all things being equal—is played out in the public sphere. There was, incidentally, a quasi-familial gesture in the way in which his most faithful students were named, the order corresponding apparently to seniority (Fédier, Hervier, Jacerme, Vezin, etc.). I was almost relieved that my name had not been omitted. The fact of finding myself at the end of the list with my friend Jean-Philippe Guinle in no way bothered me. I was neither the most senior nor the most faithful among Jean's auditors. The only unusual fact was that we were connected "to the Condorcet period." For (except for one or two times), Jean-Philippe and I had never taken classes at Condorcet. Although mentioned, the lectures from the École Normale did not seem to be really memorable! What counted most for Jean— this text shows it—was the slow work carried out in* khâgne, *with a small group of the faithful, all profoundly interested in Heidegger and in the renewed study of the great philosophers. One has to do justice to him: if Heidegger was at the center of these studies, it was in a discreet manner and in the background, for the courses never concentrated on him. It was indeed a question of the philosophical tradition, from one end to the other, undertaken in an admirable fashion.*

During the winter of 1979–80, an unexpected opportunity, my unanticipated meeting with Constantin Tacou, provided the early impetus of the Cahier de l'Herne *devoted to Heidegger. When Tacou proposed that I organize it, I was intrigued by the idea, but I quickly realized that it was something of a minefield. When I submitted the idea of the project to Jean Beaufret, without whom I could hardly see myself getting involved, I was met not by an obvious refusal but by a silence: my question was not understood or a pretext was found to change the subject. Wanting to have a clear idea on the matter, and no longer having the time to insist (it was January 1980 and I had to leave to teach in the United States), I asked François Vezin if he would be so kind as to clarify the situation. Three weeks later, while I was in Washington, I received a note from Vezin, who categorically advised me against undertaking the publication. No reason was given! This left me perplexed. Not wanting to argue with Jean, I decided to abandon the project. Only a few months later, while relating this story to Michel Haar, I suggested that he take over the project.*

Why was this Cahier *undesirable? Had someone assumed that I would not prepare it in a sufficiently "orthodox" manner? Did one prefer to adopt a "low profile" in order to avoid any return of the polemics surrounding the choice of translators or the political question? Whatever the answer might have been, the fact is that Jean Beaufret finally submitted a text when he noticed that the project was going through. Alas, he did not live to see the* Cahier *published. Perhaps, he would not have had an overly unfavorable opinion of it, for this* Cahier *offered a wide selection of excellent Heideggerian research from the time. Would it have been possible to provide a more striking testimony to the vitality of Heideggerian studies? I do not think so even today. Was it also necessary to give a voice to the most radical critiques (Bourdieu, Faye, Ferry, Renaut) as well as to the most resolute partisans (Fédier, Towarnicki, Vezin)? Probably. At that time, the choices, which were made by Michel Haar alone, seemed pertinent to me, even if—as far as I was concerned— I would personally have been tempted to go further in the direction of encouraging debate. As it stands, the* Cahier *still seems to me today to be a success—of course, it should be consulted in the original edition, and not in the paperback reprint (the cover of the latter carries the fallacious subtitle "complete edition," although certain texts have been shortened and others added).*

One will have noted that the Cahier *appeared after Jean Beaufret's death, which occurred on August 7, 1982. We must go back in time a bit, back to this event and before it. In accordance with his wishes, his resting place was Auzances, his birthplace. The funeral was simple, under the sun of the Creuse, and I remember a few moving scenes. The disciples, the friends (from the "inner circle" to Granel and Marion) were more numerous than the very small family. Notable above all was the presence of Heidegger's son and grandson, Hermann and Detlev: this young man with long blond hair seemed to symbolize the passing of the torch. In this calm town in the Creuse, Parmenides's name was heard, thanks to François Guinle, who read an excerpt from the poem before the open grave. Everything seemed to have returned to an originary peace. Yet I must ask myself: why was this life, which was for the most part happy, always inspired by work, transfigured by talent, and bathed in the happiness of teaching, why was it tarnished at its end by bitter polemics, nearly devastated by a barbaric event in which Beaufret himself never played any role? If there had been a "failing" or a compromise with Nazism, this was never the case with Jean. On the contrary, he had been in the Resistance. So? Having gone to extreme lengths in his defense of a prestigious friend, was this not clearly the origin of a problem and a darkening of the horizon? But it was also the greatness of an accepted solitude in the fidelity of friendship. Such was his destiny, sealed forever. Under the August sun and heat, these thoughts mingled with the pain of the farewell.*

To follow a path in the field of thinking seemed to me the best way to remain faithful to Beaufret's teaching. This is why Heidegger: From Metaphysics to Thought, *which appeared in 1983, was dedicated to him without intending to strictly follow in his footsteps. As far as the many years of work that culminated in* Powers of the Rational, *the question posed itself differently. If the origin of the investigation was clearly a critical revisiting of the Heideggerian question concerning technology, it was intentionally unfolded in the techno-scientific "domain," while varying the strategy of attack. The guiding thread was no longer the question of being, but rather a phenomenology of the effects of the powers of rationality, combined with its critical genealogy. The dialogue with Heidegger nonetheless reappeared when techno-science was thought as "sharing" (here one encounters Heidegger's* Geschick *again but without its ontological unification and avoiding all dualism between the "authentic" and the "inauthentic"). The issue was, and still is, one of appreciating the destinal element that governed the "mastery and possession of nature," without however failing to grasp the (ethical, political, poetical) threshold that the technicization of life, of time, and of language can and must encounter.*

In that year 1985, when this book was published and the dialogue with Heideggerian thinking seemed to unfold calmly with respect to the main concepts, a major event would shake the philosophical intelligentsia to its core: after sixty years of waiting, Being and Time *was finally published in French! But this was in the form of a daring pirate publication, by Emmanuel Martineau. Once again, controversy would rage around Heidegger . . .*

9 The Letter and the Spirit

Sixty Years Hence!

Following a sixty-year delay after the original publication of *Sein und Zeit,* two complete French translations of *Sein und Zeit* finally appeared in 1985 and 1986. How could this not be surprising? As far as the delay itself is concerned, it was rooted in (but not completely justified by) a series of coincidences. We have seen that Corbin's volume was the only thing available at that time; later, the war and Liberation were not conducive to long-drawn-out work; the Louvain pair of de Waehlens and Boehm translated the first forty-four paragraphs incredibly slowly and finally published them with Gallimard in 1964. Why was this translation (otherwise laudable) not continued? Walter Biemel, who worked during those years at Louvain, thought that the only reason for this was Boehm's departure for Gand, where he became a professor. De Waehlens did not want to continue alone, and he was then more interested in Merleau-Ponty than in Heidegger.[1] Things slowed down again, inexplicably, and inexcusably.

How, then, can we account for the two rival translations in 1985–86? There are purely anecdotal reasons, tied to personal rivalries—which cannot be ignored. Jean-François Courtine and Emmanuel Martineau proposed to take on the translation toward the end of 1979, beginning of 1980. Jean Beaufret preferred François Vezin for the task.[2] Beyond these personal issues, it is more interesting to ask what conception of translation the two publications—by Martineau and Vezin, respectively—represented. They were obviously in competition (for recognition, not for commercial success). More should be said: the choices of translation (or of nontranslation) call for justifications that themselves delimit, in both cases, the outlines of a reading of the Heideggerian text. This is the central question, which must be analyzed, apart from the "anecdotal."

There was a Gaullist dimension to Emmanuel Martineau's coup. By finally publishing the first complete translation of Heidegger's masterpiece at his own expense, he stated that he wanted to save the honor of France,[3] breaking with convention, if not with legality! Moreover, he did it in June, of all times[4] . . . The book, sent to almost two thousand people, could not be sold, due to the exclusivity clause in the contract between Gallimard and Heidegger's heirs, benefiting François Vezin, who for his part had been chosen and imposed on Gallimard by Jean Beaufret (who enjoyed the confidence of the Heidegger family, and consequently, the German publisher).

Martineau's theatrical gesture might seem megalomaniacal. How is the honor of our "dear and old country" tied to this affair? Was it necessary to dramatize the nearly sixty-year absence (unusual indeed, and more than regrettable) of a complete translation? It is indisputable that many deplored this situation as a "scandal" without completely understanding it. It was incontestable that there had been a "demand that had been long frustrated," to use Martineau's expression. I have already inquired into the reasons (that are neither excuses nor justifications) for this "extravagant delay," this "mysterious carelessness" (both Martineau's expressions).[5] What caused the latter to intervene in such an exceptional and sensational manner was—in addition to the obvious disappointment in not having been chosen despite his merits (a student from the École Normale Supérieure, and a brilliant and seasoned Germanist)—the confirmation of a new delay: the predicted Gallimard translation still did not appear![6] As for what moved Martineau to give his solitary enterprise the appearance of a matter of honor, it must be emphasized, though it is obvious, that it was his unlimited admiration for *Sein und Zeit* (that he characterized as "the book of the 20th Century"[7]). Without this admiration, the feat of having translated more than 400 difficult pages in seven months, the financial sacrifice, the energy, the time spent, would have made no sense whatsoever.

Reasonably enough, Martineau's preface contained details relevant to the specific German edition he chose, claiming at the same time readability and consistency ("rendering . . . each German word by the equivalent French word"[8]), and one understands that he refused to translate the key word *Dasein* (Heidegger himself having judged it untranslatable[9]). Nonetheless, it is surprising that he gave in to polemics, devoting the entire second part of his preface to crossing swords with his former friend, Jean-François Courtine, on the subject of the translation of two terms (albeit important): *Vorhandenheit* and *Zuhandenheit* (that he translated respectively as *être-sous-la-main* and *être-à-portée-de-la-main*). A debate among specialists, one would say. Let us attempt to reveal its stakes as clearly as possible. In making this distinction, Heidegger wanted to show[10] that constant presence, or "presence-at-hand," is not the most originary relationship to things or to beings. Thrown into the world, articulating our "surroundings," we are at first in a relation of usability and utility with respect to the objects that are the most familiar to us. The hammer, the knife, and the watch make sense in terms of their "involvement" with the environing world: What are they going to be used for? How will I use them? How can they help me? What goals will they allow me to attain? This network of signs, of calls, and of projects, constitutes structures of references that are, for the "Existents" that we are, more decisive than the presence acquired, after the fact, by these instruments or tools in theoretical term.

How, then, should one translate the two terms that denote this distinction? In essentially taking the side of de Waehlens and Boehm and of the solution they chose: *subsistance* for *Vorhandenheit*, *disponibilité* for *Zuhandenheit*, Jean-François Courtine had himself leveled a polemic[11] against Martineau's choice (who thought it was important to keep in the French the reference to the "hand"—*Hand*—in both terms).

This seemingly Byzantine dispute involved the following stakes: should one choose to render the original German as closely as possible by almost imitating its wordplays, or should one opt for a more "didactic" explanation? Neither solution is perfect—each has its own problems. The first option, chosen by Martineau, renders the difference almost "imperceptible" (as Courtine argued), and it is true that the difference between *être-sous-la-main* [*Vorhandenheit*] and *être-à-portée-de-la-main* [*Zuhandenheit*] is hard to discern, to the extent that François Fédier had originally inverted the choice. We could add that the relation between *Vorhandenheit* and theoretical knowledge disappears completely in *être-sous-la-main*. Going on the attack in order to better defend himself, Martineau replied, among other things, that *disponibilité* (chosen by Courtine for *Zuhandenheit*) in no way corresponds to the mode of being of tools.[12]

The layperson will plead for mercy before such a technical and microscopic discussion (it will nonetheless be necessary, from time to time, to address certain key points concerning issues surrounding the Vezin translation). What will be even more surprising is how differences—which are undoubtedly unavoidable and which must be discussed calmly—are caught up in the flames of heated and passionate argument. Is it really necessary to have a falling out and cry foul every time a disagreement in translation appears? On that account, the war of all against all would rage at an unprecedented level in the scientific world, thus serving as a terrible example to the uninitiated reader.

This heated exchange was only the beginning of the "Heidegger squabble" [*La guéguerre Heidegger*].[13] It was merely the early sign of the polemical outbursts that would break out on the occasion of the frontal collision of the two rivals, when in the fall of 1986, Gallimard finally published Vezin's translation.

To say that this translation had been awaited would be an understatement. Delayed for such a long time, benefiting from the prestige of Gallimard and its means of distribution, and being considered, in principle, as the "official" translation, it could not have been met by indifference or have benefited from an excessive indulgence. Would it stand up to Martineau's challenge? His "pirate" publication had intensified the suspense. Who would gain the upper hand in this veritable duel? This question is not the same as asking who would be better received by critics and the public, but rather, who, concerning the jousters them-selves, was finally more faithful to Heidegger and the most attuned to the rigor of his masterpiece?

The Vezin translation appeared with Gallimard in the *Bibliothèque de Philos-ophie* series at the end of October 1986. Opening this thick volume, one was taken aback, at first, by the words that followed the name of the translator: "based on the work of Rudolf Boehm and Alfonse de Waehlens (first division), Jean Lauxe-rois and Claude Roëls (second division)." A note on the following page clarified that "the present translation is the result of a long project carried out in many phases." The names of successive translators followed: Corbin (1938), Boehm–de Waehlens (1964), Roëls–Lauxerois (no date). However, the last phrase of this note was clear: "the definitive version of the entire translation is the work of François Vezin, who alone assumes responsibility for it." It is not surprising and it is even legitimate for Vezin to clarify things with respect to his role in a history carried out under the aegis of Gallimard. The only new element was the undated mention of a provisional version of division two; the uninitiated thus learned that Vezin took over from Jean Lauxerois and Claude Roëls, without being able to judge the extent of their respective contributions. There is much to be perplexed about here. But the major possible objection was avoided since Vezin assumed complete responsibility. One can only guess that such a "passing of the baton" could have contributed to delaying the final completion of this translation.

Dedicated to Jean Beaufret, this translation was more complete than Mar-tineau's since it included the marginal notes added by Heidegger in his own copy kept at his *Hütte* in Todtnauberg. These marginal notes, which appeared in the second volume of the *Gesamtausgabe* edited by Friedrich-Wilhelm von Her-rmann,[14] are not that numerous, but prove to be highly valuable in allowing us to judge the critical distance that Heidegger took with respect to his own text. Also noteworthy, and to the credit of the Vezin translation, no "translator's preface" comes between the reader and Heidegger's text. Vezin humbly limited his own comments to an appendix,[15] after the German publisher's afterword, preceded by this epigraph from Heidegger, translated with Braque in mind: "To head to-ward a star—this only."[16] However, Vezin's translation includes only a list of the Greek and Latin citations, no glossary and no thematic index, unlike Martineau's translation. The cursory and allusive notes in no way compensate for this highly regrettable lack. Furthermore, is the fact that there is no mention of Martineau's translation justifiable in any way? As attentive to detail as he was, even going so far as to recall scrupulously that "selections from *Sein und Zeit,* translated by Joseph Rovan, were published in the Lyon journal *L'Arbalète* in the early for-ties,"[17] Vezin made no allusion to Martineau. Taking the considerable dispro-portion in the means of distribution of the two translations into account, this omission—which cannot be attributed to chance—appears to be censorship. It is understandable that Vezin had not wanted to encumber his work with a polemic, but at the same time the debate concerning the translation choices was eliminated. Was this silence justified? It could be attributed to contempt or to rancor, perhaps also to the desire to avoid adding fuel to the fire. Nevertheless, Vezin's position would have been much stronger if he had taken the trouble to carefully discuss all of Martineau's choices (which could have been done calmly). Short of this, a simple mention of a rival translation would have been the right thing to do.

The reader thus comes to the table of contents, placed at the beginning of the work, as in the German edition. The translations of the titles and texts of the first paragraphs corresponding to the first two chapters are as expected: the differences with respect to Boehm–de Waehlens do not seem to be significant. At the most, *désobstruction* as a translation for *Destruktion* (§6) might be intriguing: here, for once, we have a word with Latin root and consonance. Why then seek out *désobstruction* that in French has more to do with the vocabulary of plumbing or of traffic flow? If Vezin is right to explain in his explicative note[18] that the word *Destruktion* is "surprising," would it not have been enough to place the French word *destruction* in quotes?[19] Was this an attempt to avoid the excessively negative connotations of the word "destruction?" But that same connotation exists in German, since Heidegger himself felt obligated to clarify that the term should be understood neither in the sense of a relativizing nor in the negative sense of a rejection of the tradition. Furthermore, Heidegger explained very clearly the sense in which the word and the project are to be taken in paragraph 6, that is to say, in the positive sense of a renewal of the possibilities of the tradition.[20]

This first difficulty is of course negligible compared to the many surprises awaiting the reader who will come upon a profusion of neologisms: *factivité*,[21] *immondation*,[22] *mondéité*,[23] *temporellité*,[24] *discernation*,[25] *conjointure*,[26] *entourance*,[27] *ouvertude*,[28] *dévalement*,[29] *util*,[30] *distantialité*,[31] *disposibilité*,[32] *temporation*.[33] All these "inventions," had they been explained, would at the most belong to an oral commentary; but, when taken as a whole, they impart the strange impression that we are dealing with a new text that has to be decrypted, and whose relation to the original is unclear. Given all this, how would it be possible to avoid the accusation of "unreadability"? No doubt it is too facile to produce unusual or even ridiculous citations, which is what many critics have done. Partisans and adversaries bombarded each other with short fragments that were increasingly jargon-laden and that, isolated from their context, amounted to pure gibberish. The public would draw the conclusion that above all *Sein und Zeit* should not be read, regardless of the translation, and that the author himself was perhaps responsible . . . Neither Martineau nor Vezin, who firmly believed that they had translated the century's masterpiece, was aiming for this "counterproductive" and catastrophic effect.

The Vezin translation provoked a veritable maelstrom. I will offer a brief account of it, in order to concentrate on the debate concerning the assumptions that led to the translation choices. Obviously, a detailed study of these would exceed the goals and the limits of the present work. We will limit ourselves to a discussion of a few significant examples, not in order to pronounce a definitive judgment, but in order to allow the reader to grasp the stakes of a confrontation that—beyond personal rivalries and side anecdotes—pointed to divergent and even antagonistic conceptions of translation, and thus of the reception of Heidegger's thought.

From the Uproar to the Issues

"Unusable,"[34] "a logic of dissimulation" and "pretentious gibberish,"[35] "caricature,"[36] "nontranslation":[37] these critiques were not even the most severe that Vezin's translation provoked. The outcry was quite widespread.[38] It would be fastidious to give a comprehensive account of it. I will nonetheless consider the article that seemed most significant, "L'ampleur du désastre" [The scope of the disaster] by Philippe Lacoue-Labarthe.[39] The language of the letter sent to *Le Monde* by Michel Haar and Roger Munier was more tame, but quite similar in its spirit.[40]

Lacoue-Labarthe wrote: "This translation is scandalous, by its assumptions, its execution and the ridiculous nature of its conceit." He was not satisfied with repeating this final condemnation. He argued as follows: this "translation" is based on the very impossibility of translation, leading to a "cockeyed" approach between "nontranslation" and the text itself. The execution was such that the result turned out to be unreadable: a plethora of neologisms and gibberish; this unreadable quality did not correspond to "*any* of the prevailing standards of modern translation"; finally, conceit and arrogance abound in the notes, reminding one of an "attitude typical of *Hypokhâgne* students." Yet that is not the worst of it: in permitting the publication of such an "unnamable thing," which will occupy the market for fifty years, one was hindering access to Heidegger's thought (and to his subtle use of the German language) and thus to philosophy itself, which a certain intellectual demagoguery tended to reduce to purely verbal games.

As severe as this article was, it was still within the deontological limits of what was admissible. Such was not the case of the new attack, of an unprecedented violence, launched by Emmanuel Martineau on December 15, 1986, entitled "Heidegger chez les cinoques"[41] [Heidegger among the crackpots]. The article was directed against the "bilingual translation," its author (surnamed Benito-the-slacker), and Fédier, his inspiration (M. Adolf Hasbeen). One has to recognize in Martineau a ferocious eloquence in the tradition of Léon Bloy, at the best moments of his essay. However, laughter quickly ended in the face of excess and vulgarity, to such an extent that the desired result risked being canceled out. In presenting a first unpublished edition of "The Origin of the Work of Art," Martineau was inviting us to think more deeply, but this "grand stylist of the insult" [*grand styliste de la Vacherie*[42]] could not bridle his grotesque excesses along with their boomerang effect.

As expected, Vezin attempted to fire back. First, before the breakout of the polemics, he presented his translation in a special issue of *Magazine Littéraire*,[43] and a response with supportive letters addressed to *Le Monde*. "Seven key words and two phrases quoted without any reference"[44]: Vezin defended himself by turning against his censors, accusing them of "pressure" and "obstructionism." He suspected them of imputing illegibility to Heidegger's own text and compared one of the incriminated sentences to the two other translations (Martineau's was finally cited): according to Vezin, the other two did not fare any better! Further, Vezin's partisans deplored "the climate of hatred and suspicion"[45] that was directed against the translation published by Gallimard and raised questions about the peremptory character of the notion of "readability."

What would a sage do, in face of such agitation? Fortified with courage, would he or she turn to the texts to form his or her own opinion? We can assume so and hope it would be the case. However, we must admit that most of the public could only have grasped the "scope of the disaster," to use Lacoue-Labarthe's expression. What remains is the possibility of attempting a reflection on the fruitfulness of a confrontation between the two translations, since the heated emotions disappeared over the years.

As we have seen, what was important for Martineau was consistency and readability. What was important for Vezin, whose justifications we have not yet examined? At the end of his translation, he presented them in a decidedly elliptical fashion, although they were complemented by notes. The only text in which Vezin described the general approach of his translation was surprisingly brief.[46] Observing that a bilingual edition of *Being and Time,* for practical reasons, was impossible, he invited the reader to carry out a "bilingual reading" and advised to use a copy of the original with a German-French dictionary. This idea of a "bilingual reading" (or even "bilateral"),[47] which would provoke Martineau's sarcasm, was hardly described or justified, apart from the acceptable affirmation that "the idea of a translation that would claim to eliminate the original text by dispensing with the need to consult it constitutes the contrary of the goal which we set ourselves." In principle, one can only accept this declaration of good intentions, at least in its first part: a translation worthy of its name cannot aim at eliminating the original text, quite the contrary; the second part of the affirmation at the beginning of the work, however, introduced a less justifiable idea, which was also ambiguous in the form in which it was presented: a translation should not replace the original by "dispensing with the need to consult it." We must weigh our words here, for their meaning will be decisive for the entire project. Vezin states the obvious: "The principle that is the basis of any *bilingual reading* is of course that priority be given to the original."[48] How can one not approve such a principle of reading, when it is not a question of a novel but of an arduous philosophical treatise, which, as we know, carries out a subtle work of displacement within the heart of the German language itself? However, it must be noted that Vezin slipped from the question of a bilingual edition to that of a bilingual reading, and finally to that of a justification for a "bilateral" *translation.*

With these nuances, which are not as negligible as they might seem, lies hidden the ferment of the bloody quarrel of the translation of *Sein und Zeit.* In fact, the question of the bilingual *edition* is relevant only to the practical conditions that—and Vezin acknowledges this more or less explicitly[49]—do not yet address the heart of the debate around the concept of translation. Bilingual editions are very convenient; there are some in the case of Heidegger's work (e.g., the *Letter on Humanism* published by Aubier), but the facility of access to the original changes nothing with respect to the intrinsic quality of the translation, its choices, its success, or its failures.

The notion of a "bilingual reading," which takes us from the practical to the hermeneutical level, especially calls for discussion. Bilingualism is an aptitude whose exercise is highly variable: in the best of cases it leads to an equal mastery of both languages; in the worst, it leads to a pidgin where each language loses its integrity and even its meaning. Vezin deserves credit for aiming at the better of the two cases: Heidegger's thought deserves and even demands a work of reading that constantly returns to the original text. It is impossible to imagine a serious seminar on *Being and Time* (or even on the other texts) that would use only translations, regardless of the ones that are chosen.

Nonetheless, acknowledging this requirement in no way justifies the application of the epithet "bilingual" to this reading, even less the concept of "bilateral translation." To read a translation in French is to read a text that is to be heard and to be understood in French. Is it necessary to repeat such an obvious thing? Why then have translations? Would we need them, if all our students and all French lovers of philosophy were to know German or were to decide to work on it thoroughly? The "Vezin doctrine," if followed literally, would lead to a refusal to translate or to a "nontranslation," showing that there is no other solution except the constant consultation of the original (Vezin's adversaries accuse him precisely of this fault). Furthermore, this attitude was expressed by Jean Beaufret when he gave this advice to his students in *khâgne:* "If you want to read *Sein und Zeit,* learn German!"[50]

Notwithstanding the fact that the argument from authority is insufficient, one must be aware of Beaufret's always abundant irony and of the fact that at the time no complete translation of the book existed. Does this quip justify, without any other form of inquiry, the concept of "bilateral translation?" Even if some of his translation choices could be debated, Jean Beaufret had always been careful to allow Heidegger's thought to be understood in French, and his inventions (for example, *désinvolture* for *Gelassenheit* or *guise* for *Weise*) aimed at catching the purest spirit of the French language.

Even though he ultimately called it "secondary" or "bilateral," François Vezin nonetheless proposed a translation and declared Heidegger translatable, with the reservations and conditions that have just been mentioned. Henceforth, could he and should he have avoided the unavoidable debate concerning the readability and pertinence of his translation? To appeal to an "idiosyncratic"[51] quality in Heidegger's German in order to fend off criticism of the unusual and disconcerting nature of certain translations seems tantamount to systematically giving oneself the facility of hiding behind a sacred text.

We have attempted to reconsider the discussion calmly and without condemnation. We now need supporting examples. Unable to lead our readers into the labyrinthine difficulties and dissensions (setting aside for the moment the nontranslation of *Dasein,* a point on which Martineau and Vezin were in agreement), I shall limit myself to examining a passage and two specific cases that were the subject of a direct polemical exchange between Vezin and his critics. My goal, it should be repeated, is not to distribute praise or blame, but to convey the nature of issues at stake on this very delicate terrain.

In his response published in *Le Monde* of February 6, 1987, Vezin only considered one contentious passage by comparing it to the two other versions.[52] It was a perilous exercise for sure, for the mentioned phrase, isolated from its context, seems as unintelligible (although less picturesque) in his adversaries' versions as in his own. For a reader without access to the German, the confusion is total. Nonetheless, one must admit that although there is gibberish everywhere, it is particularly present in Vezin. Was this effect of confusion intentional? One might be tempted to think so: Vezin seemed to admit implicitly that the three translations were more or less equivalent, but he made this apparent sacrifice (of his claim that his was better) only at the price of the effect we just discussed: if the three translations were equally dismissed, it was in order to privilege the original. At least one goal was achieved: the demonstration that translations fail, due to the same insufficiency in the face of the plenitude of the meaning of the original text. This reference back to the original text is supplemented by the following odd argument: "Except for the disparity in the vocabulary, the structure of the sentence remains the same in the three cases."[53] Can one judge the quality of a translation in abstraction from the vocabulary (here, for example, the word *bei* translated as *après*,[54] and the choice of *être en déval* for *verfallen sein*)? This is an untenable position, which was nonetheless "maintained" by Vezin, inasmuch as it was possible, when he pretended to believe that his adversaries were taking issue with the "structure" of Heidegger's sentence, and through this accusation, with "Heidegger's own text, which the signatories considered opaque and ridiculous." This, again, amounted to refusing to engage in a real discussion concerning the terminological choices by suspecting the "adversaries" of intentions that they did not have in this particular case. It was, on the contrary, in order to defend Heidegger's text that they had intervened. Yet Vezin, in turn yielding to the narrowest polemics, pretended not to realize this obvious fact. Was it really impossible to engage in a dialogue? Should one not have attempted to explain what Heidegger meant to say in the sentence in question? After having stated that "existence is always factical," Heidegger wanted to show the co-belonging, in care, of anticipation as such and the proximity with beings ready-to-hand. There is no pure anticipation; we are always already concerned with . . . Not once did Vezin attempt to provide an explanation in his "response." He only referred back to the grand text, as he did to justify the translation of *Erschlossenheit* by *ouvertude*. A quote from Heidegger is supposed to support the affirmation according to which *ouverture* and *ouvertude* are distinct: is this what we expect of a pedagogue?

Since *ouvertude* is in question, we can now examine it. Vezin himself explains it by underlining that it "constitutes one of the masterpieces of the complex terminology of *Being and Time*"[55] and goes on to thoroughly justify this neologism with an argument that I will examine in closing. The reader can draw only one thing from the Heidegger quote: barring any supplementary explication, he is not thinking of an openness in the ordinary sense, such as an opening through which a person seeks to escape from a room.[56] What then? The word *Erschlossenheit* appears on page 38 of *Sein und Zeit* to address the truth of being. What is unusual here is not the verb *erschliessen,* to open up, but the fact that Heidegger felt the need to create a noun from out of the past participle: he thus shows that the issue is not an isolated act of opening but of a state of truth (in the transcendental sense)[57] that concerns *Dasein* as well as being.[58] Is it a revelation? An *ouverture*? Or an *Ouvertude*? The first solution has an overly theophanic connotation; the second hardly presents any disadvantages: furthermore, mere quotes could well indicate that the active and banal sense of the word is not intended here. Curiously enough, Vezin rejected this solution and supported his decision with a quote from Beaufret that would, on the contrary, allow its use: it is *"the state of being open* as opposed to that which would initially be closed up on itself, shut away and closed like a box."[59] Now, the word *ouverture* can precisely designate the state of being open and even "that which makes a thing open."[60] Pretending to be unaware of this, Vezin affirmed: *"Ouvertude,* like *solitude, finitude, habitude,* designates a state." But since this was already the case for the word *ouverture,* the creation of this neologism seems purely gratuitous. In fact, it seems like a foreign body in the French language. A language, like a plant, accepts some transplants, while it rejects others; we can do nothing about this. The case for *util* is not particularly different, but even less defensible. To take recourse to this archaic word would make sense only if Heidegger himself had exhumed an ancient form. On the contrary, *das Zeug* is a most familiar term in German. Was Martineau wrong in joining de Waehlens–Boehm in translating it as *outil*? In no way. For the singularity on which Vezin rightly insists[61] is indicated by Heidegger neither by an archaic word nor by a neologism, but rather by phenomenological evidence that has nothing to do with an orthographical or pronunciation-based sleight of hand (*util* is "to be pronounced as *outile* in order to distinguish it from *outil* and from *utile!*").[62] In adding a strange prescription to an erudite quirk, did the "translator" here facilitate the reception of the thinking to which he intended to give access? I, along with many others, may have doubts. This would still not be irremediable if it were an isolated case and if the multiplication of such similar choices and so-called inventions were not discouraging to the best of good wills. If the veritable stakes were the comprehension of Heidegger's thought in *Being and Time* and beyond, should one not gain some perspective and return to what is essential: "the questions opened" by the Master of Freiburg?

The Spirit Goes Wherever It Will

Regardless of the legitimacy and even necessity of the questions concerning translation, those questions have a clearly technical character that escapes not only the larger public, but also many informed readers. Moreover, once they attain the intensity of inexpiable quarrels among schools and camps, they can only discourage earnest readers. However, the months that followed the Vezin translation would witness a rebirth of interest in Heidegger's thinking, at a time when some would discern an eclipse or a decline of his appeal to students.[63] In any case, the publication of a beautiful book by Didier Franck on *Dasein*'s embodiment,[64] Michel Haar's first book appearing in January 1987, then a "Heidegger" conference organized by the Collège International de Philosophie in March 1987,[65] and finally in the fall of 1987 the publication of the Heidegger–Kommerell correspondence concerning Hölderlin by Marc Crépon,[66] testified to a still strong and even renewed interest. Although it might seem a negligible micro-event, this last publication nonetheless deserves our full attention. Let us take it into consideration, before turning to Haar's book and the important conference just mentioned.

What is new and fascinating in the Heidegger–Kommerell correspondence is that the great literary critic puts his finger—with an intense critical lucidity, as well as a laudable honesty—on what constitutes the greatest difficulty in Heidegger's reading of the poet. In the essay in question (on the hymn "Wie wenn am Feiertage"), Heidegger clearly had the immense merit (the word is weak) of elevating the figure of Hölderlin to a destinal level,[67] but in doing so, he assumed philosophical premises (and even an "authority") that do violence to the fragile specificity of poetical saying. Heidegger did not consider the crucial and preliminary question: what is a hymn for Hölderlin? Kommerell's conclusion was not a roundabout one: "To hazard one last comment, after so much frankness: your essay could well be—I do not say that it is—a disaster."[68] Heidegger held Kommerell in the highest esteem; one can guess that this letter must have really affected him. However, his response was in the spirit of *fair play* [TN: In English in the original]: conceding a certain failure before the poet (he refused to identify with him), he nonetheless claimed "the proximity of a true thinking."[69] Was this profound humility or supreme skill? In any case, those French philosophers who had hitherto tended to accept Heidegger's readings in an uncritical, even religious, manner could not remain indifferent to the high level of this exceptional exchange.[70]

Michel Haar published his first book, at almost fifty years of age, in January 1987. The subject of the book is announced by its title, *The Song of the Earth,* but no less by its subtitle: *Heidegger and the Grounds of the History of Being.*[71] It is, however, in no way a neoromantic hymn to the Mother-Earth and rootedness. The first part bears on nature, animality, and mood (*Stimmung*), and uncovers the richness of the meanings of Earth elevated to the dignity of a concept. But it is the heart of the book, dealing with "the limits of history," that reveals its true originality. Namely, it is matter of showing that Heidegger, the thinker of the history of being, is always attentive to its reverse, the earth as soil and ground of our finitude. History is not everything. Despite troubling analogies between the two thinkers, Heidegger is not Hegel! Two limits are assigned to history: in its "end," there is a trans-historical "other beginning"; in its origin, there is the immemorial Earth that metaphysics—completing itself in technology—exploited, but that remains secretly present in us. Michel Haar's approach is quite insightful in his reading of "The Origin of the Work of Art" as a counterpart to the *Nietzsche* volumes and the texts on the completion of nihilism. Someone is bound to question the absence of the political question in this book (a significant lack, for it allows to see, as if by contrast, the shock caused the following year by Farias). Undoubtedly Haar sought to avoid regression into debates that seemed overly external and already rehashed, and above all sought to hold on to the promise in Heidegger's thought for future thinking.[72]

With respect to the quality of the participants[73] and the variety of the themes discussed, the conference at the Collège International de Philosophie (Paris, March 12–14, 1987) manifested the intent to break with the narrow polemics of the specialists and to confront the crucial problems posed by advances in international research and by the first publications of the *Gesamtausgabe* in German. In her introduction to the proceedings of this conference, Éliane Escoubas confirmed a "displacement of the stakes around Heidegger."[74] How can this displacement be characterized? It was carried out in a complex manner on three fronts: the emergence of a reading of the *Gesamtausgabe,* the opening of new questions, and a renewal of the political question in a radical philosophical manner.[75]

Thanks to a reading of the *Parmenides* lecture course of 1942–43,[76] a reading that focused on the classical Roman influence on Western political thought ("We think the 'political' as Roman i.e., imperially"[77]), Éliane Escoubas authored a pioneering work, clarifying Heidegger's "debate" with the metaphysics of the Will to Power and its misappropriation by National Socialism. Moreover, further incisive questions arose concerning the scope of the unification of the symbolic horizon of Heidegger's thought,[78] the signification of the expression "topology of being,"[79] the absence of the motif of love, which is the inverse of a "passion of facticity" in fundamental ontology,[80] and the motives behind the Adorno–Heidegger "misunderstanding."[81] Finally, with Abensour's contribution,[82] as well as that of Lacoue-Labarthe,[83] and above all with those of Levinas and Derrida—we will return to these texts later—the political question was addressed, no longer from a historiographical or biographical perspective, but rather from a resolutely philosophical point of view. What was at stake was to address the "secret core" that until then had resisted explanation—evasions or unthought complicity that must be "extracted" in order to understand and exorcise that which, in Heidegger, was more than just an ordinary "error." On the whole, this small volume, which did not benefit from a distribution as wide as the *Cahier de l'Herne* published a few years earlier, was a useful supplement to the latter, and in a clearly more critical sense.

"Dying for . . . ," the brief text by Levinas that closes the book, is extremely rich.[84] In a few pages, Levinas summarized the reasons for his unwavering admiration for *Being and Time*,[85] but also for the overcoming of ontology with a radical ethics (all the while keeping in mind "the irreversible abomination attached to National-Socialism, in which that brilliant man was somehow able—never mind how!—to take part"[86]). Levinas's admiration concerned the radical appropriation of the ontological difference: being is translated by "the adventure of being." What is then crucial is the grasping of the "verbal sense of the expression *to be*," the understanding of the "event of being"[87] that must allow for a reinterpretation of the totality of human relations in the perspective of solicitude (*Fürsorge*). But how can solicitude harden into solitude? Levinas's whole retrospective revolves around this question in order to show that the Heideggerian "being-with-others" is reducible to the relationship to the world, which is to say to the tension between the inauthenticity of the dispersion in the "they" and the resolute reappropriation of being-toward-death. Heideggerian care, without being solipsistic, is turned toward the other, "a care which is certainly assured," but remains "conditioned by *being-in-the-world*."[88] The relationship to death must be understood in a completely different manner—"the call of holiness preceding the concern for existing."[89] Beyond ontologically constitutive solicitude is an ethics of sacrifice, the radical demand of existing for the other taking priority with respect to any appropriation. It is thus at the same time the meaning of time and of death that takes on a completely different dimension than it does in Heidegger's work: that of the disinterestedness of love and of sacrifice.

In these few pages, we find the entire Levinasian effort to reverse Heidegger's radicality and rethink the event of being in order to separate it from the obsession with the authenticity of a solitary death. It is a "dying together" that becomes the absolute priority. It is not enough to record this redirection of ontology toward ethics. One must discern that the difficulty of this redirection is proportionate to its radicality. Having rethought the event of being in all of its originary rigor, Levinas assigned an altruistic destiny to it, in the most undeniable sense. However, as he reduced Heideggerian authenticity to a "worldly" ontology, did he not deny Heidegger what he himself had accorded him initially? Must one not admit, then, that the radicalization of the event of being in terms of a sacrifice for the other, far from contradicting Heideggerian authenticity, offers a possible interpretation and extension thereof? *Being and Time,* an unfinished work, leaves the self suspended, as it were, in a radically finite temporal uprooting. We can see the extent to which Levinas's contribution, aiming to deflate self-pride and to reinscribe solicitude in the "excessiveness of sacrifice,"[90] places the very Heideggerian project in question, all the while leaving the following question unanswered: Is this questioning still phenomenological or does it not introduce axiology? Can the dispossession of sacrifice be described, especially if it is a call?

A marathon lecture, which became a famous book,[91] Derrida's "contribution," as prolix as Levinas's was concise, nonetheless shared two features with the latter: the sophistication of the analyses and the critical distance. First, sophistication, since it was never a question for Derrida of accusing Heidegger, or of lowering the level of the debate; he paid utmost attention to the texts (in particular: *Being and Time,* the "Rectoral Address," and the Trakl commentary). Second, critical distance, since from the outset, the allusion to "the question" (no point in specifying which one) was transparent and spectacular: "I shall speak of ghost [*revenant*], of flame, and of ashes. And of what for Heidegger, *avoiding* means."[92] Derrida presented Heidegger's paradoxical practice of invoking spirit (*Geist*) with consummate skill (a technique that might seem no more than a textual explication): after having noted, in *Being and Time,* that this word is one that should be avoided, Heidegger invoked and laid claim to it in the "Rectoral Address": "Spirit *itself,* spirit in its spirit and in its letter, *Geist* affirms itself through the self-affirmation of the German University. Spirit's affirmation enflamed."[93] Why this (apparent?) inconsistency? If Derrida does not respond with a trivial remark such as: "Because Heidegger became a Nazi," it was not because of indulgence toward the political "error" of the new rector, but because he discerned a profound philosophical difficulty within Heidegger's gesture: rejecting biologism, Heidegger sought to ennoble his decision by giving into the most idealistic sublimation of the concept of spirit. Hence, he "capitalizes on the worst, that is, on both evils at once: the sanctioning of Nazism, and the gesture that is still metaphysical."[94] Surely, metaphysics is not an "evil" in the same sense as Nazism (Can it even be said to be one? How could Derrida have written such a phrase?). Without really addressing this considerable aporia—as he should have—Derrida preferred to pick on the features of Heidegger's text: the difficulty of freeing oneself from metaphysics, as it became "unavoidable," led Heidegger to pose the question of spirit again, in different terms. These terms are suggested by Trakl's poem, where Heidegger believes he can discern a spiritual migration beyond the Platonic Christian determinations of spirit. Impossible to summarize, Derrida's exegesis follows the meanderings of Heidegger's text, and salutes its "subtle, over-determined, more untranslatable than ever" character.[95] It is also in order to note that the shift attempted by Heidegger from the metaphysical to the more secret sense of *Geist* (as "flame") in no way liberates spirit from "the internal possibility of the worst." "Evil has its provenance in spirit itself."[96]

Emphasizing Heidegger's ambiguities in this way, even emphasizing them in an extremely subtle reading, Derrida might seem, for his part, to be avoiding a clear and definite judgment concerning both the error of 1933 and the later silence of the Master. He preferred to stage an academic dramaturgy, one by which Heidegger surrounds spirit with quotation marks in order to highlight it and then pursue his quest for a more originary *Geist*. A remarkable text and a subtle commentary, *Of Spirit* can leave those readers who expect certainty frustrated. It can even seem to entertain a strange complicity with the Heideggerian text, through the very respectful (and yet often irreverent) attention it gives it. However, one must note the fact that, in speculating on the semantic richness of *our* spirit (and here the richness of French is revealed when it thinks in its own way, without taking itself *too* seriously, regardless of what Heidegger may have said of it in "a calmly arrogant way"[97]), Derrida attempts with a certain mischievousness to conjure the return (the *revenance*) of evil. "*De l'esprit,* what the devil!"[98] There is a healthy insolence in this distancing that intervenes with subtlety, but with sufficient clarity nonetheless, in order to make Heidegger often appear peremptory, laborious, discourteous, even amusing or caricatural.[99] And yet, these are not the final words of this undefinable book. Questioning at the end the "legitimacy of the historial closure of speech,"[100] Derrida schematically outlines two paths of thinking that intersect "in Heidegger's steps."[101] One path, whose trajectory is visible in the reading of Trakl, would point to a spiritualism that is heterogeneous not only to Christianity but also to the entire language of the Western tradition; the other, the only possible path, would allow the opening onto the "*origin-heterogeneous*"[102] at the very heart of the latter, and would prepare a dialogue with the monotheistic theologies on the enigma of evil and on the promise of the "wholly other" that is touched by the Heideggerian repetition of the question concerning spirit.

The listener needed a very fine and patient ear; the reader needs a sustained attention in order to not misconstrue *Of Spirit*. The irony is that this book came out only a few months before the scandal provoked by the publication of Farias's book. In a sense, Derrida prepared the terrain (unknowingly[103]) by reposing "the question" and by suggesting that Heidegger's "crafty" practice belonged to a consummate art of "avoiding" it. There is, however, nothing in common between Derrida and Farias; the former has even been accused by the partisans of the latter of "covering for" Heidegger. With the "Heidegger affair," we descend vertiginously in the quality of the discourse: *adieu* to talented writing, *adieu* to suggestive thought! All of a sudden, the climate changed to one of a settling of accounts. Why this brutal return of a repressed violence?

Epilogue V

In a way that was radically different from the previous polemics, this chapter witnessed the outbreak of the "Heidegger war" (much more than a "skirmish"!), which was extremely violent in its first wave: the conflict between the translators of Being and Time, *in principle internal to the "Heidegger camp," largely exceeded the limits of the latter for obvious reasons. We have attempted, as impartially as possible, to recount the narrative of this conflict as well as offer an initial analysis of its tenets and outcomes: this was an extremely difficult task, it will be granted.*

To move to a more personal register in no way implies that one has appointed oneself to be the final judge, especially in questions of translation. The past continues to influence the present; it would be hypocritical to ignore it. But we must also learn from it. What I appreciated at the time in Martineau's gesture was not its violence but above all its courage: in our conformist society, it has become extremely rare for someone to sacrifice his or her energy, money, and even career, to such an extent, for a higher intellectual cause. What I also appreciated was the relative readability of the text and the coherence of the choices. Finally, the usefulness of this gesture should not to be neglected: it was an "ultimatum," and without it, we would have perhaps waited even longer for the "official" translation. Many journalists and academics were happy to receive this translation for free; others even wrote to Martineau to obtain one; those who showed him any esteem or recognition were less numerous. Human, all too human . . .

A comparable mediocrity accompanied the outcry that followed the publication of the Vezin translation. As one might have expected, it was entertaining for the onlookers, who were amused to watch philosophers tear each other apart and produce as weapons (often boomerangs) a few savory quotes of Franco-Heideggerian gibberish. In this respect, I have to plead guilty to the extent that I signed (by responding on the spur of the moment to a phone call from my friend Michel Haar) a "protest letter" against the Vezin translation. I would not do this again today, and I regret it deeply. Not that the majority of my objections—or the profound disagreements concerning the "philosophy of translation"—disappeared. But at the time I had not realized how hurtful this gesture could have been for someone whose intentions and work deserved respect and who is owed the esteem that is due to authentic philosophers, beyond all their disagreements.

I must add that, in order to be as fair as possible (to myself included), that I did all that was possible at the time in order to explain my position to Vezin and attempt to preserve our friendly relations. It was not easy, but I saved a letter from January 4, 1987, which ended: "Yours, in friendship" and in which Vezin said that "the disagreements did not trouble him" and that he expected "a debate on content with all that this required in terms of time, work, and discussion." This is why I replied on January 6, 1987 in these terms, "In your response, for which I thank you, and whose amicable serenity I appreciate, you asked for a debate on content. Here is one opportunity, even though it will not take place immediately." I then communicated to him that I was organizing my seminar for the coming year on Being and Time, *and extended an invitation for him to come and give a presentation. There was never any reply to this invitation.*

Time should heal the personal wounds that were inflicted without stifling the necessary debate on the issues: is it possible or desirable to achieve a certain readability without sacrificing faithfulness? To begin with the word Dasein, *I responded affirmatively, by declaring my disagreement on this point with Martineau as with Vezin (even with Jean Beaufret and the Master himself). Let us look again at the German: as in many other occurrences, Heidegger chose a common word and gave it a particular meaning. The specificity that the word takes on, thanks to Heidegger, is in no way automatic even in German: many of our friends from beyond the Rhine are the first to laugh, in saying that they do not understand "Heideggerian." Not translating* Dasein *in French, in no way guarantees meaning or intelligibility; on the contrary, this "nontranslation" risks turning it into a singular "object," almost extra-terrestrial, while the slippage that is taking place in German from the familiar to the unusual meaning is lost. In other words, the "untranslatable" character of* Dasein *already exists in German. There is no translation without transposition; there is no faithfulness without a risk of unfaithfulness. In order to be "faithful" to Heidegger's thought, it is not sufficient to learn German or to read him in German; one must above all listen and understand. Not to translate* Dasein *can certainly be justified in some cases, but to transform this interpretative attention into an interdiction of any attempt at translation becomes a fallacious panacea. To translate is to enable understanding, and in this respect the context is decisive. No translation is perfect; but no exclusive approach or "rigid system" (whether for translation or for nontranslation) is a definitive guarantee. In refusing once and for all to translate* Dasein, *one gained a false sense of security, believing that one was sure of having understood, whereas this understanding must always be taken up anew. The same goes for many other key words in Heidegger's language, whose effects of displacement are neutralized when one misses the twist that Heidegger gives to common words such as Zeug, Gestell, or Ereignis, to cite a few examples. Precisely, since the issue is to reveal the subtle work effectuated by Heidegger on his own language, it is not by way of a systematic recourse to neologisms that one would obtain suggestive transpositions: it is once again through a work internal to our own language, by respecting its spirit, its limits, its sound, and its readability.*

How can one not recognize, more than the trouble, the disappointment felt in the face of these difficulties of the translation of a great thinker? These are still quite negligible difficulties compared to the scandal that would shake up "the Heidegger establishment" with the publication of Farias's book, although preceded by Derrida's text Of Spirit. *Should one only retain the extraordinary "flair" that enabled him to anticipate the "scandal" by situating himself, from the outset, at an infinitely more essential level than Farias? Even more meaningful is the fact that in 1987, and in spite of many waves of polemical reflections on Heidegger's political involvement, a mind as fine as that of Derrida had understood that the "question" still harbored an unthought that deserved to be reexamined. Levinas's beautiful text and the other contributions from the conference "*Heidegger: Questions ouvertes*" attest that Derrida was not alone in addressing Heidegger's thought without any complacency. Did we really "need" Farias for posing the political question anew? Certainly not. And no one foresaw that the polemics would be reawakened with a violence that in many ways was regressive. With the passage of time, we can better determine how time itself, in doing its work, allowed what was important to emerge: thought grappling with destiny.*

10 The Return of the Repressed?

It was a scandal, and indeed a media-driven scandal, that occurred. But wherein lay the scandal? In the abomination and dishonor of a "great philosopher" suddenly put in the stocks? Or (secondarily), in the fact that the print and broadcast press carried out a media lynching of a famous person (postmortem, to be sure) without taking the trouble to verify the sources of the accusation, as if the pleasure of disparaging the man compensated for the frustration of not understanding the thinker. Finally, one will object that it is a scandal that I devoted an entire chapter to these stories and their distortions, instead of writing a genuine philosophical history.

It is the latter objection that needs to be addressed first, for if the historian of a "reception" overlooks all that seems unworthy of a great philosophy, is he still a historian? The only way of restoring a philosophical tenor to this history, to the greatest extent possible, is to include the journalistic or media frenzy (otherwise one would have to limit oneself to a work of meditation divorced from any social historical events), and to try to appreciate both the representative importance and the intrinsic pertinence of "effects," which should not be dismissed as merely superficial.

Since there was a scandal, which is incontestable, it is first necessary to go to the heart of the matter; in other words, to clarify the nature and the meaning of the "revelations" that, rightly or wrongly, alerted uninformed minds, and then unsettled an initially incredulous audience.

Lighting the Fuse

What interests us here is not to return to the discussion—which had been already conducted ad nauseum—of the validity of the existing theses in the polemical debates concerning the scope of Heidegger's political engagement: it is rather a matter of understanding what happened, that is, why Victor Farias's book caused a sensation as soon as it appeared in the fall of 1987.[1] How can this unexpected fact be explained? The author was unknown, the publisher from the provinces; in addition, the subject was not new: we already have established that the polemics concerning Heidegger's "Nazism" never really stopped brewing since Liberation, simmering, and then erupting in successive waves. Instead of entertaining the phantasmagorical hypothesis of a media-driven plot, we should rather look for the origin of the scandal in the very contents of Farias's book.

How was this book able to appear both new and disturbing? It is necessary, in a certain manner, to put ourselves in the position of a well-meaning nonspecialist, who suddenly discovers a new facet of Heidegger that is quite unworthy of a great thinker.

What caused the commotion was the radical and encompassing character of a thesis that presented itself as based upon numerous sources, which were supported by damning documents: Heidegger denounced people on two occasions![2] The facts usually cited in defense of the philosopher (his resignation from the rectorate in 1934, his marginalization and the attacks that he subsequently received from Nazis in high places) no longer worked in his favor, since they could be explained in terms of his radicalism and populism, similar to that of Roehm's SA followers, who were eliminated by Hitler in 1934 during the "night of the long knives." The thesis has thus a certain coherence: Heidegger, favorably disposed from an early age to a conservative nationalism, made a choice in 1933 that corresponded to his deepest convictions, the origins and echoes of which can be perceived in his work; not only did he pay his party membership dues until 1945, but more significantly, he never offered a word of sympathy or regret for the victims of the death camps, never renounced the "inner greatness" of the movement, and refused to make genuine honorable amends in his interview published immediately after his death in *Der Spiegel.* Heidegger a Nazi? That would be an understatement. He turned out to be more royalist than the king and wanted to be—through his Hölderlinian ideal of the spiritual homeland—more faithful to genuine Nazism than the men in power who were responsible for the catastrophic course of events.

In his preface, Christian Jambet insisted on this point by going even further than Farias: "Heidegger's biography is nothing else than the story of someone choosing the death drive."[3] Further, Jambet did so in terms that are particularly interesting to us, as they reveal the French stakes in the new polemic that was thereby launched: "It is due to the indisputable importance of Heidegger's ontology that the question of the crime merits being posed in its context. Heidegger has become, since the war, a French philosopher. It is in France that his thinking has had the most impact; it is here that it passes for being the philosophy that is most appropriate to the events of modernity. . . . For many scholars, his thinking has, more than any other philosophy in France, except for Marxism, *become unavoidable.* Ontology led to the methodical deconstruction of metaphysics as such."[4]

This citation, which reveals certain excessively "Franco-French" agendas, already goes too far: it is certain that many were pleased to find the long-awaited occasion to liquidate the intellectual hegemony of Heideggerianism in France. We will return to this apropos Jacques Derrida's delicate position in this matter. For now it is important not to be carried away by the maelstrom—or the confusion. How is one to proceed, faced with the impossibility of giving an exhaustive account of all the reactions provoked by Farias's book? For the sake of clarity, I will attend to the first and most significant press articles in order to measure the immediate impact of the book in question.

In an article entitled "Was Heidegger a Nazi?" Roger-Pol Droit devoted a whole page to this question in *Le Monde*:[5] "Implacably documented, this book is a bombshell. . . . In short, Farias's dossier is overwhelming"; these judgments in the form of a verdict condemn the "accused" without appeal. We will not, however, neglect the arguments and nuances that accompanied them: first, a reference to the old debate concerning Heidegger and his political engagement, followed by a summary of the "official" position, and then a mention of the extent of Farias's research in numerous archives, along with the admission of the fact that his conclusion ("Heidegger as an eminent and resolute member of the Nazi party") is "simple, perhaps too simple." What incontestably impressed Roger-Pol Droit is the cohesive and apparently documented solidity of Farias's thesis: from the beginning to the end of his life, Heidegger was in complicity with a conservative, agrarian ideology with anti-Semitic tendencies (his homages at an early and later age to the monk Abraham a Sancta Clara proved it); in the middle, if one can put it that way, stands the allegiance to the Nazi party, an allegiance maintained until 1945. His disillusion of 1934 is not that of a Nazi adversary, and his suspicion of the regime was "quite limited." Let us resist the temptation "to throw the complete works of the philosopher in the trash," although one must no longer ignore the links that are difficult to identify between Heidegger/Dr. Jekyl and Heidegger/Mr. Hyde. "The remaining task will be to give thought to the obscure link that unites them. The merit of Farias's inquest is that it constrains us to undertake this effort. It is a philosophical task—difficult and long."

Each newspaper has its own style. That of *Liberation* was less restrained. The title "Heil Heidegger" testifies to this, especially since it is accompanied by two striking photos of the rector Heidegger (wearing the Nazi insignia and seated in the middle of the flags with the swastika) and combatively subtitled: "From 1933 to 1945, Martin Heidegger, often considered to be the greatest philosopher of the century, was a zealous militant of the Nazi party: Victor Farias's book, published today, proves it overwhelmingly. The question is: how can anyone remain a Heideggerian?"[6] It is true that Robert Maggiori's article first gives Jean Beaufret the chance to speak, but it is in order to better refute Beaufret's official position by contrasting it with the mass of documents that "undermined his entire discourse," primarily, with the two letters of denunciation signed by Heidegger, but not without adding: "That is not, obviously, what is important in Farias's book, even if these 'anecdotes'—and many others—shed a disturbing light on Heidegger. What is crucial is that Farias's detailed inquest reveals the *consistency* of Heidegger's allegiance to Nazism." As Droit had done two days earlier, Maggiori followed Farias's argumentation, but by insisting on all that which weakened the justifications and excuses offered by Heidegger himself (he was not excluded from the conferences in Prague and Paris; he was not put "on the sidelines" after 1934; he was not forbidden to engage in scholarly activities). The invitation to consider all of that is addressed essentially to "Heideggerian posterity," in the form of a genuine challenge.

As severe as they were with Heidegger, agreeing to recognize Farias's serious documentation (a point on which their good faith had been somewhat deceived), neither Droit nor Maggiori failed to appreciate the stature of the thinker or the philosophical dignity of his oeuvre. The problem was exactly that: how to hold the two ends of the chain stretched to the breaking point, between a certain greatness of the thought and the compromises one makes in life. Is that connection even conceivable? The Heideggerians had their work cut out for them! How can one disagree with the well-grounded nature of this challenge, at least in principle? But the appeal for thoughtful reflection had little chance of being heard, considering the emotional climate that soon developed. The two articles we just considered signaled the beginning of a genuinely polemical explosion, whose most noteworthy moments must be recalled.

A Maelstrom

"Who will dare write that Martin Heidegger was a villain? That his work carried within it, better than hints, all the ingredients of a fascist thought?" It is in these unusually violent terms that Dominique Grisoni began an article entitled "M. Heidegger, Professor of Nazi philosophy" [*professeur de philonazie*].[7] He did not content himself with unabashedly lauding Farias's book. He went even further than Farias by presenting the philosopher as "the official—and recognized as such—thinker" of the Nazi regime. As we have begun to see, these formulations lack any sense of proportion, any nuance, and are rather more insults than philosophical judgments: "*Being* was Hitlerian," and Heidegger's writing "can be seen as the philosophical version of a breviary of hate." Hence the conclusion was announced straightaway in the form of this brutal question: "Should one still read this German philosopher?" This is a question that is all the more violent since the simultaneous publication of Derrida's book *Of Spirit* is referred to with the commentary, "Ironic title, Macabre Irony." But nothing further is said of Derrida's work, which deserved more attention, if not respect. It is as if Derrida himself was also guilty and should be thrown into the darkness.

The excellent Germanist and writer George-Arthur Goldschmidt, although not stylistically crude, was in the end no less extreme, since he went as far as writing this shocking sentence: "Heidegger's *thinking* is nothing but the shadow of Auschwitz, for which it has prepared the ground, and which it will carry within itself for all time as a weight."[8] Taken literally, this verdict from which there is no appeal denies the very existence of an independent Heideggerian "thought" since—through a strangely precursory lugubrious work—it is reduced to being the preparation for the Holocaust of which it would be nothing but the "shadow." An infinite and interminable malediction must accompany this pseudo-thinking, carried by the unspeakable mourning that it has itself engendered.

Christian Jambet was not far from this implacable accusation when he wrote in his preface to Farias's book, "If the core of Hitlerism is the 'final solution,' if the extermination camps and their gas chambers are the *substance* of Nazism, what does the biography of a philosopher who gives his assent to that mean?"[9] Even put as a question, the conclusion of this syllogism, not formulated but almost imposed on the reader, is as follows: "Heidegger gave his assent to the final solution." One must admit that, as in the preceding case, this extreme passage, without any proof or textual reference, amounts to libelous slander pure and simple. Heidegger is demonized and no discussion is possible. In an interview with *Art Press,* Jambet repeated these same accusations in a somewhat more circumstantial manner, but by calling Heidegger's political texts of 1933 "clearly obscene."[10]

One guesses that these hyperbolic rejections could not go without a response. To draw a detailed list of these and to undertake a complete inventory would be tedious. It is more important to analyze the responses (will insult respond to slander?) and above all to determine whether solid, precise, and serious counterarguments would be opposed to Farias. Before that, in the midst of the polemical tempest, we will be concerned less with what arises from invective, and rather more with what contributes, in spite of everything, to enriching the debate with new information.

On the full page of letters and testimonies that *Le Monde* devoted to this dossier two weeks after the article by Roger-Pol Droit,[11] partisans and adversaries were on equal footing. However, in addition to an "inept perfidy" imputed to Farias by a Heideggerian from the heart of France,[12] we learn in passing that Heidegger was the "most difficult case"[13] for the committee on denazification and—a more serious charge for Heidegger from a moral point of view—that his personal behavior toward his mentor Husserl had not always been honorable.[14]

The polemic unfolded in a paradoxical manner. As it developed, on the one hand, it revealed the weakness of Farias's book (in terms of sources but especially in terms of their interpretation), and on the other hand, it caused new information to emerge, information that would contribute to accentuating the unease that thereafter surrounded the reputation of the great philosopher.

Before returning to Farias's book, let us for the moment and for the sake of clarity consider the new elements that provided grist for the mill for Heidegger's adversaries. A particularly compromising fact seemed confirmed by the deep, long, and lasting friendship between Heidegger and Eugen Fischer, a medical specialist in human heredity, and a partisan, theoretician, and practitioner of racial eugenics. Michel Tibon-Cornillot, who devoted a long and detailed article to this question in a February 1988 issue of *Liberation*,[15] was careful not to present an excessive accusation: "We cannot infer from the deep and sustained relationship between Heidegger and Fischer a fraternity in horror similar to what linked Fischer and Mengele. No available document permits such a statement."[16] He maintained, however, that there must have been a "profoundly shared worldview" between the two men. This ideological proximity could explain Heidegger's silence on the genocide.

Fifteen days later, another significant testimony confirmed the suspicions of Heidegger's anti-Semitism: Ernesto Grassi, an Italian philosopher who had been living in Germany for a long time, known for his work on Renaissance humanism, while confessing his admiration for the thinker, judged indisputable the National Socialism of Heidegger the man. He cites as a tragic example of Heidegger's personal anti-Semitism his brutal rupture as early as 1932 with his intimate friend and disciple Szilasi, a Jew from Hungary.[17] In May, *Le Monde* reproduced the testimony of the doctor Léopoldine Weizmann, who confirmed these suspicions.[18] Finally, a year later, and to top everything, *Liberation* and *Le Monde* published a translation of a letter from 1929, previously published in *Die Zeit,* where Heidegger recommended an assistant in these terms. "Either we endow anew our German intellectual life with authentic forces and educators, emanating from the soil, or we definitively deliver it to the Jewish influence that is growing, in the narrow and broad sense of the term."[19]

The passing maelstrom did not take place without damaging the image of the great thinker. The shock produced by Farias's book seemed to have permitted specific accusations to have an impact, at least concerning certain of Heidegger's personal weaknesses, ambiguities, or failings. Did the initial shock of the scandal (an "incriminating dossier") intensify during the winter of 1987–88? This at least was the impression that the most resolute anti-Heideggerians wanted to give: namely, that this was a dossier that would not cease growing, to the point that it would silence a defense of any kind. Were the remaining faithful, confined to bed with a hot-water bottle to get through this veritable nightmare,[20] going to maintain an ontological silence in their offended dignity? Or, lacking arguments, were they limited to unleashing a barrage of invectives, and a series of insults?

After the first shock, the polemic did not in fact develop according to these extreme and caricatured hypotheses.[21] A paradoxical reversal took place: it was the defenders of this sinister master—who was presented as the (almost) "official" philosopher of Nazism, as an irrationalist, and as a hateful denunciator who was heavily anti-Semitic—who called for reason and sangfroid, and for returning to the texts, so as to carefully analyze and correct Farias's interpretive method, errors, and shortcomings. This took place in such a way that in a few months "credibility" would change camps, in view of the increasingly obvious weaknesses in Farias's book.

Seriously!

The following scathing judgment by Jacques Derrida appeared first: "The reading proposed [by Farias], if there is one, remains insufficient or questionable, at times so shoddy that one wonders if the investigator began to read Heidegger more than an hour ago."[22] Emphasizing that for more than a half century, "no rigorous philosopher has been able to avoid a *debate* with [explication *avec*] Heidegger," Derrida contrasted the seriousness of critical works by Lacoue-Labarthe, Blanchot, Levinas, and Nancy to the superficiality of Farias's book. Certainly, he thought that he himself contributed to this effort of "explication" with his two works that appeared at the time almost simultaneously: *Of Spirit: Heidegger and the Question* and *Psyche*. His position on the "question" implied a twofold reevaluation: with respect to Nazism, and without any complicity for these "regions . . . haunted by the diabolical," one must understand that it was a continent "whose roots are still obscure"; with respect to Heidegger's thought, one must recognize its "groundbreaking character," and undertake an entire work of reading with critical distance: "I have indicated my reservations in all my references to Heidegger, as far back as they go"[23] (especially with respect to the themes of the proper, the near, and the homeland). With respect to method, Derrida sought a displacement of the boundary between "external" and "internal" reading. He thought that he contributed to it, by initiating—apart from the condemnation of Nazism—a genuine "thinking" of what has happened. In the end, Heidegger was in no way to be protected; on the contrary; "by setting out from a certain deconstruction . . . one can pose, it seems to me, new questions to Heidegger."[24] Derrida finally stated that for authentic philosophical perspectives, "the debates are richer and more open abroad."[25]

Philippe Lacoue-Labarthe and the participants in a substantial dossier published in the journal *Le Débat* would also return to the letter of the documents and to the gravity of the texts.

In a text written in Berkeley as early as November 1987,[26] Lacoue-Labarthe took an extremely clear and firm position. For him, Farias had not presented anything new with respect to the basic facts of the case. That Heidegger believed in National Socialism is indisputable; that he "presented a particularly euphemistic version of his political compromise" cannot be denied. Farias's work presented the appearance of a scrupulously historical work (although it ignored, among other things, the Heidegger–Kästner correspondence and the tribulations of the relationship with Arendt). However, "this book, profoundly, is not just and I even find it—I choose my words carefully—to be dishonest."[27] So that one does not mistake the scope of these critical remarks, which in no way intended to exonerate Heidegger for what was decidedly a "moral failing" (and not a simply error in judgment), Lacoue-Labarthe clarified that Nazism was for him, as for Farias, "an *absolutely* vile phenomenon." However, concerning a complex case such as that of Heidegger, whose philosophical work is considerable, it is necessary to respect the texts and make an effort to read them honestly. Now, there are three reasons to suspect Farias's work. The first pertains to its rhetoric, and the way it presents things: all of Heidegger's acts from 1933 were supposed to be those of a "militant," and no nuance was allowed as to the nature of the acts, even if they often consisted only in passing encounters with notorious Nazi colleagues (hence the effect of "accumulative list"). At the same time, Farias systematically minimized any testimony to the contrary (the hostility of the Rosenberg clan and Heidegger's public criticism of biologism in his courses, etc.). The second reason is that in his use of texts, Farias always confused matters under the pretext of clarifying the citations through their context: thus, the brief homage of the young Heidegger to his compatriot Abraham a Sancta Clara was rendered suspect, not because of the text, which is itself harmless, but by lengthy considerations of the biography of the monk, the anti-Semitic tradition in Southern Germany, of Karl Lueger, his obituary, and so on, in a kind of strategy of "law of contamination" that "renders Heidegger responsible for what he has not said." Shockingly the contents of Heidegger's courses on Hölderlin were not seriously taken into account. Finally, and this is not surprising after what has just been established, Victor Farias has simply not read Heidegger's philosophical work, summarizing in a few pages[28] "the reflections that occupied Heidegger during the end of his life," and remaining silent—which is still more serious—on Heidegger's decisive work on Nietzsche, from 1936 on, which was designed to disengage his thought from Nazi ideology and to situate it metaphysically. Citing other significant silences, Lacoue-Labarthe concluded: where is Heidegger's thinking if not in his texts? The effect of this disproportionate "scandal" would be catastrophic if it led to forbidding the reading (and the interrogation) of a great philosophical work.

The most solid dossier on the question was presented by *Le Débat* in its issue of January–February 1988. In keeping with the tradition of this journal, the intention stated by the editor was to organize a serious discussion, compensating for the ignorance "where French opinion has remained for a long time with respect to German historical work in the matter."[29] To support this intention to document matters, the various perspectives that were solicited were accompanied by the translation of certain political texts from 1933–34, translated by Nicole Parfait and presented by François Fédier (in a spirit obviously quite different from the one that had motivated Jean-Pierre Faye at the beginning of the 1960s).[30] By all accounts, the editors of the journal (in this case Pierre Nora) had prepared the issue in close collaboration with François Fédier, avoiding any accusatory terms, any pandering to the hostile crowd, any sensational titles (the Heidegger dossier was situated next to a main section under the theme "To Save Libraries"). The choice of the contributors reflected the intent to reorient the polemic in favor of the defense: the most resolute accusers were sidelined; they invited someone who was unknown to present the excessively paradoxical thesis, "Heidegger against Nazism."[31] Only two of the seven contributions were clearly critical of the Master. Gallimard, the French publisher of Heidegger, took every precaution to avoid any conflict with the family and the philosopher's heirs. Not that a compassionate tone was adopted or that the collection gave the impression of having been programmed: one hears dissonances. Michel Deguy, in particular, did not conceal the devastating effects that Farias's book had on media coverage, but also perhaps on himself: "To hear again these harangues on the *Führung* and the *Dienst* is to hear the tone of *Sein und Zeit* imitated by its double [*sosie*], its Nazi double [*sozi*]. The merit of 'Farias' would be to remind us that each language, including that of Goethe, would be capable of confusing itself with the exaggerations provided by its caricature."[32] It is as a poet that Deguy conjured his own anxiety in the face of the ravages of the thinker's obedience (however brief) to the Nazi order. How can a principle of disobedience be found? "Discerning poetry is freedom."[33] One sees that Deguy did not directly take a position; he did better, and undertook a soul searching, which was enlightened by poetic experience, and oriented toward a new reading of Heidegger.

Let us approach now the two contributions that were explicitly "critical." They were brief and notably different from each other. Stéphane Mosès,[34] without giving any indication of any sympathy for Heidegger himself, was also quite severe toward Farias: recalling the dated status of the polemic and the best work on the question in France and in Germany, and finding Farias weak and "too systematically biased," he referred both to Derrida's studies on the "erratic trajectory of some Heideggerian motifs" and to Minder on "the profoundly conservative element" in Heidegger's thought, asking finally if it was not a fascination for *radicality* that would constitute the articulation between Heidegger's philosophy and the Nazi ideology. The article ended in an interrogative mode on the difficulty of thinking this articulation in its very possibility.

In a less thoughtful, and even quite polemical, manner, Alain Renaut took on the "French Heideggerians" for "their surprising stupidity and their extravagant dogmatism."[35] Citations from Boutot, Derrida, and Crétella were singled out. What were they accused of? They were accused of denying the new facts revealed by Farias. Renaut saluted Farias's "detailed research." Without any doubts about the details, seeming to ignore the critiques that began to be raised against the facts, even overlooking "the properly interpretive dimension of Farias's book," Renaut enumerated the three principal contributions provided by the book: the revelations on the early years of Heidegger's orientation, thanks to the study of the formative years; on his "extraordinary activism" "during and after his Rectorate" (but no date is given); and finally, the Master was the cynical and unscrupulous author of letters of denunciation. Renaut concluded the following: these "facts" render untenable the former line of defense of Jean Beaufret—who claimed that these unwelcome interrogations were mediocre—when in fact these interrogations revealed the inanity of the interpretations that played Heidegger against Heidegger by claiming that the great philosopher was misled because he was overly attached to the metaphysics of subjectivity and to humanism (it was then the author *Of Spirit* who found himself attacked once again). This hastily written text offered a strange disparity between, on the one hand, his appeal to the "facts" revealed by Farias (without any nuance, without any precise reference either to Heidegger's texts or to previous works, whether French or German) and, on the other hand, his violent final charge against Derrida's "anti-humanism." For what do the facts "prove" (insofar as they were verified) against a philosophical interpretation (which, incidentally, was much more complex than the interpretation that Renaut gave of it in a few lines)? Is it because Heidegger had written a letter of denunciation that it was no longer possible to question either the status of humanism or that of metaphysics in the evolution of his texts?

Was it chance (or a simple matter of editing) that Alain Renaut's and Gérard Granel's texts, which were diametrically opposed in both form and spirit, were published together in the same issue of *Le Débat*?[36] A joyously provocative writer with an agile pen, sparkling at times, Granel did not conceal that he wrote so as to "continue the combat" of the liberation of the possible and thus *"enraging* those who credited themselves with having buried the 'French Philosophy of the Sixties.'"[37] Renaut—coauthor of a book that bore that title—was identified by name, and one can assume that he, in particular, did not appreciate Granel's prose. Let us concede that it was too developed (because as it progressed, it evolved into an actual course on the sociopolitical theories of Rousseau and of Hume). But enough of these overly academic criticisms! Granel's text is immensely interesting by virtue of its twofold *confrontation:* first, by unmasking the genuine "spirit" of Farias's work (which was not really a historical work, but an effort to disqualify Heidegger once and for all, because he had *always* been a Nazi[38]: "an unabashedly Stalinist court"[39]) in brilliant and original terms. Next and above all, by taking seriously and reposing a fundamental question (no doubt the most decisive) with respect to the 1933 involvement (whatever its duration, its episodes, and its consequences): must one judge this involvement without making an effort to understand the *possibilities* that Heidegger had been able to discern and that must be considered as such, without stifling them under the weight of what actually took place. This mode of questioning—without implying any complicity with the Nazi horror (associating Heidegger in any way with Auschwitz is "the depth of the abjection"[40])—upsets "the blissful ignorance of our societies," whose "moral exigencies"[41] explain the attack against Heidegger. How can Heidegger's hope for the people [*das Volk*] be put in perspective? It is a question of understanding "in what sense the involvement, the rupture, the ultimate loyalty to 'something' in National Socialism, all three of them result (in different ways) from the play of a 'possible' and of a 'real': the possible and the real of the movement, in other words, of what is in motion in the movement."[42] While Farias never defined "populism" and enclosed Heidegger's thinking in a kind of ideological block where any comprehension of history is sterilized, one must understand that the "popular" could have been "the emergence in the people of an obscure consciousness of a 'lack of being.'"[43] Even if it is difficult to follow Granel in all the twists of a project that assumes its provocative character with panache, and does not fear embellishing his flaunting of a fabricated signature ("*for* general Karl-Martin-Ludwig-Geist,"[44] namely the contemporary era determined by the three "markers," Marx, Heidegger, Wittgenstein), one can appreciate his performance, while admitting that he succeeds best and reaches his goal best in the first section (where we find the high-quality polemic against Farias), while it is less convincing in the second section (where he tries to inscribe the political mirage of Heidegger's thought in a "war of secession" of the popular-revolutionary potential).

Although quite critical of Farias's project, and quite respectful toward Heidegger's philosophical work (without for that matter exploring, like Granel, the "potential" of his political adventure), Aubenque, in the same issue of *Débat*, presented a very different text, in both its configuration and its more classical formulations (its title[45] reflects an impatience shared by a number of professional philosophers faced with an "affair" that was nothing new to them). This text merits serious attention: it is without doubt the most precise, the most probing, and has the most balanced palette of the "defenses" and findings, whether passionate or more measured, all worthy of interest, that refuted or corrected the charges.

Aubenque cites Derrida's recent intervention straightaway in order to completely agree, suggesting that Farias's book is absolutely not a philosophy book (consisting in only "weak analyses") any more than it is a history (too many errors or approximations). What is it then? An indictment. But is it sound? The pages devoted to the formation of the philosopher cause us to doubt it;[46] the denunciation of the homages to monk Abraham a Sancta Clara was, frankly, the product of a "delirious interpretation."[47] Aubenque then gives two precise examples of insinuations that were nothing but "hoaxes."[48]

Once the dust settles in this "mess," we find what we already knew: during his rectorate, Heidegger "adhered to a certain idea of Nazism," but it is absolutely false to claim that he was thereby a militant (trustworthy testimonies argue the opposite).[49] It is hardly serious, and even "implausible," to connect his "personal misgivings" from 1934 to the position of the SA.[50] Conducting a properly philosophical analysis, Aubenque gives his interpretation of the way the question of the relation between Heidegger's thought and the involvement in 1933 should be posed. One sentence in this regard is surprising. "Heidegger's initial allegiance to the 'movement' was not a philosophical act."[51] Aubenque does not want to minimize the "fatal" character of this allegiance; he intends to understand it within its historical context, to the extent that it "looks like a million other cases" and in no way can be deduced from *Sein und Zeit,* which is in itself apolitical.[52] Unlike Gérard Granel, who tried courageously to defend the Heidegger of 1933, Aubenque maintained that this date represents a rupture, but that "the rupture goes both ways"[53] (between politics and philosophy): if politics overshadows philosophy in the "Rectoral Address," philosophy will reestablish its rights on a new basis, after 1935, thanks to a critical analysis of National Socialism that would no longer be considered as an historical alternative. It will become, on the contrary, one of the avatars of the forgetting of being. Of course, Farias hardly mentioned these reflections, as important as they were for Heidegger after his "turn" of 1935–36. Many, as he was, are incapable of understanding the later Heidegger's approach, which was "both lofty and cryptic," and invites us to the exigency of the "task of thinking."[54]

It would be erroneous to claim that the issue of *Le Débat* that we have read as closely as possible[55] had such an effect that it overshadowed other contributions to this discussion. This publication in no way put an end to an "affair" whose developments would unfold for several months. However, it represented a turning in the polemic: not only did it calm "hostilities," but above all it gave way to a phase of more reflective exchanges, in which philosophical arguments slowly replaced the gesticulations and invectives.

Defenders and Attackers Return to the Fray

Winter 1987–88 was the scene of intense battles in which Heidegger was the direct or indirect target. At the same time that the polemic intensified (through a shift to another level, where the odd trial of a great philosopher organized by minds eager to appear earnest was challenged, in particular by Alain Finkielkraut[56]), it was also displaced onto Jacques Derrida, whose severe response to Farias had upset more than one person. Given the fact that one of the objectives of the Farias tract (particularly perceptible in Jambet's preface) was to attack Heidegger's privileged status in the French intellectual landscape (the "clichés" of the end of metaphysics and the necessity of its deconstruction), and given that Jacques Derrida was the most renowned and the most inventive representative of that thinking, which was considered, rightly or wrongly, as "dominant," it is hardly surprising that an unanticipated event transformed, in his turn, Derrida into a target, on the occasion of the reviews of his books *Of Spirit* and *Psyche.*[57] It was, in fact, on the first of these texts that critical attention was focused. Taking advantage of the moment, the critics reduced the subtle analyses concerning the status of

Geist to the sole question of "adherences" or of "allegiances" to Nazism. But while Roger-Pol Droit conceded with reticence that Heidegger's caution with respect to the Nazi regime was "philosophically ambiguous" (attempting to render Nazism "spiritual" and refusing "biologism"),[58] Robert Maggiori launched a lively attack against Derrida's "fussing" [*les chichis*][59]: why was there still so much respect for the "letter" of Heidegger's writings? It was necessary, for Maggiori, to take an ethical position, and, as the subtitle of the article suggested, "to denounce the allegiance to Nazism" and all that which, in Heidegger's work, "has *prevented* us from thinking."[60] Fifteen days later, *Libération* published a long and sincere letter of protest that judged that Maggiori not only had been carried away by the anti-Heideggerianism of the time, but had misunderstood Derrida's ever-questioning boldness in his explication of (and with) Heidegger.[61]

That winter, which was decidedly eventful, a new development took place with the publication of an essay by Pierre Bourdieu.[62] Following an interview of his,[63] in which he insinuated that the debate about Heidegger had put Derrida "in great difficulty,"[64] Derrida had to respond forcefully, stating that Bourdieu's conceptual approach was "pre-Heideggerian": the two readings of Heidegger—external and internal—were juxtaposed and both deemed insufficient. Finally, Derrida regretted Bourdieu's "electoral sociology," which by aggressively "objectifying" the debate, had dispensed with a perhaps old-fashioned reflex that Derrida still practiced, that of "fidelity or decency in the wounded friendship."[65] Exercising his right of response in the same issue, Bourdieu briefly regretted the "unfortunate" phrase regarding "the great difficulty" in which Derrida would have found himself, but he also regretted that Derrida "was determined to remain silent concerning what is genuinely in question, while employing prophetic anathemas ('pre-Heideggerian,' etc.)." This new duel, this time between two former comrades of the École Normale Supérieure, attested to the depth of the fundamental disagreements provoked by Heidegger's thought. Certainly the polemic did not fade away.

Would a patient clarification, carefully prepared during the winter, bring the discussion to a close? It was with the title, "La parole à la defense" [The defense has the floor], that Roger-Pol Droit took account in May 1988[66] of the book François Fédier had just published,[67] which was offered with the aim of protecting "Heidegger's reputation"[68] against the slander propagated by Farias and his followers. From that point of view, his reply was no more philosophical than the attack. Assuming this limitation, he defended his position by maintaining that it was inconceivable to separate the life from the work. Is it conceivable that a great thinker be a villain? Before coming to this conclusion, and certainly before demonizing Heidegger's person, it would be better to illuminate the life through the work, instead of reducing the one to the most external or anecdotal aspects of the other. Now Heidegger has always affirmed the absolute priority of thought, whether his own or that of great classical philosophers, over any purely biographical consideration. To ignore this standard is to refuse from the outset to listen to what is most proper in Heidegger's thought.

Although not completely convinced by a highly detailed speech for the defense,[69] Roger-Pol Droit recognized that Fédier has at least one quality: he comports himself like a good attorney who, far from answering invective with slander, reconsiders the pieces of the dossier in order to demonstrate that the "method" of the accusation turns out to be more of a witch hunt than a serious and scrupulous historical inquiry: false translations, truncated citations, hasty interpretations, amalgamations, insinuations tending (with unfortunate success) to spread a "rumor," in order to draw an image of a monstrous Heidegger and to influence a gullible public unable to reference the sources. The book, in fact, only accomplished and furthered the first point that Fédier made "straightaway" in order to get it into the record, in the form of a letter to Pierre Nora dated November 4–5, 1987, and published as such in *Le Débat*.[70] What were the principal arguments advanced to prepare the dossier for the defense? First, there was the excessive nature of Farias's thesis (Heidegger was presented as more of a Nazi than the "official philosophers of Nazism"), and then the misunderstanding concerning the allusion to Sachsenhausen in Heidegger's last homage to his compatriot Abraham a Sancta Clara, a discourse that itself had been grossly "over-interpreted." Other errors or falsifications[71] left no doubt concerning Farias's constant malevolence, which was quite obvious when he used the adverb "scrupulously" with respect to Heidegger's payment of dues (pretending to ignore that in a totalitarian regime one leaves the party only at the risk of one's life). Between these first points and the spring of 1988 Fédier had himself benefited from the anti-Farias reactions that multiplied, including outside of France.[72]

Let us note, moreover, the change in the psychological climate within six months' time. The effect of the scandal had quickly abated; the seriousness of Farias's work no longer seemed at all unassailable, and consequently, the absolutely "overwhelming" character of the so-called revelations no longer imposed itself as easily. We have seen that before the publication of Fédier's book there had been no lack of interventions (and how could their various qualities be denied?) to contest Farias's factual errors and method.

Among all these responses, those that François Fédier gave in his book were, if not always the most convincing, at least very detailed[73] and careful with respect to the facts themselves, the reliability of the documents, and Heidegger's personality. After having read Fédier's book, as well as other contributions, one can no longer doubt that Farias's "method" turned out to be both unreliable and quite dangerous: certainly one is prepared to forgive some errors committed by a historian in good faith; but those of Farias were too numerous and above all betrayed such bias (along with an absence of rigor) that one is led to agree with the judgment of Pierre Aubenque: "In reality it is excessive and does not merit the attention we give it."[74] Undoubtedly some began to realize in spring 1988 that they had been too quick to lend credence to Farias's historical claims. In his account of Fédier's book, Roger-Pol Droit tried to stick to the facts. We certainly cannot expect him to unconditionally support Fédier, the most resolute defender of "the accused." We have seen that this is not the case. But among the arguments that he gave to justify important reservations, the most decisive were not, in my view, the details that he cited (for example, the case of Abraham a Sancta Clara or that of the dedication to Eugen Fischer—points on which Fédier seemed, on the contrary, convincing): the most decisive were his reservations concerning what tended, paradoxically, to "weaken the very path of Heidegger." Indeed, the excellent defense of Heidegger's "reputation," of his dignity, of his motivations, of the extenuating circumstances that one must recognize, led Fédier to accord less attention to the very core of the thought that constitutes the unique originality of the Master.

With respect to the heart of the matter, many questions remain about the link between the involvement of 1933 and Heidegger's thought; about the recognition by Heidegger himself of the "the internal truth and greatness" of the National Socialist movement, and finally about his "silence" concerning the Holocaust. Other contributors would try to situate themselves at a more philosophical level, with varying degrees of success.

In Quest of Philosophical Interpretations

One book stands out from the rest and even opens a new philosophical horizon, a more interesting phase of the debate around the "affair": Philippe Lacoue-Labarthe's *La Fiction du politique*.[75] This is the case for two reasons: not only would the book (conceived before the publication of Farias's book and without any relation to it) be the first to propose a philosophical reading that permits an understanding of the "political" of Heidegger, but that reading would also turn out to be influential: it is with or against it that other notable publications would try to rethink the question of the link between Heidegger's thought and his political involvement.

This book—which was preceded by a meditative volume on poetry, involving a probing dialogue with Heidegger[76]—was timely, which does not mean that it had always been well received or had not disconcerted some. Nor did it have the merit of offering a definitive or indisputable interpretation: it did not even claim to do so. But its virtue was that it assumed the responsibility appropriate to a philosopher: that of a rigorous thinking without complacency. Will it be said that I am giving him too much credit? It suffices, by way of justification, to circumscribe the limits that Lacoue-Labarthe himself assumed at the outset: setting forth the distinctly Heideggerian position on the closure of metaphysics and the nihilist errancy of our epoch;[77] radically questioning the core of Heidegger's "failing": his silence (or quasi-silence) on the Holocaust.[78]

These two positions—which are difficult to reconcile (Lacoue-Labarthe recognizes it)—can obviously be disputed. But to his credit, Lacoue-Labarthe first affirmed them and then above all displaced the debate by elevating it to an infinitely more meaningful level than that of knowing whether and when the Master wrote a particular letter, or took a particular position, etc. Accordingly, we arrive at the heart of a question that transcends any isolated fact, any anecdote, any politics, any psychological or ideological bias. It is a question of knowing how Heidegger was able to (and how one can after him, with or against him) "think together" a destiny of being and a "certain idea" of National Socialism.

We must confront this (quasi) unthinkable possibility, which has, until this point, been negated or denied by most interpreters (and, above all, by the core of the "faithful"): "Contrary to what one has said in a number of places, Heidegger's commitment is entirely consistent with his thought."[79] Must not this admission of a "complete consistency" *absolutely* condemn that thought? But this does not only trap that thought, since through it the crisis of our epoch is revealed, if it is necessary to admit that nihilism is its unintended truth, of which Auschwitz, that unthinkable event, was the revelatory caesura: "In the Auschwitz apocalypse, it was nothing less than the West, in its essence, that revealed itself—and that continues, ever since to reveal itself. And it is thinking that event that Heidegger failed to do."[80]

The connection between the diagnosis regarding Western history and Heidegger's thought becomes all the more inextricable as the one provides the means for reading the other, and because it turns out itself to be carried by the "failure" it denounces. Lacoue-Labarthe, in sum, claims nothing more than to be *the one who reveals* what Heideggerian thinking itself already revealed without admitting it.[81]

Does he have an excessive fascination for the paradox? Perhaps. One should not mistake two qualities in this interpretation that could remain hidden from a hasty or poorly informed reader: first, the fact that this logical paradox itself is not projected on Heidegger from outside but drawn from the source that is most intimate for him, that is, Hölderlin's thinking with respect to tragedy; second, Lacoue-Labarthe's elaboration of a theory of *mimesis,* based on Hölderlin's aesthetics.

That which actualizes this meditation, apparently quite distant from the catastrophes of the twentieth century, is the application of the concept of tragic caesura[82] to Auschwitz, and the attempt (begun by Heidegger himself) to think our modern distress (nihilist errancy) according to the exclusive reference to the

Greek model. Lacoue-Labarthe names this process of idealization, which has roots in the entire German tradition since Winkelmann, "national aestheticism," and locates therein the element of National Socialism that is foreign to any modern political rationality (even that of cynical despotism),[83] an element that contaminates Heideggerian thinking of historicity (including its determination of the essence of modern technology).

There is no need to go further into the details of the analysis of this book to establish its finesse and its authenticity: an experience of thinking led to its most paradoxical and most difficult limits. It is precisely that sophistication, guided by a tragic sense (to which the theatrical work *Sit Venia* also testifies[84]), that exposed Lacoue-Labarthe's work to lively critiques, and even sarcasm. It is, in fact, Lacoue-Labarthe who was the unnamed target at the beginning of Jean-Pierre Faye's new intervention in a debate with which he was familiar.[85] The guiding thread that he proposed on the subject of Heidegger's identification of metaphysics with nihilism (a position that he obviously challenges completely) emerged paradoxically from the accusations of Rector Krieck against Heidegger in April 1934. Those are often cited in defense of Heidegger to show that he began to be criticized by the toughest Nazis. In that respect, Faye clarified that Krieck[86] described Heidegger's philosophy as a "metaphysical nihilism" in order to demonstrate that it had nothing to do with authentic National Socialism, adding in a way that is unusual with respect to this nihilism: "as it has been represented primarily by Jewish writers." "This was a most dangerous accusation in 1934," Faye remarked appropriately, only referring to facts that he was not the only one to have published. His originality was to seize on the "incident" as a point of departure for an interpretation of Heidegger's "turn": "Heidegger's defense would consist in immediately *accepting* the Nazi equation: Western metaphysics = nihilism," while diverting the accusation toward a "fundamental event" that took place at the beginning of the history of being in Greece, Heidegger's great courses—especially those on Nietzsche—from 1935 to 1945 were nothing but the skillfully argued and disguised development of this defense, for "this obfuscation has been placed by Heidegger at the heart of European philosophy." This is an ingenuous hypothesis that Faye would develop later in *La raison narrative*[87] and to which I will return.[88]

We note in this polemic, the shifting of the debate toward the essential question of the meaning (or of the nonmeaning) of the interpretation of metaphysics as nihilism, such as Heidegger elaborated it, and as relayed by Lacoue-Labarthe. Are we then caught in the trap by our own proper destiny, led to give thought to a historical situation without precedent? Or rather, is the trap set by Heidegger's own thinking, who in this case behaves like a pyromaniac fireman? What is positive, in any case, is that the debate avoids overly personal accusations as well as simple apologies, so as to raise important questions. This more philosophically specific development, begun by Lacoue-Labarthe (following Derrida), would further develop in the work of his friend Lyotard as well as in the work of his ideological adversaries (Ferry and Renaut).

With *Heidegger and "the Jews,"* Lyotard confronted, in fact, the question of the difficult, perhaps unbearable, memory of the Holocaust and that of its repression in Heidegger's thought. Why "the Jews" since Heidegger did not speak of them? Clearly, it is not a question of Jewish people who are actual contemporary human beings, or not simply that; it is the question of the "non-people of survivors"[89] that we are, trying to face the unthinkable event in our history. Now it is precisely on this incalculable debt, this lack of thought, that the thinker of the unthought of the Western metaphysical tradition, was silent. His "failure" transcends the errors in judgment or the transgressions rehearsed by Farias, and minutely discussed by partisans and adversaries alike: it intimately concerns the relation to the Other, and to the imprescriptible law of the duty of memory.[90]

Everything Lyotard writes is by design; this text is no exception. However, in the present case, more than just some problems of presentation,[91] what makes it complex is that we are left on the edge of the abyss: what sense is there to impute a failure to Heidegger himself, if it is, in fact, the entire Western tradition of the thinking of being that is in question? The play of the quotation marks (that Derrida analyzed with such finesse in relation to the recourse to *Geist* in Heidegger's work) had become a skillful but disconcerting way of evoking major concepts (being, freedom, the Other) without defining them sufficiently, a way of accusing Heidegger (and the West) of a "failing" so fundamental that its limits remain to be determined (as the specificity of the Jews—without quotation marks—seemed erased). These are so many "perspectives," the virtues of which invite us to think beyond the ideological "settling of accounts."

Conversely, the purpose of *Heidegger and Modernity* sought to be more detailed, perhaps less brilliant but more clear. It is because Ferry and Renaut did not seek to rival the depth of a great thinker: they intended to be fair and efficacious by targeting the "French Heideggerians" (strangely said to be "gathered around Jacques Derrida"[92]) as well as their Master. The objective having been delimited in this way, the problem is simpler: how could a French Heideggerianism that masked the basic antimodernism of the Master with a sophisticated rhetoric be dispensed with, and how would humanism be philosophically reevaluated by inscribing it within a democratic project that is reconceptualized? In truth, the negative section was still substantial—no doubt too much so—in this little book where the polemic itself had trouble fixing on its moving and heterogeneous target. The censorship of the criticisms addressed to Farias attempted to save him from being completely dismissed, but did not achieve as clear a position as was hoped: while conceding that his book contained "errors" and even revealed a "certain dishonesty,"[93] they refused in principle to defend it[94] but accepted in passing certain of its easily disputable theses (for example, Farias's account of Heidegger's "militancy" before 1933 and of Heidegger's ideological affiliation with the SA wing is said to be "brilliant."[95])

What is much more interesting in this little book is the effort to understand the tensions, or even the contradictions, of this thought from within: in *Being and Time,* the ambiguity of the notion of Self [*Selbst*] that can appear after the fact as an insufficiently deconstructed subjectivity, but one that could have offered a support for the clarification of "resolute decision"; the ambivalence of the forgetting of being, which is the forgetting of a forgetting, and as such an ineluctable destiny, which is nonetheless conjured by meditative thinking; and finally, faced with modern technology, the oscillation between a "yes" (judging ineluctable the accomplishment of metaphysics in the will to power) and a "no" (managing a response, indeed a resistance in view of another future). The result was a scission with Nazism, which did not entirely "correspond" to what was expected of it (a scission that marked the difference between "correspondence" as inadequate and its meaning elaborated through a more authentic response): the acquiescence to a "correspondence" (in the first sense) between the essence of technology and modern man, coupled with the preparation of a freer relation to the very essence of technology (a response that Nazism could not give).[96]

These analyses allow us to recognize that Heidegger "developed a less than perfectly univocal interpretation of Nazism"[97] and reveal "what, in its complexity, Heidegger's assessment of Nazism"[98] had been. But instead of building on this insight to form a positive dialogue with other French interpreters, whose critical works were not always that far from their positions, Ferry and Renaut preferred to accuse them of being involved in rescue operations of Heidegger through antimodernism. Thus, in a prominent way, Derrida (whose hypothesis presented in *Of Spirit* seemed attractive and even "brilliant"),[99] was accused of practicing that rescue through antihumanism as if he had maintained that the involvement of 1933 was "a Nazi-humanistic deviation by Heidegger."[100] Now, not only did Derrida never use such an expression in *Of Spirit* but he never made such a schematic link between "spiritual" metaphysics, Nazism and humanism. It would be necessary here to return to the texts for a careful and precautionary reading. It would also be necessary to wonder whether one treats Lacoue-Labarthe fairly[101] when one ridicules the formulation, "Nazism is a humanism,"[102] while pretending to take it literally, although it supposes the understanding of the debate on the *metaphysical* character of a world such as Nazi racism. Clearly, the discussion of the direct nature of the link established by Heidegger between metaphysics and humanism is debatable, which should be carried out in a more serene and balanced way, thus sparing the authors the strangely distorted images they present of Heidegger (alleged to be led, on the one hand, by a "fanatical hatred of modernity,"[103] and credited, on the other hand, with "a *critical* attitude"[104] with respect to that same modern world). Although one notes the professed intent not to carry out a "rescue," there is, nonetheless, a certain hesitation concerning the appraisal of the Heideggerian philosophical heritage: first riddled with sarcasms, some aspects of Heidegger's work are said to offer certain resources, for example, its radical deconstruction of romantic vitalism, which "echoes the fundamental themes of criticism."[105] What finally complicates the problem—no one should doubt it—is that there is an antimodernism proper to modernity, to the extent that one of its essential traits was to constantly put itself in question. Is this regressive tension unique to Heidegger's work? Can the critical margin that it performed be recognized without being accused of "salvaging"? Because of their philosophical scope, all these questions had to be posed and have been posed effectively.[106]

Revealing Drama or Futile Quarrel?

There are scandals that never end. Is this not the case with the "Heidegger Affair," to the extent that its profound stakes are philosophical? With respect to the scandal provoked by Farias's book, we can say that a few months were sufficient for an honest person to form a relatively measured opinion regarding the value of its revelations. On this first level, one finds that a case was being "built."[107] But then the debate shifted toward interpretation, precisely where Farias was at his weakest. In the end, Farias's philosophical shortcomings were of little significance, since the effect he sought after had been achieved: the shock of a "Nazi Heidegger" had an impact; and even if, after the fact, one almost had to judge Farias philosophically worthless and historically unreliable, one simply had to undertake the interpretive work that was missing in his book. Whatever the degree of repulsion or attraction with respect to the figure of the great philosopher, or the severity or indulgence of the ethical judgment concerning his conduct, it was still necessary to understand the link or the absence of the link between his thought and what "remained" so embarrassing: that was the essential task. This is the critical point where one recognizes the contrast between the authentically philosophical texts (Derrida and Lacoue-Labarthe on one side, Ferry–Renaut on the other) that go beyond Farias's limits, and the impressionistic nature of the half-defensive, half-apologetic "description" of François Fédier. However justified it may be in the context, insofar as it simply involves respect for intellectual and moral honesty, the defense of the "reputation" of Heidegger the man becomes a dated battle for an opinion that is "maturing" and that realizes that the "true question" is situated not beyond the facts (that would be too easy) but in the refining of interpretation that must accompany and shed light on more reliable historical documentation. While subsiding for the general public, the Heidegger affair would continue to produce salutary philosophical "exchanges."

This is why the German historian Hugo Ott's apparently bemused, and in reality irritated, judgment merits our attention, but will not satisfy us completely: "In France the sky has fallen: meaning, *le ciel des philosophes* [the sky of philosophers].[108] In the dazzling presentation that the *nouveaux philosophes* [new philosophers][109] offered, along with a preface by Christian Jambet, Chilean philosopher Victor Farias' book on Heidegger made its appearance on the market, shaking the French intellectual world. It was a major affair. The clocks, we know well, work differently in France than elsewhere. We should not be surprised by the delay with which research results which had been known for some time (and in great detail) in German speaking countries, only today have reached the French audience, with the effect, it is true, that the well-ordered world of dominant philosophical schools has been caught up in a storm that turns everything *upside down*."[110]

In fact, the scope of this judgment is twofold: it concerned Farias and his effects in France.[111] With respect to Farias's book, Hugo Ott's judgment anticipated and converged with the critical path that we have taken here by following the progress of the discussion during winter 1987–88. "The merit of Farias's book lies in the compilation of new sources, and in their positive elaboration. There are many facts. His work reveals its limits, as soon as the interpretation begins, and, above all, at the point when it would be necessary to shed light on the relation between Heidegger's practical politics and his thought. This is, however, what one would be entitled to expect from a philosopher."[112] Our agreement with Ott and our respect for his sagacity does not include wholesale endorsement of the second part of his judgment concerning the specifically French aspects of the affair: namely, that we German specialists had known all that and even more (since Farias was not even up to date[113]). Was the scandal due to the ignorance of the French? In fact, Ott maintained more precisely that the intensity of the scandal was proportional to the secrecy and to the embellishment of Heidegger's behavior undertaken over the course of many years by Jean Beaufret and his disciples. Neither false nor absolutely true, Ott's vision of things seemed to ignore the successive waves of polemical discussions on the question in France itself since Liberation. One did not make a transition from the "orthodox" version to the attack leveled by Farias overnight. It is not necessary to insist on it further here: our reader has been, it seems, sufficiently instructed on the different stages of the polemic. We propose, however, the following analysis: the supplementary revelation of the facts, as compromising as they are, is not sufficient to explain the scope of the scandal. Ott is on the right track when he questions the French apologies for Heidegger, but that's as far as he goes. The situation has never been as simple as he depicts it. "And this dwelling, in which the French intelligentsia has made itself so comfortable, now appears to be uninhabitable."[114] But precisely: the French understanding (which was in no way homogeneous) was never really completely *comfortable* with the "orthodox" version concerning Heidegger. It is a question of a tense history, of rebounds, a history of a love-hate relation (an ambivalence that has existed ever since the early days of the reception and that has never stopped, perhaps even after Farias). The particularly French aspect of the Heidegger affair is far from being as sterile or as superficial as Hugo Ott thought (followed by Ferry and Renaut who, concentrating their attacks on French Heideggerians, almost seemed to envy Germany, where Heidegger "will probably long remain, along with Nietzsche, an accursed thinker"[115]). Lyotard seems to follow a more interesting path when, noting as well the French aspect of the Heidegger affair, he viewed it more favorably, inscribing it in terms of a French sensitivity to a writing "in charge of a thinking of the immemorial,"[116] from Rimbaud and Mallarmé to Artaud and Beckett (and it would be necessary to include Nerval).

As legitimate as it is within the limits of its historical competencies, Hugo Ott's judgment shows a misunderstanding that should be addressed: it involves the important question of the meaning of the quasi-fantasmatic fixation of the French intelligentsia on Heidegger.

Such a fixation is in no way limited to the admission of the defense from Jean Beaufret and his disciples, as Jeanne Hersch[117] also believed: this explanation overstates the influence of a few "sycophants" and does not permit the full dimension of the fascination provoked by Heidegger to be understood. If a comparable affective investment is often intertwined with a person of flesh and blood, how can we claim to decipher it when it animates a complex cultural formation such as the "French intelligentsia," which has a problematic identity (mythical? narrative? retrospective illusion of historians of ideas?)?

According to Freud, the return of the repressed operates through the formation of "a *compromise* between repressed elements and defense."[118] One can wonder whether all the images of Heidegger that circulated in France after 1933–34 were not "substitute formations," until the critical explosion of 1987–88, when all the substitutions collapsed. Why? Because suddenly Farias presented the king with no clothes, a Nazi Heidegger, with the oneiric clarity of a "genuine" nightmare. The question here is not whether it was true in the sense of a historic authentication (we will see constantly, from the fall of 1987, an oscillation between fantasy and fact, sleep and wakefulness): it sufficed that it briefly seemed plausible.

A preliminary question can be posed: what was the source of such a *repression* [*Verdrängung*]? What was repressed, if not the very powerful intellectual (and erotic) drive that subtends any recognition of a Master of thought and of life? In the 1930s we saw this drive of immense admiration and passionate intellectual love show itself in the work of Emmanuel Levinas and Rachel Bespaloff in particular. As early as 1934, with discreet indications, the reservations and the censorship began to appear. The scene of the psychodrama was in place: the unbearable oxymoron of that love-hate would only intensify: "great thinker/Nazi." In *Being and Nothingness*, the infernal question was censored and with cause (let us not forget the Nazi authority in Paris *allowed* the book to *appear,* where a form of self-censorship was, in a sense, already practiced). Did Sartre himself, who was in Berlin in 1933, not know more than he claimed? And were the essential matters not already known in 1933?

One saves the most violent repression for what one desires and knows all too well. But it would be necessary to conjure the repression through studied confession and through the play of corrections and denials. What complicated the affair further for the French was the infamy of the collaboration with the Nazis and the guilty conscience that followed it. France, sweet France, is there not in you one who is exhausted, excited, and defeated, who slept with a handsome German? Is your memory not inhabited by the haunting image that comes to you now and that you would like to forget? It took such a long time to get over this unavoidable past! Along with the Heidegger affair, there were the affairs of Bousquet, Papon, and Mitterrand himself . . .

But did the Heidegger affair not truly reach an intensely neurotic character when the love-hate toward the master was displaced and condensed onto Jacques Derrida, accusing him and holding him almost as guilty, simply because he had condemned Farias and had continued to take Heidegger seriously as a philosopher? Hence, Derrida became a sort of French double of Martin the Cursed [TN: A play on the French title of Fritz Lang's 1931 film *M*, which in French was titled *M le maudit* (M the Cursed One)]. Attacked for not "denouncing" Heidegger's thought, on the one hand, and for being overly subtle in understanding the ambiguities in the Master's most formidable texts, on the other hand, he was especially unsettling and upsetting for people. Was he the heir or usurper of the despised Master, a thinking that was too difficult and decidedly dangerous? With Beaufret, one had a "representative" of Heidegger in France; with Derrida, one had something even more embarrassing: a magisterial Double to adore and to hate, but without being able to exorcize completely the archaic figure of the Original Master. Will the struggle for recognition be mortgaged indefinitely by this intellectual erotic investment where Mastery is involved?

There might be a less complex and less psychoanalytic explanation for this condemnation by the self-righteous: the quite prosaic and sadly classical one that Alain Finkielkraut proposed in *Le Monde* January 5, 1988: "Ah! How sweet it must be to be anti-fascist when that frees you from phenomenology and its impossible jargon! For if Heidegger's meditation can be reduced, as Michel Polac claims, to 'a few clichés from Le Pen,' or if, as Patrick Gérard writes, 'Le Pen would make a good Heideggerian,' then there is no need to read: one has understood, 'one gets the point.' As needed, tomorrow we will organize a demonstration."[119]

One should not give this nonsense more attention than it deserves. There is a standard phase of any sustained polemic when it has to deal with the fact that some people are tired of hearing about it. Even in the streets, with any brawl, there are those who prefer to distance themselves from the fight. An intellectual and "chic" version of this attitude of disillusionment was formulated by Jean Baudrillard at the end of January 1988 in the brilliant, sophisticated, and dogmatic terms that he is known for. Is everything today not caught up in the play of the simulacra? The Heidegger affair was no different. What was essential in Baudrillard's thesis can be summed up in the first sentence: "The vain quarrel about Heidegger does not have proper philosophical meaning, it is only symptomatic of a weakness of modern thought that, failing to find new resources, returns obsessively to its origins, to the purity of its references, and painfully relives, at the end of the century, its primal scene from the beginning of the century."[120] Is this affair reduced, like the Klaus Barbie affair, to a "derisory convulsion" resulting from a "collective hallucination"?

Having agreed that the outbursts of this strange winter had an excessive, emotional, even hysterical dimension, one can understand that a strong reaction to the excessive treatment was to be expected. But Baudrillard's position was more radical, even categorical as it regarded as meaningless, if not symptomatic and pathological, the entire uproar concerning Heidegger's "Nazism." Beyond the disturbance that Baudrillard himself was able to cause at the time, we have sufficient distance now to consider things more critically. One could agree with Baudrillard only if our reconstruction of the development of "the affair" revealed "noise," furor, and vain gesticulation. By limiting ourselves to the media, or to the person on the street, we would only see a sterile "necrospective" aspect of the affair: Heidegger's name, still more famous, would attract an intense fascination, raising it to an ambiguous quasi-taboo status of a victim who symbolically atones.[121] But should we take this for granted and decide to ignore that apart from the facts (which Baudrillard seems to scorn) that what had taken place was terribly meaningful? Should one detect, with Daniel Sibony,[122] a "self-hypnosis," first with Heidegger, who was for a time captivated by his own thought taking political form, then with his disciples and adversaries who were also fascinated by the phantasm of the idol where the fetishized origin finally slips away and vanishes? If such is the case, this conjuration of a pure origin would oblige philosophers to accept this fortunately poisoned gift: a "weak and vulnerable" Master once again.

Whether or not one follows the psychoanalytic diagnosis of the "affair," should we not admit that it has allowed us to pose crucial questions—some of which have heretofore been avoided—to (and about) a decidedly labyrinthine thought? Should we pretend to be unaware that, even if it was difficult and somewhat confusing, one was better able—with a minimum of intellectual honesty—to understand events and important issues. Let us admit that January 1988 was without a doubt the time when the polemic reached its peak of intensity (or saturation) in France [123] and when one had the impression of finding oneself in a dead end. It has been established that the following months allowed a deepening of the debate.[124] The question nevertheless remains open: had the return of the repressed really been a cathartic event? If it permitted the necessary reactivation, it also produced a considerably negative effect: the occultation of a thorough attention to these texts. Thus Nicole Parfait had defended a very thorough thesis at that time on the political question and the relation between theory and practice in Heidegger's work.[125] This thesis has still not been published.[126] One can hope that it will not be too long before the thesis is published, so that the *catharsis* runs its course and reaches its end, provided that such an end can be conceived.

Epilogue VI

How could the effect produced by Farias's book be denied, at least in the first days that followed its reception? I was stunned in two senses of the word: overwhelmed by the "revelations" and the sinister light cast on Heidegger the man, and also outraged by a public fracas that ignored nuances and degenerated into intellectual terrorism. I had not recognized, at the outset, all the "tricks" that allowed Farias to demonize Heidegger in such an extreme manner; at the same time, I was aware of the huge gap between this sudden unbelievably reductive turmoil and the great texts that had inspired me and that literally inhabited me. That dramatic disjunction had to be explained, and I did not doubt within myself that the passage of time would allow this critical task to be accomplished (on both fronts: with respect to both Heidegger and his accusers).

A revealing anecdote: some days after the publication of the book, I received a call from Michel Cazenave asking me to participate in a televised debate on this issue. I did not refuse but objected that it was difficult for me to give a definite answer without having read the book. I asked him if he could be so kind as to send me the book, because I lived in the countryside and there were no bookstores nearby. He promised to mail it to me immediately. What followed? I received neither the book nor another message. The very fact of having asked for a delay for reflection and the possibility of serious discussion seemed to have been a deal breaker . . . But I do not accuse anyone and I have no regrets (at any rate, the program Océaniques *took place very well without me). In fact, this minor miscommunication allowed me to avoid taking a position too early. The polemic was launched. Everyone wanted to stir things up or calm things down.*

Another important memory: I recall having discovered, with stupefaction, large pictures of Heidegger wearing a Nazi insignia on the kiosks of the newsstands in the good town of Nice. It was a poster announcing a special edition of Bernard Pivot's literary journal, Lire. *I would never have thought that Heidegger would ever receive this redoubtable "honor," with or without insignia. And yet that actually happened.*

What remains today of this turmoil?

It would be superficial and false to think that it has completely disappeared. The whole affair has left traces and stigmas. These are not exactly what one would have expected at the time. The demonization of Heidegger has subsided. Other publications (particularly Hugo Ott's biography) have made it possible to take account of his psychological fragility, to better understand the accusation, while discriminating between insinuations and proven facts, and to put the Heidegger case in the context of the unbelievable complexity of exceptional historical circumstances during those dramatic years for Germany and for Europe. Once it subsided, the extreme agitation at the end of the '80s left a residue that needs to be carefully examined, in the same way that one would approach a chemical solution in a test tube that has cooled. On the one hand, there is no doubt that the unconditional defense of Heidegger has been marginalized, as have been the unbelievable accusations that almost transformed the thinker into a war criminal, thanks to a series of insinuations and amalgamations. On the other hand, the philosophical work has "held its ground" more than one might have feared (or conversely more than anyone hoped), but at a level of specialization in the academic world that was lost on the general public. It will be necessary to return to the scope and contours of this disassociation and to a new situation that had nothing to do with the intellectual fashions of the postwar, or even the 1960s or 1970s.

I have been able to establish, moreover, the constant divide between the media-driven agitation and the reactions of students and colleagues. Unlike what happened in 1968 and immediately after, "most people" generally remained calm, and the mention of Heidegger's name in a course rarely produced protest or emotion. It was also a generational matter with the elders: "We already knew all that." Either more or less blasé in principle or actually well-informed about the previous debates on the question, most academics of a certain age—even among the non-Heideggerians—often preferred to stay on the sidelines of the debate, going as far as minimizing or neglecting genuinely new information presented by Farias's book.

I myself hesitated for some time before writing on the affair. It was necessary to allow time for reflection in order to address the very difficult question of the secret connection that could exist between the involvement in 1933 and the very thought of the philosopher (at least some of its aspects). It was necessary to do this without taking sides, and by overcoming the overly psychological, anecdotal, or subjective aspects. But why a new intervention in the context of a "plethora" of books and articles? The weariness that overcame the public affected me as well. Nevertheless, I was unsatisfied and I felt the necessity to take up the debate again precisely where most had left it, namely, on the threshold of Heidegger's most secret philosophical hearth. The principal justification of The Shadow of That Thought—*published in 1990 thanks to Marc Richir and a courageous editor, Jérôme Millon—was less an account of the polemic than an effort to overcome its psychological and emotional aspects in order to advance a philosophical thesis: there was indeed a link between Heidegger's thought and his involvement in 1933, but this link was much more complex (and more interesting) than a circumstantial allegiance to a complete ideol-*

ogy. It was the thinking of the finitude of man in history and the radical historicity of Dasein *that exposed Heidegger to the danger of extremism: it was then a brilliant treatment of the history of metaphysics within a "historial-destinal" schema that led him to interpret Nazism as a form of the accomplishment of metaphysics as technology. The destinal dimension was not a minor appendix of historicality: the latter was explored in* Being and Time. *In fact, the thinking of the destinal character of the history of being was an achievement of the later Heidegger, the one who cast the entire history of metaphysics in terms of the Nietzschean genealogy of nihilism and reversal of Platonism.*

While Heidegger distanced himself personally from his early allegiance to Hitlerism, and imagined an outcome other than the imperial domination of men and things, he also seemed to assign an inevitable, destinal role to Nazism, which was linked to the technological accomplishment of metaphysics, without providing an account in terms of a political rationality that would be clearly defined. Heidegger's political "error" then revealed a "failure" of his thought, in the sense of a stumbling block, which was not accidental (because it pertained to the fact that the thinking of being moved away from the understanding of reality and rational possibilities). It would be necessary to draw the consequences from this by rethinking the status of the political in the era of technology in a way that was different from Heidegger's. To this end, a thinking like that of Arendt (one understands better now the extent to which she was in dialogue with Heidegger) is a great help. And one can only appreciate that this knot of questions is better known now in France (in particular thanks to the energetic work of Jacques Taminiaux).

With hindsight, it seems that these years of crisis were not entirely in vain. As limited and as partisan as Farias's book was, it had, indirectly, certain cathartic virtues. By its very excessive nature, it generated a liberation (at times hysterical, one must admit) of speech and of thought. One could be sarcastic concerning the French intellectuals, as Hugo Ott was, with the amused scorn of a scrupulous historian faced with his incorrigibly irresponsible students. First of all, why be upset about the Heidegger case as if it was so exceptional, as if the error of a philosopher was so surprising? One should stay informed about the research of the historians and classify them appropriately!

What such wisdom does not grasp is that the drama (in spite of its excess, its superficial analysis by the media, etc.) was sparked by fundamental questions caused by the effect of Nazism itself. How was the West able to arrive at such a monstrosity? This is not a problem that a historian can "resolve." One cannot criticize him or her; but must we not pose this question? Now that question intersects with the Heideggerian questioning of the destiny of Western rationality. Are we going to give thought to the Nazi horror on the basis of Heidegger's thought? Or quite the contrary, is it that thought, which was itself deluded, which impeded access to accuracy and justice? This too-brief recollection revives an anxiety and an expectation (an expectation diluted in the various revivals of the polemics since Liberation) that go well beyond the mere enumeration of facts, accurate or inaccurate, concerning the behavior of Heidegger the man. The basic question is as follows: Is this thinking a resource? Is this prodigiously intelligent and cunning little man with a disconcerting psychological profile the bearer of a message, of signs of a new thinking, of a decidedly illuminating path for our miserable lives, or is all that just rhetoric, window dressing, and language games? One could be as sarcastic as one would wish regarding the "superficiality" of others. To want to eliminate this worry, and this hope, would be to resign oneself to an incommensurable loss: the loss of the questioning of the very meaning (or the nonmeaning) of the distress of our century and of our epoch.

11 Between Erudite Scholarship and Techno-Science

THE GREATEST STORMS began to subside. Approaching the 1990s, we were sailing on relatively calm waters compared to the turbulence of the "Heidegger affair," even if the thunder could still be heard in the distance.[1]

In October 1990, the translation of a much-awaited book by the historian Hugo Ott[2] was published, a biography of Heidegger that was on the whole well received, although it contained no sensational revelations. Everyone recognized the seriousness of the historian from Freiburg, at least in terms of the establishment of the facts. Ott is not a philosopher and does not claim to be one (his work remains for the most part in the margins of Heidegger's philosophical work and barely addresses the later Heidegger). There was, with respect to this book, a general consensus that contrasted with the recent rifts; one recognized its qualities, its serious tone: but this apparent agreement concealed profound disagreements in matters of interpretation. Some found that Farias's thesis was confirmed[3] (and they were not mistaken in certain cases, for example concerning Heidegger's preparation for election to the rectorship); for others, Farias's tendentious simplifications were refuted (and this was equally true particularly with respect to the reduction of Heidegger's thought to the SA ideology or in relation to Rosenberg's growing hostility against Heidegger—which Farias had minimized or concealed). Thus, unfavorable to Farias, but trying to present a balanced account of the debate, Jean-Michel Palmier wrote in his postface with regard to the rectorate episode: "The horizon in which Hugo Ott inscribes Heidegger's Rectorate is profoundly different from that of Victor Farias, for whom nothing separates essentially the political positions of the philosopher from the most ordinary Nazism. What is interesting about Hugo Ott's approach is that he rejects equally this simplification of the 'Heidegger case' and the presentation of the facts that Heidegger himself elaborated in 1945 in order to minimize his responsibility."[4] In an effort to be fair, Palmier distanced himself from his earlier analyses, which were clearly more lenient toward Heidegger.

Let us be clear: even if one takes the inevitable gaps in memory and the effects of indifference into account, neither the philosophical world nor that of the media—broader but less homogeneous—was able or willing to ignore what had happened. In fact, nothing would be as it was before. However, what was new was that sides were taken, positions declared, arguments exchanged, camps delineated, this time much more clearly, and, to all appearances, definitively. To whoever poses the question of Heidegger's political engagement, we would respond with an understandably blasé air: "The case is closed, learn the facts!" With that, the interest in Heidegger's politics would subside;[5] or, if it remained, it would be at a more essential or more radical level than that of the polemics triggered by Farias's book.[6] It was apart from any publicity, in a journal with an unfortunately small distribution,[7] that in 1990 the debate received without a doubt its most intellectually honest and rigorous treatment: Jean Quillien, a disciple and former assistant of Éric Weil at Lille, was unwilling to simply pit his "commendable" mentor, rationalist and democrat, against the villain Heidegger, a collaborator with Nazism who was opposed to reason, modernity, and democracy. His point of departure was rather "the state of French philosophy"[8] during its very crisis: its persistent silence on "the Heidegger case" and the remarkable article Weil published in 1947, which was reinforced by a multifaceted existentialist and structuralist fascination for a Heideggerian thought treated as oracular and divorced from its social-historical context. Like Weil, Quillien labored to respect, on the one hand, the coherence and dignity proper to Heidegger's philosophy, and to grasp, on the other, the "logic" of the personal engagement of Heidegger the man, both in relation to his own work and in continuity with an entire German tradition, without ignoring the climate of the '30s. One should not confuse, as Farias did, Heidegger's philosophy with Nazism: we should learn to distinguish between Nazi ideology, on the one hand, and a certain philosophy of National Socialism, on the other hand. With respect to Heidegger's addresses and proclamations in 1933, Weil wrote: "It is Nazi language, Nazi morality, Nazi thought (*sit venia verbo*). It is not Nazi philosophy."[9] Quillien disagreed with Weil on this point: while conceding that Weil could not go further in 1947, he declared himself in disagreement with Weil's idea that the connection between *Sein und Zeit* and Nazism was arbitrary (and thus that it was necessary "to save Heidegger's philosophy, as philosophy, from Heidegger himself.")[10] How are we to understand the meaning of this connection without reducing it to Farias's hasty assumptions? By inscribing Heidegger in a certain German tradition (that he brings to its "unsurpassable completion"[11]) that, from Luther to Jacobi and Schopenhauer, challenged the domination of Reason, just as Hitler, in another way, sought to destroy the political rationality of the enlightenment thinkers. Heidegger was not an existentialist, as Weil still believed, but an essentialist who intended to think the pure violence of being, prior to and beyond onto-theology: a radicalism that accomplishes itself only "by making its own impossibility explicit."[12] Quillien's assessment of Heidegger's philosophy was thus quite severe, much more so than Weil's, but at the end of an argumentation that respected the coherence of a thought whose unsettling grandeur, resituated in its historical context, was recognized nonetheless. If it fascinated French thought, always favorably disposed toward a critical radicality, it was because of its destructive (or deconstructive) power. This would explain the silence in relation to Weil's work and his promise of construction (or reconstruction) of an ethical and political rationality. Would the end of the century allow us to turn this page? Such was the hope formulated in the conclusion: may French philosophy reconnect with positivist thought!

More generally, beyond such an account, we saw emerge, in a climate in which there was little interest in Heidegger, a number of camps that were not so much hostile as disinterested (or feigned disinterest):[13] on the one hand, there were the specialists, who worked among themselves and whose only ambition was to be recognized as such by a limited audience, that is, by other specialists, their disciples, their students, and so on; on the other hand, there were innumerable people who took Heidegger both as an established author and as "cursed" (to what degree? that is another matter), people who would be the source of interrogations, accusations, and questions that were more or less relevant, but whose central axis seemed to be what they took to be Heidegger's hostility toward the contemporary world, its science and its technology. In this way, one would observe the curious spectacle of scientists, or "neophytes," none of whom had read even one line of Heidegger, but who found it "fashionable" to mention his name (or to mention a thought that one could attribute to him), at times to legitimize their own positions, but more often as a foil. Could Heidegger not be allowed to be a philosopher "like any other"? One should not forget this question, after having taken note of the stabilization or "normalization" at the university and in scholarship, as well as a more serene climate.[14]

Within such a favorable climate, we can identify, in 1996–97, two very different accounts. The first was directed to a wide audience: the biography by Rüdiger Safranski. The French translation of his book appeared in 1996, just two years after its publication in German.[15] Neither a militant like Farias nor a historian like Ott, Safranski—who was already well-known due to a successful biography about Schopenhauer[16]—addressed himself to a wide audience. Well-informed, lively, and clear, his book did not offer anything new to specialists, neither with respect to documentation nor with respect to philosophical analysis. In this respect, nevertheless, he made a greater effort than Hugo Ott, and often with a real pedagogical talent, to clarify for his reader the thinking of the philosopher (even managing to evoke the "Zen" aspect of the elder Heidegger).[17] He was able, without being overly sympathetic, to focus on what definitively mattered in Heidegger's work: the passion of questioning and of "showing."[18] However "journalistic" this biography seemed to the specialists, it did fill a void: for the first time, the French reader had a sufficiently complete and impartial idea of the destiny of a thinker, who, despite his professional role and worldwide celebrity, perhaps retained the uncanniness of a "savage from the South Seas," with mysterious inscriptions on his body (or corpus, in the present case).[19]

Another testimony related to the "Heidegger case" was the unusual publication of two short essays by Marcel Conche,[20] which were situated at a more fundamental level and necessarily addressed to a limited group of specialists, colleagues, and friends. However, the limited nature of the distribution of these essays did not detract from their importance: the author, a distinguished and original philosopher whose work is becoming more recognized, was in no way a "Heideggerian," whether by his formation, doctrinal orientation, or style. His position, which attested to his intellectual independence, was all the more remarkable. It is necessary to consider the two essays together. Although one could believe that the second text corrected the first, it in fact completed it, not in order to condemn or approve Heidegger's political error but to understand it.[21] *Heidegger resistant:* did this title not cede too much to the belated defense of the philosopher, arguing that he had undertaken a "spiritual resistance" to National Socialism? Conche conceded that he himself should have put the epithet "resistant" in quotation marks. However, his purpose was "to exonerate Heidegger's allegiance to National Socialism for the simple reason that he was innocent of what was essential to National Socialism: racism and anti-Semitism."[22] On this point, Conche went as far as to separate himself from Éric Weil, for whom he worked as an assistant at Lille. While recognizing that Heidegger was not a "biological materialist," Weil nevertheless characterized Heidegger's "short speeches" in 1933–34 as "Nazi pieces." Conche did not agree: he argued precisely to show that, although incontestably nationalist and placing his faith in Hitler, Heidegger in no way gave in to what constituted the heart of the Nazi ideology, namely, racist ideology: "The notion of 'race' plays no role in Heidegger's thought."[23] More importantly, in his "Rectoral Address" and other writings from the "dark period"—as objectionable as they were—Heidegger clearly distinguished the tasks of philosophical thinking from the Nazi ideological claims: he separated *Dasein* from any racial or other determination. He rejected the notion of a "politicized science," refused to reduce philosophy to a "worldview," and his relation to language was not "technical," dogmatic, or based on will as was Hitler's, but rather one of questioning. Even his justification of the departure from the League of Nations conveyed no imperialist sentiment.[24] When one examines the texts carefully and without prejudice, including those concerning Nietzsche and Christianity, Heidegger was in no way a Nazi: "He is rather aligned with free thinking."[25] Why, then, his relation to the party? He believed, at least until the summer of 1934, that he could have an influence on the course of events from within and that the "movement" could be transformed: "That was his error."[26] That error is incontestable, but there was nothing criminal in it, especially if one considers the state of Germany at the time, the scope of the illusions widely shared concerning Hitler, and so on. Did certain intellectuals have the tendency to "condemn" Heidegger? One can gladly agree with Marcel Conche, whose intellectual honesty and independence deserve our respect. One is more skeptical when he went as far as to justify Heidegger's silence or "quasi silence" (including posthumously) with respect to the specific horrors of Nazism. For example, was the Holocaust Hitler's personal decision alone? Did it not have something to do with National Socialism "as such"?[27] There is certainly a discussion to be had, well beyond Heidegger's personal case, which in any case remains much less interesting than the contribution of his fundamental thinking. Even if the late intervention of Marcel Conche can seem regressive, insofar as it revives the endless discussion of the scope of Heidegger's personal responsibilities, its quality, its precision, and its high level of analysis gives us a document with which we will have to reckon.

One cannot say the same about the volume published in 1995 by François Fédier, entitled *Écrits Politiques, 1933–1966*,[28] which went almost unnoticed—a surprising fact after so many polemics. In addition to the fact that most of the texts in question were already known, the text corresponded neither to a volume in the *Collected Works* nor strictly speaking to a little book published separately in Germany by Herman Heidegger in 1983.[29] Including the translation of this latter publication, it contained the *Spiegel* interview, but also texts of self-justification or of reflection that were not explicitly political.[30] The title, *Écrits Politiques, 1933–1966*, does not quite reflect the contents. More strange still is the composition of the volume. Over 322 pages, almost half (counting the notes) are by François Fédier. In his long preface, he developed a genuine defense in favor of the accused entitled "Revenir à plus de décence" [A return to greater decency]. One would not expect him to make any other case. But does such a publication not offer us the opportunity to establish a genuine account of the debate, to elevate it philosophically and depart from the narrow context of the problem of Heidegger's personal guilt? Not only did Fédier limit himself exclusively to the famous "ten months," not only did he not envisage in any way the problem of the relations or connections between the work and the political proclamations, and did not dwell on the question of the persistent belief in the "internal truth and greatness of the movement," but he devoted two-thirds of his preface to a historical, academic, and sententious analysis, an exposé from which Heidegger was practically absent, as he addressed the crisis of the Weimar regime, Hitler's diabolical cunning, various betrayals, and so on. On the basis of all these historical references, which diluted the Heidegger case, he emphasized that there were extenuating circumstances that led the philosopher to believe in Hitler. We learn for example that "the situation was at the very least *confused.*"[31] No doubt about that, but it is all the more surprising that at the end of his heavy-handed defense, the lawyer pronounced the most severe moral judgments with respect to his "client": not only did he make a grave error of judgment, but he had indeed "tarnished"[32] and "shamed" himself.[33] What was the criterion for this sudden moral condemnation? We know nothing else about that alleged shame that Heidegger experienced during his life except on the basis of this "testimony." Fédier took great pains to maintain that Heidegger belonged to the party without enthusiasm and even that "he did not *want* to be rector [*sic*]." But what did this poor man—whom we are told was neither a hero nor a coward—want?[34] Was he a follower or was he the thinker of the will and Spirit? Is such a psychological judgment appropriate for the greatest philosopher of the century? Was it really without enthusiasm, and without intending it that he proclaimed that "the Führer alone *is* the present and future German reality and its law"?[35] If this declaration provoked shame in Heidegger himself for some time, why was the author of the preface so forgiving when others were so severe with respect to the Master? Is it only a lawyer who can accuse his client in his absence? It is in fact a strategy well known in legal procedures that an important accusation that is accepted allows the occultation of other points or the indulgence of the court in general. In the present case, does the matter receive the treatment it deserves? Is it what one expected from this Gallimard publication? Does it guarantee the seriousness, impartiality, and "decency" requested by the author of the preface, even though he managed to *black out* [TN: English in the original] the considerable debate concerning Heidegger and Nazism, both within and outside France?[36] By concluding his preface on purely psychological considerations concerning the person of Heidegger, Fédier reduced the debate to the level of 1946 when Sartre wrote: "He lacked character. That's all!" That is to take the reader of today for a fool or uninformed. Let us conclude, with respect to this publication, with a significant example: the text entitled "The menace that threatens science."[37] In principle, the idea of translating and publishing this very interesting text, until that time unpublished in French and even less known in Germany, was excellent. But the result leaves something to be desired. The translation of the title "Die Bedrohung der Wissenschaft" by "The menace that threatens science" is at the very least one-sided: literally "The menace of science" conveys the ambiguity between the subjective genitive and the objective genitive (the menace that comes from science and that which turns against it). Why was the subtle ambivalence of the original expression not respected? Was it in order to suggest that for Heidegger in 1937, it was Nazism that represented a menace weighing on science? In perplexity, let us return to the text: it is Heidegger himself who speaks of an "*internal* menace" [*innere Bedrohung*] and writes: "The true menace of science comes from itself and comes through itself."[38] To translate in a "detached" manner as did Fédier, by occulting the ambiguity of the genitive, blocks access to the richness of Heidegger's thought in a text that is still relevant.[39]

It is of course also necessary to know how to situate oneself at another level and to do justice to serious works, which, in various ways and degrees, have advanced the critical understanding of Heidegger's work in France, at the same time that new translations were being published. To consider that these works were the result of a sort of erudition is not at all pejorative, if it is true—as Chamfort thought—that "a lack of philosophy leads to a disdain for erudition; an abundance of philosophy leads one to appreciate it."[40]

The "Turn": Before and after Being and Time

The chronology that the publication and the reception of fundamental works follows is not the same as that of "scandals" and "affairs": we are once again concerned with the long-term perspective, while earlier we were situated in a "short-term chronology." In fact, this disparity of rhythms allows us to refer again conveniently to a date slightly prior to the publication of Farias's book: six months earlier, in April 1987, a book appeared titled *Le Tournant dans la pensée de Martin Heidegger,*[41] which addressed what is no doubt the most central difficulty of the work, the meaning of the famous *Kehre*. While this word is not the most mysterious one of Heidegger's terminology, it is sufficiently challenging to its interpreters. If the translation by *tournant* [turn] seems the most acceptable, the question to be determined is whether the turn is a bend or represents a complete about-face. Following Gadamer's reference to Swabian usage, the word represents "the bend in the path that goes up a mountain,"[42] but it is obvious that a *Kehre* can also be "negotiated" on the way down. The actual usage of the term is less rustic: it is part of skiing vocabulary, Heidegger's preferred sport . . .

The semantic debates do not engage the problem of interpretation. Why accord so much importance to the "turn" to the point of giving it such a celebrated status? It is indeed well-known, ever since the Master himself, in the "Letter on Humanism,"[43] and then in his preface to William Richardson's book,[44] recognized the pertinence of the term in the evolution of his path of thought. Henceforth, between "Heidegger I" and "Heidegger II," following Richardson's terminology, which was rapidly adopted in France,[45] the "turn" became the key word for any research into this work. Even the adversaries, who refused any strictly internal interpretation—Bourdieu, Faye, Ferry, and Renaut—refer to this "turn" for their own interpretation while denouncing the pitfalls of Heidegger's "self-interpretation." Is the only choice between the latter, on the one hand, and "external" interpretations" that were mostly biographical, on the other hand?

Jean Grondin's study offered a more subtle approach. With a concern for clarity, he took as his priority texts in which the *Kehre* was explicitly in question, and established that contrary to the chronology proposed by Heidegger himself (1937), and following instead the explicit indications and the internal logic of some of Heidegger's texts, this "bending" appeared much earlier: as early as the incompletion of the project of *Being and Time* and as early as the summer of 1927 (the 1930 lecture "On the Essence of Truth" was also of pivotal importance). Now, the question of the determination of the date is only preliminary to understanding what is at stake. It is on this sensitive point that Grondin did a precise and useful work, since he showed that the very meaning of this "turn" changed for Heidegger himself: first, a search for a temporal foundation of ontology (as well as for the existent henceforth understood "ek-statically"), this movement of thought then became a questioning of subjectivity and of metaphysics, a quest for "the truth of essence" (*Wesen*), and finally, the discovery that being itself is the origin and the site of the turn. From a formal perspective, one can thus distinguish five forms or "aspects" of the turn (the "vulgar" or biographical conception, the thematic conception, the "ontochronical"[46] turn, the reversal [*retournement*] of the essence of truth into the truth of essence,[47] and finally the turn in being itself).[48] But one can, after all, still recognize a continuity: "This multiplicity does not exclude a unity."[49] There is a unity of the quest for the truth of being, first in the context of *Dasein,* then on the basis of the deconstruction of the meaning of being as presence, which would lead to a more originary site, the clearing [*Lichtung*] of being resituated in its own withdrawal. Grondin succeeded then in reconstituting Heidegger's itinerary, and in maintaining his distance from the "self-interpretation" that tended to harmonize an interrupted work retrospectively. Heidegger, far from doing an about-face, radicalized his questioning from 1927, while giving this radicalization its own truth and style.[50]

A fruitful work, this study nonetheless encounters two objections. On the one hand, it lent, to an excessive degree, an "intrinsic reality" to the notion of "the turn" without preserving sufficient critical distance in relation to its hermeneutic limits. On the other hand, by maintaining that there is a philosophy of the *Kehre* and by speaking constantly of the "later philosophy" of Heidegger, Grondin maintained a position that was very close to Gadamer's. But he contradicted Heidegger himself, who rejected the use of the label of philosophy to refer to his *thought*. It would have been necessary to thematically justify this questioning of the differentiation between meditative thinking and philosophy itself. Is it too fine a point? We do not think so: it is indeed the question of the overcoming of metaphysics that is thus at issue. Either one follows Heidegger in his quest for a nonmetaphysical thinking and the "turn" is recognized (whatever its avatars) as an initial breakthrough preparing a destinal transformation, or one maintains that it restores philosophy as a radical ontology of finitude and of temporality, but in this case the "turn" was only the displacement of difficulties that were not really overcome. One discerns that Grondin leaned to the latter position, but his conclusion remained excessively elliptical: "As a figure of a new philosophical paradigm, the turn always orients the *Kehre* to a reason to which it corresponds."[51]

It is also from the hermeneutic perspective (but this time under the implicit authority of Ricoeur rather than Gadamer) that a monumental study by Jean Greisch[52] appeared some years later, offering for the first time in French more than a literal commentary on *Being and Time,* "a thorough interpretation." Although it is obviously impossible to give a detailed account of this highly technical work, we should at least characterize its spirit. The project is not only very ambitious: it is new, because it is a question for the first time of reflecting comprehensively on texts that, for the most part, were not translated into French. In this case, we are in a period prior to *Being and Time.* The publication of the courses of the young Heidegger at Freiburg and at Marburg allows us to retrace the path that led to the major work of 1927. An expert with respect to the *Collected Works,* Greisch can thus offer a close reading of *Being and Time* that is enriched by all the new information that allows for a detailed reconstitution of Heidegger's itinerary during the "phenomenological decade" (1919 to 1928). Following the text, paragraph by paragraph, Greisch undertakes to "render the 'ground plan' of *Being and Time* intelligible."[53] In this way, those who make the effort of carefully following the work will see, if not the difficulties, many of the mysteries and strange passages disappear. Greisch's concern is pedagogical (his book was originally a course) and he manages this task by avoiding jargon, by proposing schemas and even—a stimulating innovation—"excerpts" from texts (Heidegger's and others) to support his commentary. Faced with formidable translation difficulties, he proceeded with common sense and without bias, reconsidering the key terms of the original language and explaining them patiently, without hiding his preference for Martineau's[54] translation, but also citing Vezin and sometimes even agreeing with him.[55] Another innovative aspect of this work is the constant reference to the contributions of several generations of admiring readers or critics of Heidegger's major works, from Gilbert Ryle to Emmanuel Levinas and Paul Ricoeur.[56] The reader is holding "a strong hand" (with access to primary as well as secondary sources) such that one can understand how the young Heidegger made the transition from a hermeneutic of facticity to an explicitly ontological undertaking (as early as 1923), so as to arrive at a work that was "incomplete in a twofold sense,"[57] and finally (in 1928) to arrive at a first "self-interpretation" of this "failure." The repetition of the question of being did not emerge fully developed from the brain of Heidegger: the emergence of this question was gradual, but that did not deprive it of its profound interest. Certainly, the work was in some sense demystified, but was in no way diminished in terms of its importance—far from it. It was first approached as what it has become, a great classic, akin to Aristotle's *Metaphysics.*[58] Jean Greisch took a salutary distance from the French quarrels; and one can affirm without exaggerating that Greisch undeniably advanced research in France. At the international level, only the work of Theodore Kisiel[59] can be compared to it, at least from the point of view of detailed textual research, since, philosophically, it is Greisch who seems to be a better resource. But his rupture with a certain French "tradition" is perhaps excessive. It is significant that Jean Beaufret is cited only once and in passing.[60]

Nonetheless, henceforth every student and every reader of good will would have a solid research tool available to them (which is, however, not the only one to be recommended).[61] *Being and Time* is no longer to be considered as an esoteric work—a strange and unapproachable hermetic block, "fallen from an obscure disaster," as was its legend over the course of too many decades for the vast majority of the French public.

A Fragile In-Between: A Memoir of a Sojourn in Greece

At the beginning of 1992, the French translation of an essay written by Heidegger thirty years earlier, while returning from a cruise in Greece, was published with an attractive cover.[62] This short and serene text contrasts with the austerity of the vast majority of the academic works by Heidegger: it is quite readable, thanks to Vezin's translation, which avoids in this case the audacious neologisms found in his version of *Being and Time*.[63] Is the anecdotal relevant to the essential? In part, certainly; but we will see that more than a detour, these sojourns are revelatory.

Why refer to this publication as a fragile in-between? First, insofar as it does not relate directly to the principal corpus, and constitutes a sort of intermediary, it constantly engages the scientific and technological destiny of the contemporary world (multiple allusions would confirm this): it thus operates in an interval that the wide range of the work (between the ontological thematic and its technological forgetting) has not completely addressed. It is also a fragile in-between for Heidegger himself, who was uncomfortably suspended between two images of Greece: on the one hand, the ideal Greece that he sought in vain at Olympus, that he imagined at Delphi, and that he found at Delos; and on the other hand, the all-too-real Greece damaged by unregulated development, invaded and almost overrun by the tourist industry.

It can also be considered an in-between from another perspective: between the "intimate, *familial* character"[64] of these pages (written by Heidegger for his wife Elfride and offered to her on the occasion of her seventieth birthday), preserving the esotericism of a thought following its own path, and the public role that the philosopher agreed to play, more than once (from the engagement of 1933 to the posthumous *Der Spiegel* interview). As marginal as this writing may seem, it represented a sort of pleasant pause for the author, and for the reader, the unexpected occasion to hear something more personal.

Heidegger confessed to having hesitated for some time before deciding to take this trip, which had been planned in advance with his friend Erhart Kästner. The hesitations and the doubts are perceptible in the narrative itself, at Venice, Corfu, Ithaca, and even Olympus. In several cases, for example at Rhodes, but also at Cos and Patmos, Heidegger refused to leave the boat. A difficult traveler? Actually, Heidegger was not a traveler at all! A thinker inhabited by Hölderlinian Greece, as well as by the unforgettable words and visions drawn from Homer,

Pindar, and the tragic poets, he was terribly afraid of being disappointed. Which lover of ancient Greece has not felt this fear during his or her first trip? What is less banal is not that Heidegger waited until he was seventy-three years of age to undergo the experience and to take this "risk," it is rather that he had harbored the hope (the illusion?) within himself of encountering that which is "properly Greek" through a simple visit to the principal sites in the context of a comfortable cruise.[65] There is something touching, and almost pathetic (or irritating?) in his stubbornness to avoid what could be instructive, picturesque, or indeed moving in the life of the Greek people today (in distrusting the Mycenaeans[66] and even—although in careful terms—the strangeness and frivolity of the Minoans in Crete).[67] He avoided as well the human, all-too-human, activities that created the life and the destiny of an ingenious, aggressive, voyaging people, in order to almost exclusively attach himself to a certain ideal of the Hellenic divinity, an ideal that was purified by Hölderlin, and thematized by the works of Walter F. Otto.[68] He finally found his sacred places—even if through tenuous etymological analysis—on the Island of Delos (where the mind was "occupied with thinking the secret of *Aletheia*"[69]) and at Egine, at the temple of Aphaia: "what determined the sojourn of the Greeks in the world and their relationship with everything present showed itself again around the temple: namely *aletheia*, the unconcealed concealment."[70]

Is it too easy to object that Heidegger carried *his* Greece with him, an ideal homeland that shelters *Aletheia*, and in which he could find only in a few fleeting visions? He himself raised the objection: is it only an arbitrary representation or romanticism?[71] Obviously, there was no need to go to these sites to find this "original" Greece—an interpretive assumption that was acquired deep within himself after many years and that remained a *hapax*, which, for the most part, was not shared by classicists. This sojourn only played a role of illustrating belatedly his thoughts on Greece and within—perfectly respectable but quite "personal"—limits. Furthermore, if one reconsiders the thread of the Heideggerian argumentation that determines the theme of the forgetting of being, discerned as early as Parmenides, one is constrained to observe that the Greeks themselves never succeeded in thinking *aletheia*, the key word supposed to rule their existence in terms of "unconcealment"—but instead always understood it in terms of the soundness of the statement.[72] It was thus through the centuries, and not directly with their past lives, that Heidegger claimed to engage again the *essential unthought* of that existence. How could this purely intellectual matter not be even more fragile, in attempting to encounter such places—those inspired days, charged with grandeur and destiny, prior to any explicit philosophy? Is this "properly Greek essence," which the thinker carries within him, and believes he knows better than the Greeks themselves, not sheltered within the Greek language itself rather than in some places or some ruins?

It was a learned sojourn then, since place reveals its "truth" only in the light of unforgettable words and through the perspective of (or in spite of) a philosophy that conveyed almost straightaway the forgetting of that for which it was an original ethos. It was indeed a sojourn that was much more uncanny than the wise watercolors of Elfriede Heidegger, and the occasionally prosaic clarifications of the Master himself, would indicate. It was in the end a personal sojourn, a hesitant sojourn, reassured and enlightened by certain sightings (Delos, Delphi, and the Acropolis—especially its museum).

One would wrongly object that we have forgotten the other pole, that of techno-science. We have not. We just left a serene and reassured thinker. However, is there not in this work, apparent in many passages, a more distressed aspect that was unsettling for him as well as for us? In contrast with a text increasingly influenced by this "inceptual" Greece, one can discern the dark web of uncompromising critiques and hostile reactions against the technological world and the science that engendered it. There are numerous instances of irritations,[73] taken up sarcastically by Jacques Derrida: "Following the footsteps of Heidegger, who, near the very same Greek orthodox temple (Kaisariani monastery) did not fail to indict yet again in his *Aufenthalte,* not only Rome, along with its Church, its law, its state and its theology, but technology, machines, tourism, tourist attractions—and above all photography, the 'operating of cameras and video cameras' which, in organized tours, 'replaces' the authentic experience of the stay or the sojourn."[74]

The many critics of Heidegger were all too happy to conclude that his philosophy was "antimodern" and even driven by a genuine hatred toward science and technology. Was Derrida among them? Certainly not. By advocating and practicing a kind of voyage resolutely opposed to the sage path of Heidegger toward an ultimate Appropriation (it suffices to read *Counterpath* to confirm this), he was able to paradoxically indicate in Heidegger's work "a completely unheard of sense of voyage: neither literal, nor proper, the originary opening of all paths, of all destinations and all destinies."[75] But this unusual path—so elusive in the too prosaic and "ontical" course of the *Sojourns*—can in no way be reduced to a metaphor (too metaphysical): it is through a critical reconsideration of the most essential themes of Heidegger's thought that it is necessary to both follow it and question it.

Thus, an important discussion on the meaning of the destiny of the West as metaphysical sending (*Geschick*) is outlined here. The least that one can say is that *Sojourns,* accessible to a wide audience, is not one of Heidegger's more rigorous texts on the question of the essence of modern technology, in which precisely it is a matter of overcoming the subjective and arbitrary character of "attitudes" or opinions, whether optimistic or pessimistic, pro or contra.[76] Let us not forget that these *Sojourns* were the work of an elderly person and that the author did not really intend the manuscript for publication. It is entirely understandable that his wife wanted to mark the one-hundredth birthday of the Master with this pious publication. The best intentions nevertheless have their limits, and these—which are incontestable, whatever the charm of a few pages—remind us that the greatest works are not always at their optimal level. But it would be equally obtuse to refuse to heed this warning: "Modern technology together with the scientific industrialization of the world is about to obliterate any possibility of a sojourn."[77] A questioning thus emerges: What is a sojourn? What are its conditions? Has our technological civilization eliminated its possibility? These are interrogations that arise because of science and technology.

Does Science Think?

In the course of a half-century of the reception of Heidegger's thought in France, we have seen the evocation of numerous themes, and noted that nearly every intellectual circle was affected in various ways. Nevertheless, a vast domain still has not been affected by these debates: science and epistemology. And there is nothing surprising about this: even if he took a few courses in physics when he was young, and remained current in the developments in contemporary physics to the point of discussing it with Heisenberg,[78] Heidegger never presented himself—and with good reason—as an expert in these matters. Above all, the principal axis of his thought—the question of the truth of being—completely diverges from contemporary scientific research. If the majority of French scientists must have heard of Heidegger, either at the end of their secondary studies or through the press or the media, neither the name nor the work seemed to particularly retain their attention. One exception confirmed the rule: the controversy provoked by one of Heidegger's statements: "Science does not think." Even if the immense majority of the scientific community was hardly troubled (budget cuts, for example, were a matter of greater concern), this provocative phrase provoked a kind of mini-uproar, many misunderstandings, and perhaps an actual debate.

Must we see in Heidegger's formula a scandalous provocation against science, or a useful warning? The question is obviously worth posing, and all the more seriously since science has acquired a dominant position in our civilization. We are going, however, to establish that for the most part Heidegger's statement was cited out of its original context and in ignorance of the meaning that it held for its author. It is thus useful to reconstitute the context clearly and elucidate this understanding, so as to clarify the stakes of the discussion that would follow.

René Thom dates "Heidegger's chilling condemnation" in 1929.[79] This is the date of the famous lecture "What Is Metaphysics?" One will search in vain for the phrase in question,[80] which is in fact to be found at the beginning of the course given in 1951–52, "What Is Called Thinking?" Here is the passage:

> Science does not think. This is a shocking statement. Let the statement be shocking, even though we immediately add the supplementary statement that nonetheless science always and in its own fashion has to do with thinking. That fashion, however, is genuine and consequently fruitful only after the gulf has become visible that lies between thinking and the sciences, lies there un-bridgeably. There is no bridge here-only the leap. Hence there is nothing but mischief in all the makeshift ties and asses' bridges by which men today would set up a comfortable commerce between thinking and the sciences.[81]

Two things are evident from the reading of this passage: first, the use of the shocking formulation was a deliberate strategy; second, Heidegger absolutely did not want to deny that science involves a specific mode of thinking, a denial that would be an absurd falsehood. How then can the "provocation" that claims that "science does not think" be justified? Are we not obliged to recognize the obvious: science exercises a rational activity that implies deliberative consciousness, hypotheses, reasoning, verifications, and so on: all forms of thinking.

Heidegger's position seems even more radical, and paradoxical, if one wants to consider that he affirms, from the beginning of his course, that philosophy itself does not think,[82] and that, in a general sense, we still do not think! What is such a thinking that is so lofty that it seems almost inaccessible and eludes our mental skills and our ingenuity? Without any doubt, it is a meditation on what is essential. But what is that? It is a thinking of what metaphysics and science have not thought: their "unthought." It is in no way a question of rejecting the knowledge and representations that have permitted the attainment of a high level of knowledge and culture, but is a question of recognizing their limit and their scope in regard to the truth and the destiny of being. To think in this sense is not only to know, but to appraise, to reflect, or to gather through memory. The consonance of *Gedachtes* ["what is thought"], of *Gedächtnis* ["memory"] and of *Dank* ["gratefulness," "thanks"] ensures the singularity and the dignity of "thought" in the sense that Heidegger understood it henceforth, by differentiating it from metaphysical activity itself.

Whether one follows Heidegger or not in this elaboration—a careful exaltation of a meditation on the truth of being—it becomes clear that the "shock formulation" supposes, in order to be understood, the understanding of the specific meaning that Heidegger gave to *Denken*. We can identify here an explicitly circular path that is stated at the beginning of the course: "We come to know what it means to think when we ourselves try to think."[83]

What is thereby clarified is Heidegger's notion that a "leap" is necessary in order to enter into the circle, as well as the refusal of all the "beaten paths," that is to say, passages that are too rapid, too direct, and too rhetorical or opportunist, between the sciences and philosophical discourse.

Without wishing to minimize the new meaning given to *Denken*, let us note that neither the theme of the "leap" nor that of the radical difference between science and a philosophy worthy of the name is original. For Hegel, it was indeed necessary to leap from the representative sphere to that of speculative thought; and philosophy is different from specific sciences in that it is not directly concerned with an object delimited by a region of reality, but concerns itself with the Whole and its truth.[84] Kant already emphasized at the beginning of the *Prolegomena* that philosophy is distinguished from other sciences by its difficulty in establishing its constitutive limits, in an indisputable manner. The positive reverse of this aporia involves the reconsideration of its own presuppositions, a critique of the conditions of possibility that the sciences cannot undertake with such radicality.

These clarifications help us understand that Heidegger's provocative statement not only has its own coherence but can be read in such a way that it becomes reinscribed in a long philosophic tradition (going as far back as Plato to the extent that all the particular sciences must be understood and oriented in terms of the "anhypothetical" *epistēmē* of the Good). Certainly, one can judge the "superior" tone adopted by Heidegger to be excessively peremptory. But is it necessary to neglect the questions raised by (on the occasion of) his "provocation": Does science reflect upon its foundations? Does it reflect upon its effects?

These questions preoccupied René Thom. Far from opposing Heidegger, he cited him in the interest of helping or supporting his own attempt at a speculative renewal of the contemporary scientific project. Undertaking an inventory of the scientific and technological progress realized since 1950 (taking account of the fact that since that date humanity has devoted more of its resources to science than it did during the entirety of history), he noticed a diminution of technological inventiveness (that he referred to as a *bricolage*), and he diagnosed above all an "epistemological impasse."[85] For Thom, contemporary science describes rather than explains; its epistemological deficiency is due to its obsession with immediately useful results, in defiance of any theoretical knowledge. "Science must learn to think again."[86] A renewal of "natural philosophy"[87] is necessary to reverse the decline toward a catastrophic drift that is both technical and obscurantist.

There certainly remains a gap between Thom's conception of thought and that of Heidegger. The former, faithful to the enlightened tradition of the Renaissance, remained attentive to science, found its inspiration from it while orienting it at the same time, granting theory its entire interpretive dignity; we have seen the latter appeal to a "leap" that renders it more independent, but also more secret. Even if the comparison cannot prevent a misunderstanding, it was made possible by a common critique of the domination of technical efficiency. In fact, when Thom refers to "What Is Metaphysics," it is not entirely inadvertent: his own point of view agrees with the project of a regrounding of the positive sciences in a philosophy that would be revitalized. One surmises that he was ready to subscribe to Heidegger's position in 1929 ("the rootedness of the sciences in their essential ground has atrophied"[88]) and even perhaps to the call for a fundamental philosophical renewal: "Only if science exists on the basis of metaphysics can it fulfill in ever-renewed ways its essential task, which is not to amass and classify bits of knowledge, but to disclose in ever renewed fashion, through a revelation that is constantly renewed, the entire expanse of the truth of nature and history."[89] Nonetheless, in *Paraboles and Catastrophes,* after having cited Heidegger's formulation with praise, Thom also imputes the failure of "natural philosophy"[90] to the excessive claims of certain philosophers (Hegel above all), by clarifying that he would not want to be transformed into a "crypto-Heideggerian"![91] It is, according to him, the task of mathematics to provide the models of a morphological theory worthy of the name.

In this debate on contemporary science and its future, the antithesis of Thom's position was represented by epistemologists or scientists who were completely indifferent to the very thought of Heidegger, and who found in their rejection of the formulation, "Science does not think," an occasion to rail against what they perceived as an irrational antiscientism. Thus Dominique Lecourt,[92] followed on this point by Jacques Bouveresse,[93] maintained that Heidegger was the victim of a strictly neo-positivist conception of science: the science that "does not think" is that of Carnap and the Vienna Circle (at least its "inner circle," because some—like Schlick—assigned a fundamental role to philosophy).[94] Thinking he was criticizing science, Heidegger in fact was taking issue with its stylized or even caricatured image, which had been bypassed, for the most part, by contemporary science.

Jean-Michel Salanski also shared this critical perspective, although he intended to add to his refutation an account of Heidegger's hermeneutic contribution. In an article simply titled "Die Wissenschaft denkt nicht" (Science does not think),[95] he studied Heidegger's provocative phrase on several levels: in the context of fundamental ontology, it means that the scientific project is always regional with respect to the fundamental concern of philosophy; in order to understand the essence of thought, it is necessary to go to a more essential level, that of the hermeneutic envisaged according to the "circular" conception that Heidegger presented first in paragraph 63 of *Being and Time* and then rethought and deepened in many reconsiderations in his later work. This hermeneutic model of "thinking as elucidation-that-assumes-the-circle"[96] is not decisive for philosophy alone; it also offers resources to account for the aporias and interrogations that twentieth-century science, contrary to what Heidegger claimed, had elaborated. The point of contention occurred when Salanski turned the Heideggerian hermeneutic against its exclusion of science. For Salanski, it was possible and even desirable to develop a "formal hermeneutic" exploiting the most speculative reflections of logic, contemporary mathematics, and physics. This research perspective, developed elsewhere,[97] aimed to oppose a more open and deliberately "technological" hermeneutics to Heidegger's own "literal" hermeneutics (which was still too attached to a theological model).[98]

The debate did not always have this theoretical dimension. The irritation of a certain Claude Allègre during a radio interview with Alain Finkielkraut testifies to this.[99] When Finkielkraut cited various critiques of science formulated by Jünger, Heidegger, and Henry, his interlocutor did not respond regarding the contents, but only addressed one of the authors cited: "Let us not speak of Heidegger, who never understood anything related to science, or anything else for that matter. Personally I find it difficult to understand Heidegger's popularity in the philosophical world, including his positions with respect to the Jews, which is lamentable."[100] Do we expect a great scientist to be able to speak about what he does not know? One would expect that Allègre had read more than one line of Heidegger in order for him to claim that Heidegger knew nothing about anything. There were no arguments given, even concerning Heidegger's (non)comprehension of science.[101] What followed from Allègre deserves to be cited, but does not merit a commentary: "I think a man is a unity. I do not want to believe that a man who missed the point on such a serious problem can think in a proper manner on other subjects. This is my point of view on Heidegger. I have no interest in debating it."[102] After this refusal to enter into discussion, "the correct thinking" having determined *scientific correctness* [TN: In English in the original], there is indeed nothing more to say, if not perhaps: "Does *this* 'scientist' think?"

It would be too easy to remain on that point. While it was necessary to show this sort of rejection, quite simply because it exists and represents a temptation for a respectable number of scientists irritated by any philosophical questioning (an attitude that did provoke some strictly adverse reactions[103]), it is more instructive to be attentive to the efforts made by other scientists to heed Heidegger's warning, if only to disagree with him: science thinks and can even think better, but it must demonstrate it! Without strictly accepting René Thom's approach, and without agreeing to enter into the play of Heidegger's thought, this conception recognized that there is something true in the statement concerning the deficient nature of critical and philosophical reflection within contemporary scientific activity. Thus Prigogine and Stengers, while making allusion to "Heidegger's more than dangerous theses"[104] (to the extent that they directly linked the very project of rationality to the will to power), intended to demonstrate that the metamorphosis of contemporary science illustrates the contrary: the potential for a renewed listening to nature; and they give a particularly significant example of this in the recognition by contemporary physics of the plurality of times.[105] For his part, Jean-Marc Lévy-Leblond repeated the question in an apparently less ambitious, but perhaps methodologically more efficacious, way, on the basis of an explicit reference to Heidegger's formulation, in "chapter zero" of his book *Aux Contraires:* having established the "properly machine-like intellectual functioning" of science, he added, "For it is true, in a certain sense, that 'science does not think'—this is even the secret of its efficiency. Science makes a considerable effort *not to think* by perfecting remarkable symbolic and formal machines that take charge of the difficulty and fatigue of thought, just as our domestic and industrial machines support and extend our limited physical capacities."[106] This partial concession is, however, counterbalanced by a challenge quite different from Heidegger's: to restore science "to culture"; to reintroduce critical reflexivity in order to counter the hyper-specialization of disciplines and the hierarchy of functions. In this way, thanks to work on the great antinomies, a "plea for thinking *in* science"[107] takes form, seeking to illustrate the fact that the practice of science—far from excluding the exercise of thought—summons it and makes it possible.[108]

What then does it mean to think? It is not a meditation on the destinal scope of science itself, as is the case in Heidegger's work, but a reflexive and critical exploitation of the great aporias of contemporary science. One then returns to a more classical sense of the exercise of thought, thanks to the detour produced by the shock of the Heideggerian "provocation."

We are going to see that the shock must still be analyzed more fully because it involves more than questioning the constitutive limits of science: it clarifies its intimate connections with technology. If science "does not think," is it because it is entirely caught up in its technological destiny? This aspect of Heidegger's questioning has profoundly troubled contemporary French thought.

Open Season on Technology?

Heidegger, a critic of technology? This is an understatement if one considers the numerous clichés already encountered throughout this work. For most of the interpreters, it was contempt and hatred that seemed to drive him in the face of the multifaceted deployment of our technological world.

In order to reconsider the animated debate calmly and clearly, we should not forget what was just said about science. Certainly, the expression "techno-science" was not Heidegger's; it is not even found flowing from the pen of his translators. Its recent prominence[109] is justified, however, provided that the conditions of its coinage are clearly specified. The term is not understood here principally in the strict and technological sense that it might have, especially since the 1950s: information technology, for example, illustrates the extraordinary expansion of a field of interaction between programming theories and the progress of electronic equipment. In a Heideggerian context, the expression "techno-science" has a connotative range that is much more general and radical:[110] it designates not only the interdependence of science and technology, but also the fact that the scope of modern science is technological in the essential and destinal sense that Heidegger gives the word *Technik*. "The essence of technology is by no means anything technological":[111] this statement is to be understood not as a reference to "essence" in the classical sense but as a grasp of the new ontological relation that, since the beginning of the modern era, led to the mastery and domination of nature. Modern science is no longer pure knowledge; it is intimately conditioned and oriented by its technological objectives. In fact, it is pointless to refer science and technology to each other as long as one has not understood that they are both the result of a profoundly metaphysical destiny by which the relation to the real is determined on an entirely new basis.

This clarification will allow us to approach the most serious philosophical critiques formulated in opposition to Heidegger's thesis. For about a decade, we saw the emergence of a genuine "resistance," best represented, from our perspective, by Jean-Pierre Séris's book on technology.[112] A frontal ideological assault limiting itself to some clichés was no longer sufficient: one noticed that Heidegger's thesis had a philosophical coherence that had to be recognized. It was robust and even—at least in appearance—accorded "technology an unprecedented dignity in the history of thought."[113]

How did Séris formulate and articulate his critiques against the Heideggerian interpretation of technology? First, we can note that he made a real effort to characterize this interpretation while respecting its literality: he devoted a whole chapter to it,[114] including—even if reluctantly[115]—numerous citations, and not without scrupulous attention to the original German (in particular, obviously, in the case of *Gestell*). Séris did not stop there: he pursued his analysis by showing the interconnection of two themes in Heidegger's work: instrumentality and discontinuity. To instrumentalist anthropology, Heidegger answered that technology is a "concept of knowledge" and that it manifests itself as an unlimited and irresistible command. The discontinuity is that of the fundamental change of attitude toward nature, a major discontinuity that is nevertheless accompanied by a "genuine continuity" (technology as unconcealment).[116] After all is said and done, the originality of Heidegger's interpretation resides above all in the idea that contemporary technology represents "the ultimate confirmation of the closure of metaphysics";[117] this means that such originality resides in the direct link established between the essence of technology and the will to power (accomplished in the will of the will). Heidegger is therefore neither an avowed enemy of technology nor a "postmodernist." His position was very speculative, and his hopes revolved around a new (essentially poetic) relation with language.

Séris's critiques were not as developed or even as vehement as one would expect. They can be clearly grouped around two points: in the first place, the Heideggerian conception is not as original as one would claim (the rupture of modern technology in relation to *technē* and to the "arts" is generally recognized;

the affirmation of the autonomy of the development of the present technological stage has become commonplace, and remains to be discussed; finally, the character of a "theoretical mutation" of the beginnings of classical science is a correct idea, but not at all revolutionary); in the second place—and this is the properly critical part—the criticism addressed to Heidegger concerns his indifference "to the life (or the death) of human beings," as well as to work and to workers, to material life, to production, to the market, and so on. It is the "indifference of the privileged," forgetting the social place from which they speak.[118]

If one attempts to give an account of Séris's work, one sees that his verdict, however cautious it is in the end, tries not to misrecognize the philosophical dignity of Heidegger's thought and even its pertinence on certain points (the least original!). If its correctness is ultimately contested, it is not because of the usual flaws that are attributed to it (antitechnology, antirationalism[119]): it is because of its abstract character in relation to human, historical, and social complexities. For Séris, Heidegger's interpretation of technology is almost too coherent: it is in particular too schematic, preferring to eschew actual responsibility in favor of the pathos of poetic language and the destiny of metaphysics, to the detriment of a lucid vision of the social realities in which technologies are found. In sum, this is not to detract from Séris—who died too young and whose legacy is infinitely respectable—but to recognize that he did not manage to conceal his aversion to the Heideggerian project, to its alleged incantatory style, to its distance from reality, from being, and from language. One must here take into consideration a nuance that pertains to both philosophical "sensibility" (which in his work is closer to Marx and Comte) and pure argumentation; nonetheless, Séris has made a great effort to observe the rules of *fair play* [TN: In English in the original].

It is somewhat surprising to note that Jacques Bouveresse, although taking the opportunity to pay homage to Séris, appeared much less scrupulous. His text is entitled "Les Philosophes et la technique" [Philosophers and technology],[120] and Heidegger figures there only indirectly, following some generalities concerning the technophobia of philosophers. Many of them will have found in Heidegger's work the expression of their "discontent" or "refusal" of technological civilization. Thereafter, we are told about the need to address Heidegger's "case" through a long citation by Jeanne Hersch in which, claiming to make a determination about the heart of his philosophy, she sees not the expression of wonder in the face of being but a *contempt* of almost everything that constitutes the common life of human beings: rules, institutions, democracy, rationality, and so on. Bouveresse's verdict immediately follows, and without any other argumentation than Hersch's authority (which in fact extends beyond the "subject" of technology): "What is expressed in Heidegger's reflections on technology is not, from my point of view, a more profound understanding of its nature, but in effect, the lofty contempt of which Jeanne Hersch speaks."[121]

The entire Heideggerian interpretation of technology is reduced, then, to a sentiment (or rather a *ressentiment*), which, it must be said, is not the most helpful approach. We have seen that Séris was reluctant to reduce the essence of Heideggerian thinking to such a technophobia. To this reduction, Bouveresse adds an erroneous reading of Séris: "According to him, there is no philosophy of technology in *Being and Time*. And neither is there anything, in Heidegger's diagnosis and judgments, which can be considered genuinely original." It is this last sentence that misinterprets Séris's thinking (with respect to *Being and Time*, his position,[122] which is quite acceptable, is not entirely negative: Heidegger approached technology as a "question" only well after that book). Séris in no way denied Heidegger *any originality*,[123] but on the contrary situated that originality (which is often missed) in his interpretation of the accomplishment of metaphysics (and in close connection with Heidegger's reading of Nietzsche). We have noted, furthermore, that Séris's argument against the originality of certain Heideggerian theses does not exclude giving them some credit (at least regarding the nature, already noted, of the "theoretical mutation" of the beginnings of classical science).

Following an excursus on Spengler (whom he does not confuse with Heidegger and whom he associates appropriately with a Nietzschean biologism), Bouveresse pursues his severe examination of the Heidegger "case." We can see once again that he does not share, in this respect, Séris's methodological scruples. Since what is at issue is the Heidegger "case," how could the question of his "Nazism" not be addressed? Bouveresse proceeds in a way that is quite polemical and moralizing (it is a question of "moral failing"[124]). It was as if for Heidegger Nazism had been the "solution" to the "problem" of technology; finally, Heidegger was attacked for the henceforth famous sentence from 1949,[125] his only allusion—albeit problematic—to the gas chambers. "Despicable and absurd": Bouveresse's guillotine is without mercy.

What is somewhat strange in this intervention is not that Heidegger is criticized (one hardly expected Bouveresse to defend him); it is the way in which the text, an homage to Séris with a very general title, turns finally to a sort of settling of accounts with a philosopher whom Bouveresse has otherwise (nearly[126]) ignored in the rest of his work. It is as if the presence maintained by this obvious absence became too embarrassing! Furthermore, the methodology—in spite of some efforts not to be overly unfair[127]—was rather expeditious: Heidegger's thinking with respect to science was judged on the basis of the only televised interview he ever gave,[128] while no reference was made to the more significant texts (*The Question Concerning Technology, Science and Meditation* and "What Is a Thing?" among others). Admitting that he did not succeed in understanding how a "rational man" could seek the mastery of the phenomenon of technology in Nazism,[129] Bouveresse gestured toward good old common sense, but he himself had not read nearly enough of either Heidegger or Séris, who had discerned that Heidegger no longer sought the "mastery" of the technological phenomenon (which he never reduced, moreover, to a "problem"), and that the most original feature (perhaps the most "incongruous"[130]) of Heidegger's interpretation of technology was its connection to the metaphysics of the will to power.

The irritation that we just perceived in Bouveresse's work was not shared by all the ideological adversaries of Heidegger's conception of technology. If some discomfort can be perceived in the work of Dominique Lecourt in the face of the tough "resistance" of that thought, the tone is more serene: it is a question of being a fair and of analyzing the situation. Recognizing that Heidegger was "the only philosopher who had taken on . . . in a radical manner" the task of the elaboration of a general philosophy of technoscientific rationality,[131] Lecourt concedes that everything in Heidegger's work does not lead to an apocalyptic technophobia (although the pathos of "salvation" leads there eventually):[132] the methodical critique of the ordinary, anthropological, and instrumental conception of technology prepared for the meditation on the metaphysical "essence" of a radical transformation itself initiated by the mathematized theory of nature at the inception of modernity.

Whereas we expected a refutation, Lecourt proceeded rather to some pessimistic comments: the dignity accorded to technology by Heidegger is more apparent than real; for his disciples, it only offers a "pretext";[133] above all, its influence is explained by its synthetic character. Even while opposing it, Heidegger appropriates a positivist conception of science, a technical concept of technology that we all share for the most part.[134] Heidegger's prowess would be that of passing off as profound a clever recasting of the commonplace clichés, or at least deeply rooted prejudices. This is an idea that we see shared, with some variations, by the "technophile" adversaries of Heidegger's thought.[135] What is interesting in Lecourt's work is the recognition that the (ideological) "enemy" is found within us: is it not within the logic of a discourse that intends to vanquish, precisely in each of us, a very powerful feeling: fear in the face of techno-scientific progress?

This project was already that of Gilbert Hottois, who vigorously criticized "philosophical technophobia," and called for a new nonanthropological humanism, reconciled with technological expansion and its polymorphic resources. It is striking to note that Heidegger was already both questioned and relied upon in this enterprise. Accused of being one of the principal promoters of this technophobia, Heidegger was nevertheless credited with having recognized "the real scope of technology."[136] There is an ambivalence that one finds in the thinking of our author with respect to the sign and to technology: one wonders if, even while reproaching Heidegger for remaining excessively "logocentric," Hottois has not borrowed his general conception of "techno-science" as a system of operations that are essentially asymbolic from Heidegger. Even if he sought to distance himself from them, Hottois remained in the debt of the Heideggerian "provocations."[137]

Overall, in the course of our reading of the contemporary French works about Heidegger's contribution to the philosophy of technology, we have seen similar ambiguities, albeit in different forms and with different degrees of attraction or repulsion. As a whole, Heidegger is generally criticized by specialists, who are nonetheless constrained to take account—whether they like it or not—of his interpretation of contemporary technology, an interpretation that incontestably stimulated reflection.

The Exception That Proves the Rule?

The last decade of the twentieth century is characterized, for French philosophy, by a variety if not dispersion of approaches and even a certain eclecticism. Since no particular school of thought imposed itself, nor any great figure, the time belonged to encyclopedias, collective work, and conferences. An important work of translation was finally the order of the day, which does not mean that the attempts to import Anglo-American philosophy were always successful. This climate of more or less feverish work and activity corresponded well to the increasing insertion of France into Europe and into the context of the globalization of the economic and information network. Far from conflicting with each other, the demands of scholarship and those of techno-science blended well and complemented each other, as is the case in the United States. In a free-market society dominated by economism and technism, there is room for all specialties (even the most orthodox Heideggerians publish an international journal titled *Heidegger Studies*,[138] in the usual format). Why, among so many incitements offered to our developed civilizations, would Heidegger's thought eternally play the role of a troublemaker? And in the academic and encyclopedic form of the *Collected Works*, did that thought not become integrated within a system of knowledge more so than Nietzsche's disconcerting and subversive illuminations?

A desire that is quite legitimate came to light: that of establishing a serene, balanced, and documented record of the seismic shocks provoked by Heideggerian thought. Such was indeed the concern of Jean-François Courtine in an important volume published in 1990,[139] which was organized in three parts: the ontological tradition, the Husserlian institution, and perspectives on the renewal of phenomenology. From these detailed clarifications intended essentially for specialists, there are a few pages that should be discussed, some because of their phenomenological interest, and others because of their critical rigor. The first pages bear on practical themes (the hand,[140] the friend,[141] the founding of presence in equipmentality, and the fragility of the openness to the other in an existential analytic in which the Existent is above all a self). Courtine granted great significance to the work of Franco Volpi, who had shown the extent to which

Heidegger's conception of praxis, in *Being and Time*, was based on Aristotle,[142] but with nuances that need to be interpreted (in particular the emphasis on the "poietic" in relation to the practical dimension proper). But what is surprising in this detailed and careful work is the emergence of quite severe judgments: in spite of all denials, there is indeed a Platonism in Heidegger (which includes the division between the theoretical and the practical, as well as the contempt for doxa);[143] the "ontological solipsism" forbade him access to a genuine deployment of the intersubjectivity of dialogical space;[144] the rejection of "trivial" conceptions of the dialogue sublimates it (in connection with a very personal reading of Hölderlin), at the expense of its co-belonging with ethics, politics, and religion;[145] and finally, the axe falls on the last page of the book: the orientation of the later Heidegger toward a *tautological* phenomenology involves "a disastrous or catastrophic character for the very *possibility* of phenomenology."[146] Avoiding hostility and systematic thinking, as well as biases, such a critical distance was new in the work of an interpreter closely linked to the "Heidegger school." It puts him in proximity in several instances to the talented pioneers such as Jacques Derrida[147] or Jacques Taminiaux.[148]

Although, on the whole, the 1990s saw the French situation stabilize and "normalize," some residual polemics remained. Furthermore, the approach of the end of the century almost required taking account of Heidegger's influence: was Heidegger really the last thinker, and in a sense even more radical than the retrospective baptism of Sartre as the "last philosopher"?[149] Or did he prefigure the continuing resistance of "meditative thought" to the assaults of "calculative thinking"?[150]

In the category of significant polemical "flare-ups," we must mention the essays by Jean-Pierre Faye, Henri Meschonnic, and Dionys Mascolo.

While the monumental enterprise of *Langages Totalitaires* devoted itself to reconstituting the cultural milieu and the semantic variations of the entire epoch of German totalitarianism, *La raison narrative*, which is supposed to constitute the relatively abbreviated[151] second volume, accords a central importance to the collusion between Heidegger's thought and Nazism. This is not to say that Heidegger was the sole topic of the book: weaving, in his ten sections, the complex fabric of the philosophical narration with the social narration through different works and epochs, from the Hebraic Haggadah to Nietzsche, from Averroes to Spinoza, Faye analyzes the operation of all these "narrative machines" in their transformations, organization, and ruptures. This approach to reading is applied to Heidegger's thought in order to demystify it in two major respects: the "shock" of the texts pledging allegiance to Hitler in 1933 and in particular the monumental enterprise of "dissimulation" in the Nietzsche courses. It is necessary to return anew to this deciphering (whose clever nature has already been noted) in order to judge its value and discuss its pertinence. Its value cannot be denied: it consists in shedding new light—brought from the consideration of the historical context—on the Heidegger courses devoted to Nietzsche beginning in 1936: Heidegger, accused by the Rector Krieck of "metaphysical nihilism,"[152] invented a clever defense involving the identification of nihilism with metaphysics from its very origins, and including Nietzsche's thought therein, through his categories of the will to power and the eternal return. It is certain that attacks by Krieck—a powerful person in the regime—were extremely dangerous, and one cannot be indifferent to the fact that Heidegger wanted to clear himself of the charge of nihilism on the very terrain of a philosophy considered by National Socialism as almost official. Should we, however, reduce the scope of Heidegger's interpretation of Nietzsche to this clever maneuver? Do we not risk missing what is important by wishing to prove too much? If the identification of metaphysics with nihilism was thus made by Heidegger without sufficient precaution,[153] did it not depend, in spite of everything, on Nietzsche's questioning of Platonism and (as early as *The Birth of Tragedy*) of the Socratic model of "theoretical man"? Above all, Heidegger gave this thesis a new philosophical dimension that involved an entire reinterpretation of that metaphysics (Nietzsche's "five fundamental expressions" were articulated with the onto-theological structure in a tension between essence and existence). Even if the countermaneuver to Rector Krieck played a role, how could the extraordinary interpretive scope of the "turning" be explained? Even if it was only the opportunistic misrepresentation of an absurdity, Heidegger truly exhibited—giving it such a thematic coherence—the skills of a "professional" (to speak like Bourdieu) usually attributed to a magician. But with or without Krieck, does the question raised with respect to the destiny of metaphysics merit examination as such? Did it not nourish, precisely with respect to Nietzsche, a passionate debate in which Faye himself participated[154] in order to refute the entirety of the Heideggerian project? Even admitting that Faye was right with respect to the trigger mechanism (and the "response") provoked by Krieck's attacks (and if he was completely right, that would be something of a historical irony!), one can add: from small causes, big effects. Now, while debatable, those played a role in the interpretation of Nietzsche. Faye went on the attack again in 1994 in *Le piège*,[155] where he reexamined the entirety of the "Heidegger dossier," seen from the perspective of the tensions *internal to* National Socialism. The tract is fortunately supported by many documents. If it gives the impression of needless repetition (and of a sort of merciless hounding of Heidegger, and of any "deconstructionist" school), he separated a part of the work that he appreciated—the writings on the poets (Hölderlin, Rilke, Trakl) and *What Is a Thing*?—from "the infernal sequence."[156]

For his part, Meschonnic, a linguist and rhetorician, intended in principle to limit himself to the critical examination of Heidegger's treatment of language, particularly in the texts devoted to the poets: Hölderlin, Rilke, Trakl, and others. He claimed from the outset that his book "circumvents the game of being for or against Heidegger."[157] In fact, the rest of the book doubly contradicts these stated intentions: he is not only quite polemical but does not hesitate to extend his strong criticism to all of Heidegger's themes and even to the Heideggerians of all ilk (Blanchot, Derrida, Lacan, Levinas, and even the "postmoderns"). At the center of his war machine, Meschonnic situates this reproach: "Heidegger essentializes everything."[158] It is logical that this classical philosophical flaw is imputed to Heidegger's "Parmenidian tendencies." That which is most surprising is that after being charged as "indefinitely repeating Parmenides,"[159] the Master of Freiburg is at the same time accused of merely using clichés and of being unoriginal. Does Heidegger's historicism mask an essentialist abstraction? One might be more easily disposed to admit it on the basis of a precise reading of the Heideggerian corpus on history, historicity, historicality (or on the interpretation of a poem by Hölderlin, as Jean-Pierre Lefebvre, who was a pioneer in this regard, attempted[160]). In spite of numerous citations, Meschonnic seemed above all dedicated to denouncing the mirages produced by the "Heidegger effect" in contemporary thought. In passing, however, he posed some important questions: did Heidegger not overestimate language as such, but also, certainly, the German language in its very Germanness? Did he not sacrifice the syntactical to the exhibitive? Was his lack of interest in scientific linguistics not more of a hindrance than a help?

Dionys Mascolo is an author[161] who has been known for some time in other circles (above all critical Marxism) and whose interest in Heidegger was not known. It is true that this interest is entirely negative. By taking Heidegger as a "model," Mascolo did not hide his intentions or conceal his irony with an excess of rhetorical precautions. Why did Heidegger become such a loathed character? It was less a matter of having been a Nazi (some years later, Mascolo declared his dissatisfaction and his helplessness in the face of the passionate outbursts provoked by the publication of Farias's book) than a matter of the archetypical role played by the thinker in the philosophical field. Exposing Heidegger as "the incarnation of the philosophical soul,"[162] Mascolo reproached him for both his schematizing abstraction, his scholastic character,[163] his simple-mindedness [*niaiserie*],[164] and his vain wordplays,[165] and he chronicled a list of "Heidegger's foolish remarks."[166] The exercise could have been quite humorous, if it had been carried out with all the necessary precision and above all with intelligence. Unfortunately, Mascolo only listed his pet peeves in a dramatic form that detracts from their relevance.[167] Citing a confidence of Queneau to Michel Leiris ("There is no love in Heidegger's work"),[168] Mascolo added that laughter, play, sex (and women!) are equally absent in Heidegger's work, and he prefers the great boulevard of the poet vagabond of cinema (Charlie Chaplin) to Heidegger's path.[169] This is a respectable and even understandable preference, but it does not justify such a careless reading of rigorous (perhaps too "serious"!) texts where perhaps a greater sense of the play than Mascolo would believe is revealed. Most importantly, why confuse Heidegger with "the philosophical soul"? It was by wishing to encompass too much that he missed the Heideggerian "model," and misrecognized, in the end, the astonishing diversity of philosophies of the twentieth century.

On this point, on the contrary, Jeffrey Barash presented a careful account of the Heideggerian "exception" resituated in its century.[170] Barash, an American scholar who has chosen to live and teach in France, had accomplished something that is quite rare: to be accepted by the French university (he teaches at the University of Amiens). The author of an excellent thesis from the École des Hautes Études, published in English with a preface by Paul Ricoeur,[171] Barash is certainly not the only one to have written on the question of historicity in Heidegger's work. An additional drawback is that his book is a collection of articles, which seems to detract from its unity and novelty. Finally, the style is clear, but sober and discreet: there is nothing that would dazzle or scandalize the Parisian intelligentsia. This book nevertheless merits our full attention, because it is able to adopt, without being aggressive, but rather on the basis of reliable documents, an approach that clarifies the point from which one should understand Heidegger in the light of the debate with his contemporaries, in particular with post-Hegelians. Those authors (notably, Dilthey, Windelband, and Simmel), having been struck by the intellectual crisis that only worsened following the shock provoked by the war of 1914, placed historicity at the center.

By carrying out this work of "recontextualization," Barash avoided two separate pitfalls: either reducing Heidegger's thought to a Nazi ideology or considering Heidegger as an isolated great thinker, in exclusive dialogue with the giants of the history of Western philosophy. It is necessary to question the status of history and historicity in Heidegger's thought precisely because Heidegger was the one who admitted (in particular in 1936 to Karl Löwith) that his vision of historicity was the basis of his political engagement.[172] That confession in no way means that the one can be reduced to the other, but means that—if there is a link—it must be delimited and questioned. At the center of the critical studies that follow Heidegger's evolution in his difficult dialogue with Jaspers, or in his reading of Dilthey and Augustine, in his confrontation with Arendt, a principal objection takes form and meaning: if it is true that the movement of history is interpreted with an impressive unity that allows the march toward scientific mastery of phenomena to be better understood, the reverse of this interpretation entails the fragility that results from his refusal of the universal criteria of validation and of its distance with respect to the ethico-political dimension. Barash traced Heidegger's weakness to his contempt for historiography and the fact that he ignored the emergence, since antiquity, of a concern for impartiality in the work of Tacitus (but already in Thucydides). He found failure in the difficulty or incapacity to take account of the "contextual" plenitude of the historical situations as regards "a common world shared with others."[173] He even wondered whether the existential and ontological singularity, which distinguished Heideggerian historicity, did not doom the project of this thought, by cutting it (or isolating it) from the network of its determined symbolic significations, which constitute historical and social communities. The most convincing essay concerns Heidegger's ambiguous interpretation of WWII:[174] certainly that war "determined" nothing with respect to the destiny of being and only accelerated the general course of techno-scientific power; but the radical relation of this war to the most profound movement of nihilism effaces the identification of determined causes and responsibilities. This interpretation allows Heidegger to maintain unacceptable positions (a certain denial of German responsibilities, and an acerbic criticism of the "ahistorical" nature of the United States).

∗ ∗ ∗

In the light of Barash's critical reflection, Heidegger's thinking no longer appears as an absolute exception in the twentieth century, but rather as the revelation, both exemplary and symptomatic, of the difficulty of rethinking the tragic history of the century. Barash does not condemn; rather he tries to understand (and helps us in the process).[175] Recognizing the extraordinary provocation of Heidegger's thought, he intended to counter it with a critical vigilance explicitly inspired by Arendt and Ricoeur. He then testified—against the grandmaster style of Heidegger himself—that it is possible to patiently advance the critical elaboration of the very foundations of the political question, without neglecting the hermeneutic exigencies of a reappropriation of the values of the Western tradition. This critical elaboration also seemed to signify that the epoch of the ideological quarrels of the "grand" Parisian intellectuals was past or outdated. At a time when the techno-scientific competition intensified, there is a place for an erudite approach that could allow the French intellectual community to benefit from universal values that it must find again by virtue of its very vocation. While losing its fascinating singularity, "Heidegger in France" finds, within its limits, a more modest stature, but one that is capable of encouraging new research.[176]

Epilogue VII

The relatively calm and studious climate of the last decade no doubt prefigured a division of labor that needed to take place in France and elsewhere: on the one hand, a patient reading of the texts, freed from the weight of ideology, above all concerned to reveal the interaction of presuppositions and to analyze the methodological stakes; on the other hand, a recentering of the interpretations around the question bearing on the meaning of techno-science.

It was indeed in this spirit that the recasting of my own research unfolded. My reading of the texts was first focused on Being and Time. *Give honor where honor is due: since the masterwork of 1927 remained at the center of Heidegger's self-interpretation, it was important to submit the work to a richer and more detailed exegesis. Moreover, the "competition" between the two complete translations could only encourage the indispensable and constant confrontation with the German text. It was in this spirit that Jean-Paul Larthomas and I decided to organize a seminar on* Being and Time. *We wanted to invite Martineau and Vezin successively or conjointly, according to their respective wishes. This idea was obviously utopian. I recalled earlier the correspondence exchanged with François Vezin, who did not seem to rule out, and even appeared to want, a debate concerning his translation. I can only limit myself here to mentioning and regretting his silence since that time.*

The seminar on Being and Time *took place, nonetheless, from November 1987 to May 1988, with the participation of distinguished scholars. The calm atmosphere that prevailed was somewhat surprising since Farias's book appeared in October 1987. But Nice is not Paris. There were no microphones or cameras to record public comments. Above all, we decided to undertake a very basic work that took the form of interventions focused on the difficulties of method (the question of being, subjectivity, the status of discourse, everydayness, the problem of history, etc.). Jean-Pierre Cometti was kind enough to help me publish these contributions with* Éditions Sud, *in Marseille.*

I prepared for this seminar by undertaking a complete rereading of the original text of Sein und Zeit *at Tübingen during the previous summer. Forgive the frankness of the confession that will follow, which is in no way intended as an argument from authority or as exegetical necessity. It is only a question of reporting here, quite superficially, some impressions of the reading, reconstituted from memory, a memory that is at times faulty. To recall the challenging nature of the project will surprise no one. But what surprised me (and of this I am certain) was my lack of enthusiasm, my occasional irritation, my disagreements, noted in the margins of my own copy. The heaviness of the style, the repetitions, and in the end, the terribly academic tone struck me more than ever before: was it due to the fact that I had to take in the work all at once, instead of contenting myself with small doses and successive readings? I was above all troubled by the excessive schematization of everydayness and of "the they," and their opposition to a haughty and solitary authenticity. I experienced scant sympathy for the quasi-Jansenist tonality of guilt* [Schuld], *of the fall* [Verfallen], *and the return of "conscience"* [Gewissen]. *All that seemed much less innovative than I myself had previously thought. And the end of the work, where the brilliant intuitions on "ecstatic" temporality remain quite elliptical, seemed excessively historicist to me, reducing the Self to its "generation" and the choice of its "heroes." These words can seem inappropriately iconoclas-*

tic. Although sincere, they testified to a state of mind, at a given moment, and no more than that (nonetheless confirming what I have long known on the subject: unlike what was the case for leading intellectuals—Ricoeur in particular—it was the second Heidegger who captivated me, and not the reading of Being and Time*). The history of the reception of that work (including its strange detours and delays) allows us to establish the extent to which its themes were "filtered" through partial translations, commentaries, citations, and displacements (of which Sartre was the clearest example) in such a way that no French philosopher of my age directly experienced, like the pioneers of the '30s, the impact of reading* Sein und Zeit*.*

More recently, in the course of the last decade, the texts of the Gesamtausgabe *(most recently the* Beiträge*), became the topics of studious seminars with Michel Haar, Jean-François Courtine, Françoise Dastur, Éliane Escoubas, and Jean Greisch, to name a few. At Nice, no priority has ever been given to the establishment of a "Heideggerian school" because the priority was first to respond to the needs of the students (most often according to curriculum requirements and to the* Agrégation *program). On the contrary, the names that were just cited testify to the existence of a genuine intellectual community, relatively small in number, but lively and working on the reading of Heidegger's work in a spirit that one could describe as one of "faithful distance" or "critical attention." It is not really a question of a particular school, and significant differences can be discerned between two antithetical inspirations: the internal interpretation and the frankly critical reading. One who was oriented more and more clearly in the latter sense was Jacques Taminiaux: always precise and forceful, he almost became the representative for Hannah Arendt in her confrontation with Heidegger, principally concerning ethical and political thought.*

We have seen, in the course of our narrative, some who prioritize friendship or even devotion to Heidegger the man, and others who subordinate personal relations to the work on the texts. It is clear that I felt increasingly closer to the latter group. For them, the close and attentive reading of Heidegger corresponded not to a personal allegiance, but to the constancy of a philosophical reference and an inspiration. But even if we limit ourselves to the friends and colleagues mentioned, it would be necessary to add another dimension—and distinguish between those who, on the one hand, continued to consider Heidegger's thought as the best possible source for thought and those, on the other hand, who were more critical.

Furthermore, by emphasizing the question of techno-science, I do not want to say that Heidegger offered the last word on a complex series of problems and questions whose weight will only increase in the century to come (his contribution is in no way limited to this field). It is the very urgency imposed by an uncontrolled evolution of the world that should oblige us to reconsider serious questions long repressed by hyper-technical Marxism and capitalist opportunism: What is the status of science today? Can one maintain the fiction of a "pure and disinterested science"? How can one recognize the inevitable, destinal character of these changes without blindly giving into their irresistible pressure?

These questions have been instrumental in the development of renewed researches on temporality, in which the dialogue with Heidegger once again proved both indispensable and tricky. Both on the terrain of the phenomenological method and in the very contemporary research on the effects of technology, the experience of time is crucial: between the mastery of its measure and the dispossession of its meaning. A "minimalist phenomenology" does not neglect the lessons of the Heideggerian critique of the Husserlian eidetic, but it tries not to leave the authenticity of description to "tautological" repetition, completing it with a careful description articulated in an intelligible way. Not wanting to dwell on my contribution to the debate concerning these orientations of French phenomenology, I would only clarify that I am not by any means a representative of some Heideggerian orthodoxy, even if I have taken issue with various readings of Heidegger's texts. In the debate on the "theological turn," the split was not exactly between Heideggerians and non-Heideggerians. The reference to the necessary disjunction between phenomenology and theology certainly rests on two citations (one from Luther and the other from Goethe) given by Heidegger in Phenomenology and Theology; *but the renewed recourse to immanence was indeed inspired by a French practice of phenomenological description (in the work of Sartre and Merleau-Ponty). I next had to confront the following delicate question in* Phenomenology "Wide Open": *to what extent does Heidegger's thinking remain phenomenological? We saw the renewed style of listening and the new apprenticeship of the* regard *(with Heidegger's recognition at Cerisy of the beauty and depth of this French word). Even the insightful grasp of the "scope" of contemporary technology is phenomenological in this sense. But is there not more to phenomenology than that? Did the turn toward tautology, as rich as it was, not excessively divert precise articulations determined by experience? This deficiency can be felt gravely in the ethical consequences of such a phenomenology.*

It is also by posing the question of the plurality of possible styles in phenomenology that the problem of the ethical reappropriation of duration (and of long duration time span) has been posed. Why would this reappropriation not take form? There is, vis à vis the Derridean deconstruction, a difference to be noted: must the questioning of the Proper go so far as to suspend any reappropriation? Does an ethics of dissemination not dissolve itself? Must not a "Heidegger revisited" be the answer to Derrida? Unless Derrida's evolution (recognizing the character, both unconditional and undecidable, of the call of the Other) anticipated the objection.

A last word that is almost too pedestrian. In order for a critical meditation on the basis of Heidegger's work to develop, a qualitative solitary research, always unique, must find outlets. This remark arises out of experience, and it certainly does not relate to Heidegger alone. Whether it is a question of a fundamental work on the texts, of translations or critical discussions, nothing will take place without impartiality and without a shared passion. We live in the era of innumerable symposia and of constant publications. Genuine fertilization takes place through more secret, and also more lively and amicable, channels. This is why, in his time, Jean Beaufret had an influence that was infinitely superior to his "actual power." One must see things as they are: it is extremely difficult to develop emulation and organize a competent circle that is willing to work, since the degree of specialization is extreme. There will be no rich and lively reading of the Gesamtausgabe without the seriousness, impartiality, and passion of which I have spoken. Will that happen? In Paris? In Nice? On the Internet (where an Ereignis site already exists)? Time will tell.

12   At the Crossroads

OUR STORY HAVING reached its chronological end, that is to say, the end of the twentieth century, it would be possible and tempting to draw some lessons and already reach some conclusions. It seemed to us, however, that the work would be incomplete and would leave the reader particularly frustrated if we were not able to stop and cast a careful glance at the landscape we have crossed after this long journey. A philosophical accounting? This is indeed what we should attempt, not without being aware of the limits of the word "accounting," since we will never manage to establish a definitive and unquestionable inventory of the "losses" and "profits" concerning the reception of such a complex and subtle philosophical thought.

Rather than attempting this impossible accounting, we will propose a wide-ranging meditation on the different perspectives that appear at the crossroads we have reached. The idea that motivates us, as one can guess, is neither "to be done with Heidegger," nor to pretend that the future of thought will exclusively depend on him. Less authoritatively, less prophetically, more philosophically, and always in terms of the French reception, let us wonder about the sensitive questions that enable us to better delineate certain decisive limits of Heideggerian thought. Let us also envisage the limits from which a new departure is possible. "When you are able to see my limits, you will have understood me. I cannot see them":[1] as we reflect on those remarks (half-confidences or half-suggestions), let us clarify that they should be understood literally, at least as clues, even if we are aware that it is unlikely (and also beyond the scope of this book) that we could completely answer this question. We will instead and more appropriately suggest some perspectives on the basis of works or books that seem decisive to us, by disrupting, to some extent, the chronology. This rupture as regards the course of linear time will also allow us, at the same time, to complete or compensate for some of the deficiencies of our previous "narrative."

There is no limit to the possible topics that would lead to a final dialogue between French interpreters and Heidegger's thought. We have gathered the themes—in the contemporary context—that seemed the most significant and with respect to which the debate is far from being closed: the question of phenomenology, the relation to the Hebraic tradition with its connections with the possibility of a new ethics, the role of hermeneutics, the theological debate, and the legacy of a complete rereading of metaphysics.

Which Phenomenology?

Although Heidegger's thought is generally associated with phenomenology, a manifest fact should be mentioned: properly speaking, in the French context, a "Heideggerian phenomenology" did not develop on its own. Clearly, Heidegger's influence was not totally absent from phenomenological research: far from it. But what form did it take? This complex question requires a clarification.

It is in the very evolution of the phenomenological project in Heidegger's work that we should look for the origin of the dissociation that we will identify within recent French thought. Until *Sein und Zeit,* and even until the beginning of the 1930s, Heidegger still presented his thought as a phenomenology, as a phenomenological ontology, or as a "hermeneutical phenomenology." Although Heidegger inherited phenomenology from Husserl, he questioned a number of Husserl's presuppositions, principally his conception of intentionality. In fact, Heidegger never explicitly disassociated himself from the phenomenological project; he even claimed it as his own in his 1963 lecture: "My Way into Phenomenology,"[2] in which he carefully reconnected, though in a mostly autobiographical way, with this guiding thread of his work. This work of self-interpretation and self-justification was necessary because of a double rupture: the first one is obvious and relates to Husserl's legacy; the second one, which was more subtle but understandable in the context of the "turn" that decidedly guided Heidegger from 1936 and after, refers to the confrontation with Nietzsche and the entire metaphysical tradition. We have to realize that for the later Heidegger, who was a "hermeneutician" as well as a "deconstructor" of the metaphysical tradition, phenomenology (considered as an autonomous project) seemed to have lost most of its importance (such is, for example, the impression one gets when reading *The Principle of Reason,* one of the masterpieces of the later Heidegger). He opposed those who would doubt his (singular) faithfulness to phenomenology, since he himself adopted a "phenomenology of the inapparent" (or "tautological" phenomenology) and encouraged the practice of a meditative gaze enabling insight into the essential, including its very withdrawal. Realizing that "the time of phenomenological philosophy seems to belong to the past," Heidegger reasserted that the profound reach of phenomenology transcended a mere trend or a school: "The comprehension of phenomenology consists solely in grasping it as possibility."[3] Heidegger certainly managed to show the coherence of the path of thought that took him from his idiosyncratic reading of the sixth *Logical Investigation* to his "insight into that which is" (whether concerning the scope of technology or the givenness of time as such); however, he could not conceal the unintended consequences: inspiration more than method, phenomenology loses the specificity proper to the Husserlian school. Far from being an autonomous project and corpus, it is nothing but the very opening of the philosophical gaze. Heidegger recognized it explicitly: "That which phenomenological investigations rediscovered as the supporting attitude of thought proves to be the fundamental trait of Greek thinking, if not indeed of philosophy itself."[4]

It is not surprising that this legacy would lead to a dispute. The most faithful will claim that Heideggerian thought is phenomenology par excellence; the opposite position, sustained with no less conviction and even more argumentatively, is that Heidegger's thought produced a genuine "catastrophe" in the phenomenological field. In the first case, the Master's positions are addressed literally, illustrated primarily with examples, but avoiding any methodological engagement with other styles or methods belonging to the phenomenological field.[5] In the second case, on the contrary, while trying to do justice to the internal coherence of the Heideggerian quest for an original language that frees the gift of *Ereignis* (the event of appropriation, unapparent in its very appearing), one formulates very serious doubts: "Is to speak in that way not to expose oneself to ambiguity pure and simple?"; and are we not allowed to assume that "the tautological transformation of phenomenology involves . . . a disastrous or catastrophic character?"[6]

Courtine was able to raise the question with a frank acuity, but he would leave it unanswered, requiring his readers to discover the rationale and envisage the consequences of the "disastrous character" of the Heideggerian transformation of phenomenology. The question would of course deserve a comprehensive study, but our concern strictly bears on the observation and analysis of the impact of the Heideggerian "upheaval" within the recent French reception.

Phenomenology as such does not belong to anyone, and phenomenological inspiration takes many forms. Hence, it is not surprising that the opposition to Heidegger, in this context, did not challenge his "right" to practice—in particular in his late seminars—some simple "phenomenological exercises" whose pedagogical virtues were to explain, for instance, the difference between the physical body (*Körper*) and the lived-body in the phenomenological sense (*Leib*),[7] or the distinction between the direct appearance of the phenomenon (The Lubéron! René Char!) and the Cartesian (or Kantian) representations of such phenomena: "For the Greeks, things appear. For Kant, things appear to me."[8] It is not just by chance that the reference to the Greeks constantly accompanied "exercises" of the phenomenological gaze that Heidegger sought to conduct and share.

Heideggerian phenomenology thus became a "path of access to the Greek world"—an approach that was in no way nostalgic, but that rather supposed an incredible hermeneutical daring to understand the Greeks better than they understood themselves. "It is a phenomenological inquiry that should lead to an understanding of what is Greek in the Greeks."[9] The main risk is thus not anachronism; it is found in the circularity that connects the two projects, namely, listening to the Greek and the gathering of the phenomenon: "To go from the Greek to the Greek is to go from the phenomenological to the more phenomenological."[10] The first readers of *Sein und Zeit* had not detected this reciprocal implication of the two gestures: the relationship between the critique of the ontology of presence-at-hand [*Vorhandenheit*] and the "destruction" of the classical reading of Greek philosophy. This questioning recasts the problem: the hermeneutical fecundity of this new practice in phenomenology cannot be separated from the critical reinterpretation of the whole of tradition: "The Heideggerian operation thus consists in reading the reality of the metaphysical in terms of the possibility of the phenomenological."[11]

By identifying the complex radicality of the Heideggerian undertaking, Brague avoided speaking of a "disaster," but he clearly detected that the consequence of the hermeneutical challenge initiated by Heidegger was that phenomenology became "the method for all philosophy" (that is to say: for any philosophy worthy of this name), thereby losing the specificity and the autonomy of its Husserlian features. One understands, then, how Heidegger could continue praising the phenomenological inspiration while destroying the framework and the determinations of what constituted it as a "scientific" project. The close connection in Heidegger's work between his new "phenomenological" practice and the "step back" (from metaphysics) does not just prevent phenomenology from being an autonomous corpus, but it seizes its "possibilities" in a sense that is quite different from the development of research oriented toward the multiple and complex faces of intentional experience and its transcendental roots or specific expressions (logical, cognitive, emotive, etc.). Any development of phenomenological research in a positive sense is abandoned or left fallow.

The result seems obvious: did not recent French phenomenology seek a way out of the Heideggerian path? Certainly, but the situation proves more subtle: Heidegger remains in view, but as sort of a negative catalyst. In fact, phenomenological research develops, above all, in opposition to his presuppositions or suggestions.

Is this a clear opposition or a more discreet divergence? It depends. However difficult it may be to establish the definitive record of such a still-shifting terrain, it seems that the former is the case—from Levinas to Henry, from Marion to Loreau and Richir. Despite all their differences, all of these authors rejected Heidegger's presuppositions concerning phenomenology. Levinas set the tone by subordinating his faithfulness to "phenomenological inspiration" and his sustained attention to *Sein und Zeit* to his radical rupture from the phenomenology of the "there is" as well as from any philosophy of the Neutral.[12] The *differend* concerning the Heideggerian phenomenological "possible" is no less radical in

Michel Henry: constantly denouncing the "overwhelming"[13] connection between the phenomenological method and Greek phenomenology (the primacy of seeing), he devotes the first part of his last work to the "reversal of phenomenology," and he criticizes, in particular, "the ontological indigence of the appearance of the world" in Heidegger.[14] Marion undertook an intense discussion of Heideggerian themes throughout *Reduction and Givenness,* by placing the "pure form of the call" beyond Heidegger's existential reduction.[15] He pursued his search for a radical phenomenology of givenness in *Being Given* and went as far as to avow that the later Heidegger claimed that givenness "disappears in the advent [*Ereignis*]."[16] For his part, although Max Loreau—in what was to have been his final work[17]—gives serious attention to Heidegger's thought, in which he finds all the possibilities of phenomenological ontology,[18] he nevertheless devotes himself to overcoming its limits ("the spirit of retrocession"[19]) and to sketching—beyond Heidegger—a thinking of the "becoming-body-of-the-world"[20] and of its imaginary genesis in phenomenal diversity. Finally, when Richir reconsidered some of the analyses of affectivity in *Sein und Zeit* (whose genius he did not intend to contest), he reproached them for their quasi-pathological schematization under the influence of an "existential solipsism."[21] Consequently, he tried to build a "versatile" phenomenology, sensitive to the extraordinary complexity of affective life and of the dynamical structures of the experience of thinking, in a completely different way, by returning to Husserl's passive syntheses and continuing Maldiney's research.[22]

The divergences from the Heideggerian heritage were more discreet in the works of a new generation of French phenomenologists. Thus, Jocelyn Benoist, while attentive to the Heideggerian "ruptures," essentially focuses on the articulation between phenomenology and logic as it unfolded in Husserl, himself questioned on the basis of the debates that shed light on his first studies on the philosophy of arithmetic and the status of judgment.[23] For his part, Renaud Barbaras, author of a thesis on Merleau-Ponty's ontology, and already locating it "beyond Husserl and Heidegger,"[24] retains the latter's critique of transcendental phenomenology and his confrontation with nothingness. However, he orients his new phenomenology of perception in terms of the motion of life and of subjectivity as desire, which places him finally closer to Erwin Strauss (and Jacques Garelli[25]) than to Heidegger.[26] Finally, if Claude Romano at first glance seems to follow Heidegger's thematic of *Ereignis* with the term "event," he on the contrary distances himself from it, preferring to find his inspiration in the Stoics and in Nietzsche in order to understand the event in relation to birth and to the temporal diversity of human adventure, instead of reducing it to the mere question of being.[27]

The phenomenological opening of the unpredictability of the event is precisely one of the major themes of a discreet scholar whose name has not yet appeared in this book and who deserves particular attention: Henri Maldiney. His relation to Heidegger was obvious, constant, and recognized; but it was never exclusive. Inspired by plastic arts and poetry, an erudite connoisseur in Ancient Greek thought, he often referred to Heidegger, without ever simply repeating him or agreeing entirely with his views. A striking example of this free inspiration that maintains its critical distance can be found in Maldiney's book *Penser l'homme et la folie*.[28] Presenting his method as strictly phenomenological, Maldiney deals with psychotic and depressive behavior on the basis of a "reduction" that brackets them. However, beyond any anthropology, it is indeed the being-there [*Dasein*] that he questions; and he takes into account not only the existential analytic itself but also the entire tradition of *Daseinsanalysis*.[29] The extent of this debt to Heidegger only serves to make the question of the *différend*, in relation to the question of destiny more apparent. For Maldiney, Heidegger's ontology "is a 'heroic' *ethics* that interiorizes being's destiny in a legitimacy unknown to it, and which replaces the arbitrary blindness of its sheer exteriority."[30] The opening to the unpredictability of the event challenges, on the contrary, any destiny. Maldiney calls this welcome of a nondestinal novelty, transliability [*transpassibilité*], in distinction from the melancholic mood that dominates the analyses of *Sein und Zeit*. Contrary to "care," it is necessary to allow the lightness of an Angelus Silesius—reread, to be sure, with Heidegger, but from a different perspective—soar.[31]

Risking a metaphor drawn from contemporary physics, one will thus notice that the field of French phenomenology is still subject to the intense radiation of Heidegger's thought, whether it tries to escape or gain distance from it, or whether it tries to benefit from it. One has just seen that this latter case is illustrated by Maldiney's work, in the context of both psycho-pathology and aesthetics. In these domains, and especially in the second, the fecundity of research inspired by Heideggerian phenomenology continues.

From an Unthought Debt to a New Ethics

Is there a link between the silence Heidegger observed with respect to the Hebraic tradition and his refusal of any positive ethics? Is it not logical that Levinas would rediscover the former thanks to the latter? Should ethical concern not be rethought in the more subtle terms of a deconstructive thought? These questions are now going to be articulated.

Whereas in her earlier book, Marlène Zarader had followed Heidegger in his return toward the primordial words of pre-Socratic thought,[32] her subsequent approach became more radically critical and inventive.[33] She begins with Paul Ricoeur's statement concerning Heidegger's silence with regard to the Hebraic tradition.[34] Far from finding arguments in Ricoeur to fuel a direct criticism of this "omission," Marlène Zarader employed an original method that sought to respect the specificities of the case: the elaboration of the Heideggerian questions bearing on the un-thought of the Greek tradition, as well as the listening to the Judaic reading of the biblical text.

By following three leading themes (language, thought, interpretation), Zarader undertakes an inquiry that allows one to recognize troubling analogies. For Heidegger: the questioning of origin establishes a double level of inauguration (unknown and manifest) on the basis of which the Greek beginning is extracted from the traditional linear schema of the history of philosophy in order to be rethought as inaugural for the Western world as such. This hermeneutical daring is justified by a new theory of interpretation (texts speak only provided they are questioned) that makes a new approach to language possible. The latter is no longer understood principally or primarily as an instrument of signification: to name the thing is to "bring it into presence"; language makes being itself be. Thought (*Denken*) is no longer conceived as an expression of the categories of presence; it is essentially memory and welcome of what "gives" itself to it; it is gratefulness and giving thanks [*Dank*] for what is thus offered to it and withdrawn from it. Finally, interpretation cannot be reduced to a search for signification: its reading of the great texts is guided by the quest of the un-thought (in the case of metaphysical texts) and of the un-said (in the case of poems); it then penetrates a region "opened up by Heideggerian thought."[35]

Following these three themes, and almost word for word, one can identify a series of analogies. The Hebraic tradition does not conceive of language as an instrument; it practices it by exploiting its polysemic riches: speech [*davar*] is creative, not in the sense of a technical or dominating relationship with beings, but by virtue of the rhythmic plenitude of a coming into presence.[36] Language, structured by the twofold categories of call and listening, is given over to the care of a mediator: the prophet. Zarader shows that the distinguishing features of the prophet (the welcome of language, the opening to the future, the foundational role in history, the response and submission to a divine call, and the gathering of these signs so as to share them with the human community) allow close analogies with the role of the poet in the sense that Heidegger understands it.[37] As far as thought is concerned, one certainly does not find in the Bible a theoretical aim that would allow the determination of its definition and its methodical exercise: its exercise reveals itself as call, listening, memory, and faithfulness. "Hear, O Israel":[38] this call is addressed to human beings prior to any theoretical certitude; it even destabilizes it, just as Heidegger detects a call proper to thought that is more intimate than direct questioning.[39] Finally, the Judaic conception of interpretation implies an essential co-belonging of the text and the interpreter: Jewish hermeneutics does not refer to a "preexisting" set of signifieds, and even less to intangible dogmas; it inscribes itself within the scope of an infinite, inexhaustible quest; it awaits a future: for Jewish hermeneutics (just as for Heideggerian thought), the text is a potentiality.[40]

Is this an excessive comparison; does it try too hard to prove its point via the texts? Such were the main dangers to which this research was exposed. Marlène Zarader was quite aware of it. Far from trying to adjust the Hebraic tradition to Heideggerian thought, she continually emphasized, on the contrary, their differences and their specificities, and even suggested objections (the most important of which was the unquestionably Greek nature of philosophical questioning as such—a central point of the Heideggerian thematic). But she transforms what could have remained a timid attempt into an undertaking that invites further reflection: the overwhelming nature of Heidegger's silent denial of the Hebraic tradition parallels the striking accumulation of the analogies carefully identified, which include the question of the nothing and the truth of being as "withdrawal."[41]

This critical work in no way challenges Heidegger on his favorite ground (the Greek and Western traditions). On the contrary, if we take him at his word, and follow him to the heart of the un-thought of this tradition, he *reveals* another ground, another tradition that is profoundly analogical. This other tradition does not operate in the usual or "classical way" where a radical difference is maintained between the question of being and that of God (Heidegger reasserts this caesura and exploits it in relation to the radical difference between Christian faith and philosophical thought). This analogical register thus created does not oppose Heidegger in any way. But—by circumventing the Western-Greek monolith thanks to a new listening to the biblical tradition—it widens the horizon and enables not the formal repetition of the question of being, but a relaunching of the Heideggerian questioning concerning the origin, while unexpectedly disrupting the claimed "purity" of the Greek source (at least the one that Heidegger identifies as the most "proper").[42]

Henceforth, apart from the problems of influence,[43] Heidegger's denial of the Hebraic sources is questioned anew. We can now realize the progress we have made from the initial question (why this silence?). Ricoeur was the one who posed it; it is repeated with an intensified acuity. If Zarader is right,[44] Heidegger has, deliberately or not, concealed a close proximity with essential features of the biblical tradition. Zarader does not exclude the possibility that this silence (which is not total, however)[45] is "unforgivable" (one can discern a relation with the political question);[46] but her contribution to thought is greater than simply adding to the voices of those who accuse Heidegger the man: rather, her contribution is to *reveal* in his thinking the decisive *feature* of an un-thought debt. Is it an exaggeration to assert that revealing this feature improves the interpretation? We are going to verify this in the dialogue with Levinas on the question of ethics.

Levinas stubbornly wanted to have it both ways: to recognize his debt toward Heidegger, on the one hand, and to mark his irreducible opposition to the neutrality of his ontology, on the other hand. Should the delicate status of this conflicting relation not be reexamined in light of Marlène Zarader's book? If Heidegger's thought—in spite of its undeniable specificities—maintains a proximity and an unavowed "debt" to Hebraic thought, the problem becomes increasingly complicated. However, the hermeneutical situation thus created, while subtle, enables one to approach the ethical question, such as Levinas formulated it, on a new basis.

Literally indefensible, Levinas's interpretation of the later Heidegger is philosophically rich. What is literally indefensible is this "constant reduction of Heidegger's thought to the tradition from which it diverges,"[47] as if Heidegger only recapitulated and added to the ontology that on the contrary he constantly put into question. The irony of this situation is that Levinas unleashed an interpretative violence against Heidegger, the very behavior he attributed to Heidegger himself (a radicalization of difference, turning the tradition against itself), going as far as twisting key words (among others, in the very title *Autrement qu'être,* "Otherwise Than Being," the word "essence" rendered as *essance,* etc.).[48] One can only agree with Zarader when she noted "the strange alchemy" to which Levinas submitted the Heideggerian text, while adding: "It seems to me to amount to filling an abyss on one side in order better to mark the separation on the other."[49] All of Levinas's passionate talent was required to accomplish the acrobatic operation consisting in erasing the abyss Heidegger had always cultivated between the onto-theological tradition and his own thought.

When looking at it more carefully, we realize that Levinas is much closer to Heidegger than he claims, but Heidegger himself is much "closer to the Biblical tradition than he says"[50] (and the first clarification is all the more necessary in relation to the second). Isn't this a double misunderstanding? How can the promise of philosophical fecundity that we discerned in this conjunction be clarified on an ethical terrain, where Levinas excels and where Heidegger is more lacking?

One must first reconsider the question of ethics in Heidegger without neglecting the letter of the texts: although it is true that a traditional ethics in the sense of a rule-based discipline is rejected, as is the approach to ethics in terms of "values," the ethical concern is in no way sidelined.[51] On the contrary, what is proposed is an "originary ethics,"[52] rethought in terms of the (nonmetaphysical) truth of being, and a new access to the possibility of the mortals' dwelling on this earth, cultivating the sense of the sacred. Zarader rightly notes that Heidegger associates this concern with an "originary ethics" with "structures of otherness" (welcome and passivity, memory and gratitude, promise and salvation).[53] One should take this into account when engaging in dialogue with Levinas.

The latter also raised the ethical question again while eschewing any procedural, regulatory, or even practical (in the Kantian sense) consideration: he situated himself at the level of an originary call, animated by a radicalism that rivaled Heidegger on his own ground, since the claim of an infinite Transcendence directly challenges the sameness of being and its neutrality. One could even add (following Ricoeur) that the ethical command in Levinas's work only opposes the primacy of being with another "great genre" (as in Plato's *Sophist*): the Other. And yet, one should not ignore that Levinas in no way meant to separate the alterity of the Other from his or her face and flesh or from all the gestures of solicitude, respect, and love that permit the welcome, recognition, and respect of that Other.

The purpose is not here to negate or erase the distance that Levinas wanted to emphasize so vigorously in relation to Heideggerian thought. The aim is rather to rethink this distance in terms of a certain proximity: "So far and yet so near," Zarader pertinently writes.[54] Such a strained and intense relation could not be understood, and still less examined, in purely external or "topological" terms.

Henceforth, how is it possible to rethink this distance in question without excluding the proximity implied by the shared concern for a phenomenology of the originary? If this question obviously exceeds the limit of this work, it is at least possible and desirable to indicate the direction in which one should turn to attempt to answer it. The stumbling block between Levinas and Heidegger is indeed the question of the Neutral: the ethical concern in Heidegger, remaining that of a relatively indeterminate open dwelling, neither forbids nor prescribes; it involves the neutrality of conditions of possibility of a sojourn on this earth; in this sense, it remains within a phenomenology that singularizes neither the face of the neighbor nor that of God. It is precisely this indetermination that Levinas intended to challenge: his phenomenology is from the outset uprooted (or diverted) by the transcendence with respect to any sojourn, and by the return of a human singularity that is paradoxically reaffirmed in the alterity of the Other. But this very alterity remains, if not neutral, at least purified by the level of abstraction required by the phenomenological approach. Did Levinas succeed in overcoming this indetermination? His distance from positivity is not the only thing that associates him, in spite of himself, with Heidegger. It is above all the way in which the Other dispossesses the Same, from the outset, that makes Levinas's ethics an originary ethics, breaking with the Kantian or Hegelian mediations. Heidegger's refusal to classify the empirical under the sphere of "values" is appropriated in Levinas's effort to avoid the abstraction of the ought-to-be, and by short-circuiting it through a phenomenology of radical Difference.

Although one should not spare Heidegger's thought from a critical examination of its "limitations" in terms of ethics, this examination should also recognize that an originary ethical concern is in no way absent in Heidegger's work,[55] including in *Being and Time*: one can even assert that the 1933 involvement—far from indicating an ethical indifference—in fact betrays the dangers of a heroic ethics of "resolute decision" that is insufficiently attuned to the specific exigencies of ethico-political rationality.[56] As a consequence of the quest for a radical authenticity, this indetermination can be found, relatively speaking, not only in

Levinas, but still more clearly perhaps in Wittgenstein (specifically concerning Heidegger): "I can readily think what Heidegger means by Being and Dread. Man has the impulse to run up against the limits of language."[57]

Should we be surprised to find that this ethical concern, which affects, destabilizes, and disarticulates the limits of language, is also present in Derrida's later work? This is an "observation" that challenges the usual classifications, but that must be made, precisely because it concerns texts in which the approach to sexual difference, to the other's corporeity, and to the listening to the friend's voice is undertaken thanks to a close though critical reading of Heidegger. Without excluding other writings (in particular concerning the relations between the gratuity of the gift and the meaning of time[58]), it would be necessary to follow all the intricate analyses developed under the heading of *Geschlecht* (sex, race, family, generation, filiation, species, genre).[59] To challenge Heidegger with the question of difference (or the play of differentiations) that he reveals and conceals, implicitly or explicitly, is obviously an attempt to counter him. However, the question is raised patiently, with an exceptional attention to the slightest nuances of some crucial texts. Thus, since 1983,[60] Derrida questioned Heidegger's silence[61] on sexuality. While suspecting the violence of the "neutralization"[62] of *Dasein,* he locates its origin in a transcendental dispersion that characterizes the status of flesh and of corporeity in *Being and Time.* At once a general structure and a mode of expropriation (or of the "fall"), this dispersion suggests a "sexual difference that would still not be sexual duality," a difference that has not yet been set under a genre. This analysis may seem ambiguous, but it turns out to be more subtle than the harsh critique that would claim that Heidegger ignored sexuality.

This kind of deconstruction of the privilege of presence and of its theoretico-metaphysical worldview is pursued further in "*Geschlecht II:* Heidegger's Hand"[63] in a similarly precise, but also more theatrical and more critical, manner. This deconstruction was indeed more theatrical from the very beginning of the text, first given as a lecture in Chicago: "We are therefore going to speak of Heidegger. We are also going to speak of monstrosity."[64] This deconstruction was more critical as well, since the privilege given by Heidegger to the hand, to the handy or craft work, and to the gestures that mark a radical difference (or an "absolute oppositional limit")[65] between man and animality is understood as a logocentrism and a phonocentrism[66] designed to gather metaphysics (and Christianity) into a unique figure, without being able to detach itself from it (even with respect to Trakl) except in the strange form of a "repetition."[67] The critique was almost polemical, if one notes the severity of the judgments concerning Heidegger's approach, which was successively characterized as "dogmatic"[68] and hesitant,[69] following an argumentation that "takes some particularly laborious and at times very simplistic forms."[70] Henceforth, the reading of this text does not lead to a clear conclusion, and one remains perplexed, if not torn, between excessively detailed analyses (which elevate the Heideggerian text to the status of a classical reference par excellence) and harsh judgments, the scope of which range between two different kinds of risks (to compromise the entire project by discrediting the gravity of Heidegger's thought; to mitigate the admiration by camouflaging it by rhetorical casualness). As for the theatrics of "monstrosity," it rests—upon further examination—on a very narrow philological ground: while depending on the (indeed suggestive) "virtue"[71] of the translation of *ein Zeichen* by the Old French *une monstre* (in the context of Hölderlin's *Mnemosyne*),[72] it then seems to introduce and validate the translation of *ein Zeichen* by *un monstre*,[73] which is a mistake, at least if this translation is now considered as final and self-evident.[74] Nevertheless, mixing doxography and dramatization, Derrida pursued his questioning on the generic unity of humanity by following in Heidegger's footsteps: both with and, indissociably, against him.

From (Heidegger's) hand to (his) ear: the work of deconstruction continued further.[75] The extreme challenge consisted in listening to Heidegger until one paid micrological (and "otological")[76] attention to some key occurrences in which four themes were intertwined: the listening to the voice of a friend, the understanding of the philosophical tradition as erotological tension par excellence, the consonance of being as gathering, the transformation of truth into sacrifice under the authority of Heraclitus and Hölderlin. One can understand this incredible effort only if we bring to view both the final confession of the "intention" ("I thought I had to hear Heidegger")[77] and the initial epigraph of "hearing the voice of the friend whom every Dasein carries with it."[78] If one pays attention to the ambition of a text that is almost as "unreadable" as the Chicago conference was "inaudible,"[79] one can presume that Derrida thus betrayed (in the strongest and most ambiguous sense) his most intimate and passionate philosophical friendship for the one who remained his master [and "overseer" (*contremaître*)],[80] and whom he constantly sensed or felt near him, right against him, watching him.[81]

Whether exemplary or excessively singular, this listening to Heidegger defies any account: moreover, it leaves the ethical question in suspense, despite its attention to the other as friend-enemy, and its overly elliptical approval of the overdetermination of "Heidegger's sacrifice" (projected on Hölderlin's). What sacrifice? In what sense? Although Derrida does not answer these questions, one cannot deny that he went to the limits of ethics and language—philosophical paths on which Wittgenstein and Levinas had ventured before him. Has this surprising encounter (or strange proximity) been sufficiently considered, apart from the quarrels of schools or clans? If these rapprochements (and above all the thematic dialogue with Levinas) invite reflections, one can reasonably hope (or more cautiously presume) that the research to come will not limit itself to superficially opposing Levinas (or Wittgenstein) to Heidegger, but will integrate the radicality that they shared, all the while questioning the articulations to be found in the new conditions (mainly socio-technological) in which ethical concern must be inscribed. It cannot be denied that this attention to linguistic and practical articulations was the dominant axis of the hermeneutical philosophy championed in France by Paul Ricoeur.

The Place of Hermeneutics

To address the full dimension of the—mostly methodological—debate concerning the relation that Paul Ricoeur, the French master of hermeneutical thought, maintained with Heidegger's thought, a guiding thread can be found in one of Ricoeur's books on the relationship between text and practice:

> From Heidegger onward, hermeneutics is wholly engaged in *going back to the foundations,* a movement that leads from the epistemological question concerning the conditions of possibility of the "human sciences" to the ontological structure of understanding. It may be asked, however, whether the return route from ontology to epistemology is possible. . . .
>
> Ontological hermeneutics seems incapable, for structural reasons, of unfolding this problematic of return. . . .
>
> The obsessive concern with radicality thus blocks the return route from general hermeneutics toward regional hermeneutics: toward philology, toward history, toward depth psychology, etc.[82]

This text not only bears on Heidegger's case, but concerns the hermeneutical movement that it inaugurated and that Ricoeur characterized as a *return to foundations,* beginning from the epistemology of the "human sciences" and returning to the "ontological structure of understanding." Characterizing Heideggerian hermeneutics,[83] this text explicitly addresses the project and the structure of the hermeneutical path, and not praxis. But the question of method thus engaged has serious repercussions in the field that interests us. Finally, Ricoeur defends a position that would serve, after undergoing some modification, as a *working hypothesis:* the "constant preoccupation with radicality" prevents Heidegger from "making his way back"—not only from general hermeneutics to regional hermeneutics, but from the conditions of praxis (and of the deconstruction of the very concept) toward its effective (practical, ethical, and even political) implementations.

Let us follow an order that allows logic to correspond to chronology, beginning from Heidegger and his concern for the fundamental, and then addressing Ricoeur and his treatment of praxis. In a third and final stage, we will make a connection between the two positions, followed by some critical remarks.

When one returns to the impact produced between 1927 and 1930 in the philosophical world by *Being and Time,* one might be tempted to understand the existential analytic of *Dasein* as a "destruction" of an excessively abstract phenomenology (that is to say of Husserl's "theoreticism") in favor of a more concrete and practical approach. *Dasein* is no longer the Cartesian subject discovering the infinite riches of its own substance and contemplating the extended substance outside it: it is "thrown"; it is a being-in-the-world. One has to understand *Dasein* originally not in relation to what it thinks of itself with respect to itself alone, but beginning from its environment, from the referential and signifying systems surrounding it,[84] that is to say, from its involvement [*Bewandtnis*] toward things.[85]

Let us take the example of the hammer. It is first "available as a tool" (*zuhanden als Zeug*).[86] It is on the basis of "a circumspect explanation" (*aus der umsichtigen Auslegung*) that we give sense to that tool, in the set of references of our concern [*Sorge*] as beings-in-the-world.

The logico-theoretical structure of the proposition and its meaningful "content" are referred back to an originary existential-practical structure. In that case, it would therefore not be at all absurd to claim that the early Heidegger's ontology would aim to be fundamental in that it prioritizes *practical concern* over the theoretical gaze, or at least that it subordinates the latter to the former. It is in this sense that existential ontology was understood by students and interpreters, some of whom were as remarkable as Herbert Marcuse and Hannah Arendt.

However, *Being and Time* was never presented as a "practical philosophy" (neither in the Kantian sense, nor in a more general one) and the word *praxis* is itself difficult to find in the book. It does not appear in Hildegard Feick's index,[87] which, one has to admit, is not perfect. Nonetheless, one can find the expression *das praktische Verhalten* ("practical behavior") at the end of paragraph 12.[88]

What we have to remember, of course, is the confirmation of the originary character of "being-in" for theory and even more so for any theory of knowledge. Should the existential analytic be conceived of as a thought of *praxis* and for the sake of *praxis*? In the "Letter on Humanism," Heidegger warned against any strategies of reversal: an anti-metaphysical proposition remains metaphysical; and, similarly, as regards Platonism or Hegelianism (and its Marxian revision), Heidegger gave several warnings: one does not really surpass a basic philosophical position by purely and simply "reversing" it.

Does this Heideggerian mistrust (or caution) result from a kind of supererogatory style or from some devious ulterior motive (to avoid being thought of or "reduced" to Marxist or Marxian positions)? Would it not have been more honest to admit that the intention was to provide a foundation for thinking of practice (and of praxis) leading to a new approach to decision: *Entschlossenheit*?

It could have been clearer, but the price of this simplification would have been the betrayal of the cutting edge of a thought that was finding itself in *Being and Time* and that was developed subsequently more fully.

When Heidegger critiques the reduction of "practical behavior" to the "non theoretical" (or to the a-theoretical), this should not be misunderstood: it is not to the exclusive benefit of *praxis;* it is in view of a more radical and fundamental departure from the very horizon of the theory/practice dyad. It is in this more radical and more fundamental direction that the very well-known pages (but perhaps not generally read carefully enough) of the "Letter on Humanism" lead us:[89]

> We are still far from pondering the essence of action decisively enough. We view action only as causing an effect. The actuality of the effect is valued according to its utility. But the essence of action is accomplishment. To accomplish means to unfold something into the fullness of its essence, to lead it forth into this fullness—*producere* . . . [90]

When citing French expressions of Sartrean origin, such as *l'engagement dans l'action*, Heidegger does so to oppose it:

> Thinking is not merely *l'engagement dans l'action* for and by beings, in the sense of whatever is actually present in our current situation. Thinking is *l'engagement* by and for the truth of being. [*Das Denken ist nicht nur* l'engagement dans l'action *für und durch das Seiende im Sinne des Wirklichen der gegenwärtigen Situation. Das Denken ist* l'engagement *durch und für die Wahrheit des Seins.*] (*PA*, 240)

What does this mean? It means that the truth of being is substituted for action or *praxis*. But what can *l'engagement* "by and for the truth of being" mean?

It is here that we find, as it were, in real time, "this constant preoccupation with radicality" that Ricoeur was talking about. Clearly, just as the theoretical gaze in *Being and Time* was held to be "derivative," practical engagement is now considered to be insufficiently originary.

Matters become somewhat clearer when one makes the effort to read carefully through the argumentation developed by Heidegger two pages after the beginning of the "Letter on Humanism," particularly with respect to *technē, praxis*, and *poiesis*.

Trying to justify his reference to being, Heidegger states that "the history of being is never past but stands ever before; it sustains and defines every *condition et situation humaine*" [*die Geschichte des Seins trägt und bestimmt jede* condition et situation humaine].[91] It is therefore not only being in an abstract sense that is made to pertain to praxis in order to think it more radically, but it is being in its history. The word *history* is at least as important here as the word *being*. One has to consider both of them. Heidegger suggests that thinking should not be reduced to causing an effect [*das Bewirken einer Wirkung*]: "thinking accomplishes (*vollbringt*) the relation of being to the essence of the human being."[92] *Vollbringen:* "to accomplish" or "bring about" is the feature that characterizes thought, but also acting (*Handeln*): "the essence of acting is *das Vollbringen*." In this sense, thought is originary acting.

Now, to begin to understand what is thus at stake and to experience it, one has—Heidegger clarifies—to free oneself (*frei machen*) from a "technical interpretation of thought."

We thought we had understood that Heidegger wanted to free "practical comportment" from the theoretical gaze. However, he now contends that "for this reason thinking, when taken for itself, is not 'practical.'"[93] When we turn toward theory, Heidegger refers us back to practice! When we turn toward practice, he sends us back toward theory! Practice is more originary, but theory preserves the "autonomy" of thought. Theory and practice condition each other. How are we to exit this circle? By questioning the "technical interpretation" that predetermines this horizon. And how does one accomplish this? By no longer approaching thinking itself as *poiesis,* but as accomplishment, *Vollbringen.*

It is this very opposition between theory and practice that the Heideggerian radicalism means to overcome, which is confirmed by the rest of the "Letter on Humanism" concerning practical life and ethics. Does thinking remain theoretical? To this question Heidegger responds: "The answer is that such thinking is neither theoretical nor practical. It comes to pass (*ereignet sich*) before this distinction."[94]

It is time to come to a conclusion: on the one hand, the situation has been clarified, while on the other hand, it has become more complex.

It has been clarified in the sense that the refusal to favor practice over theory, and Heidegger's "reservations" with respect to any practical philosophy, can now be easily understood. The very difference between theory and practice is what needs to be rethought. The deconstruction of the one cannot be achieved without the dismantling of the other. Such is the radical exigency of returning to the foundations of metaphysical thought, which conditions any genuine renewal of thought.

It has, however, become more complex in the sense that Heidegger cannot honestly claim to have overcome the difference between theory and practice; he carried out his return to the foundations thanks to a reinterpretation of temporality (it is the freeing of the origin that frees up the possible). Yet, this opening of the possible entails a new experience: the overcoming of metaphysics is no more accomplished than the access to a new *ethos,* to a new "dwelling." The task of thought is to prepare a response to the "turn in being itself." This is indeed a task, an apprenticeship.

One knows the ethical and political consequences of this approach only too well. However subtle and enlightening it may be, the Heideggerian reinterpretation of the distinction between theory and practice runs a great risk of leaving the philosopher disarmed in the face of the exacerbated contradictions of his or her being-in-the-world in an epoch that is increasingly technological and prone to power struggles. The haughty figure of the later Heidegger, a solitary thinker disillusioned by his ideological and political engagements, certainly corresponds to the originary call of a more essential thought; but does this radical return to foundations not displace the expectation toward a future that is always withdrawn, avoiding actual praxis? Is that not a one-way ticket, and, in any case, without viable return, or without catastrophic consequences?

This question is worth being posed to the thought that itself claims to be the most questioning. This is precisely what Ricoeur has done, quite appropriately and pertinently, without yielding—for the most part—to reactive polemics, and also by taking into account the virtues of Heidegger's hermeneutic thought.[95] How is it possible to rethink *praxis* and its priority on a new basis, while integrating the lessons and the possible limits of the Heideggerian experience? Is that possible, even if it is very difficult? Let us recall briefly what Paul Ricoeur has attempted in this matter.

From the outset, Olivier Mongin[96] characterizes Ricoeur's philosophy as an "ontology of action." Indeed, Ricoeur himself characterized the unity of his thought in the same way, while also criticizing the Heideggerian theme of the "end of metaphysics": "My question is: what is human action? While asking myself this question, I find in Aristotle—but also in Spinoza with the idea of *conatus,* in Hobbes with his philosophy of passions, and in Schelling with his philosophy of powers—enough resources to re-engender metaphysics. Consequently, the latter does not appear to me as being accomplished, I would rather say it seems to me to be still unexplored."[97]

A whole dimension of this critique targets the Heideggerian interpretation of the history of metaphysics as a history of being and as "onto-theology"; there are a series of very meaningful disagreements with Heidegger's thought, as well as with Derrida's, and the undertaking of a deconstruction of the "metaphysics of presence."[98] Let us concentrate on the positive side: the priority given to human action, a question that arises prior to and beyond reflexive philosophy, but also—in the case of Ricoeur—in its midst, if it is the case that being is conceived as action.[99]

It arises prior, in virtue of the *primum vivere.* Ricoeur is well aware of this urgency of immediate *praxis.* It arises beyond it, for Ricoeur remains faithful to the philosophical ideal of a *practical* wisdom. It arises at the very core of the act of philosophizing, since Ricoeur defends the necessity of a reflexive core that must provide the thought discovering the resources of its freedom its principles of action and justification.

Is that to say that philosophy is practical through and through? It is, as we saw, an "ontology of action" whose aim is "the good life" in the Aristotelian sense, and for which being itself can be discovered and defined as *acting.*

One could add that Ricoeur always attested to this philosophy and applied it to his own life in a systematic way. The advantage of drawing a parallel between the philosophical and practical projects of Heidegger and Ricoeur is to reveal a contrast from the outset between the two philosophers (without risking a value judgment): there is *continuity* in Ricoeur and a growing concern for coherence; the metaphor of a coming and going is completely valid here: not only is Ricoeur faithful to the basic inspiration of personalism, but he was constantly involved in testifying to this inspiration and reflecting in order to draw lessons from his involvements, including from his failures.

As for Heidegger, on the contrary, the involvement of 1933—although it had been in the making for some time, as Farias and above all Ott have shown—was quite a shock (including for his closest disciples: Arendt, Gadamer, etc.); moreover, after his resignation from the rectorate, and even though Heidegger never really "renounced" his engagement, he withdrew from any political activity and even attempted to become the very incarnation of the thinker in his hut or in Freiburg. The consequence is that the involvement of 1933 remains something of an enigma, and Heidegger, far from shedding light on it, only reinforced it through unsatisfactory and partial explanations (e.g., his interview in the *Spiegel* published after his death).

Thus, one can find a stark contrast between two styles of philosophical life (which at the same time stand for two different type of relation to *praxis*). Now, precisely, what interests us most is not only the contrast between two styles; further, the risk of becoming lost in psychologism or moralism will be prevented so long as we can go back to the source of the opposition: a very profound *dissension* with respect to the heart of the matter.

Ricoeur's reservations bear less on Heidegger's radicality as such than on its stakes: being[100] as presence. Heidegger's radicality is that of a decisive return to the conditions of presence.

Ricoeur clarified his disagreement at the end of *Oneself as Another* when he questions the relation between "selfhood and ontology" and constantly referred to Aristotle: "My reticence is on a single, but essential point. Must one make presence the fundamental nexus between oneself and being-in-the-world? . . . By placing the main emphasis on the 'always already' and on the impossibility of getting away from the tie of presence—in short, on facticity- does one not diminish the dimension of *energeia* and of *dunamis* by virtue of which human *acting* and *suffering* are rooted in being?"[101]

This is to express, with considerable caution—and in the context of a discussion of Aristotle—a fundamental difference that I will now try to clarify before drawing some negative but mostly positive consequences.

A few words first on Aristotle: while Heidegger grants much importance to the overdetermination of being in Aristotle, Ricoeur reverts to a more classical interpretation by posing the equation: being = *energeia* (or act) and by giving a major role to the *dunamis-energeia* couple. The polysemy of being will be articulated not on account of being as such, or of being as presence, but of *being as acting*. The central idea is that of an "analogical unity of acting."[102]

The negative consequences of this position are twofold. Phenomenologically, Ricoeur seeks to diminish the importance of Heidegger's analyses of facticity, anxiety, and "fallenness" (the entire "passive" dimension of the existential analytic). As far as hermeneutics is concerned, he rejects the entire Heideggerian understanding of the *Schritt Zurück,* the step back and the distance intended to question and critique—for the sake of the ontological difference and of an ever more original thought—the forgetfulness of the truth of being brought about by metaphysics in its onto-theological structure, from Plato to Nietzsche.

Happily, this appropriation has very positive consequences: it allows for a philosophy of action, about which we must now provide details.

Acting is aporetic; and Ricoeur's concern is to respect this aporetic nature, to assume it, and to confront it—which first took place through an analysis of the tragic nature of acting in Jaspers's work and in a philosophy of finitude.

The immense field of acting cannot be reduced to a single principle. It is hierarchical and plural. To assign it an analogical unification is to locate it between homonymy and synonymy. Ricoeur does not want to diminish the complexity of acting: he only wants to do all that he can to preserve the coherence of meaning in a scattered world and in a society that is continually in conflict.

This philosophy of acting becomes remarkably systematic in the formulations of *Oneself as Another* and of *Réflexion faite.* With respect to the metaphysical perspective,[103] Ricoeur recognizes a "both powerful and effective ground" where Aristotle's *energeia* and Spinoza's *conatus* are conjoined. With respect to phenomenology, Ricoeur identifies practical agencies or categories enabling him to structure *praxis* in order to provide a solid ethical view that seeks to be practical wisdom. There is circularity between the meta-function and the phenomenology of acting.

* * *

To show how the resources of the practical field unfold, Ricoeur distinguishes between four instances of praxis:

language—speaking
action—doing
narrative—telling
responsibility—submitting to imputation

The investigation can proceed—he explains—at a first level, in terms of ordinary language (who speaks? who acts? etc.), then at a "greater degree of abstraction": speaking, doing, telling, imputing will be endowed with meaning and serve as an "*analogon* in various figures of acting."[104]

Let us return to the four instances to verify how each of them plays the role of referential unity:

1. With respect to language and to speech, one finds a semantic structure of the sentences that refers to actions, an investigation into the different ways one recognizes oneself as author (of narratives) and accepts moral imputation.

2. With respect to action, the point of view adopted is the performative actualization of speech itself, of narrative and of responsibility.

3. With respect to narrative, one finds the emergence of a narrative identity, in language in action and in moral and/or juridical imputation.

4. Finally, with respect to this imputation, language becomes the designation of the speaker, action assumes the free origin of causality (I accept myself as the author of my acts and I suppose the other does the same); finally, I situate myself in a network of meaning and of "references."

The priority of *praxis* in no way means, for Ricoeur, a complete rejection of theory; on the contrary, *praxis is permeated by theory* and conversely, since the mediations (speech and narrative) are symbolic.

The complexity of a philosophy that is both reflexive and hermeneutical in relation to praxis corresponds to the tragically aporetic nature of action. The conflict is always present. The "Hegelian temptation" of a total mediation is set aside, yet the concern for meaning and coherence is never abandoned. Ricoeur confronts the difficulties[105] and engages the aporias, without claiming to resolve them completely. This is a philosophy of detour, a philosophy of the "long way," of the "prolongations" (from metaphysics to morality), in contrast to the shortcuts, the short circuits, and ideological impatience.

All the features of this philosophy of action show that in contrast to Heidegger's "obsessive concern for radicality," Ricoeur has opted for another obsessive concern: the return to *praxis,* to a just *praxis,* in which the *attestation* of the self as an other can be discerned, a self opened to alterity as self, an attestation that for Ricoeur is the contrary of suspicion.

To Ricoeur's credit, let us admit—to conclude—that he put his finger on a fundamental *imbalance* that afflicts Heidegger's thought on this question of praxis: the return to foundations is always privileged over the practical implications and their exigencies. This is what Ricoeur calls the Heideggerian priority of the *aletheiological* attestation, that is, of truth and its essence. Consequently, despite his denials, Heidegger cannot overcome the theory/practice dyad; certainly he explores its limits and origins, but he cannot dispense with it without being himself reduced to a "theoreticism" that compensated for the very brutality of his engagement in 1933. As Jacques Taminiaux has shown,[106] Heidegger is much more Platonic than he claims, in particular in his political error: this so-called philosopher-king enters a domain in which he thinks he is both founder and commander. Ricoeur was right not to follow him in this direction and, on the contrary, to have exercised a critical vigilance.

However, in relation to Heidegger, Ricoeur wavered between reservations[107] (which would be emphasized and in time further explained) and a reappropriation that is at times overly forced, laborious, and even recognized as such (at the end of *Oneself as Another,* he reappropriates Heidegger's notion of Care). This corresponds to a more profound interest in the early Heidegger rather than the later one.

Ricoeur himself coined the expression "the masters of suspicion" about Marx, Nietzsche, and Freud. One could characterize him as a "master of scrupulousness." His concern for justice, his willingness to address the aporias in order to confront them, and his infinitely respectable hermeneutic efforts prevent or complicate the clear account that one would hope for—above all when it relates to such a complex figure as Heidegger.

One must go as far as recognizing that, through his vision of metaphysics and his conception of the status of reflection in the context of an ontology of action, Ricoeur is completely *opposed* to Heidegger's injunctions or suggestions. He aims at *reactivating* the treasures of metaphysical thought, from Aristotle to Kant, from Spinoza to Schelling. This attitude is quite antithetical to that of the overcoming of metaphysics, and to the idea of an "end of metaphysics" (and perhaps even more to the deconstruction of metaphysics conceived as an end).

The pages Ricoeur devoted to this question in *Réflexion faite*[108] are very illuminating. He calls the horizon common to the enormous undertaking of *hierarchization* and *differentiation* of the ontology of action, "the meta-function." Hierarchization refers to the research of principles while differentiation refers to a strategy of a semantics of the plurality of the senses of being (the metacategories such as the Same and the Other).

The situation thus seems for the most part clarified. In relation to Heidegger, the ambiguities that remain in Ricoeur seem due to his scruples and his intellectual honesty. But this does not completely excuse his misunderstanding of some of the most original aspects of the later Heidegger, in particular the questioning of technology and of the meaning of our global civilization driven by the will to power.

Finally, it is quite significant that the terrain of the debate that both separates and unites Ricoeur and Heidegger is temporality and historicity. Heidegger's masterpiece is *Being and Time* and Ricoeur's major work is *Time and Narrative*. The latter study, centered on the problem of *praxis,* seems to have forgotten the temporal axis. In fact, it always was implicit: what diverts Heidegger from determinate aporias of practice is the search for an originary time and historicity; on the contrary, by postulating that human time is a "narrated time" and by linking such narratives to a semantics of actions, Ricoeur keeps oscillating between an originary temporality and a so-called inauthentic temporality, between phenomenological time and cosmological time. On this issue, I am closer to Ricoeur rather than to Heidegger, if it is true that there is no "pure time" and that temporality always implies (historical) sharing and measure, a measure that is to a large extent socialized, and thus has a relation to action.[109] One would hope that the lessons of the Heideggerian deconstruction of time as constant presence would not be forgotten and that the most penetrating views of *Being and Time* on "ekstatic" temporality as horizon of our finitude should not be invalidated. This is what Françoise Dastur helps us understand: it is undoubtedly the most reliable explanation and interpretation yet written in French on the question.[110]

But there is, however, an area that seems to hold further difficulties, namely, the theological question, which we find to be, moreover, a central concern of our time.

The Theological Debate

Before widening the scope of our investigations, let us go back to Ricoeur's position: he adopts the critique of onto-theology, but assumes the reappropriation of the metaphysical metacategories. On this point, the relation with Heidegger reaches a state of extreme tension and complexity: Ricoeur accepts the Heideggerian critique of the God of onto-theology, while impugning the historical scheme globally applied to metaphysics. He thus intends to "save," without confusing them, the operation of the "meta-function" and the Christian God.

Perhaps Ricoeur should have emphasized his disagreements with Heidegger much earlier, by espousing the best works of onto-theology more decisively (one thinks of Schelling for example), but one cannot, in any case, accuse him of incoherence or weakness on that point. What is certain is that his intent to do justice to the ontological, existential, and even historical concerns of the Master of Freiburg increasingly prevented him from marking his opposition to an overly encompassing and reductive conception of metaphysics and his profound reservations concerning Heidegger's "paganism." However, Ricoeur did not engage in an explicitly theological debate with Heidegger's thought. One easily guesses the reason why: since the Heideggerian approach to the sacred did not fascinate or attract him, he had no reason to seek theological inspiration in a thinker who ignored the Bible and proclaimed with Nietzsche the death of God or the *Entgötterung*—the flight of the gods—while remaining deaf to the possible revival of the Christian message.

However, there was (especially among Catholics) a deep interest in the Heideggerian renewal of the question of the relation between philosophical thought and faith. We have found obvious evidence of this in the rich volume published in 1980, *Heidegger et la question de Dieu* [Heidegger and the question of God]. It seems to us that since this publication,[111] the attitude of the Catholic philosophers interested in Heidegger has changed noticeably in the direction of a more critical perspective. In what sense? In order to respond to this question, we can refer to the dense and lucid article devoted to Heidegger by Jean-Yves Lacoste in the dictionary he edited.[112]

After having recalled in detail the biographical information that testified to both Heidegger's deep Catholic roots and his subsequent decisive separation from the church, and finally to his ambiguous dialogue with theologians (an ambivalence ultimately revealed by his partially Catholic funeral), Lacoste noted the "utterly de-theologized" character of the philosophical analytic of the human being.[113] Is theology as positive a science (distinct from philosophy) as chemistry? From the lecture "Phenomenology and theology" (1927–28) to the Zurich seminar held in 1951,[114] Heidegger hammers out a warning directed toward both the theologians and the philosophers: God and being have to be radically distinguished; the attempts of "Christian philosophy" are "square circles." His advice was heeded: both Levinas and Marion intended to think God outside of any onto-theology. Yet, as Lacoste added, "the assignment of a task does not mean it will be carried out." Despite the clarity of his warnings, Heidegger could not prevent his texts devoted to language from lending themselves to a theological reading and thoughts welcoming the "event of speech" from being inspired by his reading of the poets. Better: Heidegger himself, apart from any faith or positive allegiance, did not forbid himself from speaking of the divine. In the "Letter on Humanism" (but already in the *Beiträge*), the thought of being presumes a new approach to the sacred. A kind of "theiology" is thus established, which Lacoste describes as "supremely a-theological." Hence the following question, posed with rigor but without hostility: "Would 'Heidegger's theological secret' be the quest for a substitute for the Christian experience and for the Christian delineation of what can be thought?" The answer is certainly positive. It has the merit of a disillusioned frankness: "Theology has nothing to learn here, except what it is not, which is, incidentally, a very useful lesson."

This is a lesson that merits reflection. In a sense, it remains Heideggerian, since the Christian theologian is referred back to him or herself, or rather to the specificity of the message that he or she has the calling to pursue. However, it is quite a negative message: without Kant being named, one cannot avoid thinking of the *catharsis* applied to the Protestantism of his time by the one whom the young Hölderlin hailed as the "Moses of our nation." Heidegger was no less influential, relatively speaking. But this comparison has its limits: as Kant continued to be inspired by a purified Christian tradition, Heidegger turned his eyes toward the distant star of an anonymous sacred. And it is by acknowledging this unquestionable distance that Lacoste himself, as a theologian and Christian thinker, parted with Heidegger, although he remained attached to him as a phenomenologist.

There is therefore much "unsaid" in Lacoste's remarkable article, not because what is essential is hidden in it, but rather due to the importance of a point that is clear if one resituates it in the context of the history of Heidegger's reception by the French Catholic theologians.[115] The illusion of a direct convergence or even of a constructive dialogue with Heideggerian thought has disappeared; even if the confrontation led to a "useful lesson," it resulted in a separation.

One must take a step back in order to consider the path followed thus far. In the 1950s, attempts at dialogue or rapprochement, while remaining cautious in their formulations, did not exclude ulterior motives or expectations. One finds a testimony of this in an introductory text in a journal published by the Dominicans of the Saulchoir in 1959. While avoiding "hasty baptisms," it is stressed that Heidegger's thought should not be understood as an atheism and that it encounters in the "ontological difference" the same difficulty Thomas Aquinas encountered with the analogy of being. Hence this question, seemingly sincere and unquestionably revealing: "Does it mean that the thinking of being such as Heidegger conceived of it is so foreign to us that we would be indifferent to it?"[116]

These attempts discreetly continued in the following decades, reaching a remarkable quality in 1980 in *Heidegger et la question de Dieu*. We already mentioned[117] how instructive this book is and continues to be for today's reader because it avoids no difficulty and opens the debate, to the greatest extent possible, between the scrupulous interpreters of Heidegger's thought (Beaufret and Fédier) and his opponents (Stanislas Breton, Levinas, Ricoeur). But one should complete this first approach by clarifying the intentions of Richard Kearney and Joseph O'Leary, the organizers of the conference that was at the origin of this publication, which was held at the Irish College, in Paris in June 1979. In the context of our "double belonging" to Judaism and Hellenism, while the crisis of rationalism and technological civilization worsened, the foreword noted a "strange coincidence" between Heidegger's "liberating gestures" toward the metaphysical tradition and the aspirations of a religious thought "thirsting for a more originary truth": thus "the hypothesis of a possible encounter" between them.[118]

One must also note, behind the main issue (the direct confrontation between Heidegger's thought and Judeo-Christianity), a kind of new development in the debate, introducing a questioning concerning the validity of his approach concerning the sacred within the very horizon of thought of the second Heidegger and criticizing the Master for a concept of idolatry forged from his critique of onto-theology. This was indeed Jean-Luc Marion's concern. With the title of "Double Idolatry" ["La double idolâtrie"],[119] Marion followed in Heidegger's footsteps when questioning any conceptual approach to God (but also its reverse: conceptual atheism), then—in his quest for the most divine God freed from any ontological determination—he suspected Heidegger himself of a more subtle idolatry, because of the conditions posed and intermingled that subordinate the approach to the most divine God to that of the truth of being: "Only from the truth of being can the essence of the holy be thought."[120] This passage from the "Letter on Humanism" became well-known because it gave readers so much to think about: should we identify in this an unacceptable "obstacle" placed in front of the access to the unique God of the Judeo-Christian revelation? "Here again . . . there functions *another* idolatry,"[121] Marion asserts, arguing that the authenticity of the Existent (*Dasein*) becomes the condition for any approach to God. Addressing the "unthinkable" character of God, and in order to escape any idolatry, Marion, in the end, crosses out the very name of God with a cross of Saint Andrew—a gesture that refutes Heidegger while strangely imitating Heidegger's crossing out of being.

Marion's article is followed, in the same book, by a detailed refutation of it by Maria Villela-Petit. She refutes the usage of the concept of idolatry against Heidegger because the ethical meaning of idolatry in biblical hermeneutics was overlooked. The result is that idolatry is in some way taken out of context by Marion and above all in an illegitimate manner in relation to a thinker whose entire work was devoted to a scrupulously respectful approach to the sacred and the divine. The passage in question in the "Letter on Humanism" does not impose a series of unacceptable prerequisites to monotheism: "if there are any *conditions* at all, they are phenomenological ones and are conditions of an approach to the divine God."[122] Marion does not understand that Heidegger does not situate himself at the level of abstract preconditions opposed to Revelation, but instead approaches the Divine in a henceforth nonmetaphysical way. Similarly, the lecture on "the thing" has a phenomenological scope that does not necessarily privilege the mythical sacred at the expense of biblical revelation: the suggestive evocation of the rainbow as sign of Alliance, of the various aspects of the earth (exile, passage, and the place of the promise) and of the expectation of the chosen People and of God's messengers (the angels), enables and allows a reading of "the thing" that opens on the Play of the Four in the Judaic world.[123]

"One would need to learn how to read differently than with the consternation of a *hen that would come upon silverware*."[124] For his part, Jean Beaufret neither tries to argue point by point against Marion nor to show the compatibility of Heidegger's thought with Judeo-Christian tradition: he prefers sarcasm, by referring to the Greek sense of Chaos and to Meister Eckhart's approach to the Divine.

In his response, Marion maintained that one should not minimize "the idolatrous violence of the text of the Letter,"[125] and in order to defy the "exegetes" (Fédier included), he referred to a clarification made by Heidegger himself in 1953 in Hofgeismar: "The passage in the 'Letter on Humanism' speaks exclusively of the God of the poet, and not of the God of Revelation."[126]

"So, eating crow, like fox outwitted by the chicken coop, shamed-faced, abject, ears all a-droop," Marion also refers to Jean de la Fontaine's bestiary to prevail over his opponents.[127] Actually, it is the impartial reader who may very well find him or herself, if not ashamed, at least seriously perplexed. For, if Heidegger's clarification finally satisfies Marion, should he then not have retracted his charge of idolatry? Why should one still refer to an "idolater" especially if it is not the case, since one recognizes that he was not referring to the God of the Revelation? Consequently, Marion's suspicion no longer seems justified, as it becomes clear that Heidegger did not mean to submit God to the least ontological condition. On the contrary, his constant effort (and not only in his "Letter on Humanism") consisted in freeing Christian faith from any philosophical "imperialism" and in respecting its specific requirements. Given this clarification, one can still expand the explanation: Heidegger was not personally inhabited by the Christian faith; François Fédier reported this honestly,[128] without confusing this fact with the extent to which a believer or a nonbeliever could make sense of Heidegger's approach to the sacred.

Let us return to Marion's position to observe that it takes (whatever its pertinence) a hundred-and-eighty-degree turn in his attitude toward Heidegger; Marion himself dated the end of his Heideggerianism at that time.[129] In *The Idol and Distance*,[130] a meditation on the death of God, interpreted as the death of the moral God, a constant convergence took place—with the theme of Difference—between the Heideggerian deconstruction of onto-theological metaphysics and the theological quest for a spirituality that would be respectful of the mystery of the Trinity. Heidegger was even audaciously read in a quasi-apologetic sense: the fourth dimension of *On Time and Being,* the givenness of time itself, was referred to a Giver, the Father; and the ultimate Heideggerian term, *Ereignis,* was understood as a "*medium* or *analogon* of the Trinitarian play."[131] The text on "double idolatry" marks a rupture that would be reconsidered and reconfirmed in 1982 in *God without Being.*[132] This book maintains again and in a provocative way (in the eyes of the traditional theologians) the typically Heideggerian claim of a separation between theology and ontology, but it assumes and sharpens its suspicions toward a Heideggerian "idolatry" of the truth of being and of the immanence of the thing within the horizon of the world (without taking into account the criticism addressed to Heidegger for reducing God to a being[133]). This is a strange imbroglio: the author, as early as the first page, claims affinities with Heidegger's philosophy as well as with Pascal's,[134] but he proposes "working love conceptually"[135] in intentionally speculative terms that ignore Heidegger's entire work on the deconstruction of the language of metaphysics.

Beyond these formulations and these very personal and historically situated difficulties, it would be helpful to wonder, in all serenity—the Heideggerian virtue par excellence!—what form the debate would take today. Even if it is not possible to give an account that satisfies everyone in such a delicate field, it seems that the related development of the research[136] from Heidegger's perspective as well as in the theological field proved Jean Greisch right, who, as early as 1980, sought to avoid any "strange encounters of the third kind between two discourses that are heterogeneous."[137] The double requirement of rigor that results from such an awareness is of course easier to formulate than to apply.

To what extent can a hermeneutical theology succeed in drawing some lessons from Heidegger without being caught in the opposite trap of an insufficiently critical Heideggerianism or of a new "Christian philosophy" seeking to use some Heideggerian inspirations as a means to ends that are more or less apologetic? The Dominican father Claude Geffré, aware of these risks, limited himself to strictly theological grounds, while benefiting from Heideggerian hermeneutic teachings principally drawn from a reading of *Being and Time*: the existential category of understanding (*Verstehen*) must be able to welcome the Word in its textual, linguistic inscription, and above all, in its historicity. As an initiator of the hermeneutic turn of theology in the French-speaking world, Geffré claimed to have been influenced more by Ricoeur than by Heidegger. He nevertheless accepted Heidegger's critique of metaphysics (on the condition that it does not apply entirely to Saint Thomas). On this issue, he was preceded and initiated by a German priest, one of Heidegger's personal friends, Bernhard Welte,[138] whom he had invited to come to the monastery of the Saulchoir. Since that time, he found the reading of the later Heidegger beneficial for religious anthropology, to the extent that the critique of the disenchantment of the world and the approach of a "more divine God" enabled a more open approach to non-Western religious phenomena, and facilitated an approach devoid of any "logocentrism." But what was at issue in this case was a change in the intellectual attitude, but in no way a direct integration of Heideggerian themes in Christian theology, since Heidegger himself rejected the confusion between the "passion of the cross" and philosophical wisdom. Was this tolerant overture of the Christian faith, understood in terms of nonconcealment rather than dogmatic imposition, widely shared in the Dominican order and in the Church? Claude Geffré's answer is cautious: speaking in his own name, he testified to the existence of a strand of hermeneutic theology, which had been more successful in Germany than in France. In the Dominican order, he felt rather isolated: at the end of the century, what was more important was his silence with respect to Heidegger.[139]

Jean Greisch, professor at the Institut catholique de Paris, does not have a radically different position but seems even more concerned to separate his reading of Heidegger (of whom he is a translator and above all an authoritative interpreter) from his theological and religious engagements. He presents himself as "atypical" within the French intellectual landscape. A citizen of Luxembourg, he studied theology in Austria, and he was in no way influenced—unlike the French Heideggerians of his generation—by Beaufret, Birault, Wahl, and the other Parisian "smugglers" of Heideggerian thought. He was influenced by Karl Rahner's approach to transcendentalism and studied Thomism with J. B. Lotz; later, his masters at the Institut catholique were Dominique Dubarle and Stanislas Breton, who were not at all Heideggerian. Today, while considering himself close to Ricoeur and above all interested like him by the early Heidegger, and in agreement with Ricoeur on the necessity to reactivate the "meta-function," he wanted to get the idea of a metaphysics of *Dasein* "back on the agenda" and thought there were still some hermeneutical teachings to be drawn from the *Beiträge* (which he does not, however, read without trepidation).

Asked about the subtly negative conclusion given by Jean-Yves Lacoste in his article on Heidegger in his *Dictionnaire*, neither Marion, Greffé, nor Greisch[140] disagreed with it entirely: a Christian could not find direct theological inspiration in Heidegger, whose orientation toward the "sacred" was quite unique and recognized as such. However—and far from being immaterial—each of them, in his own way, carefully tried to draw lessons from the catharsis[141] imposed by a serious reading of Heidegger: a double return to the sources is necessary for both Christian thought and philosophy. At the end of a detailed work that stands as a genuine summation of the "case," Philippe Capelle also approves the perspective of recognizing a "double irreducibility": he quite rightly shows that the relation between philosophy and theology is to be conceived as a tension that runs throughout Heidegger's work according to a threefold thematic (the relation of philosophy to New Testament theology, to onto-theology, and to the awaiting of "a more divine God").[142] The complexity of the entirety of the Heideggerian path in its relation to the theological question is also reconstituted and scrupulously analyzed in a comparable way[143] by the Jesuit Father Emilio Brito in a sweeping narrative[144] in which the fascination for the Heideggerian sense of the sacred and for the supra-conceptual mystery is balanced by a critique of the Heideggerian "weaknesses" (his ignoring of ethical imperatives and of the intersubjectivity of community, but above all his lack of openness toward the transcendence of the infinite and substantial being: God). Is neo-Thomist metaphysics capable of bringing its speculative resources to bear in order to respond to the Heideggerian quest for the "God to come"? Whatever the answer, it was no small victory, albeit posthumous, for the Master of Freiburg to have communicated his message and to have had such an impact on the Catholic thought from which he emerged.

Paradoxically, the differences between our three interlocutors seemed less clear to us in relation to theology than in relation to Heidegger's interpretation of metaphysics. Whereas Marion appropriates the critique of onto-theology while practicing a conceptuality that may seem quite metaphysical in several respects, Geffré is more accepting of the Heideggerian destruction of onto-theology; Greisch, on the contrary, remains quite reserved with respect to the "overcoming of metaphysics," which was sought by the later Heidegger: he would not deny his own ironic reflections from 1980, which bring us back to the Heideggerian conception of the history of philosophy as onto-theology: "Does the haste with which one seeks to absolve theological discourse from any complicity with a supposed onto-theo-logy (or even, in another context, from any suspicion of idolatry) not look like the furtive burial of a cadaver? 'Onto-theo-logy—or how to get rid of it?'"[145]

An Uncontested Legacy in the History of Philosophy?

For once, we must take note of a particular case: in the field of the history of philosophy, one generally recognizes that Heidegger has the qualities of a master thinker.[146] The most meaningful tributes come from "ideological" opponents.

For example, Levinas wrote: "I must underline still another crucial contribution of Heidegger's thought: a new way of reading the history of philosophy";[147] and in the evening of his life, Althusser confessed to Fernanda Navarro that he found Heidegger "fascinating," because he was "an extraordinary historian and interpreter of philosophy."[148] One could find many other similar testimonies, including from younger philosophers devoted to analytic philosophy: from the latter perspective, the tendency would be to grant Heidegger a minimal recognition on the historical ground in order to deny him practically any relevance (analytic philosophers have the tendency to consider that continental philosophy is limited to the "exclusive domain" of its own history).[149]

This quasi-consensus must nonetheless be examined with circumspection: it obviously harbors many disagreements concerning the very contents of the interpretations. To recognize Heidegger's predilection for the history of metaphysics does not mean to approve his reading of the great philosophers, but rather to concede, in most cases, its "provocative" nature.[150] The way the Heideggerian interpretations nourished—albeit indirectly—the studies in the history of philosophy in France was in fact unexpected and paradoxical. In his critique of *Kant and the Problem of Metaphysics,* Jules Vuillemin contributed to the public's awareness of the book.[151] Similarly, Dufrenne,[152] Wahl, Hyppolite,[153] Levinas, Merleau-Ponty, Birault—in their courses as well as in their publications—awakened the curiosity of the public to the Heideggerian readings of the pre-Socratics,[154] of Descartes, Hegel,[155] Husserl,[156] or Nietzsche, but without for that matter providing an exhaustive or completely favorable account of it. Jean Beaufret's publication, translation, and commentary on "Parmenides's poem" is itself paradoxical, but in a different sense. If Beaufret's enthusiasm for Heidegger is obvious, the work is also quite personal and inventive with respect to the Master's thought. In particular, Beaufret's interpretation of Kant, which allowed him to interpret the reevaluation of the "opinions" on the basis of the Kantian theory of transcendental imagination (itself reread in a Heideggerian way), is quite tenuous and anachronically "Heideggerian."[157]

From this first reception to the emergence of a genuine school of historians of philosophy inspired by Heidegger, more than a quarter of a century had to pass, the equivalent of a generation. And in this respect, there is yet another paradox: this community of inspiration has been called the "Aubenque school,"[158] although Aubenque revealed almost no Heideggerian influence in his thesis.[159] Indeed, if it was taken into account and always with a great clarity, Heidegger's interpretation of Aristotle was subjected to reservations and critiques: thus the apophantic should not be understood in the sense of un-concealment;[160] one had to go beyond the alternative between the latter and adequation;[161] Heidegger did not really see that the "fundamental" dimension in Aristotle was the theory of being as being;[162] and entelechy was not to be understood as pure presence of what is present.[163] Somewhat later, Aubenque completed his critical work in the light of new developments in Heideggerian thought: he emphasized the excessively unifying character of the understanding of the history of metaphysics on the basis of its onto-theological structure; according to him, one had to be equally attentive to the overcoming of ontology—which was announced at the end of Book 6 of the *Republic*—an overcoming that unfolded in neo-Platonism and more particularly in the Plotinian "henology."[164] It is no less true, as we have seen in the course of this work, that Pierre Aubenque recognized Heidegger's exceptional philosophical stature and vigorously opposed any politically oriented "reductionism." This is a new sign proving the fact that along with allegiances or fascinations there was room in France—more discreetly but no less decisively—for a kind of nonideological reception designed to combine interest or sympathy with a critical perspective.

Whether it is baptized "the Aubenque School" or by some other name, a hub emerged for research concerning the understanding of the unity of metaphysics on the basis of the "onto-theological constitution." These studies mainly focused on Aristotle, Suarez, and Descartes, and questioned Heidegger's theses through a return to textual sources. A historiographic approach became predominant, in particular under the direction of Jean-François Courtine, who, without taking a strictly "orthodox" position, and assuming what was at times a "desperately micrological" aporetics, recognized that his inquiries into the history of metaphysics owed much to the Heideggerian questions and provocations.[165]

Whereas in matters of the history of metaphysics, the first reception included a dominant axis of "defense and illustration" of the Heideggerian theses combined with the Nietzschean inspirations in Henri Birault,[166] illustrated by the marvelously pedagogical talent of Jean Beaufret[167] and defended (in an even more assertive way) by Gérard Granel in his two theses,[168] the new generation intended to affirm the rights and interests of a less literal faithfulness and of more erudite and concrete approaches.

Regarding the concept of "world" in Aristotle, and on what it denotes or suggests, Rémi Brague stated that he was not proposing a "Heideggerian interpretation" and claimed to have important philological reservations concerning Heidegger's reading of the pre-Socratics.[169] His project, however, was explicitly inspired by the application of the Heideggerian concept of "being-in-the-world"—with a critical intent—to Aristotle's texts. The question raised can be schematized as follows: is it not the case that the cosmological concept of world conceals its phenomenological dimension? Brague's inquiry involves three perspectives—ontological, anthropological, cosmological—and manages to reveal the complex tensions in Aristotelian philosophical research with respect to an "un-thought core," which concerns the relations between *Dasein,* facticity, and the world itself. While the project can be suspected of anachronism or illegitimate "hermeneutic violence," its detailed and nuanced achievement also offers the occasion of rediscovering Aristotle with a new eye. When he adopts a Heideggerian style, Brague does not do so naïvely or without providing justifications at each step for the gaps between his interpretative hypotheses and his results. His use of the Heideggerian notion of "world" and his recourse to the notion of an "un-thought" does not result in a mimetic adoption of the Heideggerian method or style; on the contrary, his strategy is that of a scrupulous philologist. Hence, the surprising originality of this work, which manages to critically "rework" some Heideggerian intuitions: the onto-theological structure of metaphysics is thus translated within anthropology in the form of a structure called *katholou-protological*,[170] and the Heideggerian "care" is said to be reminiscent of (and probably inherited from) the Aristotelian *phrontizein*.[171] One will forgive the technical character of these points: it was necessary in order to show the degree of precision of Brague's work.

Instead of a new reading of a great author, Jean-François Courtine chose to foreground a philosopher of lesser renown (in France): Francisco Suarez, a Spanish Jesuit of the second half of the sixteenth century.[172] It is true that Courtine undertook, at the same time, to sketch out a sweeping narrative of medieval and premodern metaphysics while pursuing the guiding thread (obviously of Heideggerian inspiration) of an inquiry into the identity of metaphysics and of its onto-theological structure. The "Suarezian moment," carefully put in perspective in the context of the horizon of the scholastic transposition of the Aristotelian project, corresponded to a systematic refoundation of metaphysics in terms of a new theory of the object in general, or "objectness" [*objectité*].[173] An heir of Ockham by virtue of his quest for a unique term that would provide an account of the whole of beings, Suarez ontologized metaphysics by rendering its "object" the correlate of knowledge, "without any appearing."[174] Suarez's metaphysics, already a quite modern undertaking in spite of its scholastic trappings, understands every being in terms of its "knowability," but does not directly confront the Thomist theory of the analogy of being: this is a difficulty that Courtine analyzed in light of a very fine distinction between the "blind spot" of metaphysics (its onto-theological constitution formalized in the theory of the analogy of being) and its structuring or systematizing accomplished or realized "after the fact" (the distinction between ontology—general metaphysics—and special metaphysics).[175] It is therefore a Heideggerian framework that allows one to truly understand this monumental work of erudition, a work that runs the risk of remaining a mystery for a reader deprived of the key that has been quite discretely inserted in the body of the text.[176]

The refinement of that same line of interpretation was also Jean-Luc Marion's project, this time concerning Descartes. Marion first tested the fecundity of what he himself named later a "wild Heideggerian methodology"[177] on the

Rules for the Direction of Mind. What does that mean? That the very idea of a confrontation between the thematics of the *Regulae* and the Aristotelian categories[178] springs from the Heideggerian notion of a transformation of the onto-logical "core" of metaphysics, without, for that matter, directly questioning the hypothesis of the onto-theological constitution of metaphysics. This broader project (this time explicitly referred to its Heideggerian source) was the one that Marion followed more systematically in his detailed analyses of the nuances of Descartes's "metaphysical prism."[179] The difficulty in this respect comes not so much from the rare use of the term "metaphysics" by Descartes as it does from the very originality of the new sense of first philosophy: the novel conjunction of a "nothingness of ontology"[180] with a "white theology."[181] Since neither beings nor God can be approached directly, it is only on the basis of thought (as *cogitatio*) that a first onto-theo-logical figure is constituted: beings as objects of thought refer to the thinking that thinks them and that thinks itself. Nevertheless, beings can be addressed more fundamentally still and more radically when treated as a cause: the Cartesian "dictate" of reason imposes the recourse to causality realized par excellence in God as *causa sui*. This second figure of onto-theo-logy does not cancel the previous one, but founds it in its turn, such that Cartesian onto-theo-logy, which, at first, was not apparent, is in fact "redoubled"[182] The Heideggerian scheme (which Marion recognized is best found in its elementary form in Leibniz and Hegel) appears, in Descartes, as "an exceptional rendition of a more complex and eventually infinitely varied game,"[183] so that—far from being refuted—it finds itself, on the contrary, to be de-multiplied, as it were.

These three examples (Brague, Courtine, and Marion) of the fecundity of Heidegger's work in the field of the history of philosophy do not correspond simply by accident to the three "moments" (Aristotle, Suarez, Descartes) that Heidegger himself had not studied as systematically and carefully as he had done with Kant and Nietzsche. Their common interest does not principally consist, however, in filling in the "blanks" in the Heideggerian program; it lies above all in the erudite and critical questioning of stimulating theses, which always ran the risk of dogmatism. In this respect, one could object that these works only exploit Heidegger's suggestions while "normalizing" them, since they have submitted themselves to the Caudine Forks of the scientific demands of academic recognition that had been, in one way or another, somewhat shaken by Heideggerian "boldness." This judgment would remain too external, unaware of the very reason for the confrontations "on the ground." Their methodological and critical purpose cannot be separated from their "transplantation" outside the original, properly Heideggerian, soil. One could almost say that this Heideggerian scheme was henceforth exploited in a "technical" way in the field of the history of philosophy. Thus adapted and applied, did it still involve essential thought in the sense the Master understood it? The question must, at least, be posed. Let us limit ourselves here to observing that even if it is vain to look for a complete consensus in a field of research that is still evolving, one cannot deny that the works that have been mentioned[184] occupy a central and strategic position for any reinterpretation of the metaphysical tradition. Heidegger's legacy can certainly be contested, here or elsewhere, but it has undoubtedly deeply transformed and enriched the French studies in the history of metaphysics.[185]

* * *

In what sense can the five inquiries that we have just conducted be said to have taken us to the crossroads? In no way exclusive from one another, they share many common points, and they do not refer to particular directions that would be exclusive from each other. Opening new paths for research, apart from the distraction of current events, they rather draw a topology that has very little to do with the early receptions of Heidegger's thought. Whether it concerns the appropriation of the two great traditions of the Western world, or the quest for a primordial ethics, or the difficult dialogue between the thought of being and a hermeneutic of action, or even the debate concerning the meaning of the sacred or the divine, or the reinterpretation of metaphysics as onto-theology, the work undertaken entailed the constant shifting of borders between the fields under consideration, as well as between the Heideggerian texts and the canonical texts of the tradition. And this thorough work escapes the more narrow problematic of the "reception" so as to converge and flow in directions we cannot yet entirely foresee. Between exegesis, ethics, hermeneutics, theology, and the history of philosophy, the crossings and the possible connections are so numerous that Heideggerian themes will bear fruit anew.[186]

Conclusion

It is the destiny of any philosophical thought, when it exceeds a certain degree of vigor and rigor, to be misunderstood by the contemporaries that it challenges.

—Jean Beaufret[1]

At the end of this study of a philosophical history that covers seven decades of our intellectual life, it is necessary to address the certainties, dissatisfactions, and perplexities, while remaining open to new developments.

With respect to the certainties, what has inspired us from the very beginning has been confirmed: the omnipresence in France of the influence, direct or indirect, of Heidegger's thought and work. Apart from the mathematical sciences and life and earth sciences, there is hardly any sector of knowledge or intellectual activity that has not been positively or negatively affected by that thought, at times marginally, often rhetorically, to be sure, but in an identifiable and significant sense, at least ideologically or negatively.

Furthermore, this omnipresence took place and spread only by diversifying itself: between existentialism and deconstruction, the critique of humanism and the renewal of the interpretation of metaphysics, to cite only the principal themes, one encounters the many faces of the "French Heidegger"! The development of our narrative has revealed that these different faces, far from having been sketched all at once, like cards thrown on a table, have emerged like unexpected masks in a drama that was intellectual, passionate, and often politicized. Like a mischievous ghost, Proteus, or evil genius, Heidegger continuously returned to the philosophical and ideological scene in new ways.

Did this happen by virtue of his own devices or thanks to his French friends or "accomplices"? It was due to both, and often concurrently. On the one hand, glorified as the great author of the master work *Being and Time,* Heidegger had not been inactive; we have followed him: attentive to the French audience, welcoming (literally and figuratively), and grasping the opportunities and the invitations extended or proposed to him—gestures that would have been less effective if they had not been sustained by a consistent work and a surprising capacity (almost up to the end of his long life, like Veronese, Goethe, Picasso, or Jünger)—to add new touches to the tableau of his thought, always reformulating, reproposing, and questioning. As for the French, it is clear that the "reception" would have been infinitely less influential if it had not been sustained and stimulated by the brightest minds, from Koyré to Levinas, from Beaufret to Birault, and from Merleau-Ponty to Derrida. This intellectual quality was also accompanied by inventiveness, for, even if at times there have been somewhat repetitive imitations, the philosophical history that we have reconstructed in no way could be reduced to a series of docile receptions (even if we have of course included in our account the strictest "orthodoxy"). Although that complex play of exchanges was often brilliant, it was also noisy, since we have seen the so-called media intervene. A preliminary hypothesis has been more than confirmed: one of the unique features of the French reception of Heidegger has been its nonacademic aspect. Heidegger has benefited from two antithetical "tracks": controversy and scholarship. Certainly, the *basso continuo* of the symphony of his reception, which at times was cacophonous, was indeed a sustained work of reading and commentary of texts, but not without a deep hostility and a stubborn resistance from influential members of the academic world (in a "climate of prohibition or intimidation that was somewhat hushed," according to Jean Beaufret).[2] And it was perhaps no accident that the patient and discreet efforts of some professors of preparatory classes[3] compensated for the reticence of the university, at least at first, because during the last three decades we have seen "Heideggerians" of diverse orientations progressively obtain university positions and responsibilities.[4] Whatever their titles or their positions, these great teachers were the mediators of Heidegger's reception in France: we can never sufficiently emphasize their influence on awakening and maintaining interest in Heidegger's thought. In the absence of the irreplaceable life of Socratic dialogue and pedagogy, that thought would have remained text-bound. In the first rank of these leading teacher-mediators were Beaufret, Birault, and Granel.[5] Our interviews have confirmed the decisive importance of these mediations and pedagogical transmissions, although there are some rare exceptions.[6]

With respect to the dissatisfactions, there is no reason to insist on the one that we must accept from the outset: one can never be certain, when it concerns such a complex and intertwined history, of not having missed something. The imperfections with regard to the understanding of the stakes would be more serious; but in this decisive matter, we cannot be both judge and judged. We have had nevertheless to constantly undertake a work of triage or selection of works and commentaries that seemed to us the most worthy of attention. And clearly, one will always be right to contest such emphases, such interpretations, or even, for example, to find that we have overly emphasized the critiques and the attacks on Heidegger, to the detriment of less sensational, more serious, and more careful readings of the texts. If this is the case, we accept this insufficiency while clarifying that it was not intentional. However, this objection requires the reexamination of a methodological problem that was noted at the beginning of the work: the very notion of "reception" presents us with a perspective that differs from that of the exegesis of the work itself. It is certainly unavoidable that paying attention to public reactions, polemics, and even echoes or "background noise" risks overshadowing the serious study of the texts. In spite of our efforts to find the right equilibrium, it is possible that the boat has been loaded too heavily on one side and that those most faithful to Heidegger's thinking would feel insufficiently recognized or praised. If such a situation turns out to be the case, it cannot be explained solely by the inevitable limitation of my personal point of view, but by some essential reasons: while the French reception has not lacked talent and creativity, nothing guarantees that a constant excellence in exegetical seriousness or careful listening will be the case. On the one hand, the proclaimed "faithfulness" cannot itself be a guarantee in the philosophical field where critical intelligence is no less important than the respect for the letter. On the other hand, the surprising developments that we have observed and described in the course of our study do not amount necessarily to a "deepening" of Heidegger's thought. Françoise Dastur even wrote: "Contrary to a widely accepted opinion, it is still in Germany, and not in France, the United States or elsewhere, that Heidegger is better read and understood."[7] Whether we agree with her or not, it is certain that this warning is useful: the "fireworks" of the most heated moments of the French reception can be misleading. There is also, where thought is concerned, a slow and more secret history, and its murmur must be heard in the background of the torrent of the present.

One dissatisfaction that is very clear and specific must also be taken into consideration: if by definition the author ("transmitter") is no longer present to censure the "receivers" (or the story of their misinterpretations, errors, or malevolence), at least we can place ourselves in his position by adopting the imperious posture of his highest ideals: to think the un-thought of metaphysics, to rise to the truth of being, to apprentice oneself to a new openness. These possibilities are always offered to us, so long as neither oppression nor inhumanity prevents us from having access to the best of that, though harbored in the folds of an immense work. The history that we have retraced is not intended as a substitute for the reading of and reflection on this corpus. Nor does it have to establish what should have been a better or ideal reception, and even less what it should be tomorrow. Were the mistakes or misunderstandings given too much attention at the expense of a more faithful listening? It would be no less illusory to believe that the intention of being faithful has always rendered one immune from mistakes and has not turned one against the author whom one wanted to understand or defend purely or unconditionally. It is important to move to another level: to appraise the path followed since the first readings of *Being and Time* and to determine the extent to which—in spite of so many tentative approaches or misunderstandings—the horizon of French thought has been modified so radically that any overly definitive "account" would be impossible.

The perplexities, finally, concern above all the judgments that will be numerous with respect to this history. In the face of innumerable difficulties, among which are so many misunderstandings, would one not be tempted to present a negative and disillusioned account, almost envying the *happy few* [TN: In English in the original] who, such as Régis Debray,[8] have (or claimed to have) escaped any influence, or any reading of Heidegger? He was not the only one among known French philosophers to have stayed away from any reception of Heidegger's thought: Clément Rosset and Michel Serres[9] are other examples. It would be ridiculous or inappropriate to apply to such free spirits a Heideggerian version of the well-known adage: "Outside the Church there is no salvation." Further, one should not support a statement such as Debray's without examination, especially if it means the rejection of an entire oeuvre: it suggests an attitude that is uncompromising and too polemical (even oppositional) to be acceptable as such. Should one feel relieved as a result of never having read Marx, under the pretext that he was unduly exploited by Stalinism? Or as a result of never having been moved by the spirit of the biblical message under the pretext that its history also includes the Inquisition? That would be to forget that risk is inherent in any intellectual exploration and that one must not give an account of an important thinking in the same way that one lists the inventory of a general's victories or of a politician's successes. Politics precisely—obviously—was and remains the Achilles' heel of Heidegger's thinking. Why? Due to its radicalism in the quest for origins? Due to its latent Platonism? Due to its excessive reliance on a certain idea of the Proper and of appropriation? Although it is fortunate that all these questions have been posed and are posed again, they should not prevent access to other resources in a work with multiple entries.

We have still not concluded with respect to the perplexities, and in particular with the importance that must be given to the fact that—in spite of the flow already noted of fascinations and passions—Heidegger remains a more or less discreet, yet persisting issue within our intellectual world. Thus, Alain Finkielkraut and Philippe Sollers, aware of going against the grain, claimed, each in his own way, Heideggerian inspirations. The first[10] has expressed it in a more discreet manner than the second, whose "new found allegiance" cannot completely erase the earlier incendiary declarations.[11]

Hence, Sollers, for example in *Studio*, referred to Heidegger as the only contemporary thinker to be in dialogue with Hölderlin and Rimbaud in the epoch of the devastation of the earth by technological nihilism. Certainly, it occurred to him to concede: "OK, fine, this kind of formulation is a bit solemn and heavy, nonetheless the (*other*) truth is there."[12] Later, he opened an issue of his journal *L'Infini* with an interview where he affirmed his debt with respect to Heidegger's *Nietzsche* ("a fundamental book that I refer to constantly") and deplored "the censorship to which Heidegger was subjected," which he attributed less to the political question than to the Heideggerian questioning of nihilism ("Heidegger's greatness was to have given thought to the exacerbation of European nihilism") and condemned the "Pavlovian movement" of the nihilists who were obsessively set against any sense of destiny, deaf to the thought of Heidegger as they are to great poetry.[13] It is precisely poetry that will now be addressed.

Thinking and Poetry: A Dialogue at the Summit

The last point evoked by Philippe Sollers indeed merits our full attention. The thinking of Heidegger II is distinguished by the decisive importance granted to poetic saying, but not to poetic saying understood simply as text or textual sequence. The poet, for Heidegger, is a partner of the thinker only insofar as he or she attains to the primordial by bringing it into language; this plunge into the "topology of being" is accomplished only by certain poets: Hölderlin,[14] first and foremost, but also Trakl, Rilke, Rimbaud,[15] and Char. It is by design that we just included two names of French poets in this prestigious list. First, in order to appreciate the full significance of a fact: although he has been reproached for the philosophical importance that he accords to his own language, Heidegger does not limit himself in this context to the German language: Nerval, Baudelaire, Mallarmé, and Valéry[16] were often on his desk.[17] Second, to address a difficulty that awaits us at the end of the present work: should we speak of a "reception" of Heidegger's thought on the part of René Char? Was there even a genuine dialogue between the poet and the thinker who became friends? Was this friendship casual, or did it convey a greater significance, one that goes beyond the personal case of René Char? Nothing guarantees that we can respond to these delicate questions completely or in a satisfactory manner. At least we must confront them.

The two first questions are connected: to respond "no" to the first and "yes" to the second is in no way a contradiction. There was no "reception" of Heidegger's thought by Char in the sense in which we spoke of "reception" in this work, that is to say, on the basis of philosophical analyses or commentaries. Char certainly read Heidegger, but he never wished to address him directly: rather than a "reception," it would be better to speak here of a silent listening. On the other hand, the second question ("was there a genuine dialogue?") calls for a positive response, at least at first. We have seen that Char, the "host" of the Thor Seminars, did not participate in the philosophical sessions.[18] At the meeting in 1966, there was nonetheless a dialogue on poetry concerning a citation from Rimbaud: "Poetry will not lend its rhythm with action. It *will be in advance*."[19]

With respect to this passage, it is the thinker who questioned the poet, whose text must be read carefully.

In his "Interrogative Responses to a Question from Martin Heidegger,"[20] René Char proceeded in small strokes: by way of forty short paragraphs that he presented as "various narrow paths" on the way toward a point of absolute justification "ahead of the word God." These are several ways of listening concerning the way poetry is in advance of action. Is a progression discernable between the first option, where poetry remains still in relation with action, guiding it, being its "mastermind," its edge, its sharp eye, and this "pure movement" that caused Rimbaud "to no longer feel nor want to be an artist"? What becomes clear at the end of the text is rather the very dated and determined political context in which Rimbaud's thought is inscribed. "From Rimbaud's perspective and that of the Commune, poetry will no longer serve the bourgeoisie, nor will it be its rhythm. It will be ahead, with the bourgeoisie the object of conquest. Poetry will then be its proper master, as it is master of its revolution; the starting signal given, the action envisaged constantly transformed into a *seeing* action."[21] These lines express in the best possible way the spirit of the brief attempt that Char did not want to present as an interpretation or a definitive reading, but rather as a set of "interrogative responses." It is important to note that he insisted, in concluding, on the political and revolutionary aspects of Rimbaud's words by alluding to "recent political actions" (no doubt he was thinking of his own protest against the installation of atomic weapons in the Albion plateau).[22]

We are fortunate to have a short text by Heidegger, written some years after the one written by Char in 1972, which also commented upon the same passage from Rimbaud. Heidegger does not allude to Char's "Interrogative Responses," but only to Char's introduction to *Pour Nous, Rimbaud*.[23] It was another poet, Roger Munier, who translated and published Heidegger's short text in the year of his death, entitled *"Aujourd'hui Rimbaud."*[24] Apart from these details, what matters is to characterize Heidegger's questions, and to establish whether they are similar to Char's. What is common to the two texts is obviously their interrogative character. However, after having praised what Char has said as groundbreaking [*Wegweisendes*],[25] Heidegger did not address in any way the historical and political context of Rimbaud's letter. He wondered, first, if "Action" simply means "acting" in the sense of *Handeln* or rather "reality in its totality," and then if "in advance" is to be understood temporally or beyond any human temporal relation. Given the development of industrial society in the modern age, was the primacy granted to poetry by Rimbaud an "error"? Referring to the letter Rimbaud sent to Izambard ("It is a question of reaching the unknown"[26]), Heidegger suggested that poetic saying "*names* the region" where the Unknown is near. "We can perhaps, by meditating on Rimbaud's word, say the following: the nearness of the inaccessible remains the region that is only reached by the few poets, and which they reveal in this way."[27] The poetic call would be "in advance" because it would already be an attuned belonging to the rhythm of the world, a rhythm that the Greeks had known. He cites two verses from Archilocus where *rythmos* is *Ver-Hältnis,* an attuned relation as well as a "reserve." One can henceforth pose the following question: "Will the word of the poet to come become a foundation on the basis of the jointure of this Relation and thus prepare the human being's new sojourn on earth?"[28] He concluded that Rimbaud remains *vivant* because he enables us to pose questions in the face of which one must remain silent in the most essential sense.

With respect to Rimbaud's saying, do the two responses—which are truly aporetic—allow us to speak of a genuine dialogue? By inquiring in this way, we do not intend to make a statement concerning the personal exchanges between Heidegger and Char: it is not for us to judge the quality or limits of a friendship whose authenticity has been confirmed, and we will not follow those who, adopting the point of view of the room servant of these great men, suspect Char and Heidegger of each having wished to profit from this mutual acquaintance (for the former, an exceptional recognition; for the latter an exoneration of his past politics). The question that on the contrary merits being examined, from the position where we intend to situate ourselves, concerns not the fact of a dialogue alone but its exemplary scope for any collaboration or confrontation between thought and poetry—and between two languages.

In fact, the relationship between Heidegger and Char was exemplary by virtue of a twofold difference: between the poet and the philosopher, and between French and German. It so happens that for Heidegger, there were two "models" in play, which far from contradicting one another, accommodate and reinforce each other: the model of mutual listening between French and Germans, outlined in the 1937 text, "Wege zur Ausprache,"[29] and the model of the assumed difference between Poetry and Thought (a thematic that was constantly addressed throughout the work of the later Heidegger). It happens that, as early as the 1937 text, the dialogue between the two languages and cultural traditions was envisaged not as a simple exchange of scientific information, but primarily in terms of the loftiest of spiritual tasks: "The fundamental form of mutual explication is the actual dialogue of the creators themselves in neighborly encounter."[30] At that time, Heidegger contemplated a dialogue between philosophers (from two traditions: the mathematical mastery of nature with Descartes and the Cartesians, and the meditation on the essence of history in German idealism). Then, on two occasions, he felt there were conditions that were favorable to the task: first, just after the war, thanks to the visit from this remarkable French philosopher, Jean Beaufret, who was determined to pursue an enduring dialogue beyond occasional visits, and then in the '50s, when he met René Char, thanks to Roger Munier and Jean Beaufret, a meeting that had already been suggested by Heidegger himself.

Whatever the circumstances were, these meetings were not the result of pure chance, since we just established that Heidegger had arranged in advance a "welcoming context" that responded to an essential necessity of his meditation on the history of the West. In this light, the dialogue with French thought in its twofold philosophical and poetic dimension took on a striking significance that forces us to rethink the excessively unilateral theme of the "reception," not only because it was infinitely more complex than a series of "reactions," but also because it was conditioned and in a way defined by a preliminary listening and expectation of the author himself. The examples of two great Germans influenced by French culture and by the spirit of its language, namely, Leibniz and Nietzsche, were constantly on Heidegger's mind. Thus it would be a complete error to depict Heidegger as enclosed and entrenched in the fortress of the German language, deaf to all that is not Germanic.

One would be right to object that, in spite of the nobility of such a conception of a mutual dialogue, its practice remained highly stylized, and that there was an emphatic sacralization that Daniel Payot brought out in the entirety of Heidegger's thinking of art.[31] Indeed, to return to its operation at the frontier of philosophical thinking and of poetry, particularly with Char, have we not begun to notice an undeniable difference in the approach to reading Rimbaud's saying: "Poetry will not lend its rhythm with action. It *will be in advance*"? Whoever rereads the two celebrated letters of May 13 and 15, 1871, cannot fail to be struck by the insolent tone ("Now, I am degrading myself as much as possible";[32] "one has to be an academician—deader than a fossil"[33]), by the revolutionary and antibourgeois fire ("mad anger drives me toward the battle of Paris"[34]), and by the extremism of "the derangement of *all the senses*,"[35] which was meant to lead to a poetic vision. Now, all these features, which were up to that point qualified as "context," in a somewhat understated way, are absolutely ignored in Heidegger's text, whose listening ennobles and purifies the poet to such an extent that Rimbaud joins Trakl (named at the end of the text) in a Region [*Gegend*] bordered by the most disincarnate silence. Char, on the contrary, restored to Rimbaud's vision its revolutionary élan, and it is he who has written, without doubt, the most unforgettable pages on Rimbaud. "With Rimbaud, *diction* precedes *contradiction* with an *adieu*. Its discovery, its incendiary date is its rapidity."[36] Char, "absolutely modern" like Rimbaud, saw him as diametrically opposed to any return to an origin: "This hope of return is the worst perversion of Western culture, its most insane aberration. Seeking to return to the sources and to renew oneself there only worsens the paralysis, only precipitates the fall and absurdly punishes its blood."[37]

To take note of the incontestable difference between the two readings of Rimbaud should not lead us to deny either the existence or the significance of a "dialogue" that one must never confuse with the conflation of the two positions. It remains that beyond the difference in the ways of listening to Rimbaud, beyond the exchange of poems or dedications,[38] beyond any question of influence, we can still legitimately inquire about what intertwines and yet nevertheless profoundly separates the poet Char from the thinker Heidegger.

Once one admits that this type of inquiry entails risks and perils with respect to interpretation, and with the constant awareness of the radical differences of languages, styles, and methods (or their absence), on what terrain does one advance? If we focus prudently on the matter of "sensitivity" alone, we discern two quite different and even antithetical approaches of the question: one conciliatory and the other conflictual.

From "The Interview under the Chestnut Tree,"[39] to his posthumous work, Jean Beaufret remained faithful to the first approach. Not that he wished to minimize the differences between the thinker and the poet. But they became definitively emblematic of a symbolic relation in which each plays his part, and expresses his signs on his own terms. Each followed his own path (we have seen the extent to which Char appreciated the fact that the philosopher did not give him any lessons). The citations of Char, the new Heraclitus, came to illustrate, emphasize, and inspire the texts of his friends the philosophers. This was not always reciprocated: Char responded only through poems, which were always addressed to Heidegger personally, and never dared to comment or even use a sentence from Heidegger, even when he dedicated the magnificent "old Impressions" to him, which he situated "at the intersection of an enduring reading, according to Jean Beaufret, of the great texts of Heidegger."[40] On the "fundamentals," the agreement seemed perfect, apart from any philosophical analysis.

Paul Veyne proposed an approach that was radically antithetical to this relation. If it merits our attention, it is not only because of the force of its critique, but above all because it was nourished by Char's texts. A few words from the poet set the tone: "I have nothing to say about Heidegger's philosophy. I am a poet, not a philosopher writing poetry; Parmenides and Plato have no place here."[41] It is necessary to return to the texts with Paul Veyne to discover a poet of ecstasis, guided in the "talismanic night" by a merciless illumination, with no possibility of gathering or consolation of a religious kind: "Lightning and blood, I have discovered, are one."[42] In the confrontation with the great natural and cosmic forces, Char's extraordinary sensitivity to the elements leads neither to God nor to being, but toward the "unknown" or to the "open void" [*vide frais*]: there is no Origin; there is, faced with the Void, our transcending without return.[43] Char himself designated his grand "predecessors" (Isaiah, Heraclitus, Villon, Hölderlin, Baudelaire, Nietzsche, Melville stand out in a sumptuous cortege that cannot be summarized here[44]), but we should not forget that in addition to Teresa of Avila, there is also Sade, because "flagellated beauty in turn tortures."[45]

Faced with this direct confrontation, one is tempted to wonder: who is the "true" Char. The question is obviously badly posed. In the same way, with Heidegger, it would be futile to overly insist on stabilizing a complex relation that one would have to be able to analyze in all of its harmonics. (Paul Veyne himself recognized, in spite of his insistence on the radical divide that separates them, that points of convergence are apparent between the poet and the thinker with respect to the dangers of modern technology, the openness to and respect for nature, and the possibility of an "entirely other" future civilization).

But there is an even more important question in the domain that occupies us here: have the "summit meetings" between Char and Heidegger been instructive, or, in more appropriate terms, have they ploughed a furrow where other thinkers and poets can come to sow? One can only respond cautiously to such a question. But it certainly seems that the Char–Heidegger "dialogue" had an exceptional character. Prévert, Saint-John Perse, Ponge, Bonnefoy, Réda, Roubaud, and many others have worked apart from the Heideggerian path. Jacottet as well.[46] Munier found a personal style of "poetic thinking" that bridges poetry and philosophy.[47] For his part, Michel Deguy did not hide his skepticism: to the question as to whether he shared Heidegger's conception of a dialogue between poetry and thought, illustrated by the relation between Char and Heidegger, he responded negatively and categorically: "I have never taken that seriously! Really, never! It is truly for show!"[48]

This, even if negatively, invites us to recognize and respect the absolute singularity of the encounter between Heidegger and Char—whether it inspires us or not. Is it not also finally in terms of singularity that it would be necessary to rethink the entirety of the tracks we have tried to retrace? Unless one adopts a theoretical position that frees philosophy from the "poeticizing suture" that was Heidegger's "stroke of genius." Let us turn now to the surprising thesis of Alain Badiou.[49] It recognizes the power of Heidegger's thought insofar as it combines a radical critique of objectivism (without falling into subjectivism) with an exceptional openness to the epochal significance of poetry: "The existence of the poets gave to Heidegger's thinking, something without which it would have been aporetic and hopeless, a ground of historicity, actuality, apt to confer to it—once the mirage of a political historicity had been concretized and dissolved in the Nazi horror—what was to be its unique, real occurrence."[50] But the "age of the poets" has ended, and the disorientation of our epoch can be addressed. Henceforth, the philosophical renewal that Badiou proposes (a Platonism of the multiple) comes to contradict, word for word, and feature for feature, the Heideggerian "commonplace,"[51] which was both praised as the pivot of contemporary thought and refuted (not without some moments of irritation or contempt).[52]

At a less theoretical level, our narrative, as any history, had to anchor itself in the proven facts, in the known tracks, in sum, in the archives worthy of attention. But there is also a secret history that risks frustrating the historian while encouraging more adventurous or inquisitive narrators, the allegedly perspicacious hermeneutists. We find this in a study entitled *Heidegger's Hidden Sources*[53]—still untranslated in French—whose author shows convincingly that the relation of Heideggerian thought to Far Eastern inspirations is much more decisive than the few references in his work to the *Tao* would suggest.[54] Although Heidegger was a disconcerting thinker with more than one secret garden, it cannot be denied that there is no mechanical imitation or simple reception among the most inventive French authors. It is as if they implicitly decided to take up the gauntlet and to be no less enigmatic than the Oracle of Freiburg. Was this an intellectual posturing or a thinker's passion? It is in that very enigma that a "French exception"—which is perhaps in the process of extinguishing itself—resides.

The End of the French Exception?

The French exception, with respect to Heidegger, has often been perceived abroad as excessively generous toward the author and overly fascinated with the work. We find unexpected testimonies concerning this fascination. Catherine Clément, an *agrégée de philosophie* who became an essayist and novelist, found a source of inspiration in the love between Hannah Arendt, a student who was at the time eighteen years of age, and her professor Martin Heidegger, almost twenty years her senior. In fact, *Martin et Hannah*[55] includes another key figure, Elfriede, the faithful and vigilant wife, who became, in spite of herself, the rival of Hannah. Arendt's last visit to the ailing philosopher in 1975 inspired a novel woven from contrasting biographical retrospectives: fifty years of passion, misunderstandings, and friendship, between the great philosopher whose destiny was to be forever marred by his Nazi foray, the brilliant intellectual Jewish exile—and Elfriede, who would finally, although not without reticence, understand and forgive.

In other venues, inquisitive minds would hardly recognize the allure and the profile of the Master in the mechanical and machine-like form of *Les Philosophes* by Jean Tinguely,[56] and would discover Heidegger's name even more unexpectedly in the comic book section. The cover of the comic book *Agrippine,* by Claire Brétecher,[57] shows the heroine, a post-68 intellectual, dressed in jeans with holes, comfortably seated between cushions, wearing a Walkman, reading (quite obviously proud of herself) *Heidegger au Congo.* This "intellectual" remake of *Tintin au Congo* (incidentally, Hergé's most—naively?—colonialist and paternalistic comic book) was missed by most, whether Heideggerians or Tintin enthusiasts. In an African setting, one discerns on the cover of *Heidegger au Congo* a little man with glasses and a moustache, who is clearly much older that Tintin, and who—obviously—depicts the Master of Freiburg as those on the left bank would imagine him. There would be no further mention of Heidegger in *Agrippine.* Neither philosophers nor Brétecher's readers (at times one and the same) complained about it. While one does not care to exaggerate this furtive appearance of Heidegger's name in this context, at least one can note that it constituted a minuscule trace, among many other no doubt more interesting celebrity publications representing an intellectual snobbery that is difficult to find anywhere but in France—and is perhaps in the process of disappearing.

In what other country in the world could these intrusions of the name and personage of Heidegger on the public stage be possible? Abroad, one is especially surprised to observe that this infatuation—far from being fleeting—has persisted and has undergone unexpected developments during more than half a century. Among discerning minds, surprise has often given way to scandalized incomprehension. Thus, Raymond Klibansky has expressed this sentiment (widely shared abroad, but also previously by quite distinguished French intellectuals, from Éric Weil to Raymond Aron, from Gaston Fessard to Gabriel Marcel). Alluding to Heidegger's statements in favor of Hitler in 1933, he indicated:

> For a long time in France, where Heidegger had many fervent disciples, an effort was made to understand all these facts as a temporary aberration. It shows that nothing has been understood. . . . Future historians will no doubt need to explain how this philosophy could have exercised such a profound influence on the countries where Romance Languages were spoken. Will one not recognize, in the submission to a thinker for whom philosophy only speaks Greek and German, the abandonment of the great traditions of the past, and a sign of weakness among many authors after the war? One will note with satisfaction that, as for the young generation in Germany, in France or elsewhere, the sobriety of critical thinking has won the day in philosophical discussions.[58]

Although we do not agree with all these formulations (we will explain why), this citation deserves to be scrupulously examined, if only because of the justified summons it addresses to the "future historian." Our work has been an effort to respond to such summons and to better understand the reasons for the fascination exercised by Heidegger on French thought. One of the lessons of our exploration of more than fifty years of intellectual life is now apparent: the French reception of Heidegger, in its meanderings and in its variety, can in no way be confused (except no doubt for a small group of the faithful) with a "submission" to a monolithic thought. With respect to the "transmitter" as well as the "receivers," things have been much more fluid and subtle (it would also necessary to take account of the impact, a posteriori, of the French reception of the German reading of Heidegger).[59] If there were several distinct "waves" of reception of this philosophy, was it not due to the very virtue of the capacity for evolution and renewal of that very thought? The existentialist enthusiasm (but also criticism and polemic) have followed the pioneering discoveries of the thirties. However, had there not been a "Heidegger II" (of the "Letter on Humanism," of *Holzwege*, etc.), the intellectual curiosity engendered by the work would have dissipated. Let us consider also the *Nietzsche* volumes, which gave, rightly or wrongly at the time,[60] the impression that Heidegger was the only one to have proposed a full interpretation of Nietzsche's genius. These examples (which in no way claim to exhaustively recapitulate our own "narrative") show clearly that one cannot maintain the superficial thesis of an "aberration" or of a quasi-pathological and extended "weakness" of the French mind. Has Heidegger written these great texts or not? Has he himself not provided the example of a renewal, at any rate of a sustained effort constantly encouraging thoughtfulness and critical thinking (and this to a greater extent than his censors recognized, who themselves, all too often, have not read him closely enough—or stopped reading him altogether—at a certain point of saturation or rejection)?

It is necessary, however, to concede an important point to Raymond Klibansky, and that point can enable a historian to better explain the very influence of "Heidegger II": the tolerance (or leniency) first manifested with respect to the engagement of 1933 led to a favorable disposition toward new publications. The thesis of a "temporary aberration" quite obviously had taken on a strategic value whose positive effects (from the point of view of the reception of Heidegger's thought) have lasted up to the death of the philosopher and perhaps even up to the publication of Farias's book. Let us imagine, indeed, that all the texts, all the documents that confirm the depth of the involvement of 1933 (and then the continued idealization of the "movement") had been known, translated, and distributed in their entirety after Liberation. Would the welcome given to the new translations in the 1950s and '60s have been the same? Certainly Éric Weil wrote something crucial at that time; but few read that work . . .

Such an approach has obvious limits; it remains too external to the very quality of the work. And this implies (in relation to the opinion formulated by Raymond Klibansky, and with all due respect to this great figure of the history of ideas) a disagreement that is no longer a matter for a historian. Is one right or wrong to consider Heidegger as a great thinker or at least as an important philosopher? Only the critical reading of these texts can settle this question. And this is exactly what Éric Weil concluded, for his part, at least in 1947, recognizing Heidegger's importance without approving his theses, but wary of ostracizing him.

Finally, even without sharing his philosophical judgment, one must be willing to concede another point to Klibansky—this one more factual—concerning the orientation of the young generation in and outside of France. Although it is always risky to pass judgment too quickly (and "without distance") on a generation, it indeed seems that young students today are attached to values and methods that are safer and more traditional than those associated with Heidegger's "hermeneutic violence." Above all, what seems undeniable is that the French situation no longer seems fundamentally different from that of the leading developed countries: Heidegger has become (or tends to become) one thinker among others in a complex landscape where historiographical and critical tasks overshadow theoretical enthusiasms. In fact, the French exception was in large part due to an extreme "ideologization" of philosophy: Marxism played, in this respect, a provocative role, which was both positive and negative. What seems particularly outdated is "the very French conjunction of a more or less ideological Heideggerianism with a kind of Marxism, as well as with a kind of Freudianism."[61] As soon as there is no longer a dominant ideology, where even the interest in the debate of ideas erodes (because the overriding concern is to insert oneself in a market society), one finds oneself in a sort of American situation: tolerance allows for many opinions; the development of the society favors a myriad of specialized studies; but indifference becomes the fate of the great majority. No doubt France still publishes (but for how long?) large print runs for two or three philosophers, but provided they are sufficiently "popularized" by the media and that their discourses are concerned with the most current ethical and political problems. These conditions are functionally different from those that prevailed during the decades that we have studied (at least up to 1990); they are, in any case, less favorable (even without taking account of the political question) to the renewal of a fascination for an important, demanding, and somewhat esoteric thinker. Even Wittgenstein, in spite of the relative favor he enjoys, does not seem able to replace Heidegger on the French intellectual scene in a comparable way.

One thing is certain: the time of leniency is over; the tendency would rather be the opposite: there is a generalized mistrust that risks giving Heidegger the ambivalent and almost contradictory status of an author who is both canonical and "cursed." While we are wary of formulating prognoses, which is always problematic, it seems now unlikely that there will be a shift in favor of a "leading thinker," whoever he or she may be; and the brilliant or disconcerting pages from the years of fascination with Heidegger seem definitively to have been turned. One can find an objective confirmation of this in the print run of the principal translations of Heidegger published by Gallimard. On the one hand, this examination reveals that Heidegger is not an author who is as "popular" as Nietzsche, since the most widely distributed pocket edition of one of his works, *Chemins qui ne mènent nulle part,* has not achieved even a sixth of the sales of *The Genealogy of Morals.*[62] The degree of difficulty of the two works is certainly not comparable, but the gap between the two authors is considerable.[63] On the other hand, the sales figures of two translations, *Écrits politiques* and *Correspondance avec Jaspers* (less technical texts with titles that would have provoked enthusiasm in another time, or at least a certain public curiosity) are respectable, but no more than that, for such a famous author.[64]

By echoing a severe judgment on these decades, we have not wished to give in to the least complacency. Our right (and even our duty) is to assume a different position, a position that has continued to take form and consistency throughout this philosophical history: if the proliferation of different forms of "Heideggerianism" has led to inevitable excess (or waste, or remains, according to the case), it has also allowed or engendered, directly or indirectly, creative transplants, some of which have still not been completely assimilated or "digested." From Sartre to Levinas, by way of Lacan and Derrida, "the French Heidegger" will have been a unique catalyst, and extraordinarily provocative: master of some, "overseer" [*contremaître*][65] of others. And what is necessary to emphasize is that French thought has been able to reverse the role that Heidegger, in a very classical manner, had assigned to it:[66] namely, to be the inheritor and representative of the great rationalism of the seventeenth century. Not only did it no longer hold this position, but it had the audacity of asking Heidegger himself questions that made him appear retrospectively as still too metaphysical, rational, attached to the Proper (whether in the form of language, homeland, or authenticity) and closed to the call of the wholly Other. Welcomed as nowhere else, Heidegger's thought has also been intensely interrogated, contested, and put into question. One could even apply a strictly critical grid to our narrative that would reveal the progress and even accumulation of resistances to Heidegger in French thought: Marxist objections as early as the '30s, spiritualist reservations, Sartrean Cartesianism, merciless sociolinguistic critiques (from Faye to Bourdieu and Meschonnic), the denunciation of Heideggerian "antimodernism" (by Ferry and Renaut), numerous displacements undertaken by the deconstructive movement, and the ethical protest against the "neutrality" of ontology, and so on. It is impossible to lay out so briefly an exhaustive treatment of the salient points of French thought engaged with Heidegger! This singularly complicates the schema according to which contemporary French philosophy would be but a series of hasty misunderstandings of Heidegger's true thinking,[67] a judgment that coincides paradoxically with certain views of the master himself and his closest disciples. However, although it is true that from the "Letter on Humanism"[68] to *On Time and Being*,[69] Heidegger sought to correct some errors or misunderstandings that originated in France, he precisely did so for the benefit of the French because he appreciated their capacity for listening. Was it an eminently ambiguous, "self-serving" gesture, seeking recognition? No doubt. He may even have thought what François Vezin went so far as to write: Sartre would have been better off translating *Sein und Zeit* than publishing *Being and Nothingness*![70] My disagreement with this sort of judgment does not concern the fact that the French readings had often been imperfect, or wrong, but concerns the interpretation of these "deviations." If Heidegger's adversaries maintained that the misunderstandings have allowed the French to "save" the thinker on several occasions, the "orthodox," for their part, boast of "saving" his reading from any misappropriations. But this would mean remaining in a game of "for" and "against." Heidegger's thought is caught in a tug of war. Our point of view is quite different: it is not a question of protecting Heidegger's work or of restoring its cursed authenticity, but of appraising (and not judging definitively) its surprisingly catalytic power. Whether one laments it or not, without Heidegger, works as original as *Being and Nothingness, Totality and*

Infinity, and *Writing and Difference* would not have been what they are. Should they only be conceived according to whether or not they are literally faithful to Heidegger? Are we forced to neglect their innovative contributions, including their "misunderstandings" (voluntary or involuntary) with respect to the Master of Freiburg? There is little doubt that he remained quite skeptical toward the free interpretations and "creative contestations" of his work in France. But skepticism does not mean indifference. Whether the attention accorded by Heidegger to the French was a tactical ruse or a sincere consideration (the two hypotheses are not mutually exclusive), it would be more fruitful for the work of thinking to adopt a vision less connected with the very person of the thinker as a person, and more open to the questions and the promises of his work, at times in spite of its intentions. In this respect, one could almost apply to the French reception of Heidegger's thought one of the conclusions of a similar research conducted by Jacques le Rider with respect to the French readings of Nietzsche: "In every case, French intellectuals have found the material for the definition of their own identity in Nietzsche, while the importation led to a transformation so profound that the French Nietzsche ended up appearing as a stranger in his own country."[71] Can one even go as far as to claim that, in both cases, "the history of interpretations henceforth belongs to the work itself?"[72] Even if this is an assumption that is more Nietzschean than Heideggerian, it poses an essential question with respect to the "re-transference" in Germany, and to the entirety of the "transferences" effectuated in France on the basis of Heidegger's work—a question that doubly exceeds (both geographically and chronologically) the present research.

Certainly, one has the right not to "agree" and to be negative about the truth or relevance of the creative grafts or contestations in the heyday of the French reception. But we will not confuse the salutary exercise of critical thinking with a sweeping censorship of the existentialist and/or "postmodern irrationalism." Notwithstanding the proponents of a *philosophical correctness* [TN: In English in the original] who reject any recourse to Heidegger's thought as irrational or aberrant (even attempting to censor the very mention of it), we believe that the French reception of this thought testifies, in its better moments, to the alliance of critical thinking and creativity.

Has this corrosive fecundity, so characteristic of what was the vitality of French intelligence, evaporated? Between the requirements of formal rigor and the openness to the most audacious intellectual provocations, it should still be possible to find a balance and thus to protect the potential of future thought and apply a reasoned judgment on the "Heidegger years" of French thought. Such were already the goals of a conference held in 1989 at the Collège International de Philosophie entitled "Thinking after Heidegger," where the French were in the minority: to break with any devotion or complacency toward Heidegger, to rise to the challenge of his thought while renouncing the "splendid isolation"[73] of

French philosophy, for example to study the major French readers of Heidegger (from Sartre to Derrida) in solidarity with Adorno and other thinkers supposed to be "adversaries" of the Master—in short, to adopt a resolutely critical and open approach. Consequently, we were told at the beginning of the conference: "We do not have to be ashamed of the French Heidegger."[74]

It is paradoxically at the very moment when one wants to bid *adieu* to this "French Heidegger"—so proteiform—that certain of his traits (and his qualities) impose themselves with the utmost clarity and brio: with Badiou, in order to recast the topology of relations between poetry and thinking;[75] with Granel, to rethink the presuppositions of the formalism and of the "logical gesture";[76] with Schürmann, to subordinate the eventual singularization of being to the twofold normative constraint of tragic knowledge.[77]

Each of these areas opens a new project on the basis of Heidegger's work, and no longer in the folds of the interpretation (or self-interpretation) of his work. Such fruitfulness is resisted both by the "orthodox" partisans and by the determined adversaries. We cannot, for now, do more than indicate its promises while also returning to a "fallback position" that is difficult to challenge. We have established, in fact, that in the context of the university it was certainly in the renewal of interest in the study of the history of philosophy that Heidegger's influence could not be disputed. The question of the unity and structure of metaphysics as "onto-theology" has formed the core of more than one good thesis. In this respect, the incompatibility that Raymond Klibansky discerned between the passion for Heidegger and the patient exercise of critical thinking seems quite unlikely. Our research confirms the opposite: the "French Heidegger" is for the most part a "critical Heidegger" (with all the ambiguity contained in this expression). What has nourished the interest and the passion for this work, despite its difficulty, is its resources first, for contesting the essentialist and idealistic tradition, and second, for the deconstruction of metaphysics as such. Even today, the opposition to globalization can find resources in the Heideggerian questioning of a technological and productivist imperialism; and at the more classical level of the studies of the history of philosophy, one is correct to conclude that the *Gesamtausgabe*—far from being completely translated into French—contains immense critical resources.[78]

Other elements that are relatively marginal but not insignificant must also be taken into account. On the one hand, the translations of the *Gesamtausgabe* do not have the spectacular or radically new character offered by the most noteworthy publications over the last half-century (however, some volumes should be distinguished from others, such as the *Sophist,* and above all the formidable volume *Contributions to Philosophy*). On the other hand, the least that one can say is that the work has not made much progress: it is far from following the pace of the *Gesamtausgabe* itself (at times producing two or three volumes per year).[79]

Above all, François Fédier, who supervises the whole project at the publishing house Gallimard, clearly intends to impose his own conception of translation. Taking on the translation of the *Beiträge* himself, he does not hesitate to propose an esoteric approach, proclaiming at the outset, "One must not fear *being misunderstood*,"[80] contesting the view that philosophy would be "*translatable* as such,"[81] and defending Vezin's translation of *Being and Time* in the strongest terms. Furthermore, Fédier has been true to his words by publishing a sample of his translation of some of the paragraphs of the *Beiträge*:[82] no effort was made to render the text intelligible to the French reader; quite the opposite. This partial publication confirms the intransigence of the previous declaration: both have the merit of clarity with respect to the pursuit of a deliberate politics of esotericism,[83] the principal effect of which has already been stated: the systematic marginalization of Heidegger's thought. If one had wanted to achieve this goal, one could not have done any better.

One final word on this issue at the conclusion of this work, that is to say, on the crucial question of translations. Beyond personal preferences or unavoidable discussions on particular translation choices, we have seen the debate focusing explicitly or implicitly on the following alternative: readability or faithfulness. Let us be clear: the partisans of readability in no way mean to sacrifice faithfulness, but they maintain—conforming to the grand classical tradition of translation—that the result must be as intelligible as possible in the recipient language, whose spirit must be respected; the inverse conception openly sacrifices readability and intelligibility to an attitude that claims to be the most faithful, by seeking, thanks to some "inventions," to follow Heidegger in his remarkable work on language. Faithfulness or fetishism? An outside observer, shall we say from Sirius, who would not have lost all common sense during his or her voyage in space, would no doubt wonder why a serene discussion is not possible in such a delicate domain where the interest in a great work should outweigh all other considerations. It is moreover in this direction that Heidegger himself seemed to tend shortly before his death, if one is to believe Roger Munier: Heidegger supported the idea of a working group open to all translators. Any dogmatism, any argument from authority, and any cliques were to be excluded. Nothing would be more absurd than to decree once and for all that one translation is better than the others because it was done by a friend, or to exclude even the mention of a translation simply because its author has been "excommunicated." This nevertheless is what happened. Our observer from Sirius would note that Heidegger's work seems to have encouraged the profusion of bizarre words, of overly stylized renderings and neologisms in French, whereas the majority of the key words in his work (*Dasein, Sein, Zeit, Zeug, Grund, Abgrund, Ereignis*, and even *Machenschaft* or *Gestell*) are not neologisms, but ordinary terms that he infused with new meaning. Logically, it would be necessary to translate them by terms that are as ordinary, even if accompanied by quotation marks. Is there no alternative to the esoteric approach? Indeed there is. Can it be avoided? Yes. The best example is the existence of André Préau's translations, which are sober, readable, and were approved by Heidegger himself as well as by Jean Beaufret. Nevertheless, neither *Essais et Conférences* nor *Le Principe de Raison* is a work that is easier than others. Why would it not be possible to work in the same spirit rather than rendering Heidegger incomprehensible, indeed ridiculous, under the pretext of being unerringly faithful? "These champions of the indecipherable translation have nevertheless an incontestable advantage over my other disciples, my brilliant Parisian admirers! Because it is to them and them alone that belongs the honor of having rendered me incomprehensible." It is in this way that Lacoue-Labarthe puts words in Heidegger's mouth through his theatrical mask.[84] No one will ever know if the "true" Master considered this.

To return to more prosaic observations, a survey of the French translations completed during the recent decades proves instructive.[85] If one attends, for example, to the published volumes, while excluding the re-editions, one has the confirmation that the existentialist reception of Heidegger was done on a very thin textual basis (given that the greatest part of the public reads only translations and that the good Germanists constitute—even among the philosophers—what was quite a limited group); one then notes a blooming of important translations from 1950 to 1960, which indeed corresponds—at least in part—to the "bright spell" that we have noted. Was it a countereffect of the events of '68 or rather of the structuralist wave?[86] Or was it perhaps the countereffect of the relative saturation of the pool of texts? One witnesses a certain diminution in the number of translations in the '70s. On the contrary, the renewal of work was impressive in the '80s and continued more modestly in the '90s. It is as if the "affair" had been a reply to the renewed interest in Heidegger studies and to a new passion for Heidegger. The number of publications during the 1990s in no way suggested a collapse, but the gap widened between the rhythm of the publication of the volumes of the *Gesamtausgabe* and the quite slow pace of translations in the series of the *Œuvres Complètes* published by Gallimard.[87] If it is to be expected that such a gap exists, given the constraints and the specific translation difficulties when it comes to Heidegger's texts, it is necessary to note that the gap is considerable, since today more than thirty volumes await publication in French.[88]

Before taking leave of the reader, it seems interesting to dwell a bit longer on the singularity of this intellectual adventure called "Heidegger in France" in order to assemble an interpretation that is closest to the thinker himself, who, as we indicated, expressed a "divine surprise" at his French success. Jean Beaufret, who replied thirty years later to the text that Heidegger devoted in 1937 to the French-German dialogue,[89] looked back with satisfaction on the path and the recognition obtained from the Master himself: "The notion that the relation of your own thought with France and the French was something essential—probably more essential than with other European or wider encounters—seemed to have come to you slowly. What was remarkable here was that a few individuals from an apparently frivolous people worked to understand your discourse, which at the outset, appeared quite strange to them. Some are still surprised by that, not always among your friends."[90] Beaufret then alluded to the many years of apprenticeship that it took him to begin to understand Heidegger and the "enormity"[91] of his work (as he himself said at times, half-joking about it).

To these touching and nostalgic memories, one may counter with the severe and even sarcastic predictions of a "progressive collapse of Heidegger's heritage and its various epigones"[92] by discerning one of the opportunities offered to future thought therein. There is, at times, in the proclamation of such "facts," a great degree of *wishful thinking* [TN: In English in the original]. It goes without saying that the author of these lines is not above such wishful thinking in spite of his concern for balance and impartiality.

What is actually the case? What has appeared incontestable to us is that the ideological and personalized fascination that marked the first decades of Heidegger's reception in France has faded. It would still be necessary to recognize the numerous "remnants" of this fascination, which turn into gestures of conjuration that are destined to exorcize the ghost: the fascination persists, but often in a negative form,[93] cultivating fantasies of rejection, or even clichés demonizing Martin the Cursed One. I will cite an example of this drawn from a literary review. In *Le Monde des Livres*, October 29, 1999, although no article or book was devoted to Heidegger, we find two important allusions in two interviews. Incidentally, the first was both beautiful and touching and concerned the memoires of Georges-Arthur Goldschmidt:[94] nothing there relates to the thought of Martin Heidegger, but the latter popped up suddenly like a jack-in-the-box with the reference to the "arrogant denigration of the French language" by certain French intellectuals, who "threw themselves into the arms of the Nazi militant par excellence: Martin Heidegger."[95] Some pages later in the same publication, Alain Renaut, questioned on the "Resources of Political Liberalism," specified that one of the volumes of his *Histoire de la Philosophie Politique*[96] is entirely devoted "to an analysis of the assaults that political rationality receives from thinkers like Heidegger, and from which, to a certain extent, political rationality has not recovered."[97] Was the "Heidegger shock" so powerful that "political rationality" still suffers from it and that at the slightest opportunity the polemic starts again? We will not discuss the pertinence of the judgments just cited, including among many others that it would have been tedious to list; they testify to the tenacious permanence of the figure of Heidegger in the French intellectual and philosophical landscape, even if negative comments seem henceforth to prevail.

Concerning "the heritage" itself, envisaged according to the different forms of a positive reappropriation, things are less clear, first for the simple reason that it is necessary at the outset to agree on the inventory, insofar as this project makes sense, which does not go without saying; second, because it is necessary to take account of the multiform penetration of Heideggerian themes into contemporary philosophy, such that the desire "to turn the page" does not itself guarantee a "total decontamination"; finally, and this is perhaps the most decisive argument for avoiding any triumphalism or doom-mongering, we are too close to "the topic"; the chronological distance is still not sufficient to draw a definitive conclusion from a story that is still too recent[98] and that remains profoundly contemporary: we are all, in different ways, both judge and judged in this affair, insofar as the debates of the twentieth century still concern us . . .

It cannot be excluded, in any case, that the intellectual and philosophical horizon changes even more radically with the progress of the new century. Globalization also bears on the reception of Heidegger. Thus there already exists an American translation of the *Beiträge*,[99] and in July 2000 an intensive seminar, exclusively devoted to this work, was organized in English.[100] The Far East should not be forgotten; even if our narcissism should suffer from it, let us be aware that there are more publications on Heidegger in Japan than in the rest of the world and that *Sein und Zeit* has been translated there in six different versions (the first appeared in 1939, almost fifty years before the first French translation).[101]

The interest in the singularity of the French reception does certainly not imply closure to other, at times neighboring, horizons,[102] or that one must exclude the possibility that radical mutations could emerge elsewhere (Germany itself, since the death of Heidegger, no longer seems to be what it had been for two centuries, the country of great philosophy). If the intellectual landscape has changed completely, this transformation should not be limited to France. At least the awareness that an important page of philosophical history seemed to have been turned nourishes the hope that our historical research and analysis would not turn out to be fruitless. Each one will judge the result for him- or herself. The precious and fragile thread that connects us to the reader, and that we wish to share with him or her, is nothing other than philosophical thinking itself, in its always renewed capacity for free questioning within (and without) Heidegger's work. We would not have undertaken this work, we would not have taken it to its conclusion, if this free inquiry and this conviction had not constantly accompanied and sustained us—along with their difficulties, but also with their participation in truth. As much as a thinker can be criticized, it is at least necessary to respect the fact that he or she makes us think. Reading him or her is the first respect that we owe him or her and that we owe ourselves, such that the sovereign exercise of free spiritual choice be made in complete lucidity.

A Singular Philosophy and Its Future

In closing, let us consider a few hopeful signs. It would be risky to make too many predictions. After all, that was not our intention. One comment is at least necessary: with the publication of the *Gesamtausgabe*, the moment of erudition and specialization has arrived. Heidegger, who is now recognized, is also on bookshelves. Just as a *grande dame* who has aged and is less courted, this work no longer provokes in a comparable way mannerisms, passion, indeed aberrations, as did the most surprising years of the French reception. From conferences to historical studies, this work now pays the price of its fame: it has been, is, will be, emptied out, dissected, analyzed, objectified, archived: having become a cultural object, it no longer really seems a path that is as adventurous as it once was for many. The work is becoming the object of a specialization among others: this is an unavoidable development that would be a mistake to lament. This is a fact and a feature of our time. Should we whisper, *'Tis your own fault, Georges Dandin,* in the shadow of the Master who has allowed his "tomb" to be erected (in the form of the *Gesamtausgabe*), which he himself recognized privately would become the "prey of many theses"?[103] This ambiguity cannot be disassociated from the intricacies of the "projects" that can be discerned in this work: to have wanted to be innovative, all the while mocking academics; to have wanted to integrate esotericism and pedagogy, the concern for history and the contempt for it. Had that thought been simpler, it would not have been as fascinating. Its destiny sealed its complexity and even its contradictions (where Kostas Axelos discerned a "double meaning" without claiming that it was always deliberate).[104]

Finally, we formulate a hope, on the basis of a confession: the author learned much while developing this book and undertook frequent reconsiderations concerning earlier certainties and methods. The hope would be that this *catharsis* would not remain his privilege alone, and that the present study would play a critical and fruitful role for readers coming from diverse orientations. May historical inquiry and philosophical reflection facilitate a more lucid, more serene relation, both more detached and more welcoming to this work, thus finding within our language (after so many attempted translations) a balance between literality and interpretation! A profound enrichment should be the result of this inquiry, as the supreme depository of thoughts whose meditation would deserve the opportunity to pass the test of time and alter its course.

One must concede to the censors that Heidegger was able to practice the art of denial with a disconcerting audacity. The most flagrant—but not the most scandalous[105]—of these pertained to philosophy itself: in the second part of his career, Heidegger always separated himself from "philosophical activity" [*das Philosophieren*], which he belittled in relation to "thought." Even if this distinction, maintained with tenacity, was not without coherence (since it was accompanied by an attempt to overcome metaphysics, itself assimilated to philosophy), under examination it revealed a paradoxical fragility. First, what rigorous philosopher has not established him- or herself by opposing him- or herself to what he or she considered to be the "commonplace" of philosophy? From this perspective, the critique of philosophizing [*Philosophieren*] seems banal. But above all, taking the ambiguity to the limit, Heidegger differentiated himself from philosophy (understood as metaphysics) only in order to return to it by meditating ceaselessly on its essence. Less of a poet than Nietzsche, incomparably less audacious in practical life than a Schopenhauer, a Marx, or a Wittgenstein, he remained in fact to a great extent—after the unfortunate exception of 1933—wisely billeted in the university and academic exercise of philosophical studies. It is not a matter of "reproaching" him, and even less so since he took teaching to a high level of mastery and was able to create a following. The point that we limit ourselves to examining here concerns the denial pertaining to "philosophy." Was his persistence to differentiate himself from philosophical activity and his claim that there was no "Heideggerian philosophy" not a mere play on words? It would be futile to deny it except on the condition of recognizing that this game has been played masterfully and that it is indeed a denial that must be analyzed. After all, this type of denial (in varying degrees of irony and systematicity) has been one of the signatures of the twentieth century, from Magritte ("ceci n'est pas une pipe") to the "non-music" of John Cage and all the forms of "non-art." However, Heidegger did not exactly propose a "non-philosophy," but rather considered "the un-thought" of philosophy itself. Although it is necessary to recognize that his main inspiration had an incontestable seminal richness that was sustained from one end of the work to the other (to unfold a thought more originary than traditional ontology), what is problematic is the provocative expression that he gave to his quest (the openly stated hermeneutic violence of the destruction of the tradition, and the overall identification of that tradition according the unified form of "metaphysics"). One can wonder (as Derrida did, at the risk of losing himself in the process) if the emphatic coherence of the "questioning" of philosophy (as metaphysics) did not mask the fullness of what remains philosophical (and thus metaphysical) in this thinking. But Heidegger's singularity resides precisely in this subtle economy of questioning: to challenge you, while putting everything into question in the most brutal manner, in order to lead you home, and to make you see everything differently. Such is indeed, we could say, the "conservative-revolutionary" spirit whose harmful aspects and associates are now well-known. Justified from a political angle, this objection is less so (or not at all justified) since what is at stake is to question the perspective of the entirety of the Western tradition. Heidegger is certainly the only thinker of the twentieth century who was able to pose the question of the scope of metaphysics in the light of its history with an unequaled radicality.

Whatever the case may be, Heidegger will not have allowed us to rest, he who showed the way to the legacy of *Gelassenheit*. And we know that we are not done with him. Beyond our personal situation, there is the future of humanity and of thought. Whether this thinking is French or francophone is unimportant, and absolutely contingent. That would mean to consider that the style of the discourse and the flesh of the words no longer matter, that only those who will borrow the operative formalisms and elementary efficiency of *basic English* [TN: In English in the original] will prevail. Such are no doubt the stakes. The question of the rootedness that has attracted more than one good soul is only the external expression of a still more essential difficulty embedded in the relation to language itself: must meaning inscribe itself in finitude in order to trace a furrow there? This inscription is the sign of our condition: it corresponds to what Heidegger named "way," which, if one avoids the fetishist trap, has, indeed, a universal scope.

Whatever the degree of interest accorded to Heidegger in France in the course of the century that is beginning, there will be (provided that the awaited publications take place) the enormous work of reading and interpretation of the numerous volumes of the *Gesamtausgabe,* still to appear in French.[106] This work must be completed in a more philosophical manner, with an awareness of the tasks called for by Heidegger's thought. We can indicate the principal axes in the following manner:

- to respond to philosophy in the context of its history;
- to rethink the being of humans;
- to confront the destiny of the power of science;[107]
- to expose the Westernization of the world to other languages and cultures;
- to pose again the question of the sacred.

These five orientations are obviously not the only possible outcomes of Heideggerian thought, which is itself given only as one "way," and which, in order to be followed, extolled virtues that have never been antirational (but that are denied by his adversaries): "the rigor of meditation, carefulness in saying, frugality with words."[108] We do not know whether the thoughts offered by the Master of Freiburg will produce new germinations or whether they will be buried, despised, and indeed forgotten; all we can do is to hope for a future, in a henceforth globalized France, in which—whatever the fortune of "Heidegger studies," great or small—the flame of thinking will not be extinguished completely, a thinking that will always be attentive, beyond any personal or scholarly interest, to the essential questions that were and remain posed to humanity.[109]

PART II
INTERVIEWS

Françoise Dastur

Interview of March 3, 2000

When did you first discover Heidegger?

I remember having read, during my last year in high school, the volume published by Henri Corbin in 1938, entitled *What Is Metaphysics?* and having been inspired by the text on Hölderlin that it contained. During my *hypokhâgne* class in Lyon, and then during my first year as an undergraduate at the Sorbonne, I continued to read Heidegger (I remember a presentation I gave during *hypokhâgne* on "Angst"). However, I did not really begin to work on Heidegger until my second year at the Sorbonne when I took courses with Ricoeur and Derrida. The year was 1962. Derrida had just published his translation of Husserl's *The Origin of Geometry,* and he had organized, for interested students, working groups in which we read and translated some of Husserl's texts. I also began to read, I should say with great difficulty, *Sein und Zeit* with the help of a student who was more advanced than I was—Jean-Louis Tristani—who was working on Heidegger. It was at the end of that year when I decided to write my master's thesis on "Language and Ontology in Heidegger's Work." Ricoeur, who at the time was giving a course on Freud, and was very interested in the phenomenon of language, agreed to direct my thesis and advised me to work on *Unterwegs zur Sprache,* which had been published in 1959.

But that book was not translated. You needed to know German!

I had received a scholarship for one year from the DAAD and of course I chose to spend a year studying in Freiburg, not only because Husserl and Heidegger had taught there, but also because I knew that Eugen Fink was teaching there at the time. Ricoeur cited him in his translation of *Ideas I,* as did Derrida in his introduction to the *Origin of Geometry.* I knew that he positioned himself "between" Husserl and Heidegger, and I wanted to study with him. I thus arrived in

Freiburg in the fall of 1963, and during the course of the first semester I had to work hard to improve my German. I began to take courses with Welte, and also with Brock, who held Heidegger's chair, and who devoted his entire course at the time to *Sein und Zeit*. I also took Fink's course on Kant. But during the second semester, when Brock retired, he was replaced not by Fink, as I had hoped, but by Werner Marx, who had returned from the United States to assume Heidegger's chair. His return was quite an event, and I recall having attended his inaugural lecture in March or April of 1964, which was devoted to German Idealism. I was struck by his strong praise of the works of the thinkers of German Idealism, in which, he claimed, "Germans aspired to the highest level of morality for all of humanity." I am very familiar with his work because some years ago I published (in 1989, some time before his death) the translation of one of his articles on Heidegger in the *Cahier du Collège international de Philosophie*.

He was a charming man, a worldly man rather than simply an academic. I attended his first seminar at Freiburg, which concerned the text *Das Ding*, but I cannot say that I learned much from him. Eugen Fink, for his part, was quite intimidating, at least for me. To my great disappointment, he had been named to the chair of education. He was giving fascinating and difficult courses, in which he never mentioned Heidegger or Husserl, but rather was developing his own thought. That year, I took his course on "Metaphysics and Death," taking copious notes, but understanding little. Distracted by my experiences at the German University, I did not complete my master's thesis during my time in Germany. The following year, in order to stay close to Germany, I taught for a year in Mulhouse as a visiting lecturer. Then I returned to Paris, and in order to complete my master's, I went with Ricoeur to Nanterre, where he had accepted an appointment. While studying Hindi in the Oriental languages program, I defended my master's thesis in June 1966 and prepared for my exams.

Your genuine introduction to Heidegger's thought really took
place, it seems, in Germany. Did you ever have the opportunity,
nonetheless, to meet Jean Beaufret and his followers?

I was not yet in touch with the French Heideggerians. I knew Beaufret only through his writings and had heard him only once at the Sorbonne, where he gave a lecture on Husserl and Heidegger, where, incidentally, there was an incredible crowd. In addition, I had completely lost all contact with Derrida for a silly reason: when I returned to Paris, he had asked me to meet with him and five advanced students to work on the translation of Husserl's *Krisis*. I was supposed to translate roughly one hundred pages, but in the process, due to both difficulties and time pressures (I was preparing at that time for the Agrégation), in the end I had to abandon it, and I did not dare contact Derrida to tell him.

Hence, I returned to Germany without having had any contact with the French Heideggerians. However, Ricoeur had liked my master's thesis and, with my permission, distributed my translations of passages from *Unterwegs der Sprache* that I had used in my thesis. This is how I came to be somewhat known among some of the Heideggerians such as Odette Laffoucrière, who attended Ricoeur's seminars. I lived again in Freiburg, where I continued to attend the university, in addition to teaching, first at Strasbourg, where I met Lacoue-Labarthe, and then at Mulhouse. Then I obtained a teaching post at the Sorbonne, where I was welcomed by Michel Haar and Henri Birault, who had heard that I was a Heideggerian.

Was it also at that time that you met François Fédier?

It was through Kostas Axelos, who was working as a teaching assistant in Belaval's team, that I contacted François Fédier—it must have been in 1971. He was in the process of translating *Unterwegs zur Sprache*. He invited me to participate in a private weekly seminar that he held in a kind of basement, at quai des Grands Augustins, and that he devoted that year to the "Rectoral Address." I attended that seminar for two to three years, discussing "On the Essence of Truth," and then the "Letter on Humanism." There were not very many of us: François Vezin, Patrick Levy, who was then translating Hannah Arendt, and occasionally Dominique Fourcade. Some of Fédier's students were there, including Marc Froment-Meurice.

I had given Fédier my translations of *Unterwegs zur Sprache,* and he returned them to me with some notes in the margins. He did not really ask me to participate in his translation, and I did not ask him about it either because I perceived in the meantime that we did not have the same conception of translation. I nevertheless had fond memories of the seminars during those years, in which the work was intense and where an atmosphere of great passion and freedom prevailed.

Later on, that seminar was open to the general public. It grew from ten participants to forty, and at times more, and after 1975 it was held, I believe, at the Maison des Lettres. At times Beaufret attended, and it was there that I met him for the first time. Fédier gave a final seminar in 1976 on Hölderlin and the question of the alternation of tones. There were some public lectures given by Beaufret as well. Then, everything was interrupted by Heidegger's death in May 1976, and I gradually lost contact with Fédier.

What happened then?

In 1981, I went to the United States with a plan to complete my thesis on "Heidegger and Language." In fact, I was no longer sure that Heidegger's thought could lend itself to an academic thesis. While in New York, where I stayed for two years, I eventually abandoned this project. Meanwhile, Beaufret died in the summer of 1982 (I was in France then and I attended the funeral). Sometime after my return to France (in 1983 or 1984), Fédier had once again organized a private seminar. This seminar took place in a private school where Claude Roëls was teaching and which was quite open: I met Éliane Escoubas and Gérard Guest there. Frédéric Postel and Nicole Parfait also attended. But the atmosphere was no longer like it was in the '70s. After Beaufret's death, Fédier had replaced him as the "overseer" of the French translations of Heidegger's works. Feeling entrusted with an almost "sacred" mission, his tendency to dogmatism increased, and the spirit of free discussion that had characterized his earlier seminars gradually disappeared.

My relationship with him had already suffered when Martineau published his "unofficial" translation of *Sein und Zeit* in 1985. This translation was perceived by Fédier, Vezin, and a few others, as a kind of major catastrophe. For several years, Vezin had indeed been the "official" translator of the text, and he was working without undue haste on his translation. The date for the publication of his translation was still not determined. This is incidentally what led Martineau to translate *Sein und Zeit* in eight months as a noncommercial publication. Vezin, then, had to work day and night in order to complete and publish his own translation the following year. Now, that year, Fédier had chosen to devote his seminar, which was then taking place at the Sorbonne, to Hölderlin, which made me particularly happy. However, when Vezin's translation came out he suddenly decided to devote the seminar to the translation of *Sein und Zeit*. I remember that there was a very unpleasant session when, compelled to choose Vezin's translation over Martineau's, and to discuss it in the course of the seminar, Éliane Escoubas and I decided to no longer attend the seminar. In the following years, Fédier constantly criticized me for not having supported the Vezin translation, which indeed I did not because I could not endorse translation choices such as "*désobstruction*" for *Destruktion*, "*disposibilité*" for *Befindichlichkeit* and "*dévalement*" for *Verfallenheit*. I never really chose between the Martineau translation, which contained a certain number of errors and infelicitous choices (such as "*échéance*" for *Verfallen*), and the Vezin translation, which is in certain places excellent, and I had refused to sign a letter distributed by Roger Munier and Michel Haar who criticized Vezin's translation in terms that seemed to me to be too harsh. My relations with Fédier and Vezin became once again distant without really being ruptured. It seems that the relations have become even worse lately, but not of my doing, as I never refused communication with Fédier. I will nonetheless have to be in touch with him since I am in the process of completing (finally) the translation of the 1925–26 course on *Logik* (volume 21 of the *Gesamtausgabe*) that Beaufret himself had entrusted to me in 1981. The official contract for the translation with Gallimard was only signed many years later and at a time when my responsibilities at the university did not allow me to devote myself to the translation of a 400-page volume, while if I had had the contract from the beginning, I could have completed the translation during my time in the United States.

Earlier you recalled all that you owe to Ricoeur and Derrida with respect to Heidegger. But did you not also work with Jacques Taminiaux?

I met Taminiaux thanks to Michel Haar, whom I met occasionally at Ricoeur's seminar during the '70s, and with whom I reconnected when I returned from the United States. At the time, my goal was to establish relations with all those in France who worked on Heidegger, because I felt that we should no longer be isolated from each other. It was for that reason that I contacted Granel, whose work I had known for a very long time without knowing him personally, and Martineau, whom I had already met on several occasions. In 1986, Michel Haar and I led a seminar together at Université de Paris IV—Sorbonne on the "first" version of *The Origin of the Work of Art* (which was, in fact, the second), the translation of which Martineau, again, had just published as a noncommercial project. I also participated, then, in Henri Birault's seminar, who had taken over the phenomenology seminar after Ricoeur's retirement. I had, in fact, regularly attended Ricoeur's seminar in the '70s. When Birault took it over, I naturally continued to attend. When Jean-François Courtine inherited the seminar, it was, especially in the early years, the occasion of an inspiring collaborative study of some of Heidegger's texts. Michel Haar arranged for me to attend a conference devoted to Heidegger at the University of Essex in 1986, where I met American Heideggerians (David Krell, John Sallis, etc.) and reconnected, after many years, with Derrida, who also attended. Subsequently, I returned to Derrida's seminar, which I had only attended once previously in 1978. At the time, there had been indeed the "Farias Affair," and it seemed to me that we had to be united against the "professional" anti-Heideggerians and that I had to show my solidarity with Derrida, who was being particularly targeted.

To return to Taminiaux, whom I met at the Collegium Phaenomenologicum in Perugia in 1988, where once again Michel Haar had arranged for me to be invited. I had the idea of asking him to be my thesis director when in 1992 I decided once again to defend a thesis based on my published work [*sur travaux*]. I had indeed followed his research at Louvain-la-Neuve in his phenomenology seminar from afar, and I shared with him a strong interest in German Idealism and Hölderlin. I was happy that he agreed to be my "sponsor" because the idea of defending at Louvain, the world center of the phenomenological movement, really appealed to me. But I nonetheless asked my first professors, Ricoeur and Derrida, to be members of the doctoral committee. It is in fact to them that I owed my first relation to Husserl and Heidegger, two thinkers that I never wanted to separate in my work. I only met Beaufret and his followers much later, as well as the last students of Beaufret: Marion, Courtine, and Martineau. I nonetheless always felt a bit estranged from the French Heideggerians, because I had done the work of learning about Heidegger on my own in Germany. I rarely used the French translations or commentaries, and, as I stated in my little book, *Heidegger and the Question of Time,* I believed that it was still in Germany that Heidegger was better read and understood.[1] It was by reading the work of Otto Pöggeler, Walter Biemel, and Friedrich von Herrmann that I really began to understand Heidegger. The work accomplished by Beaufret in the *Dialogues* is admirable, and I have a great debt to Fédier, who taught me a tremendous amount in his seminars. But I have found the work of *systematic* interpretation in the German texts alone. Certainly, Heidegger was quickly forgotten in Germany, and, even in Freiburg, with the exception of the teaching of Friedrich von Herrmann, the phenomenological tradition has hardly been continued compared to its robust quality in the 1960s. With the beginning of the '70s Germany began to abandon its own tradition and to satisfy itself with an imported philosophy, analytic Anglo-American philosophy, which literally invaded the universities. There were also very violent campaigns against Heidegger. At Freiburg, there was for instance in those years, a group of students who were distributing Bourdieu's writings attacking Heidegger's political position in the '30s and conflating it directly with his philosophy. Today Heidegger is hardly read in Germany, but he is still present in some excellent work, and a certain number of young scholars continue to work on his *Gesamtausgabe.*

I would also like to return to the question of the translation of *Sein und Zeit.* I spoke of it often with Granel and Taminiaux in the '80s. Both had translated long passages of the second division of the text for their students to use. I myself translated the chapter on *Sorge* for my classes. Taminiaux did not understand that the project of a collaborative translation had never been considered. We were, indeed, a group with a precise knowledge of the text and we could have joined our efforts. Why didn't it happen? There was something odd about it. Beaufret, for his part, was not interested in the translation, although it seemed that he should have been in charge. The translations of the "second" Heidegger were done fairly early; why did it take so long for a major work like *Sein und Zeit* to be translated, a text that determined, after all, the understanding of all that was to follow? Although there already had been for some time Spanish, English, Italian, and Japanese translations, we only had in French the translation by Boehm and Waehlens of Division I, which was published in 1963. I often asked myself why that translation, by a Germanophone and a Francophone, and for that reason eminently readable, had not been completed. Wouldn't it have been better to revise this translation, which had its virtues, and then attempt to complete it rather than try to retranslate the whole thing from scratch?

*Just before his death, didn't Heidegger consider creating
a sort of commission under René Char, to oversee the
translations? He seemed to have been very concerned.*

I indeed vaguely remember hearing something of the sort. But I do not know any more than you do. Despite my close contacts with Fédier and Vezin during those days I was not in the loop regarding the "dealings" surrounding the translation. It is clear that in this respect they did not choose to confide in me. I believe in fact that the letter criticizing the translators of *Questions IV,* which Heidegger received before his death, troubled him greatly and that he would have been happier if the translation of his work in French had not been the subject of a dispute.

Wasn't it also a blow for Jean Beaufret, since they were attacking his actions?

Indeed. But was it reasonable to commission untested translators such as Roëls and Lauxerois to translate such difficult texts as were gathered in *Questions IV?* In the '70s I myself translated *Die Technik und die Kehre.* The translation was incredibly difficult, requiring both a perfect knowledge of German but also an intimate understanding of Heidegger's thought. But with respect to Beaufret's close friends, they did not care about competence, and they were particularly suspicious of those who taught at the university. They preferred to call on the disciples, those whose unconditional loyalty to Heidegger could not be doubted. They did not invite me, for example, to participate in Heidegger's last seminar, the Zähringen seminar, which took place in 1973, although I was already following Fédier's seminar at that time, and other participants of the seminar, such as Patrick Lévy, attended. There is no doubt that they had a tendency to withhold, and not freely share, the Heideggerian "heritage," which led them to be somewhat petty. This included, for example, the opposition to the publication in *Le Débat* of Nicole Parfait's translation of some of Heidegger's political texts. I always thought that the work of translation was not sufficient in itself and that it had to be guided and accompanied by the work of interpretation. This was in a sense how Beaufret worked but not, in my view, Fédier and Vezin, who did not always give a clear explanation of the surprising translations they proposed for certain Heideggerian terms. This is particularly important in the case of *Sein und Zeit,* where the thinking still takes a systematic form, where it is imperative to have understood the theoretical articulations of Heidegger's thought in order to be able to translate it. Such a work of interpretation requires precision, a minute examination of the letter of the texts, but also an exercise of critical thought, and not a simple set of quotes that have been learned by heart.

*What are you addressing in Heidegger's work these days? Are you
interested in reading or rereading his* Gesamtausgabe *in German?*

What I would like to do in the years to come, is, above all, to work again on the
texts from the 1930s. First because they are difficult to read, which requires great
patience due to the fact that Heidegger wrote some of them solely for himself and
not for a potential reader. But also because they are the evidence of a particularly
delicate and dramatic period that one has the tendency to judge retrospectively
rather than appraise it as a period of indecision and of a "turning" precisely. The
more I read these texts, the more I realize that all was not settled, and that everything was fundamentally put into question again. But, at the same time, I admire
Heidegger for having, in spite of everything, stubbornly continued to work on
the same issues, even though things appeared to him at that time in a very different light. What seems fascinating to me about that era is Heidegger's questioning of the entirety of the Western tradition, the necessity of what he named an
"other beginning," and the gesture that led him back to an archaic Greece of the
pre-Socratics, and thus brought him to break with the usual understanding of
Greece and of the German-Greek relation that the Germans had, with the notable exception of Hölderlin, since the end of the eighteenth century. What began
to appear and develop here was the possibility of a relation of Western thought
with other traditions of thought, which Heidegger alone among Western thinkers performed with his "Dialogue with a Japanese," in *On the Way to Language*. I
find there the prelude to a fundamental task that awaits the thinkers of the twenty-first century, and Heidegger is not for me the thinker obsessed with Greece
and the return to the pre-Socratics but rather the one who began to develop anew
a dialogue with the Far East.

But I am also interested in the very early Heidegger, about which today,
thanks to the work of French and American scholars, especially Ted Kisiel and
Jean Greisch, we have an abundance of sources. I have personally begun to work
on the relationship between the young Heidegger and the neo-Kantian context
in which he first situated himself. I would especially like to investigate the figures
of Rickert and above all Lask in a more detailed manner. The guiding thread remains that of a "de-construction" of traditional logic that Heidegger undertook
very early, by following Lask and by remaining, in a certain manner, faithful to
the Husserlian idea of a "genetic" inquiry into logical concepts. I have always
intended to devote a book to this question of the relation, which pervades Heidegger's entire work, between the question of being and the question of logos.

I should however say, in order to be completely honest, that my interest in
Heidegger's work is in constant rivalry with another interest of mine, a powerful
one, which always brings me back to great works of post-Kantian German Idealism: Fichte, Schelling, and Hegel. In spite of the immense importance for me of
the thinking of finitude and of mortality that I find in Heidegger, the heights of

speculation attained by German Idealism have never ceased to fascinate me, and I continue to wonder, like Heidegger himself, if our epoch, instead of having gone beyond them has not simply abandoned the philosophical aspirations on which they rested.

In fact, it was a work of the young Hegel, The Difference between Fichte's and Schelling's System of Philosophy, *that Heidegger had assigned at the Thor Seminar in 1968.*

I would have loved to have been there. I would have only wanted to meet Heidegger in such a context, that of a course or a seminar. But I did not have this opportunity. The only year that I spent in Paris at the end of the '60s, in order to prepare for Agrégation, was the one in which the Fink-Heidegger seminar on Heraclitus took place in Freiburg. When I arrived in Freiburg in 1963, I had decided to not go to see Heidegger, to confine myself to his writings alone, since he was no longer teaching and therefore I could no longer see him *work*. I must say also that I was perfectly aware of his political attitude in 1933—the political texts had been published, for the most part, by Jean-Pierre Faye in the journal *Médiations,* that same year, 1963—and that I was a bit reticent to arrange a meeting. In the fall of 1975, when I taught for a semester at Mannheim University, I went to Freiburg with a general plan to finally meet Heidegger, but I was discouraged to do so because of his advanced age. I was told that he rarely received visitors any longer. Therefore, I never spoke with Heidegger, and in a way I do not regret it. This afforded me the freedom to read him without the interference of any sorts of feelings, whether positive or negative, with regard to his person. Moreover, I have never believed that a work can be explained on the basis of the author's psychology, something that many people forget in Heidegger's case.

Before concluding, can I ask you to put yourself in my place for a moment: how would you conceive a work on Heidegger's reception in France?

I think that your work on Heidegger's reception in France is of the greatest importance for you cover an essential aspect of everything that was done in France in terms of thinking since the '30s. I believe you are well placed to accomplish this work, because you yourself participated closely in this history. Indeed, it is not possible to narrate this history from an external vantage point. At the same time one must endeavor to try to represent everyone's point of view, which seems to me very difficult. I am at the same time struck by the fact that the history of a reception of a thought is also a history of its distortions, or its misinterpretations and its misunderstandings. I have never believed in progress in matters of the history of philosophy, and it seems to me that seventy years after the publication of *Sein und Zeit,* and although Heidegger's thought has had a huge influence on all that has taken place in philosophy in France, and not only in France, it remains nevertheless, in its fundamental significance, completely misunderstood, namely, in its fundamental critique, from beginning to end, of any anthropologism. Heidegger is for me the thinker who has recalled philosophy forcefully to its original vocation, which is that of the concern for the whole, and not only for the human sphere, in an era dominated by anthropocentrism and when, at the end of the century, first philosophy is reduced to ethics, that is to say, to a concern centered on human beings alone. This is the fundamental meaning of the return to the question of being as the *fundamental* question of philosophy, and I do not see how the question of the other, with or without a capital O, could ever take the place of such an inquiry without enclosing us at the same time in the sphere of that "human all too human" that had already been the target of Nietzsche's attacks. Heidegger's insight that the relation to being defines the being of the human being in a fundamental and original way led him to name human beings with a nontraditional name: *Dasein*, and no longer "subject" or "consciousness."

This redefinition of the human being can seem formal. Didn't you have the opportunity to test this definition in the context of a particular practice, namely that of psychiatry?

In the *Zollikoner Seminare*, the book published by psychiatrist Medard Boss in 1987, which contains the texts of the seminars that Heidegger gave over the course of ten years (1959–1969) at Zollikon, near Zurich, for a group of young psychiatrists and medical students, Heidegger explained that he sought to engage in dialogue with practitioners in the hope that they would be more open than other theoreticians had been to the "revolution in thinking" required by the task, comparable to the Galilean discovery of the natural realm—but infinitely more difficult—of unveiling the properly human domain that entails the transformation of the human being into *Dasein*. It is indeed only on the basis of such a being of the human being, essentially understood on the basis of its relation to being as such, that the relation to the other human being, in particular the therapeutic relation, could be considered. Some psychiatrists understand this quite well. Moreover, it was with the collaboration of phenomenological psychiatrists, such as Jean Naudin and Jean-Michel Azorin, who were students of professor Tatossian in Marseille, that, in 1993, I founded the French school of *Daseinsanalyse*, which is attached to the Zurich Institute founded by Medard Boss. Our monthly seminar—which has taken place for the past seven years—has brought together those interested in the phenomenological approach to mental illness and who are primarily concerned with the therapeutic relation with the ill. I often have the impression, through my contact with these practitioners, of encountering a more essential dimension of Heidegger's thought than one could find in the scholarly conferences devoted to him around the world.

Jacques Derrida

Interviews of July 1 and
November 22, 1999

When do you think you heard Heidegger's name for the first time?

I think it was probably in *hypokhâgne* and not in my high school philosophy class. I was in the philosophy class during 1947–48 and it doesn't seem to me that Heidegger's name had been mentioned at that time. In *hypokhâgne,* I am *sure* of having heard his name in lectures. I had a rather remarkable *hypokhâgne* teacher, Jan Czarneki: he gave lectures on the history of philosophy that were very synthetic and precise, in which he covered everything, from the pre-Socratics to modernity; I remember having heard him speak of Kierkegaard and Heidegger.

At the same time, I was reading Sartre, in particular, *Nausea,* and *Being and Nothingness:* Heidegger's name appeared many times in the texts. And (these are memories of texts as well as of places, and of landscapes), I remember having read, in the University of Algiers library, on the one hand, texts by Sartre—and notably a text on the history of truth published in the journal *Bifur*—and on the other hand, texts already collected and edited by Corbin in a small volume containing fragments of *Sein und Zeit* and *Was ist Metaphysik?*

But I was also very aware of him, because of classes and because of the role that I saw him play in the French intellectual landscape—with Sartre notably, and more distantly Merleau-Ponty—(but the fact is that it took place through Sartre: Heidegger's influence on Sartre, and the references in *Being and Nothingness* to Heidegger); it is there that things started, during the 1948–49 academic year. And so I read these fragments from *Sein und Zeit.* I remember, by the way, that during that year, in the written assignments, the question of the origin of negation had drawn me into these debates in *Being and Nothingness* and in *Was ist Metaphysik?* The question of anxiety, of the experience of nothingness before negation, corresponded well to my personal pathos, much more so than the cold Husserlian discipline, to which I came only later. I resonated with the pathos that was felt during that period, right after the war. One spoke of Christian Existentialism and Atheist Existentialism. The whole landscape was already there: Marcel, Sartre. Naturally, I felt that Heidegger was behind this entire edifice—both more originary and more important than his representatives, his mediators, his interpreters, his French posterity. But my reading remained both academic and preliminary.

Afterward, I entered *khâgne* at Louis-le-Grand School. I spent three years there: the first and third years, I had Borne as a teacher; the second, in the middle, Savin. But neither of the two had any affinity with or precise knowledge of Heidegger. In any case, they never showed it in their lectures. Their references to Heidegger were frequent but they were somehow "quite generic," and there were no readings of texts. In *khâgne,* one didn't read the texts; one learned how to make arguments. References were used rhetorically—but there were no demanding readings.

I read Heidegger more on my own. I would not be able to say precisely how. I do not remember having read *Sein und Zeit* directly at that time, but I have the impression that I was more interested in Heidegger—or at least, more interested than was required by the *khâgne* program.

The written assignments were often constructed on the basis of references to Sartre and Merleau-Ponty. Already, I wrote essays that Borne told me were "Plotinian." The fascination with the *epekeina tēs ousias* dates from this period. Naturally, once I came across this reference in Heidegger, my thought became connected to his discourse. I remember an essay based on a somewhat more rhetorical opposition between the Sartre of *Being and Nothingness* (who distinguished the in-itself and the for-itself and dreamed of a metaphysical synthesis of a phenomenological ontology as synthesis of a certain "human reality"—I knew already that this was a disastrous translation of *Dasein*) and Merleau-Ponty. There was, on the one hand, this Sartre, whom I allowed myself already to criticize for his Cartesian dualism etc., and, on the other hand, Merleau-Ponty, who was much more ambiguous, not deciding between or dividing up these two regions. These problems of regions of being, not at all in the sense of phenomenological regions, in Husserl's sense, but of regions of being in the Sartrean sense, kept me very busy. I already felt, at least intuitively, that these were simplifications in relation to Heidegger. I don't know to what extent I was able, at that time, to grasp this clearly.

Were you fluent in German?

This is an important and difficult question for me. German was my first foreign language. But I always had a resistance to German, which is why, in *khâgne,* my English became better than my German; I inverted the priority of my foreign languages and made English my first language and German my second. I was not competent in Greek at that time. I learned Greek at the École Normale. I did not read Heidegger directly in German. At the same time, I always referred to the German. I would do it to verify, to specify, to refine an argument or a translation.

So that is what happened in *khâgne,* where, despite everything, the rush of the written assignments, the pressure, and the anxiety of the *concours* won out over demanding readings. It was only at the École Normale, during the 1952–53 academic year, that more "responsible" readings started. In any case, this period that we are talking about is quite short: amounting to about four or five years.

A lot of things were reaching me, following trajectories that I cannot reconstitute now, by way of a sort of general porosity. At that time, Heidegger was spoken of indirectly. Sartre and Merleau-Ponty were living philosophers on the scene. Merleau-Ponty was on the entrance exam committee. One read him as a potential examiner: the *Phenomenology of Perception* as well as the texts on Cézanne and on painting. It was useful for the written assignments. He administered the orals with Jankélévitch. I would go and observe the orals where Merleau-Ponty and Jankélévitch were at work. Those were the only times when I saw Merleau-Ponty. When I made it to the oral phase, Alquié and Vuillemin were the examiners. One could write entire chapters on each one's relationship to Heidegger. Alquié took himself to be—this is visible in his books, but also in his lectures, in his spontaneous discourse—a worthy rival of Heidegger. He claimed Heidegger had somehow stolen his notion of the "nostalgia of being." He looked at it as some kind of theft. Vuillemin, too, had a relation to Heidegger: in his readings of the *Critique of Pure Reason* and of its legacy, he interpreted the Analytic in terms of Cohen and the Aesthetic in terms of Heidegger. In that case as well, we read Vuillemin because he was an examiner—and a certain Heidegger was communicated and transpired.

At that time, quite early on, there had been a debate concerning Heidegger's politics. But, so far as I can remember, for the *khâgne* students that we were, the political question concerning Heidegger did not arise. It was only later that I encountered it, at the École Normale. In the second year, I wrote my thesis on Husserl (1953–54); my reading was, in a certain way—it is difficult to show this in a preface, but I think that it is visible in the book—largely influenced by the references, sometimes implicit, sometimes explicit, to Heidegger and to a certain questioning of Husserl by Heidegger. Which is to say that this master's thesis, which eventually became a book, *The Problem of Genesis in Husserl's Phenomenology,*[1] was a work that would not have been possible without Heidegger. Sometimes I mention it, sometimes I do not, but the questions that I address to Husserl, or the type of reading that I venture at that point in time, implied a certain relation to Heidegger.

Your thesis advisor was not Hyppolite but Gandillac?

At the École, in 1952, Hyppolite was not there yet. He came the following year. I followed some classes he gave that made reference to Heidegger, and to Husserl. I know that Heidegger was quite present, but this is difficult to reconstruct; I do not have any particularly clear memories of Heidegger with Hyppolite.

It was Beaufret, finally, who came to give lectures to Agrégation students when I was at the École. His lectures were not on Heidegger. We knew that he was a great expert and friend of Heidegger's, but he gave lectures that were extremely precise, useful, etc., on Leibniz, and on Descartes, without referring to Heidegger.

What then can I say about my relationship to Heidegger during those years at the École? I think that there were, in the year ahead of me, students who were reputed to be knowledgeable about Heidegger, and that is how we looked upon them. It was also an occult atmosphere: there was Granel, Gourinat, Faucon-Lamboi, and perhaps even Grenier. There was a kind of respect for those who had an access to the original texts. This also implied a certain style of thinking, of questioning: Aubenque had come to give lectures on Aristotle and, naturally, they were not without references to Heidegger. Foucault gave lectures, but he referred more often to Husserl than to Heidegger. I am trying to bring more precise things back to memory.

Naturally, in my student assignments I referred to Heidegger. I can remember an assignment concerning time. At that moment I read Heidegger. Read, well, one never reads him enough—but I had, let us say, a more cultivated and more rigorous relation to Heidegger's texts, during those pre-Agrégation years.

In 1955, I failed the orals, but in 1956 I passed. Then, for a year, I went to the United States, to Harvard, where I had great freedom. I began to translate Husserl's *The Origin of Geometry*.

During that time, I worked a lot more on Husserl. The goal that I shared with a number of people at that time was to replace a French phenomenology (Merleau-Ponty, Sartre), which cared little for science and epistemology, with a phenomenology that would be more attuned to the sciences. The question of scientific objectivity occupied us a lot. There was also a political concern. Tran Duc Thao played a great role in this domain. I was not strictly speaking a communist, or a Marxist, but there too, it was a question of atmosphere. It was Foucault who told me about Tran Duc Tao's book, by saying, and I later thought the same thing, that the first half was very interesting, while the second half was more problematic. The first half was a relatively faithful commentary on a certain Husserl who was interested in genesis, in the problem of time. Then, the more dogmatic Marxist moment became more problematic. It was through Foucault that I heard of it. Subsequently, I read it for myself and naturally if I chose the problem of genesis then it was because I had identified in it—in that interval I read quite a bit of Husserl, notably *Ideas I*, the *Philosophy of Arithmetic,* and the *Logical Investigations*—I had been able to pre-identify there, in some way, the question of the history of science, and of the genesis of objectivity. And so the choice of this subject could be explained through this context that is both historical and academic. We were telling ourselves: "and what about science?" In the *Phenomenology of Perception,* Merleau-Ponty was occupied with the nonscientific phenomenon. Then, one has to account for ideal objectivity, for scientific ideality, and for the history of truth. So from that point on I dedicated myself to the Husserlian discipline, to which I have always remained faithful: the reductions. I became a sort of "disciplined disciple" of Husserl, despite all the questions that arose.

The "Heidegger" conference in Cerisy took place in 1955. We knew that something important was happening. The conference gathered Beaufret, Gandillac, Marcel, Goldmann, people who were part of that Parisian landscape that, after all, was ours. I was not able to go to Cerisy, but the following year, in the winter that followed, Gandillac, who had befriended me, invited me to his home. It was at his home, in the *salons* of Gandillac (I, who came from Algiers!), that I met people who, from the point of view of the history of Heidegger, were not just anyone. It was there that I met Axelos, Wahl, and Goldmann, and we spoke about Heidegger. The winter following the conference, in Madame Heurgon's apartment in Paris, there was a reception where recordings from the conference were played. I was a student at the École Normale and I heard Heidegger's voice for the first time in a *salon* in the 16th arrondissement. I remember one sequence in particular: we were all in the living room, we were listening to this voice. In those days, tape recordings were not as clear as they are today; I remember, above all, the moment in the discussion following Heidegger's talk: questions from Marcel and Goldmann. One of the two, basically, made the following objection to Heidegger: "But do you not think that this method of interpretation or this manner of reading or questioning is dangerous?"—this was a question concerning methodology, that is to say, epistemology. And I can still hear in my ear—there was a silence—Heidegger's response: "*Ja!* It is dangerous." This is a memory of a student who was about to take the Agrégation exam.

We are still in 1956. The emergence of the problem of metaphysics and Heidegger's evolution in relation to Sein und Zeit *only arose later?*

I suppose. It makes me sad, but I am not able to reconstitute this evolution and this transformation for myself, in other words, the moment I arrived at the schema of deconstruction (the word *Destruktion,* for example, I don't remember—but is my memory reliable?—having paid attention to it thematically during those years). I think it is later. I wouldn't swear to it.

Faye says, in Le piège, *that the word* déconstruction *appeared
around 1966–67 thanks to you and to Granel.*

That's true. It is in *Of Grammatology,* as far as I can remember, that the word appears, in 1965. That being said, I did *The Origin of Geometry* during the academic year 1961–62, in which there are quite a few references to Heidegger. In my reading of Levinas, "Violence and Metaphysics," in 1962–63, naturally there are many references to Heidegger.

At that moment, I was already teaching. I was an assistant at the Sorbonne and I gave courses on Heidegger. On returning from the United States, I did my military service (as a teacher in a school for children of soldiers—without wearing a uniform), and then I began to teach in *hypokhâgne,* in Le Mans, in 1959–60. I know I spoke about Heidegger in *hypokhâgne.* Then, I became an assistant at the Sorbonne from 1960 to 1964, and I gave entire courses on Heidegger: on *Kant and the Problem of Metaphysics,* and on "Irony, Doubt and the Question." It is probably during those years as an assistant that I read Heidegger most continuously, and most systematically, while referring to him. I remember teaching "What Is Metaphysics?" and lectured on possibility, and negation. And when I began to be *caïman*[2] at the École, my first course, which has never been published, was on "History in Heidegger"; that was in 1964–65.[3] At that time, incidentally, I was thinking of writing a book on Heidegger, which was announced by Éditions de Minuit. I never wrote it. The title that was announced was *The Question of History.*

The advertisement for it can be found in the journal *Critique.* Axelos was to have published it. I never wrote it, but the course itself was completely prepared. Starting in those years, obviously, my relationship to Heidegger became intense and constant. Let us say: regularly intermittent. I never stop returning to it.

Indeed, in Speech and Phenomena, *we read: "Perhaps it is already apparent
that, while we appeal to Heideggerian motifs in decisive places, we would
especially like to raise the question whether, with respect to the relations,
between* logos *and* phonē, *and with respect to the pretended irreducibility
of certain word unities (the unity of the word being or of other 'radical
words'), Heidegger's thought does not sometimes raise the same question
as the metaphysics of presence" (74n4). Heidegger against Heidegger?*

That note is a miniature photograph of a landscape or of a gesture that, in fact, never stopped repeating itself a thousand different ways.

Yet, in 1967, Ousia and Grammē *was published
first in the homage to Beaufret, right?*

As far as the text itself is concerned, it was first a seminar (what the context was, I no longer remember). In any case, the thing was written when Fédier asked me to participate in this homage to Beaufret. At first I hesitated since I actually did not feel particularly close to Beaufret, with whom I had good relations; but I did not consider myself Beaufretian nor Heideggerian in the Beaufretian mode, and since in "Ousia and Grammē" there were some troubling questions concerning Heidegger, I thought of declining. But Fédier insisted, and he was extremely kind with me (this did not last); his manner was a little seductive. I asked myself: "What if, finally, I were to publish this at least in order to establish a critical work, on the occasion of this homage to Beaufret and to Heidegger?" (it was actually a book on Heidegger). After a long hesitation, I accepted. I gave this text to Fédier, who warmly and approvingly confirmed reception. And then, one day, once he had the text, Laporte and his wife came to lunch at my house, in Fresnes, in the winter of 1967–68 (probably 1968 already). During a desultory discussion, Laporte, who had been his student, spoke to me about some anti-Semitic remarks made by Beaufret. Disturbing remarks. He reported some of them, which concerned Levinas, or the fact that the alleged exterminations of the Jews were as little believable as the rumors that circulated concerning the horrors in Belgium after the war of 1914 (that the Germans were killing and slaughtering children); and finally, he spoke to me about remarks of this type that seemed shocking to me not just because of their anti-Semitism but because of their violence. And so I was shocked and upset. Laporte was a bit surprised. Perhaps he had not predicted the effect that this could have on me.

So he hadn't mentioned it to you in order to warn you?

Oh no! He was not thinking that it would explode! And obviously, in me, it exploded. Immediately, the same day, or the next one, I wrote to Fédier (I kept this entire correspondence that I entrusted to Bident): "Listen, I have just become aware of this; I do not want to make a public scene out of it, I do not want to bring this out into the public, but allow me to withdraw my text discreetly." But voila! Fédier did not intend on keeping the matter secret. He reacted with violence: calumny, etc.! I have his letters. Obviously, I had not told him that I heard this from Laporte. After some time he found this out, but I don't know how. Laporte became the true suspect among Beaufret's friends, who closed ranks around Beaufret. There were many episodes, exchanges of all sorts, until a day when a meeting was arranged, in my office at the École Normale, between Beaufret and Laporte; a confrontational meeting unfolded. Beaufret arrived. All were pale with emotion. Beaufret and Laporte, who knew each other, were teacher and student. Beaufret arrived with Vezin. The four of us were in my office; Laporte confirmed the charge, while Beaufret, naturally, denied it violently. And that's where things remained.

Since Laporte, paradoxically, felt more and more accused—he was the one who was turning into the accused and it made him very sad (because there were protests from others who were friends of both Beaufret and Laporte like Munier, Fourcade—neither Deguy nor Granel showed themselves); he took it very badly. And it was Jacqueline Laporte who, I was told, had alerted Blanchot in order to protect her husband. Blanchot too, was in the situation of having given a text to Fédier. Obviously, the Laportes knew that Blanchot was very sensitive, irritable, and anxious about these questions. So, as soon as Blanchot was alerted, he contacted me. I didn't know him at that point. I had read him, of course; we had exchanged a few letters, but I had never met him. It was on the occasion of this affair that I met Blanchot quite frequently, during this limited period in 1968, during the "events" as one says. We met several times, asking ourselves what we should do—whether we should withdraw our texts or not. And then, after endless deliberations, we were in agreement: Beaufret did not admit to having said these things and we could not prove that he had—it was witness against witness, it was Laporte's word against his—we did not have the right to accuse Beaufret publicly of something that he denied, therefore we had to allow the promised texts to appear. But we thought, Blanchot and I, that it would be good for us to explain ourselves to other contributors to the volume—who were already informed—by saying: "Voilà, this is what we have heard, not having any proof, we are going to give Beaufret some credit; we cannot accuse him publicly and so we are leaving our texts in. But this is what happened." So we wrote this letter, we signed it together and we decided that, making as many copies as there were contributors, it would only be sent out once the book had appeared: we did not want to ruin the book's publication. The day the book came out, we mailed our letter to each contributor in order to explain our position during this process.

I happened to be in the United States in September 1968. I had typed the letters, and I had prepared them; there were eighteen or twenty copies. We had signed them and I had left them with Blanchot who was supposed to mail them the day the book came out while I was at Johns Hopkins. Thus Blanchot mailed them—and the letters never arrived. He had mailed them "in care of" the publisher. Apparently the letters had been intercepted because nobody received them. Our hypothesis or our suspicion was that Fédier intercepted them. We could not prove it, of course. In any case these letters never arrived . . .

Another thing as well: Blanchot said: "We have to talk to Levinas about this." Thus, I remember one day when I had made an appointment with Blanchot and I picked him up with my car (he lived on rue Madame in those days), and I took him to see Levinas, to whom we then revealed this whole affair, since Levinas had been involved by name, having been the subject of the comments attributed to Beaufret. Levinas took things in a very relaxed way: "Oh, you know, we are used to it." He was less emotional about the affair than we were. So there you have it! What else can I say? The book came out. Obviously the relationship with Fédier ended. Not just because of the affair but also because of this business with the letters. Fédier became increasingly hostile toward me.

I have to add another thing: my relationship with Beaufret was not seriously affected by all this. Later, after this story, I exchanged some friendly words with him, and there were a few signs, on several occasions, that indicated that he did not hold this against me and that he still respected me! As for me, I let him know that the matter was a past issue. It was long afterward that there were issues of denial.

I saw Beaufret again. I invited him to meet, if my memory serves me. I had invited him; it was Jambet who had come to see me, a Jambet who was close to me and then deferential. He was in *khâgne* at that time. He wanted to organize a talk for his *khâgne* friends on Artaud and Heidegger or on Artaud-Heidegger-Nietzsche, at the École Normale. I organized a session for him, and Beaufret came. I remember having seen Beaufret listen to this young fellow's talk. This was after the affair.

Although you were invited to contribute to L'Endurance de la pensée, *the same cannot be said for the seminars in Le Thor in 1968 and 1969?*

In 1969 I was already persona non grata! Before, I was not considered a bona fide Heideggerian nor was I one. I read Heidegger, but I was not known in those circles as someone who had a privileged connection to Heidegger.

When you published "Ousia and Grammē" in 1972, in Margins, *did you not add a note (62n37) where you criticized, simultaneously, both Heideggerian devotion and anti-Heideggerianism for the same refusal to read?*

The note was not added. One can read it already in the original volume, *L'Endurance de la pensée* (266). Because I found myself, I still find myself, with others, in the situation of a nondevotee who, at the same time, cannot stand the anti-Heideggerians. We are caught in the cross fire. I am as allergic to the Heidegger devotees as I am to the run-of-the-mill anti-Heideggerians. I strive to find a path, a line, a place where one might continue to read Heidegger seriously, to question him without giving in either to political Heideggerianism or to its opposite . . . There is nothing original in this: there are a few of us who respect this rule. I wanted to emphasize this.

In Positions, *I read: "What I have attempted to do would not have been possible without the opening of Heidegger's questions . . . but despite this debt to Heidegger's thought, or rather because of it, I attempt to locate in Heidegger's text . . . the signs of a belonging to metaphysics" (9–10). You add later: "I sometimes have the feeling that the Heideggerian problematic*

*is the most 'profound' and 'powerful' defense of what I attempt to put into
question under the rubric of the thought of presence" (55). This is in 1972.*

Indeed, I found a knot there, which at bottom I have always thought was there,
whether rightly or not. But in order to speak about this, one would have to consider things again in depth. It is less easy than telling stories!

From that moment on, in 1968, an endless *Auseinandersetzung* with Heidegger was engaged and set forth in all my texts. This is why it would be difficult
for me to speak about this because that gesture is reproduced and displaced in
all of my texts—with some regrets. Sometimes I complicate matters further. But
it would be difficult to discuss this in this informal setting. The question of presence, that's a very complicated thing, particularly in "Ousia and Grammē."

*You even told me that you had given up on the
expression "metaphysics of presence."*

Even if I wanted to defend myself against the attacks, from this moment on—I
have said this repeatedly, you can read it in *Margins*—I did not think that there
was only one metaphysics of presence, delimited by a linear circle. It is a plural
field, and this closure is not a simple one. Nonetheless, since this expression was
misleading, since it was often interpreted in polemical works and simplified as if
I ignored or neglected all sorts of internal ruptures and interior differentiations,
I abandoned it. It clarified and formalized issues at a certain moment, but I no
longer use it.

Is this also related to the question of the closure of so-called metaphysics?

I distinguish between closure and end; closure is not a unilinear closure, it is not
a closed totality. Closure is a certain type of exhaustion that does not simply imply an inside and an outside. The notion of closure is not very satisfactory either.
I no longer use these words. It is not that I deny that pedagogical or strategic moment, but I think it is inopportune to use these words any further.

*There was also the reading of Nietzsche (with and against
Heidegger) that must have played a part in this evolution?*

As early as these first texts, starting with *Of Grammatology* obviously: I addressed
the question of writing and of style. Heidegger's reading of Nietzsche, which I
have always found extremely powerful and which I worked on quite intensively
at that time, seemed very strong to me but it also misunderstood a certain gesture of Nietzsche's, which is why I tarried so long on the questions of writing and
signature.

It is in "The Supplement of the Copula," a text in *Margins,* as well as in "White Mythology," that Heidegger plays an important role, even though the conclusions, if one can speak in this way (this word is not very appropriate), are not Heideggerian. But whether the issue is metaphor, or the verb "being" in "The Supplement of the Copula," in the debate with Benveniste (the opposition between Benveniste-Heidegger-Vuillemin) or whether the issue is the concept of the human in "The Ends of Man," in each case Heidegger is a major organizing reference, but at the same time there is an opportunity to question some of his positions.

In Writing and Difference *there is a relatively corrosive expression about Heidegger: "With as much lucidity and rigor as bad faith and misconstruction" (356). Is this a conflictual relation?*

In any case, it is one of admiration, respect, recognition, and at the same time a relation of profound allergy and of irony; which is why he is always present. For example, in the book on travels that is called *Counterpath,* there are discussions of Heidegger, both in Catherine Malabou's essay on me as well as in the letters that I address to her—and there, as in *The Post Card,* there is a certain figure (a little Hebraic, for fun) of Heidegger, as a permanent witness, who always accompanies me like a ghost. For me, he is something like a watchman, a thinking that always keeps watch over me—an overseer who is always watching over me, a thinking that, I feel, has me under surveillance. It is a model—against which I naturally rebel too, I pose questions, I am ironic. There is all that, and one would have to succeed in putting all that on stage with an extreme ambivalence, and it is why I cannot tolerate either devout Heideggerians or the anti-Heideggerians.

It is a very tense relation, very singular . . .

Unique. For me, it is unique. I know of no other thinker, either in this century or in general, with whom I have had, with whom I still have, a concerned relationship of frustrated admiration. Really, I am never bored when I read him. I know it will be endless, I know that I will never ultimately settle matters with him. For me, it is an inexhaustible relationship, which is made of, again, movements of positive admiration, of recognition, of debt and then, sometimes quite severely, of critical impatience, and always very ironic.

For me, there are two images of Heidegger: there is the image of Heidegger as a great thinker, and there is the image of a slow, heavy, somewhat vulgar man, uncultivated in certain respects—from the point of view of literature, or of the arts. I remember once, in Rome, during a conference on Benjamin, and I can see myself walking down a street in Rome, at night, with Beda Alleman, who said to me: "You know, Heidegger is uneducated. He knows nothing about so many matters in German literature, in contemporary art . . ." And I was flabbergasted at having heard this man who knew Heidegger well, say to me directly, calmly: "You cannot imagine Heidegger's lack of culture!" I remember this often and I understand him even better now. I have to say that there are aspects of nonrefinement in Heidegger, and I am as sensitive to them as I am, inversely, to his extraordinary cultivation, his reading, his knowledge, his expertise in Greek thought, in German thought, and in Christian theology.

These days, what is happening for me with respect to Heidegger increasingly takes place in terms of traditions that I am not familiar with but that I intend to study: such as Eckhart, whom I know fairly well, as well as Luther, whom I am not directly familiar with. I feel more and more that Heidegger is illegible without this background. I had already identified Silesius and Eckhart, who, apparently, were familiar reading for him. And then there was the Lutheran tradition. Even the word *Destruktion*—I learned this from John Caputo—stems apparently from a Lutheran usage of *destructio,* the Latin word that designates (I haven't read the texts, I am reporting what I read in Caputo) the desedimentation, the deconstitution of a later theology that would have obscured the original biblical message. Therefore, *destructio* would consist in reconstituting, by an act of remembrance, the original biblical message by destroying and deconstructing the theological strata. Hence, we have a Lutheran gesture, a Lutheran word—this teaches us much that is useful. Heidegger often says that deconstruction is an act of remembrance, of reappropriation—not of destruction, but of reappropriation by remembrance—of a hidden originary meaning. Increasingly, I tell myself that it is by reading Luther, and Schelling as well, that one has access to a certain Heidegger whom I have not finished reading, despite frequenting the texts for multiple decades . . .

Did he conceal certain sources?

He did not conceal them, but we did not go to look for them. I cite this reference to Luther because, in fact, my endless debate with Heidegger concerns the meaning to be given to "deconstruction," the usage of this word. What concept corresponds to this word? This is an endless explication.

One of the things that has interested me the most in Heidegger is this very important moment toward which Françoise Dastur oriented me, which I evoked in a note in *Of Spirit:*[4] it is the *Zusage* that precedes, in a nonlogical and nonchronological sense of the term, the *Fragen* as *Frömmigkeit des Denkens; Zusage,* as affirmation, acquiescence. This gesture is important for me, I have reappropriated it while displacing it into other contexts, into other discursive forms. There is something "older" and more serious than the question. The question itself is carried by an affirmation that is not a precritical, dogmatic affirmation. A yes conditions even *das Fragen,* or the most critical, the most deconstructive question. It is, in my texts, a very important theme that I relate often, at least in its logical, somehow descriptive form, to Heidegger. At the point where he says, "I have often said that *das Fragen* was *die Frömmigkeit des Denkens,* but one must understand what is meant by *Frömmigkeit;* etymologically (Heidegger insists on this) it is not just piety, there is something more—neither first nor originary—that is enveloped in *das Fragen.*" And this gesture, is for me, of great use, even if I then transpose it.

And that would allow one to resume the dialogue with Levinas?

Yes, no doubt. Levinas, with whom I have an equally complicated relationship. In other ways.

But less sarcastic?

It is not the same sarcasm, it is not the same type. There are also moments of impatience. In all my texts on Levinas, there are also "negative," "critical," "sarcastic" moments. In all of them. Regardless of my admiration. I am in the process of writing a book on Jean-Luc Nancy, about the question of touching, and I encounter Levinas, who speaks of the caress and of Eros. In that book, I wrote some very "critical," somewhat mocking, sentences.

In the end, when I try to analyze or to establish a sort of typology of my relationships with respect to those people whom I consider the great thinkers of this century, Heidegger, Levinas—and Blanchot, with respect to all three there is some violence. It is not the same violence in all cases; the one who resists best is Blanchot. There are, in Blanchot, some very discrete passages on friendship, on fraternity, that I have also come to suspect (not to mention directly, the political past). There are questions, but in the end with respect to Blanchot I feel fewer tensions, fewer highs and lows.

Can we discuss Of Spirit? *What is surprising is that you anticipated in some ways, but in a more interesting manner because it was more philosophical, that great shock that took place around the political question.*

It was almost simultaneous, it is very curious. In 1987, the "Farias" book came out in a space of a few weeks from my book.

When you say at the beginning: "I shall speak of the ghost, of the flame, of ashes and of what is meant, for Heidegger, by 'avoiding,'" one is very worried!

Yes. But the whole book turns around this citation, "avoiding."

Has sufficient attention been paid to the ambiguity of avoiding?...

Clearly, the book was published at the moment that the affair broke, Farias's book created the uproar that you know, and curiously, I was identified by Farias as a Heideggerian although my approach was not at all Heideggerian, to say the least. It was very complicated from the outset. I tried to explain myself in *Le Nouvel Observateur*. I do not know how we can reconsider this tangle of knots, which were so overdetermined at that time in France. Things have abated now. But what remains?

Wasn't the result a relative disaffection among the students?
Heidegger no longer seems to be "fashionable"...

Really? I am not aware what is happening among students, but my feeling, from a distance, is that this affair, this Farias moment, has not at all hurt the reading of or the interest in Heidegger. On the contrary, I have had the impression—I do not have any statistics here—that it has not at all discouraged the reading of Heidegger, and I am glad.

Of course, it is not a huge readership, but I find no fewer students today reading Heidegger, or who are interested in Heidegger, than at the beginning of the 1980s, and this is very encouraging. I would say the same thing, *mutatis mutandis*, about Paul de Man in the United States: one could have had the impression that they were going to burn him at the stake; on the contrary, however, the good students were not impressed by the invective; they read him without dogmatism, and without being slavish . . . This will never concern the masses. Since it has been addressed by scholars, philosophers, and teachers, and since it played a productive strategic role, I have the impression that the "affair" was not at all detrimental to the consideration of Heidegger in studies that matter. There are, everywhere, philosophers who think; Heidegger's political history has not discouraged nor distracted them.

Certainly not at an essential level. But it has to play a role at the more
superficial level of relations of influence, of "academic power," for example,
when it comes to hiring. Let us say that Beaufret himself thought he had
been a victim of this, since he never had a university career...

I think this played a considerable role; I think of Beaufret's resentment, for example against philosophers who had some power, Wahl, Jankélévitch, etc. He accused them of having sidelined, or marginalized, him, based on political anti-Heideggerianism. I think that it was because of this that he perhaps let himself rail against the "great Jewish professors" of the Sorbonne who, like Jankélévitch, no longer wanted to hear talk of Heidegger. . . . Wahl, for his part, gave lectures on Heidegger and neither foreclosed nor ostracized him.

What do you think of the Gesamtausgabe, *the collected works?*

I feel guilty for not having read the ones that have appeared lately, but there is therein an incalculable future. Heidegger's future will emerge from the deciphering of these texts.

I have read the *Beiträge* but not yet seriously enough; I feel guilty for not having worked on the recent publications of the last decade as I worked on what came before.

And what do you think of my project?

"Heidegger in France" does not designate one of the possible sites of immigration or transplantation for Heidegger's thought. There is no "Heidegger in Russia," "Heidegger in England," or "Heidegger in America." "Heidegger in France" is an original outgrowth, an incomparable event, from a national point of view. In France, there was much more than a reception of Heidegger; there was something different. I think there is a Heidegger to whom we had no access. If there is a Heidegger-Event in this century, France will have counted no less than Germany. I would not say this of any other country, even if in other countries there is at times excellent knowledge of Heidegger—in Italy, in the United States, in Spain (it is there that *Sein und Zeit* was translated for the first time). Nonetheless, in none of the three countries, a fortiori anywhere else, was there an event that could be referred to in the same manner: if someone said "Heidegger in England," everyone would laugh; "Heidegger in France," that is a different story . . .

And in Germany?

Even in Germany there was little fruition. The organic metaphor, the vegetal metaphor, the metaphor of *phusis,* comes to me perhaps too quickly, but there was no flowering, no emergence of an irreducible thinking. This is because what happened in France, despite the importing or the debt, was an idiomatic event. To explain this, one has to take into account other factors as well: in the background, there is the entire French contribution. There, an incomparable transplantation took place, a hybrid—what is it called these days? A genetically modified organism. There was something of this order: Heidegger in France, a genetically modified organism—unique.

What I just said about transplantation, about the absolutely original hybrid, Heidegger would not have understood. He had no access to this. He continued to think that France was a country where people were interested in him, but he did not, in my opinion, have any access to this kind of growth, of birth. He was not interested in what was irreducibly French in French Heideggerianism. He had the following prejudice: the French are lightweights (see what Kant says). He could not take French thought seriously.

"Heidegger in France" is, in any case, a phenomenon, and its signs must be sought out not only among all those whom I have been talking about, those who cite Heidegger, refer to him, people who have explicit recourse to Heidegger (and I am among them), but even among people who do not cite him, or are in denial in relation to him, those who seldom cite him, or rarely, but who are just as much influenced by Heidegger as the others, like Foucault, Deleuze . . . Foucault said this at the end of his life without further explanation. I think that the hybridization that I am talking about is visible not just in the works of those who explicitly dedicated texts to Heidegger, but also among those who silenced the name of Heidegger but for whom he was just as important. Lyotard too. One would have to determine this further. Because in the end he is everywhere. Among journalists too, as among journalist-philosophers, it is the same thing. I have the impression that they reacted to the Farias affair as a counter-cathexis. And even if students do not read him much, or the general public for example, Heidegger definitely (one should do a study), even on the streets, is the name of a famous philosopher; even if people know nothing more, he is the most famous German philosopher. If one were to ask people on the street, "who is Heidegger?," one would be surprised, it is my hypothesis, that there would be more positive responses than for Hegel, Nietzsche, even Bergson.

For people of our generation, there was a moment when, during the last two decades, we came into contact with remarkable Heideggerians who were neither French nor German, namely, Americans. It is known that there are good readers of Heidegger in the United States. People like us have communicated with Americans and Britons, and we have come to respect a certain competence there, a certain vigilance, a watchfulness . . . The American Catholic universities were at the forefront: Notre-Dame, Loyola, and Villanova.

Coming back to the Farias affair, I would like to know what you felt when you did the interview with Le Nouvel Observateur. Was there not a sort of hostility toward you when, for example, Maggiori wrote, "Derrida keeps Heidegger at a distance"?

That interview was reprinted in *Points*. I can remember the atmosphere back then. All of a sudden, there was this, shall we say, journalistic explosion. I had just written *Of Spirit*, which, in its own way, posed political questions to Heidegger, which, I dare say, were serious and radical. And then—a chronological coincidence to which I was naturally very sensitive—the moment when I presented this talk (in an international conference on Heidegger), I felt—as in the case of all those who had been interested in Heidegger for a long time—on the one hand, that I was aware of the political question, and on the other hand, in my own way, not wanting to carry out a quick trial, I was posing substantive questions. Then the Farias book came out, and it was greeted by the press or by those in the university who have an easier time speaking in newspapers than elsewhere, as a quite scandalous revelation, the great discovery about Heidegger's shameful past! Then, I read Farias's book and I explained my position in the interview in *l'Observateur*. Besides the fact that I could not find anything fundamentally new, I was shocked, simultaneously by the claim to novelty, by the astonishment of the journalist philosophers (these journalists are philosophy professors) who not only made some fuss, which was not the worst part, but an accusatory racket not so much with respect to Heidegger, but with respect to those people in France who, according to the journalists, had cultivated their Heideggerian affiliation for a long time without any questions, and without any shame, etc. I found this to be very shocking. Maggiori's little clever line—"Derrida keeps Heidegger at a distance"—was an attempt at a play on words implying that he was quite attentive to the fact that *Of Spirit* was critical of Heidegger, in a very muted style, very discretely—basically without fireworks, and that in the end, I did not seem to be upset by the Shoah, and that I spoke calmly. "Keeping at a distance" meant that I, naturally, distanced myself from Heidegger (which is something I had always done, well before 1987) but that I respectfully continued, at the same time, to spare Heidegger, contrary to Farias. So, I found his reaction both quite odd since it was spread over two pages, with a lot of noise, and quite typical of the journalistic reaction in general. I found this gesticulating very shocking and unfair with respect to those who had been attempting to think with Heidegger for a long time—and perhaps against him—but not simply to follow him. It was unfair. It was a little heavy-handed, a little crude and naive: these people were discovering the matter; now the political question concerning Heidegger had been raised for the last thirty years! It was in that *Stimmung* that I responded to Didier Éribon's request for an interview with *l'Observateur*, where I tried to say all this in a different manner. I remember having been sarcastic and scathing about Farias, but above all I remember having tried to state my reservations concerning Heidegger's thinking, and my respect, indeed, for that thinking, as well as my feeling that if it were necessary to pose political questions without holding back, then it would have to be done with the vigilance of thought that was required. In short, that one would have to begin by reading. It is a clarification that I wanted to make as carefully as possible.

This interview, which was later translated, started an entire scandal in the United States. Let me explain the story briefly: one day, maybe two years later, I am in New York and I see a book by Richard Wolin and, in the middle of this somewhat accusatory book written in Farias's style, I find translated and published my interview, with innumerable errors in translation, serious errors, and inscribed within an interpretative paradigm that was very violent toward me. I therefore reacted against the fact that this had been published without my consent and in a context of which I could not approve, etc. This article was at the center of a major American affair, once again, and as always, it was journalistic-academic in nature. It is nonetheless interesting from a structural-typical point of view that all these affairs are managed in some way, and one can indeed say managed, by people who are neither purely or simply journalists, nor academics, but go-betweens, by philosophers who write for magazines and who always do this under conditions that are hardly respectable. And, in the United States, this was the case of Thomas Sheehan and others who wrote appalling things, unworthy of elementary deontology. Afterward, I published a response to all this in the American translation of *Points*. The leavening of all these affairs is always tabloid sensationalism. It is from the moment that things are taken up, simplified, and inflated in the press that it rises.

In Counterpath, *I see a note on page 55 where you speak*
of the attacks of an illiterate commentator who called
Heideggerians "precious damsels [précieuses ridicules]."

That was Polac. I did not want to name him; he is an expert, a specialist in this type of degradation, of denigration, of vulgar insults: resentment, hostility, and triumphant incompetence.

Things have calmed down a lot since this affair. And what of the aftermath?

Having a relatively rich experience of these stories, whether it be Heidegger or Paul de Man, I note that in both cases one has to deal with a journalistic or academic armed revolt, eager to settle a score, all sorts of scores, and not necessarily nor essentially with the accused or the dead—but with living people, all sorts of living people. But in the end, once the fight is over, and it had been ferocious, violent and discouraging, everything cools and settles down, and the essential issues remain. This does not discourage scholars from continuing to read Heidegger and de Man. I can testify to this in both cases. One might have thought, if one were to have read Maggiori in 1987, that Heidegger was going to be "shelved." But the research on Heidegger continues and it is more and more rigorous and extensive. This teaches us that we should not be impressed by eruptions in the tabloid media type. This makes me appreciate the university—it opens another time, a different duration, another filtering (it is not always the best filtering, no doubt, but there is another time, for evaluation). And when a corpus has to withstand such attacks, it resists. This is the case for Heidegger. This in no way exonerates

Heidegger of the political responsibilities we have mentioned, but it shows that there is something else that is at stake, and even from the political point of view, that it is worth continuing to work on.

I have to say that while I continue to be impressed by and drawn to Heidegger's thought in my teaching, I know that I will never stop coming back to it and that I will never be done with an infinite task. Despite all my questions, all the reservations that I might have, I continue to think that an enormous task awaits me and that I must confess that these last years, I have not succeeded in following, as I should have, all the publications, all the translations. I would like to have the time, the leisure, the freedom to start reading again: to start everything all over again. From time to time, I go and glean something, but I have not been able to carry out this work. What constitutes Heidegger's irresistible force for me is that I sense that there is still a lot in reserve. This word "reserve" must remain ambiguous: my reservations [*réserves*], his works in reserve . . .

. . . and in Counterpath *you say that Heidegger is your "overseer" [contremaître].*

As it turns out, the word "counter" [*contre*], if I may be allowed to emphasize it myself, plays a very turbulent role in this text. I am always going on about "counterparts,'" "counterexamples," "counterpaths," etc. I present myself as someone who relates to himself all the time as a counterexample—or as the counterpart of himself; someone who has to incorporate, take into account the counterpart or the counterexample of what he is, does, or thinks. I am the counterexample of myself, I am in a sort of contradiction. Thus, I say—I think it is in *Circumfession*—that deep down, I, more than anyone else (or at least as much as anyone else), am a metaphysician of presence: I desire nothing more than presence, voice, all these things I have questioned; therefore, I am, as it were, the counterexample of what I am advocating. I formalize this logic of counter-exemplarity and of the counterpart, which plays such a large role in *Circumfession*. I say that I am my own counterexample. This comes back very strongly in *Counterpath* not just because of the word "counterpath," which I try to put to work, but because of the word "counter" and of contra. When I say: *"counter to* Heidegger's order"* (*Counterpath*, 56), it is because he haunts me, in *Counterpath* as in *The Post Card;* he is always there, watching me and reproaching me for something. I do what Heidegger would not like to see being done or would not do himself, for example, traveling, taking an interest in technology, etc. I am always in the process of disobeying a Heideggerian injunction, which I, nonetheless, sense in myself. And so he is there, he haunts me like a sort of strict father and, for example, I have fun imagining him reproaching me for travelling: you can't think while traveling, its distracting. He who never travels! I do the opposite all the time—but under his watch. He is a sort of specter.

In *Athens, Still Remains* precisely, I questioned his attitude as a traveler, while I, on the other hand, have great respect for it. He takes issue with tourism and photography. And then there are these pages that he wrote in *Sojourns*, on Rome and Greece, and on Orthodox churches. There is a classic protest by him—this will bring us back to the word "counter"—against Latin and against Roman culture, which, to him, represent metaphysical decadence. Let us return to the word "counter," specifically to Latin and to Heidegger's criticism. In the passage in *Counterpath* where I say "*counter to* Heidegger's order" (*Counterpath*, 56) while underlining "counter," I was interested in the usage of the Latin word *contra* and I especially emphasized the semantics of the Latin and on everything tied up with it. "*Counter to* Heidegger's order," is not against his thinking of *Gegend*, etc., which is why I insist, as it were, on the Latin. It is also a question of writing: I have the impression that when I rely on the resources for thinking that are provided by the Latin language, and the French, then I am already betraying Heidegger. And I do it all the time. So I have fun, on this point as well, of speaking against Heidegger before Heidegger. My admiration is compensated by mocking his heavy-handedness, his inability to play, to understand literature. All these are my reservations. Heidegger is present and challenged from one end of the book to the other. In a certain way, I try not to protest against what he says of *Gegend*, or of *Begegnen*, but to reorient the thinking of traveling in terms of encounter. Because at the same time, it would be unfair to say that he is against traveling: he didn't travel; he was opposed to a certain type of tourism, but he probably had nothing against another type of travel, the "Hölderlinian" type for example. Nonetheless, there is, in my book, an atmosphere tied to the experience of traveling that is not attuned with the Heideggerian atmosphere, and so I try to account for this, to assume it. There is thus, in this passage, a play against Heidegger and at the same time an attempt to assume, in a thinking of the event as encounter of the unexpected, as what falls upon us, something of what Heidegger says about *Gegend* and *Begegnen:* a thinking of the event that is at the same time close to Heidegger and very far from him.

In what I say of the event, there is something that cannot be easily rendered in Heideggerian terms. I am on the side of dislocation, of dispersion, of dissemination. It would be unfair and a simplification to say that Heidegger negates difference, dislocation, or dissemination: one could have a reading of Heidegger that would show that he does think dislocation. But there is a force that draws him toward gathering, toward being near oneself. The difficulty is one of knowing whether one can think *Versammlung* while including in it, integrating and assimilating into it, the play of difference, of dislocation, of dissociation, or whether it is only to the extent that there is an irreducible risk of dispersion, of singularity, of dissemination, that *Versammlung* can emerge. It is a very abstract way of saying something whose stakes are found everywhere. For example—in *Specters of Marx* I speak about it with respect to justice—when Heidegger legitimately attempts to withdraw *dikē* from the Roman thinking of *jus,* he comes back to a thinking of harmony and of *Versammlung,* to *legein,* and gathering in a certain sense. I try to oppose this justice (even if it is thought or if it thinks beyond something that arrives later, namely Roman law) with the necessity of dissociation, of infinite alterity: there is no justice except where there is an insurmountable dissociation and disharmony. I would not want to give in to the pathos of the tear [*déchirement*]; nonetheless, justice, a certain thinking of justice, assumes disharmony, absolute dissonance, alterity, and absolute singularity—something that does not allow itself to be gathered. I say in a very abstract manner that there is something whose stakes are, I think, immeasurable. It is another axiomatics: thinking the One, gathering, *legein* or *Versammlung* based on the possibility of the different, of dissociation, of the incommensurable, rather than the contrary.

Here we find what you have said elsewhere regarding the retreat of metaphor.

In this case as well, we have a trace that cannot be gathered, a repetition, thus also a division. I hesitate to speak of it too quickly: I am convinced that one could find in Heidegger the means to think this difference, this dissociation. He indeed conceives of conflict as that which gathers adversaries, that which holds together two opposed poles; while I think of a difference that would not even hold together what differs. There are Heideggerian texts on *polemos,* on conflict, on the rift, adversity, and opposition, but also on that which holds enemies, or adversaries together. I try to think a difference that cannot be gathered. Obviously, the consequences of this debate extend in an incalculable fashion across the entire field of thinking, the entire positioning of the history of philosophy, of epochality.

This also puts into question the conception of history: according to
Heidegger, is not the destinal sending the unique sending of the West?

In the end, the sending is gathered. I understand the necessity of this logic, but even if Heidegger does not embrace a teleology, there is still the pole of a destination for the sending, for the dispensation that must be gathered. If one thinks this destination based on errancy or on nondestination, what I call "destinerrance," one puts into question a certain interpretation of the unity of metaphysics, and one takes technology into consideration. But I can imagine Heidegger's reply, or that of certain of his interpreters; they would say that clearly Heidegger's texts also contain this "destinerrance"—and it is true that in very early Heidegger there is this idea of "errancy," even if for him it always emerges from the horizon of a gathering, from a sending of being.

Being matters here, whatever one might say. It is being, in its difference from beings, and different from the concept of being, that gathers and harmonizes the *legein* and the *Versammlung,* and that is where things are decided. While I sense the necessity and the force of this thinking, I resist it in the name of what no longer allows itself to be gathered—alas! Alas and no, in fact, because the fact of resisting the gathering might be felt as a distress, a sadness, a loss—dislocation, dissemination, the not being at home, etc.—but it is also an opportunity. It is the opportunity of an encounter, of justice, of a relation to absolute alterity. Whereas on the contrary, there, when this risk and this opportunity do not exist, the worst can happen: under the authority of *Versammlung,* of logos, and of being, the worst can advance with its political figures. If we had the time, I would attempt to show that, on my side, the side of dissociation, obviously there are the threats of the worst, of death, but also of the best opportunity. And inversely, on the side of the gathering or of the logos of ebbing there is, clearly, the chance of gathering, but also surely the chance of a nonencounter, a certain blindness to the other, a certain cancellation of the event, a certain pure noneventfulness. That would be the argument. I can imagine that people who would polemicize or would plead Heidegger's case against what I am trying to propose could find resources in Heidegger to say things similar to what I would like to say. And they would, no doubt, be right, to a certain extent. The question is, in the end, that of emphasis, insistence, of the extent, of the stress. And there, undeniably, Heidegger stressed gathering—this is what has to be interpreted historically. Why was he led to stress *Versammlung* and not the contrary? With respect to the side to which I am drawn, not "on my side," but the side toward which I feel carried in my reservations with regards to Heidegger, the stress is instead on the side of alterity, of dissociation, of infinite distance, of dispersion, of the incommensurable, of the impossible, and of "destinerrance."

To account for this gap different arguments can be considered. One might, at first, talk of a generation gap. Historically, Heidegger is a thinker of the interwar years; the formation of his thinking belongs to a different period. This is a question of generations, but also a question of nations. On the question of Judaism, I would be very careful. I grew up in a cultural milieu that was as Christian as it was Jewish.

Since you allude to it, this might be the moment to append a question about what you think of Marlène Zarader's work (in The Unthought Debt) *concerning Heidegger's secret Hebraism.*

Basically I think that she is right. Heidegger silenced every reference to Jewish thinkers, from Spinoza to Bergson, to more originary Hebraic matters, and to what one calls the "Old Testament." One can perceive a factual violence, deliberate or not, with respect to the Jewish tradition. What Zarader says is, on the whole, convincing. It remains to be seen why, where, and how Heidegger did this. I wonder if it is because he was seeking the non-Greek or pre-Greek that would lead necessarily to the other of the Greek. Whether he did this on the basis of his background as a Catholic theologian, he knew the Bible, and the entire Protestant and Catholic traditions. Despite everything, when we speak of hearing, did he hear these texts, directly or through Protestant texts, which contain considerable Judaic material? Where did this hearing occur? He made no legible or explicit effort to refer to Judaic texts. This is indisputable. Why? This would be one of the great ideologico-political dossiers.

To come back to my humble case, what I say about the letter or about disassociation can refer either to a Judaic tradition or to Levinas. But I would be very careful, since I think the matter is more complicated; paradoxically, I am still less knowledgeable about Judaism than Heidegger was. He encountered it by way of theological texts, but I did not. I have no knowledge of Judaism—unfortunately. Even reading the Bible seriously is something that I only did later. On the other hand, Levinas, for me, is something as complicated as Heidegger. So there we have a knot, a great number of knots. In order to untie them, one would need a lot of time and a lot of care. My relation to the Jewish question is almost as complicated as my relation to Heidegger—or as complicated as Heidegger's relation to the Jewish question! None of this is clear for me.

Can we dwell for a moment on The Post Card?

We can return briefly to the relevance of the postal service and to what I tried to articulate in *The Post Card*. From the moment when one puts into question this authority of the sending, this prevalence of the destinal sending that governs, in sum, the Heideggerian interpretation of the epochality of being, then one is forced to reattribute to the technical dimension of sending—what I call "postal service" [*la poste*]—an importance that Heidegger would probably not have given it. He would have found this interest of postal, in the history of postal services, in the history of techniques of transmission, of emitting and receiving, a derivative and limited consequence of metaphysics. Thus he would not have accorded it the importance that I was driven to give it. On the other hand, if one is no longer satisfied with the gathering of the sending and if one speaks of a "destinerrance" of sending, of a sending that also depends on the addressee, that moment, clearly technological, takes on a determining dignity and is no longer just a secondary side effect. And at that moment, all of philosophy, metaphysics, and Greek philosophy, all that constitutes the corpus of Heidegger's questioning, is situated, on the contrary, in a more enveloping history of the postal service, a history of sendings, of techniques of destination. I often have a lot of fun, in *The Post Card*, in presenting the Master-thinkers as Postmasters: people who control the passing on of messages, who intercept messages, and who, in a Nietzschean gesture, attempt to mark their authority and their power by appropriating the means of transmission, in other words, with the history of the techniques and means of communication, the history of routes, and the political history of postal services. I suppose Heidegger would have considered all this some sort of technico-anthropological effect that, even if it were interesting in itself, did not have the dignity of what he calls a "sending." That is where I attempt a sort of displacement, in a constantly uneasy explication with Heidegger. In *The Post Card,* one finds basically the same scenario as in *Counterpath,* where Heidegger is present, watching over my gestures, and where I try to justify myself before him, to challenge him, and to argue against him while striving to take him seriously.

It is always the same scenario, from Heidegger the master to Heidegger the overseer: someone whom I oppose with a sort of irreverent respect. But here, the argument that I am attempting to reconstitute is a little better articulated in *The Post Card,* with respect to this history of the postal service. Obviously, *The Post Card* dates from 1980: I attempt to be consistent with what I had written about the trace much earlier, that is to say regarding separation, the fact that the trace *departs from* me, leaves me, and basically wanders errantly without a predetermined destination, or with such a destination that can only be determined based on the response of the other. Everything that I say about the trace against presence, against the gap of presence, attempts to be consistent with the history of the postal.

Heidegger himself sent letters, in particular the "Letter on Humanism," which turned into a book: did he unify them?

What is curious is, if we want to return to a form of contemporary political journalism, that the Sloterdijk affair, this business of letters, the debate with Habermas, comes back paradoxically to the premises of what we are now discussing, of course without referring to it. The thematics are clearly that of reading and that of the letter to friends. The relation between letters, postcards, and what I had called the "politics of friendship."

As far as I am concerned, I am very torn between my love for books, for the letter, and my acceptance of the machine; even if I speak about the end of the book, starting with *Of Grammatology,* I do not greet the arrival of all these machines without great concern. It was not only an immediate concern, but also a more reflexive. I realize that I belong to a time, that I do not want to give anything up, and that I would like to try to contribute to saving the book, saving everything that is associated with the culture of the book, without at the same time rejecting, condemning, or having a reactionary attitude with regard to post-book machines. Undeniably, Heidegger—even though he often criticizes what he calls literature or in any case writing in favor of the spoken word, to say it quickly—is on the side of the book. In the field that we are discussing, he is on the side of the culture of the book and not the culture of word-processing machines. I, like people of my generation, err between the two.

That is where Heidegger is very strong: he gives thought to what is happening, and even to the danger of what is happening. He spoke of cybernetics his whole life. It is certain that he has given thought to the matter, in his own way. It is necessary to have neither a taste for nor an expertise in technology in order to think technology more profoundly than the technologists and the technicians, and I think that Heidegger indeed understood what was happening with technology.

Everything that we said moments ago about the event, the encounter, the dissociation, everything that resists a certain emphasis of Heideggerian thought—all this can be transcribed in a thinking of hospitality, of unconditional hospitality, that is to say, a hospitality that is exposed, with no horizon of expectation, to the surprise of what comes. All this, in fact, takes precedence over a certain phase of the deconstruction of the metaphysics of presence, while being, I would hope, consistent with that moment. Obviously, it would be simplistic to say that there is no thinking of hospitality in Heidegger: there are many texts on *Heimat* and on welcoming, on gathering. In *Adieu to Emmanuel Levinas,* I tried to distinguish between gathering and the welcoming that is an exposition to the other rather than a gathering (this latter being on the side of reception), but naturally, if one were to be honest and sympathetic to Heidegger, one would be able to find elements of hospitality and of friendship in Heidegger. And yet, it is not at the center of his thinking. This brings us back to the question of ethics in Levinas, back to the manner in which Heidegger treats the question of ethics. On this point too I am perplexed, I would not want to give the impression of playing Levinas against Heidegger, because again, my relation to Levinas, which is also very much one of debt and admiration, is not one without reservations. It is true that in the course of these last years, it was the theme of friendship that pushed me, at the end of *The Politics of Friendship,* to question Heidegger in the texts concerning polemology, hospitality, the beyond of cosmopolitanism, and of a "democracy to come." Obviously, Heidegger is not a democrat. I, for my part, attempt to think, under the heading of a "democracy to come," a hospitality beyond the nation-state: a new international. Along all these paths that would be difficult to recollect quickly now, I no longer see Heidegger. Even an exchange with him is no longer foreseeable, and this is the case for all the books that I have written these last years, from *Specters of Marx, The Politics of Friendship,* to the little book *Of Hospitality.*

Apparently, the exchange with Heidegger has grown weaker, even if it has not been interrupted, but I think that one could reconstitute it. In *Specters of Marx,* it would be around themes of justice and *dikē;* in *The Politics of Friendship,* it would be in the very last text on polemos, on polemology. And then all my critical or "deconstructive" readings of Carl Schmitt, in this text, are inscribed in a scene where Heidegger is not absent. I do not at all want to reduce Heidegger to Schmitt: there was a truly intractable differend between them, but there was also a common space, and, in order to talk about this seriously, one would have to go back to Schmitt and to Heidegger, not on the political question, but on the question of decision, of the enemy, of war, of the state, of the nation-state, and of sovereignty. In the end, if I were to reread Heidegger now with these questions in mind, I would go and look at what he said, if he spoke of it, about citizenship, and about the nation. In the "Letter on Humanism," he says that internationalism is a sort of nationalism. How far did he pursue this line or reasoning? Today, I am interested in questioning the idea of sovereignty, the onto-theologico-political idea of sovereignty with all the contemporary stakes, in particular the death penalty. I would try to see if there is in Heidegger any trace of a reflection on the history of sovereignty, the history of the state. There are things on the *polis:* I would like to reread Heidegger from this perspective, through another prism of political questions concerning the state, citizenship—and democracy.

There might be, within an apparently circumscribed and certain field, events of thought whose effect would be to disorganize or to reorganize the entire hierarchy. A technological, biological, or techno-biological event could require a rethinking of the entire general organization and the hierarchy of the fields. It is an idea to which Heidegger was not very receptive. Neither was Husserl nor Hegel. One has to accept being provoked by things that come from places where they would not have been expected. But what we can affirm, in the fields of theory and of French thought, is that people have, in general, wanted to make a choice between, on the one hand, Husserlian, Heideggerian fundamentalism—the "serious philosophers"—and on the other hand, people like Foucault who disputed this choice, thinking that they would do all the work as historians of this or that field and in excluding Heidegger. I think both are necessary. When something happens, it is between the two. But I do not see why one should choose between a gesture of the Hegel-Husserl-Heidegger style and a more local, regional gesture. Each calls for the other. The distinctive trait of what is happening, in our time, the time of philosophy, of the sciences, and of the technologies to come, is perhaps the necessity, that we should be increasingly aware of, of this exchange (I should not say exchange, it is an awful word), of this violent, reciprocal, troubling provocation. Someone like Stiegler is seriously interested in Heidegger and also in technologies of information, and in bioengineering. This is what is calling us: that we should not choose between the style of fundamental questions and that of local questions. That is the journey.

*Do you not think that Heidegger would only accept what you
are suggesting in one domain: his dialogue with Char?*

For him, poetry was not a field, it was a "parallel" peak (one "beside the other"), at the same height as thought. It was not a region, it was another peak. But what he did for poetry, he would not do for anything else. Even if he had some knowledge of physics, or of zoology, he used it only to remind the specialists of a fundamental questioning that they were wrong to ignore or neglect.

Is there not another domain that he disdained, namely,
that of the discipline of history as a science?

The history of historians or of anthropologists. The history of sacrifice, for example. I think there is in Heidegger a fundamental, a founding, thinking of sacrifice. But he never showed any interest in anthropological studies of sacrifice. I feel I am between the two. I do not want to have to choose. In my own personal history and taste, I am more of a "fundamentalist," so to speak, on Heidegger's side; but I feel guilty enough to consider that I should be more interested in local questions. When I speak of prosthesis, I speak at a fundamental level, somewhat quickly; in order to discuss it better, one would have to go and take a closer look. I would like to read more history, more sociology . . .

If we wanted to go back to what we were saying about gathering and dispersion, the difference between France and the United States is that in the U.S., there is a great dispersion of styles and of philosophical centers, whereas in France there is great concentration. There is a model, the figure of the philosophy professor. From the point of view of society, we think we know what a philosophy professor is, whereas in the United States, a philosopher who teaches analytic philosophy is not the same as someone who teaches traditional philosophy. At the university where I teach, in California, the philosophy department is analytic, which is why, although I am part of the philosophy faculty, I teach primarily in a literature department. And yet I teach philosophy there, but as far as the philosophy department's students are concerned, it is as if they did not have the right to come and listen to me!

Éliane Escoubas

Interview of October 19, 2000

Would you please briefly retrace your "Heideggerian itinerary" since college?

At the beginning of the sixties, in the Faculté des Lettres at Toulouse, I took classes with Gérard Granel and was greatly influenced by him. His lectures on Husserl, Kant, and Hegel (I can remember a superb course on *Faith and Knowledge*), where he developed the Heideggerian interpretation of philosophy and of its history, seemed extraordinarily enlightening to me.

After passing the Agrégation, my first class at the Toulouse Lycée for young women in the fall of 1963 was an introduction to philosophy course devoted to *What Is Called Thinking?* Obviously, this was not a systematic reading of the book, but rather the sketching out of its general contours and of the questions that it suggests and generates. This did not seem to be at all inaccessible to the students, who found therein, I believe, a new world, a new questioning, and were thus placed immediately into "the matter itself" of philosophy (that was, at least, my intention, and for them I think that it was both challenging and delightful).

I entered the University of Toulouse in 1967–68 as an assistant and, at first, I taught classes in "general philosophy." Soon thereafter, at the request of students, I taught courses in "political philosophy." It was May 1968. I was quickly confronted with the thorny topic of "aesthetics and politics." That was not my first encounter with aesthetics, for I had taught a class in aesthetics (on Dufrenne's book, more specifically on the part entitled "The Aesthetic Object") during my preparation for the Agrégation, at the request of Robert Blanché (another professor who influenced me at Toulouse but who was not at all "Heideggerian"). But the link between aesthetics and politics was new to my research. It seemed to me then, as it does now, to be of an extreme difficulty. All the cookie-cutter identifications and oppositions, which abound in this discussion, are traps whose purpose is to hide and avoid the fundamental question: the question, once again, "what is called thinking?" and above all, the *genre* of this fundamental question, which, strictly speaking, is not a question to be *resolved,* or to which we must find an *answer.* This question is included in the different epochal schemes, which it itself unfolds and only unfolds within them. Nevertheless, the connection between aesthetics and politics struck me as unfathomable in the terms in which it is always presented; nor do I consider myself to have found any other more satisfactory options. We must be very prudent and daring: a conjunction of prudence and daring, which does not seem to me to characterize the majority of contemporary investigations on this issue.

Let us continue then, if you like, with my "itinerary" as concerns Heidegger. At the end of the 1970s, I began to translate Husserl's *Ideas 2* (published by PUF in 1982 in the *Épiméthée* collection) and around 1980 I began the elaboration of my doctoral thesis—defended in 1985 and published by Galilée in 1986 under the title *Imago Mundi,* subtitled *Topologie de l'art.* My thesis, built on the two philosophical pillars Kant and Heidegger, is dedicated to what I would call a phenomenological interpretation of the work of art—and for this, my investigation chose two other pillars, painting and poetry. It was on the occasion of my thesis that I met Jacques Derrida, whose texts I had been reading for some time.

Finally, two other institutional circumstances ushered me into phenomenological and Heideggerian research. On the one hand, Jean-François Courtine and Didier Franck took over the phenomenology seminar at the CNRS, and upon its relaunching in 1986–87, they invited me to join them as an associate researcher. On the other hand, I participated in the creation of the Collège International de Philosophie from 1986 to 89, where I organized, together with Miguel Abensour, the conference *Heidegger—Questions ouvertes,* the proceedings of which were published under that same title (Osiris, 1988). I would also add a third institutional circumstance, which for its part is "aesthetic" above all else: the founding in 1985 of the journal *La Part de l'œil* (and its affiliated society) by a group of artists and researchers from Brussels who invited me to join their group—the journal has published its seventeenth annual issue.

So that is how I "received" Heidegger. Should we now move on to questions that deal with the reception of Heidegger in relationship to aesthetics in France?

*In your book Imago Mundi Heidegger is doubly invoked, first with
respect to "The Origin of the Work of Art" and then in view of the
relation between language and poetry. What then constitutes the
unity of your reading of Heidegger's "aesthetic writings?"*

The core of my book *Imago Mundi* consists, as I just said, in the elaboration of what I would call a phenomenological interpretation of the work of art. I describe the artwork as a "*phainomenon*-image," but be careful! The *phainomenon*-image is not an "image" in the classical sense of the term. I aim at a sort of refoundation or transformation of aesthetics, and that is why it is necessary to rely on Heidegger's critique of aesthetics. For Heidegger is severe with regard to aesthetics, as he also is, incidentally, with regard to linguistics—for him, they are both the result of a misunderstanding and an occultation of "the thing itself," namely language or the artwork. Thus, I rely on this well-known Heideggerian critique, without, however, ignoring what in my opinion is secretly—or even dramatically—constituted in what we customarily refer to as aesthetics or linguistics. I do not adopt Heidegger's rejection absolutely in this regard, because there are, in classical aesthetics and in classical linguistics, "experiences" or "experiments" that lead to radical discoveries.

In *Imago Mundi,* I invoke Heidegger in two ways: first, via "The Origin of the Work of Art," and second, in reference to the relationship between language and poetry. What constitutes the unity of my reading? First, "The Origin of the Work of Art" is a text contemporary to Heidegger's reading of Hölderlin. This must always be remembered when working on "The Origin" or on the texts and lectures on Hölderlin. More importantly still, these are all texts that are contemporary to the *Beiträge zur Philosophie* (1937–39), which I was not familiar with at the time of *Imago Mundi* but the reading of which confirms my interpretation of "The Origin" and of the Hölderlin texts. To such an extent that I wonder today whether the *Beiträge* are not the deployment of a new "aesthetics" and whether the entire terminology of the *Beiträge* is not, precisely, "aesthetic" in a radical sense, a sense that is completely other than the one that Heidegger critiques so severely, as I already mentioned. Such a radicality would require that aesthetics and ontology no longer be distinguished from each other—it would mean the end of aesthetics in the narrow classical sense. We would then have a thinking without qualification: neither aesthetics nor ontology (undoubtedly not "politics" either). The *Beiträge* would be, in a certain sense, the other side (the positive side, if you like) of the (negative) Heideggerian critique of aesthetics. This is what I meant when I spoke of a new foundation or a transformation of aesthetics.

As far as "The Origin of the Work of Art" and the texts of the late thirties on poetry are concerned, the unity of my reading is to be found in the concepts of *Bild* and of *Einbildung*—what I call the *phainomenon*-image. This might sound surprising insofar as Heidegger does not seem to have much interest in this notion of *Bild*—far from it! And yet, I think that for Heidegger, in another text, later than the ones I have mentioned (namely in ". . . Poetically Man Dwells . . ." from 1951), the artwork is precisely that through which he defines *Bild* and *Einbildung* as "visible inclusions of the alien [*des Fremden*] in the sight of the familiar."[1] It seems to me that people did not pay attention to this. If we were to pay attention to this, we might find that the *Beiträge* is a text on aesthetics in a radical sense, and we might also be able to establish a link with the Heideggerian explanation of the political in a very different way than what is usually said of him. We would have here a "politics of the foreign."

What constitutes the unity of my reading of Heidegger's texts on language and poetry, those from the 1950s, from *On the Way to Language,* in their relation to his earlier texts? I do not think that there is a break between Heidegger's texts from these two periods. But perhaps we can simply state that "language" (*Sprache*) now explicitly plays the role that I believe to have been played by *Bild* in the earlier texts? This is what I would be tempted to say, but it would undoubtedly be too simple, and I would like, here, to pursue other avenues of inquiry.

Do you think that the late Merleau-Ponty was inspired by Heidegger as much in the aesthetical domain as in the ontological one?

The late Merleau-Ponty, the one of *Eye and Mind,* of *The Visible and the Invisible,* or of *The Prose of the World,* the author of a magnificent corpus sadly interrupted by his death, is certainly very much inspired by Heidegger in aesthetics. Not just in his analyses of the artwork, but also in his understanding of "aesthetics." For Merleau-Ponty as for Heidegger, aesthetics is neither a region nor a part of being, neither a science nor a mode of knowledge that would be defined by its particular procedures and thus by distinction from other procedures within a regional distribution of the sciences and knowledge. Aesthetics is neither a genre nor a species: it refutes all divisions of knowledge or of sciences. I believe it belongs to that which Schelling named "identity philosophy"—and I think that there is a lot of this, I mean of the Schellingian understanding of art, in Heidegger.

Merleau-Ponty was inspired by Heidegger in aesthetics as much as he was in ontology. All the concepts of the late Merleau-Ponty are, in fact, I would say, multidimensional: both have two sides—an aesthetical and an ontological one; the two being really one, which means that we can also call them unidimensional. For example, do not the "intertwining" and the "chiasm" refer, in a singular and surprising way, both to the early Heidegger of the ontological difference as well as to the later Heidegger of *Ereignis*? Do they not carry the underpinnings of the artwork and the successive structures of being according to Heidegger? Intertwining and chiasm: Is this ontology? Is it aesthetics? Doubtless, they are inseparably both. Or to take another example, the "depth" superbly analyzed by Merleau-Ponty in his reflections on Cézanne, is this not the same thing as what he calls "branches of Being?" Not to mention all the explicit references to Heidegger in *The Visible and the Invisible.* Is this to say that Merleau-Ponty could not have written without Heidegger? But does this question have to imply a devaluation? Does it imply an epigonality and a lack of originality? Absolutely not, and we must on the contrary recognize Merleau-Ponty's singularity. Indeed, these thinkers are themselves precisely in an intertwining, which means that the concept of influence is subverted at every level. I believe that what we call "history of philosophy" resides precisely in this subversion.

Which is why the reception of Heidegger's aesthetics as well as his ontology in France passes through Merleau-Ponty.

How would you characterize Maldiney's Heideggerianism, or that of Loreau?

The same thing holds for the following generation of French phenomenologists of art who contributed to the reception of Heidegger and who contributed intensively to the evolution of a Heideggerian interpretation of art, to its dynamism and its "subversion." I am thinking here, precisely, of Henri Maldiney and of Max Loreau.

We can say that for both of them, as well as for Merleau-Ponty, the central term of aesthetics is the body—and not *Dasein,* if you will, as is the case for Heidegger (even if things are not that simple). The body is, in my opinion, the core that is proper to French post-Heideggerian aesthetics.

Henri Maldiney's goal—in his principal works on art, *Regard, parole, espace* (L'Âge d'homme, 1973), *Aîtres de la langue et demeures de la pensée* (L'Âge d'homme, 1975), *Art et existence* (Klincksieck, 1985), *L'Art, l'éclair de l'être* (Éditions Comp'act, 1993), and the most recent one, *Ouvrir le rien, l'art nu* (Encre marine, 2000)—consists in the deployment of "the sensible," and this precisely through the differentiation between an "aesthetics of the sensible" and an "aesthetics of art." One of the leading threads of Maldiney's thought consists precisely in removing art from an aesthetics of "intentionality" (which would be Husserlian), as well as from an aesthetics of "projection" (which would be Heideggerian). In contrast to this we have an artwork that "exists" under the regime of the "will to form"—whereby Maldiney joins the lineage of Worringer and Riegl. Maldiney's Heideggerianism is visible in his many paths, as well as in the incidents provoked by those effects. But Heidegger's texts are never made the thematic focus of his discourse, but only the confrontation with "the thing itself" of the artwork. This led Maldiney from a thinking of the "phenomenon" to the difficult thought of the "nothing," which he elaborates in his last work, where the encounter with Heidegger is both acknowledged and overcome. To put it briefly, the "nothing" of the artwork, according to Maldiney, is an "active nothing," and not a "no thing." The "nothing" in the pictorial artwork (and here we find superb analyses of Kandinsky, Delaunay, Mondrian, Bazaine, Tal Coat, Nicolas de Stael, but also of Chinese painting, in his last book) is an "opening," which is "existence"—and, to use a term that in my opinion brings Maldiney into proximity with Schelling, an "uni-multi-dimensionality" and also "simultaneity." And this led Maldiney to think abstraction not as an emptying of everything but as reality itself.

As for Max Loreau, his principal works are *La peinture à l'œuvre et l'énigme du corps* (Gallimard, 1980), *En quête d'un autre commencement* (Lebeer-Hossmann, 1987), and *La genèse du phénomène* (Éditions de Minuit, 1988), a very important oeuvre that may have been only an "introduction" had the death of its author not transformed it into a testament. The reference to the "body" is as essential to Loreau as it is to Merleau-Ponty or Maldiney, as I just mentioned. But for Loreau the nodal term is not *aisthesis* but rather "volume." Volume is not put into place by filling up a preexisting space, for volume is the very dynamic of existence. These complex and difficult analyses can be carried out, according to Loreau, only under the auspices of a logos that breaks with the logos that philosophy has never abandoned, from Plato to Heidegger, namely the logos of "vision." It is thus this logos of "vision" that, according to Loreau, must be exhausted in order to produce "another beginning" (of thought, of aesthetics?), which for its part would be a logos of the pure word. This is a claim that Loreau pursued in his "critique" of Heidegger, which was undoubtedly not always accurate.

How can we identify the dominant traits of investigations in aesthetics today? Does Heidegger play a role here, perhaps indirectly?

Research in aesthetics today—which must absolutely be distinguished from the verbiage we are saturated with today, whether it might be good-natured or aggressive—can emerge only at the edges and surroundings of Heideggerian questions. That art is to be sought in the work, this is a first insight that is drawn from Heidegger's questions, but that most people today consider a banality. And yet few people think about this. And after all, isn't this Heidegger's greatest "lesson," and isn't this what prevents aesthetic investigations from treating art like an "occupation" among others? Must we not then affirm that the "efficacity of the work" has nothing to do with the production of so-called objects "of art?" Does not Heidegger's immense role, whether directly or indirectly, reside in this stubborn affirmation?

Are you, too, "bothered," as Philippe Lacoue-Labarthe admitted to be, by the link between "art-people-community" that still appears in the Athens lecture?

Please allow me to defer this question. I just sketched out a theoretical context in my response to your first question. Furthermore, this context is not a "theoretical" one, for me, in the "untroubled" sense of the term, but rather a profoundly dramatic sign.

Do you find Heidegger's short text "Art and Space" inspiring?

The short text "Art and Space," which was presented as a lecture by Heidegger in 1969, does indeed inspire me. It corresponds, in my view, to Heidegger's attempt to go against the grain of *Sein und Zeit.* There was a manifest tendency in *Sein und Zeit* to reduce spatiality to temporality. What appears in the other text is surely not the inverse tendency, but rather the possibility of deploying space beyond this sort of reduction. Thus, notions such as *Gegend,* already encountered in *Sein und Zeit,* are almost redefined. The Heideggerian *Gegend* in "Art and Space" must, in my opinion, be understood in terms of the "earth" of which Husserl spoke, "the earth which does not move." Is this *Gegend* not the "earth which does not move?" And are not these two that which is put to work in the artwork? Or better: does Heidegger not encounter the "alien in the sight of the familiar"—this *Bild* and this *Einbildung* of which, in the end, he spoke so little? This is why, in my opinion, this little text opens many paths. It was in full knowledge of this that I tried, in my book *L'Espace Pictural* (Encre Marine, 1995), to elaborate on a few of these paths (among which the *Gegend* brings me, I think, very close today to Maldiney's "simultaneity").

Jean Greisch

Interview of December 2, 1999

You consider yourself to be atypical: what do you mean by that?

Coming from the "wilds" of Luxemburg, and having completed training in theology before "converting" to philosophy, I consider that I am totally atypical, in the sense that I was not influenced by any tradition or by any French schools of thought. My relationship to Heidegger preexisted my encounter with the "French Heideggerian School" represented by Jean Beaufret, Henri Birault, and many others. Of course, I had read their works, but all this was in addition to a relation to Heidegger that had already been established. More significantly, I do not think that my approach to the Heideggerian texts was influenced by any particular school of interpretation. In a way, I have educated myself. I recognize, however, in retrospect, that my first encounter, which was quite indirect, my *Herkunft*, so to speak, with Heidegger's questioning, was connected to my studies in fundamental theology in 1964–65 in Innsbruck, in the shadow of Karl Rahner, if I dare say. The fact that my relationship with Heidegger involved the hermeneutic question from the very beginning was due to my work with Heinrich Schlier, who was himself a student of Bultmann, who had been my mentor in New Testament exegesis. All my later work in philosophy evolved from this initial debt.

I pursued my studies in philosophy in Paris, under the supervision of three professors who each influenced me in their own way. At the department of philosophy at the Institut Catholique de Paris, there was the memorable personality of the dean, Dominique Dubarle. He was above all interested in establishing the foundation of a "theological ontology," closer to Aquinas and Hegel than to Husserl and Heidegger. I should also mention the presence of Stanislas Breton, who was intellectually stimulating as he was humanely supportive, and under whose supervision I actually began to work on the notion of *Ereignis* in light of the Platonic and neo-Platonic notion of *exaiphnes*. For a long time, Breton's *Du Principe* guided my first foray into what the same author called the contemporary "space of the metaphysical thinkable." Breton also supervised all my academic writings until the end of my thesis, which I chose to title, somewhat mischievously, *La Parole heureuse*, to be in contrast with the text *La Parole malheureuse* that Jacques Bouveresse had just devoted to Wittgenstein. In addition, I was influenced by Paul Ricoeur, whose seminars I attended at the C.N.R.S from 1972, and where I gave my first lecture on the status of metaphor in Heidegger. I was also, of course, fascinated by Jean Beaufret, whom I met in the context of the discussions at Saint-Jacques du Haut-Pas, which were moderated by Odette Laffoucrière. However, I cannot say that he influenced me in a direct way.

Even if I consider myself a kind of Heideggerian "autodidact," I want to tell you about a twofold debt that probably makes me suspect in the eyes of some. On the one hand, my theological interests—which were very strong at the beginning, although now somewhat less so—aligned me with a particular theological school, that of the "transcendental" theology of Karl Rahner. If any tradition of reading Heidegger has influenced me more than others, in a way, without my being aware of it, it was his work: *Hörer des Wortes*.[1] Without this theological provenance, my book *La Parole heureuse* would not have seen the light of day. But this does not mean that it would be a simple transcription of crypto-theological themes into philosophical language!

Could you clarify the spirit of that tradition in relation to Heidegger?

With respect to metaphysics, I am indebted to the transcendentalism of Joseph Maréchal and his Germanic followers: Jean-Baptiste Lotz and Emmerich Coreth. I attended the latter's course on metaphysics in Innsbruck. The figure of Heidegger that I could vaguely discern through this metaphysics, which was rooted in the experience of a radical, transcendental questioning, was that of a "metaphysician," especially a metaphysician of the metaphysics of *Dasein*. It was the Heidegger of *Sein und Zeit*, of course, but read more as drawing the lineaments of a metaphysics of *Dasein* than as undertaking an existential analytic whose phenomenological presuppositions were more or less kept silent.

In this respect, I realize more and more that my approach to Heidegger and, perhaps, even to contemporary philosophy resembles the movement of a crab walking backward. In 1968, already knowing that I was going to pursue my academic studies in France, I set myself to working seriously on Gadamer's *Truth and Method*. I was reading this book while undergoing professional training in the Villeroy & Boch ceramic factory in Luxembourg. As my incompetence as a craftsperson became increasingly clear, I educated myself in the problems of a philosophical hermeneutics. It was beginning from the Gadamerian source that

I progressively ventured into the Heideggerian domain. For a long time I avoided exploring the phenomenological and Husserlian "back country" of Heidegger's thought.

This is one of the reasons that explains why, at the moment, I am much more taken by the early Heidegger, and in particular the one of the first teachings in Freiburg. One should realize that this early Heidegger has not really been addressed in France, where the debates relating to the "onto-theological" constitution of metaphysics, the critique of the metaphysics of presence, deconstruction, etc., still occupy center stage. I too knew a time when "my Heidegger" was mainly the one of the "Letter on Humanism," which remains undoubtedly an important text. In spite of this, I nonetheless concentrate now much more on Heidegger's phenomenological beginnings. This is why in my book, *L'Arbre de vie et l'arbre du savoir* (The tree of life and the tree of knowledge), I devoted myself to the task of outlining a complete interpretation of the first course in Freiburg in which Heidegger set forth the basis of what he called at that time the "hermeneutics of factical life." I would like to continue this reconstruction that is meant to be genealogical and systematic at the same time, in a style similar to the one I used in my commentary on *Sein und Zeit,* through an inquiry on the notion of a *"metaphysics of Dasein"* during the time after *Sein und Zeit,* from 1928 to 1934. In the end, it is the early Heidegger that fascinates me the most.

The reasons for my interest in the "early" Heidegger are quite complex. I feel close to Theodore Kisiel, while not being as good a "detective" as he is, since I am less focused on original sources, which demand extensive research in the archives. But, just as Kisiel and a new school of scholars, I am sensitive to a genealogical approach to Heidegger's texts. I do not think, like Ricoeur and Levinas, that one should limit oneself to *Sein und Zeit,* although I do not mean to deprive this groundbreaking work of its greatness. What I do disagree with strongly is the extravagantly theological reading that gives the impression that all the paths of Heideggerian thought should lead not to Rome, obviously, but to the Thor seminar. It is not by accident that the latest editions of Pöggeler's book, *Der Denkweg Martin Heideggers,* contain an appendix where the Heideggerian "paths of thought" appear as a *plurale tantum.*

Isn't there another reason, namely the personal interest of the young Heidegger in the Thomist tradition and Augustine's and Luther's religious thinking?

Surely, and this is also what I am interested in, of course. But unlike the orientation of Kisiel's research, which is principally genealogical, I would like to address Heidegger's early courses, not so much because of their "archaeological" interest, but because they are relevant to the present debate on the status of phenomenology and to the metamorphoses of contemporary, and in particular French, phenomenology. I am taking something of a risk by supposing that the hermeneutical importance of factical life for the first Heidegger was not purely genealogical and historical.

I have an unpublished article in my papers entitled, "Reading Heidegger with the Third Generation." It is a lecture that I presented at several places, first at the University of Lausanne, and then at the University of Memphis in the United States. In distinguishing three generations of readers of Heidegger, it is probable that I am stating the obvious. However, during my studies in philosophy, the main reading and the text of reference had become the "Letter on Humanism," whereas for a first generation, it was *Sein und Zeit,* a *Sein und Zeit* read in a more or less existentialist manner, that is to say, through the eyes of Karl Jaspers or Kierkegaard, if you will. The third generation of readers, whose work began to appear in the middle of the 1970s, was that of a phenomenological reinterpretation for which *Sein und Zeit,* inseparable from the Marburg courses, became again the primary text. Perhaps we are witnessing the emergence of a fourth generation, which is no longer mine: namely, the young thinkers who were brought up in the Levinas school before they came to Heidegger. It was in 1996, during the Conference at Cerisy-la-Salle devoted to Michel Henry, which I co-directed with Alain David, that I had the impression of discovering this new generation. It would be a nice subject for study and reflection to examine the "conflicts of intellectual generations," linked to the disparity of their respective "hermeneutical situations" in light of the concepts of "forerunners," "contemporaries," and "followers," inherited from Mannheim and Schütz.

All this does not prevent me from being interested in Heidegger after the "turn," the one of the *Beiträge,* of *Besinnung* and other texts still to be published. I will confess, however, that I read those texts with quite mixed feelings, almost as if I had to deal with kind of a *tremendum fascinosum.* The fascination I feel is great but often accompanied by an uneasy feeling; I have expressed it, among other places in my reviews of the *Feldweg-Gespräche.* The way the dialogue between two German prisoners in a Russian prison camp ignores the question of moral responsibility and addresses only the wickedness of being deeply disturbed me and continues to do so to this very day.

Your commentary on Being and Time is something completely
new in France in relation to the previous receptions and
is more similar to what has been done abroad.

What can I say, I am not French, even if I often regret it! This is the problem: I have been living in France for more than thirty years, and it would be very difficult for me to leave this marvelous country, if I ever had to. This does not prevent me from feeling that, in Parisian circles, I am only an add-on that has not been trained *à la française,* with all the intensity and grandeur this expression connotes. In the Grand Duchy of Luxembourg, in my native haunts, we do not have anything like the École Normale Supérieure of the rue d'Ulm with its great intellectual traditions and its petty feuds. The fact that I teach in an institution that belongs to a network of Catholic universities, but that, because of a strange state restriction, is not allowed to call itself a "university," increases my feeling of being a rare bird, who, for this very reason, can feel free to think whatever he wants, without any obligation to the academic authorities.

Do you feel exactly the same as Ricoeur, that is,
increasingly resistant to the second Heidegger?

No, not quite. What I agree with is that the "meta" function has not yet exhausted all its possibilities. We have not finished yet with metaphysics, not only because it does not want to die, but because it still provides resource for thought. I maintain a relationship, even if problematic, with metaphysics, precisely because of Heidegger. I do not consider myself as a "post-metaphysician," or a "post-modernist," two expressions that do not necessarily designate the same thing. Would I dare say that some ways of speaking of the "post-metaphysical" era, or of the "closure" of metaphysics, really irritate me, because one is not even capable of saying what exactly is "ended," finished, and why. If there is a lesson to be learned from Heidegger, it is the great patience we need to approach this kind of questioning.

It is also this interrogation that preoccupies me at the moment: to reinvent, to re-elaborate the meaning of the "meta" function. It is also in this sense that I part with the later Heidegger. Before returning to "the other beginning of thought," I would like, insofar as it is possible, to revisit the very idea of a metaphysics of *Dasein,* which Heidegger tried to deepen, in the wake of the fundamental ontology undertaken with *Sein und Zeit.* In my book, *Le Cogito herméneutique,* published by Éditions Vrin—the second volume of a trilogy dedicated to the idea of a hermeneutical phenomenology—I tried to propose a few hypotheses about the "meta function." I had first thought of writing a book on Ricoeur that would have been entitled *Le Cogito blessé* (The Wounded Cogito). In the process, the book has increasingly begun to resemble my own *"cogito blessé"*! I give more details on Ricoeur's contribution to hermeneutical phenomenology in my work: *Paul Ricœur: l'itinérance du sens,* which appeared with Éditions Jerôme Millon in the series *Krisis.*[2]

Ricœur was not interested in a genealogical rereading of *Sein und Zeit,* for the simple reason that Heidegger's courses during his phenomenological period have been accessible for only fifteen years or so. Moreover, he had reservations about Heidegger's views dealing with the onto-theological constitution of Western metaphysics.

My own wager is that, provided one makes the effort to restore all the links of the genesis of Heidegger's thought, one would be able to discern some possibilities that would be otherwise obscured by an overly teleological reading of his itinerary.

Further, I think it would be worth it, even if it would be a painful and time-consuming work of exegesis, to carefully examine each motif of the *Beiträge,* that is to say, the different phases of its reception of Nietzsche, etc.

In the end, what interests me most is the analytic of *Dasein* and its possible developments, even if for many philosophers it would not make it through the caudine forks of the analytic philosophy of language.

This implies, thus, that while not rejecting the whole of the Heideggerian conception of the history of being, you would remain relatively cautious?

Yes, I remain quite cautious. Let us take for example the theme of the "last God," or of the "ultimate God," to which I have devoted several studies. The last one bears the deliberately provocative title of "The Poverty of the 'Last God.'" This title, directly inspired by an expression from *Besinnung,* can be understood in two different ways. The first one is Heidegger's own understanding: the truth of being that was addressed by the later Heidegger must be approached in terms of not plenitude and overabundance, but poverty and deprivation, which has direct consequences for the post-metaphysical representation of the divine. But the way I use the expression—poverty of the last God—is meant to be provocative. What keeps troubling me is this: how does the last God intervene in the thinking of *Ereignis* that is supposed to free us once and for all from the onto-theo-logical constitution of metaphysics? Is this a "philosophical theology" in disguise? What is the philosophical status of the discourse on the "last God"? Are we closer to Schelling or to Nietzsche? Pushing this point to its limit: are we are dealing with a new kind of "theosophy"? In that case, we would not be dissimilar to Franz von Baader! I certainly know that the simple attempt to pose such questions makes many who are more orthodox Heideggerians than I am react strongly. But, you see, these are the questions that I try to address, as well as possible. The important questions for me are not the elective affinities with Schelling, Nietzsche, or Hölderlin, but rather the philosophical stakes of some of the themes that Heidegger developed in his *Beiträge* and the related pieces of work.

One point that I share closely with Ricoeur is that I too have some difficulties in accepting the sometimes critical or offhand judgments that Heidegger, in the *Beiträge,* addresses to Judeo-Christianity. To say that this is only a certain "worldview," and therefore an ideology that one can compare with Nazism or Communism, is a bit too superficial, a bit too facile! To my mind, the entire question of the conflictual relationship that the later Heidegger maintained with the Judeo-Christian tradition deserves to be examined further.

Perhaps we could move on to discuss Heidegger in terms of theology since a whole debate has been engaged, in France, between the theologians and Heidegger's thought. Do you think that there is any misunderstanding between them?

This is a difficult question insofar as I myself have theological training: I have been trained by theologians who were themselves influenced by Heidegger. So you can see how I am caught up in a "hermeneutic circle" that concerns me personally. As I have already indicated, I was influenced by a very specific theological tradition, namely, Maréchal's transcendentalism and its interpretation by metaphysicians such as Emmerich Coreth and theologians such as Karl Rahner. Their approach is not same as that of a Thomist or a strict neo-Thomist. This is what Rahner's thesis, on the metaphysics of knowledge in Thomas Aquinas, and published as *Geist im Welt,* shows. The relationship my friend Claude Geffré had with Heidegger—he has been strongly influenced by the Thomist tradition (not having myself been brought up in Thomism, our problematics are not exactly the same)—is different. The theologians have very good reasons to take Heidegger seriously, and that pleases me, as I am pleased that they formulate their questions and objections from the perspective of *intellectus fidei.* Let the Heideggerians and philosophers decide whether their questions are relevant or not! What I personally regret is the paucity of strong theological reactions. Of course the temptation is that the theologians would content themselves with merely "recycling" Heideggerian themes, in which case they would confirm the caricature that Alain conjures of theology: "a philosophy without distance."

I would like to share something with you: in 1973, at the time when I was writing my pre-doctoral thesis on *Herméneutique et grammatologie,* which Ricoeur published a short time later, Stanislas Breton advised me to send the text to Derrida and to contact him. I went to see Derrida in his office on rue d'Ulm. Anticipating a difficult time, I was completely thrown off by the question Derrida asked me *ex abrupto:* "Could you tell me under what conditions it is still possible to practice theology today?" I left the question unanswered and would be even less able to answer to it today! But this is precisely why I wish that the theologians who think they have an answer would become involved in the debate, instead of withdrawing, or simply using Heidegger's ideas. I prefer a theologian who dares to address critical questions to philosophers, however untimely, just as Karl Barth questioned a theologian who took refuge in pastoral or ecclesiastical strategies. But one could also wonder whether the French academic community is ready to listen to the voice of theologians who think critically, instead of considering them as pariahs.

Since I have been working on Heidegger, I have tried to undertake a "philological" reading, that is to say, to pay attention to the detail of the text, avoiding extrapolations and excessive generalizations. This is one of the reasons I have labored like Sisyphus to write reviews on all the volumes of the *Gesamtausgabe* in the columns of the *Revues des sciences philosophiques et théologiques*. One of the fruits of this time-consuming and patient reading is that it allows one to unmask certain argumentative strategies. It is as if, in relation to some questions, Heidegger always chose the same approach. The words may change but not the method. Take, for instance, the question of the status of eternity that I tried to analyze in an article published in English. What strikes me is that, at first, Heidegger always begins by saying that, of course, the metaphysical concept of eternity inherited from Boethius, the *sempernitas* or the *Nunc stans,* is absolutely unacceptable and that, then, eternity should be conceived on the basis of time and not the other way round. Does it mean that in a thinking of the finitude of being, there is no more room for the thought of eternity? Of course not! Second, Heidegger claims the necessity to rethink the idea of eternity in the horizon of the finitude of *Ereignis,* but one has the impression that he makes a promise he does not keep. It seems to me that he adopts a similar strategy in his relations with theologians. *Herkunft bleibt stets Zukunft:* "Provenance always remains futural." As much as the development of the *Gesamtausgabe* enables us to understand its theological provenance, the future he promises to theology remains undetermined.

How far can we trust Heidegger's self-interpretation? Even if it is an intrinsic dimension of the work (as I have shown, concerning *Sein und Zeit,* in the last chapter of *Ontologie et Temporalité*), I allow myself the right of a critical distance, instead of letting myself be blindly guided or influenced by his self-interpretation. This critical distance is relevant for the relationship to theology, as well as for other questions (for example, the retrospective judgment that Heidegger directs at his first hermeneutic works in his "'A Dialogue on Language—Between a Japanese and an Inquirer'" in *On the Way to Language*).

What would your reaction be concerning Jean-Yves Lacoste's opinion, at the end of his article "Heidegger," in the Dictionnaire critique de théologie?

Lacoste is not wrong to remind theologians who would succumb all too quickly to Heidegger's seduction (to tell the truth, they are quite rare nowadays) that the "assignment of a task does not mean it will be accomplished." But the question is: what concept of theology underlies the provocative declaration that "theology has nothing to learn here, except to learn what it is not, which would be, by the way, a very useful lesson"! Just imagine if one would say the same of the relationship between Aquinas and Aristotle! Obviously this comment involves a specific concept of theology; I would like somebody to tell me how this concept is elaborated. A Barthian would probably applaud—enthusiastically—Lacoste's comment that "man does not have the right to be near God simply by virtue of being born." Is that a sufficient reason to compare the Heideggerian hermeneutic of facticity to a "phenomenology of pagan experience," or to transform the Heideggerian *Sprachereignis* into a secularized redoubling of the theological concept of the "word of God"? Before answering, the theologian, just as the philosopher, has to allow him- or herself a very long time to understand the question. This takes us back to the question: What is the status of theology and how is it defined? How does the Catholic theologian respond to the charge of a "positivism of the Revelation" raised against Karl Barth's dialectic theology? At least in the way it is addressed at the university, theology is a rational discourse like any other with an epistemology and must be able to critically ground its own conditions of possibility.

A good example of a "positive" rather than a servile relationship with Heidegger would be a theology that aims at being as resolutely theological as that of Hans Urs von Balthasar. Von Balthasar nevertheless felt the need to graft an entire metaphysics onto his vast baroque undertaking, i.e., his three-part theological system—theological Aesthetics, divine and then Theo-logical Theatrics. The second volume of Balthasar's theological Aesthetics, where he proposes his own theological reading of the basic texts of metaphysics, ends with a theological version of the ontological difference. However theological it may be, it presupposes a particular reading of Heidegger. In the work of a theologian as close to Lacoste's heart as Balthasar, there is not only a defiant attitude toward Heidegger, inviting the theologians to manage by themselves, with the haughty assertion that we are capable of doing as well and even better without him. Balthasar, just as Rahner, was obliged to work on Heidegger at a given moment of his trajectory on the way to accomplishing his theological work. So things may be even more complex. In my view, Lacoste's defiance is only an overreaction against the "apologetic" excesses that some theologians have made of certain Heideggerian themes.

I am not fond of apologetics, and this is why I am wary of the concept of "Christian philosophy," or of the way this highly problematic expression is used. As regards this subject, I can understand Heidegger's position on Christian philosophy. Heidegger seems to have had two "pet peeves" that were probably inseparable: Christian philosophy and the analogy of being. His rejection of the analogy of being was directed toward Father Erich Przywara, a very famous Jesuit at that time, the intellectual mentor of Balthasar and Rahner (it is possible that he might have been Heidegger's music teacher during Heidegger's brief stay at the Jesuit novitiate of Feldkirch). I devoted a study to this fascinating character that I expect to take up again in the philosophy of religion that I am currently finishing entitled, *Le Buisson ardent et les Lumières de la raison*.[3] Claiming that with Karl Barth's commentary on the Roman Epistle, the "protestant vision of the world" had found its adequate metaphysical expression as dialectic theology, Przywara was proud to show that the analogy of being was the perfect metaphysical expression of the "catholic vision of the world"; an expression that he then called: "the fundamental form of Catholicism." The analogy of being becomes then the touchstone of any worldview, of a metaphysics that is inseparable from a theology. This explains why Karl Barth writes, in the preface of the *Dogmatique*, in 1927, that the analogy of being is an invention of the Antichrist and the only serious intellectual reason not to become Catholic! This is, of course, the expected response of God's Word to the shepherd of being. Przywara was an extremely important intellectual figure who acted as a foil to Heidegger. Consequently Heidegger's very negative sentences concerning the analogy of being in the course of 1932 (in 1932, Przywara published the *Analogy of Being*: one can then imagine that the students informed Heidegger, and asked him to take a position, which he did without fail, in no uncertain terms).

In all of this debate, one cannot forget the background of the Catholic theological tradition, namely the fact that the First Vatican Council established the possibility of knowing God through the light of natural reason as a truth of faith. It is in this sense that it presupposes a positive relationship between theology and philosophy. The question is, how a theology that accepts the Heideggerian thesis of the end of metaphysics, which seems to some extent similar to a Barthian intransigency, can manage such a burdensome legacy. If it is true that, undeniably, Lacoste's conception of theology is similar to that of Balthasar, Balthasar would probably not express it in the same way. The question of the relationship between theology and Heideggerian thought is and remains a complex story that could not be reduced to a simple rejection.

Does the fact that Heidegger's thought, in the United States, was better received in the Catholic schools than in the Protestant or analytic circles mean that there are connections above and beyond the historiographic aspect between Heidegger's work and the theological tradition?

This is also quite a complex question. I do not know whether the different faiths matter and to what extent. It seems to me that today, the divisions between the different intellectual traditions play a more important role. I went to a conference that took place in October 1999 at Villanova University on the theme "Religion and Post-modernism." It began with a lecture by Derrida on the theme of forgiveness. In this philosophy conference, there was a strong presence of theologians, representing different faiths, Jewish, Catholic, Anglican, Protestant, etc. What struck me most was the very strong presence of Heidegger in the debates, but a presence strongly influenced by the Derridean or Levinasian readings of Heidegger. I was one of the few contributors to directly address Heidegger's text, focusing on the theme of ipseity that I was trying to juxtapose to the Augustinian name of God, which is precisely not *Causa sui* but *Idipsum,* a very strange nomination that fascinates me deeply. As Villanova University was founded by the Augustinians, I wanted to honor this Augustinian heritage by addressing the reasons that led Augustine to elaborate that strange neologism, which, although it belongs to "onto-theo-logy," does not correspond to Heidegger's canonical definition in any way.

I do not think that one can still say that the Catholic universities steer the diffusion of Heidegger's thought. It is now already much more diffuse, in the Anglo-American world at least. We should not overlook the fact that there are hardly any departments of theology left these days since nearly all the divinity schools have been converted into departments of religious studies. At the most, if one still pursues theology in the United States, it would be likely in a department of philosophy, since there remain only three or four divinity schools where one can study theology. These institutional problems, and the division of knowledge they imply, entail considerable philosophical stakes that merit reflection.

*At the Institut Catholique de Paris, are there many students reading
Heidegger, or are there fewer students these days who are interested?*

This is a difficult question for me to answer since I am a part of it. Since my classes partly bear on Heidegger, of course my students work on him. In any case, I do not have the impression of a generalized hostility, nor do I have the feeling that Heidegger has been rejected by the theologians. This might be so, but I do not have the impression that it is the case here. In the department of philosophy and theology at the Institut Catholique de Paris, the hostile reactions do not come from "analytic philosophers" either because, in the kind of student body we have, the students are more sensitive to "continental" thought than to analytic thought.

If there are negative reactions of any kind, they rather come from some neo-Thomist circles, which vehemently call for a return to Thomism. There is today a "neo-neo-Thomism" taught in other institutions, often bound to very precise ideological orientations. There is, among some young Catholics, sort of an aspiration to a neo-Thomist lost paradise. The problem is that this is a neo-Thomism that is more or less the "unhappy consciousness" of the great Thomism of the past—*Ziehen der Linien der Sehnsucht ins Leere hinaus,* as the romantic nostalgia evoked in the *Phenomenology of Spirit*! This is the aspiration of an idealized Thomism that avoids a confrontation with the texts. What I try to show my students is how Heidegger, precisely insofar as he is our contemporary, can supply us with vital access to the great texts of the tradition, which apparently otherwise no longer speak to us. Heidegger can be an excellent *révélateur* of the significance of a text. I obviously do not use Heidegger to enhance the work of Aquinas, nor as a foil to Aquinas or to Meister Eckhart, whom I address in my class on metaphysics and ontology.

I would like to ask a question about the Gesamtausgabe,
that is to say, about the problem of translation.

It is hard for me to speak of it, as I have just finished the translation of volume 60, *The Phenomenology of Religious Life.* I gave the manuscript to François Fédier in March. It goes without saying that I am still willing to revisit my translation, but I am not ready to compromise on the terminological choices I have deemed appropriate.

Is someone holding things up?

Perhaps . . . [4]

I now have a question to ask you on the problem of
ethics, and on the hidden biblical sources.

Actually, it is rather Levinas who plays the role of "Father of the Church"! The debate is always about the question of continuity between Heidegger and Levinas. With this question, each time, I find myself before a kind of chiasm: on the one hand, I have the impression that there are two absolutely contradictory discourses, while on the other hand, I see a hidden proximity that could even, in Levinas's case, be emphasized by showing how some of Heidegger's existentials are appropriated, without being acknowledged, and with an added ethical component. The hostage, seen in a different way, could be understood as *Geworfenheit,* which is rather troubling. Something I do not accept in Levinas's critique of Heidegger is his general assertions that we are dealing with a philosophy of power. Heideggerian "care," after all, is not an existential version of Spinoza's *conatus essendi*! One can say whatever one wants about Heidegger's political wanderings, but, as for his thought, it is certainly not a philosophy of power; it is rather even a philosophy of powerlessness. The texts I am working on at the moment on the metaphysics of *Dasein* speak of a *Preisgegebenheit* [surrender] of an *Ohnmächtigkeit des Daseins* [Dasein's powerlessness], etc., and there is an entire vocabulary, on the contrary, on powerlessness. Levinas pretends not to be aware of it, which is all the more surprising since it was one of Heidegger's classes that he himself attended. This is the topic of the contribution that I have presented at the symposium on "Levinas et la phénoménologie" subsequently published by Jean-Luc Marion. I asked myself a perplexing question: we know that Levinas attended only one of Heidegger's lecture courses, *Einleitung in die Philosophie,* in 1928—his first lecture course as Husserl's successor. It was an introduction to the metaphysics of *Dasein,* and thus it was a kind of systematic commentary on the lecture "What Is Metaphysics?" I speculated about the following question: What was it that the young student Levinas understood of it at that time? What did he retain? It was precisely in this course that Heidegger strongly insisted on the *Ohnmächtigkeit* [*Dasein*'s powerlessness], the *Preisgegebenheit* [surrender] constitutive of *Dasein*'s being-in-the-world.

In Heidegger, all these terms are more ontological than ethical, in the later Levinas's sense. Rather than opposing them frontally, one should reflect on their common starting points.

Philippe Lacoue-Labarthe

Interview of June 22, 2000

Do you remember the first time you read Heidegger?

The first time that I read Heidegger must have been at the end of my *hypokhâgne* at Le Mans. I had a charming professor of philosophy, but he was not a philosopher. I had above all benefited from the teaching of a professor of French literature, Gérard Genette. The following year I left Le Mans, reluctantly, at the same time that Derrida was appointed to teach in *hypokhâgne* . . . Consequently, I never had the opportunity to be Derrida's student. Genette and I corresponded, and during that summer Heidegger's name had come up. I had told Genette that I was going trying to read Blanchot and that I did not understand him very well. I had read in a journal, probably *Les Lettres Nouvelles,* that one of Heidegger's books had just been published and that it was magnificent: *Essais et conférences* [*Vorträge und Aufsätze*]. Genette replied to me in a letter that ended playfully on a citation from Heidegger (taken from ". . . Poetically Man Dwells . . ."): "we work in the city but dwell outside it."[1] He concluded his letter with "Good luck!" I read this book and what struck me in those pages that I had great difficulty understanding, since I knew so little philosophy, were the passages where Hölderlin was invoked to justify the analysis of the thing, of building, or dwelling, etc. It was because of this reference to Hölderlin that I persisted in my reading. Soon I became a Heideggerian. Soon Heidegger became the only philosopher that I understood. Since I was a bit of a radical leftist (it is important that I clarify that I was close to the "Socialism or Barbarism" movement, perhaps even a "Situationist International"), I was reading the young Marx; I had also tried to read Hegel. I found all that magnificent but I did not understand much. In *khâgne,* I had a useless professor of philosophy, but this *khâgne,* at Bordeaux, gave me the opportunity to go listen to Gérard Granel—since the rumor was that he was a genius. Giving a course on "Poetry and Thought," he had added Bonnefoy's last book, *L'Improbable,* to the syllabus. He undertook to translate and provide a commentary on the spot for the first of Heidegger's texts on Trakl. I was tremendously impressed and continued to follow his teaching. He also gave a course on the young Marx, on the 1844 Manuscripts. At the beginning it seemed horribly difficult to me, but it was impressive, so rhetorically powerful—I say that in the best sense of the word—that I was overwhelmed by it. From the moment that I began to understand what he was saying, I was completely dazzled, and I "entered into the philosophical world." Genette really encouraged me, by the way, after a meeting with Hyppolite. Therefore I worked with Granel and thereafter with his successor Jean-Marie Pontevia, with whom I became a close friend a bit later, after I passed Agrégation and was appointed to a secondary school in Bordeaux. In 1961, when Heidegger's *Nietzsche* was published, we began to read it in German at least once or twice each week. Thereafter, I never stopped reading Heidegger, whatever the rest of my reading in the tradition of German idealism happened to be, or when I read Benjamin or Lukacs, etc. In any case, I continued to be attached to something fundamental in Heidegger's thought, which was perhaps less—although Granel maintained the contrary (and it was a subject of discussion)—a thinking of presence than a thinking of history. It was the later Heidegger, that is, the thinker of the history of being, which interested me deeply, much more so than the existential themes.

You say that you had the impression of understanding Heidegger very quickly.

Yes. First, the poetry-thought relation, and then, the history of being. Since Granel made direct reference to the German, I quickly discovered, as I knew a little German, that it was relatively simple, at least compared with the style of Hegel's *Phenomenology of Spirit* or that of Nietzsche, who has an extraordinarily rich vocabulary (which is not the case with Heidegger), and a complicated syntax. That helped enormously and I learned a lot.

Because I read so widely, I was soon part of the intellectual climate of the time. I read, as soon as they were published in *Critique* in 1962, Derrida's very first texts, and that was an illumination. I think the first was "Force and Signification," which was inspired by Nietzsche against formalism, and the prestructuralism of Jean Rousset. Then I read the first text of *Grammatology*, and also the essay on Levinas, "Violence and Metaphysics," published in *Revue de métaphysique*, which in my eyes was very different. I read everything immediately. Consequently, I distanced myself from the Heidegger of presence, that is to say, the one that I had read through the interpretations and the translations of Beaufret and Fédier.

This confirms that you did not study with Beaufret.

That's correct! I did not know him, or ever saw him or ran into him. I must have met Fédier very briefly once with Deguy, in 1965–66, before I arrived here in Strasbourg (in 1967). Then, later I read everything of Beaufret's that was available. I had a friend who attended his courses, and gave me the course notes. Among these, one on "French Philosophy" was remarkable. I was attuned to the material, but my first reservations concerned the thematic of presence as well as a certain climate of sacralization or devotion, let's call it piety to be brief. I had strong reservations: this was an old Calvinist reflex, which probably came from my education. All of these reservations emerged from my reading Derrida. In order to tell you the whole story, I told you I was a "leftist" during those years, but after the enormous shock of Hungary in 1956, I had extensive discussions with Genette, who had resigned from the Party and who steered me toward the group "Socialism or Barbarism" and toward *Arguments.* I had a profound interest in Marx, but was not a Marxist because what the communists or even diverse leftists represented troubled me. I subscribed very quickly to Heidegger's texts, which I read in German before they were published in French. I agreed with the insertion of Marx within the history of metaphysics. But my daily bread was reading Debord well before he published his book on *The Society of the Spectacle.* We had started a little journal at Bordeaux, *Notes Critiques,* situated between Lefort, Lyotard, Castoriadis, on the one hand, and by Debord, on the other . . . In addition, I came upon *Les Temps modernes* and I saw the polemic triggered at the end of the war concerning Heidegger's political engagement. Thus I knew he was involved, at the very least, with the regime. Hence, I had a strong political reticence. I vaguely began to see that what I called, for the sake of convenience, the motif of sacralization was related to this political aberration. When I discovered Derrida, I told myself that finally I had found the first "leftist" reading of Heidegger, a reading that was not submissive, or faithfully aligned, that had the right distance, and engaged critically with that thought. All of a sudden I had a direction. Without such a reading, I would not have done the work that I have done; that is clear. That has been the genesis.

We could discuss your publications in this respect.
Heidegger did not appear there immediately.

The first text was published in 1970, "The Fable," on literature and philosophy, and it bore on Nietzsche's famous text *"How the 'true world' finally became a fable: The history of an error."* But Heidegger completely subtended the work.

Next there was a text that was published in Mimesis des articulations
where you speak of philosophical madness and where Heidegger
appears already, or at least the motif of the Gestell.

I referred to a reading that still guides me to this day: Heidegger's interpretation of Jünger ("Contribution to the Question of Being") where he puts in place what I call an "onto-typology," which also pertains to Jünger. I also entitled my thesis (*soutenance d'habilitation*) "Onto-Typology," which came from my reading of Heidegger. For these politico-philosophical or philosophico-political reasons, it is a self-critical text. In fact, through Jünger, Heidegger accuses himself of Nietzscheism and thus of belonging to a "right wing lineage," "a conservative revolution," to put it succinctly. I have also used this notion of onto-typology to speak of a certain style of Heidegger's political engagement. There are stupefying sentences in his work, in the '30s and '40s, in particular in the courses on Hölderlin, on the Figures (the Types) that dominate the time: the Soldier, the Worker, the Poet, etc.

In Imitations des Modernes, a much later text, I noted a sentence that
surprised me because you did not develop it: "It happens that there
is an Oedipus for Heidegger . . . more than a year after the rupture
with National Socialism, Heidegger addresses this figure."

If there is an Antigone, there is an Oedipus. Note the 1935 course *Introduction to Metaphysics*. Oedipus is the Type par excellence, the tragic hero of the struggle against appearance and for the truth of appearing. It is only much later that Heidegger stated that the Type is the specter of the century and that *The Worker* is a book that is both prophetic and revelatory. For the most part, Heidegger traces this specter to *Zarathustra*. But, after all, Marx's Proletariat is a type; Freud's Oedipus is another, and we still are under its power and its determining force. At the same time, I think that Heidegger has perfectly circumscribed the issue, and that he was the first victim of it: he surely believed in the new man! And he also believed in the Type that must prefigure him, as an ancient *exemplum*!

I would like to ask you a more embarrassing question, not for you,
but in terms of "the thing itself": You have alluded to Heidegger's self-
criticism, but at the same time you are one of those who have criticized
him for his "silence." Is there both a self-criticism and a resistance?

Gadamer told me several times that when Heidegger was asked privately about his political "error," he responded, "It was Nietzsche who did me in." I remain convinced that the problem lay in those passages in *Being and Time* on "being-with," the choice of one's heroes, history and the destiny of peoples, which come directly from the "monumental history" of the second *Untimely Meditation* and which have been re-elaborated by Heidegger. I believe that it is that, in addition to the Germano-centrism of the German tradition, at least since Winckelmann, which is always accompanied by its reverse: Hellenocentrism. This is what largely explains the Nazi involvement, nonetheless with a tremendous philosophical distance in the texts (even the worst ones from 1933–34) in relation to party ideology: there was a complicity, but also a distance. Was there then a rupture? I would not put it that way. No one can say at this point. But there was a widening of the initial gap between Heidegger and the Nazi ideology. There was a distancing, except for certain motifs: the historicity assigned to peoples and languages; the Greek/German bipolarity; the refusal to read the Roman Nietzsche, although very important; the idea, expressed very late, that art, *Dichtung,* supposes and engages the preparation of the space of the holy in which a divinity could announce itself, the deliberate choice of the first version of "Bread and Wine," and not the last version: all that, and many other things, such as the overestimation of the people [*Volk*], or the motif of death for the community and the camaraderie of combat [*philia*?] give that thought the character—it is the right word when one speaks of a typology—of the classical thought of the German extreme right after the First World War. I am not exaggerating, but I cannot find any other terminology; and Heidegger never ceased thinking in these terms, even when he became much more cautious and even elusive after the war. Still in 1967, I believe, it was in Athens where he gave a talk on the work of art and began, "How has the people, this little people, been able, etc." and these comments were accompanied by an entire theological discourse, and thus theological-political, in relation to Athena. I believe this is something that he shared with many others, including Walter Benjamin, from 1938 to 1940: with respect to the work of art, the similarities are amazing. There was a thematic in which Walter Benjamin involved himself (including his historical or political messianism) . . . There is something of the epoch that reverberated in the Stephan George circle; including, among other things, Hellingrath's first major publication of Hölderlin. Walter Benjamin's first texts on Hölderlin resulted from this edition. This recalls one of Celan's poems, just discovered, noted in the margin of an article by Benjamin: "Port-Bou Deutsch." Benjamin's article bears on his reading of Max Kommerell, a former member of the George circle, whom Heidegger admired and who wrote extensively on Hölderlin. There is a frightening, harsh sentence: "*Niebelungen* of the left, *Niebelungen* of the right." In the end it was insightful. When Brecht "berated" Benjamin, it was because he felt that, in spite of the language borrowed from Marx, or Lukacs, etc., Benjamin thought like a man from the extreme right. In Domenico Losurdo's book *Heidegger et l'idéologie de la guerre,* one sees that people like Jaspers, Weber, and others more critical of the Nazis shared a certain number of values. Even in the "Rectoral Address," as a discourse attempting a refoundation of a university that was sinking, there is something grandiose. As in *What Is Metaphysics?* Certainly, for me the "concessions" are unacceptable, as are some of Brecht's declarations in support of the DDR. I have mentioned the source of my anarcho-syndicalist leftism! There is nonetheless a real problem there. In the same way one senses that the motif of technology was a common one, among all those people. For all the European intellectuals, the great discovery was technology, from the journal *Esprit* to Heidegger, Benjamin, and others.

We should return to Heidegger's "silence."

That silence pertains to German responsibility regarding the extermination of the Jews. He said nothing on this matter; he did not want to. He did not want to say anything against Germany. This is what Nolte's work tells us: all that, he effectively said, was the Bolsheviks' fault in the "European civil war"—an analysis that is not entirely false, and that should not conceal the fact that this "civil war" was first a German civil war between Nietzsche and Marx, or rather, Marxism and Nietzscheism, between two traditions that issued from Hegel and from idealism—which is an old story. For me, Hölderlin was one of the first centers of this division, of this internal schism: the concern with the proper, the experience of the foreign, the tearing, and the return home: this is the German schism! Hölderlin was a victim of it. It is the whole of German history since the echo or the shock that was provoked by the French revolution. It is not surprising that Nolte, who was Heidegger's student, analyzed this in this way; but Heidegger himself did not wish to say anything, nothing about the appalling system of extermination. I recognize the difference with Baeumler. Much more stupidly Nazi than Heidegger, he explained himself after the war and made an effort to claim that it was his interpretation of Nietzsche that was the problem. And he tried to address the situation, publically; Heidegger never did.

And at the same time, as you suggest, did he not refuse to hear
another Nietzsche? He seems to have had reservations with
respect to the complete edition of Colli and Montinari.

Yes, it is said that he called it "communist." When he was reintegrated into the university in 1951 or 1952 he spoke often of Nietzsche. He could have used that opportunity to say something. At least on the political appropriation of Nietzsche; but he said nothing. However, on occasion he would say something like this: "Ladies and Gentleman, there is an exhibition on German soldiers who were prisoners in the Soviet Union; you should go and see it." This is astonishing. One of our students translated a text from 1945 published in *Heidegger Studies* on poverty, *Armut.* In this work Heidegger undertakes to praise spiritual poverty—somewhat opportunistically, by stating that the problem of our time is communism. Now the text on which he relies is drawn from a collection of fragments, the most important of which is attributed to Hölderlin, "Communism of Spirits," a strange text (resembling a text by Novalis) formally translated by Armel Guerne in his *Anthologie des romantiques allemands*. In this essay, Heidegger does not explicitly mention this fragment; he carefully chooses a sentence on poverty and richness, taking just that text as if it was the same problem as the one raised by Hölderlin concerning the epochs of Western history. The realization of the Reform, said Hölderlin in the end, is that everyone is a priest! This is one of the first slogans of "reformed communism" since Boehme and Münzer. See Ernst Bloch.

We have still not approached an entirely different aspect:
the question of French Heideggerianism. It might be a
somewhat delicate matter to approach this head on.

Not at all! On this point, my position is more determined than ever. Let us not dwell on Beaufret's negationism. It belongs to a larger context. It is an operation of an ideological whitewash. It is a confiscation. I had proposed to Gallimard that I translate one of Heidegger's courses on Hölderlin because it interested me: I was rejected straightaway. Another matter is the gibberish [*patois*] of the translations. I retract nothing that I said at the time concerning the translation of *On the Way to Language* or about Vezin's translation of *Being and Time* (let us mention for instance *le déval,* which was appropriately ridiculed). I have read the latest of such projects—the translation of a few pages of the *Beiträge* in Deguy's journal *Po&sie.* It is mind boggling, incomprehensible. I defy anyone to make progress in that text. It is catastrophic. But this suits many people just fine, for example the Habermas group. It authorizes the entire Wittgensteinian invasion via America. If *we* abandon German thought, then what would remain of thought? We should read the *Beiträge* in the German: it is not so difficult. And I am not saying anything about the systematic erasure of all the political connotations of Heidegger's terminology, which is still quite evident.

As far as you are concerned, do you have the impression that your critical
distance from Heidegger has increased with (or since) La Fiction du politique?

No. But I speak now of Heidegger's "archi-fascism." The fact that Heidegger kept his Nazi party membership card does not really interest me. The fact that he stubbornly proclaimed the "truth of the movement" and that he deplored the failure of the revolution seems to me to be much more decisive.

And with respect to the interpretation of Hölderlin?

Concerning *Andenken,* for example, the exchanges with Jean Pierre Lefebvre have corroborated what I thought of Heidegger's text for some time. When I was at Bordeaux in 1965–66 I was already interested, with a German scholar, in finding documents concerning Hölderlin's stay there. He already thought that Heidegger's reading was "wrongheaded." I agreed and my opinion has not changed, except for thinking today that this reading (Heidegger's) was in fact scandalous. I also remember my first reading of Beaufret's text on *Remarques sur Oedipe, remarques sur Antigone:* there are some excellent things there, especially the interpretation on Aristotle's *mimesis.* But Fédier's notes on "Hölderlin in France" are extremely flat. I do not have the impression that I have changed. I have always had the greatest mistrust, if only with respect to the manipulation of the texts. Later, as soon as I had the chance, I wanted to translate the tragedies of Hölderlin and Sophocles . . . that is, precisely that which did not interest Heidegger.

Speaking of the theater, you have also written a play: Sit venia verbo.

It is something I did with Michel Deutsch. It is a fable in which Heidegger is the main character in the background, but it is also inspired by many other stories of collaborators from the same time—in particular Hamsun, who wrote his *Journal d'épuration* when he was in custody for a time. I also made use of one of the sons of Thomas Mann, Golo, who had returned to Germany after he obtained his American citizenship. That still is a well-known story. The first time I went to the United States I was twenty-four years old. In Monterey College, where I taught a course, there was Germanist who taught at Stanford, a Jewish German émigré who, like Golo Mann, returned to Germany with the American army. As he spoke German, the authorities asked him to oversee the de-nazification interrogations in the universities. He told me very detailed stories. He worked in the American zone. And it was on that basis that we wrote this theatrical fiction with three characters: two antagonists and the chorus. Our idea was to reduce the tragedy to the bare minimum. The three characters were as follows: a professor (held prisoner by the occupying authorities on the stage of the town theater because there was no room in the prison), his former assistant who had returned with the American army, and a German woman who brings him food every day. And who comments from time to time.

I do not believe I have changed much. What has changed is the knowledge of German history, of German ideology since 1914–18, and my knowledge of the German tradition. So I am much more accurate. But the political distrust was there from the beginning. It was also there the only time when I met Fédier; I did not really want this meeting to which I have alluded. Further, while I admired the Char of *Feuillets d'Hypnos,* I was less enamored with what came after; and I never cared for his act as the "Hölderlin from Provence." But I certainly understand how Heidegger was interested in these meetings and seminars in Provence: the French gave him a major boost!

Were you tempted, in spite of these reservations, to meet the great man?

In 1975, there was a serious plan to go to see Heidegger, who had heard of Derrida. We would have gone with Derrida, Nancy and I, and—of course—with Lucien Braun. Twice a meeting was arranged and twice Heidegger's wife canceled it because Heidegger was very tired and did not feel well.

Before his death, Heidegger had said he would leave a number of French books—that he had received—to the library of the Strasbourg Philosophy Institute. It was in part to thank Braun, who had defended him at the time of the aborted invitation to Strasbourg. Braun had been friends with Heidegger for some time. Thus, after his death, Braun and I went to collect the books. In the room where he died, I looked carefully at the books he had set aside from his large library: on the night table, apart from the etymological dictionaries and the great German histories of philosophy, there were books by Hölderlin, Goethe, and the Suhrkamp collection of Celan's poems. Of course Aristotle, Hegel, and Kant were there. But not many books, there was a shelf, and a large night table. There was a little Braque on the wall.

In the French books, were there any interesting dedications?

One by Lacan. Some books were not cut. I do not want to be inaccurate but it seemed to me that, for *Being and Nothingness,* only the first hundred pages were cut. These books have been integrated into the general library in our university and I can say that quite a few volumes have disappeared.

Jean-Luc Marion

Interview of December 3, 1999

*My first question would concern your personal
itinerary, your philosophical beginnings.*

When did I first read Heidegger? In philosophy class in high school? In *khâgne*? From Jean Beaufret? In fact, my first encounter with Heidegger was during a celebration at UNESCO in April 1964. I was there; I was not even in my senior year in high school, but was in the year before; I had read Kierkegaard or something like that. I understood nothing; I listened and that was very good; I attended this improbable thing: the session where Beaufret read a homage to Kierkegaard, a text by Heidegger that did not contain a single word about Kierkegaard ("The End of Philosophy and the Task of Thinking"). I understood nothing at all. I left telling myself: there are things that I absolutely do not understand. I did not know Beaufret, and for me Heidegger was a name in Jean Wahl's *Introduction to Existentialism*, which I had flipped through without understanding anything.

In *hypokhâgne*, I never heard about Heidegger. I read Kant's *Critique of Pure Reason* on my own, and then I read Spinoza: that, I understood. *Khâgne* was the great adventure, with Beaufret. What was very surprising was that he never spoke of Heidegger. He gave excellent courses, which were very rigorous. I learned many things, but he did not refer to Heidegger and taught no classes on him. I read a little Heidegger for the exam, *Letter on Humanism* or *What Is Metaphysics*. Basically, I had almost no exposure to Heidegger.

It was only at the École that I realized two things. First, I understood that the entire history of philosophy that I had learned had been based on Heidegger's interpretation. Without knowing it, I had imbibed a Heideggerian understanding of the history of metaphysics, far more than I had ever realized, through Beaufret's courses: I had confirmation of this when they were subsequently published.

Then, I told myself it would be necessary to learn German; I did so, and then I read *Sein und Zeit* for the first time in its entirety. But that was after Beaufret.

In a sense, I did not speak about Heidegger very often with Beaufret. I went several times to see him at passage Stendhal during my second year of *khâgne* and during my first years at the École. It was great there. But later, when he moved to rue du Temple, I felt, without really knowing why, that the atmosphere changed: there was a Praetorian guard around him, and I felt excluded, even before passing the Agrégation. I did not make an issue of it. In spite of everything, I must say that "l'Ontologie grise," for example, was an essay that responded to a question that Beaufret posed often in *khâgne:* that of the relation between Aristotle and Descartes, and how an object differs from the entity; and also a question that I have asked myself long since: how could Cartesian science be "true" without attaining reality? In order to clarify this problem, it is necessary to accept the idea that one can directly compare, without hermeneutic precaution, Aristotle's texts and Descartes's texts. I had thus acquired a somewhat unorthodox but extraordinarily efficacious Heideggerian methodology. This really was a specific approach, and it was Beaufret who taught it to me: one had to read Aristotle, and to compare, as if there was nothing to it, Aristotle to Descartes's *Regulae*—and *voila*! And thus I proceeded in this way. Why did Alquié accept such a project, such a method? Because Alquié, also in his own way, had an idiosyncratic approach to Descartes, the Descartes who spoke of a mute being and of a theory of the object without being. Thus he was quite content for me to contrast the object to the entity, when I contrasted Descartes to Aristotle. I thus was able to dedicate "l'Ontologie grise" to both Beaufret and Alquié without either of them being troubled by this, far from it. But that still did not depend on *Sein und Zeit*. When I began to become interested in the history of philosophy, just while reading Heidegger, it was often Heidegger's conception of the history of philosophy that influenced me. In a sense—it is paradoxical to say that—I was not interested in Heidegger in and for himself until 1980, after I finished *Sur la théologie blanche.*

Wasn't The Idol and Distance *before that?*

Yes, *The Idol and Distance* was in 1977, so it was well before that. But at that point I had another guiding thread in my work. The first question in *The Idol and Distance* concerned, from a theological point of view, the death of God. And in that way again I reconsidered a point of Heidegger's history of philosophy: the God of Nietzsche is the God of Metaphysics and is the figure of the moral God after Kant, etc. Certainly, I was engaging Nietzsche, but this problematic still pertained to a history of philosophy and of metaphysics influenced by Heidegger. In fact, Heidegger played only a speculative, nonhistorical role at the end of *The*

Idol and Distance, because I wanted to highlight the distance, the ontological difference and *différance.* It was only then that I worked on the enigmatic character of the ontological difference. After that I did not work on it. Even at that moment, in my mind, the discussion was centered not on Heidegger, but on the death of God. It was a short time later, when I was asked to explain the idolatry of metaphysics, the representation of God in relation to the theology of idolatry, that I specifically engaged Heidegger's decision. But finally, why did being itself become a determination of God, including within a certain part of Christian theology? I then imprudently went further into this engagement. And then I examined more attentively the case of the "'non' metaphysical God." A sentence struck me, which is found in *Die Technik und die Kehre,* page 45: "God, if he is, is a being." Right there, such questions! First the obvious, banal question, which is in fact secondary, "Does God exist?" It presupposes another question, or rather, a response prior to the question: "Must God be?" And that was too unbearable for me—as if God had any obligation, and above all the obligation to be! Hence a double refusal: of the death of God and above all that God had to be! At that moment I moved from a book against Aquinas to a book against Heidegger.

Was that God without Being?

Yes, in the 1980s. Now I am able to speak about it a bit more. I met Maurice Clavel the last year of his life. He read Heidegger at the same time that he was writing his last, little known and remarkable book, titled *Critique de Kant.* At that moment, we focused on Heidegger by comparing our works in progress. He did not find me sufficiently anti-Heideggerian, but I realized later that I became at that moment consciously anti-Heideggerian, if this expression means anything. Very curiously, this was also the time when Alain Renaut changed dramatically.

Wasn't there also a polemic with Jean Beaufret shortly before his death?

Yes. It was even included at the end of *God without Being.* I had written an article for *Heidegger et la question de Dieu,* a fine volume inspired by a conference organized by Kearney and O'Leary, which was to some extent a sort of commentary on the *Idol and Distance.* They had a conference at the Irish College in Paris, which I had not been able to attend, but for which I had given a text to which Beaufret, who had attended, had responded in a polemical manner. And I responded to Beaufret, a response that can be found in the appendix to *God without Being.* From that point on it was clearer than ever: I was no longer a Heideggerian, at least in the sense of Beaufret or Fédier.

The most curious thing was that, at the same time, my work on Descartes caused the historians of philosophy to see me as a Heideggerian. Jean-Marie Beyssade repeated (and he was only echoing the *fama*) that I had an obviously excessive Heidegger's interpretation of Descartes. In fact, I was anything but Heideggerian, but it is true that I remained faithful to the interrogation of the history of metaphysics. Nonetheless, by 1982, I had become officially a non-Heideggerian according to Beaufret's students; and that's the way things remained since.

In 1984, I arrived in Poitiers, and I resumed my work. First, I did a course on Husserl, and then, although I am not sure when, I threw myself, for the next two years, into teaching a course on the entirety of *Sein und Zeit*. I did something similar at the École with Didier Franck. When I went to Nanterre in 1988, I did a course on *Sein und Zeit* right away, doing a commentary on the entire text. I did the same when I arrived at the Sorbonne in 1995. On several occasions, I chose—truly with great joy—to provide commentaries on *Sein und Zeit,* sparing no detail for the students. This was just about the time when you invited me to participate in a volume on *Sein und Zeit* at Nice, and when there was also the issue of the Martineau translation, around which there was a productive discussion. I also published Jean Greisch's book, following this simple idea that *Sein und Zeit* is a classical text that must be treated as a classical text.

Greisch's book was published later.

Of course. But I mean to say that all of that issued from the same tactic, which was very simple, and which challenged Jean Beaufret's opinion that the university would not tolerate anyone speaking about Heidegger. As soon as I became a university professor, I therefore gave courses on Heidegger as one would for instance on Parmenides, and that was the beginning of disagreements. I have in fact worked on Heidegger from the moment that I no longer felt that I was one of the "Heideggerians."

The other moment that was determinative was the publication of *Le Prisme métaphysique,* in which I wanted to test the validity of the notion of "onto-theo-logical constitution." In fact, this took place in several stages: after my thesis, in 1982, the French Society of Philosophy had invited me to give the usual traditional lecture and I had chosen as a topic, "On Descartes' Onto-theo-logy." It was a beautiful lecture, in my view, a "metaphysical fable" for others, but I revisited it as chapter 1 of the *Prisme*... I received comments and objections on the lecture, and the book, which I strongly believe in, emerged from my response to all of them.

At the same time, Courtine was working to finish his book on Suarez. I had the idea, with respect to the methodological use of the history of metaphysics by Heidegger, that the onto-theo-logical constitution could take a flexible form, as a real hermeneutics, on the express condition that one articulate it more historiographically, and that one adapt it to each author. I believed that I was right, and others have since followed me by posing the same question: can one make use of it, and under what conditions, for specific authors (Bulnois on Duns Scotus, Carraud on the principle of reason, Bardout on Malebranche)? Frankly, I would say yes. The question remains, however: during what period? With respect to Descartes, at least, the model functions well. The proof is that if one tries to apply the model to some Cartesians, one sees clearly that the methodology works. But we still have to examine the cases of Spinoza and occasionalism. The more interesting problem would be to see how it applies to Kant, because in his case the principle of reason is no longer operative, or at least it is replaced by the "supreme principle of synthetic judgment," i.e., transcendental apperception. Then, is it not precisely the complete appropriation of the status of the onto-theo-logical constitution in the process of *cogitatio*? It is hard to say; it remains to be established and examined. We decided to organize a conference at the Sorbonne in 2004, on Kant and Descartes, to reconsider, among others, all these questions.

The problem of the status of onto-theo-logy is henceforth posed historically. For my part, I have rediscovered, by reading medieval thinkers, the validity as well as the limits of this model. Traditionally, the exceptions to onto-theo-logy are Greek theologies (Plotinus, etc., studied by Aubenque and Hadot). Personally, I have never been very convinced by the argument: to pass from being to the One remains a metaphysical gesture, by the mere conversion of the transcendentals. A failed escape!

But what is the sense of Aubenque's or of Hadot's objections? Do they suggest that onto-theo-logy is overcome, because Plotinus was a hyper-metaphysician or because he was no longer a metaphysician?

Yes, this remains quite unclear. I think the case of neo-Platonism has not been sufficiently explored. Jean-Marc Narbonne, among others, is working on it. I myself had been intrigued, when rereading Anselm, since it is clear that his celebrated argument has no metaphysical, ontological, or onto-theo-logical functions. In the context of my discussions and my belated reconciliation with the contemporary neo-Thomists, I have seen the great difficulty of speaking of an onto-theo-logy in the case of Aquinas. On numerous points, warning signs are clearly visible. On the contrary, as soon as one addresses Duns Scotus, things are in place thanks to the clear evidence of the primacy of the concept of being and of the noetic univocity.

I published an article on these matters in the *Revue thomiste* in 1995. Regarding Aquinas, there are many places in his work where onto-theo-logy is resisted. First, formally, God is not inscribed in the metaphysical domain, because it is first necessary to prove that the Christian God enters into metaphysics—which is false, at least literally, for Aquinas. Next, in Aquinas's work, there is the fact that there is absolute equivocity between what being means for creatures and what being means for God, whose *esse* remains so unknown that one is unable to speak of it (Gilson). And the analogical relations remain so detached that they reinforce the ontological unknowability of God, far from tempering the fact (as does the work of the neo-Thomists, including Suarez above all) that there is an impossibility, an obstacle. Finally, one notes the quite strange relation between God and causality; the *causa sui* is always challenged for numerous reasons; very quickly, the problem of the incompatibility of causality in God is posed as such. Some tell me that it does not prove everything: I agree, of course, but textually, one can nevertheless identify very easily some positions that, retrospectively, prevent any onto-theo-logical interpretation. There is therefore currently a decisive question in the history of philosophy (posed at some point by Alain de Libera): if there is an onto-theo-logy, if this concept has a precise meaning (nonideological, and patently clear), where and when does it operate? What depends on it and what remains completely foreign to it? This is a hypothesis that Heidegger has, incidentally, perfectly admitted: this hypothesis did not apply to thinkers like Kierkegaard or others. What cannot be refuted cannot be proved: let's be somewhat Popperian in the history of metaphysics. Likewise for the too famous "metaphysics of presence."

There is then a nondogmatic, heuristic, hermeneutic manner of using Heidegger, which permits one to see into the history of metaphysics much more clearly. So that suddenly the opposite of metaphysics becomes interesting if one can specify it. Philosophical work has much to gain. In fact, those who take a frank approach to this question turn out to be better authors than others, because the latter are reductive and do not see anything else, or persist in another vision of metaphysics that is overly narrow. I find that Heidegger's schema is the most interesting because it offers a principle of organization and of interpretation that is very open and at the same time quite efficacious, which avoids what many historians of philosophy do since Plato—and which consists in saying: everything is historical in philosophy, except *one* philosopher. This is a very metaphysical way of occluding the question of metaphysics. Who is part of it? Who is not part of it, etc.? Incidentally, this sheds an entirely new light, for example, either on medieval philosophy, which appears to be at its limit, or on authors who until then were not situated within metaphysics, and who now return to it with a vengeance. For example, at one point, Descartes was completely banished from metaphysics; there were entire periods about which one would love for there to be an inquiry, for example, into Hobbes, Spinoza, the French Enlightenment, Comte, etc.

One finds that also among contemporaries. What is the status
of metaphysics for those who critique it the most? In general,
can one respond to them at least somewhat negatively?

Absolutely. Now that we know the Vienna school better, and thus the birthplace of analytic philosophy, one sees better the immensity of the metaphysical assumptions that were admitted, without these assumptions being recognized as metaphysical. The ambivalence of Husserl or Bergson is similar.

I have remained methodologically Heideggerian, then, but especially in relation to the history of philosophy, because it is the most enlightening and fruitful method, which not only does not prevent scholarly studies, but makes the work interesting.

On this point, do you have the impression that France is an
exception? What is your experience in the United States?

Today, the history of philosophy is completely internationalized. It is not the case that the French are in their corner with their supposed French problems; the Italians, the Dutch, and the Americans work in the same way. When someone says something in France, and when it is published, it is read, approved, and reviewed by the Italians, Americans, etc. When *Le Prisme métaphysique* (so indigestible and so overly coded!) was published, it was immediately translated into Italian and English. This proves that these kinds of things are transmittable across borders. The reciprocal is true (Gregory, Garber, Frankfurt, Larmore, etc.).

Now we can discuss the phenomenological renewal with which your work
Being Given *is concerned. In that case, isn't it a bit more complicated?*

The first thing to say—this holds true for me as well as for others—is that the renewal of phenomenology in France in the 1980s was related not to Heidegger but to Husserl. Franck reopened Husserl's very question: a good period of the work of the Centre de Poitiers (that of *Phénoménologie et Métaphysique*) addressed *Logical Investigations*. Phenomenology, in fact, was renewed by a return to Husserl, which continued with good scholars (English, Benoist, Bernet, etc.). In my case, Husserl played the essential role, because I went back to write on Heidegger in terms of his relation to Husserl, the Husserl of the *Logical Investigations*. For me, the debate with Heidegger was revived, and profoundly modified, by questions like "What is intentionality?" "What is reduction?" The question of givenness emerged only when I studied the *Logical Investigations* (the article, *The Breakthrough and the Broadening*[1]), where I rejected Heidegger's and Derrida's interpretations, by maintaining that the question was not at all that of the primacy of intuition, but that the great discovery was the luminosity of givenness, whether the givenness of intuition, of signification, or that of intentionality. Incidentally, I was enlightened on this point by Franck's book, which showed in *Chair et corps,* that *Gegebenheit* dominates the distinction made in *Ideas I,* §40, between two regions supposed to be distinguished by a fundamental difference: consciousness and reality. I returned to Heidegger through the discussion of this point. On that basis, inspired by Husserl, I posed questions to Heidegger, through an exegesis of the occurrences of *Es Gibt,* which is impossible to avoid, since it is so massively present in his text. I am genuinely persuaded that what happened with this return to Husserl allowed France to avoid this kind of evanescent phenomenology devolving into a history of phenomenology that one sees elsewhere. Because these simple questions were raised anew: What is reduction? What is intentionality? Is there subjectivity or not, etc.?

We will rediscover the theological question through a return
from phenomenology to the metaphysical question.

I observe that today there are many ways to do metaphysics. Either one keeps the word and uses it in a Kantian way: this is what Husserl has done, and others after him—it is difficult but one can certainly do so. Or, one still keeps the word, while rejecting its ontological word in order to replace it with another one, for example, ethics (Levinas) or some other word. Or else, to cross out the word and the ontological stakes to discover another stakes, which is what Derrida attempted. There is above all the Heideggerian path: to speak of the question of being it is necessary to overcome metaphysics. These are clear strategies with respect to metaphysics. None of them suit me.

You omitted the destinal unity, the interpretation of metaphysics as technology.

Yes. Metaphysics as technology, indeed this is one possible path. The fact that I did not mention it proves that I am not Heideggerian, since this is a Heideggerian motif through and through.

My current position is that philosophy is perfectly open. Open by virtue of the crisis of the term "metaphysics" itself. This not a strong position; it is a provisional position.

Isn't one of Heidegger's virtues that he reopened the question of
metaphysics as such, as a question? This has happened several times in
history; for example, Hegel did not say Metaphysik *but* Wissenschaft:
the word "metaphysics" only reappeared to be rethought.

But that happened already with Descartes, from the moment that he defined metaphysics no longer as a thinking of beings as beings, but as a thinking about knowledge, as the order and principle of knowledge. That moment also reopened a metaphysics. When Descartes undertook that shift, he prefigured Kant: it is the same definition. Also, between Kant and Descartes, Baumgarten could say that he enacted these same formulations.

Perhaps we could return to theology through Lacoste's opinion of Heidegger in his article in the Dictionnaire Critique de théologie. *He says in substance that it is necessary to construct a properly Christian theology without Heidegger. Isn't this a paradoxical manner of agreeing with Heidegger after all, since it is he who led us to this gesture?*

But, curiously, he did not abide by that project: in the end, he did effectuate this departure, since he established that any thinking of God, even Christian, depends on beings. Thus he himself has not maintained this project. This is the reason I parted from him. For me, Heidegger operates absolutely and entirely only in two domains: the history of philosophy and the analytic of *Dasein*. That is already a substantial work. Then, there is the question whether one can entrust the destruction of the history of ontology to being itself, if the truth of being suffices for the abandonment of metaphysics itself. Heidegger himself refused to isolate a nonmetaphysical "truth"; he eventually admitted it somewhat bluntly. The problem remains open, and I do not see at all what Christian theology can gain from it. At any rate, it has tried many times to work with Heidegger and that has been, fortunately, a lamentable failure.

Are you thinking of particular priests?

Yes. There was Lotz, Rahner, and so many others. In the final analysis, this is still a neo-Thomist reflex, according to which being leads to God. I have never taken that path, and frankly I think that a Christian theology cannot do it: its only relation to phenomenology must remain formal. It must be able to describe formally, in all of their possibilities, in the mode of the phenomena of phenomenology, the phenomena of the Revelation. That is the only thing that they have in common. It must be said: after all, let us try to see *whether* what the biblical Revelation presents as manifestations are indeed phenomena. And let us try to describe them, to let them give their meaning.

Is it a hypothesis you are raising?

It is a question that I raise. If phenomenology is capable of constituting all that is visible (and of giving it meaning), it must be capable of letting that constitute itself.

This is all the more interesting since, as metaphysics is going toward its end, it has defined itself, very clearly, through certain of its shortcomings, through its very incapacity, its refusal or its denial to speak of a certain number of phenomena like the Revelation. This began with Hobbes's, Spinoza's, and Hume's denials of miracles. Next came Kant's and Fichte's critique of any revelation. Schelling and Hegel tried, each in his own way, to transgress or recuperate this prohibition. But they did not succeed, because clearly, they only ended up with a mythological philosophy. Their undertaking possessed a certain greatness, but what was most important was missing. In modern theology, one can see very well that, each time, one falls into a trap (Bultmann, as an example), it is because the theologian cannot describe a certain number of phenomena that nonetheless are constitutive of a Revelation, but that one cannot accept according to the positivist frame of mind. This is the decisive point. Metaphysics has clearly said that it cannot and does not want to give thought to the Revealed—this is not its domain and is not within its competence. If phenomenology really claims to go farther than metaphysics, it should be able to say something about it, or at least provide some tools of description or (nondescription). These seem to me to be the nonclassical and nonobjective phenomenological situations.

You have used the expression "end of metaphysics." Would
you thus accept that metaphysics is coming to its end?

Yes, I accept it for the purposes of a historian of philosophy. When Heidegger said, quite early, that one should no longer speak the language of metaphysics, he was thinking no doubt of what the reading of Husserl had shown. There is a perfect remark by Granel in the preface of his translation of *The Krisis:* what is striking in Husserl's work is that what he had to describe was incommensurate with Kant's properly metaphysical lexicon, in which he remained trapped. And all the philosophers, Bergson, Levinas, Wittgenstein, etc., tried not to speak of "metaphysics." In my view, the great weakness of analytic philosophers is their overwhelmingly metaphysical language. And because of this, an extraordinary imprecision occurs: when they say "being," "cause," "reality," or "truth," what can they have in mind? Even and especially when they are innovative they preserve Aristotle's language or rather the fourteenth-century Aristotelians'. What Heidegger teaches us precisely is to be historical and to know how to recognize historicity so as to not be naïve. It is when one does not want to be historical, that one is actually so.

Finally, aren't you in agreement with Lacoste's statement?

First, I do not think that, as such, Heidegger can be integrated into a theological project. I do not see how one can do it. Besides, no philosopher has done so.

Jean Greisch spoke to me of "the weakness of the last God."

For me, reading of the *Beiträge* raises nothing but doubts concerning "the last God." It is obviously not a question of God.

Perhaps you have suggestions concerning perspectives on Heidegger en France?

The question I ask myself now is how long it will take for a serious reading of Heidegger after 1934 to take place. There are two readings of Heidegger that have already been done, two phases of Heidegger that have been established: from Husserl's influence to the analytic of *Dasein;* then there was the reading of the history of metaphysics as onto-theo-logy. Now, the question remains of what there is of the best of Heidegger's work that came after, during the period that began with the *Letter on Humanism* and the Bremen Lectures. How long will it take for them to be genuinely read?

Can one speak of the end of the French exception? I mean the end of the reception that has been so distinctive since 1930. Isn't that page in the process of being turned in favor of a much more "globalized" approach?

I almost would say the contrary. When I went to Chicago the first time, ten years ago, people did not really read Husserl or Heidegger. They knew Bergson, Gilson, or Merleau-Ponty much better. And today I observe the many translations of Heidegger, and the proliferation of translations of Husserl. And in the United States there is work on French phenomenology: the reason for that—our modesty will suffer—is a historical fact: the '70s were Heidegger, the '80s were Derrida, the '90s were Levinas, and the debates that took place with these translations. In fact, it is true because I have seen it with my own eyes: the waves of translations. And the debates now are also translated. I believe that there has been a renewal, which is already in the process of being integrated into the history of phenomenology as such. I spoke about it with Vattimo. I was also struck by what is taking place in Germany, for example, in the case of French phenomenology: Waldenfelds, Casper, Kühn, and others have noted that there was a new debate in France. Thus one of the reasons why the history of philosophy makes progress is its dissemination, i.e., the fact that the information and the methods of work are the same all over the world. One proceeds in the same way in phenomenology, whereas before this there was no accumulation. In France, this strange thing happened that was constant accumulation for the last fifty years of very different scholars who were connected nonetheless: Paul Ricoeur, Levinas, Merleau-Ponty, Sartre, Michel Henry, Derrida, and the young ones: that makes quite a collection. There is no equivalent anywhere. There is a critical mass that the Americans follow with rapidity and avidity, with the awareness that one must go through it. I think that we are not at the end of the exception.

When I speak of the end of the French exception, I meant it in another sense: not the fact that we would cease being interesting, but that "Heidegger in France" will perhaps no longer have the unique status that it once had. Is it not now already somewhat passé?

In France, it played an anchoring role. When Heidegger came on the scene after the war, there were two dominant things: Marxism (with the ensuing for and against) and structuralism. Marxism was a pole of resistance to the structuralist wave until the '70s. It was these two opposing poles that made Heidegger seem overdetermined, with a function I would call ideological, indeed quasi-religious. I believe it is in the process of disappearing since the credibility of Marxism has declined and that we saw that Heidegger was nonetheless beyond that. And as a human being, he fell short of it.

If you are correct, it would correspond to a work that is more academic and more scientific. On that basis, with respect to the onto-theo-logical schema, couldn't the richness of what Heidegger inspired be more easily understood and shared?

More easily, because in the history of philosophy there are those who, in the name of the onto-theo-logical, were interested in Heidegger, because they could not avoid him, although they were not in their approach or in their language Heideggerians. For example, in your own case, you wrote your thesis, which was not a thesis on Heidegger, but the manner in which you approached Hegel was nonetheless typically Heideggerian. Now Heidegger is no longer an object of passion. This is what has changed since Granel and Birault.

Birault is a separate case. In the end, I speak about him very little in my book. Now, his place has been shown to be limited. Hasn't Jean Beaufret himself played a role that is somewhat less important than one believed?

I believe that Beaufret was much more important that Birault and even more brilliant for our generation. He really taught us how to read the texts. He put things in their context. When I arrived at the Sorbonne and even at the École, I saw, felt, and realized his absence very strongly.

Was he as successful with respect to translations?

Curiously, I think that when Beaufret's students from *khâgne* and the École Normale became professors, when, in a certain way, the door was finally open, he no longer influenced them. His vision was put into question. At that moment, for all those who had a different vision, the massive legitimization of Vezin and Fédier had a negative effect. One no longer adhered to Beaufret's approach that held that one did not need to write a thesis or enter a university.

Beaufret has an enormous responsibility for the death of a certain reception of Heidegger. In the end, it seemed to me that he did not want *Sein und Zeit* to be translated. And indeed, the official translation closed the door to the text.

A final point: shouldn't we also address the excessively negative reactions
to Heidegger, in particular from certain analytic "colleagues"? The
fact is that theses on Heidegger alone are often not approved.

Unfortunately, they are often of a poor quality. In any case, I do not advise people to write theses on Heidegger. Not because it is a taboo subject, but because it is too difficult. It is first necessary to translate the works very carefully, to go through the work of the history of philosophy. Then it is necessary to work seriously through Husserl. And then we can discuss things. The good authors write books on Heidegger only later on.

Jean-Luc Nancy

Interview of June 23, 2000

What were your Heideggerian "moorings?"

My moorings are straightforward enough. I knew nothing about Heidegger until, perhaps, 1961. I'd never heard of him before; I was a *khâgne* student in Toulouse, then at Louis-le-Grand, and Lakanal. None of the teachers mentioned him. The year at Lakanal I met François Warin, since he lived in Sceaux.

That was when you and François Warin translated
Heidegger's text on physis in Aristotle?

Yes. We translated the text in its entirety, which was then published in two issues of *Aletheia,* a journal run by students associated with Axelos. Warin suggested the project to me because I was fluent in German. We became friends and he introduced me to Heidegger, whereas at the time it was Hegel who was my passion. Warin and I remained friends, my oldest friend among philosophers. He had been a student of Beaufret's and had become associated with Fédier, and Vezin. I can't remember if he spoke to me about these people because he had already been cut off from their circle. He was, however, very much a Heideggerian and was mostly in contact with Axelos. Very much captivated and fascinated by Beaufret, he was under the ethico-political expectation of the Catholic milieu: his father was in the resistance, had been deported, and died in a camp; Warin lived with his mother and his two brothers. He also took me to a church that Ricoeur would go to sometimes. He was an uncompromising leftist. That is perhaps why there had been an initial discord with Beaufret and his followers. But Warin had introduced me to Axelos and had taken me to see him.

So it was in those years, 1963–64, that you began to read Heidegger?

In any case, my first contact with Heidegger wasn't very promising. Warin had me read the "Letter on Humanism" and I laughed out loud. I told him, this guy, with his whole peasant-pastoral motif, was ridiculous. I would put little notes in his mailbox with somewhat crass jokes about "the shepherd of being." The following year I played a trick on him, I wrote a pseudo-Heideggerian text on Auguste Comte, and I was delighted because Warin took the bait and showed the text to a few of Beaufret's followers. I had fun parodying Heidegger. I used to say that you had to hear a more originary resonance behind his spoken word, etc. That just goes to show you that I wasn't very favorably inclined toward this material.

This phase passed very quickly, however, once I realized that there was something else there besides what struck me as ridiculous. In a word: I understood the thinking of *finitude*. Warin was also very important to my education, as was Birault; but despite all that, I didn't become what one might call a Heideggerian. My contact with the Heideggerians was a bit disconnected. Warin left for Germany, then Tunisia, and he stayed abroad for a long time. Also, I never encountered Heidegger's work during the course of my studies. Then there was a leap of sorts: in 1964 I discovered Jacques Derrida's first writings: not his introduction to *The Origin of Geometry* at first, but the opening sections of *Of Grammatology.*

Which had been published in Critique, *as well as other texts later gathered in* Writing and Difference?

Yes. For me, that was another revelation. The difference between Heidegger and Derrida is that Derrida appeared more contemporary to me. I didn't know that there were people like him, right in the middle of contemporary philosophical work. I didn't have the clear feeling that Heidegger was still alive, that he was still present.

To that extent? Didn't you, given your fluency in German, have direct access to some of the Heidegger texts, but also to Nietzsche?

No. My philosophical interest at the time was Hegel, I had hardly any direct knowledge of Nietzsche, none of Husserl—and yet I had been a student of Ricoeur. He became the director of my MA thesis, which was on Hegel's philosophy of religion. My interest in religion was quite strong; I wanted to work on the question of religion. I'm returning to it now. Hegel has always been my favorite author. The first book that I wrote alone was *The Speculative Remark* in 1973. Once I passed the Agrégation, I asked to be sent to Strasbourg in order to study and get a degree in theology. I was given a *hypokhâgne* position in Colmar. I was happy. That's how I then found myself in Strasbourg. In the meantime, I had discovered Derrida's texts, and this opened up new dimensions to me. That is how I was led back to Heidegger, whom I had ignored for a while. Ricoeur offered me a job correcting his translation of *Ideas*. When I saw the size of the work I turned him down. But I stayed on good terms with Ricoeur, and I enrolled with him for a dissertation on religion. At that point I began to read Nietzsche because of Christianity. There you have it: I cannot even say what happened to Heidegger in this entire scene.

Heidegger certainly figures in your writing, but without
being the guiding thread. Is it perhaps in "Sharing Voices," in
1982, that you devoted your attention to Heidegger?

It is a commentary on what Heidegger says about hermeneutics in *Being and Time*, based on the critical distance offered by the "Conversation with a Japanese." And it is true that twenty years after my beginnings, Heidegger had become an integral part of my thought and work milieu. How did that happen? I could not say. Certainly it was through Derrida's influence; but there are not many of Derrida's texts explicitly devoted to Heidegger. The ellipses in *Voice and Phenomenon* intrigued me. And in *Positions*, Derrida simply admits: "What I have attempted to do would not have been possible without the opening of Heidegger's questions." It took me some time to realize that *différance* (with an a) was an operation carried out at the heart of the ontological difference.

Isn't your path different from that of most Heideggerians of your generation who
were influenced by an influential intermediary: Beaufret, Birault, or Granel?

My intermediary was not a professor, since it was Warin. I was initially under the influence of the spirit of left-wing Catholicism that constituted the central axis of my intellectual formation. It is even what made me become a philosopher, but with a very political style. It was first in *Esprit* that I began to write an article on Nietzsche, and then another one on Althusser. This "sensibility" didn't make Heidegger too accessible to me. However, the encounter with Philippe Lacoue-Labarthe played an obvious role. There was an important circumstance too: a study we did together around 1970–73 on Lacan. It was a little improvised because nobody here understood any of it. We wanted to take on the challenge by using a kind of academic method: reading the text itself. In *The Title of the Letter*, we found key passages where Lacan spoke of *Dasein*, of the "thing," etc. We noticed the "hidden layers" of the Lacanian text: Bataille on the one hand, Heidegger on the other. My interest in Bataille showed me that there was a much greater proximity than is usually acknowledged between Bataille and Heidegger. Bataille acknowledged this proximity, but in treating Heidegger like a professor!

Let's jump forward about fifteen years and turn to Of Divine Places.
There we read for example: "There is always a last God to be born."
Isn't this an echo of the Heideggerian theme of "the God to come?"

I don't think that the relation is very thematic or very developed. It is rather at this point, today, that I would like to take up the question of "the last God." I can remember a lecture by Courtine, here, in the '90s, where he spoke about the *Beiträge* and gave a very critical analysis of "the last God." Lacoue-Labarthe was in agreement and, paradoxically, I was the one who felt more Heideggerian. I have forgotten the arguments, and one would have to go back to them. But when Philippe said to me, "This return of the religious is despicable," I think that things are not so simple. I don't think that we can reduce this to the return of the religious. It's much more complex, just like the "affair." With respect to the latter, too, my relation has been, let's say, fairly unemotional. What I had learned before Faye's publications in *Médiations* (for example Guitton's visit to Heidegger) hadn't really shaken me. Since then, what has interested me is to understand *where* in Heidegger's thinking this takes place: where to situate not the political fault, but the philosophical problem. Philippe did very important work on this, and you as well, and Derrida, as well as Taminiaux, but there are still paths to be pursued.

What I want to say is that I am now interested in delimiting this sort of contradiction at the limits of Heidegger's perfectly legitimate thought, namely that it is in death that the highest possibility of existence presents itself, this possibility of identifying with the impossible, that it is the possibility of the end of the possible. I would say on the contrary that it is the place where *Dasein* becomes entirely *Mitsein.* And therefore, we have to take account of the others in the analysis of death, whereas Heidegger excludes them. What is a dead person if not what he or she instantly becomes in representation, in language, in the presence of others? But Heidegger neglects mourning and the presence of the dead in their tombs. There is an entire thematics therein, which I have always found interesting. Heidegger introduces "being-with" in a position that is detached from any other form of derivation of the other—no intersubjectivity, no empathy, etc. He never turned, later, in the direction indicated by Husserl's *Fifth Cartesian Meditation* (of which I am not a great fan either). Curiously, Heidegger sets up *Mitsein* as a sort of brute fact! He does not analyze the "with" [*mit*]. Not a word! "Being-with" is already given. Yet when we see where the word *mit* comes from in German, it's not at all the same as *avec,* it's not at all the idea of proximity that stands out. It's the idea of the milieu: "in the midst of." It is obvious what the later Heidegger could have done with that; but the fact that I am always with other *Dasein*s is resolved very quickly in *Being and Time,* into the relationship to the world, to equipmentality, etc. It's strange that there is no place in these analyses for other ways of being *mit,* in other words, for a phenomenology of affect, of encounter, of gaze, or of touch, etc. . . . *Fürsorge* remains rather elliptical. What is more, there is an entire tradition that comes back later: of the *Volk,* of the history of a people struggling with their spiritual identity. Of course it's very old, it goes through Hegel, and Herder . . . It is surprising to think that all those people who were not on the left in the 1930s, in Germany as elsewhere in Europe, allowed themselves to be reduced to this destiny of a people or of a nation.

There is no doubt that Heidegger already had some sympathy for the themes of the extreme right before 1933. His wife was more explicit: she was in a youth movement, or something similar.

His relationship to others, revealed by Heidegger's correspondence with Arendt and Blochmann, is very interesting. It's at the same time close to and in contrast with *Sein und Zeit.* Everything happens as if there was a certain authenticity in the relation to the other, which involved love in the case of Hannah, and loving friendship with Elisabeth. But love is absent from *Sein und Zeit,* as is sexual difference. Heidegger was a male chauvinist to an extreme, and he had a way of saying to Hannah: "You are a woman, you have to fulfill your feminine essence, etc." He did not tell her that she had to stay home, but one can sees that for him the man has a heroic, strong, virile role, etc. There are also emphases that completely corroborate the analysis of *das Man* and that are of the following type: when one is alone on the mountain, far from all the vain agitation of the city, that is when one is drawing close to authenticity. But *Sein und Zeit* doesn't suggest that. We expect something else, a different grasp of "everyday" existence.

These are tonalities that one also finds in volume 29/30 of the Gesamtausgabe (The Fundamental Concepts of Metaphysics), *where he develops the theme of boredom and of its different degrees. Should one then see in his allusions to current events an antidemocratic sensibility?*

Yes. That sort of sensibility drove many people in that period to look favorably upon everything that destabilized the Weimar Republic. The vast horizon of the Red Menace was still present. It was hard for many people to avoid being Stalinist, or Social-Democrat, or Trotskyite, it was not easy to find a "just" left . . . This has to be said because it is perfectly clear and true. We have to avoid closing ourselves up in a retrospective democratic good-conscience like that entire American movement that took great interest in showing the latent fascism of a certain number of the French. Of course there are a lot of things, good and just, to be said on this matter. But retrospective judgment should not oversimplify things . . . Should we, could we have made the same choices in 1920–30 as we would today? I am always ready to say that if I had been twenty in 1920 I have no idea what I would have become; I have to admit it honestly. I was of course captivated in the postwar years by a discourse aiming at the future with grand visions, in the style of the left. So? When we read certain texts from the '20s and '30s, the protests against "materialist" civilization, a lot of things become clear. People in general don't want to talk about it. We tried, together with Michel Surya, to dedicate an issue of the journal *Lignes* to this. We weren't able to do so. No one responded to us. It was the same situation for an issue of *Cahiers de l'Herne* that Philippe Lacoue-Labarthe and I wanted to do on Blanchot in 1985. A number of people didn't want to, under the obviously false pretense that "He is too great for me ..." People don't want to discuss the problems of democracy; they prefer to attack those who are not democrats, which remains a bit shallow.

On page 184 of your book The Sense of the World, *where you hardly speak of Heidegger, there is nonetheless a note in which we read: "It is doubtless Christianity that will have persisted in Heidegger, never really subjected to deconstruction, remaining perhaps the secret resource of the deconstruction of ontotheology." Can you discuss this point, which is alluded to only elliptically in the book?*

I believe indeed that something lies behind Heidegger's avowed anti-Christianism. It seems difficult to reduce Christianity to a Roman bastardization of the Greek heritage. It's suspicious. Is there not in Heidegger's work a secret re-elaboration of Judeo-Christian themes (*Geworfenheit, Gewissen*)—a matter in which we would also find a secret re-elaboration of Spinoza. Why nothing on Spinoza? Why pretend (in the "Letter on Humanism") that there hadn't been a treatise of fundamental ontology or of first philosophy named *Ethics*? It's staggering. The title *Ethics* says something different from ethics as separated from logic: it says something like what Heidegger wants to make it say.

I would wager that Heidegger borrows something from Spinoza (a sense of ethics prior to any division between theory and practice). And he borrowed the messianic theme from Judeo-Christianity, perhaps with the "last God," and above all a remarkably intelligent grasp of finitude as corresponding to the Christian *creature,* to Christian man. As a result we have the entire complication with respect to metaphysics, which is itself the originally Christian complication of the *intimior intimo meo.* It's a very Augustinian Christianity, a very Pascalian one. There are, by the way, striking resonances with respect to monastic life, for example in the correspondence with Elisabeth Blochmann. From another perspective, the short text of 1945, *Armut,* develops the theme of the future of (spiritual) communism based on a phrase from Hölderlin. Let us oppose spiritual communism to the vulgar political communism, and there he invokes the great Russian Orthodox spiritual tradition.

*On the way toward this detachment, Heidegger was guided
by other mystics, and by Eckhart in particular.*

A certain mysticism can even mix with anti-Christianism . . . I suspect that those who advocate anti-Christianism are those who refuse to go through to the end of the self-deconstruction that is Christianity at its heart, in other words, those who avoid to truly arrive at atheism. But even within atheism, the very need to refer finitude to the order of presence and even to the presence of a God, I don't agree that this is religion. I am not sure what this has to be called, in the end. It involves a presence to come, even if it arrives only by absenting itself, like in Heidegger's posthumous interview: "Only a God can save us"—or the absence of a God. But "salvation" is not the right category . . . It is a very complicated affair, at the heart of which we find finitude—Heidegger's fundamental contribution. I feel compelled to reread him, even though I am always troubled by *Ereignis*.

*What, in your opinion, is the future of Heidegger's thought in France? The
intellectual landscape today is quite fragmented. Are we moving toward a
marginalization of Heidegger, or even of the great German tradition?*

I am unable to make forecasts. I was recently astonished by a colleague's remark: "It is analytic philosophy which will now become prominent." It may be true on the institutional level, the juries of the exams, etc. But, as far as the *work* of thinking is concerned, how can one break with the German tradition? How many times have people said to me that I was a Heideggerian terrorist! The Nazi affair has obviously played a role, but even more there has been a lack of *work* on Heidegger. Yet, I don't want to be too optimistic, but I see signs of interest on the part of people from Eastern Europe, emerging from Communist domination, for example, or coming from Japan, from India, Latin America . . . and *even* from Germany!

*This development can certainly affect the nature of Heideggerian questions,
but perhaps most of all the style, the manner, of posing the questions?*

It is necessary to look beyond the French philosophical landscape. Whether in the United States, in Central Europe, in Italy, in Germany itself, people continue to work on Heidegger.

Is there a reshuffling of the cards?

Yes, for a more profound reason, which is tied to a surprising turn in philosophy, which leads to all kinds of developments. What prevails, in France, is another mode of the marginalization of Heidegger: the neo-Husserlian mode, which is quite strong. In France there are young philosophers, who are very gifted, who seem to mostly refer to Husserl, but who are manipulating motifs that are in fact Heideggerian *and* post-Heideggerian. Instead of going directly to Heidegger, they use tools that they borrowed from him, such as the motif of the event. The event is everywhere, but once again people are indefinitely analyzing Kant and Husserl . . . Of course I am very glad to see that Husserl-studies are concerned, for example, with passivity and the body. But after Husserl there is Heidegger. In this respect, I remain in sympathy with Granel, in particular with his introduction to the *Krisis*.

Is there some reticence on the part of the new generation to speak
about Heidegger directly? Is it opportunism, or is it prudence?

I don't know. I have been at the University of Strasbourg for thirty-two years, and Heidegger has become no more accepted than he was before. Occasionally, one may study one of his texts, no more than that. He has never been chosen as an author for the Agrégation examination program. Why is this the case? Is this because of Heidegger himself? The Nazi affair? A reaction to the Beaufret group? Against the "Derrida-effect?" But perhaps it is just and desirable that things don't get institutionalized.

Can Heidegger become an ordinary author like
any other? Why is it so hard for him?

That's a good question. I would lean in the direction of saying that the reason is extremely profound and that it has to do with what Heidegger tried to say concerning the step back from metaphysics, the *Schritt zurück*. I often like formulating this by referring to someone who is unexpected in this context: Bouveresse. In the introduction to one of his great books on Wittgenstein, he says something like: "Wittgenstein, Heidegger, and Freud together were the witnesses of what might well be called the *end of metaphysics*." I mention his comment in order to say that even someone like him can make this observation; and it is very appropriate to include Freud in this constellation. It is true: there was something that turned in between the two wars, something that took a long time to find again, on the political and social level, as a movement, a fault line; because the postwar years were dedicated to repairing, sealing off. It was then thought that they were returning to an older vein. It had not yet even become clear to what extent the 1920s–1930s had already touched the roots of what was considered as socialism and the problems tied to it. We have to return to the question of the end of philosophy and of the task of thinking: we might say that all is not lost!

It is very important to recognize that political action served as a screen: not always and not everywhere, but in a certain number of cases; in academia, it was surely a conscious and organized pretext; in other cases it was an unconscious pretext. Several years ago, in *Libération,* a journalist wrote that if you saw a Heideggerian on the sidewalk you had to cross to the other side! At about the same time, when the German translation of *The Inoperative Community* was published, there was a revolting article in the *Taz,* a leftist Berlin newspaper, titled: "*Nochmals der Führer.*" It began with "Nancy has a problem: he likes Heidegger." And it went on: "He is right in stating that there are many problems with social relations, but you know what he proposes as a solution: community, *Gemeinschaft,* so he is a Nazi!" Already in 1973–74, in Berlin, at the end of a talk with Lacoue-Labarthe, presenting *The Title of the Letter,* the first question was: "Do you know who you are talking about when you refer to Heidegger?" We were stunned, anguished. It was the time of the Baader-Meinhof gang. Things are very different today. But the result is still a gap in the education of the younger generation. I remember a graduate seminar where, about eight years ago, a student asked me what I meant by this "ontological difference." A student from the École Normale Supérieure told me that at the École people thought that there were two types of Heideggerians: the abominable fascists and the other ones, who in any case were not to be associated with.

It seems like people refuse to consider what is meant by "the end of philosophy" . . . In Germany, basically, the situation is not very different, with the reign of the Frankfurt school and of its more or less socio-psychological or "ethical" offshoots; but there are nonetheless informed and innovative young people.

I am not too pessimistic, because I have confidence in deep history and not in mundane and institutional episodes. There is an in-depth work that must rise to the surface again. But I share a different worry with you: a certain religiosity could attack philosophical questioning from a different angle. There is the Levinasian climate, which is always moralizing . . . Which leads to a question that today lacks an answer: how could Levinas have constantly and so thoroughly misunderstood the meaning of being for Heidegger?

It was a counterreaction: Levinas was almost too Heideggerian in the 1930s!

Yes, but the misunderstanding is still bizarre for someone who was so intelligent and whose thought is so widely admired.

Notes

Acknowledgments

1. *French Interpretations of Heidegger: An Exceptional Reception,* ed. David Pettigrew and François Raffoul (Albany: SUNY Press, 2008).

Translators' Introduction

1. Volume 1 of the French edition of Dominique Janicaud's *Heidegger en France* (Paris: Éditions Albin Michel, 2001), is 594 pages in length. Volume 2 of *Heidegger en France. Entretiens* (Paris: Éditions Albin Michel, 2001), is 291 pages in length, including eighteen interviews. Seven of these interviews are included in the English language edition. Hereafter the English translation is cited as *HF,* followed by the page number. Volume 2 is hereafter cited as *Heidegger en France,* vol. 2: *Entretiens.* For works cited that are not available in English, the translations are ours.

2. Ironically, in his interview with Janicaud (not included in this edition), Walter Biemel indicates that Heidegger did in fact "follow" Derrida's work, and, still according to Biemel, that he looked upon it favorably (*Heidegger en France,* vol. 2: *Entretiens,* 41).

3. Françoise Dastur, *Heidegger and the Question of Time,* trans. François Raffoul and David Pettigrew (Amherst, N.Y.: Humanity Books, 1998).

4. Jean Greisch, "The Poverty of the 'Last God,'" in *French Interpretations of Heidegger: An Exceptional Reception,* ed. David Pettigrew and François Raffoul (Albany: SUNY Press, 2008).

5. If as a whole Janicaud is particularly careful to be fair to the various protagonists, it does not prevent him, here or there, from manifesting some preferences or dislikes (for instance, he is often severe with Alphonse de Waelhens or Jean Wahl, while always complimentary to Eric Weil).

6. Dominique Janicaud, *The Shadow of That Thought: Heidegger and the Question of Politics,* trans. Michael Gendre (Evanston, Ill.: Northwestern University Press, 1996).

7. One cannot help but wonder what his reaction would have been to the recent appropriation of Heidegger's thought by the Islamic regime in Iran. One will read with interest Habermas's account of Heidegger's place in the debates within the different factions in power in Iran during the '90s. *Frankfurter Allgemeine,* June 19, 2002.

8. William J. Richardson, S.J., *Heidegger: Through Phenomenology to Thought* (New York: Fordham University Press, 2003).

9. The Thor seminars, as well as the 1973 Zähringen seminar, are now available in English as *Four Seminars,* trans. Andrew Mitchell and François Raffoul (Bloomington: Indiana University Press, 2004).

Introduction

1. See Tom Rockmore, *Heidegger and French Philosophy* (New York: Routledge, 1995), especially the introduction and chapter 1.

2. Karl Löwith, "The Political Implications of Heidegger's Existentialism," in *The Heidegger Controversy: A Critical Reader,* ed. Richard Wolin (Cambridge, Mass.: MIT Press, 1993), 168.

3. Incidentally, it was just this expression that a communist pamphleteer used after World War II as a sarcastic title to mock the French fascination with Heidegger and Jünger: see Henri Mougin, "Comme Dieu en France: Heidegger parmi nous," *Europe* (April 1946): 132–138.

4. *Frankfurter Allgemeine Zeitung,* May 19, 1999, 49: "Die Trivialisierung des Martin Heidegger. Schund, Sex und Sühne: Die neuen Abenteuer des deutschen Philosophen in Frankreich" (The trivialization of Martin Heidegger. Trash, sex, and atonement: the German philosopher's new adventures in France). I would like to thank Lucien Braun for informing me about this article.

5. This would be "a somewhat acclimated, assimilated and transformed Heidegger, who would have found in France an unknown dimension of his own thought," according to Jean Lacoste ("Heidegger et la France," *La Quinzaine littéraire* 764 [1999]: 21).

6. Theodor W. Adorno, *Jargon of Authenticity,* trans. Knut Tarnowski and Frederic Will (Evanston, Ill.: Northwestern University Press, 1973).

7. See, for example, Hans-Georg Gadamer, *Philosophical Apprenticeships* (Cambridge, Mass.: MIT Press, 1985), 142–143.

8. "Such a work would certainly be of some interest" (François Fédier, "Heidegger vu de France," in *Regarder voir* (Paris: Les Belles Lettres, 1995, 225). Evoking "the most passionate relation in the world," Alain Renault called for it to be studied in more pressing and resolute terms: "One day, someone will have to decide to write not only a history of the reception of Heidegger's thought in France, but also an account of the amazing process spanning three generations, in the course of which, in our country, in the field of philosophy and far beyond it, there has occurred a Heideggerianization of thinking that compares to nothing else in any other country" ("Sartre et Heidegger," in Jean Quillien, ed., *La Réception de la philosophie allemande en France aux XIXe et XXe siècles* [Lille: Presses Universitaires de Lille, 1994], 241. See also Alain Renault, "Heidegger en France. Une affaire de générations," in *Sartre, le dernier philosophe* [Paris: Grasset, 1993], chap. 1).

9. Rainer Maria Rilke, *Auguste Rodin,* trans. Daniel Slager (San Francisco: Archipelago Books, 2004), cited in Heidegger's *Hegel's Phenomenology of Spirit,* trans. Parvis Emad and Kenneth Maly (Bloomington: Indiana University Press, 1994), 147.

10. In an article he already titled "Heidegger en France," *Magazine littéraire,* 235 (1986): 34–38. He also noted the many varieties of this reception: see Jean-Michel Palmier, *Ernst Jünger: Rêveries sur un chasseur de cicindèles* (Paris: Hachette, 1995), 51: "The reception of Heidegger's work around 1966–1968 was as far removed from that which prevailed in 1945 as it is from the fad of which it is the object of today."

11. See Louis Pinto, *Les Neveux de Zarathoustra: La réception de Nietzsche en France* (Paris: Éditions du Seuil, 1995), and, especially Jacques Le Rider, *Nietzsche en France: De la fin du XIXe siècle au temps présent* (Paris: Presses Universitaires de France, 1999).

12. Thus, in a work by Alain De Benoist, *Vu de droite* (Paris: Copernic, 1978), the references to Heidegger are few in number and remain marginal: Nietzsche is cited far more often.

Yet, a Heideggerian inspiration can be detected in the more recent "conservative revolution" circles: see Jean-Pierre Blanchard, *Heidegger* (Puiseaux: Éditions Pardès, 2000).

13. In a meticulous and remarkable text, written in German (another paradox), Rémi Brague sketches a picture of Heidegger's influence in France, noting from the outset two distinctive features: first, Heidegger's declared interest in a dialogue with the French; and second, the fact that this dialogue continues to this day and makes Heidegger an author who is more studied and discussed in France than in Germany itself. See Brague, "Heideggers Einfluß auf das französische Geistesleben. Elemente eines Rückblicks auf die bisherige Rezeptionsgeschichte," *Theologie und Philosophie* 57 (1982): 21–42.

14. This can be seen in these excerpts from his posthumous interview in *Der Spiegel:* "I have in mind the special inner relationship of the German language with that of the Greeks and with their thought. The French continually confirm this for me nowadays. When they begin to think, they speak German, assuring that they could not get by with their own language." To the question: "Do you take this as the explanation for why you have had such a strong effect on the Romance countries, especially the French?" Heidegger responds by making the French in some way into the representatives of rationality: "Since they see that they can no longer get by in today's world with all their rationality, when it [680] comes down to understanding the world in the origin of its essence," in "*Der Spiegel* Interview with Martin Heidegger," in *The Heidegger Reader,* ed. Günter Figal, trans. Jerome Beich (Bloomington: Indiana University Press, 2009), 331. On page 69 of *Of Spirit: Heidegger and the Question,* trans. Geoffrey Bennington and Rachel Bowlby (Chicago: University of Chicago Press, 1989), Jacques Derrida addressed this passage as follows: "That the joint privilege of German and Greek is absolute here with regard to thought, to the question of Being, and thus to the spirit, is implied by Heidegger everywhere. But in the interview with *Der Spiegel,* he says it in a calmly arrogant way, perhaps somewhat naïvely, at once on his guard and defenseless, and, I would say, in 'our' language, *sans beaucoup d'esprit.*" François Vezin responded (without naming Derrida), "When Heidegger says 'the French,' it effectively means: the French friends with whom I was working the other day, chief among them being Jean Beaufret" (see *L'Enseignement par excellence: Hommage à François Vezin,* ed. Pascal David [Paris: L'Harmattan, 2000], 353).

15. His face lit up, apparently, when he crossed the border from Germany into France and darkened when he returned: according to Roger Munier's report (a broadcast by *France-Culture,* "Hommage à Heidegger," June 1976).

16. See François Fédier, *Soixante-deux photographies de Martin Heidegger* (Paris: Gallimard, 1999).

17. Already in 1857, Taine deplored the invasion of German metaphysics in the first decades of the nineteenth century in the following terms: "Soon it was a deluge. The horrible German nouns, the words as long as a fathom, drowned the elegant prose of d'Alembert and Voltaire, and it seemed that a migrant Berlin had fallen with all its weight upon Paris." *Les Philosophes français du XIXe siècle* (Paris: Pauvert, 1967), 158.

18. "Systematically mistaken," according to Tom Rockmore's own terms, in *Heidegger and French Philosophy* xi.

19. This is an expression from Jacques Derrida in our *Interviews,* see *HF,* 351.

20. See Hans Robert Jauss, *Toward an Aesthetic of Reception,* trans. Timothy Bahti (Minneapolis: University of Minnesota Press, 1982).

21. We needed a chronological endpoint for our project, and chose for this purpose the symbolic date of January 1, 2000.

1. First Crossings of the Rhine

1. Georges Gurvitch, *Les Tendances actuelles de la philosophie allemande* (Paris: Vrin, 1930).

2. Ibid., 8.

3. Ibid., 207.

4. Ibid., 209.

5. Ibid., 214.

6. Ibid.

7. Ibid., 215.

8. Ibid., 226–227.

9. Ibid., 211: "This philosophy, still in the process of unfolding, not yet completed, *Being and Time*."

10. Ibid., 210.

11. Ibid., 208.

12. Ibid., 210.

13. See Heidegger, *Sein und Zeit* (Tübingen: Niemeyer, 1927), 208; *Being and Time*, trans. Joan Stambaugh, rev. and foreword by Dennis J. Schmidt (Albany: State University of New York Press, 2010), 200. Hereafter cited as *SZ* and *BT*, followed by the respective page numbers.

14. Gurvitch, *Les Tendances actuelles de la philosophie allemande*, 227.

15. Ibid., 225; Heidegger, *SZ*, 229/*BT*, 219.

16. *SZ*, 229/*BT*, 220.

17. Gurvitch, *Les Tendances actuelles de la philosophie allemande*, 231. The "critical observations" are found from pages 228 through 234.

18. From which he was kind enough to send us some passages on the Davos meeting, more complete than those found in the published version (Maurice de Gandillac, *Le Siècle traversé* [Paris: Albin Michel, 1998], 133–134).

19. Cited in Maurice de Gandillac's manuscript (a passage abridged in *Le Siècle traversé*).

20. See Appendix, in *Kant and the Problem of Metaphysics*, trans. Richard Taft (Bloomington: Indiana University Press, 1993).

21. Jean Hering is the author of a book, *Phénoménologie et philosophie religieuse: Étude sur la théorie de la connaissance religieuse* (Paris: Alcan, 1926), which explored the possibility of a renewal of religious philosophy by means of the phenomenological method. His main sources of inspiration were Husserl and Scheler. There was at that point no mention of Heidegger.

22. See his recollections concerning the end of Husserl's teaching, "Séjour de jeunesse auprès de Husserl, 1928–1929," in *Positivité et transcendance* (Paris: Presses Universitaires de France, 2000), 3–7 (first published in *Le Nouveau Commerce* 75, [Fall/Winter 1989]).

23. Jean Hering had shown Levinas a book called *Sein und Zeit*. "But there is no Husserl in it," an astonished Levinas exclaimed. "This one goes farther than Husserl," the pastor replied. "Levinas was immediately won over and wasted no time in sharing his enthusiasm with his fellow students, including his friend Blanchot." Anne-Marie Lescourret, *Emmanuel Lévinas* (Paris: Flammarion, 1994), 74.

24. See François Poirié, *Emmanuel Lévinas* (Lyon: La Manufacture, 1987), 74. Levinas himself spoke of this youthful enthusiasm in "Fribourg, Husserl, et la phénoménologie," *Revue d'Allemagne* 43 (May 1931): 403–414, cited by Miguel Abensour, "Rencontre, silence," in *Heidegger: Questions ouvertes* (Paris: Osiris, 1988), 248–249.

25. Emmanuel Lévinas, "Fribourg, Husserl, et la phénoménologie," *Revue d'Allemagne* 43 (May 1931): 403–414.

26. Ibid., 414.

27. With respect to these details, see Jean Greisch, "Heidegger et Lévinas interprètes de la facticité," in *Emmanuel Lévinas: Positivité et transcendance,* ed. Jean-Luc Marion (Paris: Presses Universitaires de France, 2000), 184–187. Greisch consulted the archives at the University of Freiburg, which allowed him to confirm that Levinas had also attended the seminar for advanced students on "Ontological Principles and the Problem of the Categories." The course *Einleitung in die Philosophie* was published in 1996 as volume 27 of the *Gesamtausgabe.* Three decades earlier, Jean Wahl had offered an inventive commentary on it in a course at the Sorbonne: see our analyses in chapter 3, "Parisian Minds."

28. Maurice Blanchot, letter to Catherine David, "Penser l'apocalypse," November 10, 1987, published in *Le Nouvel Observateur,* January 22, 1988, 79.

29. Emmanuel Levinas, *The Theory of Intuition in Husserl's Phenomenology,* trans. Andre Orianne (Evanston, Ill.: Northwestern University Press, 1995).

30. Ibid., 154.

31. Ibid.

32. Emmanuel Levinas, "Martin Heidegger and Ontology," *Diacritics* 26, no. 1 (April 1996): 11–32. Originally published as "Martin Heidegger et l'ontologie," *Revue Philosophique* (May–June 1932): 395–432. It was partially reprinted in *En découvrant l'existence avec Husserl et Heidegger* (Paris: Vrin, 1949), 53–107. In subsequent editions, Levinas removed the first lines of the 1932 article, which are worth citing (see 395): "The prestige of Martin Heidegger and the influence of his thought on German philosophy marks both a new phase and one of the high points of the phenomenological movement. Caught unawares, the traditional establishment is obliged to clarify its position on this new teaching which casts a spell over youth and which, overstepping the bounds of permissibility, is already in vogue. For once, Fame has picked one who deserves it and, for that matter, one who is still living. Anyone who has studied philosophy cannot, when confronted by Heidegger's work, fail to recognize how the originality and force of his achievements, stemming from genius, are combined with an attentive, painstaking, and close working-out of the argument—with that craftsmanship of the patient artisan in which phenomenologists take such pride."

33. *Diacritics,* 14.

34. "De la nature de la cause" [Of the nature of cause], trans. A. Bessey, *Recherches philosophiques* (published by A. Koyré, H.-C. Puech, A. Spaier, Paris, Boivin) 1 (1931–32): 83–124. This is a translation of the short work *Vom Wesen des Grundes,* and Bessey acknowledged its clumsiness: "This translation is very imperfect. Many words and verbal relations, which are for Heidegger poetry (in the most exact sense of the term), or even revelation, could not be rendered" (83). In fact, the translations of *Grund* as "cause" and of *Satz vom Grund* as "*principe de causalité*" [principle of causality] are complete misunderstandings.

35. Ibid., 31.

36. *Conférence,* no. 6 (Spring 1998): 452–479.

37. "Lettre sur Heidegger à M. Daniel Halévy," *Revue philosophique* (November–December 1933): 321.

38. *Conférence,* no. 6 (Spring 1998): 455.

39. Ibid., 468.

40. Ibid., 472.

41. Ibid.

42. Ibid., 474.

43. Ibid., 478.

44. Benjamin Fondane, *La conscience malheureuse* (Paris: Denoël et Steele, 1936), 170.

45. Ibid.

46. Ibid., 197.

47. Jean Wahl, *Vers le concret: Études d'histoire de la philosophie contemporaine* (Paris: Vrin, 1932).

48. See Jean-Paul Sartre, *War Diaries: Notebooks from a Phoney War, 1939–1940,* trans. Quintin Hoare (London: Verso, 2011), 186: "That surge of interest for which I had my share of responsibility, and which first produced books like Jean Wahl's *Vers le concret,* had its origin in an obsolescence of French philosophy and a need we all felt to rejuvenate it."

49. Wahl, *Vers le concret,* 4.

50. Ibid., 20.

51. Ibid., 3n1.

52. Jean Wahl (ibid., 3, 5, 9, 18) refers to pages 229, 34, 56, 104, 137, 61, etc. of *Sein und Zeit.* Not all these references hit their mark: for example, the reference to a few lines on page 104 concerning the spatiality of being-in-the-world is illogical: it should have been to the whole of section 23.

53. Jean Wahl, "Heidegger et Kierkegaard: Recherche des éléments originaux de la philosophie de Heidegger," *Recherches philosophiques* (published by A. Koyré, H.-C. Puech, A. Spaier, Paris, Boivin) (1932–33): 349–370.

54. See Sartre, *War Diaries,* 186.

55. Wahl, "Heidegger et Kierkegaard,"

56. Ibid., 368. Wahl summarizes them himself. The main questions bear on the need for a more thorough analysis of freedom, on the theological background, on the perhaps excessive role of death, on the connection (still to be made explicit) between the idea of being and the revelation of the world (here, we are using Wahl's terms).

57. Ibid., 370.

58. In the letter to Jean Beaufret of November 23, 1945: "das *Missverständnis par excellence*" with respect the Jaspers-Heidegger connection (*Lettre sur l'humanisme,* trans. Munier [Paris: Aubier, 1957], 178).

59. Martin Heidegger, "Qu'est-ce que la métaphysique": translated from the German, followed by excerpts on *Sein und Zeit* and by a lecture on Hölderlin, with a foreword and notes by Henry Corbin, in *Les Essais VII* (Paris: Gallimard, 1938). "What Is Metaphysics?," in *Pathmarks,* ed. William McNeill (New York: Cambridge University Press, 1998), 82–96. Hereafter cited as *PA.*

60. Corbin himself made this clear on page 16 of the *Cahier de l'Herne: Henry Corbin* (Paris: Éditions de l'Herne, 1981).

61. Ibid., 17.

62. See Corbin's interview with Philippe Nemo, "De Heidegger à Sohravardî," in ibid., 23–37 (in particular, 29).

63. Martin Heidegger, "Qu'est-ce que la métaphysique?" translated from the German by M. Corbin-Petithenry, with an introduction by A. Koyré, in *Bifur,* no. 8 (June 1931): 1–27. This can be found at the end of the second volume of the reissue of the journal *Bifur* (Paris: Jean-Michel Place, 1976).

64. It seems that Julien Benda was behind this rejection. See Robert Sasso (*Georges Bataille: le système du non-savoir* [Paris: Éditions de Minuit, 1973], 17n12), who also reports that Corbin had Bataille read this translation before 1930. As if to make up for the *Nouvelle Revue Française*'s rejection of Corbin's translation, Koyré published in this journal a very complimentary review of the original text of *Was ist Metaphysik?:* "Heidegger's admirable work will assume a place of honor among the philosophical output of the past few years. A profound, decent, and honest thought is expressed there in a language whose density and strength are admirable" (*La Nouvelle Revue Française* [1931]: 750).

65. According to W. D. Redfern, on page 32 of *Paul Nizan* (Princeton, N.J.: Princeton University Press, 1972). The author also indicates on the same page that Nizan wrote an article for

the journal *Commune* in November 1933 (310–315) in which he attacked both young writers on the right and "Heidegger's backward-looking of an artisan society."

66. Editors' note on page 345 of *Cahier de l'Herne: Henry Corbin*.

67. *Bifur*, no. 8 (June 1931): 5.

68. Georges Gurvitch as *Les Tendances actuelles de la philosophie allemande*, Ibid., 228.

69. *Bifur*, no. 8 (June 1931): 8.

70. Ibid., 20.

71. We have seen that this text was previously translated by A. Bessey with the title "De la nature de la cause," in *Recherches philosophiques*, 83–124.

72. Translator's foreword, "Qu'est-ce que la métaphysique?," 12.

73. Martin Heidegger, *Kant and the Problem of Metaphysics*, trans. Richard Taft (Bloomington: Indiana University Press, 1990), 162.

74. Now published in volume 39 of Martin Heidegger's *Gesamtausgabe*, *Hölderlin's Hymnen "Germanien" und "Der Rhein,"* ed. Susanne Ziegler (Frankfurt am Main: Vittorio Klostermann, 1980). Martin Heidegger, *Hölderlin's Hymns "Germania" and "The Rhine,"* trans. William McNeill and Julia Ireland (Bloomington: Indiana University Press, 2014).

75. All things being equal, it was in the same context, this time in occupied Paris, that Corbin's translation of Heidegger's lecture on "Hölderlin und das Wesen der Dichtung" ("Hölderlin et l'essence de la poésie") was reprinted, in pages 131–154 of a collection published by Sorlot in 1943: *Friedrich Hölderlin: En commémoration du centenaire de sa mort le 7 juin 1843*, ed. Johannes Hoffmeister and Hans Fegers (Paris: Sorlot, 1943).

76. Translator's foreword, "Qu'est-ce que la métaphysique?," 12.

77. Ibid., 13.

78. Referring to *Miroir historial du monde*, a French translation (published in Paris in 1495) of Vincent de Beauvais's *Speculum historiale* (see translator's foreword, "Qu'est-ce que la métaphysique?," 16).

79. This book went through many editions, though it is now out of print. In all, 12,980 copies were printed, according to the report that Gallimard publishing house was kind enough to share with us. More important than any number, there are many testimonials to its influence. For example, let us cite Thierry Maulnier's *Introduction à la poésie française* (Paris: Gallimard, 1939), where one can read on page 10: "Heidegger says that one is led away from the nature and substance of poetry the more one seeks to define it as a reality common to different poets, for in this way one condemns oneself to finding only what is *indifferent* in poetry." This is an allusion to the beginning of "Hölderlin et l'essence de la poésie" (Corbin's translation, 234).

80. He explained it humorously in "*Retrouvailles*," a text published by Frédéric de Towarnicki (*À la rencontre de Heidegger: Souvenirs d'un messager de la Forêt-Noire* [Paris: Gallimard, 1993], 260–262). He relates having gently reproached Corbin for his translation of *Dasein* as *réalité-humaine*: "It was as if instead of saying 'cat,' one said 'feline reality'" (261).

81. See Joseph Rovan, *Mémoires d'un Français qui se souvient d'avoir été Allemand* (Paris: Éditions du Seuil, 1999), 148, 152, 159, 166. In Lyon, Rovan published a translation of excerpts from *Sein und Zeit* called "Fragments sur le temps" in the journal *L'Arbalète* 3/4 (1941): 34–48. An introductory note presents this attempt at translation and "adaptation" in the following terms: "We propose to contribute to the literary understanding of the present fragments rather than the systematic interpretation of Heidegger's philosophy, which would not be possible without Henry Corbin's substantial and faithful translations." The passages retained under the titles "Le temps public" (Public time) and "La finité du temps" (The finiteness of time) are respectively section 80 (excluding the first sentence) and section 65 (328–331) of *Sein und Zeit*. Without attempting to be literal (for instance, *Dasein* is rendered as "existence"),

these few pages do not lack elegance and provide a degree of readability that would be sorely lacking in later translations.

82. Sartre, *War Diaries,* 182. Sartre even calls the publication of "What Is Metaphysics?" a "*historical* event" (185).

83. Alphonse de Waelhens, *La philosophie de Martin Heidegger* (Louvain: Institut supérieur de philosophie, 1942).

84. In Jean-Paul Sartre, *Being and Nothingness: A Phenomenology Essay on Ontology,* trans. Hazel Barnes (New York: Washington Square Press, 1984), 486.

85. De Waelhens, *La philosophie de Martin Heidegger,* viii–ix.

86. *Jahrbuch der Stadt Freiburg im Breisgau,* 1937, 1:135–139 (republished in *Denkerfahrungen* [Frankfurt am Main: Klostermann, 1983], 15–22); trans. J.-M. Vaysse and L. Wagner in *Martin Heidegger: Cahier de l'Herne,* 59–62. Heidegger gave Towarnicki a typed copy during the latter's visit to Freiburg in the Fall of 1945; see de Towarnicki, *À la rencontre de Heidegger,* 31.

87. "*Der Spiegel* Interview with Martin Heidegger," in *The Heidegger Reader,* 322.

88. Victor Farias, *Heidegger and Nazism,* ed. Joseph Margolis and Tom Rockmore (Philadelphia: Temple University Press, 1989), 246, 245–250.

89. "Victor Farias, however, discovered papers in the Berlin Document Center and in the Potsdam Archives from which it emerges that Heidegger was in Paris as early as the summer of 1935 to prepare for the German participation in the congress." Rüdiger Safranski, *Martin Heidegger: Between Good and Evil,* trans. Ewald Osers (Cambridge, Mass.: Harvard University Press, 1998), 323.

90. When asked personally by Tom Rockmore, Victor Farias could not provide this evidence.

91. As noted by Safranski, *Martin Heidegger: Between Good and Evil,* 324.

92. Pascal David helpfully emphasizes this first sense of "pronunciation" ("*pronuntiatio* is given as an equivalent by the Grimm brothers") and shows that Heidegger's text retains an undeniably spiritual dimension, beyond the circumstances of 1937. See his study, "Sur les *Wege zur Ausprache* de Heidegger," *Heidegger Studies* 5 (1989): 173–179.

93. Martin Heidegger, *Denkerfahrungen* (Frankfurt am Main: Klostermann, 1983), 20–21; Michel Haar, ed., *Martin Heidegger: Cahier de l'Herne* (Paris: Éditions de l'Herne, 1983), 62. Translation modified.

94. Jean Pénard, *Rencontres avec René Char* (Paris: José Corti, 1991), 125.

95. "He revealed to us the name of this German philosopher, nearly unknown in France in 1936" (René Pomeau, *Mémoires d'un siècle entre XIXe et XXe* [Paris: Fayard, 1999], 177).

96. The allusions to Heidegger in an article on "La philosophie et les mythes," in *La Pensée,* no. 1 (April–June 1939), reprinted in Politzer, *Écrits* (Paris: Éditions sociales, 1969), 1:128–179, are very negative: "This phenomenology, which originated with Husserl, and which despite its claims to the contrary is nothing but a variety of idealism, has developed a veritable scholasticism. It is always on the lookout for neologisms, linguistic and typographical fancies: symptoms characteristic of a thought that has no content of its own and that can only resurrect old materials, fleeing the light of rational thought" (140).

97. See Henri Lefebvre, "Karl Marx et Heidegger," a discussion published in *Le Nouvel Observateur,* May 28, 1959; reprinted in Kostas Axelos, *Arguments d'une recherche* (Paris: Éditions de Minuit, 1969), 96: "My first encounter with Heidegger's thought dates back to 1930. . . . It was Paul Nizan who first spoke to me about Heidegger. Shortly thereafter, Jean Wahl loaned me *Sein und Zeit* (which I gave back to him, incidentally). . . . In Heidegger's thought, we saw a catharsis of nothingness, a sort of absolute purification through a pure and disinter-

ested contemplation. This catharsis seemed to us incompatible with our taste for action. . . . This rejection of Heidegger predated Heidegger's real or alleged involvement with Nazism."

98. Regarding the complexity of this evolution, see Robert Sasso, *Georges Bataille: Le Système du non-Savoir* (Paris: Éditions de Minuit, 1978), 19–20. Although Bataille admitted his debt to Heidegger "on a few points," did he not in the end feel a kind of "annoyed attraction" toward him? While mentioning these reservations (and even citing this sharp criticism: Heidegger's work is more of "an industrial production than a glass of sherry"), François Warin (*Nietzsche et Bataille* [Paris: Presses Universitaires de France, 1994], 329) highlights the possible rapprochements between Bataille and Heidegger: the determination of thought as "experience," the critique of logic, the return to finitude, the rejection of humanism. Bataille himself characterized his own problematic in relation to Heidegger's as follows: "This question [of the extreme rupture] is distinct from that of Heidegger (why is there being and not nothingness) in that it is only asked after all conceivable answers, aberrant or not, have been made to the successive questions formulated by understanding: thus it strikes at the heart of knowledge" (George Bataille, *Inner Experience*, trans. Leslie Anne Boldt [Albany: State University of New York Press, 1988]). In this light, we have more distance on the situation than Sartre (*Situations I* [Paris: Gallimard, 1947], 15), who accused Bataille of not having understood Heidegger, even as he wished to make use of him (especially with respect to the notion of ipseity—*Selbstheit*—that he makes the mistake of naturalizing).

99. We find evidence of it in an article by H. Thielemans ("Existence tragique. La métaphysique du nazisme," *Nouvelle Revue théologique*, no. 6 [1936]: 561–579). He himself refers to Alfred Delp, *Tragische Existenz: Zur Philosophie Martin Heidegger* (Freiburg: Herder, 1935), and notes the great effect Heidegger's teaching was having among German youth. This teaching is a metaphysics of earthly being, definitively finite, a "titanic finitism" (in Guardini's terms). Contrary to what one might expect, the author of the article did not become indignant; rather, he conceded that Heidegger "has done us a great service" by shaking up "the Bourgeois libertines trapped in the nothingness of their being" (576–577). He warns his readers, however, against choosing irrationality and breaking their bond with God.

100. Raymond Aron's influence was substantial: as early as his time at the Institut Français in Berlin in 1933 (where he was preceded by Beaufret), he read Husserl and Heidegger. He spoke to Sartre about phenomenology [see Raymond Aron, *Mémoires* (Paris: Julliard, 1983, 91)]. Some references in Sartre's *War Diaries* (185) also reveal that Sartre's reading of *L'Introduction à la philosophie de l'histoire* coincided and converged with his reading of Heidegger and, in particular, of the Corbin translation (the publication of which Aron apparently facilitated). By contrast, the case of Alexandre Kojève is altogether different: a very early reader of Heidegger, he adopted a Hegelian perspective on him: "It is only by confronting it with the work of Hegel that one can understand and appreciate the *philosophical* importance of Heidegger's work, and discover that it contains something truly new. In fact, part I of *Sein und Zeit* is only an attempt to reproduce—while correcting it—the phenomenological ("existential") anthropology of the *Phänomenologie des Geistes*, through an ontology . . . that is supposed to replace the misguided ontology of Hegel's *Logik*" (reported by Alfred Delp, *Tragische Existenz: Zur Philosophie Martin Heidegger*, Recherches philosophiques 5 [1936], 496, cited following Dominique Auffret, *Alexandre Kojève* [Paris: Grasset, 1990], 381–382).

101. In September 1933, Sartre received a scholarship from the Institut Français in Berlin, "where he followed in the footsteps of Raymond Aron and discovered phenomenology," according to Michel Contat and Michel Rybalka, *Les Écrits de Sartre* (Paris: Gallimard, 1970), 25.

2. The Sartre Bomb

1. Sartre, *War Diaries,* Ibid., 182–187.

2. Sartre, *Being and Nothingness.*

3. The *War Diaries* include a fairly large number of cursory, and often critical, allusions to Heidegger: they correspond to several passages in *Being and Nothingness.* In particular, we note Sartre's reservations about the notion of being-toward-death: "I have always had the impression that one dies out of negligence, distraction or senility, that one is free against death (and not, as Heidegger says, free for dying)." [TN: This diary entry from September 26, 1939, is in the most recent French edition and does not appear in the English translation: Jean-Paul Sartre, *Carnets de la drôle de guerre Septembre 1939–Mars 1940* (Paris: Gallimard, 1995), 56.] Also see *War Diaries,* 109–110. Let us note also a connection with Saint-Exupéry: "*Terre des hommes* has a very Heideggerian ring to it," *War Diaries,* 54.

4. Sartre, *War Diaries,* 182.

5. Ibid.

6. Ibid.

7. Ibid., 186.

8. Ibid., 182.

9. This is how Sartre's formulation in a 1939 letter to Paulhan is to be interpreted; he plans to "make a novel of Heidegger's time" (cited by Annie Cohen-Solal, *Sartre: A Life,* trans. Anna Cancogni [New York: Pantheon Books, 1987], 93; she also reports that Sartre "larded all his courses" with Heidegger, 119).

10. *War Diaries,* 183.

11. Ibid., 186.

12. At the end of that same year, Sartre taught a course on Heidegger to a group of imprisoned priests, according to Michel Contat and Michel Rybalka, *Les Écrits de Sartre* (Paris: Gallimard, 1970), 28 and 86. See also page 153 of Annie Cohen-Solal, *Sartre: A Life:* "For his part, he offers to introduce Perrin to Heidegger: a copy of *Being and Time* is sneaked into the camp by Father Etchegoyen, who works outside, in a monastery where he has struck up a friendship with an anti-Nazi German priest."

13. Sartre, *War Diaries,* 185.

14. "I read a few isolated French works dealing with the question" (ibid).

15. Even if he "had paid very little attention to Heidegger then," according to Annie Cohen-Solal, *Sartre: A Life,* 91.

16. *BN,* 41.

17. The "Otto list" excluded foreign authors, Jews in particular. See Pierre Assouline, *Un demi-siècle d'édition française* (Paris: Balland, 1984): "From September (1940) on, publishers capitulated to German demands when they did not anticipate them" (275). Further, "Gallimard surrendered to the *Propaganda Staffel* (in November 1940) . . . and the agreement was reached: Gallimard and Dr. Rahn agreed that the journal (the *Nouvelle Revue Française*) would be run for five years by Drieu La Rochelle" (280). Gaston Gallimard wrote that "Gallimard Press . . . is an Aryan publishing house with Aryan funds" (340). And: "Jean-Paul Sartre published his books and articles without suffering any censorship" (352).

18. Freud's name is glossed over on page 91 of *Being and Nothingness* and then again on page 729, in the middle of the chapter on existential psychoanalysis. When one considers the Nazis' revulsion to Freud and psychoanalysis, this is already quite a bit. It seems that it was only in Paris that German censors would look the other way from time to time.

19. In this vein, see Gilbert Joseph, *Une si douce occupation . . . (Simone de Beauvoir et Jean-Paul Sartre 1940–1944)* (Paris: Albin Michel, 1991): "Sartre participated in certain

meetings of the C.N.E. [TN: Comité national des écrivains] as early as January 1943, after having been the target of the communists who accused him in tracts of being beholden to the Germans for his repatriation from the stalag and of being a disciple of the Nazi philosopher Martin Heidegger. The communist Billoux appears to have been the one who recommended that he join the C.N.E. to put an end to this campaign" (287).

20. See Assouline, *Un demi-siècle d'édition française*: "Julien Gracq writes that 'during these years . . . publishing in France had become a propaganda tool'" (288); "Georges Politzer writes in 1941: Today in France, legal literature means 'treasonous literature'" (307).

21. See Jean Gabriel Adloff, *Sartre: Index du corpus philosophique*, vol. 1: *L'être et le néant. Critique de la raison dialectique* (Paris: Klincksieck, 1981). By this measure, there are seventy-four occurrences of Heidegger's name, or specifically Heideggerian notions. No contemporary philosopher is cited more often than he. By way of comparison, Husserl is cited forty-seven times, Bergson seventeen times, and Jaspers just once.

22. *BN*, 49–56.

23. Ibid., 50.

24. Ibid., 8–9.

25. An expression Sartre cites on ibid., 51.

26. Ibid., 133.

27. See ibid., 132.

28. Ibid., 120.

29. Ibid.

30. This is a point emphasized by Alain Renaut in his very clear analysis of the relation between Sartre and Heidegger (in *La réception de la philosophie allemande . . .*, ed. Jean Quillien, 241–252). See also Alain Renaut, *Sartre, le dernier philosophe* (Paris: Grasset, 1993), especially chapters 2 and 3. Without ignoring Sartre's mistakes or even the "misunderstandings" in his reading of *Sein und Zeit*, Renaut claims that Heidegger, for his part, unfairly reduces Sartre's humanism to a traditional metaphysics and fails to acknowledge the innovative elements of Sartre's conception of subjectivity. Conversely, for a Heideggerian reading of this debate, see Jean Launay, "Sartre lecteur de Heidegger, ou l'Être et le Non," *Les Temps modernes* 1 (Oct.–Dec. 1990): 412–435.

31. See "La liberté cartésienne," in *Situations I* (Paris: Gallimard, 1947), 314–335. In this text, Sartre acknowledges the ambiguities of Descartes's conception of freedom, but he schematizes its tensions by articulating them in overly humanistic terms.

32. "La liberté cartésienne," 334–335: "But we shall not reproach Descartes for having given to God what belongs properly to us; we shall rather praise him for having laid the foundations for democracy in an authoritarian age, for having followed to their conclusions the demands of the idea of *autonomy*, and for having understood, long before the Heidegger of *Vom Wesen des Grundes*, that the sole foundation of being was freedom."

33. *BN*, 329.

34. *SZ*, 181/*BT*, 175. "*Das Dasein existiert faktisch.*" See *SZ*, 56/*BT*, 56.

35. *BN*, 131.

36. See *SZ*/*BT* §37: "*Die Zweideutigkeit.*"

37. *BN*, 96.

38. Ibid., 101.

39. Ibid., 107.

40. Ibid., 87.

41. Ibid., 89.

42. Ibid., 98.

43. Ibid. [TN: Translation modified.]

44. See Heidegger, *Sein und Zeit,* §35, "*Das Gerede*"; §36, "*Die Neugier*"; §37, "*Die Zweideutigkeit.*"

45. *SZ,* 173/*BT,* 167.

46. *BN,* 315.

47. Ibid., 330.

48. Ibid., 333.

49. Ibid., 332–333.

50. Ibid., 336.

51. Ibid.

52. Ibid., 336.

53. Ibid., 536.

54. Ibid., 395.

55. Ibid., 795.

56. Ibid., 798.

57. Ibid., 710.

58. See ibid., 796.

59. Heidegger, *Sein und Zeit,* §56: "Der Ruf Charakter des Gewissens" [The character of conscience as a call], *SZ,* 272/*BT,* 262.

60. *BN,* 128.

61. Jean-Paul Sartre, *Notebooks for an Ethics,* trans. David Pellauer (Chicago: University of Chicago Press, 1992).

62. There are only eight occurrences according to the index included at the end of the work. Even if this index is not exhaustive and even accounting for indirect allusions, that is next to nothing for a book that is over 600 pages long.

63. Sartre, *Notebooks for an Ethics,* xxiii.

64. Ibid., 13.

65. Sartre, *Notebooks for an Ethics,* 383. Already in *Being and Nothingness* (*BN,* 498), Sartre remarked that Heidegger's *Dasein* "appears to us as asexual."

66. Sartre, *Notebooks for an Ethics,* 8.

67. See ibid., 562.

68. He accused Heidegger of wanting to "reconcile his humanism with the religious sense of the transcendent" (see *BN,* 128). This was to impute to Heidegger an imaginary humanism; nonetheless, Sartre did foresee in Heidegger a sense of the sacred that prevented him from declaring himself to be an atheist.

69. Sartre, *Notebooks for an Ethics,* 4.

70. "The book went unnoticed" (Joseph, *Une si douce occupation,* 299); "Several weeks after *The Flies,* a big book of philosophy appeared, *Being and Nothingness,* which went practically unnoticed" (Assouline, *Un demi-siècle,* 352).

3. Postwar Fascinations

1. Jean-Paul Sartre, "The Humanism of Existentialism," in *Essays in Existentialism,* ed. Wade Baskin (New York: Citadel Press, 1997), 33. [*L'Existentialisme est un humanisme* (Paris: Nagel, 1946), 16.]

2. De Towarnicki, *À la rencontre de Heidegger,* 15.

3. He claims to have been the first but gives no further chronological indications other than "Fall of 1945" (*À la rencontre de Heidegger,* 27). Maurice de Gandillac is more specific.

He left Paris on September 19th and arrived in Germany on the 21st. His visit in Freiburg probably happened on the 22nd. As for Edgar Morin, he dated his arrival in the summer of 1945. The chronological precedence is therefore in doubt.

4. See de Towarnicki, *À la rencontre de Heidegger*, 27–35.

5. Questioned by Dominique Desanti on French existentialism, Heidegger allegedly exclaimed, "holding his head in his hands": "My God, I did not want this" (*Action*, January 18, 1946). Dominique Desanti (*Les Staliniens: Une expérience politique, 1946/1956* [Paris: Fayard, 1975]) reports in the following terms her visit to Heidegger: "He received us in his unheated house in Freiburg im Breisgau, knees wrapped in a blanket, sipping a bowl of *café au lait*, without offering us any. The polite thing to do back then would have been to bring him some coffee and some powdered milk, but I was opposed to it: had he not been a Nazi? He, a genius, who was perhaps the most important innovator of his times? Had he not therefore betrayed his role as a philosopher? He denied having been a Nazi. All professors had to pledge allegiance to the regime, so to speak, by subscribing to the party. He took pleasure in setting the main representatives of French existentialism against each other, declaring Merleau-Ponty to be closer to his thought than Sartre was. What I wrote provoked the hostility of both Sartre and Merleau-Ponty who saw in it a 'communist scheme' to divide them" (22). This psychological game cannot be understood if not placed in the political context of the time: it is only under extreme circumstances that East and West allied, so as to ensure victory over Nazism. The communist side intended to immediately exploit it, and the Cold War rapidly followed the euphoria of the victory of 1945. For the communists, the "Heidegger case" offered an occasion among others to denounce the ambiguities of bourgeois thought.

6. According to him, there were several meetings, including a visit with Alexandre Astruc to the Todtnauberg hut.

7. Maurice de Gandillac, "Entretien avec M. Heidegger," *Les Temps modernes*, no. 4 (January 1946): 714–716. Within the pages of his memoirs that he was kind enough to share with me, Maurice de Gandillac condemned in retrospect his "rather inane joke" about the Master's moustache. I will return to the political dimension of this encounter.

8. Testimony of a neighbor of Heidegger, according to de Towarnicki, *À la rencontre de Heidegger*, 27.

9. They continued to take place in the following years. This is how, in August 1949, Roger Munier found himself knocking on the door of the hut in Todtnauberg, unannounced, but being very well received. The conversation was focused on being (as a dimension of transcendence rather than the transcendent) and on the approach (by way of a simple language) of its proximity. See "Visite à Heidegger," *Cahiers du Sud* 35, no. 312 (1952) (also found in Roger Munier, *Stèle pour Heidegger* [Paris: Arfuyen, 1992], 7–23).

10. "Ich spüre, soweit ich das seit einigen Wochen erst kennen gelernt habe, im Denken der jüngeren Philosophen Frankreichs einen ungeheuren élan, der darauf deutet, dass sich da eine Revolution vorbereitet." *Lettre sur l'humanisme*, trans. Roger Munier (Paris: Aubier, 1957), 178.

11. "Paul Éluard sent him dedicated poems and Towarnicki attempted to arrange a meeting with Sartre. The time of *Heidegger in France* has finally arrived, but it was not to Sartre that the 'Letter on Humanism' was *destined* but to Jean Beaufret." François Fédier, *Anatomie d'un scandale* (Paris: Laffont, 1988), 23.

12. De Waelhens, *La Philosophie de Martin Heidegger*, viii.

13. Jean Beaufret, "À propos de l'existentialisme," *Confluences*, nos. 2–6 (1945). Reproduced in Jean Beaufret, *De l'existentialisme à Heidegger* (Paris: Vrin, 1986), 11–54.

14. Dating from November 23, 1945, it is itself an answer to a previous friendly note from Jean Beaufret, passed down by a certain M. Palmer. The content of it is quoted at the end

of the Munier translation of *Lettre sur l'humanisme*, 175–181. On page 177 Heidegger wrote, "Right from the first article, in issue no. 2, I noted in what high esteem you held philosophy's essence."

15. Beaufret, *De l'existentialisme à Heidegger*, 16. Heidegger expressed satisfaction on two other points: the critique of the connection with Jaspers and the effort to understand the singularity of the key word, *Da-sein*.

16. Ibid., 11.

17. Ibid., 17.

18. Ibid., 14.

19. Ibid., 18.

20. Ibid., 29.

21. He himself reported that this reading started in Grenoble on a copy borrowed from the university's library, and was continued in Lyon thanks to his friend Joseph Rovan: see Jean Beaufret, *Entretiens avec Frédéric de Towarnicki* (Paris: PUF, 1984), 4. See Jean-Paul Aron, *Les Modernes* (Paris: Gallimard, 1984), 103–104: "During the war in Lyon, Beaufret received his copy of *Sein und Zeit* from Joseph Rovan, who was Jewish and a member of the resistance, and soon to be deported."

22. "In Lyon, I used to go to Beaufret's house in the evening to translate a few pages of *Sein und Zeit*, Heidegger's great work, and to discuss its meaning with him" (Rovan, *Mémoires d'un Français*, 183; see also 148, 166, 240). Under the name Joseph Rosenthal, Rovan published fragments of a rather loose translation of *Sein und Zeit* (that he himself presented as an adaptation). It appeared in a Lyon-based periodical, *L'Arbalète* (Summer–Autumn 1941): 33–48: the first abstract treats of "public time," and the second of "the finite nature of time."

23. Beaufret, *De l'existentialisme à Heidegger*, 14.

24. Ibid., 15.

25. Ibid., 16.

26. Ibid., 26. He adds: "where-one-has-been-overtaken-by-matters-one-encounters."

27. Ibid., 17.

28. *Action*, 27th of December 1944.

29. Beaufret, *De l'existentialisme à Heidegger*, 25. In this last paragraph, as well as in the passage before it, we are using a passage from my article "La réception de Heidegger: Jean Beaufret entre Sartre et Merleau-Ponty," in *La Réception de la philosophie allemande en France aux XIXe et XXe siècles*, ed. Jean Quillien (Lille: Presses Universitaire de Lille, 1994), 270–271.

30. To which we will return in the next chapter, under the heading "Jean Beaufret Comes to the Fore."

31. Presumably around September 10th according to Jean Beaufret, quoted by de Towarnicki, *À la rencontre de Heidegger*, 262.

32. See the account by Jean Beaufret, "Todtnauberg 1946 et la dictée de Heidegger," in de Towarnicki, *À la rencontre de Heidegger*, 253–258.

33. Translated by Jean Beaufret and reproduced in de Towarnicki, *À la rencontre de Heidegger*, 255–258.

34. "Sofort habe ich gemerkt, was da los war" (literally: "I immediately noticed what was happening." See François Fédier, "Heidegger vu de France," in *Regarder voir*, 229, who over-translated it as: "I immediately foresaw what was extraordinary in the situation").

35. On this particular point, I agree with Dominique Auffret, *Alexandre Kojève* (Paris: Grasset, 1990), 382.

36. Alexandre Kojève, *Introduction to the Reading of Hegel: Lectures on the Phenomenology of Spirit*, ed. Allan Bloom, trans. James H. Nichols Jr., assembled by Raymond Queneau (New York: Basic Books, 1969), 259n41.

37. Interviews by Henry Magnan, *Le Monde*, no. 306, December 11, 1945, 3, and no. 310, December 15, 1945, 3. Reprinted in Beaufret, *De l'existentialisme*, 141–147.

38. Beaufret, *De l'existentialisme à Heidegger*, 143.

39. Ibid., 146.

40. On this point as well as on the response concerning Nazism, see ibid.

41. Jean Beaufret provides clarifications with respect to this person and the circumstances surrounding his journey to Freiburg in the first of his *Entretiens avec Frédéric de Towarnicki*, 7. See also the account given by Jean Beaufret of the first meeting with Towarnicki, then with the aviator Palmer, at the restaurant *Le Coq d'or*, in de Towarnicki, *À la rencontre de Heidegger*, 263.

42. Alexandre Koyré, "L'évolution philosophique de Heidegger," *Critique*, no. 2 (July 1946): 182. The first article was published in issue no. 1 (June 1946): 73–82. That study was itself preceded by a brief account published in *Fontaine*, no. 52 (May 1946): 842–844, the wording of which was even more stern ("the failure" and "the helplessness" of Heidegger should quiet him).

43. It would be translated two years later by Alphonse de Waelhens and Walter Biemel for the French version, *De l'essence de la vérité* (Louvain et Paris: Nauwelaerts et Vrin, 1948).

44. Koyré insisted on this term, "despite the claims to the contrary" by Heidegger ("L'évolution philosophique de Heidegger," 180).

45. Ibid., 170n1.

46. Ibid., 179.

47. Ibid., 183.

48. Emmanuel Levinas, "Il y a," *Deucalion: Cahiers de Philosophie*, published by Jean Wahl, edition of the periodical *Fontaine* (1946): 154. A few years later, in his article, "Is Ontology Fundamental?" Levinas's opposition to the Heideggerian primacy of ontology (assimilated with the "great Western tradition" as "knowledge of the universal") appeared even more clearly with the theme of the ethical signification of the other. However, this very clear indication of the themes of *Totality and Infinity* is not expressed as a specific attack against Heidegger's work: "the return to the original themes of philosophy (and here, too, Heidegger's work remains impressive)" (Emmanuel Levinas, *Entre Nous: On Thinking-of-the-Other*, trans. Barbara Harshav and Michael B. Smith [New York, Columbia University Press, 2000], 2).

49. Emmanuel Levinas, *Existence and Existents*, trans. Alphonso Lingis (Pittsburgh: Duquesne University Press, 2001), 4.

50. Jean Wahl, *A Short History of Existentialism*, trans. Forrest Williams and Stanley Maron (New York: Philosophical Library, 1949).

51. Ibid., 27.

52. Ibid., 23.

53. See ibid., 38, where Gurvitch declares: "In Heidegger—who is not an honest thinker, but an able constructor and calculator bereft of ethics and intellectual scruples—the philosophy of existence has lost its negative sincerity: it has become a mere means dexterously used to pass from the scholastic philosophy in which he began to the Nazi philosophy."

54. Marcel was much more critical of Heidegger in a study published in 1945 ("Autour de Heidegger," *Dieu vivant*, no. 2 [1945]: 89–102), where he rails against Heidegger's excessive use of neologisms, which "flies in the face of an inviolable law of philosophical thought" (89). Marcel is sarcastic about the ambiguity of an atheism that retains an aura of piety (with the notions of fallenness and guilt) and worries about the dismissal of values and the temptations of a "false religion" of the Earth. In the end he calls for a renewal of reason.

55. Jean Wahl, *Introduction à la pensée de Heidegger* (Paris: le Livre de Poche-Librairie générale française, 1998). Contrary to what is indicated on the back cover (for which Jean

Montenot is apparently not responsible), Jean Wahl (unlike Levinas) never was Heidegger's student in Freiburg.

56. It is volume 27 of the *Gesamtausgabe: Einleitung in die Philosophie*, ed. O. Saame and I. Saame-Speidel (Frankfurt am Main: Klostermann, 1996), a course taught by Heidegger in Freiburg during the winter semester of 1928–29.

57. This comment is, of course, to be put in perspective, since the incredible delay is the result of a variety of combined circumstances. First of all, the fact that Corbin opted for a set of chosen excerpts has without a doubt contributed to the fact that Heidegger's influence extended to a larger audience and served as an extremely successful trial run for Gallimard. The quid pro quo was a delay in the full translation of *Sein und Zeit*. Then came the war, which was not favorable for enterprises as large as these. Following the war, the translator chosen by Sartre and Merleau-Ponty—co-directors of the Bibliothèque de Philosophie for Gallimard—was Alphonse de Waelhens. De Waelhens was largely responsible for the delay since he took another twenty years before publishing an incomplete translation, in 1964. The translation was executed in collaboration with Rudolph Boehm and stopped at paragraph 44. It came out under the title *L'Être et le Temps*. Again, this incomplete translation (that was going to remain incomplete since de Waelhens had given up) had the perverse effect of momentarily satisfying the public and furnished the editor with an alibi. Nevertheless, could Merleau-Ponty, director of the collection for Gallimard at the time, not have intervened with more energy to accelerate the process? His sudden death in 1961 does not allow us to say more. We will return a little later to the circumstances that led Jean Beaufret, who was a procrastinator by nature, to finally opt for François Vezin.

58. Foreword to Wahl, *Introduction à la pensée de Heidegger*, 8.

59. According to Jean Montenot, ibid., 9.

60. Kostas Axelos, who audited the course, had himself experienced at the time a similar disappointment: "It was pedestrian and also a paraphrase." See our interview with Kostas Axelos in *Heidegger en France*, vol. 2: *Entretiens*. [TN: This interview with Kostas Axelos was not included in the English edition.]

61. We must keep in mind, however, that his dactylogram is likely to not have been as complete as the version we now have thanks to volume 27 of the *Gesamtausgabe*.

62. Wahl, *Introduction à la pensée de Heidegger*, 240.

63. Ibid., 246 (see also 240). Heidegger demonstrates the profound connection between the two problems: "The problem of being unfolds as the problem of the world, the problem of the world in turn deepens into the problem of being" (*GA 27*, 394).

64. Wahl, *Introduction à la pensée de Heidegger*, 247–248. See also 115.

65. However, Wahl is wrong in seeing in Heidegger a "disdain for sheltering" (ibid., 248).

66. Ibid., 211.

67. Emmanuel Levinas, *Time and the Other*, trans. Richard A. Cohen (Pittsburgh: Duquesne University Press, 1987).

68. Ibid., 35, 34.

69. Emmanuel Levinas, *En découvrant l'existence avec Husserl et Heidegger* (Paris: Vrin, 1949). An abridged version appeared in English as *Discovering Existence with Husserl*, trans. Richard A. Cohen and Michael B. Smith (Evanston, Ill.: Northwestern University Press, 1998). Levinas specified in the foreword to the 1949 edition that his work does not have "the dubious ambition" to plead "for a philosophy that does not always promise wisdom." He added: "However, whether we like it or not, the themes introduced by Heidegger have opened new possibilities for philosophical thought, and have shed a new light on old ones."

70. See ibid., 18, 39, 57, 89.

71. Maurice Merleau-Ponty, *Phenomenology of Perception*, trans. Colin Smith (New York: Routledge 1962), vii.

72. Ibid, vii.

73. Ibid., 369.

74. Ibid., 374.

75. Ibid., 407.

76. "Zusammenhang *des Daseins*" (*SZ*, 388/*BT*, 369). The expression "Zusammenhang des Lebens," however, does appear on page 373 of *Sein und Zeit*; it is accurately quoted by Merleau-Ponty at 407n1 of *Phenomenology of Perception.*

77. Its title is: "The Historicity of Dasein and World History" (*Die Geschichtlichkeit des Daseins und die Welt-Geschichte*).

78. See ibid., 372.

79. Ibid., 410. Citation from *SZ*, 331/*BT*, 316: "Der Sinn des Daseins ist die Zeitlichkeit" (the meaning of Dasein is temporality).

80. Ibid., 412. Merleau-Ponty made mention of this thought only once, although a core theme of *Sein und Zeit.*

81. Ibid., 420 ("temporality temporalizes itself as a future that makes present in the process of having-been": *SZ*, 350/*BT*, 334).

82. See our *Chronos* (Paris: Grasset, 1997), 154–157.

83. Merleau-Ponty, *Phenomenology of Perception*, 417–420.

84. It is remarkable that Merleau-Ponty would be sensitive to the Heideggerian notion of *Augenblick*, even if he associated it excessively to subjectivity: "there is at the core of time a gaze" (ibid., 422). He also cites (ibid., 421) *Kant und das Problem der Metaphysik* (not yet published in French) and a comment from Corbin (ibid., 424).

85. Ibid., 422.

86. Ibid., 427.

87. Wahl, *Introduction à la pensée de Heidegger*, 249. The preceding sentences are no clearer: "It would be a matter of understanding whether Heidegger had a full awareness of the moment of history he was living and had used his freedom appropriately; everything depends, if you will, on figuring out who the philosopher is. It is indeed an acutely existential question."

88. Michel-Antoine Burnier, *Les Existentialistes et la politique* (Paris: Gallimard, 1966), 53. In fact, these attacks began much earlier, since Sartre reacted to them as early as 1943 to Claude Morgan: "'So,' he noted with a smirk, 'it would seem I am a henchman of National Socialism because I have quoted and worked on Heidegger's phenomenology. If I'm not mistaken, the promulgator of this idiocy is a certain Marcenac'" (from Annie Cohen-Solal, *Sartre: A Life*, trans. Anna Cancogni [New York: Pantheon Books, 1987], 194). Sartre must justify himself again in his "statement" in *Combat* in December 1944: "What do you reproach us for? To begin with, for being inspired by Heidegger, a German and a Nazi philosopher" (ibid., 221).

89. Jean-Paul Sartre, "A More Precise Characterization of Existentialism," in *The Writings of Jean-Paul Sartre: Selected Prose*, trans. Richard C. McCleary (Evanston, Ill.: Northwestern University Press, 1974), 156.

90. Simone de Beauvoir confirmed the virulence of these communist attacks: "Soon *Les Lettres françaises* became sectarian. *Action* remained more open-minded. . . . We were very surprised when Ponge, who ran the cultural section, told us that a mountain of articles against Sartre was piling up on his desk . . . he was criticized for drawing inspiration from Heidegger: the political position Heidegger had taken did not retrospectively invalidate all his ideas." Simone de Beauvoir. *La force des choses. I.* (Paris: Gallimard, 1963), 20. Sartre's clarifications did not curb the communist attacks: a few months later (in *Action*, no. 40 [June 8, 1945]), Henri Lefebvre renewed the attacks, "no longer imputed Sartre 'with having been a disciple of the Nazi Heidegger.'" Michel-Antoine Burnier, *Choice of Action: The French Exis-*

tentialists on the Political Front Line, trans. Bernard Murchland (New York: Random House, 1968), 44.

91. "While walking by the Flore, I caught sight of Albert Camus. . . . He did not have any particular enmity toward Heidegger, but still . . . Heidegger was not his cup of tea and he had been a national-socialist" (de Towarnicki, *À la rencontre de Heidegger,* 37).

92. Even on this topic, documents and testimonies were not numerous: de Waelhens did not even allude to the fact that Heidegger was a member of the National Socialist Party: "In 1933, Heidegger becomes rector of Freiburg's university, and his inauguration was marked by a resounding speech: 'Die Selbstbehauptung der deutschen Universität'" (*La Philosophie de Martin Heidegger,* viii).

93. Henri Mougin, "Comment sauver les intellectuels nazis?," *La pensée,* no. 5 (October–December 1945): 121–125. This article was mainly aimed at Jünger, but mentioned that Heidegger was "not looked down upon" by the regime, since all the philosopher's works were sold in bookshops. Mougin renewed his attacks in the same periodical (no. 7 [June 1946]: 111) in these terms: "We have blown the whistle on the tendency of late to attempt to save Heidegger. The campaign has continued: Heidegger's words have been gathered religiously. It is only natural under these conditions that they became more outlandish. It is therefore useful to remind you of the speech pronounced by the philosopher on May 27, 1933, when he received from the Hitlerian government his position at the head of Freiburg's university." This inaccurate comment (since Heidegger was elected by his colleagues) is followed by a few quotes from *The Rectoral Address,* which Mougin considered quite self-explanatory since he did not comment on them.

94. See our interview with Edgar Morin in *Heidegger en France,* vol. 2: *Entretiens.* [TN: This interview with Edgar Morin was not included in the English edition.]

95. *Les Temps modernes,* no. 4 (1946): 713.

96. Ibid., 713–716.

97. Ibid., 717–724.

98. De Towarnicki, *À la rencontre de Heidegger,* 22.

99. *Ibid.,* 32.

100. "Professor, Sir, some people say, in Paris, that you have authorized, in 1933, a book-burning, that you have forbidden Husserl from accessing the university's library and let some students display a *Plakat* against Jews in it." Ibid., 33.

101. Ibid.

102. Ibid., 33–34.

103. *Les Temps modernes,* no. 4 (January 1946): 715–716.

104. Ibid., 716.

105. In the second issue of the *Revue socialiste* (June 1946): 149–154 (under the title "Vers une critique marxiste de l'existentialisme"), Beaufret sarcastically responded to the rationalistic and nationalistic attacks from Julien Benda and Armand Cuvillier. Without devoting his entire article to parrying their attacks, he contrasted them with Lachelier's and Boutroux's Kantianism; he stressed that although the German influence was not new, it would be narrow-minded to critique the demonization of existentialism in general and Heidegger in particular by appealing to a "good German thought." He asserted that Heidegger, as was the case for Plato (under whose authority De Maistre and L. Brunschvicg placed themselves, although in contradictory ways), was a genuine philosopher whose thoughts were much richer than he was given credit for. Benda had bemoaned in *Lettres françaises* (Dec. 23, 1944) the fact that existentialism ensured "an absolute triumph in the spiritual order" for Nazi and German thought. Cuvillier developed in 1945 a similar assault, under the alias Pervicax, in an article published in the first issue of *Revue socialiste,* titled "Les infiltrations germaniques

dans la pensée française." The untroubled answer made by Beaufret was in line with Marxist inspiration, as is shown by the following conclusion: "It is . . . certain that the simple exercises in lucidity to which we invite our readers can only be embraced by Marxism, because Marxism has no other motto than a respect for truth" (154). The alias Pervicax would in turn answer in October 1946, in the same periodical: "l'Existentialisme de Heidegger," reproduced in A. Cuvillier, *Parti pris sur l'art, la philosophie et l'histoire* (Paris: A. Colin, 1956), 160–172. Faced with the attempts to "clear" Heidegger, he maintained that "this philosophy of the irrational is no more than a philosophy of *fascism,* in the broad sense of the term" (171).

106. Sartre, "The Humanism of Existentialism," in *Essays in Existentialism* [*L'Existentialisme est un humanisme*].

107. Ibid., 21. The references to "forlornness" on pages 29 and 51 are in the same spirit.

108. One example of it is the caricatural page Paul Foulquié devoted to Heidegger in a *Que sais-je?* that was widely used in high schools, whose lack of depth was organized around the following "argument": "This system being quite abstruse, and Jean-Paul Sartre having given a much clearer adaptation of it in French, we will limit ourselves to mentioning its basic theses" (*L'Existentialisme* [Paris: PUF, 1947], 51). Once these limitations became clear, the editor much later asked Jacques Colette to write under the same title and in the same series an entirely different text (published in 1994).

109. One should keep in mind that Emmanuel Mounier's point of view was fairly marginalized in this debate. In his *Introduction aux existentialismes* (Paris: Denoël, 1947), Mounier devoted himself to restoring "the forgotten scope" (8) of the existential tradition, which, in his opinion, was mostly religious and Christian (from Augustine and Pascal to Gabriel Marcel, and including Kierkegaard). Without being hostile to Heidegger, he seemed to not know his work very well and merely devoted a few general pages to "being-with."

110. Indeed, in the *Critique of Dialectical Reason,* Heidegger and his philosophy are mentioned only five times, according to Jean Gabriel Adloff's index, *Sartre: Index du corpus philosophique,* part 1: *L'Être et néant: Critique de la Raison Dialectique* (Paris: Klincksieck, 1981).

4. Humanism in Turmoil

1. Martin Heidegger, *Platons Lehre von der Wahrheit: Mit einem Brief über den "Humanismus"* (Berne: Francke, 1947); *Lettre Sur Humanisme,* trans. R. Munier (Paris: Aubier, 1957). In fact, a first version of Munier's translation was published in 1953 in the *Cahiers du Sud.* An important fragment had already appeared, translated by Joseph Rovan, in the journal *Fontaine,* no. 63 (November 1947), preceded by a study by Jean Beaufret on "Martin Heidegger et le problème de la vérité." Previously, in note 58 of the same journal, in 1947, Joseph Rovan had published a first partial translation of "La remontée au fondement de la métaphysique" (The way back into the ground of metaphysics) before its publication in German as a postscript to "Was ist Metaphysik?"

2. "*Wir bedenken das Wesen des handelns noch lange nicht entschieden genug.*" "Letter on Humanism," *PA,* 239).

3. Ibid., 241. The question is cited in French by Heidegger.

4. The German word is even stronger [*Unheil*]: it ascribes the decline of language to the loss of the sense of the sacred.

5. "Letter on Humanism," in *PA,* 275. The question is also cited in French in Heidegger's text.

6. Beaufret, *De l'existentialisme à l'humanisme,* 47.

7. A lecture given by Jean Beaufret at Club Maintenant in Paris.

8. A report by Jean Wahl in *Fontaine* (May 1946): 840. Let us also note this severe judgment on the same page: "Some truths appeared gradually in a lecture overly filled with a spirit of conciliation in which, under the features of existentialism, we were presented with the clichés of traditional philosophy: the role of consciousness, freedom, the subjective . . . opposed to the objective."

9. See my article "La réception de Heidegger: Jean Beaufret entre Sartre et Merleau-Ponty," 270–272.

10. Maurice Merleau-Ponty, *Humanism and Terror: An Essay on the Communist Problem*, trans. John O'Neill (Boston: Beacon Press, 1990).

11. Citation from *A Contribution to a Critique of Hegel's Philosophy of Right*, given by Maurice Merleau-Pontry in *Humanism and Terror*, 101.

12. Ibid, 187. This allusion to the Moscow trials was reconsidered in a manner no less contestable by Georg Lukacs, *Existentialisme ou marxisme?* (Paris: Nagel, 1948), for whom the universe of the convicts corresponds to that of *Sein und Zeit*, "'this *theatre of the grotesque* of philosophy,' as Henri Lefebvre said it so rightly" (23).

13. "Communist behavior has not changed: it is still the same attitude of conflict, the same warlike cunning, the same methodical wickedness, the same distrust, but underwritten less and less by class spirit and revolutionary brotherhood" (Merleau-Ponty, *Humanism and Terror*, xx–xxi).

14. Ibid., 185–186.

15. Heidegger, "Letter on Humanism," in *PA*, 259.

16. "Die Heimatlosigkeit wird ein Weltschicksal," in *PA*, 258.

17. Löwith, "The Political Implications of Heidegger's Existentialism," 167–185. Many important passages of this account can be found in the same author's book, *My Life in Germany before and after 1933: A Report*, trans. Elizabeth King (London: Athlone Press, 1994).

18. Löwith was a close friend of Heidegger and did his "Habilitation" with him. See *My Life in Germany*, 44–47. See also Gadamer, *Philosophical Apprenticeships*, 168–175.

19. Löwith, "The Political Implications of Heidegger's Existentialism," 172.

20. Ibid., 175.

21. Ibid., 178.

22. Ibid., 176.

23. Ibid., 172, 176.

24. Ibid., 182.

25. Ibid., 169.

26. Éric Weil, "Le cas Heidegger," *Les Temps modernes* (July 1947): 128–138. Reprinted in the journal *Lignes*, no. 2 (February 1988): 139–151.

27. Weil, "Le cas Heidegger," 128.

28. Ibid., 129.

29. Ibid., 131.

30. Ibid., 131–132.

31. Ibid., 135.

32. Ibid., 137.

33. Alphonse de Waelhens, "La philosophie de Heidegger et le nazisme," *Les Temps modernes* (July 1947): 115–127.

34. Ibid., 116.

35. Ibid., 117.

36. Ibid., 115.

37. "Réponse à M. de Waelhens par K. Löwith," *Les Temps modernes* (August 1948): 370–373.

38. Ibid., 371.

39. Alphonse de Waelhens, "Réponse à cette réponse," 375.

40. "Réponse à M. de Waelhens par K. Löwith," 373.

41. The list is not exhaustive, of course. We will have the opportunity to expand it. Let us not forget from the outset to add, for example: Jean Wahl, Georges Canguilhem, and Dina Dreyfus, with whom he quarreled in the mid-fifties.

42. "And one day, I arrived in Germany, and I met Heidegger. This was in September 1946, but neither he nor I remember the exact date, although we agreed that it must have been around September 10th" (Beaufret, *Entretiens avec Frédéric de Towarnicki*, 7).

43. He would only later be honored in 1957 in the *Tableau de la philosophie contemporaine*, ed. Alfred Weber and Denis Huisman (Paris: Fischbacher, 1957), 373.

44. Beaufret, *Entretiens avec Frédéric de Towarnicki*, 10.

45. This excerpt, published after Jean Beaufret's article in *Fontaine*, no. 63 (1947): 786–804, begins with the following sentence: "You ask: '*How can we restore meaning to the word "humanism"?*'" It corresponds to the last part of the "Letter on Humanism," in *PA*, 262–263.

46. *Fontaine*, no. 63 (November 1947): 758–785. This text was reproduced ten years later in Weber and Huisman, *Tableau de la philosophie contemporaine*, 352–373.

47. Thanks to the first contact between Heidegger and Jean Beaufret, which was facilitated by Palmer: see Beaufret, *Entretiens avec Frédéric de Towarnicki*, 7.

48. Beaufret, *Fontaine*, no. 63 (November 1947): 759; Weber and Huisman, *Tableau de la philosophie contemporaine*, 354.

49. According to Beaufret, this was the beginning of the first conversations with Heidegger. See *Entretiens avec Frédéric de Towarnicki*, 8.

50. Beaufret, *Fontaine*, 765; Weber and Huisman, *Tableau de la philosophie contemporaine*, 358.

51. Beaufret, *Fontaine*, 770; Weber and Huisman, *Tableau de la philosophie contemporaine*, 361.

52. See Beaufret, *Fontaine*, 777; Weber and Huisman, *Tableau de la philosophie contemporaine*, 367.

53. Beaufret, *Fontaine*, 785; Weber and Huisman, *Tableau de la philosophie contemporaine*, 372.

54. Jean Beaufret, *Le poème de Parménide* (Paris: PUF, 1995).

55. Beaufret even corrected Alphonse de Waelhens, who was so naïve as to believe that Heidegger did not know the phenomenological reduction (see Weber and Huisman, *Tableau de la philosophie contemporaine*, 358).

56. Louis Althusser, *The Future Lasts Forever: A Memoir*, ed. Olivier Corpet and Yann Moulier Boutang, trans. Richard Veasey (New York: New Press, 1995), 176.

57. It remains one of Heidegger's most widely read works in France, and the inquiry into the meaning of humanism is still relevant today. As a testimony to this, Bruno Pinchard organized a symposium at the University of Tours on "Heidegger et la question de l'humanisme. Nouvelles lectures de la *Lettre sur l'humanisme*," March 30–31, 2001.

58. Jean-Paul Sartre, *Truth and Existence*, trans. Ronald Aronson (Chicago: University of Chicago Press, 1995). See Arlette Elkaim-Sartre's preface, xiv: "In fact, Sartre remains quite distant from Heidegger's thought because their objectives differ."

59. Ibid., 13.

60. Ibid., 2.

61. Ibid., 44.

62. This date is cited according to the chronology given by Michel Contat and Michel Rybalka in *Les écrits de Sartre*: "Gives a long lecture in Freiburg-im-Brisgau and visits Heidegger" (34). However, Simone de Beauvoir dates this lecture (if it is indeed the same one)

at the end of Fall 1953 [see Simone de Beauvoir, *Hard Times, Force of Circumstances*, vol. 2: *1952–1962*, trans. Richard Howard (New York: Paragon House, 1992), 288–289.]

63. He had almost gone to Freiburg in the fall of 1945, but the plan for the trip by Frédéric de Towarnicki had failed at the last moment. At that time, Heidegger had written Sartre a friendly letter (dated October 28, 1945), the text of which can be found, along with the narration of its circumstances, in de Towarnicki's book *À la rencontre de Heidegger*, 83–85.

64. De Beauvoir, *Hard Times, Force of Circumstances*, vol. 2: *1952–1962*, 289. And Sartre would have added, "his eyes wide": "Four thousand students and professors toiling over Heidegger day after day, just think of it!" (ibid.).

65. See Jean Cau, *Croquis de mémoire* (Paris: Julliard, 1985), 253; Sartre adds: "His small town is the magic Mountain. At the bottom are the students, higher up the teachers' houses, still higher those of the administrators of the University and, at the top, the old man's villa. The old man of the mountain, exactly. . . . He vomits engagement. I told him about it. He was looking at me with infinite pity. At the end, I was talking to his hat."

5. The Bright Spell of the '50s

1. Among them, we note Walter Biemel who published in 1950 *Le Concept de monde chez Heidegger* (Louvain-Paris: Vrin-Nauwelaerts, 1950). This quite austere and precise volume takes after the work of Alphonse de Waelhens (with whom Biemel collaborated): it essentially consists in a reading of key passages of *Sein und Zeit* and does not limit itself to the technical problems of the relation between space and "worldliness." This is why this little book was widely read, in the fifties, by students who were frustrated at being unable to study *Sein und Zeit* in German and were eager to complete their reading of Alphonse de Waelhens's book.

2. One can read an example of this in Jean-Toussaint Desanti, *Introduction à l'histoire de la philosophie* (Paris: Éditions de la Nouvelle Critique, 1956), who was very critical of Heidegger's interpretation of Kant: "You could call that way of writing history 'impressionistic.' Every philosophy is taken in its singularity as if it were absolute. . . . This 'impressionism' does not only leave you at the mercy of charlatans. He himself plays a part in the falsification and easily becomes dishonest."

3. Éric Weil, *Logique de la philosophie* (Paris: Vrin, 1987).

4. Ibid., 391, see note 3.

5. Ibid., 377.

6. Ibid.

7. "He paid a visit to Heidegger, perched on his eyrie, and told him how sorry he was about the play Gabriel Marcel had just written about him. That was all they talked about, and Sartre left after half an hour" (Simone de Beauvoir, *Hard Times, Force of Circumstance*, vol. 2, 288–289). The play was broadcast on the *Chaîne nationale* of French radio on October 17, 1953.

8. Gabriel Marcel, *La Dimension Florestan* (Paris: Plon, 1958), 11. It is important to clarify that the expression *Die Wacht am Sein* is an exact copy of a patriotic German song, *Die Wacht am Rhein* (The watch of the Rhine). Let us also note that the names of the characters are not accidental: *Dolch* means "dagger" or "*stiletto*"; *Schmuck* means "finery" or "ornament."

9. Ibid.

10. Ibid., 32. *La pêche* is both a piece of fruit (peach) and the act of fishing in French. The corresponding verb is *pêcher*.

11. Martin Heidegger, *Vorträge und Aufsätze* (Pfullingen: Neske, 1954), 163–186. One reads, among other things, on page 179: *Das Ding dingt Welt*, literally *La chose chosise le*

monde ("the thing things the world"). Préau translates in a more elegant way: *La chose rassemble le monde* ("the thing gathers the world"). Heidegger, *Essais et conférences* (Paris: Gallimard, 1958), 215.

12. *Jahrbuch der Akademie, Band 1, Gestalt und Gedanke* (München: Oldenbourg, 1951), 128.

13. Those reservations, shared by many, were strongly expressed a few years later in a resounding book in which the hermeticism of Heidegger's thought was ridiculed. In particular, the distinction between being and beings was presented as the typical example of empty verbosity, sterile and divorced from human realities: see Jean-François Revel, *Pourquoi des philosophes?* (Paris: Julliard, 1957), 56–59.

14. In a lecture held in spring 1957 in Germany and published much later ["Ma relation avec Heidegger," in *Présence de Gabriel Marcel*, Cahier 1 (Paris: Aubier, 1980)], Marcel explained that since his meeting in Cerisy, his opinion had changed: what struck him about Heidegger's work was "a kind of naïveté, and a quite unusual simplicity" (25). At the philosophical level, he went as far as asserting: "I deeply admire the Heidegger's heroic attempt to restore the sacred" (36), but he maintained important reservations about the terminology, about the danger of abstraction and "substantification" of being, about the self-closing before death and about a "disturbing" ambiguity toward Christianity.

15. Etienne Gilson, *L'être et l'essence* (Paris: Vrin, 1948), 226.

16. Ibid., 331.

17. There is a very allusive passage connecting him with Kierkegaard: ibid., 233.

18. "Réponses à quelques questions," in ibid., 352.

19. As suggested by Jean-François Courtine, "Gilson et Heidegger," in *Étienne Gilson et nous: la philosophie et son histoire*, ed. Monique Couratier (Paris: Vrin, 1980), 114n2.

20. "*Étant* is a term that, at that time, was not considered acceptable French" (Beaufret, *Entretiens avec Frédéric de Towarnicki*, 8).

21. Gilson, *L'être et l'essence*, 365.

22. A valid expression from Jean-François Courtine ("Gilson et Heidegger," 103) that nevertheless seems to be minimizing Gilson's efforts in the appendix of *L'être et l'essence* to recognize Heidegger's philosophical stature and open a discussion.

23. Martin Heidegger, "Introduction to 'What Is Metaphysics': The Way Back into the Ground of Metaphysics," in *PA*, 277–290. "*Le retour au fondement de la métaphysique*," trans. Roger Munier, *Revue des sciences philosophiques et théologiques* 43, no. 3 (July 1959): 401–433.

24. "Die onto-theo-logische Verfassung der Metaphysik," in *Identität und Differenz* (Pfullingen: Neske, 1957), 35–73; "The Onto-Theological Constitution of Metaphysics," in *Identity and Difference*, trans. Joan Stambaugh (Chicago: University of Chicago Press, 2002), 42–74. The French translation would appear only in 1968 in *Questions I*.

25. Gilson, *L'être et l'essence*, 365.

26. Ibid.

27. Ibid., 371.

28. Although he stresses the difference between the Aristotelian contemplation of being as such and the "position" of modern ontology. Ibid., 367–368.

29. Ibid., 369.

30. Ibid., 366.

31. Aquinas sought to "go beyond beings from within," which Heidegger contests: see ibid., 370.

32. Ibid., 376.

33. Ibid., 377.

34. Courtine, "Gilson et Heidegger," 114n4.

35. "Le retour au fondement de la métaphysique," ibid., 403.

36. Ibid. (The author of the presentation dissociates himself, on that point, from Henri Birault, who perceived an "awaiting of God" in Heidegger.)

37. Ibid., 404. One finds the same ambiguous attitude of support and reticence in the study of the Dominican Maurice Corvez ["La place de Dieu dans l'ontologie de Martin Heidegger," *Revue thomiste,* no. 1 (1953): 287–301], who managed a "Heideggerian chronicle" in the same journal (see ibid., 591–619).

38. "Le retour au fondement de la métaphysique," 405.

39. *Philosophies chrétiennes: Recherches et débats,* no. 10 (Paris: Fayard, 1955). Birault's text is on pages 108–132.

40. It would be published in its entirety only in 1970 in Tübingen by Klostermann under the title *Phänomenologie und Theologie.* However, a French translation appeared in 1969 in *Archives de Philosophie* 32, no. 3 (1959): 356. The second part of the 1927 lecture, translated as "Théologie et philosophie," was then published in an appendix of Ernst Cassirer—Martin-Heidegger, *Débat sur le kantisme et la philosophie et autres textes de 1929–1931* (Paris: Beauchesne, 1971), 101–131.

41. See Henri Birault, "La foi et la pensée d'après Heidegger," in *Philosophies chrétiennes: Recherches et débats,* no. 10 (Paris: Fayard, 1955): 117.

42. Ibid., 131.

43. Ibid., 132.

44. Henri Birault, "Existence et vérité d'après Heidegger," *Revue de métaphysique et de morale* (January–March 1951): 86–87. Birault's attitude, characterized by an eloquent clarity in his exposition of Heidegger's theses and his attention to the questions of the Christian circles, gained him their support, at least in the 1950s. Unlike Beaufret, Birault is then quoted favorably by Gabriel Marcel as well as by Father Jeannière. His spiritual quest would become less Christian and more Nietzschean.

45. See Jean Guitton, *Le Clair et l'Obscur* (Paris: Librairie Auguste Blaizot, 1962), 72–98 and especially, 91. This text, first published as "Visite à Heidegger," in *La Table ronde,* no.123 (March 1958): 143–155, apparently brought about a rapprochement between Beaufret and Guitton. This is not simply due to the fact they are both from the Creuse region of France. Since he was on bad terms with Jean Wahl, Jean Beaufret asked Jean Guitton to be his new thesis advisor. This choice did not fail to surprise many of his friends, but was made by Jean Beaufret as a protest against the anti-Heideggerian attitude of the majority of the professors in the Sorbonne and of French academics.

46. Jeannière wrote a prudent and scrupulous text about Heidegger a few years earlier, clearly differentiating him from Sartre's atheism and concluding with a laudatory reference to Birault, who placed the thinking of being in the context of an awaiting of God: see Abel Jeannière, "L'itinéraire de Martin Heidegger," *Études* (January–March 1954): 64–74.

47. This is my own account since I attended this session. See *HF,* epilogue 1, 108.

48. According to Aron, *Les Modernes,* 105.

49. See de Gandillac, *Le Siècle traversé,* 347.

50. Marcel, Postscript to *La Dimension Florestan,* 161.

51. Ibid., 62.

52. One finds confirmation of this in Marie-Madeleine Davy, *Un philosophe itinérant: Gabriel Marcel* (Paris: Flammarion, 1959), 103: "*La Dimension Florestan* (followed by the "*Crépuscule du sens commun*" [Twilight of common sense]) is born from a theatrical reflection on Heideggerian language. It should not be understood as a play on Heidegger himself, which would be a mistake, but on an incomprehensible terminology that appears burlesque."

53. Ibid., 169.

54. That is certainly why Gabriel Marcel—undoubtedly annoyed by the "snobbery" of certain religious authorities—places in his play a Priest near Professor Dolch.

55. Jean Beaufret, "En France," *Erinnerung an Martin Heidegger* (Pfullingen: Neske, 1977), 9. Heidegger says: "I am indeed in Paris," and then answering his wife: "I am surprised— about myself!"

56. See our interview with Kostas Axelos in *Heidegger en France*, vol. 2: *Entretiens*. [TN: This interview with Kostas Axelos was not included in the English edition.]

57. These details were given by Jean Beaufret in *Dialogue avec Heidegger,* vol. 4 (Paris: Éditions de Minuit, 1985), 86.

58. "While in France," Heidegger wrote, "*I would really like to meet Georges Braque and René Char.*" Jean Beaufret, "L'entretien sous le marronnier," *L'arc,* no. 22 (Summer 1963): 1.

59. Confirmed by the recollections of Kostas Axelos and Roger Munier in our interviews in *Heidegger en France*, vol. 2: *Entretiens*. [TN: These interviews were not included in the English edition.]

60. Beaufret, "En France," 9.

61. Ibid.

62. According to Jean Beaufret, Heidegger made the following comment just after dinner. He found "what Char told him striking: *Treffend was Char sagte. This is the entire difference between thought and poetry. Poetry goes forward, but thought is essentially memory, even if poetry remains its* viaticum" ("En France," 9).

63. Quoted by Beaufret, "L'entretien sous le marronnier," 2.

64. Ibid., 2. Also see Beaufret, "En France," 10.

65. Jacques Prévert, quoted by George Braque and Jacques Prevert, *Varengeville* (Paris: Maeght, 1958), 5.

66. See *Entretiens* with Kostas Axelos in *Heidegger en France*, vol. 2. [TN: This interview with Kostas Axelos was not included in the English edition.]

67. Ibid.

68. "Heidegger stayed at *La Prévôté,* then visited the Cathedral at Chartres. Lacan drove his car with the same speed as his psychoanalytic sessions. Seated in front, Heidegger did not flinch, but his wife could not stop complaining. Sylvia conveyed her dissatisfaction to Lacan. But to no avail: the master drove faster and faster. On the way back, Heidegger remained silent, while his wife's protests grew louder and Lacan pressed down still harder on the gas-pedal. The trip came to an end, and each of the passengers went his or her own way." Elisabeth Roudinesco, *Lacan and Co. A History of Psychoanalysis in France 1935–85,* trans. Jeffrey Mehlman (Chicago: University of Chicago Press, 1990), 299.

69. This detail was provided by de Gandillac, *Le Siècle traversé,* 345.

70. This offer was encouraged by Heidegger himself who "had hoped for a series of meetings in France," according to de Gandillac (ibid.).

71. According to Aron, *Les Modernes,* 99.

72. One of the most enthusiastic participants was Walter Biemel: "The session that had been organized so judiciously as to include time for conversations during strolls and trips was essentially attuned to Heidegger's style of interpretation. All the participants felt the same fascination that I had myself felt fifteen years earlier during my first seminars in Freiburg" ("Le professeur, le penseur, l'ami," in *Martin Heidegger: Cahier de l'Herne,* 135).

73. One finds a list, with sarcastic commentaries, in Jean-Paul Aron's book (*Les Modernes,* 105–106), which confirms fifty-six participants. Apart from Marcel, Gandillac, Goldmann, and some religious figures (R. F. Fessard, Kleiber, Léger, the Canon Dondeyne, the Abbots Morel and Pépin), other names stand out such as Axelos, Ricoeur, de Waelhens, Biemel, Starobinski, Philonenko, Allemann, and Deleuze. Maurice de Gandillac (*Le Siècle traversé,* 345) also informs us of the presence of Gilbert Kahn, a translator of Heidegger, and of Pierre Burgelin. Let us also note the participation of Mlle Jeanne Hersch, Mme Parain-Vial, and Mme Simone Pétrement.

74. Some absences should be mentioned: Hyppolite, Merleau-Ponty, Sartre, and Jean Wahl. The latter, who did not show any philosophical hostility toward Heidegger in his *Traité de métaphysique* (Paris: Payot, 1953), in which chapter 4 focused on *"L'idée d'être"* (the notion of being), would devote a whole course, in his highly interpretative style, to the *Introduction to Metaphysics* (which had not been translated yet), which appeared in *Vers la fin de l'ontologie* (Paris: SEDES, 1956). However, he made a point of expressing his reservations about the reprinting in the German edition of *Einführung . . .* of Heidegger's pronouncement on "the inner truth and greatness of this movement" (National Socialism). Wahl specified: "There is a page (152) that is really embarrassing for those who admire Heidegger the philosopher. . . . What is typical but also quite disturbing with respect to both Heidegger and Germany, is that he thought it was appropriate to reprint that sentence as such" (ibid., 5).

75. Martin Heidegger, *What Is Philosophy?*, trans. W. Kluback and J. T. Wilde (Lanham, Md.: Rowman & Littlefield, 2003).

76. According to Jean-Paul Aron in *Les Modernes*, 106.

77. As reported to the author by Jean Beaufret.

78. De Gandillac, *Le Siècle traversé*, 346.

79. See Biemel, "Le professeur, le penseur, l'ami," *Cahier de l'Herne*, 135.

80. I am indebted to Françoise Dastur and Frédéric Postel for their kind provision of the preliminary transcripts of the tape recording from the "Decade" (the ten-day conference at Cerisy). Those transcripts seem to be the work of Alexis Philonenko. The clarifications or brief quotations that made it possible to reconstitute the course of the work came from typed documents that had been circulating for many years in specialized circles.

81. This text was to be published in 1957 as Heidegger, *Qu'est-ce que la philosophie?*, trans. Kostas Axelos and Jean Beaufret (Paris: Gallimard, 1957).

82. Heidegger, *What Is Philosophy?*, 45. We will refer to the main themes of this lecture a bit later.

83. See Immanuel Kant, *The One Possible Basis for a Demonstration of the Existence of God*, trans. Gordon Treash (Lincoln: University of Nebraska Press, 1994), 53.

84. Ricoeur deplored that method in his *Critique and Conviction* (New York: Columbia University Press, 1998), 21, and declared he had a "bad memory" of Cerisy: Heidegger was "literally guarded by Axelos and Beaufret, and he behaved like a schoolmaster."

85. Kant, *The One Possible Basis for a Demonstration of the Existence of God*, 59.

86. We borrow this expression from the later work where Heidegger reconsidered and developed his interpretation: see "Kant's Thesis about Being," in *PA*, 337–363.

87. It is noteworthy that Ricoeur, while distancing himself from Heidegger's theses, nonetheless showed an interest in them, not only by his presence at Cerisy, but above all by the orientation of his questions, which were more a request for clarifications than strong objections. A short time earlier, he had written the chapter on Heidegger that concluded Bréhier's *Histoire de la philosophie allemande* (Paris: Vrin, 1954), a well-informed and balanced text that concluded on a confession of perplexity concerning Heidegger's thought of the sacred: "As his esoteric language testifies—Openness, Clearing, Domain, Dwelling, Revelation, Mystery, Benediction, Simplicity—this thought is organized around the theme of the sacred and with all the equivocations that proceed from it" (257).

88. During the same intervention, Heidegger also responded to two other lectures; he confessed not to have understood the lecture by the Spanish professor Marias; and more seriously, he declared to Lucien Goldmann that the debate with Marxism would require a penetrating interpretation of Hegel, going beyond a "simple reversal"; it would also be necessary for Marxism to free itself from its dogmatism.

89. A comment from Jean-Paul Aron who gives a picturesque account of those days in *Les Modernes*, 106–107.

90. G. W. F. Hegel, *Science of Logic*, trans. A. V. Miller (New York: Humanity Books, 1969), 82.

91. G. W. F. Hegel, *Phenomenology of Spirit*, trans. A.V. Miller (London: Oxford University Press, 1977), 38.

92. Ibid., 38: "This conflict between the general form of a proposition and the unity of the Notion which destroys it is similar to the conflict that occurs in rhythm between meter and accent. Rhythm results from the floating center and the unification of the two."

93. Walter Schulz, *Die Vollendung des Deutschen Idealismus in der Spätphilosophie Schellings* (Stuttgart: Kohlhammer, 1955).

94. Georges Braque, *Le Jour et Nuit* (Paris: Gallimard, 1952), 9.

95. Those objections came from Gabriel Marcel, Paul Ricoeur, and Lucien Goldmann: see Aron, *Les Modernes,* 106. On the political question, see Biemel's account (ibid.): "Lucien Goldmann took Heidegger to task one afternoon about the events of 1933. Heidegger answered calmly and in a very precise manner, by indicating that his work had nothing in common with national-socialism." See also our interview with Kostas Axelos in *Heidegger en France,* vol. 2: *Entretiens.* [TN: This interview with Kostas Axelos was not included in the English edition.]

96. Beaufret, *Dialogue avec Heidegger,* vol. 4, 83.

97. See this text in *PA*, 277–290.

98. "I say—into *a* path. Thereby we admit that this path is certainly not the only one." Heidegger, *What Is Philosophy?*, 21.

99. The beginning of the "Translators' Notes" is relevant as regards the denial that we have begun to analyze and that represented one of Jean Beaufret's favorite themes: without being literally false, this note intended to put Heidegger's lecture beyond the reach of any "view-point" or "interpretation." One can read for oneself: "The pages that precede are not a historico-philosophical interpretation of the history of philosophy from Heidegger's perspective. These pages do not even reveal the full extent of Heidegger's meditation on the *truth of being* (which relates to the definition of philosophy as metaphysics)." *Questions I,* 53.

100. Ibid., 31.

101. Ibid., 33.

102. Ibid., 63.

103. Ibid., 95.

104. Should we go so far as to see, with Henri Crétella, the beginning of a poetic "revolution" of thought, asserting that the Greek and French "double history" of philosophy as truth and clarity has ended? Should we also consider with him that the transcriptions of the tapes from *La Décade de Cerisy* show that Heidegger's interlocutors missed the point of the lecture "What Is Philosophy?" despite Heidegger's "indulgent generosity" toward Gabriel Marcel? Should we above all propose a political interpretation (reconsidered in relation to the "error" of 1933) of the Heideggerian reading of Hegel's speculative proposition? Should we draw a parallel between the Hölderlinian illusions regarding Bonaparte (in his poem *Celebration of Peace*) and the Heideggerian delusion concerning Hitler? We have proposed a more cautious interpretation of the *Décade de Cerisy,* but we fully agree with Henri Crétella when he puts the question of language and of "sayability" at the heart of an encounter in which Heidegger was respectful of both the Hebraic tradition and the French language: see Henri Crétella, "Heidegger à Cerisy," in *L'enseignement par excellence. Hommage à François Vezin,* ed. Pascal David (Paris: L'Harmattan, 2000), 131–153.

105. Thus in *La Nouvelle Revue française:* "Le sentier," preceded by a brief introduction by the translator Jacques Gérard, "Heidegger et ses lieux" (January 1954): 41–46. "Sur l'expérience de la pensée," (February 1954): 236–239; "Georg Trakl," trans. Jean Beaufret and Wolfgang Brokmeier (January and February 1958): 52–75 and 213–236. In the *Cahiers du Sud,*

in addition to "Hegel et les Grecs," see "Hebel l'ami de la maison," trans. Annie Li Carrillo, no. 355 (1960): 383–396.

106. Except in the case of *Kant und das Problem der Metaphysik* (Bonn: F. Cohen, 1929).

107. Martin Heidegger, "On the Essence of Truth," trans. John Sallis, in *PA*, 136–154.

108. Which does not always avoid misunderstandings: for instance, the interpretation of *Verbergung* proposed on page 47 of the Introduction renders Heidegger's daring undertaking banal: "Un-concealment is only ever partial, particular."

109. Martin Heidegger, "On the Essence of Truth," in *PA*, 145.

110. Ibid., 148.

111. Ibid. "Die Verborgenheit versagt der Aletheia das Entbergen . . ."

112. See *Le Robert* entry on *obnubiler*.

113. See Heraclitus: *Phusis kruptesthai philei* (generally translated as: "Nature loves to hide"), Diels-Kranz, *Die Fragmente der Vorsokratiker* (Berlin: Weidmann, 1960), 1:178, fragment 123.

114. Contrary to what is affirmed in the introduction to the French translation.

115. Thus *Geheimnis* is reduced to a "mystery"; the key word "*Gelassenheit*" becomes a *souple douceur*; the *caractère originaire* [*Anfänglichkeit*] of truth is difficult to recognize in its "originariness." See *PA*, 152–154.

116. In which, as we have seen, Jean Beaufret proved quite brilliant and suggestive but refrained from engaging in precise and "technical" explanations of Heidegger's essay. Levinas also published an account, albeit much later, and he did not really develop a technical discussion. He recognized the serious work of the translators, even paid tribute to Beaufret, but ended with a radical critique: "Is not the real outcome of the understanding of being, for Heidegger, this movement towards death?" (*Revue philosophique* 149 [1959]: 563).

117. De Waelhens and Biemel, Introduction to Martin Heidegger, *De l'essence de la vérité* (Louvain-Paris: Nauwelaerts-Vrin, 1948), 7.

118. "When a philosophical text uses a new or foreign vocabulary, we are accustomed, in order to interpret it, to translate this language into the language with which we are most familiar. This is both unavoidable and dangerous. We can only avoid this problem if, in addition to the assimilation of the vocabulary, there is a corresponding effort to perform a 'leap' within the very problematic." Ibid.

119. See Martin Heidegger, *Kant et le problème de la métaphysique*, trans. A. de Waelhens and W. Biemel (Paris: Gallimard, 1953), 256.

120. Ibid., Introduction, 50.

121. Translator of *Lettre sur l'humanisme* (Paris: Aubier, 1957).

122. Translator of *Essais et conférences* (Paris: Gallimard, 1958).

123. Translator of *Introduction à la métaphysique* (Paris: PUF, 1958).

124. Thus, among others, *éclairement* for *Lichtung* ("Lettre sur l'humanisme," 75), *absence de patrie* for *Heimatlosigkeit* (ibid., 99), the *dam* for *das Unheil* (ibid., 133), the *lieu de combat* for *das Strittige* (ibid., 153). The final glossary evaluates those choices. Some are particularly felicitous: thus *injonction* for *Fügung* and the distinction between *histoire* and *chronique* to restitute the difference between *Geschichte* and *Historie*.

125. Jean Beaufret's comment in his preface to *Essais et conférences*, xv.

126. Heidegger, *Essais et conférences*, 260; *Vorträge und Aufsätze* (Pfullingen: Neske, 1954), 216.

127. Heidegger, *Essais et conférences*, 215; *Vorträge und Aufsätze*, 179. On the same page, Préau translates *Das Ding dingt Welt* by *La chose rassemble le monde* and not as *la chose chosifie le monde* ("the thing things the world" would be an utter mistranslation)

128. Heidegger, *Essais et conférences*, 217; *Vorträge und Aufsätze*, 180.

129. See Heidegger, *Essais et conférences*, back cover.

130. Gilbert Kahn's Foreword to *Introduction à la métaphysique*, 3.

131. For example: *latence* for *Verborgenheit*, *mésinterprétation* for *Misdeutung*, *la dignité de question* for *die Fragwürdigkeit*, *l'obédience* for *die Hörigkeit*, *le recueillement* for *die Sammlung*, and *perdominer* for *Walten*.

132. Somewhat ahead of its time, it offered elements of a debate on Heidegger's translations, which would resurge later violently.

133. Martin Heidegger, *Einführung in die Metaphysik* (Tübingen: Niemeyer, 1953).

134. Wahl, *Introduction à la pensée de Heidegger*.

135. Ibid. Also see Jean Wahl, *Vers la fin de l'ontologie* (Paris: SEDES, 1956).

136. See note 71.

137. *Vers la fin de l'ontologie*, 240.

138. Heidegger, *Einführung in die Metaphysik*, 152.

139. Wahl, *Vers la fin de l'ontologie*, 5. What is even odder is that Wahl mentions *die Höhe* although the term does not appear in the printed text.

140. "Namely, the encounter between global technology and modern humanity" [*nämlich mit der Begegnung der planetarisch bestimmten Technik und des neuzeitlichen Menschen*], Martin Heidegger, *Introduction to Metaphysics*, trans. Gregory Fried and Richard Polt (New Haven, Conn.: Yale University Press, 2000), 213.

141. Wahl, *Vers la fin de l'ontologie*, 256.

142. Martin Heidegger, *Was heisst denken?* (Tübingen: Niemeyer, 1954); *Qu'appelle-t-on penser?*, trans. Aloys Becker and Gérard Granel (Paris: PUF, 1959); *What Is Called Thinking?*, trans. J. Glenn Gray (New York: Harper Perennial, 2004).

143. Heidegger, *Qu'appelle-t-on penser?*, 16.

144. Beda Allemann, *Hölderlin et Heidegger: Recherche de la relation entre poésie et pensée*, trans. François Fédier (Paris: PUF, 1959).

145. However, the inverse trajectory (toward Hölderlin) remains more problematic. This is what Paul de Man, prior to the publication of the French translation of Allemann's essay, emphasized in "Les exégèses de Hölderlin par Martin Heidegger," *Critique* (September–October 1955): 800–819. See Paul de Man, "Heidegger's Exegesis of Hölderlin," in *Blindness and Insight*, 2nd ed. (Minneapolis: University of Minnesota Press, 1983), 246–266. While recognizing the value of that work, he opposed the idea that the Heideggerian "turn" could be understood "by analogy" to Hölderlin's poetry. For him, Hölderlin *"says exactly the opposite of what Heidegger makes him say"* (ibid., 254–255). This is an over-interpretation of the texts that transforms the poet into a herald of dwelling in the *parousia* of being and into an harbinger of the overcoming of Western metaphysics.

146. As an example, see "Georg Trakl: Situation de son DICT," trans. Jean Beaufret and Wolfgang Brokmeier, *La Nouvelle Revue française* (January 1958): 66 and 68, a beautiful and careful translation in which, however, *Die Abgeschiedenheit* is rendered by the neologism *le Dis-cès* and in which *der Ab-geschiedene* becomes *le Dis-cédé*. Heidegger chose a fairly ordinary word to make it resonate with a new, more radical, and more singular sense: in the present case, placing a hyphen after the prefix *Ab*, he writes *Ab-geschiedenheit;* but he used a word that any German can understand: this is a separation, a setting aside, a withdrawal. On the contrary, forging a neologisms such as *Dis-cès, dis-cédé* does not offer any familiarity or intelligibility in French. Of course, it is a studied transposition, which is not gratuitous since it refers to a more originary separation than a simple departure or death; but it is so abstruse that it obliges the reader to refer to the German. In other words, this is no longer a translation: it is a referral to the origin, which leaves in the French text the esoteric seal of a *non possumus*. We will return to the meaning of such a choice when discussing later polemics.

147. Jean Beaufret, *Le poème de Parménide* (Paris: PUF, 1995), 11n54.

148. Such is the title of a study that Dufrenne admitted was "audacious and for some sacrilegious" and at the end of which he aimed to preserve the conquests of rationalism and even of Marxism ["La mentalité primitive et Heidegger," *Les Études philosophiques* (1954): 284–306]. In that same issue, Jean Hyppolite is much more cautious by offering a few pedagogical pages on "Ontologie et phénoménologie chez Martin Heidegger," 307–314.

149. Alphonse de Waehlens, *Chemins et impasses de l'ontologie heideggérienne* (Paris-Louvain: Desclée de Brouwer-Nauwelaerts, 1953). The title suggests a more critical reading than is actually the case. In fact, it is a paraphrase that goes through the themes of *Holzwege* without taking a position, except in the final questions, the last of which is a good example: "How can we understand the signification of the human being's privilege if he of she does not exercise it?" (52).

150. Edgar Morin has confirmed the importance of this influence: see our interview with Edgar Morin in *Heidegger en France,* vol. 2: *Entretiens.* [TN: This interview with Edgar Morin was not included in the English edition.]

151. "Le principe d'identité," trans. Gilbert Kahn, *Arguments* (April–May 1958): 2–8; "Le mot de Nietzsche *Dieu est mort,*" trans Wolfgang Brokmeier, *Arguments* (1960): 27–33; "Principes de la pensée," trans. François Fédier, *Arguments* (1960): 27–33; "Au-delà de la métaphysique," trans. Roger Munier, *Arguments,* no. 24 (1961): 35–39.

152. This discussion, which took place in February and March, was partially published in the issue of May 28, 1959, of the *Nouvel Observateur.* The original version was reproduced in Kostas Axelos's book, *Arguments d'une recherche* (Paris: Éditions de Minuit, 1969), 93–105.

153. See ibid., 101.

154. Ibid., 104.

155. *Revue internationale de philosophie,* no. 52 (1960). In addition to Birault, the issue included Rudolf Boehm ("Pensée et technique"), Alphonse de Waelhens ("Identité et différence: Heidegger et Hegel"), Jean Paumen ("Heidegger et le thème nietzschéen de la mort de Dieu"), as well as elements of a bibliography of Heidegger's works.

156. *Revue internationale de philosophie,* no. 52, 135–162.

157. Ibid., 135. [See Kojève, *Introduction to the Reading of Hegel,* 259n41.]

158. Ibid., 136.

159. Ibid., 162.

160. He and Maurice Blanchot are the only French authors to be in the *Festschrift* offered to Heidegger for his seventieth birthday (see "La Fable du monde," in *Martin Heidegger zum siebzigsten Geburtstag* [Pfullingen: Neske, 1959], 11–18).

161. "During the three years following Cerisy, Heidegger visited Aix-en-Provence three times. After having been in 1956 and 1957 warmly welcomed in the *Faculté des Lettres,* he gave, on March 20, 1958, his lecture on 'Hegel and the Greeks'" (in *PA,* 323–336). Let us clarify that this lecture was not given at the initiative of the department of philosophy but at the invitation of Professor Sagave, of the Department of German Studies.

162. See the first version of this text, translated by Jean Beaufret and Pierre-Paul Sagave, *Cahier du Sud,* no. 349 (1958): 355–368, and, in particular, the introductory note on page 355.

163. Pierre Aubenque, "*Martin Heidegger (1889–1976). In memoriam,*" *Les Études philosophiques,* no. 3 (1976): 259. François Fédier, commenting on the two photographs of the event published at the beginning of his compendium, gives a different interpretation of the same anecdote: Frederic II in Potsdam is the one who would have pointed out the presence of Bach in the audience: see photos no. 1 and no. 2 and caption, in Fédier, *Soixante-deux photographies.*

164. "Hegel and the Greeks," in *PA,* 323–336

165. See the complete text in Fédier, *Soixante-deux photographies.* See caption of the first photograph.

166. Who had introduced Heidegger's lecture one year earlier, evoking the sojourns of the philosopher in the *pays d'Aix* in the following terms: "Heidegger is very happy every time he returns to the serenity of the countryside of Provence. He likes Cassis where he celebrated his birthday; he enjoys visiting the villages perched on our hills. But what is essential for him is the countryside of Aix, the road of Cézanne, where he took his daily walk during his sojourns among us." Pierre-Paul Sagave, "Martin Heidegger à Aix," *Cahiers du Sud,* no. 344 (1957): 31.

167. "Georg Trakl," *La Nouvelle Revue Française,* 52.

168. Beaufret, preface to Heidegger, *Essais et conférences,* ix.

169. Jean Wahl, "Pages de journal," *Les Temps modernes,* (March–April 1958): 1710 (concerning a lecture by Beda Allemann on Hölderlin).

170. Ibid., 1713.

171. Wahl is referring explicitly (in ibid., 1713) to an article published in *Les lettres modernes* (no. 57, 1958), the complete version of which is reproduced in Axelos, *Vers la pensée planétaire* (Paris: Éditions de Minuit, 1964), 217–225. Referring to the lecture Heidegger gave in Cerisy ("What Is Philosophy?"), Axelos emphasized the following ideas: there is no Heideggerian philosophy; philosophy has Greek origins and speaks Greek; modern humanism presents the human being as absolute subject at the expense of listening to the truth of being. He then insists on Heidegger's "humility": he "only aimed at preparing the path for the thought to come" (221), and in this respect, he initiated a productive dialogue with Marx. He then alluded to the national socialist involvement, noting its brevity but without concealing its gravity, and rejecting the accusation of anti-Semitism: "He was lacking and he lacks political sense" (224). Then he emphasized that Heidegger had advised him not to content himself with a repetitive paraphrase of his work and that he had asked that one "abandon the use of Heideggerian language" in order to engage in "the tasks of a thought to come" (225). In a similar vein, see an account ("Deux livres sur Marx") reproduced in Axelos's book *Arguments d'une recherche* (78–85) in which the latter ironically elaborates on the following scene: "In Freiburg-im-Brisgau—during the twentieth century—lived a man used to spend most of his time in the Black Forest. Almost everybody used to call him a national-socialist and an ontologist and mistreated him as much as they could. Churches, political parties and universities denounced his atheism, his nihilism, his conformism or non-conformism, etc., before a conspiracy of silence was established. The deep reasons for these attack remained, however, well-hidden" (ibid., 81). Axelos identified those reasons elliptically: Heidegger recognized the historical scope of Marx's thought for the planetary era of the accomplishment of metaphysics in technology.

172. Jean Wahl, "Autres pages de journal," *Les Temps Modernes* (October 1958): 755–762. The critique of Char and Ponge, referred to as "little poetizers" (*poètereaux*) is found on page 757.

173. See the January 1959 issue of the *Nouvelle Revue française,* 153–155. Char had the mischievous pleasure of quoting (154) Wahl's incredibly mediocre "verses," imprudently close to the cited pages ("Did I forget my pencil/ in my dressing gown/that I had so carefully placed there yesterday, etc."). The complete text of Char's "open letter" is the following: "With you Sir, the shit no longer climbs up on the horse, as Kierkegaard enjoyed saying, it falls down to the pot. . . . I will from now on see you seated on that round thing, with some soft obelisk hanging loosely from mouth to nostril, such as those with which you fill the pages of your pitiful journal. Your ugly recent lines against Heidegger, your gobbling of a fool, about the marvelous, spring-like Ponge, perfectly translates your state of mind, you, philosopher of public opinion!"

174. "For dawn, the coming day is disgrace; for dusk, the disgrace is the night that engulfs. Long ago there used to be people of dawn. At this time of fall [*tombée*], perhaps we are here.—But why crested like larks?" (poem by Char in *Martin Heidegger zum siebzigsten*

Geburstag [Pfullingen: Neske, 1959], 299). The beautiful text by Jean Beaufret on Leibniz ("La fable du monde") appeared at the beginning of the same book (11–18).

175. This discussion, published in the issue of *France-Observateur* dated from May 28, 1959, is reproduced in Kostas Axelos's *Arguments d'une recherche*, 93–105.

176. Ibid., 93.

177. Ibid., 101.

178. Ibid.

179. Ibid., 93.

180. [TN: *Hypokhâgne* and *khâgne* are part of a two-year program of preparatory classes for the entrance examination to the École Normale Supérieure.]

181. [TN: a student of the École Normale Supérieure.]

182. [TN: A *caïman* is an expression (jargon) at the École Normale Supérieure to designate any teacher who prepares the students for the Agrégation exam.]

6. Renewed Polemics, New Shifts

1. For example, Kostas Axelos's *Marx penseur de la technique* (Paris: Éditions de Minuit, 1961). Axelos situates Marx in the planetary development of a technology characterized by its "errancy": alienation and the forgetting of being are rethought together. Understanding Marx's thought as a "technology" (the word is used by Marx himself to characterize "the active relationship of man towards nature"), Axelos does not reduce it to the exhilaration of its conquests but opens it to the planetary totality that is forming: Heidegger's thought then becomes one of the sources of an interrogation still to be pursued. But this was a critical and antidogmatic approach that could not possibly satisfy the Marxists or "doctrinaire" Heideggerians. Let us also note, on a completely different and resolutely poetical level, the translation (done by a team composed of Jacques Bellefroid, Michel Deguy, François Fédier, Julien Hervier, and Godofredo Iommi) of a text given by Heidegger on February 24, 1951, at Bühlerhöhe that ends with these words, as an echo of one of Sappho's poems: "The beautiful starlings of this sacred service are closer to the essential than all the feathercocks spreading in their inanity." See *Revue de Poésie* (October 1964): 52–57.

2. Martin Heidegger, *Chemins qui ne mènent nulle part* (Paris: Gallimard, 1962); *Holzwege* (Frankfurt am Main: Klostermann, 1957). Wolfgang Brokmeier, who signed the translation, and François Fédier, his "editor," did not work in constant collaboration: the former developed a first version, which was inspired though somewhat "rough," such that the latter had to "smooth it out." The result was good. The French title, drawn from a verse by Rilke, emphasized the sense of *Holzweg* as a dead end, or path to nowhere. However, as the "Editor's note" on page 8 honestly signals, the first sentence of the prologue of the German edition has not been translated: "Holz lautet ein alter name für Wald" [Wood is an old name for forest]. The French translation of the title [*Chemins qui ne mènent nulle part*] leaves out the connotation associated with "forest" in *Holzwege*. The paths in question do not exactly lead "nowhere" as if their only function was to lead one astray, but they lose themselves in the heart of the forest, which the rest of the prologue clarifies (7). The result is a careful and inspired translation even if its daring innovations can sometimes mislead the reader. Let us give but one example, apparently minor, but significant. On page 449, one reads: "Then thinking must take dictation at the hive of being," which is the French translation of "Dann muss das Denken am Rätsel des Seins dichten" (*Holzwege*, 343). If "to take dictation" is a new finding for *dichten* in that context, the "hive of being" is a magnificent metaphor that masks

a complete mistranslation (*Rätsel* means "enigma," "problem," or "riddle"). [TN: The English reads, "Then thinking must poeticize on the enigma of being." Martin Heidegger, "Anaximander's Saying," in *Off the Beaten Path,* ed. and trans. Julian Young and Kenneth Haynes (Cambridge: Cambridge University Press, 2002), 281.]

3. Let us also mention the inspired translation of *Der Satz vom Grund* (Pfullingen: Neske, 1957) by André Préau [*Le principe de raison* (Paris: Gallimard, 1962)]. Jean Beaufret praised its "dynamism" in his preface (a very beautiful variation on the theme of the genealogy of reason on the basis of "the radiant creation of the Greek world . . . still dependent on an origin hidden and latent within it" (ibid., 21). The conclusion of this text is worth noting: less because of the attack against the "intellectuals" than because of the great prudence of the last sentence evoking Heidegger as follows: "And thus he goes, alone, with the step of a peasant, on the path of thought he has chosen for himself, that path which is only a path, not the only path, and of which nothing assures us that it is what one ordinarily understands by 'path'" (ibid., 34).

4. Claude Lévi-Strauss, *The Elementary Structures of Kinship,* ed. Rodney Needham (Boston: Beacon Press Books, 1969); *Structural Anthropology,* trans. Claire Jacobson (New York: Basic Books, 1974).

5. While recognizing this fact, Sartre refused to interpret it as a rallying of Merleau-Ponty to Heidegger: for him, it was because of personal circumstances, in particular because of the loss of his mother, that Merleau felt the need to "to rejoin the imperatives of ontology" and to read Heidegger more closely "to understand him better, but not to be influenced by him." And he added: "Their paths crossed, that was all. Being is the only concern of the German philosopher. And in spite of a philosophy which they at times share, Merleau's principal concern remained man." "Merleau-Ponty vivant," trans. Benita Eisher, in *The Debate between Sartre and Merleau-Ponty,* ed. Jon Stewart (Evanston, Ill.: Northwestern University Press, 1998), 617. That being said, in the "opening towards being" that is central to Heidegger's thought, Sartre perceives "a sense of alienation" (ibid., 617).

6. This was reported by Jean Beaufret (*Dialogue avec Heidegger,* vol. 4, 86): "He (Merleau-Ponty) had henceforth committed himself to stopping what he considered to be a scandal and, since he was a professor at the Collège de France (where Heidegger had just been publicly vilified), he told me, on April 5th 1961, that he had asked the assembly to invite Heidegger. His letter, which I have in front of me, ended symptomatically in the following way: 'Finally, not a word of all this, please, it is better to have a strategy of surprise.'" The attacks mentioned against Heidegger were most probably coming from Robert Minder.

7. See Michel Foucault, *Madness and Civilization: A History of Insanity in the Age of Reason,* trans. Richard Howard (New York: Random House, 1965).

8. Foucault's relation to Heidegger is, however, more secret, although Marcel Gauchet rightly detects a deep, although not declared, Heideggerianism in the fact that reason constitutes itself as exclusion: see François Dosse, *Histoire du structuralisme* (Paris: La Découverte, 1991), 1:454.

9. One finds a trace of this in the following reflection offered by Jacques Rancière: "The generation preparing for the Agrégation included the old guard Heideggerians; for Jean Beaufret, Heidegger's disciple, it was his last year of teaching" (*Histoire du structuralisme,* 1:355).

10. This latent hostility has never ceased. However, at the beginning of the decade with which we are concerned, Jean Beaufret experienced it in the following way: "In 1959, at a dinner at which Lacan and his daughter Judith were present—together with Maurice de Gandillac, Jean Beaufret and Dina Dreyfus, Lévi-Strauss's second wife—a lively argument arose about Heidegger's past. Dina Dreyfus refused even to consider his philosophy, while Beaufret

argued that it had nothing to do with Nazism." Elisabeth Roudinesco, *Jacques Lacan: An Outline of a Life and History of a System of Thought,* trans. Barbara Bray (Cambridge: Polity Press, 1997), 231.

11. Aimé Patri, "Un exemple d'engagement. Martin Heidegger et le nazisme," *Le Contrat social* (January–February 1962): 37.

12. This was a research project that led to his books, *Théorie du récit* and *Langages totalitaires,* both published in 1972 by Hermann.

13. Guido Schneeberger, *Ergänzungen zu einer Heidegger-Bibliographie* (Berne: Francke, 1960), 27 pages and an illustration.

14. See our interview with Jean-Pierre Faye in *Heidegger en France,* vol. 2: *Entretiens.* [TN: This interview with Jean-Pierre Faye was not included in the English edition.]

15. See *Médiations. Revue des expressions contemporaines,* no. 3 (Fall 1961). Heidegger's texts and proclamations are on pages 139–150. Jean-Pierre Faye's commentary ("Heidegger et la *Révolution*") is on pages 151–159.

16. Apart from the one that has just been quoted, these texts include: "German Students," Nov. 3, 1933; "German Men and Women!" Nov. 10, 1933; "Declaration of Support for Adolf Hitler and the National Socialist State," Nov. 11, 1933; "Schlageter," May 26, 1933.

17. Faye, "Heidegger et la *Révolution,*" 152.

18. Ibid., 153.

19. Ibid.

20. Ibid., 154.

21. Ibid., 158 and 159.

22. On both these points, see ibid., 154.

23. Ibid., 159.

24. Faye seems to us, in fact, to avoid—at least in this text—treating Heidegger's thought in a reductive manner. Let us mention this example (ibid., 155): "We do not intend to suggest that Heidegger's project can be reduced to that of Jünger, and that, gradually, step by step, the latter's could be reduced to the cruel myths of the Third Reich, of Rosenberg or of Krieck—whose offices and publications launched several waves of attack against Heidegger. The question is whether their language finds, in the speeches and calls of the latter, a muffled echo, accidentally blended into his own words, or, whether, by these untimely documents, we gain unexpected access to Heidegger's own discourse, as they reveal a thoughtful response to the human condition shaped by modernity."

25. A testimony of this improvement of the climate, in Germany itself, was the ovation that saluted the end of the lecture on "The Question Concerning Technology" on November 18, 1953, in Munich, according to Heinrich Petzet (*Auf einen Stern zugehen* [Frankfort, 1983], 81): "I had the feeling that the ring of defiance and hatred that had surrounded my master and friend had finally been broken."

26. Patri, "Un exemple d'engagement," ibid., 37.

27. "Husserl, under the pressure of the nazi regime, had to abandon his chair in Freiburg, where Heidegger succeeded him." Jean-François Lyotard, *La Phénoménologie* (Paris: PUF, 1954), 11–12. On this point, Aimé Patri ("Un exemple d'engagement," ibid., 38) is right to recall that Husserl had already become professor emeritus by 1928.

28. Aimé Patri (ibid., 37) repeats a quotation from Faye's commentary (in *Médiations,* no. 3, 154) clearly admitting Heidegger's rejection of Hitlerian anti-Semitism.

29. "In quite a confusing way, Faye's commentary juxtaposes the arguments of the defense, of the prosecution and of the balanced judgment, and does not help distinguish between them" (Patri, "Un exemple d'engagement," 39).

30. See ibid., 42.

31. Ibid., 37: "from November 1933 to January 1934." In fact, Heidegger was elected on April 21, 1933.

32. See the clarifications given in our interview with Jean-Pierre Faye, in *Heidegger en France,* vol. 2: *Entretiens.* [TN. This interview with Jean-Pierre Faye was not included in the English edition.]

33. Guido Schneeberger, *Nachlese zu Heidegger. Dokumente zu seinem Leben und Denken* (Berne: Francke, 1962), 288.

34. François Fédier, "Trois attaques contre Heidegger," *Critique,* no. 234 (November 1966): 883–904.

35. The French translation by Éliane Escoubas would only appear with Payot in 1989.

36. Fédier, "Trois attaques contre Heidegger," 885.

37. Ibid., 889.

38. Ibid., 892: "But was Adorno's goal to *understand* Heidegger?"

39. Paul Hühnerfeld, *In Sachen Heidegger: Versuch über ein deutsches Genie* (Hamburg: Hoffmann & Campe Verlag, 1959).

40. Fédier, "Trois attaques contre Heidegger," 900.

41. *Critique,* no. 237 (February 1967): 284–297.

42. Robert Minder, "Langage et nazisme," ibid., 284.

43. Ibid., 285.

44. See ibid. Minder nonetheless concedes the "metaphysical impulse" of the first works and the fact that Heidegger was "a remarkable philosophical technician" (ibid., 287).

45. Ibid., 287.

46. Jean-Pierre Faye, "La lecture et l'énoncé," in *Critique,* no. 237 (February 1967): 288–295.

47. Ibid.

48. Ibid., 291.

49. Ibid., 293.

50. Ibid., 295.

51. Ibid. Faye's response is followed in *Critique* (296–297) by a rather embarrassed clarification by Aimé Patri regretting "the polemical tone" of his first intervention and trying to place himself above the fray: "I am not concerned with all the controversy of M. Faye and Mlle. Lenk with Beaufret, the addressee of the famous 'Letter on Humanism,' his disciples and his friends. It does not concern me and I could not possibly bother with it."

52. François Fédier, "À propos de Heidegger: une lecture dénoncée," *Critique,* no. 242 (July 1967): 672–686.

53. Ibid., 674.

54. Ibid., 675–677. The German text is as follows: "Verwahrt es als den notwendigen Urbesitz des führerischen Menschen in den völkischen Berufen des Staates." [Preserve it as the necessary primal possession of the leader (*führerischen Menschen*) in the *völkisch* professions of the State]. Martin Heidegger, "German Students," trans. William S. Lewis, in *The Heidegger Controversy: A Critical Reader,* ed. Richard Wolin (Cambridge, Mass.: MIT Press, 1993), 46.

55. See the conclusion: Fédier, "À propos de Heidegger: une lecture dénoncée," 686.

56. It is indeed difficult to follow François Fédier when, refusing to translate *Schrecken* by *terreur* [terror], he adopts the word *sursaut* [shock], erasing the incontestable element of fear and fright that the word evokes, after his own admission (ibid., 678). All the same, should we agree to minimize (as he does: ibid., 681–682) the passage in the "Rectoral Address" where the *Erd- und Bluthaften Kräfte,* the "forces that are anchored in blood and soil," were extolled, under the pretext that Buber had made an allusion once to the spiritual character of "blood" in a completely different context?

57. There will also be a more serene epilogue in April 1968 in *Critique*. Fédier ("A propos de Heidegger: Le point," no. 251, 433–437) acknowledged that François Bondy did recognize his mistake: Heidegger never forbade Husserl access to the university library; those apologies resulted in Heidegger's responding to Bondy, indicating that Husserl's daughter, Mrs. Rosenberg, was ready to bear witness: "She knows that during my short year as Rector, and during the four succeeding years, her father, then emeritus, never experienced any problems." While saluting François Bondy's reaction, Fédier did not mention the philological and philosophical critiques that accompanied the clarification in question (Bondy reproached Fédier for having granted too much importance to Hühnerfeld, while neglecting the important work of Schwan, and for having ignored Fourquet's clarification concerning the word *völkisch,* and finally for having given "an excessively narrow definition of national-socialism").

58. Jean-Pierre Faye took up the issue again in a short note in the journal *Études germaniques* ["Heidegger: ou la chaîne de la 'dureté'" (1968): 283–286] where he mocks the "comical depth" of some of Fédier's translations (for example, *Schrecken* becoming "*sursaut*") and argues that his choice for the "hard line" (*ligne dure*) in his own translations was "dictated by the text" (285).

59. This is allegedly what Paul Ricoeur would have said after Levinas's doctoral defense, according to Anne-Marie Lescourret, *Emmanuel Lévinas* (Paris: Flammarion, 1994), 218.

60. These pages are reprinted in Emmanuel Lévinas, *Difficile liberté* (Paris: Albin Michel, 1963), 299–303. See *Difficult Freedom, Essay on Judaism,* trans. Sean Hand (Baltimore: Johns Hopkins University Press, 1997), 231–235.

61. Ibid., 231.

62. Ibid., 232. A beautiful sentence on the same page merits our attention: "The mystery of things is the source of all cruelty towards men."

63. Emmanuel Levinas, *Totality and Infinity,* trans. Alphonso Lingis (The Hague: Martinus Nijhoff, 1979).

64. Ibid., 21.

65. Ibid., 45.

66. Ibid.

67. Ibid., 46.

68. The opposition to the "Heideggerian conception" is explicit on this point: ibid., 27–28.

69. Ibid., 135.

70. Ibid., 284.

71. One should not forget, indeed, that Jacques Derrida's decisive text "Violence et métaphysique. Essai sur la pensée d'Emmanuel Lévinas" already appeared in 1964 in the third and fourth issues of the *Revue de métaphysique et de morale.* It was reprinted as "Violence and Metaphysics: An Essay on the Thought of Emmanual Levinas," in *Writing and Difference,* trans. Alan Bass (Chicago: University of Chicago Press, 1980), 79–153.

72. Ibid., 88.

73. Ibid., 118.

74. Ibid., 133.

75. Ibid., 137.

76. Ibid., 142.

77. Ibid., 143.

78. See ibid., 146–147, 151–152.

79. See Christophe Bident, *Maurice Blanchot partenaire invisible* (Paris: Champ Vallon, 1988), 37.

80. Maurice Blanchot, *Thomas the Obscure,* trans. Robert Lamberton (New York: Station Hill Press, 1988), 29.

81. See ibid. Maurice Blanchot, *The Space of Literature*, trans. Ann Smock (Lincoln: University of Nebraska Press, 1982), 46.

82. Emmanuel Levinas, "The Poet's Vision," in *Proper Names*, trans. Michael B. Smith (Stanford, Calif.: Stanford University Press, 1996), 139.

83. On this influence, in particular in "Literature and the Right to Death," see Bident, *Maurice Blanchot*, 248–249.

84. Bident (ibid., 444) remarks that Blanchot attended the defense of this thesis at the Sorbonne. He above all notes, in addition to the themes that the two friends had in common (radical exteriority, the critique of ontology), those that separated them: "radical atheology, the interruption of any subjective thought" in Blanchot's work.

85. Thus Blanchot, in *The Writing of the Disaster*, trans. Ann Smock (Lincoln: University of Nebraska Press, 1995), 95, proves sensitive to the fact that the translation of *Unverborgenheit* by *désabritement* "leads back to errancy, to the meaning that Plato had suggested in the *Cratylus*."

86. "It put in Hitler's service the *very* language and the *very* writing through which, at a great moment in the history of thought, we had been invited to participate in the questioning designated as the most lofty—that which would come to us from *Being and Time*." Maurice Blanchot, *The Infinite Conversation*, trans. Susan Hanson (Minneapolis: University of Minnesota Press, 1993), 451n4.

87. I will return to this question in the conclusion, "Thinking and Poetry: A Dialogue at the Summit."

88. Maurice Blanchot, "L'attente," in *Martin Heidegger zum siebzigsten Geburstag* (Pfullingen: Neske, 1959), 217–224.

89. Ibid., 221.

90. Ibid., 217.

91. See the translations of Heidegger's commentary on Aristotle (*Physics*, B1) in a few issues of the journal *Aletheia* (January 1964, May 1964, May 1966) published by Axelos's younger colleagues. See our interview with Jean-Luc Nancy.

92. See Jacques Derrida, *The Problem of Genesis in Husserl's Philosophy*, trans. Marion Hobson (Chicago: University of Chicago Press, 2003). (This was Derrida's *Diplôme d'études supérieures*, written in 1953–54, under the direction of Maurice de Gandillac.)

93. See Derrida's interview in this volume. This teaching, following that of Wahl and (much earlier) that of Gurvitch, and preceding the brilliant lectures of Birault and Granel in the 1960s and 1970s, attests that Heidegger was never absent from the lecture courses in the French university, even before the next generation including Rémi Brague, Jean-François Courtine, Françoise Dastur, Éliane Escoubas, Jean-Luc Marion, and Marlène Zarader.

94. Reproduced in Jacques Derrida, *Margins of Philosophy*, trans. by Alan Bass (Chicago: University of Chicago Press, 1984), 1–29.

95. Ibid., 27.

96. Ibid.

97. The last text in the *Holzwege* (296–343). See *Off the Beaten Track*, trans. and ed. by Julian Young and Kenneth Haynes (Cambridge: Cambridge University Press, 2002), 242–281.

98. Derrida, *Margins*, 23.

99. This play was initiated by Heidegger himself in his famous letter to Ernst Jünger, "Über 'die Linie'" This has been included in the essay "On the Question of Being," trans. William McNeill, in *PA*, 291–322.

100. *L'endurance de la pensée: Pour saluer Jean Beaufret* (Paris: Plon, 1968).

101. No name appears on the title page of the book. François Fédier's name appears only as a translator of Heidegger's lecture "On Time and Being."

102. Much more numerous than the pure philosophers, "the literati" (authors, critics, historians, or poets) bear mention: Beda Allemann, Jean-Paul Aron, Jacques Berque, Maurice Blanchot, Michel Butor, Michel Deguy, Dominique Fourcade, Marcel Jouhandeau, Roger Laporte, Henri Mathieu, Roger Munier, and Eugène Vinaver. As for the French philosophers, there are only three of them (Kostas Axelos, Jacques Derrida, and Gérard Granel), while others, from several generations of Jean Beaufret's former students—younger or older—could have been asked to give testimonies of an exceptional pedagogical influence. On the other hand, and no doubt on purpose (but in that case, the operation could only have made things worse for those concerned), one cannot find any well-known philosophers from the French university of those years: Alquié, Aubenque, Canguilhem, Foucault, Gandillac, Hyppolite, Gouhier, Wahl, to name but a few.

103. Gadamer's name is glaring in its absence, while one notes the name of only one philosopher—obviously apart from Heidegger—known within academic circles: Hartmut Buchner, along with a personal friend of Heidegger (Heinrich Wiegand Petzet), and Ingeborg Krummer-Schroth, authors of contributions that were more aesthetic than philosophical.

104. The word *pareonta* has disappeared from Parmenides's quotation at the beginning of the volume, such that the sentence cited literally (and strangely) invites thought to turn toward what is absent, although the complete verse means: "But what is absent, you see, in spite of everything, forecloses presence." Beaufret, *Le Poème de Parménide*, 80–81.

105. Related in these very words in an entire chapter of Christophe Bident's book, *Maurice Blanchot*, 463–468 ("Entre deux formes de l'inavouable: L'affaire Beaufret, 1967–1968"). Contrary to what Bident asserts (468), Laporte's name was not removed from the summary (7) of *L'Endurance de la pensée*. It also appears in the table of contents.

106. On that *affaire*, see Derrida's interview in this volume.

107. "Ousia and Grammē: Note on a Note from *Being and Time*," in *Margins of Philosophy*, 29–69.

108. *SZ*, 432–433n30/*BT*, 410n30.

109. This is Hegel's expression (*Zusatz*, in *Philosophy of Nature: Encyclopedia Part Two*, trans. A. V. Miller [Oxford: Clarendon Press, 1970], sec. 258, 36), used by Derrida, in *Margins*, 36.

110. *Margins*, 38.

111. Ibid., 49.

112. Ibid., 67.

113. See ibid., 62n37, translation modified.

114. Michel Foucault, *The Order of Things: An Archeology of Human Sciences* (New York: Vintage Books Editions: 1994), 42.

115. Hubert L. Dreyfus and Paul Rabinow, *Michel Foucault: Beyond Structuralism and Hermeneutics* (Chicago: University of Chicago Press, 1982).

116. "The Return of Morality," trans. Thomas Levine and Isabelle Lorenz, in *Michel Foucault. Politics, Philosophy, Culture: Interview and Other Writings, 1977–1984*, ed. Lawrence D. Kritzman (New York: Routledge, 1988), 250, translation modified.

117. We refer here to the excellent work of Béatrice Han, *L'ontologie manquée de Michel Foucault* (Grenoble: Millon, 1998). Béatrice Han, *Michel Foucault's Critical Project: Between the Transcendental and the Historical* (Stanford, Calif.: Stanford University Press, 2002), in particular 13, and 188–198.

118. According to Elisabeth Roudinesco, *Jacques Lacan: An Outline of a Life and History of a System of Thought*, 224.

119. Ibid., 225. "Still pursuing his recasting of Freud in the light of Lévi-Strauss, he adopted a different approach to Heidegger's writing from that he had favored before the war. To all

intents and purposes, he accepted Beaufret's interpretation while rejecting Sartre's philosophy of freedom. The clearest evidence of Beaufret's influence is to be seen in the 'Rome Discourse,' written two months after the end of the analysis."

120. Jacques Lacan, *Écrits: The First Complete Translation in English*, trans. Bruce Fink (New York: W.W. Norton, 2007).

121. The text in question is the translation by Lacan of Heidegger's lecture "Logos," in the journal *La Psychanalyse*, no. 1 (1956): 59–79. Alain Juranville's *Lacan et la philosophie* (Paris: PUF, 1984), 127n, mentions it only in passing. Elisabeth Roudinesco (*Lacan*, 226–231) pays more attention to it, but refers to this translation only through the commentaries of others. I will return to this.

122. Lacan, *Écrits*, 50.

123. The text would be published only in 1995, by Galilée in *Études*, 45–62.

124. He did not conceal, even minimally, the inaccessibility felt by Heidegger himself before the "baroque" character of the Lacanian text: see the letter to Medard Boss of December 4, 1996, quoted by Gérard Granel, *Études*, 48n.

125. Ibid., 59.

126. Ibid., 62.

127. Let us mention, however, in addition to the allusions already noted, this excerpt (drawn from *Scilicet*, no. 4, 7–8) reported by Gérard Granel (*Études*, 52): Lacan notes, as regards the close connections between *aletheia* and *Verborgenheit*: "Thus I did not deny the fraternity of this saying, since I only repeat it from a practice that, belonging to another discourse, renders it unquestionable."

128. *Écrits*, 438. "But please don't be content to classify the fact that I am saying so as a case of Heideggerianism, even prefixed by a 'neo-' that adds nothing to the trashy style by which it is common to spare oneself any reflection with the quip, 'Separate that out for me from its mental jetsam,'" ibid.

129. Ibid.

130. A fact noted by Elisabeth Roudinesco. André Préau, translator of "Logos" in *Essais et Conférences*, indeed makes no allusion to it.

131. Fragment 50 in the Diels-Kranz edition, a first translation of which (quite similar to Snell's, used by Heidegger in "Logos") would be: "When you have listened not to me but to the Meaning / It is wise within the same Meaning to say: *One* is All." "Logos" (Heraclitus, Fragment D50), in *Early Greek Thinking: The Dawn of Western Philosophy*, trans. David Farrell Krell and Frank A. Capuzzi (San Francisco: Harper, 1984), 59.

132. This is a quite literal translation adopted by André Préau for *die lesende Lege* (*Essais et Conférences*, 260).

133. In note 1 of Lacan's translation, he writes: "We have undertaken . . . this translation in search of equivalences, which were at times in our view bold enough, so that we decided not to publish it without the German text on the facing page so that Professor Martin Heidegger would honor us by reading it and approving it." "Logos" in *La Psychanalyse*, 59.

134. See Jacques Lacan, ibid., 61n1. Stating a pedantic mistake of the sixteenth century, Lacan adds: "We will see the unexpected convergence of derivations such as to allege (*alléguer*) or to relegate (*reléguer*), with German verbs related to *legen* and we will use the word lay (*lais*) in its older form to translate *Lege*, which will have to be distinguished in the latter part of the text."

135. Jean Bollack, quoted by Elisabeth Roudinesco, *Jacques Lacan*, 228. However, it is impossible to follow Elisabeth Roudinesco when she claims that the paragraph added by Heidegger in 1954 to the version of 1951 (translated by Lacan) clearly expressed the doctrine (of the superiority of the German language over all the others) (ibid., 228): first, this is not

a paragraph but the last pages of the definitive version, and, above all, any reader can see that this "doctrine" is literally not to be found in those pages (see Heidegger, "Logos," in *Early Greek Thinking,* 76–78). It seems that Elisabeth Roudinesco has taken for granted the peremptory conclusion of a subtle essay by Nicholas Rand: "Heidegger's linguistic thought is connected to his Nazi involvement" ["Logos cryptophore," in *Le Cryptage et la vie des œuvres* (Paris: Auber, 1989), 146]. But it is precisely because this connection is not explicitly asserted by Heidegger, at least in this text, that Rand needs all his skills to decipher it through the homophony of *legein* and *lesen.* There are numerous textual indications that Heidegger granted the German language a privileged "vocation in thinking." Does this justify making such a direct connection with his political involvement? The risk is then to reduce what Lacan perceived, on the contrary, as a new beginning of thought by and through language to a lying and politically shameful fiction. The homophony between *legein* and *lesen* was not presented by Heidegger as the only way to listen to Logos, but rather borrowed from the Latin *legere* (in relation to which the French finds all its resources). It remains that while Heidegger engaged in bold etymological ventures, the riches he found, in this case in the Greek *legein,* are confirmed by any good dictionary, as Rand himself had to concede (ibid., 136), quoting Chantraine's *Dictionnaire étymologique de la langue grecque* (Paris: Klincksieck, 1974), 625–626. Incidentally, Elisabeth Roudinesco has later noted that "it is only in the second version of his commentary on Logos, that is to say, after the publication of Farias' book, that Rand showed that the Heideggerian text bore traces of his Nazi involvement" ["Vibrant hommage de Jacques Lacan à Martin Heidegger," *Lacan avec les philosophes* (Paris: Albin Michel, 1991), 236]. In this contribution, Roudinesco insists on the fact that Jacques Lacan's tributes to Martin Heidegger did not prevent the psychoanalyst from disassociating himself from the philosopher, going as far as to be "sacrilegious" (232) in his translation of Logos. Later, between both men, a silence ultimately prevailed, as during the last meeting in 1975 in Freiburg, when Lacan presented his theory of knots, without receiving any response (235).

136. Lacan, "Logos," *La Psychanalyse,* 68.

137. See Bollack's reply: "No truer being manifests itself (or unveils itself) through language." "Réflexions sur les interprétations du logos héraclitéen," in *La Naissance de la raison en Grèce,* ed. Jean-François Mattéi (Paris: PUF, 1990), 184.

138. Jean-Luc Nancy and Philippe Lacoue-Labarthe, *The Title of the Letter: A Reading of Lacan,* trans. François Raffoul and David Pettigrew (Albany: State University of New York Press, 1992), 141. The conclusion of this essay, however, contains a double nuance: on the one hand, one has to take into account the "extreme caution" of the very Heideggerian text on the question of truth; on the other hand, Lacan does not follow Heidegger up to the "laborious, although systematic, blurring of the *aletheia/homoiosis* opposition." (143)

139. Mikkel Borch-Jacobson, *Lacan: The Absolute Master,* trans. Douglas Brick (Stanford, Calif.: Stanford University Press, 1991), 107: "Formally, the Lacanian definition of the 'truth of the subject' is nothing other than truth as subjective certainty—which, by the same token, takes us far from Heidegger" (107).

140. The expression of an "anguished greeting" (*salut déchiré*) was formulated by Axelos on September 25, 1964, in a talk during a France-Culture broadcast on the occasion of the seventy-fifth birthday of the Master: "The anguished greeting that I address to Martin Heidegger for his 75th birthday would wish to encounter his own anguish without being devastated by what is extremely difficult to bear. Heidegger taught me that what was at stake was not to be Heideggerian." This homage is reproduced in Axelos, *Arguments d'une recherche,* 106–107. With respect to these circumstances, see our interview with Kostas Axelos in *Heidegger en France,* vol. 2: *Entretiens.* [TN: This interview with Kostas Axelos is not included in the English edition.] Axelos would not receive any thanks for his homage, and the personal relations

between the two philosophers did not continue. See Éric Haviland, *Kostas Axelos: Une vie, une pensée—une pensée vécue* (Paris: L'Harmattan, 1995), 49–53.

141. In the preceding chapter, we have noted the rapprochement between Jean Beaufret and Jean Guitton. The latter confirmed his interest in Heidegger's thought in "Chemins de campagne. Méditations sur Heidegger," *La Table ronde*, no. 162 (June 1961): 9–15. It is in this excellent journal (which presents itself as a "Revue européenne de recherche chrétienne" [European journal of Christian research]) that Stanislas Fumet published a very lively interview with "a brilliant monk, Dom Jourdain Vermeil," in which Heidegger is praised as a genius who refused atheism, "who seems to go to Mass," and belongs to the family of great mystics. See Stanislas Fumet, "Heidegger et les mystiques," *La Table ronde*, no. 182 (1963): 82–88. In the same issue of the journal, there is a brief contribution by Jean Beaufret on "La pensée du néant dans l'œuvre de Heidegger," 76–81.

142. A little known example of this atmosphere in the 1960s was the unsuccessful attempt to invite Heidegger to the University of Strasbourg in 1963. Lucien Braun had arranged it and had obtained Heidegger's unofficial agreement (the latter wanted to use the occasion to speak about his relations with Husserl). This idea met resistance from the president of the Société de Philosophie, Pierre Burgelin, as soon as it was proposed ("What will they think of this in Paris?"), and encountered even more blatant opposition (André Neher even declared that if Heidegger were to come, he would block him from the entry to the university). The official invitation was therefore never sent. We obtained these details from Lucien Braun (in a conversation on June 22, 2000).

7. Dissemination or Reconstruction?

1. Jacques Derrida, *Dissemination*, trans. Barbara Johnson (Chicago: University of Chicago Press, 1983).

2. See Luc Ferry and Alain Renaut, *French Philosophy of the Sixties: An Essay on Anti-Humanism*, trans. Mary H. S. Cattani (Amherst: University of Massachusetts Press, 1990).

3. Otto Pöggeler, *Martin Heidegger's Path of Thinking*, trans. D. Magurshak and S. Barber (Atlantic Highlands, N.J.: Humanity Books, 2000). This book is a highly rigorous presentation of Heidegger's work. It has the advantage of being faithful to the texts and nuanced in its judgments, and of taking into account the most recent developments at that time (even referring to the unpublished manuscript of the *Beiträge*). However, the reader seeking original inspiration or biting critique would be disappointed. All things being equal, this book would become a primary resource in France, similar to Alphonse de Waelhens's book published thirty years earlier in 1942 in Louvain.

4. Paradoxically, the first volume in this series was *Questions III* in 1966 (This was probably because it included texts already published in French: "Le chemin de campagne," "De l'expérience de la pensée," "Hebel," "Lettre sur l'humanisme"). Two volumes appeared in 1968: *Questions II* (devoted to Greek thought) in March and *Questions I* in November. The latter gathered texts that were already known and previously published ("Qu'est-ce que la métaphysique?" with the introduction and the postscript, "Ce qui fait l'être-essentiel d'un fondement ou raison," "De l'essence de la vérité"), but it also included two new texts: "Identité et différence" (1957), translated by André Préau, and particularly "Contribution à la question de l'être" (1955), a homage to Ernst Jünger, translated by Gérard Granel. It is in this text that the term "Dé-construction" appears as a translation for the *Abbau* of metaphysics (see *Questions I*, 240), which appeared almost simultaneously in the writings of Jacques Derrida and

subsequently enjoyed the reception that is well known. On this issue, see the clarifications by Jean-Pierre Faye, in *Le piège* (Paris: Balland, 1994), 175–187.

5. Jean-Michel Palmier, *Les Écrits politiques de Heidegger* (Paris: Éditions de l'Herne, 1968). Palmier may even have had some sympathies toward Maoism: see Christophe Bourseiller, *Les Maoïstes* (Paris: Plon, 1996), 135, 293.

6. Himself the author of a *Présentation d'Herbert Marcuse* (Paris: Plon, 1968), Palmier saw in Marcuse "the sole authentic disciple of Heidegger with respect to the problem of the completion of metaphysics in the essence of technology" (*Les Écrits politiques*, 287n1).

7. Ibid., 8.

8. Ibid., 9.

9. "In 1968, the worst attacks have failed," wrote Frédéric de Towarnicki (*L'Express*, December 2–8, 1968, 131), even attributing to Claude Lévi-Strauss the following praise of Palmier's book: "This work made me want to read [Heidegger's work] more deeply."

10. François Chatelet, *"Heidegger politique,"* in *La Quinzaine Littéraire* (December 1–15, 1969): 3 and 4.

11. See Jean Beaufret, "Heidegger et la pensée du déclin," in *Dialogue avec Heidegger*, vol. 3: *Approche de Heidegger* (Paris: Éditions de Minuit, 1974), 155–182.

12. In paragraph 38 of *Sein und Zeit*.

13. See Heidegger, *Einführung in die Metaphysik* (Tübingen: Niemeyer, 1958), 139. Translated as "downfall," *Introduction to Metaphysics*, 194.

14. Beaufret, *Heidegger et la pensée du déclin*, 180. Concerning the term "decline" in this context, see my article, "Déclin," in *Vocabulaire de la philosophie contemporaine de la langue française, Les Cahiers de Noésis*, no. 1, Paris, Diffusion Vrin (Printemps 1999): 82–84.

15. Originally from the Creuse, and the son of a teacher who was the socialist mayor of Aubusson, Beaufret had a particular fondness for this town.

16. Their *La Pensée 68* appeared in 1985.

17. In his essay, *Pour l'homme* (Paris: Seuil, 1968), Mikel Dufrenne denounced the convergence between Heideggerian antihumanism and positivism, in two ways: the "bracketing out of beings or of reality" and the "dispossession of the human being" (see 27).

18. *French Philosophy of the Sixties*, 6–12.

19. See the claim according to which "most of the currents of 68 philosophy" belong to "the Heidegerian perspective," ibid., 208.

20. Ibid., 122.

21. *Entretiens Paul Ricœur-Gabriel Marcel* (Paris: Aubier-Montaigne, 1968). Marcel's critiques concerned the reduction of existence to an object of inquiry (12) and the excessive importance accorded to anxiety at the expense of joy (87). Recognizing, however, that he shares with Heidegger the position of a "guardian of the threshold," he declares himself in agreement with Heidegger's thought in its denunciation of the spirit of abstract reasoning and in the welcome accorded to the "sacral dignity of being" (104–105).

22. Paul Ricoeur, *The Conflict of Interpretations*, ed. Don Ihde (Evanston, Ill.: Northwestern University Press, 1974), 223–235.

23. Ibid., 234, 235.

24. Ibid., 223–224. Ricoeur nonetheless minimizes the Heideggerian critique of the cogito by reducing it to its refutation of "an epistemological principle" and by pretending that the issue is less one of a "critique of the *cogito* as such than of the metaphysics that underlies it." Ibid., 224. But how can one dissociate the two critiques?

25. This fact, mentioned by numerous witnesses, was confirmed for us by Jacques Orsoni, who in September 1966 chatted with René Char (among other things about sports and rugby) while the "philosophers" were working.

26. Curd Ochwadt, translator of the German edition of the seminars, noted that René Char participated personally only in the last session of 1966. See Heidegger, *Vier Seminare* (Frankfurt am Main: Klostermann, 1977), 143. Martin Heidegger, *Four Seminars,* trans. Andrew Mitchell and François Raffoul (Bloomington: Indiana University Press, 2004), 87. Although this last session is dated September 9 in the protocol of *Questions IV* (ibid., 207–212) where Jean Beaufret reported on the dialogue between the poet and the philosopher concerning the triple sense of *Kosmos* in Heraclitus, Beaufret himself mentioned the afternoon of September 10 in the heretofore unpublished notes written later and published subsequently by Frédéric de Towarnicki: "A la lisière des lavandes," *Magazine littéraire,* no. 340 (February 1996): 49–54.

27. Jean Beaufret, "Martin Heidegger (1889–1976)," *La Quinzaine littéraire,* no. 235 (June 16–30, 1976): 21. Concerning these places and these circumstances, see Fédier, *Soixante-deux photographies,* in particular, photographs 23–26 with their commentary.

28. Vezin provided the precise details of Heidegger's itinerary during his visit to France in 1966: August 30, departure; stop in Dijon, then in Saint-Didier-sous-Riverie (Rhône), summer residence of Beaufret who joined the trip; arrival in Le Thor September 1, and stay at the Chasselas Hotel until September 12; Heidegger returned home on the 13th, after a stop in Besançon. Vezin comments: "I do not think I am exaggerating when I say that he was delighted by his trip." He also describes the daily schedule: seminar (initially improvised) in the morning; a walk with Char in the afternoon. As far as the discussions are concerned, where French and German alternated, "Jean Beaufret was almost always Heidegger's principal interlocutor." See François Vezin, "Philosophie française et philosophie allemande," in *L'Enseignement par excellence,* ed. Pascal David (Paris: L'Harmattan, 2000), 352–353.

29. Let us not forget that in 1966 Heidegger was already seventy-seven years old.

30. See the interview with Kostas Axelos, in *Heidegger en France,* vol. 2: *Entretiens.* [TN: This interview with Kostas Axelos was not included in the English edition.]

31. The published photographs allow us to recreate the relatively "collegial" atmosphere of these seminars. See François Fédier, *Soixante-deux photographies;* photos 23 to 35 specifically pertain to the 1966 seminar. There were only a few participants: "Vezin, Fédier, Beaufret were joined by two young friends from Italy, Ginevra Bompiani and Giorgio Agamben" (*Questions IV,* 197). The German edition notes that Dominique Fourcade and Roger Munier joined the seminar for a session or a weekend (*Vier Seminare,* 150; *Four Seminars,* 91).

32. "*Das Seminar von 1966* war nicht geplant" (*Vier Seminare,* 142). "The 1966 Seminar was not planned" (*Four Seminars,* 86).

33. Martin Heidegger and Eugen Fink, *Heraclitus Seminar,* trans. Charles H. Seibert (Evanston, Ill.: Northwestern University Press, 1983).

34. Heidegger, *Questions IV,* 197. The protocols from the 1968 and 1969 seminars, reproduced in *Questions IV,* were first privately printed as a pamphlet in limited number, "with the willing generosity of Roger Munier."

35. *Four Seminars,* 2.

36. Ibid., 5.

37. We are referring here to the "protocol" of the session proposed by Jean Beaufret: *Questions IV,* 207.

38. This is an allusion to a posthumous text by Beaufret, published by Fréderic de Towarnicki in *Le Magazine littéraire,* no. 340 (February 1996): 49–54. Beaufret emphasized this encounter at Les Busclats.

39. François Fédier (*Soixante-deux photographies*) noted that the seminar on that day concerned the Heraclitean "Day-Night" fragment, and that the small book on the table (photographs 28 and 29) was the Walzer edition.

40. *Four Seminars,* 9.

41. The German edition adds the following details: Heidegger read his lecture on "Hölderlin's Earth and Heaven," and there was a discussion of Rimbaud, based on his second letter on poetry (May 15, 1871): "Poetry will not lend its rhythm with action. It *will be in advance*" [*La Poésie ne rythmera plus l'action; elle sera* en avant (*Four Seminars,* 87)]. Furthermore, Heidegger mentions seven questions submitted to him by Roger Munier (ibid., 44), of which he cites only the first: "In *Gelassenheit* you speak of a 'power concealed in modern technology.' What is this power that we still do not know how to name and that is 'not made by man'? Is it positive in its origin? Does it belong to that open region (*Gegnet*) in which the human freely unfolds his essence?" (ibid., 88).

42. See ibid., 6, where a quote from *Feldweg* directly illustrates the "singular presence" of Heraclitean opposites.

43. Ibid., 3 and 6.

44. See Fédier, *Soixante-deux photographies;* photos 36 to 50 pertain to the sessions and the walks from September 1968.

45. Once again, these details are not found in the French version but only in the German: *Vier Seminare,* 143. Also see *Four Seminars,* 87.

46. The following participated in all sessions in 1968: Jean Beaufret, François Fédier, François Vezin, Michel Deguy, Gérard Granel, Godofredo Iommi, Federico Camino, Jacques Bontemps, Giorgio Agamben, Patrick Lévy, Michel Podgorny. Participating for only a few sessions were: Roger Munier, Robert Davreu, Dominique Janicaud, Pierre Badonal. This is the list as furnished in the German edition (*Vier Seminare,* 150; see *Four Seminars,* 91). It should be noted that this list does not follow alphabetical order, but rather a sort of implicit hierarchical order. See Epilogue III at the end of this chapter for the author's personal recollections.

47. The German edition notes: "In regard to this last seminar of Heidegger's, held outside the university, the participants came together in a free and friendly agreement" [*in freier freundschaftlicher Übereinkunft*] (*Vier Seminare,* 147; see *Four Seminars,* 89).

48. *Four Seminars,* 63.

49. Ibid., 10.

50. Of course the context of this allusion concerns a specific "phenomenological'" exercise, namely the reinterpretation of a Hegelian aphorism (the usual version of which is "a mended sock is better than a torn sock") that Heidegger reverses as "a torn sock is better than a mended one," while emphasizing the ambiguity of self-consciousness in the part of the sentence that follows: "Not so with self-consciousness [*Selbstbewusstsein*]" (or with consciousness certain of itself?) (*Four Seminars,* 11)

51. *Four Seminars,* 14. See G. W. F. Hegel, *Differenz des Fichte'schen und Schelling'schen Systems der Philosophie* [Philos. Bibl. 62a (Hamburg: Meiner Verlag, 1962)]. English translation: G. W. F. Hegel, *The Difference between Fichte's and Schelling's System of Philosophy,* trans. H. S. Harris and Walter Cerf (Albany: State University of New York Press, 1977), 91: "*Wenn die Macht der Vereinigung aus dem Leben der Menschen verschwindet und die Gegensätze ihre lebendige Beziehung und Wechselwirkung verloren haben und Selbstständikeit gewinnen, entsteht das Bedürfnis der Philosophie.*"

52. *Four Seminars,* 12.

53. Ibid., 24. Heidegger responded in a very interesting manner to the objection according to which the ontological difference would already be present within metaphysics and in particular in Aquinas (in the form of the difference between the *actus purus essendi* and beings). Heidegger's answer consists first in an apparent concession: yes, the ontological difference is formally present in Aquinas, but God as "pure act" is still conceived of as a supreme being; however, the difference is not thought of *as* difference.

54. Ibid., 27. See Hegel, *The Difference between Fichte's and Schelling's System of Philosophy*, 114.

55. *Four Seminars*, 29.

56. Hence the "icy" and even "formal" aspect of this seminar: see our interview with Michel Deguy in *Heidegger en France,* vol. 2: *Entretiens.* [TN: This interview with Michel Deguy was not included in the English edition.]

57. *Four Seminars*, 9. This advice is followed in 1969 (ibid., 51): "It is a matter for a few of us to untiringly work outside of all publicness to keep alive a thinking that is attentive to being, knowing that this work must concern itself with laying the foundation, for a distant future, of a possibility of tradition."

58. On this occasion, the group included: Jean Beaufret, François Fédier, François Vezin, Barbara Cassin, Patrick Lévy, Jean-François Grivas, and for one or two sessions: Roger Munier, Julien Hervier, Robert Davreu, and Franz Larese (*Four Seminars*, 91). See François Fédier, *Soixante-deux photographies;* photos 51 to 56 are related to the 1969 seminar.

59. This was a choice he had already made, for, as we have seen in chapter 5, he had already chosen this text as one of the main references for the meeting at Cerisy.

60. *Four Seminars*, 35.

61. See Kant, *The One Possible Basis for a Demonstration of the Existence of God.* "The concept of position or positing is totally simple and on the whole identical with the concept of being in general" (ibid., 59).

62. *Four Seminars*, 35. Heidegger is referring, somewhat mistakenly and without reference, to Wittgenstein's proposition in the *Tractatus Logico-philosophicus, I.* trans. D. F. Pears and B. F. McGuinness (New York: Routledge & Kegan Paul, 1974), 5: "The world is all that is the case."

63. *Four Seminars*, 35.

64. For the session of August 30, 1968: François Fédier; August 31: Patrick Lévy; September 1: François Vezin; September 2: Michel Deguy; September 4: Jacques Bontemps; September 5: Michel Podgorny; September 6: Frederico Camino; September 8: Gérard Granel. The private printing of the 1969 seminar is not as precise, noting simply: "By: Barbara Cassin, François Fédier, Julien Hervier, Patrick Lévy, François Vezin."

65. The German edition appeared in 1977, one year after the French publication and Heidegger's death.

66. The noncritical character of the edition of these seminars was questioned at the time of the publication of *Questions IV.* A comparison of the private printing of the protocols of 1968 and 1969 with the published text of *Questions IV* shows that some modifications were made. The protocols were slightly edited and "smoothed out" (the names of the protocol recorders were removed). Thus, the protocol for September 8, authored by Gérard Granel, undoubtedly bore the style of the latter in its original version, if only in its ending: "On the silence created by the wind of speculation the session ended, each person content and satisfied." These final words were removed for the edited version. The same holds for the earlier phrase "Director," which is replaced by "Heidegger." In the penultimate paragraph, the allusion to Meister Eckhart was added. These corrections, all in all, were minor.

67. Gilles Deleuze and Felix Guattari, *Anti-Oedipus: Capitalism and Schizophrenia,* trans. Robert Hurley, Mark Seem, and Helen Lane (New York: Penguin Classics, 2009). It is worth recalling that Deleuze's dissertation appeared (was it ironic?) in 1968 with PUF: namely, *Difference and Repetition,* undoubtedly his masterpiece, incidentally a text that is stylistically quite traditional.

68. Jean-François Lyotard, *Libidinal Economy,* trans. Iain Hamilton Grant (London: Continuum, 1984) and a collection of earlier texts, *Driftworks,* trans. Roger Mckeon (New York: Semiotext(e), 1984).

69. Concerning these various aspects of the Parisian intellectual climate immediately following 1968, one can benefit greatly from consulting the excellent text of Vincent Descombes, *Le même et l'autre* (Paris: Éditions de Minuit, 1979), chap. 4, "La fin des temps."

70. One must, for example, mention the publication of posthumous material by Lucien Goldmann under the title *Lukács et Heidegger* (Paris: Denoël/Gonthier, 1973). Goldmann presented a parallel between the early Lukács and the Heidegger of *Being and Time,* while insisting on the fact that both break with the idealist tradition and that they share common positions: "a return to the Hegelian tradition, the rejection of the transcendental subject, a conception of the human being as inseparable from the world of which he or she is a part, and the definition of his or her place in the universe as historicity" (ibid., 67). However, Heidegger's evolution is considered as a return to "romanticism" and his involvement of 1933 is strongly condemned. See, in this regard, the precise observations in the introduction by Youssef Ishagpour (ibid., 37, 38, 42, 45) on the state of the debate concerning the relations between Heidegger and National Socialism.

71. The reason for this is more obvious today: Derrida decided to provide his contribution to *L'endurance de la pensée,* a homage to Jean Beaufret, in spite of a controversy with the latter in 1967–68 concerning the "affair" mentioned in the previous chapter. Nonetheless, explanation is not justification: one can well imagine how the encounters at Le Thor could have assumed a "supplementary" interest (of another style), if Derrida had been invited, even if only once and "discreetly."

72. This footnote, number 37 of *Margins of Philosophy,* 62 (see next note), which was already present in "Ousia and Grammē," a text published in 1968 in the homage to Beaufret, is worth citing in its entirety: "Only such a reading [of the Heideggerian text], on the condition that it does not give authority to the security or structural closing off of questions, appears to us capable of undoing *today, in France,* a profound complicity: the complicity which gathers together, in the same refusal to read, in the same denegation of the question, of the text, and of the question of the text, in the same reeditions, or in the same blind silence, the camp of Heideggerian devotion and the camp of anti-Heideggerianism. Here, political 'resistance' often serves as a highly moral alibi for a 'resistance' of an other order: *philosophical* resistance, for example, but there are other resistances whose political implications, although more distant, are no less determined."

73. All these books appeared in 1972, the first with Seuil and the two others with Minuit.

74. Derrida, *Dissemination,* 17.

75. "Plato's Pharmacy" first appeared in *Tel Quel,* nos. 32 and 33 (1968), as did "The double session," nos. 41 and 42 (1970). The first version of "La dissémination" appeared in *Critique,* nos. 261–262 (1969).

76. Derrida, *Dissemination,* 20.

77. Ibid., 165.

78. Ibid., 206 (the reference to the essay "Moira" from *Early Greek Thinking: The Dawn of Western Philosophy* is here explicit).

79. Ibid., 388 (concerning "the crossing of a line").

80. See our analyses of "Différance" and of "Ousia and Grammē" in the preceding chapter in the section "The Text Makes the 'Différance,'" *HF,* 125–129.

81. Jacques Derrida, *Positions,* trans. Alan Bass (Chicago: University of Chicago Press, 1981), 9. Also 54: "I do maintain . . . that Heidegger's text is extremely important to me, and that it constitutes a novel, irreversible advance, all of whose critical resources we are far from having exploited."

82. Ibid., 54.

83. He does not, at this point, put into question the idea of a unity or of a language of metaphysics. See *Margins*, 16: "This privilege is the ether of metaphysics, the element of our thought that is caught in the language of metaphysics."

84. *Margins*, 27: "There will be no unique name, even if it were the name of being."

85. *Positions*, 55.

86. See his statement on Freud and Lacan (not without reference to Heidegger): *Positions*, 107–113.

87. For example, there was disruption by leftists, which forced him to interrupt a seminar at the École Normale Supérieure that had been organized by Emmanuel Martineau. However, the ethos of 1968 is absent from the *Haut-Pas* discussions organized by Odette Laffoucrière where Beaufret entered into dialogue with Aubenque, Axelos, Bollack, Mgr. Pézeril, and Father Tillette. Beaufret also participated on several occasions in the private seminar given by François Fédier at the Lycée Pasteur and rue Érasme. See our interview with Jean-François Courtine in *Heidegger en France*, vol. 2: *Entretiens*. [TN: This interview was not included in the English edition.]

88. One opportunity was an interview with Roger-Pol Droit in *Le Monde* of September 27, 1974 (18), in which Beaufret summarized with particular clarity his interpretation of Heidegger's political involvement: "His relations to Nazism were thus limited to ten months of administrative collaboration and of publicly proclaimed allegiance. One might think this was already too much. But one cannot forget that these few months were followed by twelve years of exclusion during which his professorial teaching and his silence made him sufficiently intolerable to the authorities such that in 1944 he was forced from the university."

89. Jean Beaufret, *Dialogue with Heidegger: Greek Philosophy*, trans. Mark Sinclair (Bloomington: Indiana University Press, 2006); Jean Beaufret, *Dialogue avec Heidegger*, vol. 2: *Philosophie Moderne* (Paris: Éditions de Minuit, 1973); Jean Beaufret, *Dialogue avec Heidegger*, vol. 3: *Approche de Heidegger* (Paris: Éditions de Minuit, 1974). Jean Beaufret, *Dialogue avec Heidegger*, vol. 4: *Le Chemin de Heidegger* (Paris: Éditions de Minuit, 1984).

90. Beaufret, *Dialogue with Heidegger: Greek Philosophy*, 15–18.

91. It is in this spirit, both meditative and pedagogical, that Jean Beaufret presented his third volume in response to questions from Éryck de Rubercy and Dominique Le Buhan at the beginning of *La Quinzaine Littéraire*, no. 196 (October 16–31, 1974): 3–5, entitled: "Heidegger ouvre le chemin." The following themes were addressed: metaphysics as a thesis about being, the return to the Greeks, the critique of "Christian philosophy," and the essence of technology.

92. Alain Renaut, "Vers la pensée du déclin," *Les Études philosophiques*, no. 2 (1975): 203. Renaut, who presented himself at that time as a guardian of Heideggerian "orthodoxy," took the liberty of addressing a few respectful criticisms to Beaufret concerning the conception of the divine (an allusion to the "simplicity of the Gospels" seemed unfaithful to the Heideggerian preparation of a new experience of the sacred on the basis of a new encounter with being) and concerning the meaning of the decline of the truth of being (which Beaufret was said to have mistakenly understood along the lines of a succession). But he presented (almost too skillfully) these discrepancies between the Master and his principal interpreter as proof that there was indeed a dialogue between Heidegger and Beaufret, and not just a repetition. The critical exchange that he had hoped for with his former professor did not take place.

93. Quoted by Jean Beaufret, *Dialogue with Heidegger: Greek Philosophy*, xxv.

94. Gérard Granel, "Remarques sur l'accès à la pensée de Martin Heidegger, *Sein und Zeit*," in *La philosophie au XXe siècle*, ed. François Châtelet (Paris: Hachette, 1973), 173–215. This text was written in June 1969 and was first published in *Traditionis Traditio* (Paris: Gallimard, 1972), 114–153.

95. "… like Egyptian figures that move forward with the head turned and looking back" (ibid., 115).

96. "The world is called 'transcendent' exactly in the sense in which Dasein, or in which *Sein* itself, are called 'transcendent.' The same transcendence is in play 'in' each of them" (ibid., 204).

97. Ibid., 135.

98. Ibid., 214.

99. Let us recall here Jean-Pierre Faye's monumental work, *Langages totalitaires* (Paris: Hermann, 1972), wherein Heidegger is quoted (about twenty times) in a relatively marginal way (and mostly with respect to the language of his "Rectoral Address"). This work presents itself as a critique of narrative reason (and economy), and investigates in meticulous detail the ideological narratives of the "conservative revolution" and the "semantic oscillators" of German totalitarian ideology. We shall see (in chapters 10 and especially 11) that Faye would return to the specificity of the "Heidegger case" and apply his method of analysis.

100. Jean-Pierre Cotten, *Heidegger* (Paris: Seuil, 1974).

101. Ibid., 25.

102. See ibid., 41: "All this takes place within a problematic where the pre-analytical data cannot be transcended."

103. Ibid., 106.

104. Ibid., 142.

105. Emmanuel Levinas, *Otherwise Than Being or Beyond Essence*, trans. Alphonso Lingis (Dordrecht: Kluwer Academic Publishers, 1991).

106. See ibid., 182, 189n28.

107. This is noted already on ibid., xli.

108. Ibid., 163–164.

109. Ibid., xlii.

110. This, at least, is the title indicated on the cover of issues 5–6 of the *Actes de la recherche en sciences sociales*, November 1975. The actual title that one finds on pages 109–156 is: "L'ontologie politique de Martin Heidegger" ["Martin Heidegger's Political Ontology"].

111. William J. Richardson, *Heidegger: Through Phenomenology to Thought* (New York: Fordham University Press, 2003).

112. Pierre Bourdieu, "Heidegger: un professeur ordinaire," 156. See also: *The Political Ontology of Martin Heidegger* (Stanford, Calif.: Stanford University Press, 1991), 95: "The specific interests of the interpreters, and the very logic of the field which guides toward the most prestigious works the readers with the greatest vocation and talent for hermeneutic hagiography, are not sufficient to explain why Heidegger's thought could have been recognized at one point, in the most divergent sectors of the philosophical field, as the most *distinguished* accomplishment of the philosophical ambition."

113. *The Political Ontology of Martin Heidegger*, 102.

114. See "the family album" and in particular the picture "with Jean in front of the house" on pages 148–149 of the original French version of the article cited in *Actes de la recherche en sciences sociales*.

115. An appropriation that was especially apparent. See Bourdieu, *The Political Ontology of Martin Heidegger*, 8–10.

116. Ibid., 70–87.

117. "Heidegger: un professeur ordinaire," 121. *The Political Ontology of Martin Heidegger*, 92. [TN: The expression "scientific reason" does not appear in the English edition.]

118. See *The Political Ontology of Martin Heidegger*, 81 ("unconscious content to the declared content of discourse"), and 7: "Heidegger is right to affirm that his thinking reflects a critical point."

119. Ibid., 47.

120. One could draw up an impressive inventory of this. For example: mimicry (ibid., 73), making things easy (86), the verbal and pastoral fetishism ("Heidegger: un professeur ordinaire," 118), the interaction (92), the "priestly prophecy" (96), "the professional tricks and tics" (96), the "alchemy of philosophy" (104).

121. Ibid., 83.

122. We find this expression on ibid., 101.

123. The protocol of this seminar, known as the "Zähringen seminar" (the name refers to a neighborhood on the outskirts of Freiburg where Heidegger resided), was published in *Four Seminars* (64–81). This seminar, originally designated by Heidegger as the *Vogesen-Seminar,* was to be held precisely in the Vosges at Le Lyaumont, on Roger Munier's property. Due to his age and fragile health, Heidegger chose to give the seminar at his home. Curd Ochwadt gives the details in Heidegger, *Vier Seminare,* 89–90.

124. These are Roger Munier's terms (in a letter to the author dated October 2, 1998).

125. The volume was published in February 1976. The translators were Jean Beaufret, François Fédier, Jean Lauxerois, and Claude Roëls.

126. The signatories to the letter, dated March 20, 1976, were Ysabel de Andia, Henri Birault, Lucien Braun, Dominique Foucher, Michel Haar, Henri Mongis, Roger Munier, Alain Renaut, and Jacques Taminiaux. Emmanuel Martineau published in the same year a translation of Rudolf Boehm's *La Metaphysique d'Aristote. Le fondamental et l'essential,* with Gallimard, preceded by a learned and brilliant introduction. This erudite Heideggerian recital was not without bold and even baroque translations: foremost among them was *das Wesentliche* rendered as *l'essential.*

127. The contents include the very important lecture "On Time and Being," the protocol of a seminar on this lecture, some marvelous pages on "Art and Space," the lecture (read by Jean Beaufret at UNESCO) on "The End of Philosophy and the Task of Thinking," and three clarifications on the relations to phenomenology, and finally the protocols of the Le Thor and Zähringen seminars.

128. Here is the text of the letter: "*Die Unverborgenheit* translated as 'the Open without withdrawal,' or *das Offene ohne Entzug* (!), which suggests a full presence without concealment, in the metaphysical sense. 'The state of not being in withdrawal' is not better, for the notion of *state* eclipses the temporality of presence."

129. Let us cite the letter again: "*Zur Sache des Denkens* is rendered by 'straight to the question' [*gerade zur Frage*]. The idea of straightness or rectitude designates a metaphysical sense of truth. *Sache* has hitherto been translated as *affaire* [the matter] conforming to the explication which you have given for this term at the beginning of *The Onto-theo-logical Constitution of Metaphysics.*"

130. On this point, the letter presents no argument. In fact, the Beaufret translation is accused of introducing the idea of "retrocession," which is literally absent from "step back." On this point I do not agree with the accusers, for the properly Heideggerian distancing from metaphysics is coupled with an appropriation of its essence. The translation in question does not present any misinterpretation. At most, it overdetermines the German expression, but it is thought-provoking.

131. In the letter addressed to Roger Munier alone, March 27, 1976, Heidegger apologized for not being able to express himself on the "difficulties" in question, suggesting that his French was insufficient and that all the forces of his old age were required for the preparation of his *Gesamtausgabe.* He approved Munier's earlier proposal to put together a translation lexicon shared by all translators. He even suggested that René Char act a as 'mediator' in this project [*Vielleicht könnte René Char, der mit Ihnen wie mit Beaufret gleicherweise befreundet ist, als Vermittler wirken*]. Furthermore, Roger Munier confided to me that Heidegger had

previously expressed, in his presence, the hope that translation questions would be handled by all the translators collaboratively.

132. However, François Vezin published a laudatory review of *Questions IV* in *La Nouvelle Revue Française,* no.284 (August 1976): 80–87. He made no allusion to the criticisms but saluted Jean Beaufret as a "distinguished translator" (80) and proclaimed: "It is an auspicious time for translating Heidegger into French" (86).

133. Emmanuel Martineau, who claimed to be the most faithful of the faithful, as far as issues of content were concerned, did not agree with this characterization. Perhaps one should speak, forcing the comparison with Gaullism, of a "free Heideggerianism."

8. Death and Transfiguration?

1. "Bread and Wine" (4th strophe), "To the Germans" (1st and 2nd strophes), "The Conciliator, Whom None Had Ever Believed . . ." (vv. 1–13), *The Titans* (vv. 1–3), "Bread and Wine" (vv. 41–46). See "Vers de Hölderlin choisis par Heidegger et lus dans cet ordre, selon son vœu par son fils Hermann devant sa tombe ouverte," translation by Michel Haar, in *Martin Heidegger: Cahier de l'Herne,* 120–123. Concerning the burial see Hugo Ott, *Martin Heidegger: A Political Life,* trans. Allen Blunden (New York: Basic Books, 1993), 369–371.

2. Jean Beaufret, "Martin Heidegger (1889–1976)," *La Quinzaine littéraire,* no. 235 (June 16–30, 1976): 21.

3. Numbered 078, dated May 26, 1976, coming from Bonn, this dispatch was signed by Serge Arnold, and was meant to be synthetic and impartial. Some of its more significant passages are worth citing, in the sense that they set the tone for the reception of the time: "He who was one of the most important philosophers of the 20th Century, and whose life corresponds well to the image one has of wise-men detached from worldly realities, making himself understood only in an esoteric language, will not, in the eyes of many, have succeeded in effacing the infamy of a temporary allegiance to the theses and myths of National-Socialism." After a short review of a life "for the most part ordinary" (the involvement of 1933 put aside), the dispatch noted the incomplete nature of *Being and Time* and the fact that Heidegger subsequently devoted essential texts to "the works of others." The reason is the following: "for him, a philosophy is almost impossible as a discourse that would speak the truth of the world and of existence. We are only able to pose questions and the failure of all philosophies is to have forgotten it." In its conclusion, the dispatch tried to balance out the severity ("Heidegger thus appeared as the man of the most useless, most laughable thinking, which searches and which knows that it will not find") with the affirmation of his immense influence: "He has been able to inspire new and profound reflections, to the extent that today one can only think either for or against Heidegger: the representatives of the latest philosophy in France, Gilles Deleuze, Michel Foucault, have read Heidegger . . . and the world's philosophy departments have been filled already during his lifetime by 'Heideggerians.'" My thanks to Claude Roëls for a copy of this dispatch.

4. And on all of page 8 of the same issue.

5. Jean-Michel Palmier ("Heidegger et le national-socialisme," in *Martin Heidegger: Cahier de l'Herne,* 337) nonetheless singled out "this Trotskyite journalist, who, in an article written on the occasion of Heidegger's death, saw in the determination of the human being as being-towards-death the old rallying cry of the Spanish fascists: *Viva la muerte!*"

6. This was the title of Lacroix's article in *Le Monde* of May 28, 1976. He recalled, in a deliberately impartial manner, the great themes of Heidegger's philosophy while insisting on

his influence: "It would be an understatement to say that his immense work has profoundly marked our times."

7. In the section "Repères," a rather neutral summary of the philosopher's career mentioned the following: "For a brief period, he manifested his support for the National-Socialist regime through speeches and articles that would be held against him for a long time. . . . In 1945, a special tribunal ruled that he had been a Nazi 'sympathizer' but not an activist."

8. Thus Guitton noted: "As we might say in France, Heidegger rolled his eyes."

9. Titled: "Vers la fin de la métaphysique." *Le Monde*.

10. *Les Nouvelles littéraires*, no. 2535 (June 3, 1976): 3. Henri Mongis recalled his visits to Heidegger in 1972 and in 1976. The Master was weak, but always very courteous toward his guests. One detail is of interest: "He remained curious about the state of French philosophy. He showed interest in Sartre's evolution. But he told me that he knew nothing about Derrida. I did not know whether his confession was honest or mischievous." Also participating in this issue were Henri Birault, Michel Haar, and Michel Deguy.

11. My thanks to Henri Mongis for having sent me a recording of this program from April 1976. The other participants were Kostas Axelos, Henri Birault, Michel Haar, and Roger Munier. The general tone of the program, titled "Homage to Heidegger," was at the same time didactic and respectful. Nonetheless, things turned clearly polemical with Axelos, who railed against the philosophical movements that were then holding sway in Paris (structuralism, Lacanian psychoanalysis, Althusserian Marxism, etc.). Birault, for his part, took issue with the cliquish culture and the all-too-devout and academic repetitions of Heidegger's thought.

12. *Martin Heidegger interrogé par* Der Spiegel: *Réponses et questions sur l'histoire et la politique*, trans. Jean Launay (Paris: Mercure de France, 1977).

13. He thus maintained having forbidden the burning of books in the university, rejected the charge that he removed the books of Jewish authors from the library, or forbade Husserl access to the philosophy school and its library. "*Der Spiegel* Interview with Martin Heidegger," in *The Heidegger Reader*, 318–320.

14. This is the case for the *Revue Internationale de philosophie, Archives de philosophie,* and *Revue philosophique de Louvain* (1976): 496–497, a simple bio-bibliographical note without commentary, but also for the *Revue philosophique* where we find a brief note signed P.-M. S. (Pierre Maxime Schuhl), in which he managed to make two errors (concerning the date and the title of *Was ist Metaphysik?*) and to conclude with the bizarre euphemism that Heidegger's influence "has reached several philosophers in France," *Revue philosophique*, no. 3 (1976): 381.

15. See the balanced and careful homage by André Doz, "Martin Heidegger," *Revue de métaphysique et de morale*, no. 4 (1976): 433–437.

16. Pierre Aubenque, "Martin Heidegger (1889–1976). *In Memoriam*," *Les Études Philosophiques*, no. 3 (1976): 260.

17. Ibid., 267.

18. Ibid., 262. Concerning the return to the great texts, Aubenque noted that it is "regrettable that this task is misrepresented in French, and at times reversed in a caricatural way, due to the inevitably laborious and awkward element in the translations."

19. The neo-Platonists were, according to Aubenque, the "least metaphysical of the Greek thinkers." This suggestion was often contested by Beaufret, which had not escaped Aubenque's attention ("Even if I have to irritate certain orthodox Heideggerians on this point," ibid., 265).

20. He rejected Bourdieu's "gratuitous insinuation and calumny." The former alluded to what he thought was "the discretely anti-Semitic over-determination of the whole Heideggerian relation to the intellectual world," in his book *Martin Heidegger's Political Ontology*, 120.

21. Pierre Aubenque, "Martin Heidegger (1889–1976). *In Memoriam,*" 269.

22. "Heidegger aujourd'hui," *Magazine littéraire,* no. 117 (1976): 7.

23. Jean-Marie Benoist, "De Héraclite à la Forêt-Noire," *Magazine littéraire,* no. 117 (1976): 9.

24. Ibid., 10.

25. Ibid.

26. Respectively by François Laruelle, Youssef Ishaghpour, and Gérard Legrand.

27. "Le langage des origines," a conversation between Lionel Richard and Robert Minder, *Magazine littéraire,* no. 117 (1976): 21–22.

28. Ibid., 23.

29. This poem was only published three years later in the booklet "Aisé à porter," quoted by Beaufret in *Dialogue avec Heidegger* IV, 128.

30. René Char's letter from May 28, 1976, reproduced by Éryck de Rubercy and Dominique Le Buhan, *Douze questions posées à Jean Beaufret à propos de Martin Heidegger* (Paris: Aubier, 1983), 79.

31. Martin Heidegger, *On the Way to Language,* trans. P. Hertz and Joan Stambaugh (New York: Harper & Row, 1971).

32. Jean Beaufret and Wolfgang Brokmeier translated "Die Sprache im Gedicht," while the other texts were translated by François Fédier, who was also responsible for reviewing the whole text. This translation, begun in 1962, was undertaken with great care. But it was challenged, at its very core, by Philippe Lacoue-Labarthe ("De l'impossibilité de connaître Heidegger en français," *La Quinzaine littéraire,* no. 264 [October 1–15, 1977]: 18–20). According to Lacoue-Labarthe, this translation is a "pure and simple *scandal,*" not because of the lack of competence of the translator, but because of "the ideology of translation" that it follows. The latter obeys "the logic of the gloss" and carries many paraphrases, which are often specious: "How can one distinguish—which is after all indispensable . . . —between what Heidegger actually wrote and what the 'translator' added?" Among the numerous examples given by Lacoue-Labarthe, we can mention *Wesen,* which was rendered, not without any argument, as *déploiement* [unfolding], but without letting the reader know that the word is usually translated as "essence" (this initial choice, incidentally, was not always respected: *Wesen* is translated on page 16 as "existence," and on page 228 as *manière d'être* [way of being]. Lacoue-Labarthe gives other examples: *die Unverborgenheit des Seins* becomes *la retraite de l'être* [the withdrawal of being] (25) and (even more incomprehensible) *die Stimmung* becomes *la corde* [the string] (154).

33. "For René Char, with thanks for the poetical abode during the time of the Thor seminar, with friendly salutations."

34. André Glucksmann, *The Master Thinkers* (New York: Harper Collins, 1980).

35. Ibid., 240.

36. Ibid., 182.

37. Ibid., 183. See also on the previous page this passage: "Heidegger made pro-Nazi speeches during a few months of 1933. . . . Let us leave to those learned men, who are so fortunate as to have avoided this wretchedness the task of showing that it is exclusively a German wretchedness—that we ought to burn Heidegger at the stake for his six months' sympathy with National-Socialism, while glossing over the fifty years spent by others in hailing the (national) socialism of the fatherland of the Gulag Archipelago."

38. Ibid., 183. See also the references to Heidegger in the notes on pages 300, 301, 302.

39. Jean Beaufret, "A propos de *Questions IV* de Heidegger," *Les Études philosophiques,* no. 2 (1978): 235–245. Reprinted in *Dialogue avec Heidegger* IV, 75–87.

40. Alain Renaut, "La fin de Heidegger et la tâche de la philosophie," *Les Études philosophiques,* no. 4 (October–December 1977): 485–492.

41. Ibid., 485–486.

42. Ibid., 487.

43. Ibid., 492. This return to Hegel is accompanied by a critique of Heidegger who is taken to be trying to "*desperately* find an outside to the concept" (ibid., 490).

44. This article, published in *Études Philosophiques,* no. 2 (1978), was reprinted in *Dialogue avec Heidegger* IV, 75.

45. Ibid., 79. Concerning the translation of *Gefahr* by *péril,* no justification is offered either by Renaut (who was opposed to it) or by Beaufret (who was in favor). On the disputed translation of *Nachstellen* as *traque* [hunt], Beaufret emphasized that *traquer* can mean "being in pursuit of" and is in no way limited to the technical sense of a trap set for animals (*das Hetzen*).

46. Ibid., 77 and 80.

47. Ibid., 80.

48. "As for the rest, I strictly have nothing to say." Ibid., 75.

49. "Monsieur Renaut speaks today as Gabriel Marcel did more than twenty years ago when, at Cerisy, he amusingly said of Heidegger: 'He excels in confusing everything.'" Ibid., 83.

50. Ibid., 86.

51. Luc Ferry and Alain Renaut, "*Heidegger en question: Essai de critique interne,*" *Archives de philosophie* 41, no. 4 (October–December 1978): 597–639.

52. Henri Birault, *Heidegger et l'expérience de la pensée* (Paris: Gallimard, 1978).

53. It must be recalled that in 1976 Renaut was still publishing two extraordinarily "orthodox" Heideggerian texts, in a tone inspired by Jean Beaufret: "The decline (*Verbergung*) . . . harbors unearthed wealth and is the promise of a treasure that awaits nothing else that its discovery." Such is the conclusion of the essay "La nature aime à se cacher" [Nature loves to hide"], *Revue de métaphysique et de morale* (March 1976): 111. See also the long essay "Qu'est-ce que l'homme? Étude sur le chemin de pensée de M. Heidegger," *Man and World* 9 (1976): 3–44.

54. The essays by Cotten and Bourdieu have been previously cited. The one by Jean-René Ladmiral is called "Adorno contra Heidegger," in *Présences d'Adorno* (Paris: Plon, 1975), *Revue d'esthétique,* 1.

55. Ferry and Renaut, "*Heidegger en question: Essai de critique interne,*" 603.

56. Ibid., 637.

57. Ibid., 638.

58. The monumental and detailed reconstruction of Heidegger's itinerary by Arion L. Kelkel in *La légende de l'être: Langage et poésie chez Heidegger* (Paris: Vrin, 1980), shows a similar spirit. A scrupulous rereading, which clarifies many details, this enterprise remains nonetheless on the threshold of critical confrontations, which it addresses in its concluding questions (see ibid., 611–624): Must not the dialogue with the thinking of language be supplemented by a (more objective) study of the language of thought? Must philosophy become "philo-logy" to the point of concentrating exclusively on the "source words?" Does Heidegger, *nolens volens,* not become a metaphysician?

59. Birault, *Heidegger et l'expérience de la pensée,* 138.

60. Ibid., 221–273.

61. Ibid., 184.

62. I am making here use of formulations and notions taken from a critical study that I dedicated to this book under the title "Henri Birault et l'expérience de la pensée," in *Les Études philosophiques,* no. 2 (1979): 229–234.

63. George Steiner, *Martin Heidegger,* trans. Denys de Coprona (Paris: Albin-Michel 1981). English edition: *Martin Heidegger* (Chicago: University of Chicago Press, 1991).

64. "It is his complete silence on Hitlerism and the Holocaust after 1945 which is very nearly intolerable" (ibid., English edition, 123). Yet Steiner does not limit himself to this: "To which one ought, in fairness, to add the possibility that the enormity of the disaster and of its implications for the continuance of the Western spirit may have seemed to Heidegger, as it has to other writers and thinkers, absolutely beyond rational comment. But he could, at the very least, have said *this,* and the interest he took in the poetry of Celan shows that he was fully aware of the option" (ibid., 125). Next to this crucial clarification, it seems negligible (although indispensable) to note a factual error that casts a shadow on the end of the book: the "Biographical Note" mentions the Thor seminars given "to a group of French admirers and disciples, which includes the painter Georges Braque and the poet René Char" (ibid., 159). Braque received Heidegger on a visit only once, in 1955, at his home in Varengeville in Normandy, and obviously attended no seminars! As far as Char is concerned, we have seen that he received Heidegger as a friend and outside of the philosophical work sessions.

65. Jacques Derrida, *The Post Card: From Socrates to Freud and Beyond,* trans. Alan Bass (Chicago: University of Chicago Press, 1987).

66. Ibid., 54.

67. See ibid., 63–66.

68. "[T]here is no longer A metaphysics," (ibid., 66).

69. Ibid., 63.

70. See ibid., 477–479, and the entirety of the final essay, "Le facteur de la vérité," 411–496. See also "Freud and Heidegger, Heidegger and Freud," 357.

71. Martin Heidegger, *Die Selbstbehauptung der deutschen Universität: L'auto-affirmation de l'université allemande,* trans. Gérard Granel (Mauvezin: T.E.R., 1982). See "Rectorship Address: The Self-Assertion of the German University," in *The Heidegger Reader,* 108–116.

72. Gérard Granel, "Pourquoi avons-nous publié cela?" in *De l'Université* (Mauvezin: Éditions T.E.R., 1982), 99–143.

73. Ibid., 107.

74. "To say nothing of the Church and of Western democracies, rushing to recognize the new power and to making all sorts of compromises with it," (ibid., 106).

75. On the necessity of this questioning, see Heidegger, "The Rectorship Address," in the *Heidegger Reader,* 111–112.

76. Granel, *"Pourquoi,"* 136.

77. Ibid., 142.

78. Ibid., 123.

79. Among these, there is an apparently minor fact that merits our attention (Raymond Klibansky pointed it out to me): Heidegger's translation of the passage from the Republic (497d) that concludes the address: (*ta megala panta episphalē,* "Alles Grösse steht im Sturm" [All that is great stands in the storm]). Chambry translates more plainly: "great undertakings are always hazardous," but Heidegger gives a serious "emphasis," overly determined by the circumstances, to the adjective *episphalès* ("unsteady," "unstable," "slippery," "even dangerous"). Furthermore, it should be noted that this passage concerns the way in which the State is to treat philosophy: one cannot dare think that this is a coincidence.

80. See ibid., 143.

81. Reiner Schürmann, *Heidegger on Being and Acting: From Principles to Anarchy,* trans. Christine-Marie Gros in collaboration with the author (Bloomington: Indiana University Press, 1987).

82. Ibid., 1.

83. As a committee member, together with Pierre Aubenque and Emmanuel Levinas, I among others raised this objection to Reiner Schürmann at his oral defense at the Sorbonne in June 1981.

84. Schürmann, *Heidegger on Being and Acting*, 6.

85. Ibid., 3.

86. Ibid., 43.

87. See ibid., 168–181 (*Eon, Physis, Aletheia, Logos, Hen, Nous*).

88. See ibid., 182–202 (Will to Power, Nihilism, Justice, Eternal Return of the Same, the Transmutation of all Values, the Overman).

89. See ibid., 203–229 (Ontological Difference/World and Thing, 'There is'/Favor, Unconcealment/Event, Epoch/Clearing, Nearness/Fourfold, Corresponding/Thinking).

90. Particularly the ones that were raised at his oral defense.

91. Schürmann, *Heidegger on Being and Acting*, 4.

92. Ibid., 17n46.

93. It is even oddly noted by the *Le Canard Enchaîné* (Wednesday, September 29, 1982, 7), in an article titled "Ask Inside about What You Don't Find on Display," which interprets the book as an inquiry into the extent of Heidegger's allegiance to Nazism, and takes advantage of this in order to delve into Heidegger's personal life, including his relationship with Hannah Arendt.

94. Evoked by Gérard Granel in "Pourquoi avons-nous publié cela?," 103, in an allusion to three publications: Philippe Lacoue-Labarthe's 1981 study, "Transcendence Ends in Politics," in *Typography*, trans. Christopher Fynsk (Stanford, Calif.: Stanford University Press, 1998), and the 1982 special issue of *Exercises de la patience* and of *Nouvelle École*.

95. Lacoue-Labarthe, "*Transcendence Ends in Politics*," 269.

96. Ibid., 268.

97. "No concept of the political is powerful enough to broach the Heideggerian determination of the political in its essence" (ibid., 287).

98. Ibid., 297.

99. Ibid.

100. Ibid.

101. Luce Irigaray's book, *The Forgetting of Air in Martin Heidegger*, trans. Mary Beth Mader (Austin: University of Texas Press, 1999), is worth singling out. Atypical (insofar as it is neither an academic nor a thematic study), this essay is a dense and difficult reflection that assumes Heidegger's concern for the "clearing" (*Lichtung*), but disputes its grounding in the earth, interpreted as still metaphysical. The aim: "To take away from him this solid ground, to rid him of the 'illusion' of a path that holds up under his step—even if it goes nowhere—and to bring him back not only to thinking but to the world of the pre-Socratics" (2).

102. This is the title of a volume published by Grasset in 1980 (it would deserve a reprinting); the initial occasion was a conference organized in Paris at the Collège des Irlandais, June 24, 1979. Organized by Richard Kearney and Joseph Stephen O'Leary, this anthology, divided into three parts ("Thinking God," "Thinking the Tradition," and "Dialogues"), also contains texts by Heidegger on the question of God and is ripe with tension between Heideggerian orthodoxy (especially Beaufret and Fédier) and the "non-convergence" taken note of and emphasized by Levinas (invoking the God of monotheism beyond its philosophical idea to which Heidegger remained ultimately attached). An undisputable attestation to this remarkable critical openness is offered by the "Introductory Note" written by Paul Ricoeur. The latter spared no words in deploring Heidegger's "systematic avoidance of the confrontation with the entirety of Jewish thought" and his reduction of ethical thought to a "thinking of values." "This misunderstanding seems to me to parallel Heidegger's inability to take 'a step back' in a way that would allow us to adequately think all dimensions of the Western tradition" (ibid., 17). In chapter 12, I will return to the substantive question concerning the possibility of an encounter between Heideggerian thought and the Christian message.

103. In Paris, August 7, 1982.

104. This is the title of the fourth volume of Jean Beaufret's *Dialogue avec Heidegger* (Paris: Éditions de Minuit, 1985). Claude Roëls, who directed this publication, noted that Beaufret "had reviewed and corrected all the gathered texts in this fourth volume." Of the last two, from which the title is drawn, let us note that "En chemin avec Heidegger," which appeared in the *Cahier de l'Herne,* was originally a lecture delivered at the Paris Goethe Institute, January 8, 1981, and presented again at the University of Freiburg, May 7, 1982, three months before Beaufret's death.

105. Beaufret, *Dialogue avec Heidegger* IV, 13.

106. Ibid., 70.

107. Eryck de Rubercy and Dominique Le Buhan, *Douze Questions posées à Jean Beaufret à propos de Martin Heidegger;* Jean Beaufret, *Entretiens avec Frédéric de Towarnicki.* Published one year after Beaufret's death, these two books correspond nonetheless to conversations that would need to be carefully dated. The *Douze Questions* appeared first in 1974, in issue 5 of the journal *Les Lettres Nouvelles,* and were later modified. The *Entretiens* were recorded in May 1981, at the instigation of Yves Jaigu, who was then director of France-Culture, and were broadcast on that radio station in July 1983.

108. Beaufret, *Entretiens avec Frédéric de Towarnicki,* 81.

109. "Pythagoras would have shouted, it's madness! Now Mr. Descartes, calm down!" (ibid., 80).

110. Ibid., 21.

111. Ibid., 32.

112. Ibid., 77. These last lines borrow from the end of an article that I had dedicated to these *Entretiens* in *Le Figaro* of May 11, 1984, 29.

113. The article by François Fédier, "Heidegger, l'édition complète," *Le Débat* (November 1982): 31–40, is dedicated to this task. This text is as it were a technical presentation of the planned edition. Nonetheless, Fédier responded to the objections made by Hans Martin Sass and Hartmut Buchner, who protested against the nonscientific character of this edition (which obscured, according to them, the sources). He maintained that "Heidegger wanted his Collected Works to be his last path" (38) and that "the refusal of a scientific edition is not a *refusal*" (ibid.), in the sense that it did not show "animosity towards the scientific method." Announcing further the planned translation of volumes 21, 24, 26, 32, 39, and 51, as well as the Vezin translation of *Sein und Zeit,* he concluded in the following way: "Everything seems thus ready for a decisive renewal of Heidegger studies in France" (40).

114. *Exercices de la patience,* nos. 3/4 (Spring 1982). This issue, prepared by Francis Wybrands, gathered important contributions (from Munier, Levinas, Birault, Vattimo, Lacoue-Labarthe, Nancy, etc.). It did not attempt to be as encyclopedic or as carefully balanced as the *Cahier de l'Herne* would be.

115. Concerning this whole paragraph, see Michel Haar's preface to *Martin Heidegger: Cahier de l'Herne,* 11–13.

116. Ibid., 20–24.

117. Ibid., 17.

118. Ibid.

119. Ibid., 333–353.

120. This dossier would continue to grow during that same year, 1983, with Fédier's translation of the text written by Heidegger in 1945, although not initially intended for publication: "Le rectorat 1933–1934. Faits et réflexions," *Le Débat,* no. 27 (November 1983): 73–89.

121. See Jean-Michel Palmier, "Heidegger et le national-socialisme," in *Martin Heidegger: Cahier de l'Herne,* 334.

122. Ibid., 339.

123. Ibid., 341.

124. Ibid., 351.

125. Roger-Pol Droit, "Le long voyage de Heidegger," *Le Monde,* Friday, February 24, 1984, 17: "With . . . precision and objectivity, a complete dossier by Jean-Michel Palmier on 'Heidegger et le national-socialisme' renders justice to all the misunderstandings and wild claims provoked by the ten months."

126. "The enormous volume that the *Cahier de l'Herne* dedicated to Heidegger, which was edited by Michel Haar, avoided the trap of hagiography as well as the absurdity of a final assessment, ignored the obscure jargon used by different factions as well as reductive classifications. Neither a mausoleum nor a melting pot, this *Cahier* is already indispensable for any reading of Heidegger that is more attentive to his words than to his reputation" (ibid).

127. "La réserve de l'être," in *Martin Heidegger: Cahier de l'Herne,* 255–268. Chrétien had just published another excellent article, "De l'espace au lieu dans la pensée de Heidegger," in *Revue de l'enseignement philosophique* (February–March 1982): 3–21. Starting from the critique in *Sein und Zeit* of Cartesian extension, he shows the richness of the analyses of the spatiality of *Dasein,* not without noting the paradox of the Heideggerian thinking of place: "It is essentially unifying and gathering, whereas it seems to be, from the perspective of a unique space, closer to a fragmentation and a splintering" (ibid., 50). But the "gift of the open-region" grants the chances of a thought that itself would be "spacious" (20–21).

128. "Histoire de la métaphysique," "La pensée de l'être," "L'époque de la technique," "Politique," "La question de Dieu," "Signes et Chemins."

129. *Martin Heidegger: Cahier de l'Herne,* 414.

130. The expression *der kommende Gott* is found at the end of the third strophe of Hölderlin's hymn "Brot und Wein."

131. See Heidegger, "The Origin of the Work of Art," in *Off the Beaten Path,* 10–14.

132. Jacques Derrida, *The Truth in Painting,* trans. Geoff Bennington and Ian McLeod (Chicago: University of Chicago Press, 1987), 255–382. The first part of this text appeared in the journal *Macula,* in a dossier entitled "Martin Heidegger et les souliers de Van Gogh." The same issue of the journal also contained Schapiro's critical essay on Heidegger: "La nature morte comme objet personnel" (see Derrida's indications in *The Truth in Painting,* 257–259)

133. Derrida, *The Truth in Painting,* 276.

134. Ibid., 301.

135. Ibid., 311.

136. Ibid., 306.

137. Ibid., 309.

138. Ibid., 318.

139. Ibid., 306.

140. Ibid., 354.

141. Ibid., 381.

142. Ibid., 284.

9. The Letter and the Spirit

1. See the interview with Walter Biemel in *Heidegger en France,* vol. 2: *Entretiens.* [TN: This interview with Walter Biemel was not included in the English edition.] According to Claude Troisfontaines, professor at the University of Leuven, the complete translation of *Sein und Zeit* was almost finished, but de Waehlens and Boehm were no longer on very good

terms and not in agreement as far as the translational choices were concerned. Boehm was less and less interested in Heidegger and suggested terms that were too "sophisticated" for de Waehlens (personal conversation of the author with M. Troisfontaines, March 22, 2000).

2. It was indeed in January 1980 that the Gallimard contract with François Vezin was signed, according to the latter's account in his lecture of November 1999, "Vingt ans après, philosophie et pédagogie de la traduction," in a conference held at Jean Moulin University of Lyon. See also our interview with Jean-François Courtine in *Heidegger en France*, vol. 2: *Entretiens*. [TN: This interview with Jean-François Courtine was not included in the English edition.]

3. These are the very terms he used in the note included with each copy, which are worth citing in full:

Dear readers,

After a 58 year delay, here is the book of the 20th Century, *Sein und Zeit*, 1927, in a new and complete translation.

I am happy to offer you a copy of this private publication (none are for sale nor will they be).

Because its limited print-run cannot satisfy the long frustrated demand, which you know to be growing, I would ask you to make its existence at least known to as many of our compatriots and Francophone friends as possible.

What is at stake is not just my personal honor, but also the honor of our country.

I continue to hope that the house of Gallimard, which owns the translation rights to the work, will one day publish it. I leave it up to you to determine if you can contribute to convincing them.

Friends of philosophy, help me!

4. Martin Heidegger, *Être et Temps*, trans. Emmanuel Martineau (Paris: Authentica, 1985). The print run was completed on June 4, 1985.

5. Ibid., "Translator's Preface," 13.

6. "Before his death in 1982, Jean Beaufret asked his disciple François Vezin to translate the masterwork, which had remained inaccessible to those who could not read German. François Vezin, assisted by François Fédier, thus signed a contract with Gallimard in 1980, and was to submit his translation in 1984. The year 1984 came and went, and no manuscript was submitted to Gallimard. François Vezin obtained a four year extension, and that brought us more or less to Easter 1986" (Nicole Casanova, in *Le Quotidien de Paris*, June 10, 1986). Given the date referenced by the journalist, it seems that the extension was for two rather than four years.

7. Or also: "the *chef-d'œuvre* of the Century" (Heidegger, *Être et Temps*, "Translator's Preface," 7).

8. Ibid., 8.

9. Ibid.

10. See especially *Being and Time*, §15–18, and 22.

11. In his note to the French translation of Heidegger, *Les problèmes fondamentaux de la phénoménologie* (Paris: Gallimard, 1985), 12–13.

12. Heidegger, *Être et Temps*, "Translator's Preface," 10.

13. This is the title of an article by Robert Maggiori in *Libération*, March 12, 1987, 30–31.

14. See Martin Heidegger, *Être et Temps*, trans. François Vezin (Paris: Gallimard, 1986), 509.

15. Ibid., 515.

16. Ibid. See Heidegger, *Aus der Erfahrung des Denkens* (Pfullingen: Neske, 1954), 7. French translation by André Préau, *Questions III,* 21. "To head towards a star—this only." In "The Thinker as Poet," in *Poetry Language Thought,* trans. Albert Hofstadter (New York: Harper & Row, 1971), 4. Hereafter cited as *PLT.* See Georges Braque, *Le jour et la nuit* (Paris: Gallimard, 1952), 35. "To head towards a star: those who are ahead are the shepherds, those who march behind carry the whip. On the sides, the unfortunate rearguard."

17. Heidegger, *Être et Temps,* trans. Vezin, 579.

18. Ibid., 535. Vezin suggests that one must think here of Mallarmé writing to Eugène Lefébure on May 17, 1867: "Destruction was my Béatrice." A very nice reference, but one that actually opposes *désobstruction.* It is indeed the French word *destruction* that preserves the magnificent Mallarmean sense. In a rich and precise text going beyond the questions of translation, "Remarques sur la destruction," Gérard Guest credits Vezin with having tried to restore to *Destruktion* its expressive force and its reappropriation of the tradition. But in use, it seems to him that "an essential feature of *Destruktion* risks being *erased*: precisely the 'destructive' moment in 'destruction'" (*L'Enseignement par excellence,* 106).

19. Incidentally, Vezin recognized that the translation of *Destruktion* by *destruction* "is not entirely impossible," as in the case of *Erschlossenheit* rendered as *ouverture* [openness]. Also see François Vezin, "Ouverture, ouvertude," *Heidegger, Semaine de Chexbres, Genos,* I, Lausanne, 1992, 58.

20. See *BT,* §6, 21–22.

21. *Être et Temps,* trans. Vezin, 89.

22. Ibid., 101.

23. Ibid., 98.

24. Ibid., 383.

25. Ibid., 118.

26. Ibid., 120.

27. Ibid., 141.

28. Ibid., 65. It is the only translator's choice to which Vezin later dedicated a brief remark ("Ouverture, ouvertude," 57–58). He maintained that the Heideggerian term (which one cannot find in any dictionary) does not designate an act but a "state"; it is above all not to be taken in the ontic sense, which is the risk with *ouverture.* Translating by *ouvertude,* a neologism (formed on the model of *béatitude, désuétude,* or *plénitude*) thus has the merit of being clear, in the case of a "technical term." However, Vezin must concede at the beginning and at the end of his note that the choice of *ouverture* was also possible, but he withdrew this concession by concluding—with no further explanation—that it would have been a "far-fetched translation." This is an odd statement, for it calls the most eloquent solution in French "far-fetched," and leaves unsolved the question of whether it is desirable to multiply neologisms in an already difficult text.

29. Ibid., 223.

30. Ibid., 104.

31. Ibid., 169.

32. Ibid., 178.

33. Ibid., 363.

34. Maggiori, "La guéguerre Heidegger." Roger-Pol Droit is no more favorable to the Vezin translation in his article in *Le Monde* of December 12, 1986: "Peut-on traduire Heidegger?"

35. Luc Ferry, "Ne laissons pas Heidegger aux heideggériens!" [Let's not leave Heidegger to the Heideggerians!] in *L'Événement du Jeudi* (January 22–28, 1987): 81.

36. Alain Renaut, "Heidegger à la poursuite de l'être," *L'Express,* January 16–22, 1987, 87.

37. Marc B. de Launay ["Note critique sur *Être et Temps, trans. Vezin,*" *Revue de métaphysique et de morale,* no. 3 (July–September 1987): 428–430] does not undertake a detailed criti-

cism but attacks the very project of a "bilingual reading" recommended by Vezin (page 515 of his translation). He finds Vezin's justifications "unacceptable or false." In a lecture given in Lyon ("Vingt ans après," page 11 of the typewritten manuscript cited in note 2), a pleasant chat really in which he *almost* did not address the problems in his translation, Vezin took issue with de Launay, accusing him of "of not wanting to read," and confusing "bilingual reading" with nontranslation. But this polemical reply, which is perhaps to be expected, remains very general.

38. Jean Lacoste is an exception: in an article that attempts to be balanced, he acknowledges that the Vezin translation is "complete, legal, and, given the difficulty of the task, more of a success than the preceding polemics and rumors would have allowed one to believe." He does not criticize the project of a "bilingual reading," because "the work of acclimatization begun by Beaufret is successfully continued by Vezin." Nonetheless, he regrets the absence of a glossary, of an index, and of meaningful notes for the second part of the book [see "*Sein und Zeit* enfin au complet," *La Quinzaine littéraire,* no. 476 (December 11–16, 1986): 9–11.]

39. See *Libération,* Thursday, March 12, 1987, 31.

40. "À propos de Heidegger," *Le Monde,* January 16, 1987. The text is followed by this remark: "This letter was signed by Henri Birault, Lucien Braun, Jacques Colette, Marc Froment-Meurice, Dominique Janicaud, Philippe Lacoue-Labarthe, Jacques Rivelaygue, Jacques Taminiaux, Pierre Trotignon, Francis Wybrans, all of whom are commentators and translators of Heidegger."

41. See Martin Heidegger, *De l'origine de l'œuvre d'art* [The origin of the work of art], first version (Paris: Authentica, 1987). Martineau's satirical text was published at the end of the preface, on pages 9–18, titled: "Post-scriptum (December 1986): D'une 'traduction bilingue' ou Heidegger chez les cinoques."

42. This is Roger-Pol Droit's expression, in "D'un temps pamphlétaire en philosophie," *Le Monde,* Friday, March 20, 1987, 20.

43. "L'horizon de la traduction," François Vezin interviewed by Frédéric de Towarnicki, *Le Magazine Littéraire,* no. 235 (November 1986): 30–33.

44. "Toujours à propos de Heidegger," *Le Monde,* February 6, 1987.

45. Pascal David, "Toujours à propos de Heidegger," *Le Monde.* The other defenders of Vezin's translation were Dominique Fourcade, Henri Crétella, and Gérard Guest.

46. "Au sujet de la traduction," in *Être et Temps,* trans. Vezin, 515–518.

47. Ibid., 517.

48. Ibid., 515.

49. "One receives a lot of practical advice" (ibid., 516).

50. Ibid., 515.

51. Ibid., 516.

52. Referring to page 192 of *Sein und Zeit,* Vezin writes: "Let us compare the existing translations. In de Waehlens and Boehm, we have: "*L'être-déjà-au-monde-en-avant-de-soi-même implique essentiellement l'être en déchéance auprès de l'étant disponible, offert à la préoccupation intérieurement au monde.*" [The being-already-in-the-world-ahead-of-itself implies essentially the fallen *being alongside* usable entities, offered to innerworldly concern.] In Martineau: "*Dans l'être-déjà-en-avant-de-soi-dans-un-monde est essentiellement impliqué l'être échéant auprès de l'à-portée-de-la-main intra-mondain dans la préoccupation.*" [In the being-already-ahead-of-oneself-in-a-world is essentially implied the fallen *being alongside* the intraworldly ready to hand in concern.] I, for my part, wrote: "*Dans l'être-en avance-sur-soi-déjà-en-un-monde est essentiellement inclus aussi l'être en déval après l'utilisable intérieur au monde en préoccupation.*" [In the being-in-advance-of-oneself-already-in-a-world is essentially included the declining *being after* the innerworldly usable in concern.] We can com-

plete this little dossier with the original text: "*Im Sich-vorweg-schon-sein-in-einer-Welt liegt wesenhaft mitbeschlossen das verfallende* Sein beim *besorgten innerweltlichen Zuhandenen.*"

53. "Toujours à propos de Heidegger," *Le Monde*, February 6, 1987.

54. Mistaken or overly clever? The summary (on page 543 of Heidegger, *Être et Temps*, trans. Vezin) that refers to the fourth and tenth sense of *après* in the Littré dictionary makes us lean toward the second hypothesis.

55. Heidegger, *Être et Temps*, trans. Vezin, 538.

56. This citation was alluded to by Vezin, and drawn from the seminar given by Heidegger with Fink on Heraclitus. Martin Heidegger and Eugen Fink, *Heraclitus Seminar*, trans. Charles H. Seibert (Evanston, Ill.: Northwestern University Press, 1993), 17. See François Vezin, "Ouverture, ouvertude," in *Genos*, 57.

57. This corresponds literally to the following formulation: "Phänomenologische Wahrheit (Erschlossenheit von Sein) ist veritas transcendentalis."

58. At issue is an "opening of being" in the subjective as well as the objective sense of the genitive. On this point, we are not in disagreement with François Vezin. "Explicative Note," in Heidegger, *Être et Temps*, trans. Vezin, 538.

59. Beaufret, *De l'existentialisme à Heidegger*, 21, quoted by Vezin, "Explicative Note," in Heidegger, *Être et Temps*, trans. Vezin, 539.

60. See the article on *Ouverture*, I and II. *Le Petit Robert, Dictionnaire de Langue Française* (Paris: Le Robert, 2014).

61. Heidegger, *Être et Temps*, trans. Vezin, 546–547.

62. Ibid., 546.

63. "It is rare to meet a student in Germany or in France who is particularly familiar with Heidegger. Eclipse or decline? Difficult to say" (Jean-Michel Palmier, "Heidegger en France," *Magazine Littéraire* [November 1986]: 38).

64. Didier Franck, *Heidegger et le problème de l'espace* (Paris: Éditions de Minuit, 1986). Scrupulously rereading *Being and Time*, Franck notes an "overestimation of time" and an underestimation of space in its irreducible relation to the flesh. Through the themes of the hand, of touch, of embodied anxiety, the issue is one of showing that "the existential analytic presents a space constituted otherwise (than as *res extensa*)" (90) and of indicating (apparently in the spirit of Merleau-Ponty) the extent to which "the flesh is spatializing as intertwined with and by another flesh" (97). This careful and subtle reading of Heidegger belongs to a thoroughly "immanent" critique.

65. Held on March 12, 13, and 14, 1987 in Paris. The proceedings were published a year later: *Heidegger: Questions ouvertes* (Paris: Osiris, 1988).

66. Max Kommerell and Martin Heidegger, Correspondance, trans. Marc Crépon, *Philosophie*, no. 16 (Fall 1987): 3–16.

67. See Kommerell's terms, ibid., 11.

68. Marc Crépon scrupulously notes: "*Disaster* [*désastre*] translates, somewhat excessively, but in conformity with the tone of the letter, the German term *Unglück*" (ibid., 14). Translating by "misfortune" would no doubt have been more literal. Furthermore, in a letter to Gadamer, Kommerell humorously described Heidegger's essay as a "productive trainwreck" (ibid., 4).

69. Ibid., 16: "You are right. This text is a disaster. *Sein und Zeit* was also a disastrous accident. And any immediate presentation of my thinking today would be the greatest of disasters. Is there perhaps here a first indication that my attempts sometimes approach a true thinking?"

70. "The analogy with religious practices is all the more appropriate since one of the most widespread modes of Hölderlin's reception in France was precisely that of veneration—not

just among poets but also, and perhaps above all, among philosophers, who tended to assimilate, following Heidegger, Hölderlin's 'sacred word' to a 'revelation'" (Isabelle Kalinowski, "Une histoire de la réception de Hölderlin en France: 1925–1967," Doctoral thesis defense, University of Paris XII, May 1999, 5). However, this judgment can be accepted only in the light of an inventory. For example, the *Cahier de l'Herne* on *Hölderlin,* published in 1989 under the direction of Jean-François Courtine, hardly allows this religiosity to appear. Heidegger's influence is clearly present but within limits; and even the texts gathered under the title "Hölderlin et Heidegger" are mostly aporetical. Thus, in his contribution that precisely bears on "Heidegger and Hölderlin's God" (503–511), Michel Haar did not fail to note Heidegger's "hierocentrism" and his studious avoidance of the theme of the Hölderlinian Christ. Heidegger's interpretation is in no way accepted and even less religiously reappropriated: "The intimate tension of the Hölderlinian hymn does not reside first between the immediate evidence of the Sacred and the melancholy of the 'absence of God' or nostalgia for the 'vanished God,' but rather between the joyful feelings of the continual return of the Celestials, between the undeniable overabundant presence of the supreme God and the extreme *difficulty* of celebrating them" (510).

71. Michel Haar, *The Song of the Earth,* trans. Reginald Lilly (Bloomington: Indiana University Press, 1993).

72. Michel Haar published two important books in the following years: *Heidegger and the Essence of Man,* trans. William McNeill (Albany: State University of New York Press, 1993), in which he took issue with Heidegger's antihumanism and Western anthropocentrism; and *La fracture de l'histoire,* (Grenoble: Millon, 1994), in which he reexamined the question of the "overcoming" of metaphysics in light of the Heidegger–Nietzsche debate and of the interpretation of contemporary nihilism.

73. In addition to the following: Gianni Vattimo, *"Nietzsche, interprète de Heidegger"* [Nietzsche, reader of Heidegger]; François Laruelle, *"Sur la possibilité d'une déconstruction 'non-heideggérienne'"* [On the possibility of a 'non-Heideggerian' deconstruction]; Françoise Dastur, *"La fin de la philosophie et l'autre commencement de la pensée"* [The end of philosophy and the other beginning of thinking]; Jeffrey Barash, *"L'image du monde à l'époque moderne"* [The image of the world in the modern era].

74. *Heidegger: Questions ouvertes,* 7. According to Éliane Escoubas, it was Miguel Abensour who conceived of this conference and basically chose the speakers. In order to avoid any incident, this conference was carried out on the basis of invitations alone.

75. Not counting the "French dimension, the Franco-German chronicle in which we are *situating* Heidegger during this conference," following Jacques Derrida's remark. Derrida, *Of Spirit,* 4.

76. Martin Heidegger, *Parmenides,* trans. André Schuwer and Richard Rojcewiz (Bloomington: Indiana University Press, 1992) was published in 1982 by Klostermann.

77. Heidegger, *Parmenides,* 63. "Wir denken das 'Politische' römisch, d.h. imperial."

78. Marc Richir, *"Ereignis,* temps, phénomènes," in *Heidegger: Questions ouvertes,* 13–36 (see above all 24–25).

79. Jacques Garelli, "Temporalité poétique: Topologie de l'être," in *Heidegger: Questions ouvertes,* 37–62.

80. Giorgio Agamben, "The Passion of Facticity," in *Rethinking Facticity,* ed. François Raffoul and Eric S. Nelson (Albany: State University of New York Press, 2008), 89–112.

81. Guy Petitdemange, "Adorno-Heidegger: quelle més-entente?" in *Heidegger: Questions ouvertes,* 97–111.

82. Miguel Abensour ("Rencontre, silence," in *Heidegger: Questions ouvertes,* 247–254) introduced Emmanuel Levinas's lecture and emphasized Heidegger's "unforgivable silence" on the Holocaust in front of Paul Celan, who had come to pay him a visit.

83. Philippe Lacoue-Labarthe, *Heidegger, Art, and Politics: The Fiction of the Political,* trans. Chris Turner (New York: Blackwell, New York, 1990). We shall come back later to this remarkable text, actually published early 1988.

84. According to Éliane Escoubas, this was Levinas's first public intervention about Heidegger since the end of the war.

85. This is a point on which Levinas never wavered, as many can attest. Thus, in his conversations with François Poirié [*Emmanuel Lévinas: Qui êtes-vous?* (Lyon: La Manufacture, 1987)], he noted the following: "Everything seemed unexpected with Heidegger, the wonders of his analyses of affectivity, the different modes of access to the everyday, the difference between being and beings, the well-known ontological difference. The rigor with which all that was thought in the spark of brilliant formulations was absolutely impressive. Until now, this was more important for me than the later speculative consequences of this project: the end of metaphysics, the themes of *Ereignis,* of the *es gibt* in its mysterious generosity" (75). Levinas emphasized that "one would have needed the gift of prophecy" to anticipate the Hitlerian involvement in Davos. However, he added, "I deeply regretted, during the Hitler years, having sided with Heidegger in Davos" (78). See also *Ethics and Infinity: Conversations with Philippe Nemo,* trans. Richard A. Cohen (Pittsburgh, Pa.: Duquesne University Press, 1985).

86. Emmanuel Levinas, "Dying For . . . ," in *Entre Nous: On Thinking-of-the-Other.* trans. Michael B. Smith and Barbara Harshav (New York: Columbia University Press, 1998), 179.

87. Ibid., 181, translation modified.

88. Ibid., 186.

89. Ibid., 187.

90. Ibid., 188.

91. Derrida, *Of Spirit.*

92. Ibid., 1.

93. Ibid., 31.

94. Ibid., 40.

95. Ibid., 86.

96. Ibid., 97.

97. Ibid., 69.

98. Ibid., 69.

99. See, for these different descriptions, ibid., 11, 48, 70, 52.

100. Ibid., 101.

101. Ibid., 112.

102. Ibid., 107.

103. Jacques Derrida confirms this: he was not at all aware of the upcoming publication of the book by Farias. See our interview with Derrida in this volume.

10. The Return of the Repressed?

1. Victor Farias, *Heidegger and Nazism,* ed. Joseph Margolis and Tom Rockmore (Philadelphia: Temple University Press, 1989).

2. In the cases of Staudinger and Baumgarten, see ibid., 110–111 and 119–121.

3. Victor Farias, *Heidegger et le Nazisme* (Paris: Éditions Verdier, 1987), 8. [TN: This passage from the French preface was not translated and published in the English edition.]

4. Ibid., 13–14.

5. *Le Monde,* Wednesday, October 14, 1987, 2.

6. *Libération,* Wednesday, October 16, 1987, 40 and 41.

7. *L'Événement du Jeudi*, October 28 to November 4, 1987, 124–125.

8. *La Quinzaine littéraire*, no. 496 (November 1–15, 1987), 10.

9. Farias, *Heidegger et le Nazisme*, 9.

10. "Martin Heidegger: achèvement de la métaphysique et politique d'extermination" [The end of metaphysics and the politics of extermination], interview with Christian Jambet by Jacques Henric and Guy Scarpetta, *Art Press*, December 1987, 41–44.

11. *Le Monde*, Friday, October 30, 1987, 19.

12. Henri Crétella, professor at the Lycée of Montauban, found the anti-Semitism attributed to Heidegger slanderous, judging exorbitant the importance given by Farias to two secondary texts devoted to Abraham a Sancta Clara, which were written fifty years apart: because Heidegger "has twice celebrated the work of a preacher from the end of the 18th century without saying anything about Sancta Clara's anti-Semitic diatribe, he would be himself, it is suggested to us, something like an advocate and herald of the Holocaust. One much pinch oneself to accept that *Le Monde* had published such an inept perfidy." We note that the preacher in question was of from the seventeenth century and not the end of the eighteenth.

13. Testimony from Jacques Lacant, "curator of the University of Freiburg," who was a member of that committee (*Le Monde*, Friday, October 30, 1987).

14. The testimony of Jean Lassner (ibid.) citing Mrs. Husserl, Christmas 1934: "Heidegger (Husserl's assistant at that time) had been an intimate friend of the family, seeking care and staying with them when he was sick, etc., although he had removed Husserl's portrait at the university, no longer greeted him and crossed the street in order to avoid him. Is it necessary to recall that the dedication to Husserl was removed from editions of *Sein und Zeit* published between 1933 and 1945?"

15. "Heidegger: le chaînon manquant" [Heidegger: The Missing Link], *Libération*, Wednesday, February 17, 1988, 41–42.

16. Ibid., 42.

17. "Heidegger, la piste italienne" [Heidegger, the Italian Trail], Ernest Grassi's comment reported by Charles Alunni and Catherine Paoletti, *Libération*, Wednesday, March 2, 1988, 40–41.

18. *Le Monde*, Wednesday, May 6, 1988, 22. This testimony, published first in the journal *Études*, attests that Heidegger refused in April 1933 to oversee the promotion of a certain Ms. Minz, because she was Jewish, and that, as early as since the Spring of 1932, he allegedly made comments about the philosophy library: "It was the Jews Husserl and Kohn who made a mess there."

19. *Libération*, Thursday, February 8, 1988, 35; "The Heidegger Affair (continued)," *Le Monde*, Friday, February 23, 1990, 27.

20. Further reinforced by the publication of Jean Beaufret's letters to the revisionist historian Robert Faurisson: see Michel Kajman, "Heidegger et le fil invisible" [Heidegger and the invisible thread], *Le Monde*, Friday, January 22, 1988, 1 and 18.

21. Which included, of course, developments on television. The most notable was the broadcast of *Océaniques*, hosted by Michel Cazenave, December 7 and 14, 1987, on FR3 with the participation of George Steiner, Jean-Pierre Faye, François Fédier, and André Glucksmann. Here is the report on the first show in *Libération*, Monday, December 7, 1987, 43: Steiner paid homage to the greatness of the philosophical work while insisting on the infinitely troubling character of Heidegger's silence on the Holocaust. Fédier responded "a bit sheepishly": "I have no information on this silence which has tormented me for a long time. Presumably he did not have anything adequate to say on the matter." Glucksmann, transposing Heidegger's famous sentence, "Science does not think," turned the formulation against its author: "Heidegger denkt nicht" [Heidegger does not think] (with respect to the relation between Nazism and the Holocaust).

22. An interview with Jacques Derrida, "Heidegger, The Philosophers' Hell," reprinted in *Points . . . Interviews 1974–1994*, ed. Elizabeth Weber, trans. Peggy Kamuf et al. (Stanford, Calif.: Stanford University Press, 1995), 181, initially an interview with Didier Éribon, *Le Nouvel Observateur*, November 6–12, 1987, 170. This interview is reprinted in *Points de Suspension* (Paris: Galilée, 1992), 193–202, and followed (203–207) by a brief clarification titled, "How to Concede, with Reasons?" where Derrida rebels against "the gravest and most obscurantist confusions" arrived at on the basis of Farias's book, while suggesting that the critical reading of Heidegger must meditate on the scope of the exchange between the philosopher and Max Kommerell in 1942 concerning Hölderlin: in particular on the shrewd manner in which Heidegger conceded a certain failure of his reading and claimed that "the experience of the disaster" is beyond any "immediate presentation" of his philosophy (see "Correspondence between Martin Heidegger and Max Kommerell," trans. Marc Crépon, *Philosophie*, no. 16 [Fall 1987]).

23. Derrida, "Heidegger, the Philosophers' Hell," 183.

24. Ibid., 186.

25. Ibid., 189.

26. Published in January 1988 as "Heidegger: les textes en appel," *Le Journal littéraire*, no. 2: 115–117.

27. Ibid., 116.

28. Farias, *Heidegger and Nazism*, 288–89.

29. *Le Débat*, no. 48 (January–February 1988): 112.

30. "Martin Heidegger: textes politiques 1933–1934," 176–192. The translation by Nicole Parfait was completed as early as 1984 and delayed at the request of François Fédier, who explained the reasons (ibid., 176). On this point, as well as on the consequences of this affair, I refer to Nicole Parfait's account in her interview in *Heidegger en France*, vol. 2: *Entretiens*. [TN: This interview was not included in the English edition.] She defended a very comprehensive thesis at the University of Paris I, June 6, 1986, on Heidegger and politics: "Théorie et pratique chez Heidegger: Histoire d'une erreur" [Theory and practice in the work of Martin Heidegger: History of an error]. Unfortunately, this thesis has not been published (see *HF*, 484n125 and 485n126). One can get a general sense of it in Nicole Parfait, "Heidegger and Politics: Hermeneutics and Revolution" [Heidegger et la politique: herméneutique et révolution], *Le Cahier du Collège international de philosophie*, no. 8 (1989): 105–108. Heidegger's political error resulted from his teleological and even totalitarian thinking of history; certainly the philosopher seemed to distance himself from this thinking at the end of his work, but he abstained from any radical critique of his previous conception. "It is this abstention from thinking that constitutes the major failure, because with it the unthought becomes the unsaid" (154). The same issue of the journal also contained texts on Heidegger by John Sallis, Werner Marx, and Karl Löwith, edited by Miguel Abensour and Éliane Escoubas and titled "Heidegger: Questions ouvertes II," which was not based on a conference as was the first *Questions ouvertes*.

31. Such is the title of an article by Henri Crétella, a professor of philosophy who is not unknown to readers of this chapter since we just saw him express strong support for Heidegger in the letters to the editors of *Le Monde*, October 30, 1987.

32. Michel Deguy, "Le sozi de Heidegger" [Heidegger's Nazi double], *Le Débat*, no. 48 (January–February 1988): 132.

33. Ibid., 134.

34. Stéphane Mosès, "Radicalité philosophique et engagement politique" [Philosophical radicality and political engagement], *Le Débat*, no. 48 (January–February 1988): 169–171.

35. Alain Renaut, "The Heideggerian 'deviation'?" [*La déviation Heideggérienne?*], *Le Débat*, no. 48 (January–February 1988): 172.

36. Gérard Granel, "La guerre de Sécession ou *Tout ce que Farias ne vous a pas dit et que vous auriez préféré ne pas savoir*" [The War of Secession, or *Everything that Farias has not told you and that you would have preferred not to know*], *Le Débat*, no. 48 (January–February 1988): 142–168.

37. Ibid., 168.

38. Granel also denounces the misuse of the abbreviation "Nazi" and the "*short circuiting . . . at work in Abkürzung as an abbreviation*" (ibid., 146n3).

39. Ibid., 143.

40. Ibid., 145.

41. Ibid., 147.

42. Ibid.

43. Ibid., 156.

44. The printed version does not bear the first name Ludwig because of a production error that was fortunately corrected on my personal copy.

45. "Encore Heidegger et le nazisme" [Again Heidegger and Nazism], *Le Débat*, no. 48 (January–February 1988): 113–123.

46. Farias places the most antinomical movements (traditionalist Catholicism, anticlericalism) in the same basket in order to foster the belief that the young Heidegger was in some way "predestined" to Nazism! See Aubenque, "Martin Heidegger," 114.

47. Aubenque finds these texts insignificant and recalls that the Augustinian monk was a "Rabelais of the pulpit," whose talents had been recognized by, among others, Goethe and Schiller. He did not appear to them as an "anti-Semitic" author, and his diatribes against the Jews (as well as against the Turks) need to be put in the religious and political context of the time. Similarly, the connection of Sachsenhausen, a suburb of Frankfurt, with the concentration camp of the same name, is either ignorance or dishonesty. See ibid., 115.

48. See ibid., 116. The first insinuation consists in attributing an intervention to Himmler that permitted the publication of "Plato's Doctrine of Truth" in *The Annual* edited by Ernesto Grassi. (See Farias, *Heidegger and Nazism*, 236.) The second, which can be attributed to Christian Jambet (page 10 of the preface in the French edition), referred to "murdered militants" in Freiburg during Heidegger's rectorate, with Heidegger making no effort to respond to the complaint: hence the very serious accusation of "complicity in a crime" that Aubenque asked Jambet to retract in future editions.

49. Aubenque cites the accounts of Ochsner and Biemel, Heidegger's students in Freiburg. The latter affirmed that "Heidegger's entourage at the University was the only one in which open criticism of the regime was permitted" (Aubenque, "Martin Heidegger," 117). Also see our interview with Walter Biemel in *Heidegger en France*, vol. 2: *Entretiens*. [TN: This interview with Walter Biemel was not included in the English edition.]

50. On the one hand, Heidegger in no way aligned himself with the populist "old guard" of this movement; on the other hand, Krieck's attacks against Heidegger began as early as February 1934, "and one finds nothing there that prefigured the specific condemnation of the revolutionary 'adventurism' of Röhm" (ibid., 118).

51. Ibid., 119.

52. In spite of "a few attempts by Heidegger in his 1933 speeches that attempted to establish a kind of correspondence, after the fact, between certain themes in *Being and Time* (for example, with respect to work) and his political 'program' at that time" (ibid., 119).

53. Ibid., 120.

54. Ibid., 123.

55. Apart from François Fédier's article, which we prefer to examine at the same time as his book, published in the spring of 1988.

56. Alain Finkielkraut, "Heidegger: la question et le procès" [Heidegger: The question and the trial], *Le Monde*, Tuesday, January 5, 1988, 2.

57. Jacques Derrida, *Of Spirit: Heidegger and the Question*, and *Psyche: Inventions of the Other*, ed. Peggy Kamuf and Elizabeth Rottenberg (Stanford, Calif.: Stanford University Press, 2007).

58. Roger-Pol Droit, "Jacques Derrida et les troubles du labyrinthe" [Jacques Derrida and the challenges of the labyrinth], *Le Monde*, Wednesday, December 4, 1987, 24.

59. Robert Maggiori, "Derrida tient Heidegger en respect" [Derrida keeps Heidegger at a distance], *Libération*, Wednesday, November 27, 1987, 40–42.

60. Ibid., 42.

61. "Written before the publication of Farias's book, this text [*Of Spirit*] is in fact quite bold since it attempts to do what Farias announced but never accomplished. It engaged that which, in Heidegger's writing, thinking, and his *language itself*, tended toward Nazism, went to its encounter and sustained *it*. It did not avoid it: it questioned the avoidance itself" ["Unthinkable thought" (Pensée impensable), letter of M. Moscovici, *Libération*, Tuesday, December 15, 1987, 45].

62. Pierre Bourdieu, *The Political Ontology of Martin Heidegger*, trans. Peter Collier (Stanford, Calif.: Stanford University Press, 1991).

63. "Heidegger by Pierre Bourdieu: The Philosophical Genius" [Heidegger par Pierre Bourdieu: le krach de la philosophie], interview with Robert Maggiori, *Libération*, Thursday, March 10, 1988, vi–vii.

64. It so happens that Derrida already had to intervene a few days earlier concerning the case of Paul De Man, comparable in certain respects to the Heidegger affair [See "A Letter from Jacques Derrida" (Une lettre de Jacques Derrida), *Libération*, Thursday, March 3, vii.]

65. "Derrida-Bourdieu: débat," *Libération*, Saturday and Sunday, March 19 and 20, 1988, 36.

66. Roger-Pol Droit, "Heidegger: la parole à la défense" [Heidegger: The defense has its day in court], *Le Monde*, Wednesday, May 27, 1988, 2.

67. François Fédier, *Heidegger: anatomie d'un scandale* (Paris: Laffont, 1988).

68. Ibid., 31.

69. Roger-Pol Droit even wrote that "this defense is marked by many weaknesses." "Heidegger: la parole à la défense," 2.

70. "Harmful intent" [L'intention de nuire], *Le Débat*, no. 48 (January–February 1988): 136–141.

71. Ibid., 138–139.

72. We point in particular to Hugo Ott's article published in the *Neue Zürcher Zeitung* (November 28–29, 1987): 67. Gérard Guest circulated a French translation before its publication titled "Heidegger et le Nazisme: Chemins et fourvoiements" [Heidegger and Nazism: Paths and errancy], *Le Débat* (March–April 1988): 185–189.

73. Let us note in particular the point-by-point refutation of the so-called new character of the thirteen "discoveries" that Farias had claimed to make (in order to respond to Jacques Derrida's critiques). See Fédier, *Anatomie*, 138–146.

74. Aubenque, "Martin Heidegger," 116.

75. Published in January 1988 with Bourgois, this essay (with the subtitle: *Heidegger, l'art, et la politique*) was originally the written presentation of the thesis dossier *Sur travaux* by Lacoue-Labarthe. As he indicated in his foreword (11–12), a first version with limited print run was published by the Association des Publications près les Universités de Strasbourg. See also "La césure de la pensée," *Exercices de la patience*, no. 8 (Fall 1987): 181–199. The article in *Le Journal Littéraire* critical of Farias mentioned above is reproduced as an appendix (123–137) in Lacoue-Labarthe, *Heidegger, Art and Politics*.

76. Philippe Lacoue-Labarthe, *Poetry as Experience,* trans. Andrea Tarnowski (Stanford, Calif.: Stanford University Press, 1999). A very tense dialogue indeed, through a reading of Celan, which is in no way resolved in the final pages, for the pain caused by Heidegger's silence on the Holocaust is evoked ("Heidegger's irreparable offense," 122).

77. Referred to as "incontestably the greatest thinker of the age" in Philippe Lacoue-Labarthe's *Heidegger Art and Politics,* 9, Heidegger determines the horizon of the problematic: the completion (or closure) of metaphysics: "Philosophy is finished/finite (*La philosophie est finie*); its limit is uncrossable" (ibid., 4). Lacoue-Labarthe nonetheless protests that he is in no way a Heideggerian while accepting Heidegger's claim that "there is no Heideggerian philosophy"! On nihilism, see ibid. 37; 52.

78. Once again, we find a twofold demand where one attempts to reconcile the irreconcilable: to think the abyssal severity of Heidegger's "human failing," not in terms of a constituted ethics (see 31), but on the basis of the historical and destinal "fault" of any ethics: "That is why this event—the Holocaust—is for the West the terrible revelation of its essence" (ibid., 37).

79. Ibid., 19.

80. Ibid., 35.

81. "That God died at Auschwitz is clearly what Heidegger never *said.* But everything suggests that he could have said it if he had wanted, that is if he had agreed to take a certain step which is, perhaps, that of courage" (ibid., 39n4).

82. Ibid., 45–46. This application is itself hyberbolic, since it is an event that is "beyond tragedy."

83. Ibid., 66–67.

84. This play, written by Michel Deutsch in collaboration with Philippe Lacoue-Labarthe, premiered April 20, 1988, in Grenoble and was published with Bourgois that same year. Under the name of Erwin Meister, it presents Heidegger confronted by his former assistant, who had become an officer in the American army, Wolfgang Lerner, during the "denazification" proceedings that took place during the winter of 1945–46. Apart from the change of names and the fiction of the imprisonment of the great thinker in a theater, the "content" refers to the Heidegger case: the philosopher, who only wants to think about ascending to summits or about trivial details, obstinately refuses to recognize a responsibility in his involvement with the Nazis and remains silent in relation to the essential issues. The title, which is quite intriguing and which literally signifies "pardon the expression!" seems to us to be an allusion to a passage from a special article by Éric Weil on "the Heidegger Case": "It is Nazi language, Nazi morality, Nazi thinking (*sit venia verbo*), Nazi feeling, it is not Nazi philosophy" (ibid., 129).

85. Jean-Pierre Faye, "Heidegger, the 'black hole' and the future" [Heidegger, le 'trou noir' et le futur], *Le Monde,* Friday, March 25, 1988, 2.

86. In issue 4 of the Nazi journal *Volk im Werden.*

87. Jean-Pierre Faye, *La raison narrative* (Paris: Balland, 1990).

88. See *HF,* chapter 11, 259. See also "Entretiens with Jean-Pierre Faye" in *Heidegger in France,* vol. 2. [TN: This interview was not included in the English edition.]

89. Jean-François Lyotard, *Heidegger and "the Jews,"* trans. Andreas Michel and Mark Roberts (Minneapolis: University of Minnesota Press, 1990), 93.

90. "Freedom is owed not to the Law but to being. And by this error Heidegger's thought reveals itself, quite despite itself, as, in its turn, the hostage to the Law. Such is its true 'failing'" (ibid., 89, translation modified).

91. Discovered by Robert Maggiori, "Heidegger au nom de la Loi" [Heidegger in the name of the law], *Libération,* Thursday, April 28, 1988, xi.

92. Luc Ferry and Alain Renaut, *Heidegger and Modernity,* trans. Franklin Philip (Chicago: University of Chicago Press, 1990), 2. We are following the chronological order, since the book was available for sale in April 1988, a month after Lyotard's book.

93. Ibid., 21.

94. "The point is not to defend Farias's book," ibid., 22.

95. Ibid., 28 and 118n34.

96. Ibid., 65–66.

97. Ibid., 71.

98. Ibid., 79.

99. Ibid., 44.

100. Ibid., 53.

101. As well as Élisabeth de Fontenay (ibid., 115n16 and 120n29) as regards her text, "Fribourg-Prague-Paris. Comme l'être, la détresse se dit de manières multiples," *Le Messager Européen,* POL, no. 1 (1987).

102. Ibid., 2–3.

103. Ibid., 108.

104. Ibid., 109.

105. Ibid., 95.

106. They would also be posed in Germany thanks to Habermas who, in his presentation of Farias's book to the German public, attempted to adopt a balanced position, salvaging the autonomy of the work with respect to biographical data. The French translation of that work was published in September 1988 [Jürgen Habermas, *Martin Heidegger l'oeuvre et l'engagement,* trans. Reiner Rochlitz (Paris: Éditions du Cerf, 1988)]. In fact, Habermas drew from the work of Pöggeler and Ott, much more than from Farias. Avoiding the temptation to discredit a work that he still considered to be deeply creative (especially through the deconstruction of subjectivity that took place in *Being and Time*), he concentrated his critique against the "essentializing abstraction" through which Heidegger separated the history of being from historical political events and dissolved his own responsibility (and his own disappointment toward the actual Nazism) in an idealizing and "fatalistic" historicism (see 53).

107. This does not exclude the pursuit of research and thereby the enrichment of the historical record: see Jacques Le Rider's article in *Le Monde,* October 14, 1988, 18: "Le dossier d'un nazi 'ordinaire'. Les archives du Quai d'Orsay s'entrouvent aux chercheurs. Jacques Le Rider y a consulté le 'dossier Heidegger'." [The case of an 'ordinary' Nazi. The Archives of the Quai d'Orsay are open to scholars. Jacques Le Rider consulted the 'Heidegger File']. This file shows that even in 1938 Heidegger was not considered to be politically suspect, even though he was attacked by some Nazis such as Rector Krieck.

108. In French in the German text.

109. In French in the German text.

110. Ott, "Heidegger et le Nazisme," 185 (see *HF,* 481n72). We find a more ironically severe reaction to the French success of Farias's book (qualified as a "pseudo-event") in *Die Welt* (Thursday, October 29, 1987): "Things are seen quite differently in Paris."

111. Which, in turn, have also had important repercussions abroad: see Robert Maggiori, "Heidegger mondial" ["Heidegger worldwide"], *Libération,* Monday, December 7, 1987, 42–44.

112. Ott, "Heidegger et le Nazisme," 188.

113. According to Ott, Farias's book, completed in 1985, does not take account of two essential publications from 1986: the Heidegger–Kästner correspondence and Karl Löwith's book, *Mein Leben in Deustchland.* In English as *My Life in Germany before and after 1933: A Report,* trans. Elizabeth King (London: Athlone Press, 1994).

114. Ott, "Heidegger et le Nazisme," 186.

115. Ferry and Renaut, *Heidegger and Modernity*, 15.

116. Lyotard, *Heidegger and "the Jews*," 5.

117. In her account, "Les enjeux du débat autour de Heidegger," published in *Commentaire*, no. 42 (Summer 1988): 474–480, Jeanne Hersch considered that the French debate has been "superficial." Having lived through the summer semester in Freiburg in 1933, she appreciated, on this topic, "the accurate and cautious" accounts provided by Farias's book. On the other hand, she admitted that the book in question was often more indicative of the circumstances than of Heidegger's actual thinking. In this respect, she did not intend to incriminate the person of the philosopher (she did not accuse him of anti-Semitism) but characterized his philosophical approach as "contemptuous" of all that is not wonder before being and as "hugely ambitious" concerning the role of the philosopher. She denounces "a manner of philosophizing that is at once dictatorial and irresponsible" (479). Contrasting him to the great figure of Jaspers, she concluded implacably that Heidegger "is not a true philosopher."

118. See Jean Laplanche and Jean-Bertrand Pontalis, *The Language of Psychoanalysis*, ed. Masud R. Khan (London: Hogarth Press, 1973), 411.

119. Finkielkraut, "Heidegger: la question et le procès."

120. Jean Baudrillard, "Nécrospective autour de Heidegger," *Libération*, Wednesday, January 27, 1988, 2.

121. This extreme ambiguity (affecting the intellectual fascinated by Heidegger) is also noted by Jean-Michel Besnier in *Raison présente*, no. 89 (1989): 126: "Toppling Heidegger's statue no doubt paralyzes the intellectual critic, depriving him or her, with the question of being, of the ultimate transcendent point of view from which to denounce the modern world. But the figure of the pathetic intellectual, who used to think he or she could avoid the malaise by joining with the movement of his or her time, is also affected."

122. "Heidegger, la pensée fascinée," *Libération*, Tuesday, February 16, 1988, 7.

123. For example, one can refer to the publication of a large dossier by the *Nouvel Observateur* (January 22–28, 1988) on "Heidegger and Nazi thought" with this subtitle: "The facts are there. The Heidegger affair is a tragedy for thought, a tragedy one has only just begun to consider." In this dossier prepared by Catherine David, we find contributions by Maurice Blanchot, François Fédier, Hans-Georg Gadamer, Philippe Lacoue-Labarthe, and Emmanuel Lévinas. Let us consider the conclusion of the latter: "The diabolical is thought provoking," as well these lines from Maurice Blanchot: "Heidegger's silence on the Shoah is his irreparable failing. His silence or refusal, faced with Paul Celan, to ask forgiveness for the unforgivable, was a refusal that cast Celan into despair and made him ill. Celan knew that the Shoah was, for the West, the revelation of its essence, and that he had to preserve the shared memory, even if at a great cost, to safeguard the possibility of the relation to the other."

124. See a text by Paul Veyne published a few months after Farias's book: "Responsibilité politique ou hagiographie du philosophe?" *Raison présente*, no. 87 (1988): 27–38. Rising above the narrow polemics for or against Heidegger, Veyne deplores that the "current French debate" is a "false debate." According to him, the political opinions of the man Heidegger, reactionary and petit bourgeois, must be completely separated from his philosophy, the greatness of which cannot be denied and which deserves to be discussed on its own terms, without however, avoiding the suspicion concerning "unrealistic aspects" that can be found therein (34).

125. See *HF*, 479n30. This thesis for a Doctorat d'État of close to one thousand pages directed by Jean-Toussaint Desanti has the following title: "Théorie et pratique chez Heidegger: Histoire d'une erreur" (the *et* is in fact crossed out to indicate the effort of overcoming the opposition of theory and practice). Showing the extent to which Heidegger's thought belongs

to the German tradition of *Gründlichkeit,* she gives a detailed account of the relation between the texts from 1933–34 and *Sein und Zeit* (especially the last paragraphs on historicity). She insists on the continuity of Heidegger's thought despite the thematics of the turn that appeared after the war (in the "Letter on Humanism"). Heidegger's thought is indeed at the heart of the 1933 involvement (the conception of the human being as *Dasein,* of history as destiny, of the situation as opening of authentic possibilities), but its core has nothing to do with the racism that is the heart of Nazi ideology (see "Théorie et pratique chez Heidegger," 923–994).

126. Regarding the various interventions and events that led to this blocking of the publication of her thesis (and also regarding the translations of the "political texts" included in the fourth volume of the thesis), see vol. 2, *Entretiens* with Nicole Parfait. [TN: This interview was not included in the English edition.]

11. Between Erudite Scholarship and Techno-Science

1. A long and detailed study by Nicolas Tertulian on the *Beiträge* ("Histoire de l'être et révolution politique," in *Les Temps Modernes,* no. 523 [February 1990]: 109–136) provoked a reply from Miguel de Beistegui, followed by a rejoinder from Tertulian. While conceding that Heidegger partially disassociated himself from the Nazi regime (in particular regarding the biological racism), Tertulian showed the close connections between Heideggerian thought and a certain idea of National Socialism: "If he never renounced his political views, it was because they were too intertwined with the foundations of his thought" (135). In the no. 529–530 from August–September 1990 (198–213) of the same journal, in an article titled "Qui craint Heidegger?" [Who is afraid of Heidegger?], Miguel de Beistegui accused Tertulian of a strictly reductive and tendentious interpretation of Heidegger's more meditative writings: "Ladies and gentlemen, do not allow the Tertulians of the world to prevent you from reading Heidegger!" (213). Exercising his right to respond in a text titled "Qui a peur du débat?" [Who is afraid of the debate?] (ibid., 214–240), Tertulian justified himself by arguing that in the *Beiträge,* Heidegger continued to pursue the ideal of a radical revolution and maintained the illusion of "guiding the Guide," following Jasper's expression (see in particular, ibid., 229). We should note also in the February 1990 issue of *Les Temps Modernes* (89–108) the article by Myriam Revault d'Alonnes ("Lecteurs de la modernité: Heidegger, Carl Schmitt, Hannah Arendt"), who, while recognizing "the unavoidable character of Heidegger's thought," considered it to be too intimately linked to a deep historical amnesia by the philosophical tradition of the conditions of a refoundation of politics.

2. Ott, *Martin Heidegger.*

3. It is the case of Thomas Ferenczi in *Le Monde,* November 16, 1990: "Twelve years in Heidegger's life. The German historian Hugo Ott confirms that from 1933 to 1945, the philosopher remained faithful to Hitler's regime." This opinion was challenged by Pascal David and Henri Crétella, in *Le Monde,* December 14, 1990 ("Réponse à Hugo Ott," 24).

4. Jean-Michel Palmier, "Heidegger face à l'histoire," in Hugo Ott, *Martin Heidegger: Éléments pour une biographie* (Paris: Payot, 1990), 396. Palmier's postface is not included in the English edition.

5. Without completely disappearing of course. A proof of this is the translation of the book by the American scholar Richard Wolin, *The Politics of Being: The Political Thought of Martin Heidegger* (New York: Columbia University Press, 1990). Presenting itself already as the final account of the impassioned discussions of the end of the '80s, this book argues that the 1933 involvement is rooted in the deep tendencies of Heidegger's work, without claiming,

however, that there is a direct link between these works and Nazism. The thought of the second Heidegger is understood as a self-criticism, but one that was undermined by the denial of his personal responsibilities in favor of the "destiny of being." Ultimately, Wolin turns out to be quite close to Habermas and to the works of Pöggeler and Ott, in relation to whom he does not add much. From the perspective of the French reception, let us note his rejection of the postmodern and deconstructionist readings of Heidegger; in fact he situates himself in the wake of Bourdieu's work to which he explicitly intends to provide a "philosophical supplement" (ibid., 12).

6. Jacob Rogozinski shows in his essay "Dispelling the Hero from Our Soul," *Research in Phenomenology* 21, no. 1 (1991): 73, that if the theme of the hero at the end of *Sein und Zeit* exposes Heidegger to the political adventure, it represents also for *Dasein* "an original, irredeemable alteration which breaks the circle of its solipsistic self-affection." This meditation on the limits of the ontological formalism is taken up again in "*Hier ist kein Warum*: Heidegger and Kant's Practical Philosophy," in *Heidegger and Practical Philosophy,* ed. François Raffoul and David Pettigrew (Albany: State University of New York Press, 2002), 43–64.

7. Jean Quillien, "Philosophie et Politique: Heidegger, le nazisme et la pensée française," in *Germanica* 8 (1990): 103–142.

8. Ibid., 103.

9. Éric Weil, cited by Quillien, ibid., 117.

10. Ibid.

11. Ibid., 127.

12. Ibid., 135.

13. One of the signs of this relatively new situation, characterized by a topology of the "distribution of influences," can be seen in an issue of the journal *Le Débat* with the catchy title, "La philosophie qui vient," no. 72 (November–December 1992). Among twenty-one contributions, only three (Brague, Courtine, and Marion) can be said to have been influenced by Heidegger. The others are silent on Heidegger. The remaining allusions are sarcastic (Vincent Descombes, 94), reserved (André Laks, 149), or openly critical (Marc Richir, 227).

14. A sign among others of the stabilization of this atmosphere can be found in the article "Heidegger (Case)," in *Le Dictionnaire des intellectuels français*, ed. Jacques Julliard and M. Winock (Paris: Éditions du Seuil, 1996). After having summarized the main elements of the polemic by presenting the various points of view, and not without noting "errors and approximations" in Farias, Joël Roman raises the debate, "beyond the factual issues," opening to broader and more fundamental questions concerning Nazism, modernity, and the "political responsibility proper to the thinker (of the writer)."

15. Safranski, *Martin Heidegger: Between Good and Evil*. The original edition was published in 1994 with Carl Hanser Verlag. Its title (*Ein Meister aus Deutschland*) is an allusion to a poignant poem by Paul Celan, "*Todesfuge*" [Death fugue].

16. Rüdiger Safranski, *Schopenhauer and the Wild Years of Philosophy*, trans. Ewald Osers (Cambridge, Mass.: Harvard University Press, 1991).

17. Safranski, *Martin Heidegger: Between Good and Evil*, 429.

18. Ibid., 430.

19. An allusion from Safranski (ibid., 431) to Queequeg, the harpooner, who in *Moby Dick* has a coffin made for him with the inscriptions he bore on his body.

20. Marcel Conche, *Heidegger résistant* (Treffort: Éditions de Mégare, 1996); *Heidegger inconsideré* (Treffort: Éditions de Mégare, 1997).

21. See the conclusion of *Heidegger inconsidéré*, 34.

22. Conche, *Heidegger résistant*, 8.

23. Ibid., 13.

24. On all these points, see Conche, *Heidegger résistant*, 11–17.

25. Ibid., 24.

26. Conche, *Heidegger inconsidéré*, 23.

27. Ibid., 33.

28. Martin Heidegger, *Écrits politiques 1933–1966*, trans. and ed. François Fédier (Paris: Gallimard, 1995).

29. Martin Heidegger, *Die Selbstbehauptung der deutschen Universität: Das Rektorat* (Frankfurt am Main: Klostermann, 1983). Let us recall that "The Self-Assertion of the German University" was published in France and translated as early as 1982 by Gérard Granel with TER publishing house.

30. This is especially the case of the text "Why Do I Stay in the Provinces?" in Thomas Sheehan, ed., *Heidegger: The Man and the Thinker* (New Brunswick, N.J.: Transaction Publishers, 2010), 27–30.

31. Heidegger, *Écrits politiques 1933–1966*, "Préface," 69.

32. Ibid., 95.

33. Ibid., 90.

34. See the conclusion of "Préface," 96.

35. An English language translation of this text can be found in Richard Wolin, ed., *The Heidegger Controversy: A Critical Reader* (Cambridge, Mass.: MIT Press, 1993), 47.

36. The bibliography of this voluminous dossier is systematically ignored. Very rare allusions to Ott and Pöggeler should not mislead us in this respect.

37. Heidegger, *Écrits politiques 1933–1966*, 165–192. The German publication of this reference is: "Die Bedrohung der Wissenschaft," in *Zur philosophischen Aktualität Heideggers*, vol. 1: *Philosophie und Politik*, ed. D. Papenfuss and O. Pöggeler (Frankfurt am Main: Klostermann, 1991), 5–27.

38. "Die eigentliche Bedrohung der Wissenschaft kommt aus ihr selbst und geschieht durch sie selbst" ("Die Bedrohung," 8); Heidegger, *Écrits politiques 1933–1966*, 169. Fédier translates as follows: "The true menace that weighs upon science comes from within itself and takes place through science itself," which again changes the understanding of such menace in terms of a determined, present, and external event, while the paragraph in question bears on the radical transformation of modern science in relation to the science of the middle ages and antiquity.

39. See also the indefensible translation of *Zwiespältigkeit* by "incoherence" (ibid., 177); "Die Bedrohung" (ibid., 15). Heidegger does not state that the relation between National Socialism and science is "incoherent"; he describes it as split and contradictory (one could translate this as schizoid), as what follows confirms (on the one hand, the concern of being close to life, on the other hand, planning and social control). Additionally, Fédier does not give (not even in the notes) the German pagination. At times he forgets to mention his editing of the text (thus in the translation on pages 133 and 176; "Die Bedrohung," pages 11 and 14). In 1996, answering without naming him someone who had referred to his "crestfallen appearance" during the revelation of Heidegger's comportment in the Nazi years [see Philippe Batsale, "Le rêve de Bourdieu," *L'infini*, no. 53 (Spring 1996): 112], Fédier preferred that one speak of his "profound consternation" by the extent to which Heidegger was misunderstood, and he presented his 1995 preface as the suggestion of another hypothesis than that of the definitive guilty involvement: that of a deliberately conditional engagement ["S'il s'agit de rendre justice à Heidegger," *L'Infini*, no. 56 (Winter 1996): 36].

40. Chamfort, *Maximes et pensées* (Paris: Jean-Jacques Pauvert, 1960), 108.

41. Jean Grondin, *Le Tournant dans la pensée de Martin Heidegger* (Paris: PUF, 1987).

42. Cited in ibid., 7.

43. Martin Heidegger, "Letter on Humanism," in *PA*, 250. The essential passage is retranslated correctly by Grondin: "Ici le tout se retourne" [*Hier kehrt sich das Ganze um*]. The failure of the turning from *Being and Time* to "On Time and Being" is in part avoided by the reversal found in "On the Essence of Truth." What is henceforth at stake, according to Heidegger, is "the language of metaphysics." These chiasmic reversals are not in themselves sufficient to cancel its destinal power. They are themselves part of the general movement of the "turning."

44. Richardson, *Heidegger: Through Phenomenology to Thought*, viii–xxiii: "Die Kehre spielt im Sachverhalt selbst" ([The reversal] is inherent in the very matter), xviii.

45. Richardson's book, in and of itself, has a value that is more documentary in nature than properly philosophical. It was more the preface by Heidegger that has contributed to making the book known. Its own value has not seemed sufficient to warrant a translation.

46. Corresponding to the deepening of the problematic of temporality of being: see Jean Grondin, *Le Tournant*, 121.

47. "Not without some mannerisms," as he himself recognized, Grondin described that phase as "aletheic-essentialist." See ibid., 32.

48. This is one of Heidegger's greatest conceits: to dare to believe that his 1927 work is so essential that it is itself a destinal sending, a transformation of the truth of being, and that it announces a shift in history itself (or even outside of it).

49. Ibid., 123.

50. See ibid., 14.

51. Ibid., 127.

52. Jean Greisch, *Ontologie et Temporalité: Esquisse d'une interprétation intégrale de "Sein un Zeit"* (Paris: PUF, 1994).

53. Ibid., v.

54. See ibid., 70.

55. For example, ibid., 77.

56. Ibid., 70.

57. According to an expression by Jean-François Courtine (ibid., 423), referring—in addition to the nonpublication of the third section of *Being and Time*—to the absence of the three great thematic deconstructions that were announced (Kant's schematism, Descartes *Cogito*, Aristotle's treatment of time).

58. Ibid., 1.

59. Theodore Kisiel, *The Genesis of Heidegger's "Being and Time"* (Berkeley: University of California Press, 1993).

60. See Greisch, *Ontologie et Temporalité*, 473, regarding the moment of the appearance of the "ontological difference," but without any specific reference to a text by Beaufret himself. Let us also note, despite an undeniable effort to be thorough, the absence of any allusion to the book that I co-edited with Jean-Pierre Cometti in 1989: *"Être et Temps" de Martin Heidegger: Questions de méthode et voies de recherche* (Marseille: SUD, 1989).

61. See in particular the proceedings of the conference organized at the University of Paris-Sorbonne by Jean-François Marquet in November 1994 and published by Jean-François Courtine as *Heidegger 1919–1929. De l'herméneutique de la facticité à la métaphysique du Dasein* (Paris: Vrin, 1996), with contributions—in addition to the two authors already cited—by Franco Volpi, Michel Haar, I. Schüssler, Françoise Dastur, Jean Greisch, M. Rudgenini, Jean Grondin, Theodore Kisiel, C. Jamme. One must also mention the solid work of Jacques Taminiaux, *Heidegger and the Project of Fundamental Ontology*, trans. and ed. Michael Gendre (Albany: State University of New York Press, 1991), which shows, always precisely on the basis of the texts of the existential analytic, how Heidegger reads and reappropriates Husserl, Kant,

Aristotle, Hegel, Descartes, and Nietzsche. This very careful and critical reading is not a polemic, although it refuses to compromise with respect to the political allusions in the 1934–35 courses on Hölderlin (ibid., 275–278). From the same perspective, Taminiaux accentuates his critical distance from Heidegger in *The Thracian Maid and the Professional Thinker: Arendt and Heidegger,* trans. and ed. Michael Gendre (Albany: State University of New York Press, 1997), the guiding thread of which is the recourse to Arendt's work (and in particular to *The Human Condition*) as a response to the Heideggerian neglect of the phenomenological articulation of the *vita activa*.

62. Martin Heidegger, *Séjours-Aufenthalte,* ed. François Vezin (Paris: Éditions du Rocher, 1992). Martin Heidegger, *Sojourns: The Journey to Greece,* trans. John Panteleimon Manoussakis (Albany: State University of New York Press, 2005).

63. Apart from the translation of *das Gewesene* by *être été* [TN: Literally: "being been"], which Vezin attempts to justify on pages 101–102: while recognizing the "unusual" character of the expression, he argues that it allows one to distinguish *das Gewesene* from the simply bygone past. The problem is that *"l'être été,"* strictly speaking, means nothing in French.

64. As François Vezin indicates on page 89.

65. See, on this point, our interview with Kostas Axelos in *Heidegger en France,* vol. 2: *Entretiens.* [TN: This interview Kostas Axelos was not included in the English edition.]

66. Heidegger, *Sojourns,* 19.

67. Ibid., 22–23.

68. The main publications in French of this great Hellenist, who was greatly admired by Heidegger, include: *Les Dieux de la Grèce* (Paris: Payot, 1981); *Dionysos* (Paris: Mercure de France, 1969); *Essais sur les mythes* (Mauvezin: TER, 1987).

69. Heidegger, *Sojourns,* 36.

70. Ibid., 48.

71. Ibid., 37.

72. It was to Heidegger's credit that he recognized this, in the explicit terms of a self-criticism. *Zur Sache des Denkens* (Tübingen: Niemeyer, 1979), 78. *On Time and Being,* trans. Joan Stambaugh (Chicago: University of Chicago Press, 1992), 71.

73. Martin Heidegger, *Sojourns,* 1–3, 5–6, 9–10, 17–18, 26, 34–36, 38–39, 43–44, 53–56.

74. Jacques Derrida, *Athens: Still Remains,* trans. Pascale-Anne Brault and Michael Naas (New York: Fordham, 2010), 11. Cited in *Counterpath: Traveling with Jacques Derrida,* trans. David Wills (Stanford, Calif.: Stanford University, 2004), 126.

75. *Counterpath,* 130.

76. We are thinking here, among other texts, not only of "The Question Concerning Technology" but also of a much neglected text, "Science and Reflection" (see Heidegger, "Science and Reflection," in *The Question Concerning Technology and Other Essays,* trans. William Lovitt (New York: Harper & Row, 1977), 3–35 and 155–182.

77. Heidegger, *Sojourns,* 56.

78. See Catherine Chevalley, "La physique de Heidegger," in *Les Études philosophiques* (July–September 1990): 299. This remarkably precise and pertinent contribution shows how (in a 1935 course, assembled in the text *What Is a Thing?*) Heidegger took the modification of objectivity in contemporary nuclear physics into account. This theoretical perspective is nevertheless in contradiction with what Heidegger wrote in 1938 about modernity in "The Age of the World Picture." Why did Heidegger seem to ignore his earlier findings? Even if object and subject disappear to the benefit of their relation, what does remain as the most decisive is the "calculative project concerning things." Despite the shattering of its classical concept, contemporary physics continues to "seek" the unity of a picture of the physical world: there is a break between its explicit discourse and its fundamental project. It is the latter that

Heidegger wants to rethink beyond any epistemology, with the expression the "essence of technology."

79. René Thom, "La Science en crise?," *Le Débat*, no. 18 (January 1982): 39.

80. The passage that most directly announces the expression from 1951–52 is as follows: "For this reason no amount of scientific rigor attains to the seriousness of metaphysics. Philosophy can never be measured by the standards of the idea of science." "What Is Metaphysics?," in *PA*, 96. "Daher erreicht keine Strenge einer Wissenschaft den Ernst der Metaphyik. Die Philosophie kann nie am Masstab der Idee der Wissenschaft gemessen warden."

81. Heidegger, *What Is Called Thinking*?, 8.

82. Ibid., 5. "It is no evidence of any readiness to think that people show an interest in philosophy."

83. Ibid., 3.

84. See G. W. F. Hegel, *The Encyclopedia Logic: Part One of the Encyclopedia of the Philosophical Sciences*, ed. Ernst Behler (London: Bloomsbury Academic, 1991).

85. Thom, "La science en crise?," 35.

86. Ibid., 40.

87. A sign of his interest for natural philosophy is Thom's participation at the conference on "Aristotle's Physics," held from June 27 to 29, 1986, in Nice, as part of the *Séminaire d'épistemologie et d'histoire des sciences*.

88. Heidegger "What Is Metaphysics," in *PA*, 83.

89. Ibid., 95.

90. See René Thom, *Paraboles et catastrophes* (Paris: Flammarion, 1983), 56–58.

91. At the end of his article, "Halte au hazard, silence au bruit," *Le Débat*, no. 3 (July–August 1980): 119–132, René Thom wonders whether the "vagueness" that often prevails within French philosophy with respect to the sciences should be imputed to the "fundamentally subjectivistic and a-scientific character of academic tradition issued from Husserl and Heidegger" (132).

92. Dominique Lecourt, "De l'antiscientisme à l'antiscience," *Alliage*, no. 10 (Winter 1991): 6–7.

93. Also concerning the connection with Spengler, see Jacques Bouveresse, "Les philosophes et la technique," *Zouila* (Winter 1998): 21–22.

94. As Jacques Bouveresse notes, ibid., 22.

95. Jean-Michel Salanskis, "Die Wissenschaft Denkt Nicht," *Revue de métaphysique et de morale*, no. 2 (1991): 207–231.

96. Ibid, 215.

97. See Jean-Michel Salanskis, *Le Temps du sens* (Orléans: HYX, 1997).

98. See Salanskis, "Die Wissenschaft Denkt Nicht," 227–231. One should note that the interest of Salanskis's article is somewhat diminished by a certain generality in his approach: I am thinking less about the final allusion to Heidegger's silence on the Holocaust than about the fact that the sentence "Die Wissenschaft denkt nicht" is examined outside of the context in which it appeared in "What Is Called Thinking?" (8), a work that Salanskis mentions only in passing.

99. "Promesses et menaces de la science" (France Culture, *Répliques*, February 17, 1996, with François Lurçat), transcript published in *Alliage*, no. 27 (Summer 1996): 3–12.

100. Ibid., 9.

101. As for his "positions with respect to the Jews," one needs to ask: where are they developed in Heidegger's *philosophical* work? One would like to have a more precise idea than the vague memory of accusations or insinuations read one day in *Libération*.

102. France Culture, *Répliques*, February 17, 1996.

103. Thus, for example, echoing earlier works, Jean-Paul Dollé, "La haine de la pensée," *L'Observatoire de la télévision,* no. 14 (October 1999): 24, takes "without acrimony or obscurantist fervor" Heidegger's famous statement as its point of departure, in order to denounce the censors Sokal and Bricmont. These physicists, according to him, were trying to impose a "correct" thinking ("*korrekt* as Hitler's followers used to say"), patterned after a scientific model uniquely concerned with exactitude and efficiency, by attacking creative thinking, especially that of Deleuze, without understanding it.

104. Ilya Prigogine and Isabelle Stengers, *La Nouvelle Alliance* (Paris: Gallimard, 1979), 38. [TN: This passage was omitted in the English edition, Ilya Prigogine and Isabelle Stengers, *Order Out of Chaos: Man's New Dialogue with Nature* (New York: Bantam New Age Books, 1984)].

105. Prigogine and Stengers, *Order Out of Chaos: Man's New Dialogue with Nature,* 225. From the same authors, see *Entre le temps et l'éternité* (Paris: Payard, 1988).

106. Jean-Marc Lévy-Leblond, *Aux contraires: L'exercice de la pensée et la pratique de la science* (Paris: Gallimard, 1996), 16.

107. Ibid., 21.

108. In addition, Jean-Marc Lévy-Leblond and I organized a seminar on the theme of "Does Science Think?" together at the University of Nice, 1989–90. It was focused not on Heidegger's thought but on the opening of new perspectives or new intersections along the "common border" between science and philosophy. The participants included Henri Atlan, Jean-Pierre Dupuy, Jean-Yves Girard, Marc Richir, Clément Rosset and Isabelle Stengers.

109. Gilbert Hottois, *Le Signe et la Technique* (Paris: Aubier, 1984), seemed to be the principal promoter of the expression.

110. As Alain Boutot showed in *L'Invention des formes* (Paris: Odile Jacob, 1993), 108–111.

111. Heidegger, *The Question Concerning Technology and Other Essays,* 4; *Vorträge und Aufsätze,* 13: "So ist denn auch des Wesen der Technik ganz und gar nichts Technisches."

112. Jean-Pierre Séris, *La Technique* (Paris: PUF, 1994).

113. Dominique Lecourt, *Contre la peur* (Paris: Hachette, 1990), 144.

114. Chapter 7, "Métaphysique et essence de la technique: Heidegger," in Séris, *La Technique,* 288–305.

115. "The many citations that we had to use, in order to preserve the evocative power of Heidegger's language, despite translations that rarely correspond to the genius of our language, at least allowed one to dismiss the baseless criticisms that one hears too often" (ibid., 299–300).

116. Concerning the intertwining of these two motifs, a critique of instrumentalism and a critique of discontinuism, see ibid., 287–291.

117. Ibid., 302.

118. Concerning these criticisms, see ibid., 303–305.

119. Despite the interest and the quality of his book, *Pour la connaissance philosophique* (Paris: Odile Jacobs, 1988), Gilles-Gaston Granger devotes only two brief pages to Heidegger (192–193), where he denounces, with respect to the "The Question Concerning Technology," "the arbitrary nature" of Heidegger's "approach to language." These two pages are in their own way more a "denunciation" that a refutation, reducing Heidegger's thought to a series of "myths." "Thus anything is permitted," he even writes (193).

120. Bouveresse, "Les philosophes et la technique."

121. Ibid., 14.

122. See Séris, *La Technique,* 285–287.

123. Since Bouveresse insisted, even claiming to correct Séris on something he did not exactly say ("Séris is perhaps not entirely correct when he claims that Heidegger's diagnosis is

in no way original," in "Les philosophes et la technique," 17), it may not be unhelpful to recall the very terms used by Séris: "The true originality does not lie in this diagnosis. . . . Heidegger is not the only one who is saddened by the metamorphoses of nature . . . his originality lies elsewhere." This originality is clearly indicated further on: *La technique,* 302–3. ("The idea that modern technology is the ultimate closure of metaphysics.")

124. Bouveresse, *Les Philosophe et la technique,* 19.

125. "Agriculture is now a mechanized food industry, in essence the same as the production of corpses in the gas chambers and extermination camps, the same as the blockading and starving of countries, the same as the production of Hydrogen bombs": Martin Heidegger, *Bremen and Freiburg Lectures,* trans. Andrew J. Mitchell (Bloomington: Indiana University Press, 2012), 27 (cited in Bouveresse, *Les Philosophe et la technique,* 23, following Lacoue-Labarthe, *Heidegger, Art and Politics,* 34). Since Bouveresse raised the question, "but what does 'the same thing' exactly mean?" (ibid., 23), it is not unhelpful to clarify that upon scrutiny of the original text nothing permits the justification of the translation by "the same thing" for *Das Selbe,* which Heidegger always distinguished from the identical *Das Gleiche.* "Ackerbau ist jetzt motorisierte Ernährungsindustrie, im Wesen das Selbe wie die Fabrikation von Leichen in Gaskammern und Vernichtungslagern, das Selbe wie die Blokade und Aushungerung von Ländern, das Selbe wie die Fabrikation von Wasserstoffbomben" (*GA,* 79, 27).

126. In the preface to the second edition to his thesis, *La Mythe de l'intériorité* (Paris: Éditions de Minuit, 1987), Bouveresse describes (11) the "insurmountable apprehension that continues to provoke" in him "the idea of risking any affirmation whatsoever with respect to this author" (Heidegger).

127. See ibid., 18, where Bouveresse agrees with Heidegger that positivism à la Carnap cultivated a naïve idea of the opposition between science and metaphysics; he also mentions that it is necessary according to Heidegger to understand the problem of technology on the basis of the history of metaphysics. Further, he considers that it is necessary to recognize that Heidegger "did not make the mistake of explicitly reducing science to technology" (ibid., 20).

128. This is the interview with Richard Wisser on the occasion of his eightieth birthday (the translation of which can be found in the *Martin Heidegger: Cahier de l'Herne,* 93–97). Let us grant to Bouveresse that the "pedagogical" formulation that Heidegger himself gives of the sentence "science does not think" is not the best one: he wanted to show that this expression is not a "reproach" against science but a statement regarding its "internal structure": "science does not operate *in the dimension of philosophy.*" Conceding to Heidegger that it is not possible to say what physics is through the method of physics (which is not an insignificant concession), Bouveresse nonetheless gets on his high horse, as it were, by advancing two arguments ("Les Philosophe et la technique," 22): a neo-positivist like Schlick was quite capable "of admitting that science is philosophical"; further, the theory of relativity has been "a conceptual and philosophical revolution." Schlick's counterexample (Schlick was in no way a representative of science as such!) simply proves that he was not an "ordinary" positivist! The second argument is much more interesting, to the extent that it leads one to wonder what was "thought" or "not thought" (and in what sense) in general or special relativity, as well as in the other conceptual revolutions brought about by the science of the twentieth century. It is clear that one cannot be satisfied with the "trivialized" formulation of Heidegger's statement, itself modeled by the author himself on a classical philosophical position (expressed for instance by Hegel in the letter to Goethe from February 24, 1821: "It is true that Newton expressly warned physics to beware of metaphysics." *Hegel, the Letters,* trans. Clark Butler and Christian Seiler (Bloomington: Indiana University Press, 1984), 700. If, however, Bouveresse had referred to "What Is Called Thinking?" in order to situate the statement in question in

its context and put it in relation to the whole range of implications that Heidegger gives it, he could have engaged the discussion in a much for rigorous manner.

129. Bouveresse, Preface to the second edition, *La Mythe de l'intériorité*, 17.

130. See Séris, *La Technique*, 302.

131. Lecourt, *Contre la peur*, 139.

132. See ibid., 142. In addition, Lecourt notes that the connection with Spengler encounters a major objection: Heidegger does not share the "philosophy of life" of the author *The Decline of the West* (ibid., 144). Another crucial difference that must be taken into account: there is no cyclical conception of history in Heidegger. Consequently, the connection itself seems quite tenuous, and Lecourt went too far when he wrote that "Heidegger borrows most of his conception of technology" from Spengler (ibid., 143).

133. Ibid., 144.

134. See ibid., 145.

135. Among which one must also include François Guéry. In *Heidegger rediscuté: Nature, technique et philosophie* (Paris: Descartes & Cie, 1995), he first attempts to avoid any "demonization" concerning Heidegger by admitting that "the Heidegger lesson is useful both for knowledge and for experience" (79), especially in the domain of ecology. But the "provincial" attachment to nature seems to him completely conservative (to the Heideggerian attitude he opposes [30] "republican France!"), as is Heidegger's lack of understanding of the industrial world ("Heidegger is like the prophet Philippulus!" 125). Reproaching Heidegger for his "hysterical style" (99), Guéry even seems to have a hard time remaining calm and moderating his discourse when discussing an author he describes as follows: "Despite his contortions designed to go against current opinion, in the end he can only paint with a deceptive coating all the platitudes and bad ideas of the century, under the excuses of medieval ontology and the theology of faith: long ways long lies!" (102).

136. Hottois, *Le Signe et la Technique*, 11 and 114

137. This ambiguity is also perceptible, though in a more complex way, in the work of Bernard Stiegler, *Technics and Time*, vol. 1: *The Faculty of Epimetheus*, trans. Richard Beardsworth and George Collins (Stanford, Calif.: Stanford University Press, 1998), and *Technics and Time*, vol. 2: *Disorientation*, trans. Stephen Barker (Stanford, Calif.: Stanford University Press, 2009), who refers almost constantly to Heideggerian schemes while reworking them in terms of both Leroi-Gourhan's anthropology and Derrida's deconstruction.

138. This journal, published in German, English, and French by Dunker and Humboldt in Berlin, was organized by François Fédier and François Vezin.

139. Jean-François Courtine, *Heidegger et la phénoménologie* (Paris: Vrin, 1990).

140. "Donner/prendre: la main" (ibid., 283–304).

141. "La voix (étrangère) de l'ami. Appel et/ou dialogue" (ibid., 327–354).

142. See, in particular, ibid., 328, 332–333. See Franco Volpi, *Heidegger e Aristotele* (Padua: Daphne, 1984).

143. See "Le platonisme de Heidegger," in Courtine, *Heidegger et la phénoménologie*, 129–160.

144. Ibid., 338–339.

145. Ibid., 353.

146. Ibid., 405.

147. A proximity that was recognized (concerning the role of the hand): ibid., 292.

148. See ibid., 328.

149. See Alain Renaut, *Sartre, le dernier philosophe* (Paris: Livres de Poche, 2000).

150. One expected such an assessment from a mathematician who had proposed a somewhat Heideggerian reading of the formal sciences in his book, *Herméneutique formelle*

(Paris: Éditions du C.R.N.S., 1991) and who proposed, as we saw earlier, an interesting interpretation of the memorable statement, "science does not think." Unfortunately, Jean-Michel Salanskis disappoints our expectations in his *Heidegger* (Paris: Les Belles Lettres, 1997), which for that reason we cannot recommend to students as a reliable study. Certainly, this is only an introduction on the basis of the two themes of existence and ontological difference. But the didactic character of the work does not justify serious mistakes that escaped the author (thus for instance the translation of *Being and Time* by Vezin is attributed on pages 14 and 153 to François Fédier; we read on page 8 that Heidegger left the Nazi party in 1934 when he resigned from the rectorate, when recent research has shown the contrary). But these are details when compared with the liberties the author takes by his own admission (12) in relation to the thought to which he is supposed to introduce the reader (for instance *Being and Time* is presented on page 32 as "the novel of existence," and the existential category of the understanding is evoked on page 24 in reference to the cartoons *Rahan* and *Pif*). But the most problematic was to have adopted in the end a reading that is resolutely external of Heidegger's four "themes" (technophobic, hermeneutic, historical, and Nazi). To strangely conclude with this last motif could lead one to believe that it is still present and even that it represents the truth of Heidegger's thought. Salanskis denies this in two ways: first by refusing to minimize Heidegger's philosophical importance (150) and also by explaining his engagement in terms of his "avoidance" of the primacy of ethics (144). However, in the final analysis, this kind of engagement would in part "belong to that of philosophy in general" (145). This is to say too much or not enough . . .

151. Thus the complete title of *La Raison Narrative: Langages Totalitaires: Critique de l'économie narrative*.

152. The key sentence of Krieck's attack against Heidegger in *Volk im Werden* in 1934 is as follows: "The meaning of this philosophy is an explicit atheism and a metaphysical nihilism, as has been represented previously in our country by Jewish authors, that is to say, a mixture of disintegration and dissolution for the German people" (see Jean-Pierre Faye, *Le piège: La philosophie heideggérienne et le nazisme* [Paris: Balland, 1994], 101). See our interview with Jean-Pierre Faye in *Heidegger en France*, vol. 2: *Entretiens*. [TN: This interview with Jean-Pierre Faye was not included in the English edition.]

153. Faye even produces a text by Nietzsche where nihilism is clearly distinguished from metaphysics: "Morality protected from nihilism *those who turned out badly* by granting *everyone* an infinite value, a metaphysical value, and placing them in an order which did not correspond to that of worldly power and hierarchy: it taught submissiveness, humility, etc." "European Nihilism," June 10, 1887, in *The Nietzsche Reader*, ed. Keith Ansell Pearson and Duncan Large (Malden, Mass.: Blackwell, 2006), 387–388. See Faye, *Le piège*, 124–125.

154. Jean-Pierre Faye, *Le Vrai Nietzsche* (Paris: Hermann, 1998).

155. Faye, *Le piège*, 155.

156. Ibid., 20.

157. Henri Meschonnic, *Le Langage Heidegger* (Paris: PUF, 1990), 5. I have devoted a critical review to this book from which I borrow a few elements: See "Heidegger entre polémique et philosophie," *Les Études philosophiques*, no. 2 (1991): 229–234.

158. Meschonnic, *Le Langage Heidegger*, 8.

159. See ibid., 385.

160. See Jean-Pierre Lefebvre, "Auch die stege sind Holzwege," in *Hölderlin vu de France*, ed. Bernhard Böschenstein and Jacques Le Rider (Tübingen: Günter Narr, 1987), 53–76. Contrary to Heidegger, who developed a reading oriented toward Greece and India of the hymn *Andenken* ("Remembrance"), Lefebvre presents very convincing arguments to interpret it as a poem of a voyage to the West. He summarizes (ibid., 60) the spirit of his "counter reading"

in the following way: "I do not want to defend this maritime hypothesis in a unilateral way: I even remain convinced that it plays a part in the poem in a tension with the other voyage, the one that Heidegger suggests and that I would call here the voyage of the intertext."

161. Dionys Mascolo, *Haine de la philosophie: Heidegger pour modèle* (Paris: Jean-Michel Place, 1993).

162. Ibid., 131.

163. See ibid., 91.

164. See ibid., 121.

165. See ibid., 112.

166. Ibid., chapter 5 ("Éléments pour un sottisier heideggèrien").

167. We will limit ourselves to two examples. In the commentary proposed by Heidegger in *The Principle of Reason* on Angelus Silesius's saying ("The rose is without why"), Mascolo sees only a "scandalous stupidity" (*Haine de la philosophie,* 121): skimming over the details of the analyses, paying no attention to the subtle displacement of the "all-powerful principle," he believes (or pretends to believe) that Heidegger only wanted to say that the rose is different from the human being. One of Heidegger's most subtle meditations is thereby reduced to a trivial banality. The second example is no less significant: to claim that Heidegger betrayed Nietzsche's originality is neither original nor scandalous (Faye showed that in a better-argued passage), but Mascolo merely claims that Heidegger rejects Nietzsche with "contempt" and judges his thought as "the perfect symptom of the general decadence" (127). These allegations are false and even caricatural: Heidegger always put Nietzsche on a pedestal; the metaphysical character of his thought corresponds, according to Heidegger, to the deepest destinal necessities.

168. Ibid., 149.

169. Ibid., 155.

170. Jeffrey Andrew Barash, *Heidegger et son siècle: Temps de l'être et temps de l'histoire* (Paris: PUF, 1992).

171. Jeffrey Andrew Barash, *Martin Heidegger and the Problem of Historical Meaning* (Dordrecht-Boston: Nijhoff, 1998).

172. See Barash, *Heidegger et son siècle,* 13. One finds the same conviction in the very well documented study by Domenico Losurdo, *Heidegger et l'idéologie de la guerre,* trans. J.-M. Burée (Paris: PUF 1998), which in no way aims to reduce Heidegger's thought to that ideology, but which shows the extent to which the shock of WWI was determinant for an entire generation that shared with Heidegger, *mutatis mutandis,* the theme of heroic community, sacrifice before death, the spiritual vocation of the German people, and the radical critique of modernity.

173. Barash, *Heidegger et son siècle,* 184.

174. Chapter 8, "La Deuxième Guerre mondiale dans le mouvement de l'histoire de l'être," ibid., 168–179.

175. We should also note an interesting position against the translation (although largely or broadly accepted) of *geschichtlich* by *historial.* Barash argues that with this neologism one makes Heidegger speak "—in French only—a language that distances him from his predecessors." This is a perfectly justified remark that should be taken into account by the translators. However, Barash himself is not immune from criticism when he, on several occasions, translates Heidegger's *Verborgenheit* with the factual brutality of the word *opacité.*

176. This conclusion seems to be a case of *"wishful thinking"* [TN: In English in the original]. It should not obscure the fact that the "Heidegger case" continues to inspire virulent reactions that are moral rather than hermeneutical. Thus, while denying (112) that he is "judging Heidegger" and conceding that he is "one of the greatest philosophers of our cen-

tury," Christian Delacampagne devotes an entire chapter (with the significant title "Papon, lecteur de Heidegger") of his book *De l'indifférence* (Paris: Odile Jacob, 1998) to very severe attacks on Heidegger's explicit or implicit political behavior across different phases. The fact that Foucault is also condemned for having argued that a certain racism is an unavoidable component of biopower in no way diminishes the emblematic importance given from the outset to Heidegger as a "moral pariah." Even if we cannot blame Delacampagne for having emphasized, as others, the grave nature of Heidegger's silence (or quasi-silence) concerning the Holocaust, it remains that the case is presented in a one-sided manner.

12. At the Crossroads

1. Reported by Jean Beaufret, *Dialogue with Heidegger: Greek Philosophy*, trans. Mark Sinclair (Bloomington: Indiana University Press, 2006), xxv.

2. Heidegger, "My Way into Phenomenology," in *On Time and Being*, 74–82.

3. Heidegger makes this clarification in the supplement from 1969, ibid., 82.

4. Ibid., 79.

5. Such is the attitude adopted by François Fédier in his book *Regarder voir* (Paris: Les Belles Lettres, 1995)..

6. These two questions are asked by Jean-François Courtine at the end of his text, "Phénoménologie et/ou tautologie," in *Heidegger et la phénoménologie*, 399, 405.

7. *FS*, 32.

8. *FS*, 36.

9. Rémi Brague, "La phénoménologie comme voie d'accès au monde grec," in *Phénoménologie et métaphysique*, ed. Jean-Luc Marion and Guy Planty-Bonjour (Paris: PUF, 1984), 249.

10. Ibid.

11. Ibid., 250.

12. Levinas, *Totality and infinity*, 298.

13. Michel Henry, *Phénoménologie matérielle* (Paris: PUF, 1990), 112.

14. Michel Henry, *Incarnation: Une philosophie de la chair* (Paris: Éditions du Seuil, 2000), 35–132, especially paragraph 4.

15. Jean-Luc Marion, *Reduction and Givenness: Investigations of Husserl, Heidegger, and Phenomenology*, trans. Thomas A. Carlson (Evanston, Ill.: Northwestern University Press, 1998), 197–202.

16. Jean-Luc Marion, *Being Given: Toward A Phenomenology of Givenness*, trans. Jeffrey L. Kosky (Stanford, Calif.: Stanford University Press, 2002), 37.

17. Max Loreau, *La Genèse du phénomène* (Paris: Éditions de Minuit, 1989). With respect to Max Loreau, see our interview with Éliane Escoubas.

18. Ibid., part 4, 243–410.

19. Ibid., 374.

20. Ibid., 528.

21. Marc Richir, *Méditations phénoménologiques* (Grenoble: Millon, 1992), 42–51.

22. Marc Richir, *L'Expérience du penser* (Grenoble: Millon, 1996), and more particularly the critique of Heidegger, 469–470.

23. Jocelyn Benoist, *Phénoménologie, sémantique, ontologie: Husserl et la tradition logique autrichienne* (Paris: PUF, 1997).

24. See the "Prière d'insérer" by Renaud Barbaras, in *De l'être du phénomène: Sur l'ontologie de Merleau-Ponty* (Grenoble: Millon, 1991).

25. From Jacques Garelli, a poet and a phenomenologist who was very much influenced by the later Merleau-Ponty, see *Rythmes et mondes* (Grenoble: Millon, 1991). His critiques toward Heidegger (183–208, 267–310) essentially concern the unity of *Ereignis* in relation to the play of the world and the selfhood of *Dasein*.

26. Renaud Barbaras, *Le désir et la distance: Introduction à une phénoménologie de la perception* (Paris: PUF, 1999).

27. Claude Romano, *Event and World*, trans. Shane Mackinlay (New York: Fordham University Press, 2009), in particular, §3, and *L'Événement et le temps* (Paris: PUF, 1999).

28. Henri Maldiney, *Penser l'homme et la folie: À la lumière de l'analyse existentielle et de l'analyse du destin* (Grenoble: Millon, 1991).

29. Let us mention the existence of a French Society of *Daseinsanalyse*, directed by Françoise Dastur. See our interview with Françoise Dastur.

30. Maldiney, *Penser l'homme et la folie*, 419.

31. Ibid., 421.

32. See Marlène Zarader, *Heidegger et les paroles de l'origine* (Paris: Vrin, 1986).

33. Marlène Zarader, *The Unthought Debt: Heidegger and the Hebraic Heritage*, trans. Bettina Bergo (Stanford, Calif.: Stanford University Press: 2006).

34. Paul Ricoeur's introductory remarks to Richard Kearney and Joseph Stephen O'Leary, eds., *Heidegger et la question de Dieu* (Paris: PUF, 2009), cited by Zarader, *The Unthought Debt*, 7: "What has often astonished me about Heidegger is that he would have systematically eluded, it seems, the confrontation with the block [*bloc*] of Hebraic thought. He sometimes reflected on the basis of the Gospels and of Christian theology, but always avoided the Hebraic cluster [*massif*], which is the absolute stranger to the Greek discourse."

35. Ibid., 106.

36. Ibid., 45.

37. Ibid., 56: "In the first place, the majority of traits that characterize the poet in Heidegger's approach are found in the biblical prophet, and vice versa."

38. Deuteronomy 6:4.

39. See *The Unthought Debt*, 67–68.

40. See ibid., 96.

41. Concerning the "nothing that is not nothing" and the analogies with the abyss of the Midrash and of the Kabbalah, see ibid., 130. On the parallel between the hidden God and the withdrawal of being, see ibid., 133–135. Is it necessary to evoke, in this respect, the Kabbalist Louria's thought on the doctrine of the Tsim-Tsoum, since "there is no other God in the Bible but the *hidden* God" (ibid., 134)? Verse 45:15 of Isaiah ("Truly you are a hidden God") is thus translated in Luther's Bible: "*Führwahr, Du bist ein verborgner Gott.*" We know that, with Heidegger, the key word referring to the withdrawal of being is precisely *Verborgenheit*.

42. Concerning the ambivalence of the Heideggerian treatment of *logos*, the questioning was relaunched in a different, though comparable, way by Denise Souche-Dagues: "The ambivalence of Heideggerian thought consists in that it avoids, *but without actually betraying it*, the Judeo-Christian ground on which it actually rests" (*Du "Logos" chez Heidegger* [Grenoble: Millon, 1999]), 122.

43. Zarader does not ignore this, since she devotes interesting pages to the early courses in which Heidegger interprets the New Testament and Paulinian texts. *The Unthought Debt*, 152–159.

44. One can even push her "arguments" further. For example, in his *Philosophie et théologie dans la pensée de Martin Heidegger* (Paris: Éditions du Cerf, 1988), 238, Philippe Capelle is surprised that Zarader does not mention *L'âme de la vie* (1824) by Rabbi Hayyim de Voloshym, the Jewish *Schekinah*, and even some mystical Islamic schools.

45. If one takes this declaration seriously in the dialogue with the Japanese: "Without this theological background I should never have come upon the path of thinking. But origin always comes to meet us from the future" (*On the Way to Language*, 10). This theological origin implies, among other things, the reading of Luther's Bible, which, for Heidegger, as he confided to Jean Beaufret, is the book that establishes modern German.

46. Marlène Zarader already mentioned this in the foreword to the French edition: Zarader, *La Dette impensée,* 11. See also 202 of the English edition.

47. Zarader, *The Unthought Debt,* 142.

48. This example is given by Zarader, ibid., 235n129.

49. Ibid., 143.

50. This is a formulation that we borrow from Zarader, ibid., 144.

51. See Heidegger, "Letter on Humanism," in *PA,* 268, "The desire for an ethics presses ever more ardently for fulfillment as the obvious no less than the hidden perplexity of human beings soars to immeasurable heights."

52. See ibid., 271: "Then that thinking which thinks the truth of Being as the primordial element of the human being, as one who eksists, is in itself originary ethics."

53. See Zarader, *The Unthought Debt,* 145.

54. Ibid., 146.

55. This is what Jean-Luc Nancy has also emphasized in a very convincing way: see Jean-Luc Nancy, "Heidegger's 'Originary Ethics,'" in *Heidegger and Practical Philosophy,* ed. François Raffoul and David Pettigrew (Albany: State University of New York Press, 2002).

56. This is the position I argued for in my book: *The Shadow of That Thought: Heidegger and the Question of Politics,* trans. Michael Gendre (Evanston, Ill.: Northwestern University Press, 1996).

57. Ludwig Wittgenstein, "On Heidegger on Being and Dread," in *Heidegger and Modern Philosophy. Critical Essays,* ed. Michael Murray (New Haven, Conn.: Yale University Press, 1978), 80. Wittgenstein's citation ends as follows: "This running-up against the limits of language is *Ethics.* I hold that it is truly important that one put an end to all the idle talk about ethics—whether there be knowledge, whether there values, whether the Good can be defined, etc. In Ethics one is always making the attempt to say something that does not concern the essence of the matter and never can concern it" (ibid, 80–81).

58. See Jacques Derrida, *Given Time,* vol. 1: *Counterfeit Money,* trans. Peggy Kamuf (Chicago: University of Chicago Press, 1992). Regarding Heidegger, see 18–24 and 80–81.

59. To follow the list of the possible translations of this key word, provided by Jacques Derrida himself, in "*Geschlecht:* Sexual Difference, Ontological Difference," in *A Derrida Reader: Between the Blinds,* ed. Peggy Kamuf (New York: Columbia University Press, 1991), 401n1.

60. Ibid., 380–402.

61. A silence that Derrida judges, rightly or wrongly, to be of "great importance" (ibid., 382).

62. Ibid., 388.

63. "*Geschlecht II:* Heidegger's Hand," trans. John P. Leavey Jr., in *Deconstruction and Philosophy: The Texts of Jacques Derrida,* ed. John Sallis (Chicago: University of Chicago Press, 1987), 161–196.

64. Ibid., 161.

65. Ibid., 173.

66. Ibid., 189.

67. Ibid., 193.

68. Ibid., 174.

69. Ibid., 174n69

70. Ibid., 194.

71. See ibid., 167.

72. *Ein Zeichen sind wir, deutunglos:* literally "we are a sign deprived of meaning."

73. For example, "*Geschlecht II:* Heidegger's Hand," ibid., 168. This "overtranslation" is due to Aloys Becker and Gérard Granel (see Heidegger, *Qu'appelle-t-on penser?* (Paris: PUF, 1959), 90), who sometimes put *monstre* in quotation marks (92).

74. In German, a monster is *Missgeburt* or *Monstrum.*

75. Jacques Derrida, "Heidegger's Ear: Philopolemology (*Geschlecht IV*)," in *Reading Heidegger: Commemorations* (Bloomington: Indiana University Press, 1993), 163–218.

76. From the Greek *otos,* "ear."

77. Derrida, in *Reading Heidegger,* 215.

78. "Hören der Stimme des Freundes, den jedes Dasein bei sich trägt" [In hearing the voice of the friend whom every Dasein carries with it (*SZ,* 163/*BT,* 158)]. Cited by Derrida in *Reading Heidegger,* 164. One should almost translate *bei sich* by "right against oneself" [*tout contre soi*] to echo the ambivalence of the Heideggerian "philopolemology."

79. I attended the conference at Loyola University in September 1989, and saw that the lecturer made no accommodation for the general—and quite large—audience. However, the consequence of this "performance," which lasted for almost two hours and a half, was the obvious difficulty (for an increasingly diminishing public) of following a very difficult talk, which was punctuated by German passages.

80. This is the way he himself names him (see Catherine Malabou and Jacques Derrida, *Counterpath: Traveling with Jacques Derrida,* trans. David Wills [Stanford, Calif.: Stanford University Press, 2004], 54). [TN: Translation modified.]

81. On the theme of "surveillance," see our interview with Jacques Derrida.

82. Paul Ricoeur, *From Text to Action: Essays in Hermeneutics 2,* trans. Kathleen Blamey and John B. Thompson (Evanston, Ill.: Northwestern University Press, 1991), 295–296. The pages that follow, concerning Ricoeur's relationship to Heidegger, were sketched out in a lecture on "Freedom and Praxis" given at the University Charles de Gaulle-Lille 3 (Professor Quillien's seminar) on February 15, 1996.

83. In particular §32 of *Sein und Zeit,* "Understanding and Interpretation" ["Verstehen und Auslegung"]. On the relations between phenomenology and hermeneutics in relation to Ricoeur's dialogue with Heidegger's thought, see Françoise Dastur's contribution, "De la phénoménologie transcendantale à la phénoménologie herméneutique," in the proceedings of the 1988 Cerisy symposium, which testified to the importance of Ricoeur's thought: Jean Greisch and Richard Kearney, eds., *Les métamorphoses de la raison herméneutique* (Paris: Éditions du Cerf, 1991), 37–50. See in the same volume (381–403) Ricoeur's text, "L'attestation," which addresses the Heideggerian *Selbst* (397).

84. *BT,* §17.

85. Ibid., §18.

86. Ibid., §33.

87. Hildegard Feick, *Index zur Heideggers "Sein und Zeit"* (Tübingen: Niemeyer, 1961).

88. *BT,* 59. One can find a serious mistake in Martineau's French translation in which one reads "theoretical" instead of "practical" on page 65 of his edition.

89. Heidegger, "Letter on Humanism," in *PA.*

90. *PA,* 239.

91. Ibid., 240.

92. Ibid., 239.

93. Ibid., 240. "Deshalb ist das Denken, wenn es für sich genommen wird, nicht 'praktish.'"

94. Ibid., 272. In the German text: "Die Antwort lautet: dieses Denken ist weder theoretisch noch praktisch. Es ereignet sich vor dieser Unterscheidung."

95. We will see that this fundamental disagreement concerning metaphysics renders this claim problematic.

96. Olivier Mongin, *Paul Ricœur* (Paris: Éditions du Seuil, 1994).

97. Christian Bouchindhomme and Rainer Rochlitz, *"Temps et récit" de Paul Ricœur en débat* (Paris: Ed. du Cerf, 1990), 22.

98. This entire discussion is reexamined in the light of a critique of the circularity of Heideggerian hermeneutics in Christian Ferrié, *Heidegger et le problème de l'interprétation* (Paris: Kimé, 1999).

99. This is the case, for Ricoeur, as early as the *Philosophy of Will*.

100. Being itself is referred to *A-letheia* as un-concealment. Let us recall that Heidegger finally crossed out being and rethought its truth more originally from *Ereignis*.

101. Paul Ricoeur, *Oneself as Another,* trans. Kathleen Blamey (Chicago: University of Chicago Press: 1992), 314–315.

102. Ibid., 19, 312–313.

103. Ricoeur himself speaks of a "meta function." We will return to this.

104. See Paul Ricoeur, *Oneself as Another,* 67. *Analogon* means here a referential as a "family resemblance" in Wittgenstein's sense.

105. This is an attitude inherited from Emmanuel Mounier: see his book *L'affrontement chrétien* (Paris: Seuil, 1951).

106. See Jacques Taminiaux, *Heidegger and the Project of Fundamental Ontology,* and *The Thracian Maid and the Professional Thinker: Arendt and Heidegger.*

107. We saw how at Cerisy Ricoeur was annoyed by Heidegger's "schoolmaster" manner; but this did not prevent him from recognizing that the Heideggerian readings of the poets were "magnificent," that he had been impressed by Heidegger's genius and "caught up in the Heidegger wave" (see Paul Ricoeur, *Critique and Conviction: Conversations with François Azouvi and Marc de Launay,* trans. Kathleen Blamey [New York: Columbia University Press, 1998], 21–22).

108. Paul Ricœur, *Réflexion faite* (Paris: Éditions Esprit, 1995), 100.

109. See Dominique Janicaud, *Chronos: Pour l'intelligence du partage temporel* (Paris: Grasset, 1997).

110. Françoise Dastur, *Heidegger and the Question of Time,* trans. François Raffoul and David Pettigrew (Amherst, N.Y.: Prometheus Books, 1998). On the notion of horizon, see 58–59.

111. We also have to draw attention to a previous work that, while scrupulously respecting the letter of Heidegger's text, is clearly oriented toward the quest for a convergence between Heideggerian eschatology and Christian soteriology: Ysabel De Andia, *Présence et eschatologie dans la pensée de Martin Heidegger* (Paris: Éditions universitaires-université de Lille III, 1975).

112. Jean-Yves Lacoste, ed., *Dictionnaire critique de théologie* (Paris: PUF, 1998). The following citations are from the article "Heidegger" (522–523) written by Lacoste himself.

113. One can of course analyze these characterizations in terms of compromise or division. Indeed, as Lacoste recalls, the philosopher's funeral in Messkirch only partially observed the Catholic ritual. We saw that this symbolic division represented by the person of Welte (both priest and philosopher) and appeared in the choice of texts read at the burial: the Lord's Prayer and excerpts from Hölderlin. As for the gravestone, it does not bear a cross, but a little star, whereas the neighboring gravestones of Mrs. Heidegger and of his brother do have crosses (we learned this from Didier Franck; see also Béatrice Commengé, "Le tombeau de Heidegger: De Messkirch à Todnauberg," *L'Infini,* no. 53 [Spring 1996]: 51: "Only Martin had a star"). This neighboring of crosses and a star constitutes one final difference (in contiguity).

114. Martin Heidegger, *The Zollikon Seminars,* trans. Franz Mayr and Richard Askay (Evanston, Ill.: Northwestern University Press, 2001).

115. See our Interviews with Jean Greisch, Jean-Luc Marion and Claude Geffré. [TN: Geffré's interview was not included in the English edition.]

116. Roger Munier's introduction to Heidegger's "Le retour au fondement de la métaphysique," *Revue des sciences philosophiques et théologiques* 43, no. 3 (July 1959): 401–405.

117. See *HF,* chapter 8, 180.

118. "Foreword" to *Heidegger et la question de Dieu,* 9–10.

119. Jean-Luc Marion, "Double Idolatry," in *God without Being,* trans. Thomas A. Carlson (Chicago: University of Chicago Press, 2012), 25–52.

120. Martin Heidegger, "Letter on Humanism" in *PA,* 267. "Only from the essence of the holy is the essence of divinity to be thought. Only in the light of the essence of divinity can it be thought or said what the word 'God' is to signify" (ibid., 267).

121. Marion, "Double Idolatry," 41.

122. Maria Villela-Petit, "Heidegger est-il idolâtre?," in *Heidegger et la question de Dieu,* 82.

123. Ibid., 87–89. The rest of this very rich text also shows that Heidegger did not subordinate the approach to the Divine to *Dasein* and that it is by no way certain that the "inscription of God (or of the god) as a being" would be "necessarily idolatry" (92).

124. Jean Beaufret, "Heidegger et la théologie," in *Heidegger et la question de Dieu,* 30; reprinted in *Dialogue avec Heidegger,* vol. 4, 46.

125. Jean-Luc Marion, "Note on the Divine and Related Subjects," in *God without Being,* 52.

126. A clarification offered by Françoise Dastur in her excellent article, "Heidegger et la théologie," *Revue philosophique de Louvain* (May–August 1994): 242–243. See also "Dialogue avec Martin Heidegger" (notes from a session of the Evangelical Academy that took place in early December 1953 in Hofgeismar), trans. Jean Greisch, in *Heidegger et la question de Dieu,* 336. One can wonder, however, whether the clarification in Hofgeismar put an end to any question, in the light of the "confession" made to Roger Munier on August 14, 1949: "Die Grundfrage der Theologie muss rein aus dem Wesen des Seins neu gefragt werden. / Die erste und letzte Frage hat den Charakter der Antwort gegenüber 'dem Wort'" (The fundamental question of theology should be raised anew strictly on the basis of the essence of being. The first and last question has the character of an answer given in response to "the Word.") Roger Munier, *Stèle pour Heidegger* (Paris: Arfuyen, 1992), 13–14.

127. Jean de La Fontaine, "The Fox and the Stork," in *The Complete Fables of Jean de La Fontaine,* trans. Norman R. Shapiro (Urbana: University of Illinois Press, 1985), 22.

128. "We start from a fact: Heidegger has no faith" (François Fédier, "Heidegger et Dieu," in *Heidegger et la question de Dieu,* 37).

129. See our interview with Jean-Luc Marion.

130. Jean-Luc Marion, *The Idol and Distance: Five Studies,* trans. Thomas A. Carlson (New York: Fordham University Press, 2001).

131. Ibid., 247.

132. *God without Being.*

133. See the following text by Heidegger: "For the god also is—when he is—a being and stands as a being within Being and its coming to presence, which brings itself disclosingly to pass out of the worlding of world" (Heidegger, "The Turning," in *The Question Concerning Technology and Other Essays,* 47; "denn auch der Gott ist, wenn er ist, ein Seiender . . . ," *Die Technik und die Kehre* [Pfullingen: Neske, 1962], 45).

134. Next to the expected reference to the Pascalian order of charity, one find this Heideggerian passage: "If I were to write a theology—to which I sometimes feel inclined—then the word Being would not occur in it. Faith does not need the thought of Being" (Marion, *God without Being,* vi).

135. Ibid., 47.

136. This development of the field of reflection is illustrated by the translation of the book by Johannes B. Lotz, *Martin Heidegger et Thomas d'Aquin,* trans. Philibert Secretan (Paris: PUF, 1988).

137. Jean Greisch, "La contrée de la sérénité et l'horizon de l'espérance," in *Heidegger et la question de Dieu,* 170.

138. One can find some of Welte's texts in French (they show an immense respect toward Heidegger and a great interpretative prudence in the connections he makes with Christian thought).

139. For this entire paragraph, see our interview with Claude Jeffré in *Heidegger en France,* vol. 2: *Entretiens.* [TN: The interview with Claude Jeffré was not included in the English edition.]

140. See our interviews with Jean Greisch and Jean-Luc Marion.

141. Hans Jonas invites Christian theologians to a comparable *catharsis* by insisting on Heidegger's "immanentism" and neo-paganism in a beautiful text: see Hans Jonas, "Heidegger et la théologie," trans. Louis Evrad, *Esprit* (July–August 1988): 172–195. Let us note that although Jonas knew the work of the early Heidegger quite well, as he was his student, he was not attuned to themes after the "turn" and, in particular, to the step back from metaphysics as ontotheology (see my essay "En guise d'introduction," ibid., 169–171).

142. See Capelle, *Philosophie et théologie dans la pensée de Martin Heidegger,* 241. The three issues corresponds to the three moments of Heidegger's thought, although they do coexist to a large extent in the second Heidegger. In the end Capelle emphasizes an essential lesson drawn from Heidegger: it is on the basis of the "thinking from the step back" that the irreducible tension between philosophy and theology can be articulated.

143. The convergences between Capelle and Brito, particularly as regards the critiques of the relationship between the philosophical and the theological in Heidegger, have been identified by Emmanuel Tourpe, in "L'esprit pontife," *Revue philosophique de Louvain* (February 2000): 123n10.

144. Emilio Brito, *Heidegger et l'hymne du sacré* (Louvain: Peeters, 1999).

145. Jean Greisch, "La contrée de la sérénité et l'horizon de l'espérance," in *Heidegger et la question de Dieu,* 170.

146. In this field, as in others, however, unanimity was not reached: thus Michel Henry declared that Heidegger's conception of the history of metaphysics "does not hold up" (during the debate organized by the Collège international de philosophie for Didier Franck's book, *Nietzsche et l'ombre de Dieu,* December 4, 1999). Henry did not limit his remarks to such declarations since he argued in a very detailed manner against Heidegger: see in particular his refutation of the Heideggerian understanding of the Cartesian *cogito* in chapter 3 of his *Genealogy of Psychoanalysis,* trans. Douglas Brick (Stanford, Calif.: Stanford University Press, 1993): "If we return to Descartes's text, however, we find no allusion whatsoever to any problematic like the one developed in *Nietzsche* in which ipseity is tributary to and comprehensible through the structure of representation" (75–76). Another example: one discovers in the foreword of the thesis of the sorely missed Gérard Lebrun a critique of a "resolutely dogmatic *history of being.*" *Kant et la fin de la métaphysique* (Paris: Colin, 1970), 9.

147. Emmanuel Levinas, *Ethics and Infinity: Conversations with Philippe Nemo,* trans. Richard A. Cohen (Pittsburgh: Duquesne University Press, 1985), 43.

148. Louis Althusser, *Sur la philosophie* (Paris: Gallimard, 1994), 116. While he remained silent about Heidegger in *For Marx* and in the noted militant theoretical writings from the 1960s and the 1970s, Althusser was far from having a negative attitude toward Heidegger: "Nietzsche and now Heidegger have become established figures," he wrote in *The Future*

Lasts Forever (181), where one finds other rather favorable allusions to Heidegger (107, 172, 178), despite an obvious allergy to his tendencies as a "negative theologian" (171) or even a "priest" (*Sur la philosophie,* 123). According to other texts from the end of his life, Althusser read Nietzsche and Heidegger fairly closely, though with more difficulties for the latter than for the former, to the point that he confessed on August 6th 1984: "I am tired of Nietzsche and I am afraid of Heidegger" (ibid., 111). However, he went as far as to see in Heidegger (ibid., 42) the last inspiration of a "materialism of the encounter, of contingency, that is, of *unpredictability,*" even more authentic than the materialisms of the rationalist tradition, including those that have commonly been attributed to Marx, Engels, and Lenin!

149. See Pascal Engel, *La Dispute* (Paris: Éditions de Minuit, 1997).

150. Paul Ricoeur, whose opposition to Heidegger concerning the philosophy of action was discussed early, also expressed strong reservations toward the category of "metaphysics," qualified as an "after-the-fact construction of Heideggerian thought, intended to vindicate his own labor of thinking and to justify the renunciation of any kind of thinking that is not a genuine overcoming of metaphysics." Ricoeur added, almost reactively: "It seems to me time to avoid the convenience, which has become a laziness in thinking, of lumping the whole of Western thought together under a single word, metaphysics." See Paul Ricoeur, *The Rule of Metaphor* (New York: Routledge, 2003), 368.

151. Jules Vuillemin, *L'Héritage kantien et la révolution copernicienne, Fichte-Cohen-Heidegger* (Paris: PUF, 1954). In this book, the "existentialist" interpretation of Heidegger is presented as a "displacement" of Kantian concepts (§23) in terms of a finite ontology of temporality. Consequently, "the whole of the Transcendental Logic, Dialectic and Analytic is but the wormy bark of Kantianism" (14). However, in order to reach and understand the "fruit," namely the transcendental Aesthetic, one has to reinterpret the theory of intuition in terms of a metaphysics of finitude. The existentialist intuition, or originary understanding, plays the role of intellectual intuition in Fichte. This is an unacceptable compromise for Vuillemin: "A new formal ontology appears where the reduction to time is perpetually compensated for by the contrary reduction of time to eternal temporalization" (295). If this clever critique can be questioned, what is certain is that Vuillemin saw the change in Heidegger's position between *Sein und Zeit* and the *Kantbuch:* Kant is no longer referred back to Descartes nor to "the metaphysics of the infinite in general" (289).

152. See Mikel Dufrenne, "Heidegger et Kant," *Revue de métaphysique et de morale* (January 1949): 1–28; "La mentalité primitive et Heidegger," *Les Études philosophiques* (July–September 1954): 284–306. In both of these articles, Dufrenne presented Heidegger's thought without espousing it. With respect to Kant, he suggested that Heidegger had ignored the practical scope of the doctrine of autonomy. But his reservations were even stronger at the end of the second text, in which he rejected any return to primitive thought and affirmed his attachment to rationalism.

153. In her foreword to the texts edited by Jean Hyppolite, *Figures de la pensée philosophique,* 2 vols., (Paris: PUF, 1971), Dina Dreyfus mentioned that a course on Heidegger was given by Hyppolite at the Sorbonne in 1953–54. Also see in the second volume of this book, "Note en matière d'introduction à *Que signifie penser?*" (607), "Ontologie et phénoménologie chez Martin Heidegger" (615), and "Étude du commentaire de l'introduction à la *Phénoménologie* de Hegel" (625).

154. However, without explicitly criticizing Heidegger, Kostas Axelos, in his 1959 complementary thesis published in 1962 by the Éditions de Minuit with the title *Héraclite et la philosophie,* presents an open, ironical Heraclitus, with a "fragmented and fragmentary totality." The opposition to Heidegger's reading (that tends to unify on the basis of an origin) becomes explicit and more philologically argued in Jean Bollack and Heinz Wismann, *Héraclite ou*

la séparation (Paris: Éditions de Minuit, 1972), 28–32 and 405: "Following Reinhardt, he [Heidegger] confines Heraclitus to the language of a nascent ontology." This argumentation is used by Bollack and Wismann under the form of a critical analysis of the Heideggerian "strategy" of a dismemberment of syntax in "Heidegger l'incontournable," *Actes de la recherche en sciences sociales,* no. 5/6 (1975): 157–161.

155. Hegel's case would deserve a specific and complex study insofar as Heidegger did not immediately develop a thematic interpretation of this author. As Denise Souche-Dague wrote about the first Heidegger ("Une exégèse heideggérienne: le temps chez Hegel d'après le §82 of *Sein und Zeit,*" *Revue de métaphysique et de morale* (January–March 1979): "The brief and summary nature not only of his reading of Hegel's texts, but of the judgment he makes about them, contrasts with the care that, at that time, he applied to Kantian thought" (119). Concerning the Heidegger-Hegel *gigantomachia,* see my essay "Heidegger-Hegel: un 'dialogue' impossible?," in *À nouveau la philosophie* (Paris: Albin Michel, 1991), 151–174.

156. The study of the relations between Heidegger and Husserl did not, at first, escape the reductive clichés, as shown in a study by Rev. Fr. Przywara, "Husserl et Heidegger," in *Les Études philosophiques* (January–March 1961): 55–62, according to which Husserl remains "idealistic" while Heidegger is "romantic," both announcing the "last hour" of philosophy.

157. Jean Beaufret recognized it after the fact. See the critique by Barbara Cassin in Parmenides, *Sur la nature ou sur l'étant* (Paris: Éditions du Seuil, 1998), 19: "The *dokounta* bathe in the love of this world: Beaufret went so far as to interpret insolently the *dokounta,* in the most anti-Platonic manner, as 'the things themselves'" (33). More generally, Barbara Cassin distanced herself from the Heideggerian reading of Parmenides and from his "ontological nationalism": see ibid., 14–19; 66–67.

158. See Franco Volpi, "Wittgenstein et Heidegger," in *La métaphysique,* ed. J.-M. Narbonne and L. Langlois (Paris-Québec: Vrin-PUL, 1999), 71.

159. Pierre Aubenque, *Le Problème de l'être chez Aristote* (Paris: PUF, 1962).

160. Ibid., 112.

161. Ibid., 167.

162. Ibid., 417n.

163. Ibid., 441.

164. See Pierre Aubenque, "Plotin et le dépassement de l'ontologie grecque classique," in *Le Néoplatonisme* (Paris: C.N.R.S., 1971), 101–108.

165. See Jean-François Courtine, "Phénoménologie et métaphysique," in *Le Débat,* no. 72, 88–89. See also our interview with Jean-François Courtine in *Heidegger en France,* vol. 2: *Entretiens.* [TN. This interview with Jean-François Courtine was not included in the English edition.]

166. See *HF,* chapter 8 (172–175), the section "Between Critique and Hermeneutics," where we noted that the technique of "double-reading" enabled Birault to expose the confrontation between Nietzsche's and Heidegger's thoughts. In general, Birault's style is the opposite of an erudite critique. Even if he did not always follow Heidegger with the faithfulness of a Jean Beaufret, Birault promoted and practiced lofty thinking, more faithful than simple allegiances. He preferred meditative thinking to pedantic critique. Hence his penchant for textual commentaries, which almost become philosophical prayers in Nietzsche's "grand style." See the foreword of his *Heidegger et l'expérience de la pensée,* 621–623, which ends with a magnificent retranslation of paragraph 296 of *Beyond Good and Evil.*

167. Besides the four volumes of the *Dialogue avec Heidegger* that we already have mentioned, one can find another example of it in the publication by Philippe Fouillaron of two posthumous volumes by Jean Beaufret, *Leçons de Philosophie* (Paris: Seuil, 1998) in which the thematic exposé of Heidegger's thought is almost entirely sacrificed to the benefit of the

careful explanations of the great classical works from Plato and Aristotle to Nietzsche and Husserl.

168. Gérard Granel, *Le sens du temps et la perception chez E. Husserl* (Paris: Gallimard, 1968), and *L'Équivoque ontologique de la pensée kantienne* (Paris: Gallimard, 1970). In both cases, an ontological reading (not dictated in detail, but profoundly inspired by Heidegger) wants to be the battering ram that would shake and deconstruct the citadel of traditional readings (enclosure of phenomenology within the horizon of perception in Husserl, reduction of Kantian philosophy to a theory of the possibility of representation) to the benefit of a questioning of phenomenality as such. With his vigorous and personal style, never that of an epigone, Granel characterized his project as follows: "What we have to do is thus clear, we for whom Heidegger's work has precisely opened the greatest understanding of the question of the meaning of being: we must attempt to 'repeat' the interpretation, which should remain *as close as possible to its own possibility* and thus reveals the texts *more manifestly and more completely to themselves* and themselves alone" (*L'équivoque ontologique*, 26). This is indeed a new application of the Heideggerian method of "hermeneutical violence" that reveals both what Kant and Husserl "meant to say," and also what they could not have said, and kept concealed.

169. Rémi Brague, *Aristote et la question du monde* (Paris: PUF, 1988), 54–55.

170. See ibid., 110, 194, 271, 391, 513–515.

171. Ibid., 150.

172. Jean-François Courtine, *Suarez et le système de la métaphysique* (Paris: PUF, 1990).

173. Ibid., 406. "Suarez's greatness, which in one way justifies his outstanding reputation, is to have been able to face, in his own way, the basic problematic in which Aristotle's *Metaphysics* unfolds, and to have inaugurated a new concept of metaphysics, and re-founded it while giving it a new form that had remained unknown until then."

174. See ibid., 536.

175. Ibid., 534–535.

176. One finds hardly more than ten references to Heidegger in the entirety of this 550-page single-spaced volume. However, and this is not to diminish the immense importance of this work, the decisive motivation for the volume does indeed seem to come from Heidegger and even more precisely from the allusion to Suarez's *Disputationes metaphysicae* on page 22 of *Sein und Zeit*, where Heidegger mentions the work of great importance that remains to be accomplished in order to understand the metamorphoses of metaphysics between its Greek advent and its transcendental refoundation.

177. See our interview with Jean-Luc Marion.

178. A confrontation that was set into motion in Marion's first book, *Sur l'ontologie grise de Descartes* (Paris: Vrin, 1975).

179. Ibid. Jean-Luc Marion, *On Descartes' Metaphysical Prism: The Constitution and the Limits of Onto-theo-logy in Cartesian Thought*, trans. Jeffrey L. Kosky (Chicago: University of Chicago Press, 1999).

180. See ibid., §6, 73.

181. An allusion to Jean-Luc Marion's thesis, *Sur la théologie blanche de Descartes* (Paris: PUF, 1981).

182. See Jean-Luc Marion, *On Descartes' Metaphysical Prism*, §10, 118, and the schema, on 121.

183. Ibid., 121.

184. To which one should add the following works, until a full inventory can be completed: Vincent Carraud, *Pascal et la philosophie* (Paris: PUF, 1992); Jean-Christophe Bardout, *Malebranche et la métaphysique* (Paris: PUF, 1999); Olivier Boulnois, *Être et representation: Une généalogie de la métaphysique moderne à l'époque de Duns Scot* (Paris: PUF, 1999).

185. One can also find signs of this in other readings. Thus for example the personal reflections in Jean-François Marquet's *Singularité et événement* (Grenoble: Millon, 1995) contain quite a number of allusions to Heidegger, either finding inspiration in them (for instance, 82, 103 with respect to *Ereignis* and the unique character of being), or differentiating himself from them ("metaphysics" as "Heideggerian myth": 101).

186. One could object that the themes that have been singled out in this chapter do not represent an exhaustive list and that we should have made room for other themes, in particular for deconstruction. We had to choose: we did so with the awareness of the unavoidable limits of a subjective perspective, given that the chronological distance does not exist anymore. As for deconstruction, it is in no way missing from our reflection in other parts of this book. We wanted to exclude it here as a theme because of a scope that appears to have much more support in the United States than in France. In France, deconstruction as such did not enjoy outside of the philosophical field a fortune comparable to that which it has known in the United States, especially in literary criticism and in comparative literature. It did not become a movement independent of the person and work of Jacques Derrida. The deconstructionist "network" (in the American sense) has very little relation to its Heideggerian origins. Therefore one had to limit oneself to a narrow dialogue with Derrida (and with some of his associates), which we believe we have done in the body of the present work.

Concerning the enrichment of the aesthetic field by Heidegger's thought, one should read our dialogue with Éliane Escoubas in our interviews. As for literary criticism, it seems to have received Heideggerian inspiration only indirectly or episodically. Let us single out, however, as an exception to confirm the rule, the little book written by Alfred Bonzon, *Racine et Heidegger* (Paris: Nizet, 1995), in which some connections are attempted, though rapidly and not in a convincing way, on the basis of themes such as truth, the simplicity of language, and the temporal meaning of "anticipatory resoluteness" (see, concerning this last point, 77, where the unity of time in *Andromaque* is interpreted in terms of the "fourth dimension" of temporal givenness according to Heidegger).

Conclusion

1. "Martin Heidegger et le problème de la vérité," *Fontaine* (November 1947): 758.

2. *Dialogue avec Heidegger*, vol. 4, 86.

3. In the lineage and the tradition of Jean Beaufret, let us mention his former students or disciples: Serge Boucheron, François Fédier, Gérard Guest, Pierre Jacerme, and François Vezin.

4. This is a point that Jean-Luc Marion understandably emphasizes in his interview. Since the 1950s the situation has evolved considerably in this regard, and even if the French university is quite far from being won over by some Heideggerian "cause," one finds nothing like the exclusion experienced by Jean Beaufret in the 1950s and '60s (about which Louis Althusser had been aware).

5. It would also be necessary to mention other names, in particular those of Françoise Dastur, Michel Haar, and Jacques Rivelaygue.

6. Among these, we note the cases of Alain Boutot and Didier Franck. The first told me that he discovered Heidegger "almost by chance" through his readings. The second defined himself, in response to our questions, as an autodidact in Heideggerian studies: he discovered Heidegger's thought in his last class in high school through a reading of Kojève, but

it was more by virtue of his readings than the classes he took at Nanterre that he began to assimilate Heideggerian themes, before following the seminar of Jacques Derrida.

7. Françoise Dastur, *Heidegger et la question du temps* (Paris: Presses Universitaires de France, 1999), 126. [TN. Françoise Dastur's statement is in a bibliographic note in the French edition that was not included in the English edition.] Dastur then refers principally to the works of Biemel, Pöggeler, Walter, and von Herrmann (especially to the latter's *Die Selbstinterpretation Martin Heideggers* [Meisenheim am Glan: Hain, 1964]).

8. See Régis Debray, *Contretemps: Éloges des idéaux perdus* (Paris: Gallimard, 1992), 70, where he pays homage to his former professor Muglioni: "Snobism distinguishes the leaders from the peons. I like 'leaders' in literature but in philosophy I firmly remain on the side of the 'peons.' Those who advance step by step in the limpidity of the day and of the words are more illuminating to me than those who fulgurate in the night. . . . And since, like Jean-Jacques, I prefer to be a man of paradox than a man of prejudices, let me thank Muglioni for having kept me away me from Heidegger." See also from Debray, in a similar vein, "Un maître à l'ancienne," in *Par amour de l'art: Une éducation intellectuelle* (Paris: Gallimard, 1998), 13–86.

9. In *Atlas* (Paris: Julliard, 1984), does Serres criticize Heidegger's ontology, "existence conceived as *Dasein*"? See Pierre Lévy's suggestion in *Qu'est-ce que le virtuel?* (Paris: La Découverte, 1995), 150. If such was the case, this criticism would arise from a misunderstanding regarding *Dasein*, radically different from any other entity and essentially "ecstatic," and therefore "outside." In fact, the only explicit allusion to Heidegger in *Atlas* (70) refers to a "blunder" that Heidegger would have shared with Bergson: having connected geometry with measure and overlooking topology; now, the argumentation that follows addresses only Bergson, and cites no precise reference in Heideggerian matters.

10. It is above all with respect to global technology as a form of "thoughtlessness" that Finkielkraut makes reference to Heidegger: see *La Défaite de la pensée* (Paris, Gallimard, 1987), 146. We note that the journal *Le Messager Européen,* edited by Finkielkraut, has been judged "militantly Heideggerian" by Alain Renaut in Jean Quillien, ed., *La Réception de la philosophie allemande en France aux XIXe et XXe siecles* (Lille: Presses universitaires de Lille, 1994), 243.

11. Thus, in 1972, Sollers congratulated Denis Roche for freeing Holderlin "from the sinister Zimmer and his cousin Heidegger," cited by Jean-Claude Pinson, *Habiter en poète* (Seyssel: Champ Vallon, 1995), 33.

12. Philippe Sollers, *Studio* (Paris: Gallimard, 1997), 154. See also pages 152, 153, 183.

13. See ibid. "*Heidegger en passant,*" remarks gathered by Yannick Haenel and François Meyronnis, in *L'Infini* (Fall 1999): 17–23. This interview was significantly followed by a brief article by François Fédier, "Hannah Arendt à propos de Heidegger," ibid., 25–28.

14. It is particularly difficult to give a "final account" of the French discussions of Heidegger's interpretations of Hölderlin. The Germanist Jean-Pierre Lefebvre attempted to do so in these terms: Hölderlin, after the war, finally found in France "the philosophical dignity that he had been denied." "Hölderlin was finally recognized as a thinker, an intellectual engaged at least in thinking. This was Heidegger's contribution, which was not negligible. However, this philosophical dignity does not abolish the myth, quite to the contrary. Maurice Blanchot thus writes of 'the sacred speech of Hölderlin.' The entire ontological pathos of French Heideggerianism crystallizes around the myth of Hölderlin: Heidegger's discourse itself contaminates the translation and confirms Walter Benjamin's remarks on translation. The poetical is supposed to surge from the uncanny. It is paradoxically that uncanny that must be saved in the translation, following the model of what Hölderlin attempted in translating Sophocles and Pindar. The Hölderlin of the Pléiade, for example (edited by Philippe

Jacottet), has very few notes and privileges the translators-poets like Gustave Roud. François Fédier, a translator of Heidegger, pushes the principle of literality to the extreme, going as far as reproducing in French the disjunction of verb and particle proper to German. Thus 'to descend' [*herunter gehen*] becomes '*aller en bas*,' etc. There is in this approach a neo-religious dimension: the sacred is celebrated." I thank Jean-Pierre Lefebvre for having permitted me to cite this excerpt from his habilitation thesis (47–48).

15. See the citation by Heidegger of a passage from *Illuminations* on page 39 of *On Time and Being*.

16. Thus Heidegger cites a passage from "La crise de l'esprit," in Paul Valéry, *Œuvres*, Bibliothèque de la Pléiade 1 (Paris: Gallimard, 995), in "Hölderlins Erde und Himmel," *Hölderlin-Jahrbuch* 11 (1958–60): 35.

17. See Jean Guitton's testimony, "Visite à Heidegger," *La Table Ronde* 123 (March 1958): 145, 154.

18. See *HF*, chapter 7, 145–146.

19. Arthur Rimbaud, "Letter to Paul Demeny, May 15, 1871," in *Rimbaud: Complete Works, Selected Letters*, trans., intro. and notes Wallace Fowlie (Chicago: University of Chicago Press, 1966), 309.

20. René Char, *Œuvres complètes*, Bibliotèque de la Pléiade 308 (Paris: Gallimard, 1983), 734–736.

21. Ibid., 735.

22. See ibid., in 1965: "A plaque: *La Provence point oméga* (Imprimerie Union, Paris) testifies to the protest campaign that was organized following the installation of an atomic missile base in Haute-Provence. A sketch was drawn by Pablo Picasso."

23. René Char, *Pour nous, Rimbaud* (Paris: GLM, 1956). See "Arthur Rimbaud," in Char, *Œuvres Complètes*, 727–734. Char's text also serves as preface to Rimbaud, *Poésies* (Paris: Gallimard, 1973).

24. *Archives des lettres modernes*, no. 60 (1976): 12–17. This text is reprinted under the title "Rimbaud vivant" in *GA* 13, 225–227.

25. Heidegger, *GA* 13, 225.

26. Arthur Rimbaud, "Letter to Georges Izambard, May 13, 1871," in Rimbaud, *Complete Works, Selected Letters*, 303.

27. *GA* 13, 226: "Dürfen wir, Rimbaud's Wort bedenkend, vielleicht sagen: Die Nähe des Unzugangbaren bleibt die Gegend, dahin die selten gewordenen Dichter einkehren, dahin sie nur erst weisen?"

28. *GA* 13, 227: "Wird das Sagen des kommenden Dichters am Gefüge dieses Verhältnisses bauen und so dem Menschen den neuen Aufenthalt auf der Erde bereiten?"

29. "Wege zur Ausprache" (*GA* 13, 15–21).

30. "Die Grundform der Auseinandersetzung ist das wirkliche Wechselgespräch der Schaffenden selbst in einer nachbarlichen Begegnung" (*GA* 13, 20).

31. Daniel Payot, *La Statue de Heidegger* (Belfort: Circé, 1998). In this very careful study of key texts by Heidegger, from the commentary of the chorus in Antigone to later contributions on art, space, and technology, Payot shows both that Heidegger magnifies the work as a revelation of the truth of Being (and of the world) and that he also gestures toward a dimension that lets "sovereignty occur with figure" (111). Hence, on the basis of the observation that Heidegger never could (or wanted to) emancipate the work of art from its "sacralizing reappropriation," the following question is posed: "But why should the thinking of the open necessarily be a thinking of foundation"? (116).

32. Rimbaud, *Complete Works, Selected Letters*, 303.

33. Ibid., 309.

34. Ibid., 303.

35. Ibid.

36. Char, *Œuvres Complètes*, 268.

37. Ibid., 732. Even if Heidegger never conceived of the return to the Greeks in a literal sense or in a mechanically mimetic way, it is undeniable that the theme of the *Wieder* runs through his work, from the "repetition" of the question of being (*Wiederholung*) in *Being and Time* to this exclamation from his poem *Language* (1972): "When will words / Again be word?" See "Language," trans. Thomas Sheehan, *Philosophy Today* 20, no. 4 (1976): 291.

38. If the attention of the public mostly focused on the short poems by Char that were dedicated to Heidegger, as testimonies to their friendship, one should not neglect, inversely, the seven "thinking poems" by Heidegger in homage to Char: see "Temps," "Chemins," "Signes," "Site," "Cézanne," "Prélude," and "Reconnaissance," in *René Char: Cahier de l'Herne* (Paris: Éditions de l'Herne, 1971), German text with French translation by Jean Beaufret and François Fédier, 169–187. Two translations seem problematic to us: on pages 182–183, "ein Zusammengehören des Dichtens und des Denkens" is translated as "une commune présence du poème et de la pensée" [a common presence of the poem and the thought]. (The translators wanted to pay homage to Char's title but in this way they erased the difference included in the co-belonging of *Zusammengehören*.) Of greater concern, on pages 186–187, the translation of "die Entbergung der sich entziehenden Befugnis" by "déclore permis de s'échapper" seems to us very far from the German and literally incomprehensible in French.

39. This is the title of Jean Beaufret's article in *L'Arc* already cited about Char's and Heidegger's first meeting in Paris. See *HF*, 88–90.

40. Char, *Œuvres complètes*, 742–744. The dedication on page 742 confirms the admiration and friendship that Char held for Heidegger.

41. From September 5, 1984, reported by Paul Veyne, *René Char en ses poèmes* (Paris: Gallimard, 1990), 310.

42. Cited by Paul Veyne, "René Char et l'expérience de l'extase," *La Nouvelle Revue française* (November–December 1985): 16.

43. "We encounter once again the deep opposition between Char and Heidegger." Veyne, *René Char en ses poèmes*, 521. However, the antithesis should not be taken too far either, for paradoxically it supposes the possibility of a comparison of the "worldviews" that both Char and Heidegger would have rejected.

44. See Char, "Page d'ascendants pour l'an 1964," in *Œuvres complètes*, 711–712.

45. Paul Veyne, "Char et Sade," *La Nouvelle Revue française* (March 1984): 18.

46. With respect to Jacottet, Jean-Claude Pinson, *Habiter en poète*, 172, writes, "To the poetics of height, which, influenced by the 'Heidegger-effect,' claim to directly convey the oracles of Being, he opposes the way of an indirect poetic ontology, aware that the light of Being only shines in order to withdraw in the beings that diffract it."

47. His Heideggerian inspiration is made explicit in "La pensée du Même" and "L'eau d'oubli." Roger Munier, *Stèle pour Heidegger* (Paris: Arfuyen, 1992), 25.

48. See our interview with Michel Deguy in *Heidegger en France*, vol. 2: *Entretiens*. [TN. This interview with Michel Deguy was not included in the English edition.]

49. Alain Badiou, *Manifesto for Philosophy*, trans. and ed. Norman Madarasz (Albany: State University of New York Press, 1999). See a fuller elaboration in Badiou's *Being and Event*, trans. Oliver Felpham (London: Continuum, 2005). In particular, see chapter 3 ("Being: Nature and Infinity. Heidegger/Galileo").

50. Alain Badiou, *Manifesto for Philosophy*, trans. and ed. Norman Madarasz (Albany: State University of New York Press), 74.

51. This expression corresponds to the vulgate that Badiou hastily designates as the "*current* Heidegger" in chapter four ("Heidegger Viewed as Commonplace") of the *Manifesto for Philosophy*, 47.

52. Particularly when it comes to the texts on technology, which are said to be pompous and spun from "reactionary nostalgia" (ibid., 53). His irritation is clear with respect to the relation between Heidegger and Char (ibid., 76): Heidegger "exceeded the poetic jurisdiction" and Char takes "the pose."

53. Reinhard May, *Heidegger's Hidden Sources,* trans. Graham Parkes (London: Routledge, 1996).

54. With respect to his interpretation of the nothing (*Nichts*), Heidegger himself opposes the availability of a Far Eastern approach to its nihilistic interpretation in the West. See his letter to Roger Munier, in *Le Nouveau Commerce,* cahier 14 (Summer–Fall 1969): 55.

55. Catherine Clément, *Martin et Hannah* (Paris: Calmann-Levy, 1998). Claude Roëls also told me about the thriller by Gérald Messadié, *Ma vie amoureuse et criminelle avec Martin Heidegger* (Paris: Robert Laffont, 1994).

56. Heidegger indeed figures in *Les Philosophes,* a Jean Tinguely exhibition, at the Jean Tinguely Museum of Bâle (July 10 through October 24, 1999, in Fort Carré, Antibes).

57. Claire Brétecher, *Agrippine* (Paris: Éditions France Loisirs, 1987).

58. Raymond Klibansky, "L'Université allemande dans les années trente (notes autobiographiques)," *Philosophiques: Revue de la Société de philosophie du Québec* 18, no. 2 (Fall 1991): 153–154.

59. A particular example of such a reaction is the effect produced by the "pirate" publication by Gerard Granel of a bilingual edition of the "Rectoral Address" in October 1982 (ibid.). At first threatened with a lawsuit by the publisher Klostermann, Granel was de facto "absolved" by Hermann Heidegger, who then considered that the time had come for a German re-edition in the spring of 1983 (the first edition of 1933 had been out of print for some time). An even more eloquent and significant example is the German publication of *Vier Seminare* (Frankfurt am Main: Klostermann, 1977), a text that was translated by Curd Ochwadt from the French transcripts of the seminars held by Heidegger in Provence and in Zähringen: this was an unprecedented case in which the German philosopher—who as we know was extremely attached to his own language—saw, postmortem, his thinking translated from the French, with the original forever lost.

60. From 1971 on, the date of the publication of the Klossowski translation of the two volumes of *Nietzsche.*

61. See Marc Richir, "La république des philosophes," *Le Débat,* no. 72 (November–December 1992): 222.

62. Respectively, 55,321 copies of *Chemins* and 385,000 of *La Généalogie de la morale.* See Jacques Le Rider, *Nietzsche en France: De la fin du XIXe siècle au temps présent* (Paris: Presses Universitaires de France, 1999), 242.

63. Although Gallimard reproduced most of Heidegger's works in its paperback edition "Tel."

64. Both were published in *La Bibliotèque de Philosophie,* and had a print run of 4,000 and 3,000, respectively. The first was published in September 1995, the second in January 1997. As of November 30, 1999, they were still not sold out. For this information provided by Gallimard concerning these figures, we thank Eric Vigne and Marie-Paule Llorens.

65. An expression from Jacques Derrida in Malabou and Derrida, *Counterpath,* 54. [TN: translation modified.]

66. In his already mentioned 1937 text, *Wege zur Aussprache.*

67. Which is judged, incidentally, to be "inconsistent," at least with respect to the question of humanism, which is the guiding thread of Thomas Rockmore's *Heidegger and French Philosophy,* 181.

68. If his main target was Sartre's existentialism, Heidegger also targeted the other contemporary forms of humanism (Marxism in particular), which he knew full well were flourishing in France.

69. See *On Time and Being,* 48, where Heidegger takes issue with "some of the grossest misunderstandings which [his] thinking encountered in France."

70. François Vezin, "Philosophie française et philosophie allemande," in *L'Enseignement par excellence: hommage à François Vezin,* ed. Pascal David (Paris: L'Harmattan, 2000), 370.

71. Le Rider, *Nietzsche en France,* 252.

72. Ibid., 255.

73. Jacques Poulin's presentation at the conference titled *Penser après Heidegger* (held September 25–27, 1989). [TN. This was later published as Jacques Poulain and Wolfgang Schirmacher, eds, *Penser après Heidegger* (Paris: L'Harmattan, 1992), 6.]

74. Wolfgang Schirmacher, ibid., 10.

75. Alain Badiou, "Le statut philosophique du poème après Heidegger," ibid., 263–268. Badiou credits Heidegger with having delimited historically the respective functions of the poem and of thinking, but he criticizes the "historical construction" that made him miss the scope of the Platonic gesture and fail to reactivate the poetic Sacred.

76. Gérard Granel, "Que l'on peut, que l'on doit penser après Heidegger—et comment," ibid., 89–121. Gérard Granel sketches the contours of a thinking "epistemology" that could articulate a phenomenology of originary forms along with a reflection on the actual presuppositions of each determined science. This text was reprinted as "Après Heidegger," in Gérard Granel, *Écrits logiques et politiques* (Paris: Galilée, 1990), 85–125.

77. Reiner Schürmann, *Broken Hegemonies,* trans. Reginald Lilly (Bloomington: Indiana University Press, 2003), 25–39. Schürmann distinguishes (613–614) three senses of transgression ("fiat," "trans-" and "co-normativity"). It is this last "double bind" that Heidegger brought to its paroxysm in the *Beiträge.* We recognize here the thematic of Schürmann's great work, *Broken Hegemonies,* the last part of which, "The Diremption: On Double Binds without a Common Noun (Heidegger)," 511–620, is a critical commentary on the *Beiträge.*

78. See our interview with Jean-François Courtine in *Heidegger en France,* vol.2: *Entretiens.* [TN: This interview with Jean-François Courtine was not included in the English edition.]

79. Regarding the publication of the translation of volume 60 of the *Gesamtausgabe,* see the clarifications provided by Jean Greisch in his interview. The translation of volume 19 (*Platon: Le Sophiste,* ed. Jean-François Courtine and Pascal David) appeared in 2001. More generally, the situation in January 2000 reveals the small number of the published volumes of the *Gesamtausgabe* that have been translated by Gallimard. Without including already translated works, whether partially or in their entirely, in different forms (for example the courses of Nietzsche), the number of volumes still to be published in French was then thirty-two! This number provides a good idea of the extent of the "reception" still to come for an indeterminate length of time, but which, at this current rate, could take several decades.

80. François Fédier, "Traduire les *Beiträge,*" in *Regarder voir* (Paris: Les Belles Lettres, 1995), 83.

81. Ibid., 97.

82. Heidegger, *Beiträge* §§238–242, trans. François Fédier, *Po&sie,* no. 81 (October 1997): 9–21. The extreme difficulty of translating the *Beiträge* being well-known, it is interesting to compare the spirit of Fédier's translation with another version by Jean Greisch offered earlier (translation of §267 in *Rue Descartes,* no. 1 [April 1991]: 213–224).

83. An example was provided with the translation of *Nichts* by *néent* and *Ereignis* by *amêmement:* see Fédier's translation of Heidegger's text "Die 'Differenz' und das Nichts" (not

yet published at the time), in *L'Enseignement par excellence: Hommage à François Vezin,* ed. Pascal David (Paris: L'Harmattan, 2000), 10–13. Let us analyze, with these two examples, the basis of an interpretation that claims, with the best intentions, to "shed light" on a brief text by Heidegger to justify the spelling of *néent* (or *ce qui néentit* for *das Nichtende*). Fédier argues that it directly reveals "what is not an entity" (*ens*), making the negation more dynamic. One could object that this graphic artifice reveals nothing *directly,* since it supposes an intellectual detour toward the *ens,* and that in addition it corresponds to nothing in the original German (*Nichts,* the usual word)—unlike the case where it is a matter of indicating the passage from *Sein* (*être*) to *Seyn* (*estre*). Furthermore, Sartre had already used and abused the verb *néantir* to avoid understanding the nothing in an abstract or static sense. The new spelling of *néent* thus has the appearance of a sheer *mimesis* of certain Heideggerian gestures, themselves mimetically displaced by a French philosopher (*différance* with Derrida and the crossed-out God with Marion). It is even more difficult to justify the neologism *amêmement* to render *Ereignis,* for not only is the bizarre noun not French (when it is a question of translating an ordinary German word) but what it evokes ("the coming to oneself that leads to the same") certainly relates to the Heidegger theme of the *Selbst,* but completely misses the innovative thinking that Heidegger develops on the basis of the root *eigen* and the play between *Ereignis* and *Eraugnis.* François Fédier, so preoccupied with the Heideggerian *letter,* must have thought of the following passage from "On Time and Being": "What remains to be said? Only this: Appropriation appropriates. Saying this, we say the Same in terms of the Same about the Same" (ibid., 24). Now, this sentence, which invites the reader to conceive of *Ereignis* from itself, in no way establishes its *equivalence* with the Same. As Rémi Brague had noted once while discussing a choice of the same translator, it is not a question of contesting his competence, quite the contrary. What is contestable is *over*-translating. See Rémi Brague, "Heideggers Einfluß auf das französische Geistesleben. Elemente eines Rückblicks auf die bisherige Rezeptionsgeschichte," *Theologie und Philosophie* 57 (1982): 35.

84. In the play written in collaboration with Michel Deutsch, *Sit venia verbo* (Paris: Bourgois, 1988), 17.

85. This account of published translations (excluding reprints) is as follows: the 1930s: 1; the 1940s: 1; the 1950s: 6; the 1960s: 7; the 1970s: 5; the 1980s: 10; the 1990s: 8.

86. About which one will have noted that we did not attribute its "paternity" to Heidegger, unlike a few authors who dilute the influence of Heidegger to the point of discerning it in the work of Lévi-Strauss. The only perceptible convergence between Heidegger, on the one hand, and Foucault and Althusser, on the other (and not "structuralism" as a whole), concerns the critique of humanism: and it operates on the basis of a displacement of the assumption and modes of application of this critique.

87. Of the seven volumes announced in 1982 by François Fédier in *Le Débat* (ibid., 40), two had still not appeared at the time of this writing: volume 21 (Françoise Dastur) and volume 26 (Gérard Guest). Let us also recall that the translation of volume 60, submitted by Jean Greisch in March 1999, is still not out at the time of this writing. [TN: The volume came out in 2012.] See the interview with Jean Greisch. However, the year 2001 marked a new beginning of the publications of translations of Heidegger's work.

88. As an example, and without claiming to be absolutely exhaustive (excluding the case of the volumes such as *Wegmarken* whose texts were published in parts), the list of the *Gesamtausgabe* volumes still not published in France at the time of this writing are: 1, 13, 16, 17, 20, 21, 22, 26, 27, 28, 38, 45, 47, 48, 49, 50, 52, 53, 54, 55, 56–57, 58, 59, 60, 61, 63, 65, 66, 67, 68, 69, 75, 77, 85. [TN: GA 17, 20, 22, 38, 50, 54, 59, 60, 63, 65, and 68 have since appeared in French.]

89. "Wege der Ausprache," already cited in chapter 1, *HF,* 30–31.

90. Beaufret, *Dialogue avec Heidegger,* vol. 1, 16–17.

91. See ibid. Also see "L'énormité de Heidegger," interview with Roger-Pol Droit, *Le Monde*, September 27, 1974, 18.

92. See Marc Richir ("La république des philosophes," *Le Débat*, no. 72 [November–December 1992: 227]), who adds: "Heidegger is indeed the one who, in our century, covered this drift with his authority by manipulating, in turn, great categories such as 'metaphysics,' 'science,' 'technology,' etc. One would need, one day, to investigate Heidegger's work as a *symptom* of the discontent of our civilization." In an unexpected manner, this violent condemnation in terms of "pathology" converges with similar criticisms, although coming from different horizons: Richir is no doubt the most anti-Heideggerian among the phenomenologists.

93. Thus the reference to Heidegger still paradoxically unifies, in a completely negative mode, philosophical orientations whose unity was still problematic. See this remark by Régis Debray in *Introduction à la médiologie* (Paris, PUF, 2000), 178: "We shall say that there is no mediological School (in the sense of a collective allegiance to a common doctrine), but a network of connected bodies of knowledge, perhaps even of strong disagreements, which implicitly draws the contours of an archipelago or scholars having a common goal: to understand technology otherwise than Heidegger." One can wonder whether, *mutatis mutandis,* this contrarian position does not also apply to the "analytic school" in France today.

94. See Georges-Arthur Goldschmidt, *La Traversée des fleuves* (Paris: Éditions du Seuil, 1999).

95. "Donner la parole aux silences," an interview by Pierre Deshusses with Georges-Arthur Goldschmidt, *Le Monde des Livres*, Friday, October 29, 1999, v. In *Le Monde*, January 6, 2001, 15 ("Un scandale intellectuel français"), Goldschmidt relaunched his attack blatantly by treating Heidegger as an emblematic figure of French "Germanomania."

96. See Alain Renaut, ed. *Histoire de la philosophie politique*, 5 vols. (Paris: Calmann-Lévy, 1999).

97. "Les ressources du libéralisme politique," an interview by Nicolas Weill with Alain Renaut, in *Le Monde des Livres*, Friday, October 29, 1999, ix.

98. Further, the violence of many of the critiques we have cited prior to the "condemnation" formulated by Richir shows indeed the extent to which Heidegger's thought remains an intense, often emotional question, in relation to which calm must be progressively restored, a task to which our whole effort is devoted.

99. Martin Heidegger, *Contributions to Philosophy,* trans. Parvis Emad and Kenneth Maly (Bloomington: Indiana University Press, 1999). [TN: A subsequent translation has also appeared: Martin Heidegger, *Contributions to Philosophy (Of the Event)*, trans. Richard Rojcewicz and Daniela Vallega-Neu (Bloomington: Indiana University Press, 2012).]

100. Gathering an international audience, mostly American, this session of the Collegium Phaenomenologicum took place from July 7 to 27, 2000, in Città di Castello, Italy, under the direction of John Sallis and Charles Scott.

101. According to Graham Parkes, preface to R. May, *Heidegger's Hidden Sources,* ix.

102. See an important publication on the Italian reception edited by Marco Olivetti, *La recezione italiana di Heidegger* (Padoue: Cedam, 1989). This substantial volume of 600 pages includes the most prestigious names (from Ernesto Grassi to Gianni Vattimo and Massimo Cacciari) and testifies to the richness and diversity of thought that touched three generations. The range of the themes addressed is quite wide (the existential analytic, the ontological difference, the phenomenological method, the question of language, nihilism, the sacred, the reading of Nietzsche, the confrontation of Heidegger with Gentile, Pareyson, etc.), but the general orientation of this volume is mostly historiographic (in the best sense of the word). The critical intelligence and the objective distance prevail throughout. One hardly perceives

the conflictual positions and the creative displacements that specifically characterize the French reception.

103. See our interview with Kostas Axelos in *Heidegger en France,* vol. 2: *Entretiens.* [TN: This interview with Kostas Axelos was not included in the English edition.] It is moreover not certain that Heidegger truly *wanted* this monumental edition. It rather seems that old age and illness deprived him of the ability to oppose it forcefully. This hypothesis seems confirmed in our *Entretiens* with Biemel. [TN: The interview with Walter Biemel was not included in the English edition.]

104. Kostas Axelos, *Métamorphoses* (Paris: Éditions de Minuit, 1991), 16–17: "Heidegger's case is extremely complex and contradictory. There are even uncertainties, ambiguities and ambivalences . . . further, Heidegger, the thinker of the truth of being, often lies . . . He follows various paths, almost simultaneously. . . . Does Heidegger play a double game? Yes and no. He remains in the between, in the split, which is not only metaphysical. Being and beings keep referring to one another. Beings often contaminate the saying of being. Heidegger is altogether—the *whole* being *fractured*—a great thinker and a *petit-bourgeois.* There is no impermeable separation between the text and the context. Both are to be questioned, as well as their relation."

105. The most stupefying denial was formulated at the time of a plebiscite organized by Hitler, November 11, 1933, to gain support for his spectacular break with the League of Nations: "The German people has been summoned by the Führer to vote; the Führer, however, is asking nothing from the people. Rather, he is giving the people the possibility of making, directly, the highest free decision of all: whether the entire people wants its own existence [Dasein] or whether it does *not* want it." See "Address presented by Heidegger at an election rally held by German university professors in Leipzig in support of the upcoming plebiscite," in *The Heidegger Controversy: A Critical Reader,* ed. Richard Wolin (Cambridge, Mass.: MIT Press, 1933), 49. The confrontation of this lofty speech with the facts is cruel: "Speeches abound, the radio, the press, and the cinema have been unleashed. On November 12, the answer is given in a peremptory way. Those who voted: 96%, the 'Yes votes': 95%; Forty million six hundred thousand votes for the government, 661 seats for the Nazis, but the vote is secret in theory only." Pierre Gaxotte, *Histoire de l'Allemagne* (Paris: Flammarion, 1963), 2:494. One should nonetheless add, in order to allow for a balanced judgment on this matter, that the citation in question does not belong strictly speaking to Heidegger's philosophical corpus: it is an excerpt of a speech given in Leipzig on November 11, 1933. In the interview with *Der Spiegel* that appeared posthumously, Heidegger would clarify with respect to another declaration of allegiance to Hitler: "Today, I would no longer write these cited sentences. Even by 1934 I no longer said such things." "*Der Spiegel* Interview with Martin Heidegger," in *The Heidegger Reader,* 317. Even if one accepts these statements, what remains to be questioned is the form of the "denying schema" applied in other cases and other contexts in the face of common sense, or of the theses that Heidegger seeks to refute.

106. Let us recall the dates that will mark the pursuit of Heidegger's reception in the twenty-first century: in 2026, the Heidegger Archives will be opened in Marbach; in 2046, the entirety of Heidegger's work will be in the public domain. We are grateful to Marc de Launay for this information.

107. According to Jean Beaufret, it is on the question of the relation to science that Heidegger's "enormity" is the most noticeable (see the interview with this title in *Le Monde,* September 27, 1974, 18): "For him, what is important in the course of history is much more the effect of philosophy on science that the alleged influence of science on philosophy."

108. "Letter on Humanism," in *PA,* 276: "die Strenge Besinnung, die Sorgfalt des Sagens, die Sparsamkeit des Wortes." Jean Beaufret liked to refer to these qualities: see his *Introduc-*

tion aux philosophies de l'existence, de Kierkegaard à Heidegger (Paris: Denoël/Gonthier, Bibliothèque Médiations, 1971), 112.

109. There is, however, one condition for any qualitative philosophical listening (this is obvious but one must state it in our times, where almost everything is given to us visually and immediately): work, considerable work.

Françoise Dastur

1. TN: Françoise Dastur's statement is in a bibliographic note in the French edition that was not included in the English edition. In her note, Dastur writes that "contrary to a widely accepted opinion, it is still in Germany, and not in France, the United States, or elsewhere, that Heidegger is better read and understood." Françoise Dastur, *Heidegger et la question du temps* (Paris: Presses Universitaires de France, 1999), 126.

Jacques Derrida

1. TN: Jacques Derrida, *The Problem of Genesis in Husserl's Philosophy,* trans. Marian Hobson (Chicago: University of Chicago Press, 2003).
2. TN: A *caïman* is a slang expression that is used at the École Normale Supérieure to designate any teacher who prepares students for the Agrégation exam.
3. TN: The course to which Derrida is referring, titled, "Heidegger: La question de l'être et l'histoire," has since been published by Editions Galilée in 2013. The English language translation is forthcoming as *Heidegger: The Question of Being and History,* trans. Geoffrey Bennington (Chicago: University of Chicago Press, 2015).
4. Derrida, *Of Spirit,* 129–130n5.

Éliane Escoubas

1. Martin Heidegger, *Poetry, Language, Thought,* trans. Albert Hofstadter (New York: Harper & Row, 1971), 225.

Jean Greisch

1. Karl Rahner, *Hearer of the Word: Laying the Foundation for a Philosophy of Religion,* trans. Joseph Donceel (New York: Continuum, 1994).
2. Jean Greisch, *Paul Ricœur: l'itinérance du sens* (Grenoble: Jérôme Millon, 2001).
3. [TN: Jean Greisch, *Le Buisson Ardent et les lumières de la raison,* tome 1: *Héritages et héritiers du XIXe siècle* (Paris: Le Cerf, 2002).]
4. [TN: The translation appeared in January 2012.]

Philippe Lacoue-Labarthe

1. Martin Heidegger, *Poetry, Language, Thought,* trans. Albert Hofstadter (New York: Harper & Row, 1971), 215.

Jean-Luc Marion

1. Marion, Jean-Luc, "The Breakthrough and the Broadening," in *Reduction and Givenness,* Translated by Thomas A Carlson (Evanston, IL: Northwestern University Press, 1998).

Selected Bibliography

Works by Martin Heidegger

German Works

Gesamtausgabe. Frankfurt am Main: Vittorio Klostermann, 1978–.

Gesamtausgabe. Vol. 2: *Sein und Zeit* (1927). Edited by Friedrich-Wilhelm von Herrmann. Frankfurt am Main: Vittorio Klostermann, 1977.

Gesamtausgabe. Vol. 3: *Kant und das Problem der Metaphysik* (1929). Edited by Friedrich-Wilhelm von Herrmann. Frankfurt am Main: Vittorio Klostermann, 2010.

Gesamtausgabe. Vol. 4: *Erläuterungen zu Hölderlins Dichtung* (1936–68). Edited by Friedrich-Wilhelm von Herrmann. Frankfurt am Main: Vittorio Klostermann, 1981.

Gesamtausgabe. Vol. 5: *Holzwege*. Edited by Friedrich-Wilhelm von Herrmann. Frankfurt am Main: Vittorio Klostermann, 1977.

Gesamtausgabe. Vol. 6.1: *Nietzsche 1* (1936–9). Edited by Brigitte Schillbach. Frankfurt am Main: Vittorio Klostermann, 1996.

Gesamtausgabe. Vol. 6.2: *Nietzsche 2* (1939–46). Edited by Brigitte Schillbach. Frankfurt am Main: Vittorio Klostermann, 1997.

Gesamtausgabe. Vol. 7: *Vorträge und Aufsätze* (1936–53). Edited by Friedrich-Wilhelm von Herrmann. Frankfurt am Main: Vittorio Klostermann, 2000.

Gesamtausgabe. Vol. 8: *Was heißt Denken?* (1951–2). Edited by Paola-Ludovika Coriando. Frankfurt am Main: Vittorio Klostermann, 2002.

Gesamtausgabe. Vol. 9: *Wegmarken*. Edited by Friedrich-Wilhelm von Herrmann. Frankfurt am Main: Vittorio Klostermann, 1976.

Gesamtausgabe. Vol. 10: *Der Satz vom Grund* (1955–1956). Edited by Petra Jaeger. Frankfurt am Main: Vittorio Klostermann, 1997.

Gesamtausgabe. Vol. 11: *Identität und Differenz* (1955–1957). Edited by Friedrich-Wilhelm von Herrmann. Frankfurt am Main: Vittorio Klostermann, 2006.

Gesamtausgabe. Vol. 12: *Unterwegs zur Sprache*. Edited by Friedrich-Wilhelm von Herrmann. Frankfurt am Main: Vittorio Klostermann, 1985.

Gesamtausgabe. Vol. 13: *Aus der Erfahrung des Denkens*. Edited by Hermann Heidegger. Frankfurt am Main: Vittorio Klostermann, 1983.

Gesamtausgabe. Vol. 14: *Zur Sache des Denkens*. Edited by Friedrich-Wilhelm von Herrmann. Frankfurt am Main: Vittorio Klostermann, 1962.

Gesamtausgabe. Vol. 15: *Seminare*. Edited by Curd Ochwadt. Frankfurt am Main: Vittorio Klostermann, 1981.

Gesamtausgabe. Vol. 24: *Die Grundprobleme der Phänomenologie*. Edited by Friedrich-Wilhelm von Herrmann. Frankfurt am Main: Vittorio Klostermann, 1997.

Gesamtausgabe. Vol. 25: *Phänomenologische Interpretation von Kants Kritik der reinen Vernunft*. Edited by I. Görland. Frankfurt am Main: Vittorio Klostermann, 1995.

Gesamtausgabe. Vol. 29/30: *Die Grundbegriffe der Metaphysik: Welt-Endlichkeit-Einsamkeit*. Edited by Friedrich-Wilhelm von Herrmann. 3rd ed. Frankfurt am Main: Vittorio Klostermann, 2004.

Gesamtausgabe. Vol. 31: *Vom Wesen der menschlichen Freiheit: Einleitung in die Philosophie*. Edited by H. Tietjen. Frankfurt am Main: Vittorio Klostermann, 1994.

Gesamtausgabe. Vol. 32: *Hegels Phänomenologie des Geistes*. Edited by I. Görland. 3rd ed. Frankfurt am Main: Vittorio Klostermann, 1997.

Gesamtausgabe. Vol. 34: *Vom Wesen der Wahrheit: Zu Platons Höhlengleichnis und Theätet*. Edited by Herrmann Mörchen. Frankfurt am Main: Vittorio Klostermann, 1988.

Gesamtausgabe. Vol. 39: *Hölderlins Hymnen "Germanien" und "Der Rhein."* Edited by Susanne Ziegler. Frankfurt am Main: Vittorio Klostermann, 1980.

Gesamtausgabe. Vol. 40: *Einführung in die Metaphysik*. Edited by Petra Jaeger. Frankfurt am Main: Vittorio Klostermann, 1983.

Gesamtausgabe. Vol. 43: *Nietzsche: Der Wille zur Macht als Kunst*. Edited by Bernd Heimbüchel. Frankfurt am Main: Vittorio Klostermann, 1985.

Gesamtausgabe. Vol. 47: *Nietzsches Lehre vom Willen zur Macht als Erkenntnis*. Edited by E. Hanser. Frankfurt am Main: Vittorio Klostermann, 1989.

Gesamtausgabe. Vol. 48: *Nietzsche: Der europäische Nihilismus*. Edited by Petra Jaeger. Frankfurt am Main: Vittorio Klostermann, 1986.

Gesamtausgabe. Vol. 53: *Hölderlins Hynme "Der Ister."* Edited by Walter Biemel. Frankfurt am Main: Vittorio Klostermann, 1982.

Gesamtausgabe. Vol. 55: *Heraklit*. Edited by Manfred S. Frings. Frankfurt am Main: Vittorio Klostermann, 1994.

Gesamtausgabe. Vol. 61: *Phänomenologische Interpretationen zu Aristoteles: Einführung in die phänomenologische Forschung* (1921–22). Edited by Walter Bröcker und Käte Bröcker-Oltmanns. Frankfurt am Main: Vittorio Klostermann, 1985, 2nd ed. 1994.

Gesamtausgabe. Vol. 65: *Beiträge zur Philosophie (vom Ereignis)*. Edited by Friedrich-Wilhelm von Herrmann. Frankfurt am Main: Vittorio Klostermann, 1989.

Gesamtausgabe. Vol. 78: *Der Spruch des Anaximander* (1942). Edited by Ingeborg Schüßler. Frankfurt am Main: Vittorio Klostermann, 2010.

Gesamtausgabe. Vol. 79: *Bremer und Freiburger Vorträge*. Edited by P. Jaeger. Frankfurt am Main: Vittorio Klostermann, 1994.

Gesamtausgabe. Vol. 89: *Zollikoner Seminare*. Edited by Medard Boss. Frankfurt am Main: Vittorio Klostermann, 2006.

Translations

The Basic Problems of Phenomenology. Translated by A. Hofstadter. Bloomington: Indiana University Press, 1982.

Being and Time. Translated by Joan Stambaugh. Revised and with a foreword by Dennis J. Schmidt. Albany: State University of New York Press, 2010.

Bremen and Freiburg Lectures. Translated by Andrew J. Mitchell. Bloomington: Indiana University Press, 2012.

Contributions to Philosophy (Of the Event). Translated by Richard Rojcewicz and Daniela Vallega-Neu. Bloomington: Indiana University Press, 2012.

De l'origine de l'œuvre d'art. Paris: Authentica, 1987.

Early Greek Thinking: The Dawn of Western Philosophy. Translated by David Farrell Krell and Frank A. Capuzzi. San Francisco: Harper, 1984.

Écrits politiques 1933–1966. Translated and edited by François Fédier. Paris: Gallimard, 1995.

Elucidations of Hölderlin's Poetry. Translated by Keith Hoeller. Amherst, N. Y.: Humanity Books, 2000.

The Essence of Human Freedom. Translated by Ted Sadler. London: Continuum, 2002.

Être et Temps. Translated by Emmanuel Martineau. Paris: Authentica, 1985.

Four Seminars. Translated by Andrew Mitchell and François Raffoul. Bloomington: Indiana University Press, 2004.

The Fundamental Concepts of Metaphysics World, Finitude, Solitude. Translated by William McNeill and Nicholas Walker. Bloomington: Indiana University Press, 1995.

Hegel's Phenomenology of Spirit. Translated by Parvis Emad and Kenneth Maly. Bloomington: Indiana University Press, 1994.

The Heidegger Reader. Edited by Günter Figal. Bloomington: Indiana University Press, 2009.

Hölderlin's Hymn "The Ister." Translated by William McNeill and Julia Davis. Bloomington: Indiana University Press, 1996.

Hölderlin's Hymns "Germania" and "The Rhine." Translated by William McNeill and Julia Ireland. Bloomington: Indiana University Press, 2014.

Identity and Difference. Translated by Joan Stambaugh. Chicago: University of Chicago Press, 2002.

Introduction to Metaphysics. Translated by Gregory Fried and Richard Polt. New Haven, Conn.: Yale University Press, 2000.

Kant and the Problem of Metaphysics. Translated by Richard Taft. Bloomington: Indiana University Press, 1993.

Nietzsche. Vol. 1: *The Will to Power as Art.* Edited and translated by David F. Krell. New York: Harper & Row, 1979.

Nietzsche. Vol. 2: *The Eternal Recurrence of the Same.* Edited and translated by David F. Krell. New York: Harper & Row, 1984.

Nietzsche. Vol. 3: *The Will to Power as Knowledge and Metaphysics.* Edited by David F. Krell. Translated by Joan Stambaugh. New York: Harper & Row, 1987.

Nietzsche. Vol. 4: *Nihilism.* Edited by David F. Krell. Translated by Frank A. Capuzzi. New York: Harper & Row, 1982.

Off the Beaten Path. Translated and edited by Julian Young and Kenneth Haynes. Cambridge: Cambridge University Press, 2002.

On the Way to Language. Translated by P. Hertz and Joan Stambaugh. New York: Harper & Row, 1971.

On Time and Being. Translated by Joan Stambaugh. Chicago: University of Chicago Press, 1992.

Parmenides. Translated by André Schuwer and Richard Rojcewiz. Bloomington: Indiana University Press, 1992.

Pathmarks. Edited by William McNeill. New York: Cambridge University Press, 1998.

Phenomenological Interpretation of Kant's Critique of Pure Reason. Translated by Parvis Emad and Kenneth Maly. Bloomington: Indiana University Press, 1997.

Phenomenological Interpretations of Aristotle: Initiation into Phenomenological Research. Translated by Richard Rojcewicz. Bloomington: Indiana University Press, 2001.

Poetry, Language, Thought. Translated by Albert Hofstadter. New York: Harper & Row, 1971.

The Principle of Reason. Translated by Reginald Lilly. Bloomington: Indiana University Press, 1991.

The Question Concerning Technology and Other Essays. Translated by William Lovitt. New York: Harper & Row, 1977.

Sojourns: The Journey to Greece. Translated by John Panteleimon Manoussakis. Albany: State University of New York Press, 2005.

What Is Called Thinking? Translated by J. Glenn Gray. New York: Harper Perennial, 2004.

What Is Philosophy? Translated by W. Kluback and J. T. Wilde. Lanham, Md.: Rowman & Littlefield, 2003.

The Zollikon Seminars. Translated by Franz Mayr and Richard Askay. Evanston, Ill.: Northwestern University Press, 2001.

Heidegger, Martin, and Eugen Fink. *Heraclitus Seminar.* Translated by Charles H. Seibert. Evanston, Ill.: Northwestern University Press, 1993.

Works by Others

Adorno, Theodor W. *Jargon of Authenticity.* Translated by Knut Tarnowski and Frederic Will. Evanston, Ill.: Northwestern University Press, 1973.

Allemann, Beda. *Hölderlin et Heidegger: Recherche de la relation entre poésie et pensée.* Translated by François Fédier. Paris: PUF, 1959.

Althusser, Louis. *L'avenir dure longtemps.* Paris: Stock/Imec, 1992.

———. *The Future Lasts Forever: A Memoir.* Edited by Olivier Corpet and Yann Moulier Boutang. Translated by Richard Veasey. New York: New Press, 1995.

———. *Sur la philosophie.* Paris: Gallimard, 1994.

Aron, Jean-Paul. *Les Modernes.* Paris: Gallimard, 1984.

Aubenque, Pierre. *Le Problème de l'être chez Aristote.* Paris: PUF, 1962.

Axelos, Kostas. *Arguments d'une recherche.* Paris: Éditions de Minuit, 1969.

———. *Héraclite et la philosophie.* Paris: Éditions de Minuit, 1962.

———. *Marx penseur de la technique.* Paris: Éditions de Minuit, 1961.

———. *Métamorphoses.* Paris: Éditions de Minuit, 1991.

———. *Vers la pensée planétaire.* Paris: Éditions de Minuit, 1964.

Badiou, Alain. *Being and Event.* Translated by Oliver Felpham. London: Continuum, 2005.

———. *L'Être et l'événement.* Paris: Éditions du Seuil, 1998.

———. *Manifeste pour la philosophie.* Paris: Éditions du Seuil, 1989.

———. *Manifesto for Philosophy.* Translated and edited by Norman Madarasz. Albany: State University of New York Press, 1999.

Barash, Jeffrey Andrew. *Martin Heidegger and the Problem of Historical Meaning.* Dordrecht-Boston: Nijhoff, 1998.

Barbaras, Renaud. *De l'être du phénomène: Sur l'ontologie de Merleau-Ponty.* Grenoble: Millon, 1991.

———. *Le désir et la distance: Introduction à une phénoménologie de la perception.* Paris: PUF, 1999.

Bataille, Georges. *Inner Experience.* Translated by Leslie Anne Boldt. Albany: State University of New York Press, 1988.

Beaufret, Jean. *De l'existentialisme à Heidegger.* Paris: Vrin, 1986.

———. *Dialogue avec Heidegger.* Vol. 1: *Philosophie grecque.* Paris: Éditions de Minuit, 1973.

———. *Dialogue avec Heidegger.* Vol. 2: *Philosophie moderne.* Paris: Éditions de Minuit, 1973.

———. *Dialogue avec Heidegger.* Vol. 3: *Approche de Heidegger.* Paris: Éditions de Minuit, 1974.

———. *Dialogue avec Heidegger.* Vol. 4: *Le Chemin de Heidegger.* Paris: Éditions de Minuit, 1985.

———. *Dialogue with Heidegger: Greek Philosophy.* Translated by Mark Sinclair. Bloomington: Indiana University Press, 2006.

———. *Entretiens avec Frédéric de Towarnicki.* Paris: PUF, 1984.

———. *Le poème de Parménide.* Paris: PUF, 1995.

Benoist, Jocelyn. *Phénoménologie, sémantique, ontologie: Husserl et la tradition logique autrichienne.* Paris: PUF, 1997.

Biemel, Walter. *Le Concept de monde chez Heidegger.* Louvain-Paris: Vrin-Nauwelaerts, 1950.

Birault, Henri. *Heidegger et l'expérience de la pensée.* Paris: Gallimard, 1978.

Blanchot, Maurice. *The Infinite Conversation.* Translated by Susan Hanson. Minneapolis: University of Minnesota Press, 1993.

———. *The Space of Literature.* Translated by Ann Smock. Lincoln: University of Nebraska Press, 1982.

———. *Thomas the Obscure.* Translated by Robert Lamberton. New York: Station Hill Press, 1988.

———. *The Writing of the Disaster.* Translated by Ann Smock. Lincoln: University of Nebraska Press, 1995.

Borch-Jacobsen, Mikkel. *Lacan: The Absolute Master.* Translated by Douglas Brick. Stanford, Calif.: Stanford University Press, 1991.

Bourdieu, Pierre. *The Political Ontology of Martin Heidegger.* Translated by Peter Collier. Stanford, Calif.: Stanford University Press, 1991.

Boutot, Alain. *Heidegger et Platon: Le problème du nihilisme.* Paris: PUF, 1987.

Bouveresse, Jacques. *Le Mythe de l'intériorité.* Paris: Éditions de Minuit, 1987.

Capelle, Philippe. *Philosophie et théologie dans la pensée de Martin Heidegger.* Paris: Éditions du Cerf, 1998.

Char, René. *Œuvres Complètes.* Bibliotèque de la Pléiade 308. Paris: Gallimard, 1983.

Cohen-Solal, Annie. *Sartre.* Paris: Gallimard, 1985.

———. *Sartre: A Life.* Translated by Anna Cancogni. New York: Pantheon Books, 1987.

Cotten, Jean-Pierre. *Heidegger.* Paris: Seuil, 1974.

Courtine, Jean-François, ed. *Heidegger 1919–1929: De l'herméneutique de la facticité à la métaphysique du* Dasein. Paris: Vrin, 1996.

———. *Heidegger et la phénoménologie.* Paris: Vrin, 1990.

Dastur, Françoise. *Heidegger and the Question of Time.* Translated by François Raffoul and David Pettigrew. Amherst, N.Y.: Prometheus Books, 1998.

De Beauvoir, Simone. *Hard Times, Force of Circumstances.* Vol. 2: *1952–1962.* Translated by Richard Howard. New York: Paragon House, 1992.

———. *La force des choses.* Vol. 1. Paris: Gallimard, 1963.

———. *La force des choses.* Vol. 2. Paris: Gallimard, 1963.

De Gandillac, Maurice. *Le Siècle traverse.* Paris: Albin Michel, 1998.

De Man, Paul. *Blindness and Insight.* 2nd ed. Minneapolis: University of Minnesota Press, 1983.

De Towarnicki, Frédéric. *À la rencontre de Heidegger: Souvenirs d'un messager de la Forêt-Noire.* Paris: Gallimard, 1993.

De Waelhens, Alphonse. *Chemins et impasses de l'ontologie heideggérienne.* Paris-Louvain: Desclée de Brouwer-Nauwelaerts, 1953.

———. *La philosophie de Martin Heidegger.* Louvain: Institut supérieur de philosophie, 1942.

Deleuze, Gilles, and Felix Guattari. *Anti-Oedipus: Capitalism and Schizophrenia.* Translated by Robert Hurley, Mark Seem, and Helen Lane. New York: Penguin Classics, 2009.

Derrida, Jacques. *Athens: Still Remains.* Translated by Pascale-Anne Brault and Michael Naas. New York: Fordham, 2010.

———. *Dissemination.* Translated by Barbara Johnson. Chicago: University of Chicago Press, 1983.

———. *Given Time.* Vol. 1: *Counterfeit Money.* Translated by Peggy Kamuf. Chicago: University of Chicago Press, 1992.

———. *Margins of Philosophy.* Translated by Alan Bass. Chicago: University of Chicago Press, 1984.

———. *Of Spirit: Heidegger and the Question.* Translated by Geoffrey Bennington and Rachel Bowlby. Chicago: University of Chicago Press, 1989.

———. *Points . . . Interviews, 1974–1994.* Edited by Elizabeth Weber. Translated by Peggy Kamuf and others. Stanford, Calif.: Stanford University Press, 1995.

———. *Positions.* Translated by Alan Bass. Chicago: University of Chicago Press, 1981.

———. *The Post Card: From Socrates to Freud and Beyond.* Translated by Alan Bass. Chicago: University of Chicago Press, 1987.

———. *The Problem of Genesis in Husserl's Philosophy.* Translated by Marion Hobson. Chicago: University of Chicago Press, 2003.

———. *Psyche: Inventions of the Other.* Edited by Peggy Kamuf and Elizabeth Rottenberg. Stanford, Calif.: Stanford University Press, 2007.

———. *The Truth in Painting.* Translated by Geoff Bennington and Ian McLeod. Chicago: University of Chicago Press, 1987.

———. *Writing and Difference.* Translated by Alan Bass. Chicago: University of Chicago Press, 1980.

Desanti, Jean-Toussaint. *Introduction à l'histoire de la philosophie.* Paris: Éditions de la Nouvelle Critique, 1956.

———. *Les Staliniens: Une expérience politique, 1946/1956.* Paris: Fayard, 1975.

Descombes, Vincent. *Le Même et l'Autre.* Paris: Éditions de Minuit, 1979.

Dosse, François. *Histoire du structuralisme.* Paris: La Découverte, 1991.

Dreyfus, Hubert L., and Paul Rabinow. *Michel Foucault: Beyond Structuralism and Hermeneutics.* Chicago: University of Chicago Press, 1982.

Farias, Victor. *Heidegger and Nazism.* Edited by Joseph Margolis and Tom Rockmore. Philadelphia: Temple University Press, 1989.

Faye, Jean-Pierre. *Langages totalitaires.* Paris: Herrmann, 1972.

———. *La raison narrative.* Paris: Balland, 1990.

Fédier, François. *Heidegger: anatomie d'un scandale.* Paris: Laffont, 1988.

———. *Interprétations.* Paris: PUF, 1985.

———. *Regarder Voir.* Paris: Les Belles Lettres, 1995.

———. *Soixante-deux photographies de Martin Heidegger.* Paris: Gallimard, 1999.

Ferry, Luc, and Alain Renaut. *French Philosophy of the Sixties: An Essay on Anti-Humanism.* Translated by Mary H. S. Cattani. Amherst: University of Massachusetts Press, 1990.

———. *Heidegger and Modernity.* Translated by Franklin Philip. Chicago: University of Chicago Press, 1990.

Figal, Günter, ed. *The Heidegger Reader.* Translated by Jerome Beich. Bloomington: Indiana University Press, 2009.

Foucault, Michel. *Madness and Civilization: A History of Insanity in the Age of Reason.* Translated by Richard Howard. New York: Random House, 1965.

———. *The Order of Things: An Archeology of Human Sciences.* New York: Vintage Books Editions: 1994.

Franck, Didier. *Heidegger et le problème de l'espace.* Paris: Éditions de Minuit, 1986.

Gadamer, Hans-Georg. *Philosophical Apprenticeships.* Cambridge, Mass.: MIT Press, 1985.

Gilson, Étienne. *L'être et l'essence.* Paris: Vrin, 1948.

Glucksmann, André. *The Master Thinkers.* New York: Harper Collins, 1980.

Greisch, Jean. *Ontologie et Temporalité: Esquisse d'une interprétation intégrale de "Sein un Zeit."* Paris: PUF, 1994.

Grondin, Jean. *Le Tournant dans la pensée de Martin Heidegger.* Paris: PUF, 1987.

Gurvitch, Georges. *Les Tendances actuelles de la philosophie allemande.* Paris: Vrin, 1930.

Haar, Michel, ed. *Heidegger and the Essence of Man.* Translated by William McNeill. Albany: State University of New York Press, 1993.

———. *La fracture de l'histoire.* Grenoble: Millon, 1994.

———. *Martin Heidegger: Cahier de l'Herne.* Paris: Éditions de l'Herne, 1983.

———. *The Song of the Earth.* Translated by Reginald Lilly. Bloomington: Indiana University Press, 1993.

Han, Béatrice. *Michel Foucault's Critical Project: Between the Transcendental and the Historical.* Stanford, Calif.: Stanford University Press, 2002.

Hegel, G. W. F. *The Difference between Fichte's and Schelling's System of Philosophy.* Translated by H. S. Harris and Walter Cerf. Albany: State University of New York Press, 1977.

———. *The Encyclopedia Logic: Part One of the Encyclopedia of the Philosophical Sciences.* Edited by Ernst Behler. London: Bloomsbury Academic, 1991.

———. *Phenomenology of Spirit.* Translated by A. V. Miller. London: Oxford University Press, 1977.

———. *Philosophy of Nature: Encyclopedia Part Two.* Translated by A. V. Miller. Oxford: Clarendon Press, 1970.

———. *Science of Logic.* Translated by A. V. Miller. New York: Humanity Books, 1969.

Henry, Michel. *Genealogy of Psychoanalysis.* Translated by Douglas Brick. Stanford, Calif.: Stanford University Press, 1993.

———. *Incarnation: Une philosophie de la chair.* Paris: Éditions du Seuil, 2000.

———. *Phénoménologie matérielle.* Paris: PUF, 1990.

Irigaray, Luce. *The Forgetting of Air in Martin Heidegger.* Translated by Mary Beth Mader. Austin: University of Texas Press, 1999.

Janicaud, Dominique. *Chronos: Pour l'intelligence du partage temporel.* Paris: Grasset, 1997.

———. *Phenomenology and the "Theological Turn": The French Debate.* New York: Fordham University Press, 2000.

———. *The Shadow of That Thought: Heidegger and the Question of Politics.* Translated by Michael Gendre. Evanston, Ill.: Northwestern University Press, 1996.

Janicaud, Dominique, and Jean-Pierre Cometti. *"Être et Temps" de Martin Heidegger: Questions de méthode et voies de recherche.* Marseille: SUD, 1989.

Juranville, Alain. *Lacan et la philosophie.* Paris: PUF, 1984.

Kant, Immanuel. *The One Possible Basis for a Demonstration of the Existence of God.* Translated by Gordon Treash. Lincoln: University of Nebraska Press, 1994.

Kearney, Richard, and Joseph Stephen O'Leary, eds. *Heidegger et la question de Dieu.* Paris: PUF, 2009.

Kelkel, Arion L. *La légende de l'être: Langage et poésie chez Heidegger.* Paris: Vrin, 1980.

Kisiel, Theodore. *The Genesis of Heidegger's "Being and Time."* Berkeley: University of California Press, 1993.

Kojève, Alexandre. *Introduction to the Reading of Hegel: Lectures on the Phenomenology of Spirit.* Edited by Allan Bloom. Translated by James H. Nichols Jr. Assembled by Raymond Queneau. New York: Basic Books, 1969.

Kritzman, Lawrence D., ed. *Michel Foucault: Politics, Philosophy, Culture: Interview and Other Writings, 1977–1984.* New York: Routledge, 1988.

Lacan, Jacques. *Écrits: The First Complete Translation in English.* Translated by Bruce Fink. New York: W. W. Norton, 2007.

Lacoue-Labarthe, Philippe. *Heidegger, Art, and Politics: The Fiction of the Political.* Translated by Chris Turner. New York: Blackwell, 1990.

———. *Poetry as Experience.* Translated by Andrea Tarnowski. Stanford, Calif.: Stanford University Press, 1999.

———. *Typography.* Translated by Christopher Fynsk. Stanford, Calif.: Stanford University Press, 1998.

Laplanche, Jean, and Jean-Bertrand Pontalis. *The Language of Psychoanalysis.* Edited by Masud R. Khan. London: Hogarth Press, 1973.

Le Rider, Jacques. *Nietzsche en France: De la fin du XIXe siècle au temps présent.* Paris: Presses Universitaires de France, 1999.

Lévi-Strauss, Claude. *The Elementary Structures of Kinship.* Edited by Rodney Needham. Boston: Beacon Press Books, 1969.

———. *Structural Anthropology.* Translated by Claire Jacobson. New York: Basic Books, 1974.

Lévinas, Emmanuel. *Difficult Freedom: Essay on Judaism.* Translated by Sean Hand. Baltimore: Johns Hopkins University Press, 1997.

———. *Discovering Existence with Husserl.* Translated by Richard A. Cohen and Michael B. Smith. Evanston, Ill.: Northwestern University Press, 1998.

———. *Entre Nous: On Thinking-of-the-Other.* Translated by Michael B. Smith and Barbara Harshav. New York: Columbia University Press, 2000.

———. *Ethics and Infinity: Conversations with Philippe Nemo.* Translated by Richard A. Cohen. Pittsburgh: Duquesne University Press, 1985.

———. *Existence and Existents.* Translated by Alphonso Lingis. Pittsburgh: Duquesne University Press, 2001.

———. *Otherwise Than Being or Beyond Essence.* Translated by Alphonso Lingis. Dordrecht: Kluwer Academic Publishers, 1991.

———. *The Theory of Intuition in Husserl's Phenomenology.* Translated by Andre Orianne. Evanston, Ill.: Northwestern University Press, 1995.

———. *Time and the Other.* Translated by Richard A. Cohen. Pittsburgh: Duquesne University Press, 1987.

———. *Totality and Infinity.* Translated by Alphonso Lingis. The Hague: Martinus Nijhoff, 1979.

Loreau, Max. *La Genèse du phénomène.* Paris: Éditions de Minuit, 1989.

Löwith, Karl. *My Life in Germany before and after 1933: A Report.* Translated by Elizabeth King. London: Athlone Press, 1994.

———. "The Political Implications of Heidegger's Existentialism." In *The Heidegger Controversy: A Critical Reader.* Edited by Richard Wolin. Cambridge, Mass.: MIT Press, 1993.

Lyotard, Jean-François. *Heidegger and "the Jews."* Translated by Andreas Michel and Mark Roberts. Minneapolis: University of Minnesota Press, 1990.

———. *La Phénoménologie.* Paris: Presses Universitaires de France, 1954.

———. *Libidinal Economy.* Translated by Iain Hamilton Grant. London: Continuum, 1984.

———. *Phenomenology.* Translated by Brian Beakley. Albany: State University of New York Press, 1991.

Malabou, Catherine, and Jacques Derrida. *Counterpath: Traveling with Jacques Derrida.* Translated by David Wills. Stanford, Calif.: Stanford University Press, 2004.

Maldiney, Henri. *L'Art, l'éclair de l'être: Traversées.* Seyssel: Éditions Comp'Act, 1993.

———. *Penser l'homme et la folie: À la lumière de l'analyse existentielle et de l'analyse du destin.* Grenoble: Millon, 1991.

———. *Regard, Parole, Espace.* Lausanne: L'Âge d'homme, 1973.

Marcel, Gabriel. *La Dimension Florestan.* Paris: Plon, 1958.

Marion, Jean-Luc. *Being Given: Toward a Phenomenology of Givenness.* Translated by Jeffrey L. Kosky. Stanford, Calif.: Stanford University Press, 2002.

———, ed. *Emmanuel Lévinas: Positivité et transcendance.* Paris: Presses Universitaires de France, 2000.

———. *God without Being.* Translated by Thomas A. Carlson. Chicago: University of Chicago Press, 2012.

———. *The Idol and Distance: Five Studies.* Translated by Thomas A. Carlson. New York: Fordham University Press, 2001.

———. *On Descartes' Metaphysical Prism: The Constitution and the Limits of Onto-theology in Cartesian Thought.* Translated by Jeffrey L. Kosky. Chicago: University of Chicago Press, 1999.

———. *Reduction and Givenness: Investigations of Husserl, Heidegger, and Phenomenology.* Translated by Thomas A. Carlson. Evanston, Ill.: Northwestern University Press, 1998.

Marquet, Jean-François. *Singularité et événement.* Grenoble: Millon, 1995.

May, Reinhard. *Heidegger's Hidden Sources.* Translated by Graham Parkes. London: Routledge, 1996.

Merleau-Ponty, Maurice. *Humanism and Terror: An Essay on the Communist Problem.* Translated by John O'Neill. Boston: Beacon Press, 1990.
———. *Phenomenology of Perception.* Translated by Colin Smith. New York: Routledge, 1962.
Meschonnic, Henri. *Le Langage Heidegger.* Paris: PUF, 1990.
Mounier, Emmanuel. *Introduction aux existentialismes.* Paris: Denoël, 1947.
Nancy, Jean-Luc. *Being Singular Plural.* Translated by Robert Richardson and Anne O'Byrne. Stanford, Calif.: Stanford University Press, 2000.
———. *A Finite Thinking.* Edited by Simon Sparks. Stanford, Calif.: Stanford University Press, 2003.
———. *The Sense of the World.* Translated by Jeffrey Librett. Minneapolis: University of Minnesota Press, 1997.
Nancy, Jean-Luc, and Philippe Lacoue-Labarthe. *The Title of the Letter: A Reading of Lacan.* Translated by François Raffoul and David Pettigrew. Albany: State University of New York Press, 1992.
Ott, Hugo. *Martin Heidegger: A Political Life.* Translated by Allen Blunden. New York: Basic Books, 1993.
Palmier, Jean-Michel. *Les Écrits politiques de Heidegger.* Paris: Éditions de l'Herne, 1968.
Pettigrew, David, and François Raffoul, eds. *French Interpretations of Heidegger: An Exceptional Reception.* Albany, N.Y.: State University of New York Press, 2008.
Pinto, Louis. *Les Neveux de Zarathoustra: La réception de Nietzsche en France.* Paris: Éditions du Seuil, 1995.
Pöggeler, Otto. *Martin Heidegger's Path of Thinking.* Translated by D. Magurshak and S. Barber. Atlantic Highlands, N.J.: Humanity Books, 2000.
Poirié, François. *Emmanuel Lévinas.* Lyon: La Manufacture, 1987.
Prigogine, Ilya, and Isabelle Stengers. *Order Out of Chaos: Man's New Dialogue with Nature.* New York: Bantam New Age Books, 1984.
Raffoul, François. *Heidegger and the Subject.* Amherst, N.Y.: Prometheus Books, 1999.
Raffoul, François, and Eric S. Nelson, eds. *Rethinking Facticity.* Albany, N.Y.: State University of New York Press, 2008.
Raffoul, François, and David Pettigrew. *Heidegger and Practical Philosophy.* Albany: State University of New York Press, 2002.
Richardson, William J. *Heidegger: Through Phenomenology to Thought.* New York: Fordham University Press, 2003.
Richir, Marc. *L'Expérience du penser.* Grenoble: Millon, 1996.
———. *Méditations phénoménologiques.* Grenoble: Millon, 1992.
Ricoeur, Paul. *The Conflict of Interpretations.* Edited by Don Ihde. Evanston, Ill.: Northwestern University Press, 1974.
———. *From Text to Action: Essays in Hermeneutics 2.* Translated by Kathleen Blamey and John B. Thompson. Evanston, Ill.: Northwestern University Press, 1991.
———. *Oneself as Another.* Translated by Kathleen Blamey. Chicago: University of Chicago Press: 1992.
———. *The Rule of Metaphor: Multi-Disciplinary Studies in the Creation of Meaning in Language.* Translated by Robert Czerny with Kathleen McLaughlin and John Costello. New York: Routledge, 2003.
Rockmore, Tom. *Heidegger and French Philosophy.* New York: Routledge, 1995.

Romano, Claude. *Event and World.* Translated by Shane Mackinlay. New York: Fordham University Press, 2009.

Roudinesco, Elisabeth. *Jacques Lacan: An Outline of a Life and History of a System of Thought.* Translated by Barbara Bray. Cambridge: Polity Press, 1997.

———. *Lacan and Co.: A History of Psychoanalysis in France 1935–85.* Translated by Jeffrey Mehlman. Chicago: University of Chicago Press, 1990.

Rovan, Joseph. *Mémoires d'un Français qui se souvient d'avoir été Allemand.* Paris: Éditions du Seuil, 1999.

Safranski, Rüdiger. *Martin Heidegger: Between Good and Evil.* Translated by Ewald Osers. Cambridge, Mass.: Harvard University Press, 1998.

———. *Schopenhauer and the Wild Years of Philosopher.* Translated by Ewald Osers. Cambridge, Mass.: Harvard University Press, 1991.

Sartre, Jean-Paul. *Being and Nothingness: A Phenomenology Essay on Ontology.* Translated by Hazel Barnes. New York: Washington Square Press, 1984.

———. *Carnets de la drôle de guerre: Septembre 1939–Mars 1940.* Paris: Gallimard, 1995.

———. *Essays in Existentialism.* Edited by Wade Baskin. New York: Citadel Press 1997.

———. *L'être et le néant: Essai d'ontologie phénoménologique.* Paris: Gallimard, 1943.

———. *Notebooks for an Ethics.* Translated by David Pellauer. Chicago: University of Chicago Press, 1992.

———. *Situations I.* Paris: Gallimard, 1947.

———. *Truth and Existence.* Translated by Ronald Aronson. Chicago: University of Chicago Press, 1995.

———. *War Diaries: Notebooks from a Phoney War, 1939–1940.* Translated by Quintin Hoare. London: Verso, 2011.

———. *The Writings of Jean-Paul Sartre: Selected Prose.* Translated by Richard C. McCleary. Evanston, Ill.: Northwestern University Press, 1974.

Schürmann, Reiner. *Broken Hegemonies.* Translated by Reginald Lilly. Bloomington: Indiana University Press, 2003.

———. *Des hégémonies brisées.* Mauvezin: TER, 1996.

———. *Heidegger on Being and Acting: From Principles to Anarchy.* Translated by Christine-Marie Gros. Bloomington: Indiana University Press, 1987.

Sheehan, Thomas, ed. *Heidegger: The Man and the Thinker.* New Brunswick, N.J.: Transaction Publishers, 2010.

Steiner, George. *Martin Heidegger.* Chicago: University of Chicago Press, 1991.

Stiegler, Bernard. *Technics and Time.* Vol. 1: *The Fault of Epimetheus.* Translated by Richard Beardsworth and George Collins. Stanford, Calif.: Stanford University Press, 1998.

———. *Technics and Time.* Vol. 2: *Disorientation.* Translated by Stephen Barker. Stanford, Calif.: Stanford University Press, 2009.

Taminiaux, Jacques. *Heidegger and the Project of Fundamental Ontology.* Translated and edited by Michael Gendre. Albany: State University of New York Press, 1991.

———. *The Thracian Maid and the Professional Thinker: Arendt and Heidegger.* Translated and edited by Michael Gendre. Albany: State University of New York Press, 1997.

Thom, René. *Paraboles et catastrophes.* Paris: Flammarion, 1983.

Veyne, Paul. *René Char et ses poèmes.* Paris: Gallimard, 1990.

Volpi, Franco. *Heidegger e Aristotele.* Padua: Daphne, 1984.

Wahl, Jean. *Introduction à la pensée de Heidegger.* Paris: le Livre de Poche-Librairie générale française, 1998.

———. *A Short History of Existentialism.* Translated by Forrest Williams and Stanley Maron. New York: Philosophical Library, 1949.

———. *Vers la fin de l'ontologie.* Paris: SEDES, 1956.

———. *Vers le concret: Études d'histoire de la philosophie contemporaine.* Paris: Vrin, 1932.

Warin, François. *Nietzsche et Bataille.* Paris: Presses Universitaires de France, 1994.

Weil, Éric. *Logique de la philosophie.* Paris: Vrin, 1987.

Wittgenstein, Ludwig. "On Heidegger on Being and Dread." In *Heidegger and Modern Philosophy: Critical Essays.* Edited by Michael Murray. New Haven, Conn.: Yale University Press, 1978.

———. *Tractatus logico-philosophicus.* Translated by C. K. Ogden. London: Routledge & Kegan Paul, 1922.

Wolin, Richard, ed. *The Heidegger Controversy: A Critical Reader.* Cambridge, Mass.: MIT Press, 1993.

———. *The Politics of Being: The Political Thought of Martin Heidegger.* New York: Columbia University Press, 1990.

Zarader, Marlène. *The Unthought Debt: Heidegger and the Hebraic Heritage.* Translated by Bettina Bergo. Stanford, Calif.: Stanford University Press: 2006.

Index

DOMINIQUE JANICAUD was Professor of Philosophy at the University of Nice-Sophia-Antipolis, where he began teaching in 1966. He was a former student of the École Normale Supérieure and Agrégé de Philosophie. From 1983 to 1998 he directed the Centre de recherches d'histoire des idées, in Nice. He was a visiting professor at several universities in the United States, including the Pennsylvania State University and Stony Brook University. Professor Janicaud was a critical and inventive reader of Heidegger. His many books include *Powers of the Rational* (IUP, 1994), *Heidegger from Metaphysics to Thought* (1995), *The Shadow of that Thought* (1996), *Phenomenology and the Theological Turn* (2001), and *Phenomenology Wide Open* (2010). His book *Heidegger en France,* the crowning achievement of his philosophical work, was published by Éditions Albin Michel in 2001. Born November 14, 1937, in Paris, Professor Janicaud passed away August 18, 2002.

DAVID PETTIGREW is Professor of Philosophy at Southern Connecticut State University, where he has taught since 1987. He has co-edited a number of volumes, including *French Interpretations of Heidegger: An Exceptional Reception* (2008) and *Heidegger and Practical Philosophy* (2002). He is also the co-translator of Françoise Dastur's *Heidegger and the Question of Time* (1998), among other works. Pettigrew has authored essays on the ethical implications of Heidegger's thought that have appeared in French and Arabic. In addition, he has authored a number of essays on the work of French thinkers such as Jacques Derrida, Jacques Lacan, Maurice Merleau-Ponty, Jean-Luc Nancy, and J-D. Nasio. He is co-editor (with François Raffoul) of a book series at SUNY Press devoted to Contemporary French Thought.

FRANÇOIS RAFFOUL is Professor of Philosophy at Louisiana State University. He is the author of *Heidegger and the Subject* (1999), *A Chaque fois Mien* (Paris, 2004), and *The Origins of Responsibility* (IUP, 2010). He is completing a new manuscript entitled *Thinking the Event*. He is the co-editor of a number of volumes, including *Disseminating Lacan* (1996), *Heidegger and Practical Philosophy* (2002), *Rethinking Facticity* (2008), *French Interpretations of Heidegger* (2008), and *The Bloomsbury Companion to Heidegger* (2013). He has co-translated several French philosophers, including Jacques Derrida and Jean-Luc Nancy. He is the editor (with David Pettigrew) of a book series at SUNY Press, Contemporary French Thought.